A Revelation of Jesus

David Lackey

AB ASPECT Books
www.ASPECTBooks.com

Copyright © 2016 David Lackey

Copyright © 2016 ASPECT Books
ISBN-13: 978-1-4796-9392-3 (Paperback)
ISBN-13: 978-1-4796-0393-0 (ePub)
ISBN-13: 978-1-4796-0394-7 (Mobi)
Library of Congress Control Number: 2015911754

Scripture (except from the book of Revelation) taken from the New King James Version®. Copyright © 1982 by Thomas Nelson. Used by permission.

Unless otherwise noted, all Scripture from the Book of Revelation is taken from the American King James Version (Public Domain)

Cover art: "A woman clothed with the sun...bore a male Child [Jesus] who was to rule all nations...And her Child was caught up to God and His throne" Revelation 12:1-5. Woodcut by Albrecht Durer, 1498

Published by

ASPECT Books
www.ASPECTBooks.com

Table of Contents

"The Four Horsemen of the Apocalypse."
Woodcut by Albrecht Durer 1498

Introduction

The Book of Revelation is the most exquisitely fascinating yet frustratingly elusive book ever written. By today's standards it would hardly be considered a book, with just 10,300 words, but despite the fact that it is small and written with simple vocabulary, its meaning is still largely a mystery. It is the only book of the Bible in which there is no consensus as to its general theme, organization, time frame or target audience, and if you have read other commentaries about Revelation you have probably come away feeling frustrated and unsatisfied.

A major problem of most interpretations of Revelation is the reference material that has been used. Some theologians have compared Revelation with other ancient secular and Christian documents. Others have arbitrarily assigned its meaning to a particular era and then have compared it with the history of that time. Many have guessed and speculated about the meaning of its symbols or have tried to "plug in" the current international trends and headline news. But the source material that God inspired the apostle John to use was the Bible itself. Revelation is packed with references and allusions to verses, themes, and stories from the Bible, primarily the Old Testament, and it is only by praying for insight and then comparing the themes and symbols of Revelation with the inspired Scriptures that we can hope to understand this book that is so vital now.

The Book of Revelation ends with the statement, "The Lord God of the holy prophets sent his angel to show to his servants the things which must soon take place" (Revelation 22:6). The evidence all around us indicates that "the things" that John was shown will "soon take place" and that the vast majority of the people of this world are completely unprepared.

A Revelation of Jesus presents and explains the well-known themes of the Book of Revelation that everyone expects—the mark of the beast, 666, the Battle of Armageddon, the 144,000, the Millennium and the Four Horsemen of the Apocalypse. It also explores lesser known but important subjects such as the seven churches, seven seals, and seven trumpets, the two witnesses, the beast from the bottomless pit, the woman clothed with the sun, the great harlot, the seven-headed beast from the sea and the two-horned beast from the earth.

A Revelation of Jesus identifies the roles of the United States and the European Union, Islam, the Roman Catholic, Orthodox, Protestant and Pentecostal Churches, the King of the North and the King of the South, the Jews and the Twelve Tribes of Israel, the remnant church and the Antichrist. And it delves into current controversial themes such as the secret rapture, the charismatic movement, modern Babylon, the ecumenical and new age movements, the Sabbath controversy, the immortal soul and the nature of heaven and hell.

The Book of Revelation is not just a collection of interesting symbols and metaphors—it reveals in symbolic language Jesus and His great enemy who are engaged in a very real spiritual battle between good and evil that has been raging since "Lucifer, son of the morning...said in [his] heart...I will be like the Most High" (Isaiah 14:12-14). At the dawn of creation "that ancient serpent" succeeded in bringing the battlefield to planet earth. This is a battle to the death that has no neutral ground, even though the majority of the world's people know nothing about it. A *Revelation of Jesus* unmasks the great deceiver and exposes his fatal traps, tricks and agents.

But the Book of Revelation is not about Satan—it is "the Revelation of Jesus Christ" (Revelation 1:1). Jesus is the hero and His complete victory and the eradication of evil is the great theme. The purpose of this book is to present Jesus as He is revealed in the Book of Revelation, so that in seeing Him more clearly, we may fall in love with Him more than ever before.

"And in the midst of the seven lampstands One like the Son of Man." Revelation 1:13
Woodcut by Albrecht Durer 1498

14

Chapter 1

Revelation 1:1-20

1:1 The Revelation of Jesus Christ, which God gave to Him, to show to His servants things which must shortly come to pass; and He sent and signified it by His angel to His servant John:

1:2 Who bore record of the word of God, and of the testimony of Jesus Christ, and of all things that he saw.

1:3 Blessed is he that reads, and they that hear the words of this prophecy, and keep those things which are written therein, for the time is at hand.

1:4 John to the seven churches which are in Asia: Grace be to you, and peace, from Him who is, and who was, and who is to come; and from the seven Spirits who are before His throne;

1:5 And from Jesus Christ, who is the faithful witness, and the first begotten of the dead, and the prince of the kings of the earth. To Him that loved us, and washed us from our sins in His own blood,

1:6 And has made us kings and priests to God and His Father; to Him be glory and dominion for ever and ever. Amen.

1:7 Behold, He comes with clouds, and every eye shall see Him, and they also which pierced Him; and all tribes of the earth shall wail because of Him. Even so, Amen.

1:8 "I am Alpha and Omega, the beginning and the end," said the Lord, who is, and who was, and who is to come, the Almighty.

1:9 I John, your brother, and companion in tribulation, and in the kingdom and patience of Jesus Christ, was on the isle that is called Patmos, for the word of God, and for the testimony of Jesus Christ.

1:10 I was in the Spirit on the Lord's day, and heard behind me a loud voice, as of a trumpet,

1:11 Saying, "I am Alpha and Omega, the first and the last," and, "What you see, write in a book, and send it to the seven churches which are in Asia: to Ephesus, and to Smyrna, and to Pergamos, and to Thyatira, and to Sardis, and to Philadelphia, and to Laodicea."

1:12 And I turned to see the voice that spoke with me. And being turned, I saw seven golden lampstands;

1:13 And in the midst of the seven lampstands One like the Son of man, clothed with a garment down to the feet, and girded about the chest with a golden sash.

1:14 **His head and His hair were white like wool, as white as snow; and His eyes were as a flame of fire.**

1:15 **And His feet were like fine brass, as if they burned in a furnace; and His voice was as the sound of many waters.**

1:16 **And He had in His right hand seven stars, and out of His mouth went a sharp two edged sword, and His countenance was as the sun shines in his strength.**

1:17 **And when I saw Him, I fell at His feet as dead. And He laid his right hand on me, saying to me, "Fear not; I am the first and the last:**

1:18 **I am He that lives, and was dead; and, behold, I am alive forever more, Amen; and I have the keys of Hades and of death.**

1:19 **Write the things which you have seen, and the things which are, and the things which shall be hereafter.**

1:20 **The mystery of the seven stars which you saw in My right hand, and the seven golden lampstands: the seven stars are the angels of the seven churches, and the seven lampstands which you saw are the seven churches."**

1:1 A Revelation of Jesus

Dragons, bizarre creatures, epic battles, and an intimate love story laced with malicious treachery. This could be the tag line of a blockbuster movie, but instead it is a thumbnail sketch of the concluding chapters of the all-time international best-seller. During the past nearly two thousand years millions of people have had the chance to read the Book of Revelation, the last book of the Bible. Many have wondered if Revelation will show them in advance what will happen in the future. Some churches have used it to support their interpretation of current world events. Influential Christian teachers and even whole denominations have basically considered it to be "off limits," a book whose message is so cryptic that it is of little value, or even dangerous. It is no wonder that the vast majority of readers have come away scratching their heads and wondering, "what on earth was that all about?"

"The Revelation of Jesus Christ, which God gave to Him, to show to His servants things which must shortly come to pass; and He sent and signified it by His angel to His servant John" (Revelation 1:1). The first sentence of Revelation

hints that "what on earth…?" may be the wrong question; the Book of Revelation is first and foremost a **"Revelation of Jesus Christ."** Jesus is the central figure, and whatever else we may learn about world events in the past or the future can only find its true context in a deeper understanding of Jesus Christ. The world is full of misconceptions and even blatant lies about Jesus. The fact that there are hundreds of denominations and diverse religions that all claim Jesus as their central figure shows that the world needs a much deeper "Revelation of Jesus." Millions have wondered where Jesus was when they needed Him, why He allowed tragedies to ruin their lives, why He doesn't seem to help them with their problems when they do what their church tells them. The Book of Revelation explains all of this within the context of a cosmic battle between good and evil that affects every person on earth.

Although written by John,[1] Revelation perhaps more than any other book of the Bible reveals that God is the real author. There is very

---

1 Most commentators believe that the author was John the beloved disciple who also wrote the Gospel and three Epistles of John.

little commentary or dialogue by John; even the messages directed **"to the seven churches which are in Asia"** (Revelation 1:4) are direct quotations of what Jesus said. John basically described the visions he saw along with the commentaries given by Jesus or **"His angel"** as he had been instructed: **"Write the things which you have seen, and the things which are, and the things which shall be hereafter."** (Revelation 1:19).

The first thing Jesus reveals about Himself is His relationship to the human race: **"The Revelation of Jesus Christ, which God gave to Him to show to His servants"** (Revelation 1:1). God the Father, the Source of everything, gives to Jesus, who in turn gives to **"His servants."** Jesus is our link to the invisible heavenly reality. The patriarch Jacob "dreamed, and behold, a ladder was set up on the earth, and its top reached to heaven; and there the angels of God were ascending and descending on it" (Genesis 28:12). Nearly two thousand years later Jesus revealed to His disciples that He is the ladder connecting heaven and earth: "you shall see heaven open, and the angels of God ascending and descending upon the Son of Man" (John 1:51).

In the Book of Revelation Jesus is revealed within the context of prophecy. Jesus shows **"His servants things which must shortly come to pass."** Revelation, more than any other book of the Bible, reveals the things that will take place in the future. When Revelation was written the future included, of course, events which are now history, and these are an important part of the book. But Revelation focuses upon a particular part of the future called "the time of the end." The time of the end itself is largely a preparation for a specific, short but very intense period called "the time of trouble" (Daniel 12:1) or "the great tribulation" (Matthew 24:21)—Jesus said, "There will be great tribulation, such as has not been since the beginning of the world until this time, no, nor ever shall be" (Matthew 24:21). The fulfillment of

a number of Bible prophecies (which will be presented in this book) show that this fearsome time is about to break upon the unsuspecting world, and those who are unprepared will be plunged into unimaginable distress. One of the important purposes of Revelation is to help God's people understand and navigate the time of the end, and particularly the great tribulation.

The prophet Daniel, who saw visions similar to John's, was instructed to "shut up the words, and seal the book until the time of the end" (Daniel 12:4). In contrast, Revelation is a book to be read and understood—**"Blessed is he that reads, and they that hear the words of this prophecy, and keep those things which are written therein"** (Revelation 1:3). One of the purposes of Revelation is to unseal the prophecies of Daniel that were to be sealed until the time of the end. And Revelation adds vital information that is not found in any of the Old Testament prophecies. The angel who showed the visions to John specifically directed him "Do not seal the sayings of the prophecy of this book" (Revelation 22:10). Those who claim that the Book of Revelation is too complex and obscure to be understood are contradicting the very purpose of the book which is **"to show His servants the things which must shortly come to pass"** (Revelation 1:1).

However, the meaning of Revelation is not simple or obvious. It is the only book of the Bible that does not have a general consensus by theologians as to its theme, its structure, the outline of its main sections and the meaning of the major symbols. It is a book that requires deep study, with the insight of the Holy Spirit, and it deserves much more than a quick glance to see what the mark of the beast is and if there is anything that relates to the current headline news. A study of Revelation requires slow, thorough and repeated reading, looking up texts and wrestling with scriptural comparisons to uncover the mysteries that are there. But it is definitely worth the effort—**"Blessed** [fortunate, happy] **is he who reads…this prophecy and keeps those things which are written therein."**[2]

1:2,3 Source

"And He sent and signified it by His angel to His servant John, who bore record of the word of God, and of the testimony of Jesus Christ, and of all things that he saw" (Revelation 1:1,2). John did not "dream up" Revelation as a means of teaching systematic theology—he shared what he had seen and heard. There are a number of keys to understanding the meanings of the prophecies God revealed to him.

First of all, John bears witness **"to the word of God,"** which in John's time were the Old Testament Scriptures. There are hundreds of scriptural references in Revelation, and in fact the majority of the verses have some Old Testament link. Those who consider the Old Testament to be a part of the "old covenant," irrelevant to Christians, will not be able to understand the Book of Revelation.

John also bore witness to **"the testimony of Jesus Christ."** The testimony of Jesus is defined in Revelation chapter 19 by the angel who presented the visions to John: "I am your fellow servant, and of your brethren that have the testimony of Jesus…for *the testimony of Jesus is the spirit of prophecy*" (Revelation 19:10). Jesus has a testimony (a message) which He wants to share with each one of us, but He illuminates the meaning of the Biblical messages through the same "spirit of prophecy" (the Holy Spirit) that inspired

the prophets who wrote them. Only those whose minds are illuminated by His Holy Spirit will be able to understand His testimony. The apostle Paul put it this way: "No one knows the things of God except the Spirit of God. Now we have received, not the spirit of the world, but the Spirit who is from God, that we might know the things that have been freely given to us by God" (1Corinthians 2:11,12).

Many people who read the book of Revelation find only a confusing jumble of seemingly unrelated and incomprehensible symbols. The basic prerequisite to understanding Revelation is not a course in theology or Biblical languages, but being filled with the Holy Spirit. John was **"in the Spirit"** (Revelation 1:10) when he wrote the Book of Revelation. We also must be in the Spirit in order to understand it.

This is not to say that the Holy Spirit will interpret the prophecies with no effort on our part. The **"word of God"** and the **"testimony of Jesus"** go together. As we make an effort to compare the verses in Revelation with their links in other parts of the Bible, using modern resources to check the ancient language and praying for insight from the Spirit, we will be amazed to find that previously incomprehensible prophecies begin to make sense.

This book will analyze the meaning of the Book of Revelation verse by verse, but before we do that we will see how Revelation uses symbols, how it is structured and organized, and how the various phases of the vision fit into a chronological timeline.

Use of Symbols

The Book of Revelation is a series of visions that John saw, with the messages encapsulated in dramatic images and symbols. Symbols convey a rich, multifaceted message that touches both the intellect and the emotions. But symbols must be interpreted correctly, or the entire meaning

---

2 Notice that the blessing is not for those who simply have a Bible on their bookshelf or who read Revelation at some time in the past. The Greek participle *anaginoston* may be better translated "Blessed is the reader…of this prophecy", implying regular, continuous reading. This word is used in the Old Testament to characterize those who read or heard and then responded to the message (Ezra 4:23, 2Chronicles 34:14-21, Nehemiah 8:1-3, 5:8,12). This thought is echoed in Revelation, "those who read and hear…and keep those things which are written" (Revelation 1:3).

is misconstrued. Some commentators have assigned meanings to symbols based on logic, imagination and the preconceived ideas of their own prophetic interpretations. It is important to let the Bible interpret its own symbols, and there are some simple principles which apply specifically to apocalyptic prophecies.

First of all, the interpretation of a symbol in the Book of Revelation should be found, whenever possible, in the Book of Revelation itself. For example, in Revelation 17:1 an angel said to John, "come here, I will show you the judgment of the great harlot that sits on many waters." In verse 15 the interpretation for water is given: "The waters which you saw, where the harlot sits, are peoples, and multitudes, and nations, and tongues." In Revelation 12:15 water is again used as a symbol—"And the serpent cast water out of his mouth like a flood after the woman." Instead of guessing or searching elsewhere in the Bible for the meaning of this water, we should use the definition in Revelation—the "serpent" pursued the "woman" with "peoples, multitudes, nations and tongues."

Often the symbols are not clearly interpreted in the Book of Revelation. The next place to look is in other apocalyptic prophecies, such as Daniel or Zechariah. For example, in Revelation chapter 13 John saw a beast like a leopard. Although Jeremiah used the leopard as an example of how impossible it is for us to change our sinful characters ("can the leopard change his spots?" Jeremiah 13:23), Jeremiah would not be the first place to look for the meaning of apocalyptic symbols. The apocalyptic prophecy of Daniel 7 portrayed a leopard which symbolized the ancient Greek Empire under Alexander the Great (Daniel 7:6, see appendix 11), and this is where we should start in our attempt to understand the leopard of Revelation 13.

If a symbol cannot be found in the apocalyptic books the search should be expanded to the rest of the Bible, starting with the Old Testament since these were the Scriptures of John's time. This often results in multiple meanings, in which case the context of the passage in Revelation should be matched as closely as possible to the context of the Old Testament passages. It is also important to consider all the texts which use the symbol and try to find a consensus or underlying theme, rather than picking out an isolated example that fits with a pet theory.

Historicist Model of Interpretation

Theologians use general models of interpretation to try to correlate the visions of Revelation with events on earth. The most common models are preterism, which sees the visions as applying to the time they were written (first and second centuries),[3] futurism, which applies most of Revelation to the future "time of trouble,"[4] and historicism, which interprets the prophecies as covering the span of history.

Obviously the model used will make a tremendous difference in the interpretation, so rather than speculate, we should find out how other apocalyptic prophecies in the Bible relate to world events. The book of Daniel is the book

---

3 Preterism was a development of higher criticism/enlightenment of the post-reformation era that denied that prophecy could supernaturally predict the future, so they consider the prophecies to be symbolic commentaries and predictions based on the political, social and religious issues of their time. See footnote in 2: *To the Seven Churches* for a brief discussion of problems of the preterist interpretation.

4 Futurism was developed as a reaction to the Protestant reformers who identified the pope as the antichrist, and pushed the time of the antichrist into the indefinite future. In recent years it has been embraced and developed by dispensationalist writers such as Hal Lindsey and Tim LaHaye (the *Left Behind* series of books and movies) and often includes unbiblical elements such as the "secret rapture" (see Appendix 4). See Wikipedia contributors, "Futurism (Christianity)," *Wikipedia, The Free Encyclopedia,* http://en.wikipedia.org/w/index.php?title=Futurism_(Christianity)&oldid=624492918 (accessed October 21, 2014).

of the Bible that is most similar to the Book of Revelation, so its visions can provide a helpful model. The vision of the multi-metal image of Daniel 2 is typical. The various metals comprising the image represent the progression of world empires which oppressed the people of God from the time of Daniel (Babylon, Persia, Greece, Rome, Papal Europe, see appendix 11). But the greatest emphasis of the vision is on "what will be in the latter days" when "the God of heaven will set up a kingdom which shall never be destroyed" (Daniel 2:28,44).

Likewise, in chapter 7 Daniel was in vision "and four great beasts came up from the sea." Again, the progression of the beasts (lion, bear, leopard, monster, horn) represents the progression of the oppressive empires through the ages. But the most important emphasis is the time of the end when "the court was seated, and the books were opened…and the time came for the saints to possess the kingdom" (Daniel 7:10,22). The vision of Daniel chapter 8 (the ram, the goat and the "little horn") follows the same pattern.[5]

This fits best with the historicist model of interpretation, which sees the apocalyptic prophecies as spanning the course of history but focusing on the time of the end, a model held by most theologians until fairly recently.[6] A careful study of the prophecies of Daniel shows the principles of the historicist model of interpretation, which can be applied to the Book of Revelation.

First of all, with each new vision the prophet begins by giving his own personal context (for example, Daniel received the vision of chapter 7 in "the first year of Belshazzar…while on his bed," Daniel 7:1). Likewise the prophet John gives his personal context, as being in exile **"on the isle that is called Patmos…on the Lord's Day"** (Revelation 1:9,10). We should notice that the book of Daniel is comprised of a series of parallel visions with a repeating theme, each beginning with Daniel's personal context, interspersed with stories from Daniel's life (such as Daniel in the Lion's Den). Revelation, on the other hand, only has one personal context at the beginning, so it is more like one of the *visions* of Daniel than like the *book* of Daniel with its repetitive visions.

Secondly, the time frame of each vision begins at the time it is given. For example, the dream with the metal image of Daniel 2 was given "in the second year of Nebuchadnezzar's reign," which was the golden age of Babylon when its power was at its peak, and the vision begins by representing Babylon as a "head of gold." The other visions of Daniel also begin chronologically at the time the visions were given.[7] So we would expect the events of the Book of Revelation to start around the time it was written, which most scholars believe to be the last decade of the first century, rather than at the Cross or at the time of the end.

Each of Daniel's visions then makes a basically linear progression through the important facts of world history that pertain to God's people. History is dealt with briefly, as the main focus is on the establishment of God's kingdom. There may be a shifting of scenes, such as in Daniel 7:8,9 where the scene shifts from earth, where the "Little Horn" is destroying kingdoms, to heaven where the heavenly judgment is beginning. There

---

5 Appendix 11 gives more details about the visions of Daniel.

6 Wikipedia contributors, "Historicism (Christianity)," *Wikipedia, The Free Encyclopedia,* http://en.wikipedia.org/w/index.php?title=Historicism_(Christianity)&oldid=612757913 (accessed June 26, 2014).

7 The vision of chapter 7, given "in the first year of Belshazzar" (the last king of Babylon), begins by picturing Babylon as a lion who is forced to stand up like a man and have his wings plucked (showing the weakness which now characterized the kingdom). By the time the vision of chapter eight was given "in the third year of the reign of King Belshazzar" when the Babylonian Empire was just about to end, Babylon is not even mentioned in the vision, but it starts with Persia, the empire that succeeded Babylon.

may also be explanatory passages such as Daniel chapter nine, which clarifies aspects of chapter eight that Daniel had not understood.

In a similar fashion, we would expect the Book of Revelation to cover the span of history from the time of John, but for the emphasis to be on the time of the end. We would expect some changes of scene and explanatory passages, within a basically linear progression. We will see below (section 1: *Chronological Organization*) that this is indeed how the Book of Revelation is constructed.

Chiastic Literary Structure

Readers of the Book of Revelation have noticed that words, phrases and symbols that appear at the beginning of the book also appear at the end, and often nowhere else. Further investigation of this phenomenon has uncovered one of the keys to understanding the Book of Revelation: its remarkable literary organization. Revelation is not a chaotic jumble of incomprehensible symbols; it is highly organized in its presentation of the theme of God's resolution of problem of sin. The book is organized in a chiasm, which is a literary structure that divides a passage of literature into two halves with sections that are mirror images of each other, reaching a climax in the middle of the passage. A chiasm looks like this:

```
      E-1   E-2
     D-1       D-2
    C-1          C-2
   B-1             B-2
  A-1               A-2
```

In the Book of Revelation this chiastic structure is comprised of a progressive series of sections in the first half that are mirrored by corresponding sections in the second half. Each section has a theme that is related to the theme in the corresponding section. In each section there are characteristic words, phrases and symbols that are also found in the corresponding section of the chiasm. In many cases the paired elements are unique to these passages in the Book of Revelation or even in the whole Bible. The sections can be easily identified because each section (except for the prologue and epilogue) begins with a scene from the heavenly sanctuary, with sanctuary elements such as God's throne, the lampstand and the altar of incense that were in the earthly sanctuary, or the four living creatures, twenty-four elders and the myriad of angels who surround the heavenly throne. The sanctuary scenes that introduce the chiastic sections have a remarkable progression through the stages of the Old Testament sanctuary services that confirms the interpretations of the corresponding sections that they introduce (see Appendix 1: *Progression of Sanctuary Scenes*).

The following table shows the corresponding sections and their mirror elements, as well as the sanctuary scenes that introduce each of the sections. Then follows a chart that depicts the chiasm with its sections and themes. You will understand this much better as you read the book and see how the chiastic sections help in its interpretation.

* This Phrase appears in Revelation only in these two verses.

** This Phrase appears in the Bible only in these two verses.

Prologue (1:1-10)	Epilogue (22:5-21)
1. ** "To show his servants things which must shortly come to pass" (1:1). 2. ** "Blessed is he that reads, and they that hear the words of this prophecy, and keep those" (1:3). 3. ** "The time is at hand" (1:3). 4. "He is coming with clouds" (1:7). 5. Book (of Revelation) sent to the seven churches (1:11). 6. "Alpha and the Omega, the first and the last" (1:11). 7. "I [John] fell at His feet" (1:17).	1. ** "To show His servants the things which must shortly take place" (22:6). 2. ** "Blessed is he who keeps the words of the prophecy" (22:7,10,18). 3. ** "The time is at hand" (22:10). 4. "I am coming quickly" (22:12,20). 5. Angel sent to testify (through the Book of Revelation) to the churches (22:16,18). 6. "Alpha and the Omega…the first and the last" (22:13). 7. "I, John…fell down to worship before the feet" (22:8).

Church on Earth (1:10-3:22)	Church in the Kingdom (21:1-22:5)
Sanctuary Scene: 1:12-15 Jesus among the lampstands 1. * The tree of life (2:7). 2. "To him that overcomes I will give" (2:7,17,etc.). 3. "Shall not be hurt by the second death" (2:11). 4. "Behold I am coming quickly" (3:11). 5. "I will write on him My new name" (3:12). 6. Overcomers are pillars in God's temple (3:12). 7. ** "New Jerusalem…comes down out of heaven from my God" (3:12). 8. Overcomers sit with Christ on His throne as He sits on His Father's throne (3:21).	Sanctuary Scene: 21:2-5, 22 New Jerusalem, God is the temple 1. * The tree of life (22:2). 2. "He that overcomes shall inherit" (21:7). 3. "There shall be no more death" (21:4). 4. "Behold I am coming quickly" (22:7). 5. "His name shall be in their foreheads" (22:4). 6. God and the Lamb are the temple (21:22). 7. ** "New Jerusalem coming down from God out of heaven " (21:2,10). 8. Servants of God reign and serve God and the Lamb as they sit on Their throne (22:1,3,5).

Investigative Judgment (4:1-8:1)	Executive Judgment (19:1-20:15)
Sanctuary Scene: 4:1-5:14 Open door of the sanctuary, throne of God	Sanctuary Scene: 19:1-8 Voices heard from the sanctuary and throne
1. "A door was open in heaven" (4:1).	1. "I saw heaven opened" (19:11).
2. "Behold, a throne was set in heaven and one sat on the throne" (4:2).	2. "I saw a great white throne and Him that sat on it." (20:11).
3. Central theme: opening the sealed book (5:1-9).	3. "Books were opened. And another book was opened, which is the Book of Life" (20:12).
4. Redeemed to be kings and priests and reign (5:9,10).	4. Those resurrected are priests and reign (20:6).
5. * "A white horse, and He that sat on him… went forth conquering and to conquer" (6:2).	5. * "A white horse. And He who sat on him… judges and makes war." (19:11).
6. ** Death and Hades (6:8).	6. ** Death and Hades (20:13,14).
7. Souls of martyrs (6:9,10).	7. Souls of martyrs (20:4-6).
8. "How long…will You not judge and avenge our blood?" (6:10).	8. "He has judged…and has avenged… the blood of His servants" (19:2).
9. Second coming, emphasizing the wrath of the Lamb (6:12-17, esp. 16,17).	9. Second coming, emphasizing the wrath of Almighty God (19:11-19, esp. 15).
10. Kings, great men, rich men, commanders, mighty men, slaves and free men plead to be killed (6:15,16).	10. Kings, captains, mighty men, all people, free and slaves, are killed (19:17,18).
11. * Great multitude (7:9).	11. * Great Multitude (19: 1,6).

Trumpet Plagues (8:2-11:19)	Seven Last Plagues (15:1-18:24)
Sanctuary Scene: 7:9- 8:5 Golden censer ministry with smoke ascending in the sanctuary	Sanctuary Scene: 15:1-8 Ministry finished, sanctuary filled with smoke
1. First trumpet plague falls on the earth (8:7).	1. First plague falls on the earth (16:2).
2. Second plague falls on the sea, a third becomes blood (8:8).	2. Second plague falls on the sea, it becomes blood (16:3).
3. A third of the creatures in the sea die (8:9).	3. Every living creature in the sea dies (16:3).
4. Third plague falls on the rivers and springs (8:10).	4. Third plague falls on the rivers and springs (16:4).
5. Fourth plague affects sun, moon and stars (8:12).	5. Fourth plague affects the sun (16:8).
6. "Woe to the inhabitants of the earth" (8:13).	6. "The Inhabitants of the earth have been made drunk" (17:2).
7. Fifth plague darkens the sun and air (9:2).	7. Fifth plague darkens kingdom of the beast (16:10).
8. "The beast that ascends out of the bottomless pit" (11:7).	8. "The beast...shall ascend out of the bottomless pit" (17:8).
9. * Sixth plague releases angels bound at river Euphrates (9:14).	9. * Sixth plague dries up the river Euphrates (16:12).
10. "Three plagues...out of their mouths" (9:17,18).	10. "Three unclean spirits...out of the mouths" (16:13).
11. They did not repent of their murders, etc. (9:21).	11. They did not repent of their deeds (16:14).
12. A great earthquake and a tenth of the city fell (11:13).	12. A great earthquake and the cities of the nations fell (16:18,19).
13. Seventh plague a loud voices announce the kingdoms of the world have become Christ's (11:15).	13. Seventh plague a loud voice announces "it is done!" (16:17).
14. Lightenings, noises, thunderings, an earthquake and great hail (11:19).	14. Noises, thunderings and lightenings, a great earthquake and great hail (16:18,21).

Satan's Ultimate Demonstration (11:19-13:18)	God's Ultimate Demonstration (14:1-14:20)
Sanctuary Scene: 11:15-19 Throne room of the temple opened, ark of the covenant seen 1. * Those "who keep the commandments of God and have the testimony of Jesus Christ" (12:17). 2. Beast given authority over every tribe, tongue and nation (13:7). 3. ** "Here is the patience and the faith of the saints" (13:10). 4. Command to worship the beast (13:12). 5. Image of the beast (13:14,15). 6. Mark of the beast (13:16,17). 7. Mark on their hands or foreheads (13:16).	Sanctuary Scene: 14:1-5 Lamb and 144,000 before the throne 1. * "Those who keep the commandments of God and the faith of Jesus" (14:12). 2. Gospel preached to every nation, tribe, tongue and people (14:6). 3. ** "Here is the patience of the saints" (14:12). 4. Invitation to worship the creator (14:7). 5. Image of the beast (14:9,11). 6. Mark of the beast (14:9,11). 7. Father's name on their foreheads (14:1).

See Diagram 1.1 to view the chiastic structure

Diagram 1.1

CHIASTIC STRUCTURE OF REVELATION

SATAN'S ATTACKS ON GOD AND HIS PEOPLE   GOD'S VICTORY OVER SATAN AND HIS FORCES

PROLOGUE
1:1-10

CHURCH ON
EARTH
1:10—3:22
God's church
struggles against
the attacks of the
enemy.

Messages to the
seven churches.

INVESTIGATIVE
JUDGMENT
4:1—8:1
The sinless
universe assesses
candidates for
eternal life.

Courtroom in
heaven, lamb and
the scroll, seven
seals, sealing of
144,000, the great
multitude.

TRUMPET
PLAGUES
8:2—11:19
God's protection of
the world is
withdrawn, Satan
is allowed to cause
chaos.

Seven trumpets,
seven thunders,
measuring the
temple, the two
witnesses.

SATAN'S
ULTIMATE
DEMONSTRA-
TION
11:19—13:18
History and future
of Satan's activity.

Dragon and the
woman, war in
heaven, beasts
from the sea and
the earth, mark of
the beast

GOD'S
ULTIMATE
DEMONSTRA-
TION
14:1-20
Worldwide
proclamation of the
gospel, ultimate
outcome.

144,000, Three
angel's messages,
the two harvests

SEVEN LAST
PLAGUES
15:1—18:24
Close of probation,
plagues of God
upon the
impenitent

Temple closed, 7
last plagues, battle
of Armageddon,
judgment of
Babylon

EXECUTIVE
JUDGMENT
19:1—20:15
Christ comes for
His people, judges
systems and people
who have rebelled
against him.

Second coming of
Christ, millennium
binding of Satan,
Great white throne
judgment

CHURCH IN
THE KINGDOM
21:1—22:5
God's church
glorified in His
eternal Kingdom.

New heaven and
earth, New
Jerusalem.

EPILOGUE
22:5-21

The chiastic structure was not a literary challenge that John undertook to impress his readers—it was given by inspiration in order to help readers understand the meaning of Revelation. As you can see on the diagram, the Book of Revelation has an even number of sections (five in each half). This means that instead of building up to one climax of an overall theme, there are two climaxes, one for the first half of the book and another for the second half. This shows that there are actually two sub-themes within the context of the overall theme of the book.

The climax of the first half is Revelation 13:11-18, which presents the image of the beast, the mark of the beast, the number of the beast and the death decree against those who refuse to submit to the beast. This is the climax of Satan's long war against God's people, so we would expect the theme of the first half of the book to be Satan's efforts to defeat God's people.

The climax of the second half is Revelation 14:1-5, which presents Jesus as the Lamb with His victorious people in heaven. This represents God's ultimate victory over sin and Satan, which is the theme of the second half of the book.

Thus it can be seen that the overall theme of the Book of Revelation is the great controversy between God and Satan (for a detailed explanation of this controversy see chapter 12). The first half of the book is concerned with Satan's attacks on God and His church, both in history and in the future. The second half of the chiasm reveals God's victory over sin, Satan and his followers.

Chronological Organization (Timeline)

One of the controversial aspects of the Book of Revelation is its chronological context and organization. Some of the confusion stems from the fact that certain events, such as the plagues, the judgment and the Second Coming of Christ seem to appear in a number of scattered passages. However, these difficulties can be resolved with the understanding that there are two parallel timelines which give two perspectives on the same events, one on earth and the other in heaven.

Both the "on earth" and the "in heaven" timelines give a basically linear progression that starts at the time of the apostle John and continues until the final eradication of sin and establishment of God's people in His eternal kingdom. The "on earth" timeline is quite detailed and tied to specific dates and events. It is interrupted by the fairly extensive, parallel, "meanwhile in heaven" sections that explain what is happening in heaven while events unfold on earth.

There are also two extensive elaborations that depart from the chronological timelines in order to explain vital background information. The first, found in chapters 12-14, elaborates on the history of the great controversy between good and evil from its beginning when there was "war in heaven" through its conclusion with "the two harvests". The second elaboration in 17:1-19:4 details the characteristics, fall and judgment of Babylon.

The following diagram presents a chronological timeline for the Book of Revelation (see diagram 1.2). This chart will probably not make much sense without reading the detailed explanations in the chapters that follow, so please reserve judgment until you have read the supporting material. Please note that the timeline has two lines, one "on earth" and the other "in heaven". In order to fit it all on a single page it was necessary to break them, so there are four lines on the chart, but the lower two are a continuation of the upper two.

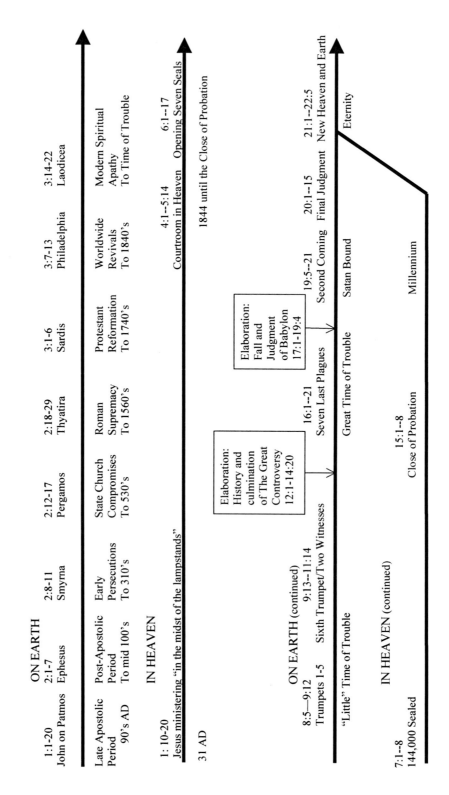

Diagram 1.2

REVELATION TIME LINE

1:4-6 A Message from Jesus

"John to the seven churches which are in Asia: Grace be to you, and peace, from Him who is, and who was, and who is to come; and from the seven Spirits who are before His throne; and from Jesus Christ, who is the faithful witness, and the first begotten of the dead, and the prince of the kings of the earth." (Revelation 1:4,5).

"The Revelation of Jesus Christ" begins by showing who He is. The idea that the one-and-only God is also three persons, the Father, Son and Holy Spirit, was not the philosophical invention of Byzantine theologians; it permeates the Scriptures. The messages "to the seven churches" are from all three persons. "Him who is and who was and who is to come" is the Father,[8] and this title emphasizes His eternal nature. The "seven Spirits" refer to the fullness and completeness of the Holy Spirit, the third person of the Godhead.[9] But the greatest emphasis is upon Jesus. Even though He is fully man, "the first begotten of the dead" and "the prince of the kings of the earth," He is also completely and fully God.

Why does the Book of Revelation especially focus on Jesus? It is He "who loved us, and washed us from our sins in His own blood, and has made us kings and priests to His God and Father" (Revelation 1:6). This is not to say that the Father and the Spirit have any less love for

sinful mankind; "God so loved the world that He gave His only begotten Son" (John 3:16). But Jesus loves us in a unique way: with the unity of the human and the divine. "The Word" existed from eternity with the Father and the Spirit, but 2000 years ago "the Word became flesh and dwelt among us" (John 1:14). Jesus did not cease to be God, but He is forever the "Son of Man," eternally identified with the human race which He died to save.

God the Father, Son and Holy Spirit sent Revelation as a message "to the seven churches." The number seven is used throughout Scripture to represent fullness and completeness, so the message is to the full and complete body of Christ. Many denominations and Christian organizations have tried to limit the church, claiming that they only are the "true church." But God's message in Revelation is unlimited and totally inclusive, directed toward all believers everywhere at all times. "Whoever believes in Him" (John 3:16) has the privilege of being a part of His kingdom; all who accept His offer of forgiveness can be "kings and priests to His God and Father." This is not to say that any of us deserve to be a king or a priest—we are all sinners, no matter what religion or denomination we belong to. But Jesus with "His own blood" took upon Himself the death that we deserve for our sins, giving us hope and assurance that we can be a part of the eternal kingdom forever. "To Him be glory and dominion forever and ever! Amen" (Revelation 1:6).

1:7-9 The Great Controversy

"Behold, He is coming with clouds, and every eye shall see Him, and they also which pierced Him; and all tribes of the earth shall wail because of Him. Even so, Amen" (Revelation 1:7). Verse 7 alludes to what will turn out to be one of the major themes of Revelation. Even though Jesus loves everyone and wants

---

8 Some have assumed that since He "is to come" that this title refers to the Son. However, in the other three texts where this title appears it becomes clear that this is God the Father. In Revelation 1:8, He "who is and who was and who is to come" is called "the Almighty," a title of the Father. Again in Revelation 4:8, before the lamb is introduced, the four living creatures sing "Holy, holy, holy, Lord God Almighty, Who was and is and is to come!" Also in Revelation 11:15-19 it is clear from the context that God the Father, "Lord God Almighty," Whose wrath and judgment has come, Whose temple is opened, is "the One who is and who was and who is to come" (v.17).

9 See chapter 4:5 *Seven Lamps, Seven Spirits.* The seven Spirits of God are also mentioned in Revelation 3:1 and 5:6.

all to become **"kings and priests to His God,"** not everyone accepts His love. There are those **"who pierced Him."**[10] There are the **"tribes of the earth"** who **"shall wail because of Him."** Revelation 6:15 portrays those who cry out to the mountains and the rocks to fall on them and hide them from the face of Jesus when He comes. Chapters 16 and 19 show the "nations" and "kings of the world" arrayed against Him in the Battle of Armageddon. As incredible as it may seem when we consider His infinite goodness and love, Jesus has enemies.

There are two sides in a great controversy that has been raging since "war broke out in heaven" (Revelation 12:7) with the rebellion of Lucifer (see chapter 12). This war is being waged here on planet earth. John himself was caught up in this great controversy, both a victim and a victor: **"I John, your brother, and companion in tribulation, and in the kingdom and patience of Jesus Christ, was on the isle that is called Patmos, for the word of God, and for the testimony of Jesus Christ"** (Revelation 1:9). John was exiled to Patmos[11] (and, according to tradition, he survived being boiled in oil) because he was on God's side of the great controversy.

The resolution of this controversy between God and Satan and the total eradication of sin and evil is the theme of the Book of Revelation. This theme is not just of academic interest; the Book of Revelation presents the world as being divided into two great camps. There are those whose names will be found in the Book of Life and those whose names will not (Revelation 20:15). There are those who are with the Lamb and those who are with the beast (Revelation 14:4,11).

The choice of allegiance is infinitely more important than the choice of what political party to belong to or what sports team to support; and it is a personal choice. No one is a follower of Christ just because they were born into a Christian family or in a Christian society, and no one becomes a Christian just because their parents chose to have them baptized as an infant.

There is no choice that is more important. It is a matter of eternal destiny, with those on the Lamb's side destined for eternal life and those on the beast's side destined for eternal destruction. The Book of Revelation (as well as the rest of the Scriptures) does not present a great unaligned majority who haven't made up their minds—everyone has been infected by sin and is by default on the wrong side of the controversy. But the fearsome scenes as well as the awesome promises presented in Revelation are both a solemn warning and an encouraging reminder that everyone has the privilege of choosing to transfer his allegiance to God's side. We can all be a part of the "new heaven and new earth" (Revelation 21:1).

1:10 The Lord's Day

"I was in the Spirit on the Lord's day, and heard behind me a loud voice, as of a trumpet" (Revelation 1:10). John was **"in the Spirit."** The general biblical meaning of this expression is to be filled with the Holy Spirit—"You are not in the flesh but *in the Spirit*, if indeed the Spirit of God dwells in you" (Romans 8:9). It can refer to the everyday, moment by moment experience of the born again Christian ("walk in the Spirit" Galatians 5:16), but when this expression is used

---

10 1 Thessalonians 4:18 makes it clear that the righteous will arise and see Christ coming. Revelation 20:5 makes it clear that "the rest of the dead" will not be resurrected until the 1000 years (the Millennium) are finished, in other words, the unsaved will not see Christ coming with the clouds. However, this verse shows that there will be exceptions. "Those who pierced Him," in other words, those who had a special part in His death (which could also include those who "pierced Him" by persecuting His children) will have a special resurrection. This is what Jesus meant when He said to Pilate, "hereafter you [Pilate] will see the Son of Man sitting at the right hand of the Power, and coming on the clouds of heaven" (Matthew 26:64).

11 Patmos is a small Greek island in the Aegean Sea just off the coast of Turkey and about 60 miles southwest of Ephesus where John lived (according to tradition) before and after his exile.

in Revelation it refers to John's being carried off in vision, for example, "And he carried me away *in the spirit* to a great and high mountain, and showed me that great city, the holy Jerusalem" (Revelation 21:10, see also Revelation 4:2, 17:3).

John said, **"I was in the Spirit on the Lord's day."** In every other instance of its use in Revelation, the passage specifies where John was carried to **"in the Spirit."** This passage specifies that he was carried in vision to **"the Lord's day"** (*i kuriaki imera*). This particular Greek phrase is unique in the Bible, and although later in the second century[12] it was applied to Sunday,[13] there is no biblical evidence to support this usage. In fact, the day that the Lord Jesus Christ refers to as *His day* is the day of His coming: "For as the lightning that flashes out of one part under heaven shines to the other part under heaven, so also the Son of Man will be in *His day*" (Luke 17:24).[14] Thus **"the Lord's day"** may simply be another way of saying "the Day of the Lord,"[15] which is clearly the day when Jesus comes to rescue His people who have been waiting for Him amidst the persecution and the death decree that will take place during the final crisis.[16]

This interpretation is supported by the fact that John, **"in the Spirit on the Lord's day,"** heard **"a loud voice, as of a trumpet."** The trumpet was used in ancient Israel to call God's people to attention when a great event or threat was at hand, and it is particularly associated with the Day of the Lord: "Blow the trumpet in Zion, and sound an alarm in My holy mountain! For the *Day of the Lord* is coming, for it is at hand" (Joel 2:1, see also Zephaniah 1:14-16, 1 Thessalonians 4:16). The primary focus of Revelation is "the Lord's day"—the "Day of the Lord"—when God steps in to take control of human affairs.

1:10,11 Messages to the Seven Churches

John heard the message before He saw the messenger. **"I heard behind me a loud voice, as of a trumpet, saying, 'I am Alpha and Omega, the first and the last,' and, 'What you see, write in a book, and send it to the seven churches which are in Asia: to Ephesus, and to Smyrna, and to Pergamos, and to Thyatira, and to Sardis, and to Philadelphia, and to Laodicea.'** (Revelation 1:10,11).

---

12 The first clear application of the Greek word *kuriaki* to Sunday is in the apocryphal *Gospel of Peter*, written in the second half of the second century.

13 In the New Testament, Sunday is consistently referred to as *the first day of the week*, even in the Gospel of John which was written by the same author at about the same time (eg. John 20:1).

14 Some commentators have suggested that the Lord's day is the Sabbath. This view also has valid scriptural support. Jesus said, "the Son of Man is Lord even of the Sabbath" (Matthew 12:8). Likewise Isaiah 58:13 says "Call the Sabbath a delight, the holy *day of the Lord*." At any rate, there is no biblical support for the idea that the Lord's day is Sunday. This theory finds its support in church tradition, which was heavily influenced by the need of second century Christian to distance themselves from the Jews and "their" Sabbath because of persecution of the Jews by the Romans. For a thorough discussion of this subject see "From Sabbath to Sunday" by Samuele Bacchiocchi, Pontifical Gregorian University Press (available from Biblical Perspectives, Berrien Springs, MI).

15 "I will pour out My Spirit in those days. And I will show wonders in the heavens and in the earth: Blood and fire and pillars of smoke. The sun shall be turned into darkness, and the moon into blood, before the coming of the great and awesome *day of the Lord* and it shall come to pass that whoever calls on the name of the Lord shall be saved" (Joel 2:29-32). "But the *day of the Lord* will come as a thief in the night, in which the heavens will pass away with a great noise, and the elements will melt with fervent heat (2 Peter 3:10. See also Isaiah 2:10-21, Joel 2:1, 10,11, Zephaniah 1:14-17, Malachi 4:5, 1 Thessalonians 5:2-4).

16 See Chapters 13 and 14 for an explanation of the persecutions and death decree.

The messages to **"the seven churches"** are important on three levels. First of all, they were specific messages to specific churches that existed at the time of John in Asia Minor. It is important to understand the messages, as much as possible, in terms of the understanding of the first-century Christians they were addressed to.

Secondly, the messages have an application to all Christians in every era who face similar problems and challenges. The problem of Christians losing their first love (Revelation 2:4) or being luke-warm in their devotion to God (Revelation 3:16) are not unique to the first century. The church has had to face persecution (Revelation 2:10) and internal heresy (Revelation 2:13,20) at many times in her history. Thus there is a universal application, and the messages are relevant to all Christians everywhere.

Finally, many commentators have seen in the messages to the seven churches a prophesy of what will happen to the Christian church from the time of John until the end of time. There is valid scriptural support for this position,[17] reflected in Jesus' instruction to John, **"Write the things which you have seen, and the things which are, and the things which shall be hereafter"** (Revelation 1:19). Keeping this in mind, a comparison of the messages to the seven churches (as presented in chapters 2 and 3) with the history of the Christian church from the time of the Apostles to the present shows a remarkable correlation that is convincing evidence that God indeed knows "the end from the beginning" (Isaiah 46:10). When we realize that God knew and predicted the history of the world before it took place,[18] we can also be sure that He already knows about our present and future situation, and His promises to bless and save His followers are sure.[19]

1:12-15 Jesus Among the Lampstands

"And I turned to see the voice that spoke with me. And being turned, I saw seven golden lampstands; and in the midst of the seven lampstands One like the Son of man, clothed with a garment down to the feet, and girded about the chest with a golden sash. His head and His hair were white like wool, as white as snow; and His eyes were as a flame of fire. And His feet were like fine brass, as if they burned in a furnace; and His voice was as the sound of many waters" (Revelation 1:12-15).

Jesus, the majestic Son of Man, is portrayed **"in the midst of the seven golden lampstands"** (Revelation 1:12),[20] which symbolize **"the seven churches"** (Revelation 1:20). He is dressed in **"a garment down to the feet"** (Greek *potheres*)

---

17 The fact that there are seven churches implies a message to the fullness of God's church, not only in all places but for all time. Series of seven consistently have a prophetic application in Revelation, speaking of events future to the time of John (for example, the seven seals, trumpets, thunders and plagues are all prophetic). Moreover, the seven churches that the messages were addressed to were not the only churches in Asia, or even the ones closest to where John was on the island of Patmos (Troas, Miletus and Colossae are three that are specifically mentioned in the New Testament). This implies that they were chosen for their symbolic representation of a larger theme (such as a historical period).

We would expect that the Book of Revelation would follow the pattern in the book of Daniel, the Old Testament book most similar to Revelation, in which each vision begins with a survey of history followed by a focus on the end of time. According to this pattern, the messages to the seven churches would be a survey of history. For a more thorough analysis see chapter two where the messages are evaluated.

---

18 Isaiah 46:9,10

19 Daniel's first historical survey, for example, was the metal image of chapter 2. He identifies the world empires that will arise through history, but the central message is that at these empires will come to an end and "the God of heaven will set up a kingdom which shall never be destroyed" (Daniel 2:44).

20 Again the inseparability of the Father and the Son is shown by the fact that "the Son of Man" (Jesus) announces that He is "the first and the last" (verse 11). But in the Old Testament the title "the first and the last" is clearly applied to God— "I am the first and I am the last; besides Me there is no God" (Isaiah 44:6).

which is the same Greek word[21] used for the garments worn by the high priest as he ministered in the ancient Hebrew sanctuary (Exodus 28:31-35, 39:22-26). This amazing picture shows the depth of Jesus' love—**"in the midst"** indicates the most intimate relationship. Jesus is by nature "holy, harmless, undefiled, separate from sinners...higher than the heavens" (Hebrews 7:26), and yet He is pictured as High Priest in the very midst of the polluted church. Some of the largest Christian denominations teach that the church, being the body of Christ, is perfect and cannot err.[22] But the Book of Revelation does not depict the church as perfect, but to the contrary, as defective and defiled. This is the church that has lost her first love (Revelation 2:4), holds false doctrines (Revelation 2:14,15), tolerates Jezebel and her immorality (Revelation 2:20), is spiritually dead (Revelation 3:1), and disgustingly self-satisfied (Revelation 3:16,17).

But despite her pollution, Jesus is willing to leave the holy atmosphere of heaven and minister **"in the midst"** of her! In His earthly incarnation Jesus never separated Himself from sinful humanity and He still doesn't. We can "come boldly to the throne of grace, that we may obtain mercy and find grace to help in time of need" (Hebrews 4:16). It is never necessary to "clean up our act" before we come to Jesus; in fact, only He can make us clean.

When we come to Jesus He transforms us into the **"lampstand"** that we were intended to be. **"The seven lampstands which you saw are the seven churches"** (Revelation 1:20). A lampstand has no other function than to hold a lamp. Jesus is the lamp, the "light of the world" (John 9:5), but the world can only see Jesus if we, His church lift Him up and reveal Him. This is why Satan attacks the church so ruthlessly, as we will see in the messages to the seven churches.

1: 16-20 Jesus, Our Awesome High Priest

"He had in His right hand seven stars, and out of His mouth went a sharp two edged sword, and His countenance was as the sun shines in his strength. And when I saw Him, I fell at His feet as dead. And He laid his right hand on me, saying to me, 'Fear not; I am the first and the last: I am He that lives, and was dead; and behold, I am alive forever more, Amen; and I have the keys of Hades and of death" (Revelation 1:16-18).

Although John was so overwhelmed by the vision of Jesus in His glory that he **"fell at His feet as dead,"** he was able to remember some of the details of His appearance. John noticed that Jesus had seven stars in His hand. An angel explained that **"the mystery of the seven stars which you saw in My right hand...the seven stars are the angels of the seven churches"** (Revelation 1:20). Although the Greek word for angel (*aggelo*) is often used for heavenly beings, the basic meaning is "messenger, one who is sent" and can also refer to a person who has a message from God. This is obviously the meaning here, because in chapters two and three John is commanded to write

21 Although the Old Testament was written in Hebrew, the Septuagint is a version of the Old Testament which was compiled by Greek scholars in Alexandria more than a hundred years before Christ. Despite its inaccuracies, it allows some comparison of New Testament words (such as in Revelation) with their Old Testament equivalents.

22 For example, the Orthodox Church teaches, "Christ and the Holy Spirit cannot err, and since the church is Christ's body, since it is a continued Pentecost, it is therefore infallible...In the words of Dositheus: 'We believe the catholic church to be taught by the Holy Spirit...and therefore we both believe and profess as true and undoubtedly certain, that it is impossible for the catholic church to err, or to be at all deceived, or ever to choose falsehood instead of truth." Timothy Ware, *The Orthodox Church* (New York, NY Penguin Books, 1997), p. 248. Also the Roman Catholic Church teaches, "As the Divinely appointed teacher of revealed truth, the church is infallible...in matters of both faith and morals." George Joyce, "The Church." *The Catholic Encyclopedia* http://www.newadvent.org/cathen/03744a.htm, accessed June 26, 2014

"To the angel of the church of (Ephesus, Smyrna, etc.)." John was not addressing his letters to heavenly beings, but to the earthly "angels" (elders) of the churches who had the responsibility of bringing God's messages to the church members.

The messages to the seven churches which are given in Revelation chapters two and three show that God's people would pass through fearsome times of trial, temptation, persecution and often failure. But even though His people have often stumbled, they have not been defeated, because they are following their leader the Lord Jesus Christ, who symbolically represents himself in these verses as the ultimate victor—**"out of his mouth went a sharp two-edged sword"** (Revelation 1:16).

We see this symbol of a sword in the mouth of Jesus again in chapter 19. There Jesus is portrayed at His Second Coming as a heavenly warrior riding a white horse, and "out of His mouth goes a sharp sword, that with it He should smite the nations; and He shall *rule them with a rod of iron*" (Revelation 19:15). This image, taken from Psalm 2, emphasizes His complete and permanent victory over His enemies. Jesus here in the opening scene of His revelation of Himself assures His church, which will face nearly two thousand years of trials and sometimes deadly persecution, that ultimately there will be victory and deliverance. John, who was suffering on an island prison, along with all of Christ's followers throughout the ages who have been oppressed and who sometimes felt abandoned are reassured, **"Fear not; I am the first and the last. I am He that lives, and was dead; and, behold, I am alive forever more, Amen; and I have the keys of Hades and of death"** (Revelation 1:17,18). Persecution, ridicule and defeat will not last forever, and the prison of death will be opened by the one who is **"alive forevermore"** and holds **"the keys."**

When John saw the face of Jesus in all its glory he **"fell at His feet as dead"** (Revelation 1:17).

This is the same reaction that other great men of God had when they saw Jesus in His heavenly glory.[23] Mortal, sinful man cannot look upon Jesus in the fullness of His divine glory and holiness unless He supernaturally imparts strength to endure the sight. Jesus **"laid his right hand on [John], saying to [him], 'Fear not"** (Revelation 1:17), and John was strengthened and was able to witness the greatest revelation of God, heaven, Jesus and His kingdom that had ever been seen by anyone.

Someday we too will see God as He is, but if we saw His glory and holiness now we would be so overwhelmed that His presence would be fatal. God in His mercy has "veiled" himself from sinful humanity, revealing Himself to us through His Word and through Jesus, who took upon Himself humanity so that we could bear to see God. But the day is coming when **"every eye will see Him"** (Revelation 1:7), the day "when the Lord Jesus is revealed from heaven with His mighty angels in flaming fire" (2 Thessalonians 1:8).

That will be a terrifying day for those who have comforted themselves with the thought that they can ignore Jesus, live their lives as they please, or even worse, mock God and His followers. With the stresses of the final crisis they could unwittingly end up fighting against God; John saw those who had persistently rejected God crying out "to the mountains and the rocks, 'fall on us, and hide us from the face of Him who sits on the throne'" (Revelation 6:16).

On the other hand, those who have been seeking Him with all their hearts will know Him through His Spirit living in them and will rejoice to see Him coming. "And it will be said in that day: 'Behold this is our God; we have waited for Him, and He will save us; we will be glad and

---

23 See for example Daniel 8:18, 10:8-19, Isaiah 6:1-5, Ezekiel 1:1-28, 3:14,15.

rejoice in His salvation" (Isaiah 25:9).

The Book of Revelation is the story of how God is preparing the world for the full revelation of His glory. "But truly, as I live, all the earth shall be filled with the glory of the Lord" (Numbers 14:21). **"Behold, He is coming with clouds, and every eye shall see Him"** (Revelation 1:7). God is doing everything He can now to prepare us for that day.

The rapid fulfillment of the prophecies found in the Book of Revelation indicate that "the Day of the Lord" is near; we are about to witness events more awesome than any that have ever happened, events that we could not imagine if they were not revealed to us in the symbolism of the Revelation of Jesus Christ. The messages of Revelation have been given so that we can be ready. **"Blessed is he that reads, and they that hear the words of this prophecy, and keep those things which are written therein, for the time is at hand"** (Revelation 1:3).

"Do not fear any of those things which you are about to suffer." Revelation 2:10
Woodcut by Albrecht Durer 1498

Chapter 2

Revelation 2:1-29

2:1 "To the angel of the church of Ephesus write: These things said He that holds the seven stars in His right hand, who walks in the midst of the seven golden lampstands:

2:2 I know your works, and your labor, and your patience, and how you cannot bear those who are evil, and you have tested them who say they are apostles, and are not, and have found them liars;

2:3 And have borne, and have patience, and for my name's sake have labored, and have not fainted.

2:4 Nevertheless I have somewhat against you, because you have left your first love.

2:5 Remember therefore from where you are fallen, and repent, and do the first works; or else I will come to you quickly, and will remove your candlestick out of its place, unless you repent.

2:6 But this you have, that you hate the deeds of the Nicolaitans, which I also hate.

2:7 He that has an ear, let him hear what the Spirit said to the churches; To him that overcomes will I give to eat of the tree of life, which is in the midst of the paradise of God.

2:8 "And to the angel of the church in Smyrna write: These things said the First and the Last, who was dead, and is alive:

2:9 I know your works, and tribulation, and poverty (but you are rich), and I know the blasphemy of those who say they are Jews, and are not, but are the synagogue of Satan.

2:10 Fear none of those things which you shall suffer. Behold, the devil shall cast some of you into prison, that you may be tested; and you shall have tribulation ten days. Be faithful to death, and I will give you a crown of life.

2:11 He that has an ear, let him hear what the Spirit said to the churches; He that overcomes shall not be hurt by the second death.

2:12 "And to the angel of the church in Pergamos write: These things said He which has the sharp sword with two edges:

2:13 I know your works, and where you dwell, even where Satan's seat is; and you hold fast My name, and have not denied My faith, even in those days wherein Antipas was my faithful martyr, who was slain among you, where Satan dwells.

2:14 But I have a few things against you, because you have there those who hold the doctrine of Balaam, who taught Balak to cast a stumbling block before the children of Israel, to eat things sacrificed to idols, and to commit fornication.

2:15 So you have also those who hold the doctrine of the Nicolaitans, which I hate.

2:16 Repent; or else I will come to you quickly, and will fight against them with the sword of my mouth.

2:17 He that has an ear, let him hear what the Spirit said to the churches; To him that overcomes will I give to eat of the hidden manna, and will give him a white stone, and on the stone a new name written, which no man knows except he that receives it.

2:18 "And to the angel of the church in Thyatira write: These things said the Son of God, who has His eyes like a flame of fire, and His feet are like fine brass:

2:19 I know your works, and love, and service, and faith, and your patience, and your works; and the last are more than the first.

2:20 Notwithstanding I have a few things against you, because you allow that woman Jezebel, who calls herself a prophetess, to teach and to seduce My servants to commit fornication, and to eat things sacrificed to idols.

2:21 And I gave her space to repent of her fornication; and she did not repent.

2:22 Behold, I will cast her into a bed, and those that commit adultery with her into great tribulation, unless they repent of their deeds.

2:23 And I will kill her children with death, and all the churches shall know that I am He who searches the minds and hearts; and I will give to every one of you according to your works.

2:24 But to you I say, and to the rest in Thyatira, as many as do not have this doctrine, and which have not known the depths of Satan, as they call them, I will put on you no other burden;

2:25 But that which you have already, hold fast till I come.

2:26 And he that overcomes, and keeps my works to the end, to him I will give authority over the nations.

2:27 And he shall rule them with a rod of iron; like the vessels of a potter they shall be broken to pieces, even as I received of My Father.

2:28 And I will give him the morning star.

2:29 He that has an ear, let him hear what the Spirit said to the churches."

To the Seven Churches

"He [God] put all things under His [Christ's] feet, and gave Him to be head over all things to the church, which is His body, the fullness of Him who fills all in all" (Ephesians 1:22,23). "The Revelation of Jesus Christ" tells the story of His body on earth, the church of God, as it has faced the challenges of a world filled with sin while being relentlessly attacked by Satan and his followers.

Revelation chapters two and three consist of messages "to the seven churches which are in Asia" (Revelation 1:4).[24] Are these messages primarily intended for the first-century churches they were addressed to, as preterest theologians claim? This would limit their value to us, because although there is some historical information about the cities where the churches were located, there is essentially no information about the churches themselves.[25] Moreover, there are serious problems inherent in the preterest view[26] which underscores the need for a more universal approach.

As we saw in chapter one, the context of the introduction to the messages to the seven churches emphasizes universality. Jesus is portrayed as the great High Priest in the heavenly sanctuary, walking among seven lampstands. Jesus explained, "the seven lampstands which you saw are the seven churches" (Revelation 1:29). Jesus is in the midst of the universal church, in all places and at all times. Likewise, He had in His hand seven stars, which are "the angels of the seven churches." Again, seven is a number used to represent fullness and completeness. Jesus in His priestly ministry has the angels of the whole church in His hand, not just of seven first-century churches in Asia Minor.

The Book of Revelation is most like the Old Testament book of Daniel. Each of the four major visions in Daniel begins at the time of the prophet and then gives an overview of history extending to and focusing on the events of the last days (See

---

24 The number seven is repeatedly and consistently used in Revelation to signify fullness and completion. For example, in Revelation 15:1 "I saw another sign...seven angels having the seven last plagues, for in them is filled up the wrath of God."

25 Much has been written about the ancient cities where the seven churches were located. Although there is quite a bit of historical information about these *cities*, we have essentially no information about the actual *churches* in Asia at the time Revelation was written. Some theologians have assumed that characteristics of the cities would apply to some extent to the churches, and have made assumptions about them based upon this. But these kinds of speculations would be analogous to assuming that since Las Vegas is the city of gambling, the church of Las Vegas must have a gambling problem. Obviously, members of the Las Vegas church would be upset if assumptions were made about them based upon the characteristics of their city!

Likewise, while trying to find the meaning the messages had to the first-century Christians they were written to, it is not particularly helpful to speculate about the characteristics of their churches based on the scanty information in Revelation combined with historical information (often unreliable) about the cities. It is more helpful to try to determine how the original readers in these churches would have interpreted messages that applied primarily to the universal church.

---

26 Many theologians teach that we should find the meaning of a Bible text by determining what it meant to the people it was written for. Preterist interpreters go farther and insist that the chronological context of Revelation is around the time it was written, citing texts like Revelation 1:1,3 "The Revelation of Jesus Christ which God gave to Him to show His servants things which must shortly come to pass." When evaluating this text it is important to keep in mind that the God of eternity does not view "shortly" the same way that we do (see 5:7,8 *Then He Came—When?*). The preterist view cannot be harmonized with such obviously end-time themes as the mark of the beast, the Second Coming of Christ and the Millennium. A more helpful principle is that Revelation uses language and symbols which had meaning for first-century Christians, but the messages rarely have their primary application in that time period.

There are verses in the messages to the seven churches that are difficult to place in a first-century context. For example, the church of Philadelphia was promised, "Because you have kept My command to persevere, I also will keep you from the hour of trial which shall come upon the whole world, to test those who dwell on the earth" (Revelation 3:10). This reference to the great time of trouble obviously did not take place in the first century.

1: *Historicist Model of Interpretation*).[27] With this model in mind, we would expect that Revelation would also begin by reviewing the span of history from the time it was written at the end of the first century until the time of the end. It is amazing to see how the messages to the seven churches have accurately predicted what would happen to God's people through the ages. [28]

Some readers may be frustrated by what seems to be an inordinate focus on history in chapters two and three. But keep in mind that God has a purpose in focusing on history, as the Apostle Paul stated: "All these things happened to them as examples, and they were written for our admonition, upon whom the end of the ages have come" (1Corinthians 10:11). Edmund Burke put it another way: "Those who do not learn from history are destined to repeat it."

---

27 In Daniel 2, the multi-metal image shows the progression of world empires culminating in the setting up of God's kingdom. In chapter 7, the four beasts and the little horn again show the progression of empires and the attack on God's people and his law, culminating in the day of judgment. In chapter 8 and 9, the ram, goat and little horn again depict the political powers from the time of Daniel but focus on the attack on Christ's ministry in the heavenly sanctuary culminating in the cleansing of the sanctuary. Chapters 10-12 detail the long war between the King of the North and the King of the South and the setting up of the abomination of desolation, culminating in the great time of trouble and deliverance of God's people.

28 It is the belief of this author that the events of history that would be important enough to be mentioned in a universal book such as Revelation would not be obscure details but rather the major critical events which would be found in any good encyclopedia or history of Christianity. The classic "The History of the Christian Church" by Williston Walker (New York, NY, C. Scribner, 1918, reprint available from Amazon.com) has been quoted from extensively in this book, but any standard, objective history will give the same basic information. Wikipedia.com has also been used repeatedly, not because of its authority but because of its availability so that readers can do further research. And the Catholic Encyclopedia has been used extensively because of its exhaustive scholarship from a Roman Catholic perspective and its availability online (newadvent. org/cathen/).

Ephesus
2:1-5 First Love

"To the angel of the church of Ephesus write: These things said He that holds the seven stars in His right hand, who walks in the midst of the seven golden lampstands: I know your works, and your labor, and your patience, and how you cannot bear those who are evil, and you have tested them who say they are apostles, and are not, and have found them liars; And have borne, and have patience, and for my name's sake have labored, and have not fainted" (Revelation 2:1-3).

At first glance the church of Ephesus looks pretty good. They are doing good works, laboring to spread the gospel, patiently enduring trials, and maintaining the purity of the church, protecting it from evil liars and false apostles, and all this with perseverance, not growing weary. Jesus commends them for this.

But something essential is missing that spoils all of their good works. **"Nevertheless I have somewhat against you, because you have left your first love"** (Revelation 2:4). This lack of love is not a minor issue; it is so serious that Jesus warns, **"Remember therefore from where you are fallen, and repent, and do the first works; or else I will come to you quickly, and will remove your candlestick out of its place, unless you repent"** (Revelation 2:5). The Ephesian Christians are in danger of losing their salvation because of a lack of love.

The first-love experience of the early church is described in the first chapters of the book of Acts. The early Christians loved God with all their hearts, and this resulted in love for their neighbors. The disciples "were all with one accord in one place," continuing "with one accord in prayer and supplication" (Acts 1:14, 2:1). "All who believed were together, and had all things in common" (Acts 2:44). They had continuous fellowship with one another and took care of each others' needs.[29]

But as the years passed and most of these early Christians died, including the apostles, the church began to struggle with the issue of love. John, the last of the apostles, wrote his epistles to the church shortly before he wrote the Book of Revelation (around AD 95), apparently while living at Ephesus. It seems that the problem of lack of love was serious, because one of his major themes is the need for love—just one of many examples is his thought-provoking statement, "Let us love one another...He who does not love does not know God, for God is love" (1 John 4:7,8).[30] With few records, it is impossible to know in detail the conditions of the church from the time of John's writing of Revelation into the second century, the time period represented by the message to the church of Ephesus. However, there is one love problem that is apparent from the few writings that remain: the developing hatred of the Jews by the church.

On a human level this hatred is understandable. It was the Jews who conspired with the Romans to murder Christ. The Jews carried out the first persecutions (Acts 8) and hounded the apostles, particularly Paul, who was driven from city to city by Jews who were jealous of his ministry and zealous for their traditions.[31] However, following the teaching of Jesus to love our enemies and do good to those who hate us (Matthew 5:44), Paul could honestly say, "I have great sorrow and continual grief in my heart...for my brethren, my countrymen according to the flesh, who are Israelites...Brethren, my heart's desire and prayer to God for Israel is that they may be saved" (Romans 9:1-4, 10:1).

What a contrast with the attitude of prominent Christian writers during the "Ephesus" era of the early second century! According to the so-called epistle of Barnabas, probably written in the AD 130's, "The Jews are 'wretched men' who were deluded by an evil angel and who 'were abandoned by God' because of their ancient idolatry."[32] Likewise Justin Martyr, a Christian philosopher who wrote during the first half of the second century, asserted that "the Jews are a ruthless, stupid, blind, and lame people, children in whom there is not faith." In a dialogue with Trypho, a Jew, he asserted that "the custom of circumcising the flesh, handed down from Abraham, was given to you as a distinguishing mark, to set you off from other nations and from us Christians. The purpose of this was that you and only you might suffer the afflictions that are now justly yours; that only your land be desolated, and your cities ruined by fire, that the fruits of your land be eaten by strangers before your very eyes...it was by reason of your sins and the sins of your fathers that, among other precepts, God imposed upon you the observance of the Sabbath as a mark."[33] This hatred of the Jews and

---

29 "Continuing daily with one accord in the temple, and breaking bread from house to house, they ate their food with gladness and simplicity of heart" (Acts 2:46). "Nor was there anyone among them who lacked; for all who were possessors of lands or houses sold them, and brought the proceeds of the things that were sold... and they distributed to each as anyone had need" (Acts 4:34,35).

30 The need for love is the central theme of the first epistle of John: "In this the children of God and the children of the devil are manifest: whoever does not practice righteousness is not of God, nor is he who does not love his brother...he who does not love his brother abides in death...By this we know love, because He laid down His life for us, and we also ought to lay down our lives for the brethren. But whoever has this world's goods, and sees his brother in need, and shuts up his heart from him, how does the love of God abide in him? My little children, let us not love in word or in tongue, but in deed and in truth...beloved, let us love one another, for love is of God, and everyone who loves is born of God and knows God. He who does not love does not know God, for God is love" (1 John 3:10-4:12).

31 Acts 13:45, 50, 14:2, 19, 17:5, 13, 18:12, 21:27, 23:12.

32 These statements are quoted in Samuele Bacchiocchi, *From Sabbath to Sunday*, (Rome, Pontifical Gregorian University Press, 1977) p. 219.

33 *Ibid.*, pp. 226-228.

the desire of Christians to distinguish themselves from them led to serious doctrinal errors,[34] and has been a blight and a disgrace on the Christian Church right up to the present time.[35]

2:2,6 False Apostles and Nicolaitans

"You have tested them who say they are apostles and are not, and have found them liars...But this you have, that you hate the deeds of the Nicolaitans, which I also hate" (Revelation 2:2,6). The Ephesus period saw the beginnings of some of the heresies that would later be accepted by the church—the doctrines of the "false apostles" and the **"Nicolaitans."** Paul

warned, "After my departure savage wolves will come in among you, not sparing the flock. Also from among yourselves men will rise up, speaking perverse things, to draw away the disciples after themselves" (Acts 20:29,30). "The mystery of lawlessness is already at work" (2 Thessalonians 2:7). The Apostle John warned, "Even now many antichrists have come, by which we know that it is the last hour" (1 John 2:18).

Although the apostles predicted apostasy in the church, we see that in general the church of the Ephesus period rejected the messages of the false apostles—**"You have found them liars."** The seeds of the false doctrines would spring up later in the heresies of the synagogue of Satan (2:9), the throne of Satan (2:13), the Nicolaitans (2:15), the doctrine of Balaam (2:14) and Jezebel (2:20). But during the Ephesus period the church was successfully struggling to maintain moral and doctrinal purity—**"But this you have, that you hate the deeds of the Nicolaitans, which I also hate"** (Revelation 2:6).

What were the **"deeds of the Nicolaitans"** that the false apostles were promoting? Irenaeus, a second-century theologian, asserted that the Nicolaitans considered it irrelevant if Christians committed adultery or ate foods which had been offered to idols since it was the soul and spirit that were important, not the deeds of the body.[36] This is supported by the description in the book of Jude of the heresies which were developing during the last part of the first century: "Certain men have crept in unnoticed...who turn the grace of our God into lewdness...these dreamers defile the flesh, reject authority, and speak evil of dignitaries...these are sensual persons, who cause divisions, not having the Spirit" (Jude 4,8,19). Peter also predicted that "there will be

---

34 For example, from early times there have been attempts to characterize the Ten Commandment law as a "Jewish" institution which does not apply to Christians. The rejecting of the validity of the Ten Commandments has led in turn to the acceptance of the worship of idols and icons, which is forbidden by the second commandment and the change of the Sabbath to Sunday, a violation of the fourth commandment. As will be brought out later, the Sabbath itself was an obvious commonality with the Jews that caused Christians to be identified with them, so that the hatred-inspired desire to differentiate themselves from the Jews and "their Sabbath" was a strong motivation to reject the validity of the whole law. While it is true that our salvation is based on Christ's perfect life and sacrifice for sinners and that no one will be saved by keeping the commandments, it is also true that "He who says 'I know Him' and does not keep His commandments is a liar, and the truth is not in him" (1 John 2:4). See Bacchiocchi, *From Sabbath to Sunday* for a more detailed analysis.

35 The first ecumenical council of the Christian church at Nicea (AD 325) codified contempt of the Jews in the decision to adjust the date of Easter so that it would never coincide with the Passover of the Jews. The emperor Constantine summed up the attitude, "It appeared an unworthy thing that in the celebration of this most holy feast we should follow the practice of the Jews, who have impiously defiled their hands with enormous sin, and are, therefore, deservedly afflicted with blindness of soul...Let us then have nothing in common with the detestable Jewish crowd...who are our adversaries" Wikipedia contributors, "Constantine the Great and Judaism," *Wikipedia, The Free Encyclopedia*, http://en.wikipedia.org/w/index.php?title=Constantine_the_Great_and_Judaism&oldid=612077553 (accessed June 25, 2014). Persecution of the Jews through the centuries up to the holocaust has been tolerated or even approved by the church on the basis that "it was the Jews who killed Jesus."

36 Wikipedia contributors, "Nicolaism," *Wikipedia, The Free Encyclopedia*, http://en.wikipedia.org/w/index.php?title=Nicolaism&oldid=607624752 (accessed June 26, 2014).

false teachers among you who will secretly bring in destructive heresies…who walk according to the flesh in the lust of uncleanness and despise authority…having eyes full of adultery and that cannot cease from sin, enticing unstable souls… for when they speak great swelling words of emptiness, they allure through the lusts of the flesh, through lewdness, the ones who have actually escaped from those who live in error. While they promise them liberty, they themselves are slaves of corruption" (2Peter 2:1,10,14,18,19).

A picture emerges of false apostles and prophets who teach that behavior doesn't matter, who offer a deceptive promise of liberty expressed through "great swelling words of emptiness." Gnosticism was such a religion that posed a serious threat to Christianity during this period. Based on Babylonian and Persian magic, Greek philosophy and borrowing from the "mystery" religions,[37] it transformed itself into a number of forms of "Christianity," some of which included gross immorality. During the Ephesus period these ideas were circulating widely, but the church as a whole was still rejecting them—**"you hate the deeds of the Nicolaitans."** Unfortunately, by the time of the church of Pergamos the **"doctrine of the Nicolaitans"** had invaded the church in a surprising way (see 2:14: *Nicolaitans*).

The messages to the seven churches, with a few bright exceptions, is a story of a downward spiral of compromise, heresy and defeat, with repeated calls to repent, or at least to hold onto what they still had. It is true that the church is the body of Christ, and "Christ also loved the church, and gave Himself for her" (Ephesians 5:25). But the reality in this world is that the church has an enemy, Satan, who works vigilantly, "secretly

bringing in destructive heresies" (2 Peter 2:1).

"To him that overcomes will I give to eat of the tree of life, which is in the midst of the paradise of God" (Revelation 2:7). The great hope in the messages to the churches is for those believers who accept the victory God has promised them. "Thanks be to God, who gives us the victory through our Lord Jesus Christ" (1Corinthians 15:57). Despite the pressures of life and of the enemy we can be overcomers because victory, just like faith, grace and forgiveness, is a gift of God that we can claim. **"To him that overcomes"** one of the most beautiful promises of scripture is given, access to **"the tree of life, which is in the midst of the Paradise of God."** This is full restoration to the original state of perfection that Adam and Eve enjoyed in the Garden of Eden, where we will have intimate and eternal communion with our Creator.

Smyrna
2:8,9 Tribulation, Poverty, Synagogue of Satan

"And to the angel of the church in Smyrna write: These things said the First and the Last, who was dead, and is alive: I know your works, and tribulation, and poverty (but you are rich), and I know the blasphemy of those who say they are Jews, and are not, but are the synagogue of Satan." (Revelation 2:8,9).

The early church grew rapidly during the second and third centuries. In contrast to other religions of the era, it was not an elitist body with mysterious rituals open only to the rich and powerful. Within the church everyone was equal, even slaves, so the poor and disenfranchised

---

37 The most popular of the Oriental religions of the time included the Great Mother, which originated in Asia Minor, Isis and Serapis from Egypt, and Mithras from Persia. Elements of these were mixed in a multitude of forms.

flocked into the church.[38] This apparent weakness and poverty was actually their source of strength (**"but you are rich!"**). Lacking social and political power, they relied upon God and He blessed them with spiritual power.

Jesus recognized the positive in the church of Smyrna, but even here it is obvious that there had been a deterioration compared with the Ephesus period. Ephesus was commended for **"your works, your labor, your patience, that you cannot bear those who are evil,"** for testing false apostles, and for hating the deeds of the Nicolaitans. The church of Smyrna has a much shorter list: **"Your works, and tribulation and poverty."**

As the church grew, Christians faced continuous persecution (**"I know your...tribulation"**), some of it from the Romans, but much of it from the Jews, which resulted in the mutual hatred between Christians and Jews that developed during the Ephesus period.[39] Despite these bad relationships, Jesus did not condemn the Jews, but rather those **"who say they are Jews and are not."** The apostle Paul clarifies this thought in Romans 2: "For he is not a Jew who is one outwardly, nor is circumcision that which is outward in the flesh; but he is a Jew who is one inwardly; and circumcision is that of the heart" (Romans 2:28,29). In other words, born again, Spirit-led Christians are the true Jews. These are contrasted with "you who are called a Jew" who

"boast in God,...know His will, being instructed out of the law," who "boast in the law" but "dishonor God through breaking the law" (vs. 17-23). Of these false Jews he concludes that "the name of God is blasphemed among the Gentiles because of you" (v.24).

Paul's words condemning legalism, hypocrisy and law-breaking are mirrored in the message to Smyrna. Jesus says, **"I know the blasphemy of those who say they are Jews and are not, but are a synagogue of Satan."** By the time of the Smyrna period (mid second through early third centuries) the church was dividing into two categories: those who were **"rich"** in faith (despite their **"tribulation and poverty"**) and those who were a **"synagogue of Satan."** The synagogue was the Jewish "church" where the Jews met for instruction in the laws and traditions of Moses. During the Smyrna era some of the church leaders (**"those who say they are Jews and are not"**) were attempting to create a new "Christian" synagogue; in other words, a church with a focus on laws and traditions rather than on Jesus and the Spirit.

The great curse of the church has never been those outside; it is those inside, who call themselves Christians but are not. Lacking a living relationship with Jesus, they substitute legalism and pressure to conform to the church's standards. The law of God has an important role in the Christian life, "for by the law is the knowledge of sin" (Romans 3:20); "the law was our tutor to bring us to Christ" (Galatians 3:24). However, no one will ever be declared righteous or worthy of eternal life because he faithfully kept the law or the traditions of the church.

The key concept of the gospel is that it is "by grace you have been saved through faith, and that not of yourselves, it is the gift of God" (Ephesians 2:8). Paul condemned legalism in the book of Galatians: "We have believed in Christ Jesus, that we might be justified by faith in Christ

---

38 "For you see your calling, brethren, that not many wise according to the flesh, not many mighty, not many noble, are called" (1Corinthians 1:26).

39 The first persecution of Christians was by the Jews after the stoning of Stephen (Acts 8), and the first persecution by the Romans, during the reign of Nero in AD 64, was incited by the Jews who suggested to him that he blame the Christians for the burning of Rome. Around AD 80 the Jews started to include a curse upon Christians in their daily prayers in the synagogues, and this was used as a test to detect covert Christians in their communities, who were then persecuted. The book "Sabbath to Sunday" by Samuele Bacchiocchi details the antagonistic relationship between the early Christians and the Jews.

and not by the works of the law; for by the works of the law no flesh shall be justified" (Galatians 2:16). But the false teachers "set aside the grace of God" (v.21), trying to substitute rituals, ceremonies and rigorous dietary restrictions, long vigils, pilgrimages and detailed rules and laws instead of a life led by the Spirit.

These false brethren are called **"a synagogue of Satan."** During the second and third centuries the church waged a fierce battle against the Gnostics, who claimed that secret spiritual knowledge, imparted to the elect few, could rescue them from this evil physical world. Although the church rejected the most serious errors of gnosticism, it still had a legalistic influence.[40] The basis of salvation was gradually changing from a personal union with Christ ("life is in His Son. He who has the Son has life" 1John 5:11) to a focus on membership and participation in the church and its liturgies ("There is no salvation except in the church").[41] The legalistic influences in the church of Smyrna were kept in check by **"tribulation and poverty,"** but the steady development of these doctrines led to more serious compromises during the next period of the church, Pergamos, when the **"synagogue of Satan"** became

the throne of Satan (Revelation 2:13).

2:10 Persecution

"Fear none of those things which you shall suffer. Behold, the devil shall cast some of you into prison, that you may be tested; and you shall have tribulation ten days. Be faithful to death, and I will give you a crown of life" (Revelation 2:10).

As the Christian church was growing rapidly among the poor and disenfranchised, the Roman government began to be alarmed. Here was an organization which taught the poor that all were equal, which taught the slaves that all were free, which taught that "we ought to obey God rather than men" (Acts 5:29). The church also had by this time a highly organized hierarchy of bishops, elders and deacons. This was a period of disarray and decline for the Roman empire, with 60 different men proclaimed emperor between AD 235 and 284. In that year Gaius Diocletian was proclaimed emperor and he immediately began to consolidate his power and to try to bring control and stability to the empire. His attention was soon fixed on the Christians as the cause of the evils of the time because they offended the traditional Roman gods and refused to worship the emperor. In AD 303 Diocletian forbade Christian worship, ushering in the "great persecution," the last and most severe persecution of Christians in the Roman Empire. The reign of terror continued for 10 years until AD 313 (the **"ten days"** of tribulation).[42] By that time Constantine the Great had become emperor. He realized that political control of the church would be more effective than attempts to eradicate it, so he granted Christians

---

40   See Walker, *History of the Christian Church*, pp. 92-96. "Christians of the last half of the second and the third centuries lived in an atmosphere highly charged with influences sprung from the mystery religions…The church came to be more and more regarded as possessed of life-giving mysteries, under the superintendence and dispensation of the clergy." In particular, during the Smyrna period baptism was changing from being a *symbol* of an inner change which had already taken place in the life of the believer (Romans 6:3-5, Colossians 2:12) into an *initiation ritual* of purification and rebirth into eternal life, appropriate for infants to free them from "original sin." The exact wording of the Apostles Creed and the Lord's Prayer came to be seen as sacred, secret knowledge. The Lord's Supper was transformed from a memorial of Christ's death for our sins, shared by common Christians whenever they met, into "the medicine of immortality, and the antidote that we should not die, but live forever," a sacrifice offered to God by a priest (Ignatius of Antioch quoted in Walker, *History of the Christian Church*, p. 98).

41   This famous and much-quoted statement originated with Cyprian, Bishop of Carthage from AD. 248-258.

42   This is an example of the "day -for-a-year" principle of prophecy. See Appendix 5 for a full explanation.

freedom of worship.[43]

Painful though these persecutions were, they kept the church relatively free of hypocrites. Jesus did not condemn the church of Smyrna, even though the Nicolaitan and synagogue-of-Satan heresies were beginning to show their presence; He simply encouraged the church in the face of persecution to **"be faithful unto death."** Death is often considered to be the ultimate enemy, but Jesus had told his disciples, "do not be afraid of those who kill the body, and after that have no more that they can do" (Luke 12:4). Now He repeats that promises, and reveals the rich reward to those who make the ultimate sacrifice: **"He who overcomes shall not be hurt by the second death... and I will give you the crown of life"** (Revelation 2:11,10).

Pergamos
2:12,13 Throne of Satan

"And to the angel of the church in Pergamos write: These things said He which has the sharp sword with two edges: I know your works, and where you dwell, even where Satan's throne is" (Revelation 2:12,13). In the previous Smyrna period Satan invaded the place of worship (the **"synagogue of Satan"**) through legalism and the desire of the leadership for power and control. But in the Pergamos era Satan ascended from the place of fellowship to the throne of rulership—**"you dwell even where Satan's throne is."**

A throne is a symbol of governing authority and is the source of the principles of government of the kingdom—"Righteousness and justice are the foundation of [God's] throne" (Psalm 97:2). **"Satan's throne"** on the other hand is "the

throne of iniquity, which devises evil by law" (Psalm 94:20). The devising of "evil by law" was a prime characteristic of the Pergamos era, as the emperor Constantine made Christianity the official religion of the Roman Empire in the early fourth century.

The persecutions of the Smyrna period had tended to strengthen rather than weaken the church. Astute politician as he was, Constantine recognized that the persecution policy was a failure. While on the battlefield Constantine claimed to have had a vision in which he saw a cross with the inscription, "in this sign conquer." Taking this to mean that he should embrace Christianity, he "baptized" his troops by marching them through the river, and had them write the Greek initials for Christ on their shields. He soon began to pass laws favoring Christianity over other religions, and by AD 321 heathen sacrifices had been outlawed as well as work on Sunday. Gifts were made to the clergy, and great churches were erected in Rome, Jerusalem, and especially in Constantinople, the new capital of the empire.

Besides favoring the "true believers" with funds from the royal treasury, Constantine organized church councils to deal with heresy, took an active role in the decisions made, and banished and persecuted those who were declared heretics. Thus the union of church and state was established, which would be the model both in the Byzantine Eastern Orthodox Church and in the western Roman Catholic Church until the Reformation over 1000 years later. "The imperial church came into existence, and a policy of imperial interference was fully developed. Departure from official orthodoxy had become a crime."[44]

For the official church it seemed like a dream come true. They were finally not only legal but favored, so that they could get on with the

---

43 Wikipedia contributors, "Diocletianic Persecution," *Wikipedia, The Free Encyclopedia,* http://en.wikipedia.org/w/index.php?title=Diocletianic_Persecution&oldid=613282469 (accessed June 25, 2014)

44 Williston Walker, *The History of the Christian Church* (New York, NY, C. Scribner, 1918) p. 128

mission Christ had given them to preach the Gospel in all the world. New "believers" were pouring into the church, and the wealth and power of the empire were at their disposal to create the kingdom of God on earth. They never dreamed of what a corrupting effect the union of church and state would have, or what kinds of heresies the half-converted pagans would bring with them into the church.

Antipas

Although the church was becoming an official state religion there was still a fair bit of independence of the bishops and their churches in major Christian centers such as Antioch and Alexandria, with heated debate and sometimes violent disagreement over theological issues such as the nature of God and Christ. The message to Pergamos seems to be directed to those Christians who were still resisting some of the false theology that was gaining traction within the state church—**"you dwell, even where Satan's throne is; and you hold fast My name, and have not denied My faith, even in those days wherein Antipas was my faithful martyr, who was slain among you, where Satan dwells"** (Revelation 2:13).

According to Orthodox tradition[45] Antipas was the Bishop of Pergamos during the reign of Emperor Domitian (81-96 AD). Pergamos was a center of Pagan worship, and Antipas had a busy ministry casting out demons from former pagans who were accepting Christ as their Lord. The pagan priests began to have dreams in which demons appeared and told them that they were so afraid of Antipas that they were fleeing the city.

The priests aroused the idolaters of the city to seize Antipas and take him to the governor, who tried to force him to worship their idols. Antipas urged them to learn from the demons who fled from a simple Christian that their faith in idols was in vain. Enraged, they cast him into a red-hot copper idol of an ox, where he continued in prayer until he died.[46]

Antipas thus symbolized those faithful Christians who were actively resisting the inroads of idolatry during the Pergamos era (the fourth through the mid-sixth centuries). This was a time when idolaters were flocking into the new state church, seeking new "Christian" idols to take the place of their old pagan idols. The custom of honoring those who had died as martyrs began to provide an outlet for the popular need for gods who were more real, and thus worship of the saints was coming into the church from the grassroots level.[47] In particular, the worship of the Virgin Mary[48] was becoming popular, and the theologians of the time were busy trying to fit the cult of Mary, with its popular title "theotokos" (Mother of God), into their speculative theologies about the nature of Christ.[49] In the midst of this descent into idolatry Nestorius is a flawed but prominent example of the "Antipas" spirit of

---

45 Simeon Metaphrastes (900-984 AD) was a Byzantine hagiographer and statesman who compiled a 10 volume collection called the Menologion which preserved the legends and traditions about the early eastern saints. The legend of Antipas was included and April 11 is still dedicated to the memory of St. Antipas by the Orthodox Church.

46 Summaries of the legend of Antipas can be found on a number of Orthodox websites, such as the Orthodox Church of America or Comeandseeicons.com.

47 Herbert Thurston, "Devotion to the Blessed Virgin Mary," *The Catholic Encyclopedia,* http://www.newadvent.org/cathen/15459a.htm (accessed June 25, 2014).

48 Although Catholics claim that their tradition comes in an unbroken chain from the Apostles, they themselves admit that this is not always the case, as in the worship of the Virgin Mary. "Devotion to Our Blessed Lady is not contained, at least explicitly, in the earlier forms of the Apostle's Creed, so there is perhaps no ground for surprise if we do not meet with any clear traces of the cultus of the Blessed Virgin in the first Christian centuries." *Ibid.*

49 The basic premise was that Christ had one nature, divine and human, not two natures (one divine and one human). Since Christ's nature was indivisible, Mary was mother of His full nature, both divine and human, and thus the mother of Divinity.

resistance.

The theological issues of the time had to do with the relationship between the human and divine natures of Christ. Nestorius represented the Antioch school, which emphasized the human nature of Christ, while the Alexandrian school, represented by Cyril, emphasized the divine nature of Christ. When Nestorius was made patriarch of Constantinople in AD 428 he not only continued the dispute over the nature of Christ but also got involved in the jealousies and rivalries between Constantinople and Alexandria over power and prominence.[50]

All of this might have remained in the realm of theological and political competition except that Nestorius saw in the popular term "Mother of God" the inroads of idolatry. His bottom line was: "If Mary is called the Mother of God, she will be made into a goddess."[51] But goddess worship can be very popular, and any criticism enrages the worshipers. "In preaching against this expression [mother of God] Nestorius seemed to be resisting the popular piety and the rising religious reverence for the Virgin. Cyril saw his opportunity to humiliate the rival see of Constantinople and the school of Antioch at one blow."[52] A council was convened and Nestorius was condemned, banished and died in exile. The controversies over the nature of Christ continued, eventually splitting the eastern church,[53] and the title "Mother of God" became more popular than ever, along with the developing worship of Mary, the saints and icons.

It is true that Nestorius is best known for his erroneous position on the nature of Christ.[54] But his courageous opposition to idolatry is an example of the Antipas spirit, which grew during the next few centuries until it became a powerful force during the iconoclast controversy of the eighth and ninth centuries.[55] The eastern church was almost freed from idolatry, but in the end, with the support of the Roman Church, the image worshipers prevailed and the resistance movement was stamped out (see 2:18-20 *You Tolerate Jezebel*).

2:14 Doctrine of Balaam

"But I have a few things against you, because you have there those who hold the doctrine of Balaam, who taught Balak to cast a stumbling block before the children of Israel, to eat things sacrificed to idols, and to commit fornication" (Revelation 2:14).

The story of Balaam and his attempts to curse the children of Israel is found in Numbers 22-24. As a prophet he knew the voice of God, and God had shown him that he was not to respond to

50   Wikipedia contributors, "Nestorianism," "Monophysitism" "Nestorius," *Wikipedia, The Free Encyclopedia,* http://en.wiki-pedia.org/w/index.php?title=Nestorianism&oldid=600806550, http://en.wikipedia.org/w/index.php?title=Monophysitism&oldid=604305191 , http://en.wikipedia.org/w/index.php?title=Nestorius&oldid=612390801, (accessed June 25, 2014).

51   John Chapman, "Nestorius and Nestorianism." *The Catholic Encyclopedia,* http://www.newadvent.org/cathen/10755a.htm, accessed 5 June 5, 2014.

52   Walker, *The History of the Christian Church*, p. 147.

53   The eastern church split into Nestorian churches (emphasizing Christ's human nature) in Persia and India, Monophysite churches (emphasizing Christ's divine nature) in Syria and Egypt, and Orthodox (who adopted the Roman two-natures position at the council of Chalcedon) based in Constantinople.

54   In fact, all the church leaders of the time were speculating about a theme (the nature of Christ and God) that is incomprehensible to man. The Antiochan emphasis on the human nature of Christ was extreme and incomplete, but it was more in harmony with the Bible than the Alexandrian position that minimized the human nature: "Every spirit that does not confess that Jesus Christ has come in the flesh is not of God. And this is the spirit of the antichrist" (1John 4:3).

55 Wikipedia contributors, "Byzantine Iconoclasm," *Wikipedia, The Free Encyclopedia,* http://en.wikipedia.org/w/index.php?title=Byzantine_Iconoclasm&oldid=595944193 (accessed June 25, 2014).

the offer of money from Balak, the king of Moab, who wanted a curse pronounced upon Israel. But Balaam "loved the wages of unrighteousness" (2Peter 2:15) and willfully ignored God's command. Because God protected His people, Balaam was not able to curse Israel and instead pronounced a series of blessings.

Disappointed, "Balaam rose and departed and returned to his place" (Numbers 24:25). But apparently on the way home he had a new thought: if the children of Israel could be enticed into sin they would forfeit their divine protection and the Moabites could defeat them. "[Moabite] women caused the children of Israel, *through the counsel of Balaam*, to trespass against the Lord in the incident of Peor, and there was a plague among the congregation of the Lord" (Numbers 31:16). "They [the Moabite women] invited the people to the sacrifices of their gods, and the people ate and bowed down to their gods. So Israel was joined to Baal of Peor, and the anger of the Lord was aroused against Israel…and those who died in the plague were twenty-four thousand" (Numbers 25:2,3,9). Balaam exploited the spiritual weakness and love of sin of the people of Israel and enticed them into idolatry for his own personal profit.[56]

This shameful practice entered the church during the Pergamos era when the monks and priests began to exploit the shrines of the saints and their relics for the sake of monetary gain. "The veneration of martyrs and their relics runs back to the middle of the second century…With the conversion of Constantine, however, and the accession to the church of masses of people fresh from heathenism, this reverence largely increased." By the end of the fourth century the martyrs had become unofficial saints—"they were prayed to as intercessors with God, and as able to protect, heal and aid those who honored them. Special days were dedicated to the saints, and on these days their icons and relics were displayed. The superstitious multitudes were taught to believe that offerings given on these days could secure God's favor for themselves or their departed loved ones."[57]

Mary and the saints became the friends and advocates of the people, while God the Father and even Jesus were seen as distant and severe. Lavish gifts were given to build shrines to the saints and buy icons of them. Stories of miracles performed by the saints or even by their icons made the common people even more anxious to "buy" access to them.

Along with the worship of the saints there developed reverence for all manner of relics associated, it was believed, with Christ, the Apostles, and the saints. These included pieces of the Cross, articles and bones of the saints, and icons that were reputed to have miraculous healing power. Great value was placed on long and difficult pilgrimages to places where the relics were preserved. The idolatrous tendencies of the masses were exploited to enrich the church and enhance the power and prestige of the bishops and monks who were conservators of the relics and "sacred sites." Instead of "fleeing from idolatry" (1Corinthians 10:14), the theologians and church leaders embraced it and exploited it for financial gain. "This Christianity of the second rank [of the masses] had its heartiest supporters in the monks, and it was furthered rather than resisted by the great leaders of the church, certainly after the middle of the fifth century. It undoubtedly made the way from heathenism to Christianity easier for thousands, but it largely heathenized

---

56 In the end Balaam did not get to enjoy his ill-gotten gains—"Balaam the son of Beor they also killed with the sword" (Numbers 31: 8).

57 Walker, *The History of the Christian Church*, p. 147.

the church itself."[58] The "Balaam" practices of monks, priests and church leaders encouraged the "spiritual adultery" of idolatry, which became firmly entrenched during this period.

Nicolaitans

"So you have also those who hold the doctrine of the Nicolaitans, which I hate" (Revelation 2:15). The Nicolaitans were one of the Gnostic sects. The basic idea of Gnosticism was that the material world is evil, but through secret knowledge the enlightened ones could escape to a higher sphere. Jehovah, the God of the Jews, was considered evil because He created matter, but Jesus came with secret knowledge that would lead back to the realm of the good God. Since the physical nature was hopelessly evil, there was no point in trying to resist temptation.[59] Thus the followers of this sect rejected the holistic biblical view of man, splitting the "holy" mind and spirit from the corrupt and immoral body as if the one had no effect on the other. Although the church officially rejected Gnosticism during the Ephesus and Smyrna periods, an unexpected version of the Nicolaitan heresy entered the church during the Pergamos period with the development of asceticism and monasticism,[60] which split the body of Christ into corrupted commoners and "holy" priests and monks.

Many of the great "church fathers" such as Origin and Tertullian practiced exceedingly strict, ascetic lifestyles,[61] and this became the ideal for serious Christians who wanted to be "holy." But rather than insisting on holiness for everyone, they began to draw a distinction between the "advice" and the "requirements" of the gospel, asserting that Jesus taught[62] a very high standard of poverty and celibacy that was optional "advice" for those who were serious about their religion, but which was different from the lower "requirements" that applied to the common people. "While the requirements of Christianity are binding on all Christians, the advice is for those who would live the holier life...voluntary poverty and voluntary celibacy were, therefore, deemed advice impossible of fulfillment by all Christians, indeed, but conferring special merit on those who practiced them."[63] Naturally the common people who had not chosen the way of the spiritually elite had the tendency to feel that the lower standards of the "requirements" made it unnecessary or even impossible for them to live a holy life.

A number of trends contributed to the dividing of the church into the "holy" elite and the "profane" masses. As the official religion of the empire, the church was attracting large numbers of heathen converts who were Christian in name only. Many more became Christians because their parents had them baptized, never making a decision themselves to follow Christ. Since "everyone" was a Christian now, it was easy for the general selfishness and worldliness of society to

---

58 *Ibid*

59 John Arendzen, "Gnosticism" *The Catholic Encyclopedia* http://www.newadvent.org/cathen/06592a.htm, accessed June 25, 2014.

60 Monasticism is the way of life typical of monks or nuns, in which they withdraw entirely or in part from society to devote themselves to prayer, solitude, and contemplation and is often characterized by asceticism, which is severe austerity and self-denial.

61 Origin, for example, "was ascetic in the extreme, and to avoid slander arising out of his relations with his numerous inquirers he emasculated himself, taking Matt.19 as a counsel of perfection" (Walker *The History of the Christian Church*, p. 79).

62 "There are eunuchs who were made eunuchs by men, and there are eunuchs who have made themselves eunuchs for the kingdom of heaven's sake. *He who is able to accept it, let him accept it*" (Matthew 19:12) "*If you want to be perfect, go sell what you have and give to the poor*" (Matthew 19:21).

63 Walker *The History of the Christian Church*, p. 104.

be considered normal.[64]

"Serious" Christians reacted to this by adopting the monastic lifestyle of extreme asceticism and withdrawal from the world. This asceticism shared with Gnosticism the idea that the material world is evil, and that only the select few can escape to a higher sphere (in the monastery). The unfortunate consequence is that this promotes a double standard of Christian morality. The ordinary "Christian" understood that immorality was evil, but since he was not taking part in the pure monastic life, he could not be expected to overcome his sinful physical nature. The monks themselves did not expect the common people to live a moral life since they had rejected the optional "advice" to be holy. The result was the **"doctrine of the Nicolaitans"** on a church-wide scale: the church was divided into a "pure and holy" elite who withdrew from the "world" in the monasteries, and the masses of ordinary "Christians" who lived worldly and immoral lives.

But even among the priests and monks the doctrine of celibacy, which was codified during this period,[65] resulted in a split "Nicolaitan" life. On the one hand they engaged in nearly constant prayers, liturgies and fastings, but on the other hand fell into perverse and immoral behavior as a result of the inhumane and unbiblical requirement of celibacy.[66] Immorality between monks and nuns, sexual exploitation by priests of those who came to them for confession, homosexuality, and child abuse have been a tragic pattern that unfortunately has been a curse in the church not only during the Pergamos era but all through the centuries until the present day. It is no wonder that Jesus condemned **"the deeds of the Nicolaitans, which I also hate"** (Revelation 2:6).

2:16,17 Repent, or Else

"Repent; or else I will come to you quickly, and will fight against them with the sword of my mouth" (Revelation 2:16). In Revelation 19:15 the sword which comes out of the mouth of the Lord strikes the nations as He "rules them with a rod of iron." In Psalm 2:8,9 this same phrase means breaking the nations and dashing them to pieces. This warning was carried out against the imperial church, which did not repent of its idolatry. The worship of saints, relics and religious art (icons and images) became more entrenched as the centuries passed, and God allowed the sword to ravage the church.

In the east Islam developed, in part as a reaction to the idolatry of Byzantine Christianity, particularly the worship of Mary. Convinced that Christians were idolaters who must come into subjection to Allah,[67] Muslims continued their relentless attacks against the Christian Byzantine Empire from the middle of the seventh century until Constantinople finally fell in AD 1453.

In the west **"the sword"** came earlier. Repeated waves of barbarian invaders swept

---

64 *Ibid*, p. 103.

65 The first church council to decree celibacy was the council of Elvira, at the beginning of the fourth century. Herbert Thurston, Herbert "Celibacy of the Clergy." *The Catholic Encyclopedia*, http://www.newadvent.org/cathen/03481a.htm, accessed June 25, 2014.

66 Peter and the other apostles had wives (1 Corinthians 9:5). Bishops and elders were to be "the husband of one wife" (1 Timothy 3:2, Titus 1:5,6). One of the "doctrines of demons" is "forbidding to marry" (1 Timothy 4:1,3).

67 Muhammad's chief objection to the religions around him was that they worshiped a multitude of gods instead of the one God, Allah. Although he taught through the Koran that Christians had received a true revelation from God through the great prophet Jesus, he maintained that the Christian scriptures had been corrupted with doctrines such as the Trinity, which he violently opposed as polytheism. Tragically, the Trinity he understood from the Byzantine Christians around him was the Father, the Son and the Virgin Mary. "And then God said, 'O Jesus, son of Mary, did you say to the people, take me and my Mother as two gods apart from God?' He said, 'Glory be to you, I cannot say what is not my right to say'" (Quaran 5:116) Thus the Quran says that Jesus himself rejected the Trinity as God, Mary and Jesus" George Braswell, *What You Need to Know About Islam and Muslims*, (Nashville, TN, Broadman & Holman, 2000) p. 125. Used by permission.

down from Northern Europe, deposing the last of the western Roman emperors in AD 476. These invading tribes followed the teachings of Arius, who had been condemned as a heretic for his views on the nature of Christ by the Catholic Church. Now these barbarian "heretics" were ruling Rome, and although they did not destroy the papal church, they severely limited its political power and influence.

"He that has an ear, let him hear what the Spirit said to the churches; To him that overcomes will I give to eat of the hidden manna, and will give him a white stone, and on the stone a new name written, which no one knows except he that receives it" (Revelation 2:17). "Hidden manna" and "a new name written which no one knows" both emphasize the development of "hidden" or secret Christians who increasingly had to go underground in the face of rejection and persecution by the official state church, which was comprised of false "Balaam" leaders supported by immoral "Nicolaitan" masses. This division of the church became even more pronounced in the next Thyatira period, in which the official church is characterized as Jezebel and the true church went underground.

Thyatira
2:18-20 You Tolerate Jezebel

"And to the angel of the church in Thyatira write: These things said the Son of God, who has His eyes like a flame of fire, and His feet are like fine brass. I know your works, and love, and service, and faith, and your patience, and your works; and the last are more than the first. Notwithstanding I have a few things against you, because you allow that woman Jezebel" (Revelation 2:18-20). The message to Thyatira starts with a surprising development: the church has recovered the virtues of the Ephesus period (works, service, faith, patience) and has even

developed the love that the Ephesus Church had lost, and this during what is considered the darkest period for the church—the Middle Ages.

The explanation is that the official state church had gone so far in its departure from Christ that the message is no longer addressed to her. In the Pergamos era the Lord declared that the faithful Antipas Christians **"have there those who hold the doctrine of Balaam"** and **"have those who hold the doctrine of the Nicolaitans,"** in other words, these heretics were a part of God's church. In the Thyatira age there has been a separation; the true church[68] does not "have" Jezebel, rather it "allows"[69] her.

Jezebel is a fitting symbol of the visible church of the Middle Ages. Jezebel was the wife of Ahab, a king of Israel who "did evil in the sight of the Lord, more than all who were before Him" (1 Kings 16:30). Previous to Ahab, the ultimate in iniquity was "the sins of Jeroboam" who had divided the kingdom and set up calf idols in the territory of Ephraim and Dan. But Ahab, "as though it had been a trivial thing to walk in the sins of Jeroboam…took as wife Jezebel the daughter of Ethbaal king of the Sidonians" (v.31). Jezebel became the effective ruler, manipulating weak king Ahab to do her will.

Their first act was to "set up an altar for Baal in the temple of Baal, which he had built in Samaria" (v.32). She had an army of idolatrous priests—"the four hundred and fifty prophets of Baal and the four hundred prophets of Asherah, who eat at Jezebel's table" (1 Kings 18:19). Later Jezebel "massacred the prophets of the Lord" (1 Kings 18:4) and arranged to have Naboth, an innocent man, murdered in order to seize his property. "So there was no one like Ahab who

---

68 The true church in Revelation is called "the remnant" (see 12:17 *The Remnant*).

69 The Greek verb is *eaos* which means to permit, to allow one to do as he wishes, not to restrain, tolerate.

sold himself to do wickedness in the sight of the Lord, because Jezebel his wife stirred him up" (1Kings 21:25).

In like manner the medieval church officially embraced idolatry and manipulated the state to persecute the true children of God. In both the east and the west the worship of images of Jesus and the saints became more and more entrenched, despite the fact that it is condemned by the scriptures.[70] Early in the eighth century the Byzantine emperor Leo III initiated the iconoclastic controversy, vigorously opposing any artistic representations of Christ or the saints. For more than a hundred years the controversy raged, with church councils deciding for and against the worship of images.[71] In AD 787 the Second Council of Nicea made an official decision to continue the use of icons,[72] and in the ninth century finally rejected the last attempt to put a stop to the use of images, an event that ironically is still celebrated as "the triumph of Orthodoxy."[73]

Meanwhile in the west, at the end of the Pergamos era the western Roman Empire was overrun by barbarian "heretics" who severely limited the political power of the Papacy. The powerful Byzantine emperor Justinian changed that, sending his armies to liberate not only Rome but also to reclaim much of the western Roman Empire. In order to do this he needed the support of the influential Bishop of Rome. The pope and the bishop of Constantinople had been involved in a long-standing rivalry as to who would have precedence. But in AD 533 Emperor Justinian settled the controversy by issuing a decree in the form of a letter to the pope, in which he declared him "head of all the churches" and "the true and

---

70 John of Damascus and Theodore of Stoudios were the leading theologians who defended icon worship in the iconoclast controversy. "John of Damascus carefully distinguished between the relative honour of veneration shown to material symbols and the worship due to God alone" Timothy Ware, *The Orthodox Church*, (London, Penguin books, 1997) p. 32. However, the masses of worshipers were not able to make such a distinction, and their "veneration" is identical to actual worship, including bowing, kissing, prayers, liturgies, shrines, special days, processions, and all that would be involved in worship. John of Damascus asserted, "Of old God the incorporeal and uncircumscribed was not depicted at all. But now that God has appeared in the flesh and lived among humans, I make an image of the God who can be seen. I do not worship matter but I worship the Creator of matter, who for my sake became material and deigned to dwell in matter, who through matter effected my salvation. I will not cease from worshiping the matter through which my salvation has been effected" Ibid, p.33. But this argument does not recognize that God had already sanctified matter in His original creation as it came forth from His hand, but He always forbade its being used to depict God or being worshiped in any way (Exodus 20:4,5, Deuteronomy 4:15-18, Deuteronomy 27:15, Isaiah 44:9-20, Acts 17:29). The many strong prohibitions against using images to depict an object of worship demand clear scriptures to show that this had been changed, not just the arguments of a philosopher or theologian.

71 Both Orthodox and Roman Catholics insist that they do not worship the images, distinguishing between worship (Greek *latreia*—adoration) and veneration (Greek *proskinisi*—bowing down to show allegiance or reverence). But the second commandment forbids both worship and veneration of any image of anything of the creation (Exodus 20:4,5). Although Jesus, being divine, allowed *proskinisi*, Peter and the angels did not (Acts 10:25,26, Revelation 19:10, 22: 8,9). Angels insisted twice in Revelation, "see that you do not do that (*proskinisi*) for I am your fellow servant...Worship God" (Revelation 19:10, 22; 8,9). Every one of the 60 times the word *proskinisi* is used in the New Testament refers either to worship of God or Jesus, a condemnation of false worship of idols or "the beast," or a rebuke of those who tried to worship men or angels. Icon and statue worshipers claim that they do not worship the wood, paint and stone, but the one who is depicted. But this is even worse, since it is usually a human being (one of the saints or the Virgin Mary) who is depicted and worshiped.

72 The Nicean council of AD 787 which permanently approved of the use of Icons was the seventh and last ecumenical council.

73 Basic information about the iconoclastic controversy can be found in the Wikipedia article Wikipedia contributors, "Byzantine Iconoclasm," *Wikipedia, The Free Encyclopedia*, http://en.wikipedia.org/w/index.php?title=Byzantine_Iconoclasm&oldid=629127454 (accessed November 25, 2014).

effective corrector of heretics."[74] It took many years for the Papacy to fully establish her own political power, but when she did she became the **"Jezebel"** of prophecy, establishing idolatry and destroying all who opposed her.

By the thirteenth century this had become a fearsome reality. Innocent III (1198-1216) organized the Inquisition, a cooperation of church and state, to root out heresy. "Pope Innocent III held that heresy, as treason against God, was worse than treason against the king…The Inquisition became a most formidable organ. Its proceedings were secret, the names of his accusers were not given to the prisoner, who, by a bull of Innocent IV in 1252, was liable to torture. The confiscation of the convict's property was one of its most destructive features, and as these spoils were shared by the lay authorities, this feature undoubtedly kept the fires of persecution burning where otherwise they would have died out."[75] Jezebel had influenced the king to exterminate God's prophets, and had Naboth murdered in order to seize his property. Her despicable actions were reproduced in the medieval Papacy, which controlled the kings of Europe and used them to war against God's faithful followers.[76]

The True Church

Obviously the official "Jezebel" church of the Middle Ages is not the church that Jesus commends in the message to Thyatira. So who were the true people of God during the Thyatira era? They are described as having **"works, love, service, faith, and…patience."** They also **"allow"** Jezebel—to some extent they are influenced by her and do not effectively protest against her. But with the passage of time they become more effective in rejecting her—**"as for your works, the last are more than the first."**

The names of individuals and groups that rejected the papal system and were true to God are lost in the mists of legend and history, and much of what is known comes from those who accused them of heresy. The Paulicians, Cathari and Waldensians were among those who rejected some of the worst errors of the papal church. These movements, particularly the Cathari, had serious doctrinal errors, and naturally the question arises, why would these groups with their doctrinal errors be considered the "true church of God" rather than the papal church, which had a different set of doctrinal errors?

The answer is that God can and does tolerate many conflicting doctrinal positions, but the characterization of the papacy as Jezebel shows what He will not tolerate. Jezebel introduced the worship of false gods and slaughtered the priests of God who challenged this false worship. The papal church did the same, promoting the worship of the saints and viciously persecuting those such as the Cathari and Waldensians who rejected idolatry and corruption and attempted to follow the scriptures rather than church

---

74 Codex Justiniani as quoted in Uriah Smith, *Daniel and the Revelation* (Hagerstown, MD, Review and Herald 1972).

75 Walker, *The History of the Christian Church*, p. 254.

76 An example was the inquisition against the Cathari. "This war pitted the nobles of the north of France against those of the south. The widespread northern enthusiasm for the Crusade was partially inspired by a papal decree permitting the confiscation of lands owned by Cathars and their supporters…this made the region a target for northern French noblemen looking to acquire new fiefs. The barons of the north headed south to do battle." Wikipedia contributors, "Catharism," *Wikipedia, The Free Encyclopedia*, http://en.wikipedia.org/w/index.php?title=Catharism&oldid=613221344 (accessed June 25, 2014).

tradition.[77] They were forced to retreat further and further into remote mountain areas, and finally, "thanks to the Inquisition...the Cathari were utterly rooted out in the course of a little more than a century, and the Waldenses greatly repressed."[78]

But just as prophesied, **"as for your works, the last are more than the first."** The true church became more biblical in her doctrines and more effective in her resistance to the Jezebel abuses of the Roman Catholic system. John Wycliff (1320-1384) defied the papacy, translating the scriptures into English and denouncing the Papal and monastic systems, even going so far as to identify the pope as antichrist. His followers became known as Lollards, and they carried the translated scriptures throughout England, where they were noticed by university students and taken to Europe, particularly to Bohemia where they had an influence on John Huss. His heroic martyrdom in AD 1415 was an example for the reformers who followed.

---

77 In the middle of the seventh century the Paulicians arose, who "rejected monasticism, the external sacraments, the cross, images, and relics...The Catholic hierarchy they repudiated. They opposed the externalism of current orthodox religious life." (Walker, *History of the Christian Church*, p. 235). "The Cathari seem to have been men and women of uprightness, moral earnestness and courageous steadfastness in persecution." These groups had some serious doctrinal errors, which to a certain extent were corrected by the Waldenses, who arose near the end of the twelfth century.

The fundamental teaching of the Waldenses was that the Bible is the sole rule of belief and life. "As unbiblical, they rejected masses and prayers for the dead and denied purgatory...they believed prayer in secret more effective than in church. They defended lay preaching by men and women...At the Reformation they readily accepted its principles, and became fully Protestant" (*Ibid* 251-253).

At first the Roman church sent missionaries to try to convert the Waldenses and Cathari. An alternative movement, the *Pauperes Cathokici*, was set up with many of the same practices of the Waldenses, but under strict supervision by the church. Although many were won back to the church, the "heretic movement" continued to grow and spread, threatening the stability of the church in southern France, northern Italy and northern Spain. A crusade was organized against them in 1209 which led to twenty years of destructive warfare. The result was the extermination of the Cathari.

78 *Ibid* p. 254

2:21-23 Jezebel's Sickbed

In the meantime another aspect of the prophecy against Jezebel was being fulfilled—**"I gave her space to repent of her fornication; and she did not repent. Behold, I will cast her into a bed [sickbed, NKJV], and those that commit adultery with her into great tribulation, unless they repent of their deeds. And I will kill her children with death; and all the churches shall know that I am He who searches the minds and hearts; and I will give to every one of you according to your works."** (Revelation 2:21,22).

The "sickbed" of the eastern church followed their acceptance of image worship in the iconoclastic controversy. The official acceptance of idolatry (the "triumph of Orthodoxy") marked the end of universal church councils and was followed by five centuries of decline and defeat at the hands of the Turks and even by the "Christian" crusaders. Estranged from the western church and the European powers, Constantinople and the Byzantine empire finally fell in 1453 (**"kill her children with death"**) and the eastern Orthodox Church was oppressed and subjugated by the Muslim Ottoman Empire.

In the West the papacy reached the pinnacle of power in the thirteenth century and then began a long and steady decline (her **"sickbed"**). Corruption and power struggles weakened the authority of the church,[79] but particularly damaging were the increasing financial demands to pay for grandiose projects such as the building of

---

79 In 1378 the College of Cardinals elected a new Pope, only to find in a few months that he was unacceptable, so they elected a second Pope, causing "the Great Schism"—two rival Popes, each condemning the other. The schism continued for nearly forty years with a series of Popes and anti-popes. Europe was divided and scandalized, and the Papacy lost a great deal of the esteem it had once held. The Renaissance, which began in Italy during the fourteenth century, emphasized the present life, beauty, and satisfaction, rather than a future heaven or hell, and wrenched the minds of thinking Europeans from narrow medieval theological disputes.

St. Peter's Cathedral in Rome.

One of the favorite means of raising money was through the sale of indulgences. According to Catholic teaching, sins committed after baptism had to be paid for by good deeds. Christ and the saints, with their sin-free lives, had a large oversupply of good deeds which they did not need personally since they had lived holy lives. The average sinner either had to perform his own good deeds (which never seemed to be enough) or he would have to pay for his sins in purgatory (a place where the souls of those who have died are tortured until they are pure enough for heaven). However, by benefiting the church with a donation he could have access to the good deeds of Christ and the saints, either for his own sins, or for those of a loved one who would need them to shorten his time in purgatory. This system obviously led to much abuse, and Martin Luther's protest against it was a precipitating factor in the Protestant Reformation.

Luther grew up thoroughly immersed in the Catholic system, and with a strong sense of his own personal sin, entered a monastery to try to escape feelings of condemnation. He attempted to appease God through fasting, vigils and scourgings, but with no relief. Finally a wise abbot of the monastery taught him that true repentance does not involve self-inflicted penances and punishments but rather a change of heart. Thus began a long journey of spiritual growth, including a disillusioning visit to Rome, culminating in His appointment as a professor of theology at the University of Wittenburg. As he prepared studies in the book of Romans he was powerfully impressed by the idea that our salvation and righteous standing before God is of God's grace through faith, not by any works we perform. This concept was summed up by Paul's statement "The just shall live by faith" (Romans 1:17).

This new revelation was in striking contrast to the selling of indulgences, and as the Papal representative approached Wittenburg in 1517, Luther reacted by posting his famous Ninety-five Theses which exposed the fallacies of the Catholic system of salvation. These proved to be a spark that touched off a massive wave of protest and reform throughout Europe. The leaders involved in the Protestant Reformation are a listing of the great heroes of spiritual history; Melanchthon, Zwingli, Farel, Berquin, Calvin, Tausen, Tyndale, Knox, and a host of others extended and spread the reformation. As they struck blow after blow to the Jezebel system they did indeed **"kill her children with death,"**[80] snatching long-held strongholds away from the Roman authority. Although imperfect in their understanding and methods, they initiated a revolution which permanently changed the course of history.[81]

2:24-29 Hold Fast

"But to you I say, and to the rest in Thyatira, as many as do not have this doctrine, and which have not known the depths of Satan, as they call them, I will put on you no other burden; but that which you have already, hold fast till I come." (Revelation 2:24,25).

This verse confirms the location of Thyatira in history. The phrase **"the rest in Thyatira"** uses the Greek word *loipos* (remnant), the same word that is used in Revelation 12 to describe the faithful few that remained after the fierce persecution of the Middle Ages: "And the dragon was wroth with the woman, and went to make war with *the remnant of her seed*, which keep the commandments of God, and have the testimony of Jesus

---

80 Besides the loss of territory, prestige and subjects to the reformation, the Roman Catholic empire also suffered massive loss of life in the religious wars of that period (eg. the Thirty Years' War).

81 In chapters 13 and 17 we will see that "Jezebel" is the same as the beast from the sea of Revelation 13 and the destructive horn of Daniel 7 and 8. We will also see that as the culmination of Jezebel's "sickbed" the papal church received a "deadly wound" (see 13:3 *The Deadly Wound*).

Christ" (Revelation 12:17). The use of the Greek word "remnant" in both of these passages links them to the struggle of God's faithful people against the "Jezebel" persecution of the oppressive state church.

For more than a thousand years the faithful underground church struggled with the corrupting influence of the Roman Catholic Church. Through heroic sacrifice and at a high cost the church wrenched herself away from the papal system, in the end refusing to tolerate the idolatry of Jezebel, even though it meant facing her wrath. The false doctrines that support the Catholic tradition represent the **"depths of Satan,"** based as they are on subtle but fatal anti-Christian philosophy and theology (see chapter 18). Although the Protestant Reformation did not totally recover the "faith which was once for all delivered to the saints,"[82] it did make significant progress. Jesus, knowing the counterattack that Satan would carry out, admonished the church to **"hold fast what you have."** Unfortunately it was not to be. The church of the next period, Sardis, has a name of being spiritually alive but is actually dead, and even the remnant is about to die (Revelation 3:1,2).

"And he that overcomes, and keeps my works to the end, to him I will give authority over the nations. And he shall rule them with a rod of iron; like the vessels of a potter they shall be broken to pieces, even as I received of

My Father" (Revelation 2:26,27). This promise demonstrates the justice of God. For centuries **"the nations"** persecuted those who wanted to be true to God. This should not be surprising—"all who desire to live godly in Christ Jesus will suffer persecution" (2Timothy 3:12). But God promises that someday the tables will be turned. Those very nations which condemned the saints of God will be judged by them—"Do you not know that the saints will judge the world?" (1Corintians 6:2). Those who were slaughtered by the rulers of this world will themselves rule—"Then I saw the souls of those who had been beheaded for their witness to Jesus and for the word of God…and they lived and reigned with Christ" (Revelation 20:4). "And all those who despised you shall fall prostrate at the soles of your feet" (Isaiah 60:14,15).

"And I will give him the morning star. He who has an ear, let him hear what the Spirit said to the churches" (Revelation 2:28,29). Jesus himself is the morning star (see Revelation 22:16). Those who in the darkest ages have believed in Him and lived for Him and died for Him have done so believing in "the prophetic word…as a light that shines in a dark place, until the day dawns and the morning star rises in your hearts" (2 Peter 1:19). Someday soon those who beheld **"the morning star"** in the darkness will rise to everlasting life on that day when "all the earth shall be filled with the glory of the Lord" (Numbers 14:21).

---

82 Jude 1:3

"The hour of trial which shall come upon the whole world." Revelation 3:10
Woodcut by Albrect Durer, 1498

Chapter 3

Revelation 3:1-22

3:1 "And to the angel of the church in Sardis write: These things said He that has the seven Spirits of God, and the seven stars: I know your works, that you have a name that you live, but you are dead.

3:2 Be watchful, and strengthen the things which remain, that are ready to die; for I have not found your works perfect before God.

3:3 Remember therefore how you have received and heard, and hold fast, and repent. If therefore you do not watch, I will come upon you as a thief, and you will not know what hour I will come upon you.

3:4 You have a few names even in Sardis which have not defiled their garments; and they shall walk with Me in white, for they are worthy.

3:5 He that overcomes, the same shall be clothed in white raiment; and I will not blot out his name out of the Book of Life, but I will confess his name before My Father, and before His angels.

3:6 He that has an ear, let him hear what the Spirit said to the churches.

3:7 "And to the angel of the church in Philadelphia write: These things said He that is holy, He that is true, He that has the key of David, He that opens, and no one shuts; and shuts, and no one opens:

3:8 I know your works. Behold, I have set before you an open door, and no one can shut it; for you have a little strength, and have kept My word, and have not denied My name.

3:9 Behold, I will make those of the synagogue of Satan, who say they are Jews, and are not, but do lie; behold, I will make them come and worship before your feet, and to know that I have loved you.

3:10 Because you have kept the word of My patience, I will also keep you from the hour of trial, which shall come upon all the world, to test those that dwell on the earth.

3:11 Behold, I come quickly; hold that fast which you have, so that no one takes your crown.

3:12 He that overcomes I will make a pillar in the temple of My God, and he shall go out no more, and I will write on him the name of My God, and the name of the city of My God, which is New Jerusalem, which comes down out of heaven from My God. And I will write on him My new name.

3:13 He that has an ear, let him hear what the Spirit said to the churches.

3:14 "And to the angel of the church of the Laodiceans write: These things said the Amen, the Faithful and True Witness, the Beginning of the creation of God:

3:15 I know your works, that you are neither cold nor hot; I would that you were cold or hot.

3:16 So then because you are lukewarm, and neither cold nor hot, I will spew you out of my mouth.

3:17 Because you say, I am rich, and increased with goods, and have need of nothing; and do not know that you are wretched, and miserable, and poor, and blind, and naked.

3:18 I counsel you to buy from Me gold tried in the fire, that you may be rich; and white raiment, that you may be clothed, and that the shame of your nakedness may not appear; and anoint your eyes with eye salve, that you may see.

3:19 As many as I love, I rebuke and chasten; be zealous therefore, and repent.

3:20 Behold, I stand at the door, and knock. If anyone hears my voice, and opens the door, I will come in to him, and will dine with him, and he with Me.

3:21 To him that overcomes will I grant to sit with Me on My throne, even as I also overcame, and sat down with My Father on His throne.

3:22 He that has an ear, let him hear what the Spirit said to the churches."

Sardis
3:1, 2 The Dead Church

"And to the angel of the church in Sardis write: These things said He that has the seven Spirits of God, and the seven stars: I know your works, that you have a name that you live, but you are dead. Be watchful, and strengthen the things which remain, that are ready to die, for I have not found your works perfect before God." (Revelation 3:1,2).

The message to the church of Sardis is perhaps the harshest rebuke of all. Except for the "few names...who have not defiled their garments" (v.4), the Lord has nothing to commend them—even that which they have is "ready to die." Worst of all they "have a name" of being alive, but are actually "dead." The strangest thing is that historically Sardis represents the period just following the Protestant Reformation, which brought a tremendous increase in spiritual light, whereas during the previous "Thyatira" period,

which represents the darkness of medieval Europe, the church was highly commended.

As we saw in chapter two, the Thyatira church that was commended was the underground church, the "remnant," which rejected the false doctrines and illicit political relationships[83] that characterized "Jezebel," the official papal church. Although at first she "allowed" (did not actively work to counteract) the misrepresentation of Christ, her "last works [were] more than the first." By the time of the reformers she was aggressively protesting against the abuses of the state church, spreading the true gospel throughout Europe and presenting a radically different model of Christianity.

In the Sardis period the Papacy ("Jezebel") is not part of the description, having been rejected by the Protestant ("remnant") churches. The formerly underground church has become "official,"

---

83 Revelation 17:2.

but tragically God says that now she is dead. But that's not all the bad news. In the Thyatira/medieval period there was a remnant that remained faithful and was the hope for keeping the gospel message alive. Now the remnant[84] is itself **"ready to die!"** This desperate situation is what calls forth the harshest rebuke of all the seven churches—now there are only **"a few names"** to be witnesses for the "truth as it is in Jesus." This characterization of a dead official church and a dying remnant describes the tragic history of the Protestant churches after the Reformation.[85]

Protestant Formalism and Intolerance

Martin Luther boldly protested against the Catholic system of "righteousness by good works," insisting that it is God's unmerited grace, offered in the sacrifice of Jesus, which allows the sinner to be free of his deserved condemnation and death sentence. To Luther "salvation is a new relationship with God, based not on any work of merit on man's part, but on absolute trust in the divine promises."[86] However, even within his own lifetime this emphasis on relationship began to slip back into the medieval model of a

government-supported church that demanded conformity to a set doctrinal formula. The Lutheran theologians became obsessed with academic arguments over issues such as the wording of creeds, the role of good works and the physical presence of Christ in the Lord's Supper. These disputes tended to alienate the common people who could not understand the philosophical arguments that absorbed the attention of the theologians.[87]

The Lutheran princes turned the cause of the gospel into a political tool to further their own ambitions. Germany became a battlefield, the Catholics attempting to consolidate the areas under their control, and the Protestants doing the same in the areas where the prince was a Protestant, setting up a Lutheran state church in the place of the old bishop-ruled Catholic churches. The Lutheran cause degenerated into military battles for territory, political battles for influence, and theological battles over creeds.

In Switzerland the prominent reformer Huldreich Zwingli rejected tradition in favor of the Bible as the only binding source of authority for the Christian. In some points he went farther than Luther, insisting on a symbolic rather than actual physical presence of Christ in the Lord's Supper. Luther and Zwingli agreed on many points, particularly salvation by faith alone, but their disagreement concerning the Lord's Supper became so bitter that it split the Protestant Church. "To Zwingli Luther's assertion of the physical presence of Christ was a remnant of Catholic superstition…Luther declared that Zwingli and

---

84 The phrase "the things which remain" (Revelation 3:2) is the same Greek word for remnant that is used in Revelation 2:24 and 12:17.

85 The Eastern Orthodox Church was also "dead" during this period. Constantinople, the capital of the Christian Byzantine Empire, was defeated by the Turks in 1453. Under Turkish rule the Orthodox Church was not only a legal entity, but also the political representative of the defeated Greeks. "The Muslims drew no distinction between religion and politics…The Orthodox Church therefore became a civil as well as a religious institution…The ecclesiastical structure became an instrument of secular administration…Church administration became caught up in a degrading system of corruption and simony…What was once said of the Papacy was certainly true of the Ecumenical Patriarchate under the Turks: everything was for sale" Timothy Ware, *The Orthodox Church* , (London, Penguin Books, 1997) p. 90.

86 Williston Walker, *History of the Christian Church* (New York, NY, C. Scribner, 1918), p.338

87 "Emphasis was on pure doctrine and the sacraments, as the sufficient elements of the Christian life. For the vital relationship between the believer and God which Luther had taught had been substituted very largely a faith which consisted in the acceptance of a dogmatic whole. The layman's role was largely passive, to accept the dogmas, to listen to their exposition from the pulpit, to partake of the sacraments and share in the ordinances of the church…It was a tendency often called 'dead orthodoxy' (*Ibid*, p. 495).

his supporters were not even Christians…their disagreement unfortunately split the Evangelical ranks."[88]

In Zurich where Zwingli lived a debate arose concerning baptism. The "Anabaptist" movement took the position that infant baptism was unscriptural. When adult leaders began to be rebaptized Zwingli and the Zurich city council rose up in fierce opposition. "The Zurich government ordered Anabaptists drowned, in hideous parody of their belief. Everywhere the hand of the authorities, Catholic and Evangelical, was heavy on the Anabaptists."[89] Imprisonment, torture and burning, the classic tools of the Papacy, were used against them. The Protestant movement, which had suffered so much under Catholic church-state persecution, began themselves to look to the oppressive power of the state to enforce "orthodox" religious doctrine.

Calvinism, English "Reformation"

John Calvin was one of the most influential reformers and with his brilliant, logical writings he sought to prove that righteousness and salvation are by faith alone, not dependent on the initiative, efforts or good works of the sinner or of the priest. In his efforts to establish righteousness by faith Calvin developed a doctrinal system that unfortunately misrepresented the character of God and contributed to the **"dead"** condition of the Sardis Church.

In his famous *Institutes* Calvin developed five cardinal doctrines. An underlying assumption was the sovereignty of God, that He, being omnipotent, omniscient and omnipresent, accomplishes all that He wills. While this is true

from one point of view, a wrong understanding[90] leads to the erroneous conclusions that Calvin developed in his five cardinal doctrines.[91] Calvin insisted that no one can respond to God unless God calls him,[92] but since God is omnipotent His call will always be effective and the person will of necessity come to Christ.[93] Since not all come to Christ, this means that not all are called

---

88 *Ibid* p. 364

89 *Ibid* p. 367

90 There are some things God cannot do—he cannot lie, for example (Titus 1:2) or do anything else contrary to His character. The question is, can God save humans (who have the freedom of choice) if they do not want to be saved? Although He wants to, He cannot without changing them into another kind of creature. But through His grace He can He give those who are spiritually dead the true freedom to choose life.

91 For an examination of the tenets of Calvinism see Robert Shank, *Elect in the Son*, (Bloomington, MI, Bethany House 1989)

92 *(1) Because of the fall, humans are totally depraved, and thus completely unable to respond affirmatively to God except by a divine dispensation of Grace.* While this is true, God also at the time of the fall put within mankind a "way of escape"—"I will put enmity between you and the woman, and between your seed and her Seed" (Genesis 3:15). God has put within all people something which responds to Him—"That [Christ] was the true Light which gives light to every man" (John 1:9).

93 *(2) Since God is sovereign and accomplishes all that He wills, His grace, which is designed to bring man to repentance will of necessity bring all to repentance to whom it is extended—in other words, God's grace, as reflected in His call to salvation, is irresistible.* Many scriptures show that humans can resist God. For example,"You stiff-necked and uncircumcised in heart and ears! You always resist the Holy Spirit" (Acts 7:51). "The Pharisees and lawyers rejected the will of God" (Luke 7: 30). God bids everyone, "come unto me," but many refuse. See also Matthew 23:37, Romans 1:19, 13:2. God allows resistance because of the value He places on the freedom of the human will. The fall of man shows that man can resist God. He said "of the tree of the knowledge of god and evil you shall not eat" (Genesis 2:17)—a clear expression of His will, and in defiance Adam and Eve ate.

to salvation[94] and that Christ's sacrifice was not intended for all people.[95] Since God wants those who have been called to be saved, they will of necessity continue in faith and cannot later lose their salvation. [96]

Although it is true that salvation is totally a gift of God's grace, it is not a grace that takes away human freedom. God does not "flip a switch" or "pull strings" in people's minds to get them to do what He wants.[97] The miracle of grace is that it enables totally depraved humans to make a choice for or against God, even as Adam did in the Garden of Eden. But the Calvinist doctrine denies that choice and makes man a puppet in the hands of an arbitrary God, excusing His apparently unjust behavior by insisting that we cannot understand Him.

Worst of all, the Calvinists did not repudiate the Catholic doctrine of the immortality of the soul and the eternal torment of the wicked. According to Calvinist belief, God continues to bring creatures into existence who are unable to make any choices that would enable them to avoid eternal damnation, and He does nothing Himself to save those who are not a part of "the elect" from this terrible fate![98]

Despite its misrepresentation of the love and justice of God, this doctrinal system was highly effective against its opponents because of its logic, organization and clever use of proof texts, and so it became widely accepted in the Protestant Churches. Although Calvin's vast influence provided a tremendous boost for the Protestant cause, his doctrine of predestination produced a fatal misconception of God's character.

In England the "Protestant Reformation" was established on the false foundation of lust and political ambition. Henry VIII, desiring a new wife who could bear him a son to sit on his throne after him, was not able to win the approval of the Catholic establishment for a divorce. Exploiting the popular opposition to foreign influence, he

---

94 *(3) Since God's call is irresistible and yet not all are saved, God obviously does not call everyone to salvation, but only those elected or predestined through God's eternal purposes. Those not called, being totally depraved, are unable to positively respond to God and are thus consigned to eternal reprobation.* This doctrine of unconditional election requires radical redefinition of such plain texts as 2Peter 3:9, "The Lord is...not willing that any should perish but that all should come to repentance" See also 1Timothy 2:4-6, Titus 2:11, John 3:14-17, 6:33, 51, 12:32, 1John 2:2, 2Corinthians 5:19, Romans 5:18. It also denies the fact that the offer of saving grace is just as extensive as the damaging effects of sin—"Therefore as through one man's [Adam's] offense judgment came to all men, resulting in condemnation, even so *the free gift came to all men*, resulting in justification of life" (Romans 5:18, see also vs. 12-21).

95 *(4) Since God's sovereign acts accomplish their purpose, and not all men are saved, the atonement provided by Christ on the cross must be limited, efficient only for the elect.* This doctrine does not harmonize with such plain scriptures as 1John 2:2, "He Himself is the propitiation for our sins, and not for ours only but also for the whole world." Christ bought salvation through His sacrifice even for those who will be destroyed: "There shall be false teachers among you, who will secretly bring in damnable heresies, *even denying the Lord who bought them, and bring upon themselves swift destruction*" (2 Peter 2:1). See also 2Corinthians 5:19, I Timothy 2:4-6, John 3:16, John 12:32, John 6:33, 51, John 1:29, Titus 2:11, I John 2:2, 4:14, Romans 5:18, Hebrews 2:9.

96 *(5) Since it is God's sovereign will that calls individuals to salvation, they will of necessity persevere and cannot later lose their salvation.* This doctrine takes away the free will of man and ignores the many scriptures that clearly teach that those who have been saved by Christ can later abandon Him and be lost. See Hebrews 6:4, 10:26, 35-38, 1Timothy 1:19, 6:20,21, Matthew 18:23-35, Ezekiel 18:24, Romans 11:17-24, 1Corinthians 9:27, 15:2, Colossians 1:2. Hebrews 6:4, 10:26, 35-38, 1Timothy 1:19, 6:20,21, Matthew 18:23-35, Ezekiel 18:24, Romans 11:17-24, 1Corinthians 9:27, 15:2, Colossians 1:22,23, 1 Thessalonians 3:8, 2 Peter 1:10, 2:20,21, 3:17, 1John 5:12,13, Revelation 2:4,5.

---

97 Many have been disappointed because God allowed someone to commit undesirable behavior. Others have prayed for someone to believe in God, or to do or stop doing something, and have been disappointed when their prayers did not seem to be answered. But God really has given humans true free will, including the freedom to choose what He doesn't want, because only free-will beings can choose to love God.

98 See chapter 20 for an examination of the scriptures related to the eternal fate of the impenitent.

set about through political maneuverings to make himself the head of the Church of England. "In November, 1534 Parliament passed the famous Supremacy Act, by which Henry and his successors were declared 'the only supreme head in earth of the Church of England'...it practically put the King in the place of the Pope."[99]

The leaders of the country used religion as a political tool. When they needed help against powerful Catholic forces such as France and Spain the "Ten Articles" were drafted which reflected Protestant sentiment in order to seek political support from German Protestants. Later when the Catholic powers had to be appeased the "Six Articles" were formulated which affirmed Catholic doctrine. Whatever the prevailing sentiment, all who were in opposition were persecuted and there were many martyrs.

Papal Response

The Roman Church was slow to respond to the Protestant threat, but by the mid-sixteenth century had taken up the battle in earnest. The Council of Trent, one of the most important in Catholic history, essentially confirmed all the Catholic doctrines, particularly the authority of tradition, and rejected the Protestant beliefs.

One of the most effective weapons against the Protestants was the formation of the Society of Jesus (Jesuits). Ignatius Loyola conceived the idea of a military-style company, with strict discipline and obedience to the Papacy, to fight the battles of the church against infidels and heretics. The Jesuits molded the minds of future political leaders with their excellent schools. Through diligence and sacrifice they made themselves indispensable political advisers. In Catholic countries they brought about a new emphasis on the confessional, thus gaining influence over the people

through the dark secrets they were aware of.

The Inquisition was reorganized where the Catholic Church could manipulate government policy, stamping out the fledgling Protestant movement in Italy and stopping its progress elsewhere. Spain became the military arm of the church, exterminating thousands of Protestants in the Netherlands, France and Germany. The savage St. Bartholomew's day massacre in 1572 epitomized the ruthless crushing of Huguenot Protestantism in France. But Catholicism was looking beyond its traditional European domain; in an era when whole new continents were opening up to European influence, the Jesuits in co-operation with monastic orders were in the vanguard to establish the Catholic system in the Americas, Africa and Asia.

To summarize, the **"dead"** Sardis Church was Protestantism from the later period of the reformers (the 1520's) through the mid eighteenth century. In England and Lutheran Germany the protesting underground church had become an official state church, with a focus on political and territorial struggles. Lutheran theologians were absorbed with scholastic, technical creeds, while Calvinists produced a false doctrinal system based on the theory of unconditional election; none of this was comprehensible to the common man. The various Protestant factions fought with each other, even persecuting one another and resorting to military might rather than faith and sacrifice, and Protestants lost ground to the newly aggressive Catholic opposition.

3:3-6 Hold Fast and Repent

"Remember therefore how you have received and heard, and hold fast, and repent. If therefore you do not watch, I will come upon you as a thief, and you will not know what hour I will come upon you." (Revelation 3:3). If Protestants had remembered and incorporated the heart of the message of the reformers, they

---

99 Walker, *History of the Christian Church*, p. 404.

could have avoided the political and military catastrophes which came upon them **"as a thief."** One of the most tragic aspects of this period was that millions of people lost their lives prematurely, cut off in the bitter and unholy passions of religious wars.[100]

Jesus' warning that **"I will come upon you as a thief, and you will not know what hour I will come upon you"** recalls what He said concerning His Second Coming: "Watch therefore, for you do not know what hour your Lord is coming. But know this, that if the master of the house had known what hour the thief would come, he would have watched and not allowed his house to be broken into" (Matthew 24:42-44). The reformers "rediscovered" the promises of the second advent of Christ and preached His soon coming.[101] Unfortunately this great truth was lost again by their **"dead"** followers and it was not until the Philadelphia era that the church woke up and proclaimed with power the Second Coming.

"You have a few names even in Sardis which have not defiled their garments; and they shall walk with Me in white, for they are worthy" (Revelation 3:4). In this period of darkness for the true church there were still some champions of faith. In England, Tyndale translated the scriptures and died a martyr's death, along with John Frith, Nicholas Ridley, Hugh Latimer and others. John Knox in Scotland stood boldly for the Protestant cause in the face of the plots and political intrigues of the Catholic Mary Queen of Scots. The Puritans were hounded from country to country for their fidelity to their faith in the Bible, with some of them, the "Pilgrims," eventually establishing their colonies in America. Most of the **"few names"** will only be known in eternity; on this earth they were persecuted by Catholics and Protestants alike.

"He that overcomes, the same shall be clothed in white raiment; and I will not blot out his name out of the Book of Life, but I will confess his name before My Father, and before His angels. He that has an ear, let him hear what the Spirit said to the churches" (Revelation 3:5,6). In His closing message to the church of Sardis Jesus warns of the great danger facing those who have **"a name that [they] are alive"** but who have not **"overcome:"** their names would be **"blot[ted]… from the Book of Life."** Jesus was here directing attention to the Philadelphia era that would come next, when the judgment that takes place in heaven would begin, a judgment in which the lives of those whose names were written in the Book of Life would be examined and their names would be either retained or blotted out.

Philadelphia 3:7 Revival

"And to the angel of the church in Philadelphia write: These things said He that is holy, He that is true, He that has the key of David, He that opens, and no one shuts; and shuts, and no one opens: I know your works. Behold, I have set before you an open door, and no one can shut it; for you have a little strength, and have kept My word, and have not denied My name." (Revelation 3:7).

---

100 The Thirty Years' War (1618-1648) is an example; it was a particularly brutal territorial struggle between Protestants and Catholics in Europe. "To Germany the Thirty Years' War was an unmitigated and frightful evil. The land was ploughed from end to end for a generation by lawless, plundering armies. Population had fallen from sixteen million to less than six. Fields were waste, commerce and manufacturing destroyed. Above all, intellectual life had stagnated, morals had been roughened and corrupted, and religion grievously maimed. A century after its close the devastating consequences had not been made good. Little evidence of spiritual life was manifested in this frightful time of war" (Walker, History of the Christian Church, p. 451).

101 For example, John Knox wrote, "Has not our Lord Jesus carried up our flesh into heaven? And shall He not return? We know that He shall return, and that with expedition." Other reformers made similar statements. See White, Ellen "The Great Controversy," (Pacific Press) Pg. 303.

In contrast to all the other churches, the Philadelphia Church is not condemned for anything.[102] This period, from the mid-eighteenth through the mid-nineteenth centuries, was one in which the Christian church woke up from their **"dead"** Sardis condition and with their **"little strength"** they **"kept [His] word,"** triggering the greatest revivals since Pentecost.[103]

One of the first to come to life was the Moravian Church, arguably the first protestant denomination. The Moravians arose in the fifteenth century through the influence of John Huss but had been scattered and disheartened by fierce persecution. In 1727 a small group of Moravian Christians received a "visitation by the Holy Spirit" and "learned to love one another."[104] The revived Moravian Church grew rapidly, being zealous about sharing the gospel and willing to go anywhere in the service of Christ. One of their projects was in the American colony of Georgia among the Indians, and a providential encounter of Moravian missionaries with John and Charles Wesley on a ship to Georgia helped to prepare the way for a remarkable reformation in England.

The Wesleys were the sons of an Anglican clergyman and from an early age had a deep interest in religious purity. John became a priest, while Charles formed a club at Oxford University which was dedicated to the pursuit of holiness; it was derisively called the "Holy Club" and later the "Methodists" because of their painfully methodical efforts to be pious. Although they had a deep sense of spiritual inadequacy, the Wesley brothers were zealous and energetic, and in 1735 accepted a call to go to America to be missionaries in Georgia. While on the journey the ship encountered a fierce storm, which terrified all of the passengers (including the Wesleys) except for a group of Moravian Christians. The humiliating contrast of the Moravians' faith with his own fears made a deep impression on John Wesley.[105]

After a fairly fruitless ministry in America the Wesleys returned to England where they again came in contact with Moravian Christians. One evening in 1738 at a small meeting John Wesley heard the reading of Martin Luther's description of the change that God works in the heart through faith in Jesus Christ. "I felt my heart strangely warmed. I felt I did trust in Christ, Christ alone, for salvation; that He had taken away my sins, and saved me from the law of sin and death." Charles had already had a personal experience with Jesus three days earlier during a serious illness, and they now worked tirelessly to bring the gospel to the common people.

The Wesleys took their message directly to the poor and organized the new converts into small groups for spiritual growth. Rather than relying on professional clergy the members themselves were trained to be responsible for leadership and even for preaching. Their movement swept through England and transformed

---

102 The Smyrna church is not explicitly condemned for "the blasphemy of those who say they are Jews and are not, but are a synagogue of Satan," but this book takes the position that this was a developing trend within the church rather than a threat from outside.

103 This period corresponds to the end of the 1,260 years of persecution, when the "beast from the sea" which "made war with the saints and overcame them" received a "deadly wound" (see 13:3 *The Deadly Wound*). This gave the remnant Christian church some breathing room in which she could come back to life.

104 Wikipedia contributors, "Moravian Church," *Wikipedia, The Free Encyclopedia,* http://en.wikipedia.org/w/index.php?title=Moravian_Church&oldid=614604778(accessed June 27, 2014).

105 Walker *History of the Christian Church* p. 511.

British society.[106]

One of the most powerful preachers among Wesley's associates, George Whitefield, took the message to America. In 1740 under the influence of his stirring sermons the "Great Awakening" took place, a powerful revival which swept through New England and the middle colonies. In 1780 the Sunday school movement began, teaching the fundamentals of Christianity to all levels of society, and in 1804 the Bible Society was founded, resulting in massive distribution of the scriptures.

Missionary and Advent Movemements

In 1792 William Carey helped to organize The Baptist Society for Propagating the Gospel among the Heathen. Carey was sent to India, and his letters inspired a whole host of mission societies to be formed. The missionary movement of the 1800's sent wave after wave of teachers, doctors and evangelists to Africa, Asia, South America and the Islands of the Sea, often to a premature death from illness or martyrdom.[107]

One of the last reforms was the advent movement, a worldwide focus on the soon return of Christ. Many people were convinced that a series of unusual events were signs of the soon coming of Christ as prophesied in Revelation 6:12, "there was a great earthquake; and the sun became black as sackcloth of hair, and the moon became as blood; and the stars of heaven fell to the earth." In 1755 the Lisbon earthquake caused massive destruction in Portugal, Spain and North Africa, and damage in a much larger area; it was the most destructive earthquake that has ever struck in Europe. Twenty-five years later on May 19, 1780 an unnatural darkness which became known as the "dark day" covered much of New England. Then on November 13, 1833 the most spectacular display of meteorites ever seen took place. These events convinced many that the end of the world was at hand .

Particularly in America the preaching of William Miller stirred up a deep interest in the scriptures related to the Second Advent. One of the key passages of interest to the "Adventists" (believers in the soon coming or advent of Christ) was Daniel 8, which portrays a "little horn" (the medieval papacy) which "exalted himself as high as the Prince of the host; and by him the daily sacrifices were taken away, and the place of his sanctuary was cast down" (v. 11). One of the angels who presented the vision to Daniel asked, "How long will the vision be? (v. 13). The Adventists believed that the answer, "For two thousand three hundred days, then the sanctuary shall be cleansed" (v. 14) identified the time of the Second Coming of Christ. Thus attention was directed to the study of the sanctuary and the priestly ministry of Christ, a theme that is central in the message to the Philadelphia Church .

3:8, The Key of David, the Open Door

Jesus presents Himself to the church of Philadelphia as **"He that has the key of David, He that opens, and no one shuts; and shuts, and**

---

106 Wesley made sure that those who were serious about leading a new life were channeled into small groups for growth in discipleship. These "class meetings" turned out to be the primary means of bringing millions of England's most desperate people into the liberating discipline of Christian faith.

"Other reformers looked upon these decadent neighborhoods and threw up their hands in despair. It seemed hopeless that the plight of the poor could be remedied. Wesley looked at the same miserable conditions and saw a situation which was ripe for evangelism. Instead of abhorring their miseries and vices from a comfortable and safe distance, he eagerly sought the foulest circumstances in which to work…the nation was shaken to its foundations by a spiritual awakening. Historians…generally agreed that the transformation of English society was largely due to the impact of Wesley and the movement he spawned." D. Michael Henderson, *John Wesley's Class Meeting*, (Nappanee, IN, Evangel 1997) p. 28

107 Walker *History of the Christian Church* p. 523

no one opens." This verse quotes from Isaiah 22, which tells the story of the transfer of the royal stewardship to Eliakim the son of Hilkiah. God declared through the prophet, "I will call My servant Eliakim the son of Hilkiah...*The key of the house of David* I will lay on his shoulder; *So he shall open and no one shall shut; and he shall shut and no one shall open*" (Isaiah 22: 19-22). A study of 1Chronicles 9 shows that the key of David was for opening "the chambers and treasuries of the House of God," in other words, for the opening of the sanctuary.[108]

Thus Jesus, **"who has the key of David,"** is opening the chambers and treasuries of the sanctuary to the church of Philadelphia. This introduces one of the most important themes of Revelation—**"See, I have set before you an open door, and no one can shut it"** (v.8). This theme of the **"open door"** is so important that it is repeated as the introduction to the seven seals, one of the longest, most critical and most poorly understood sections in the Book of Revelation: "After these things I looked, and behold, *a door standing open in heaven*" (Revelation 4:1). The original Greek wording shows first of all that the open door of Revelation 4:1 is the same open door that was set before the church of Philadelphia. It also shows that this is not a door *into* heaven, but instead, the door is open *in* heaven, as if there is some kind of building with doors in heaven. And indeed, the book of Hebrews tells us of just such a "building," the heavenly sanctuary: "We have such

a High Priest [Jesus], who is seated at the right hand of the throne of the Majesty in the heavens, a Minister of the sanctuary and of the true tabernacle which the Lord erected, and not man" (Hebrews 8:1,2).

Although the book of Hebrews tells us a few things about the heavenly sanctuary, we can learn more by studying the earthly sanctuary, because it was a "copy and shadow of the heavenly things" (Hebrews 8:5).[109] The tabernacle[110] was built with two rooms: an outer sanctuary (the Holy Place) where daily sacrifices were offered, and an inner sanctuary (the Most Holy Place) where the yearly ritual of the Day of Atonement took place. There were two doors in the tabernacle, one into the Holy Place, and the other going from the Holy Place into the Most Holy Place (Ezekiel 41:23, 1Kings 6:31-35).

The special **"open door"** that was **"set before"** the Philadelphia Church would not refer to the door into the Holy Place, which was open every day as the priest performed the daily ceremonies

---

108 1 Chronicles 9 describes the 212 gatekeepers of the Temple. "David...appointed them to their trusted office. So they and their children were in charge of the gates of the house of the Lord" (v. 22). Of these there were four who had a special position: "in this trusted office were four chief gatekeepers...They had charge over the chambers and treasuries of the house of God...and they were in charge of *opening* it every morning" (v. 26, 27). The Hebrew word for "opening," *metsolaw*, is the same word that is translated "key" in Isaiah 22:22 ("the *key* of the house of David"). The chief gatekeepers were in charge of opening (with the key of David) the chambers and treasuries of God's sanctuary.

109 Detailed descriptions of the wilderness sanctuary and its services are given in Exodus chapters 25-40, most of the book of Leviticus, and Numbers chapters 8,9,15,28,29. The temple planned by David and built by Solomon is described in 1Kings chapters 6-8, 1Chronicles 22, 28 and 2Chronicles 2-5. This temple was destroyed by the armies of Nebuchadnezzar, king of Babylon and its treasures were hauled away (Jeremiah 52). The prophet Ezekiel was given detailed plans for a new temple (Ezekiel 40-48) but no details have been given of the actual temple that was built after the Babylonian captivity during the time of Ezra and Nehemiah. This last temple, enlarged and beautified by Herod, suffered the fate predicted by Jesus, ("not one stone shall be left here upon another, that shall not be thrown down") being destroyed by the Roman army in A.D. 70, never to be rebuilt. The earthly tabernacle and its priestly ministry is compared with the heavenly sanctuary and the ministry of Jesus in Hebrews 8-10. All through the book of Revelation are references to the temple (1:11,12, 2:1, 3:8,12, 4:1-10, 5:1-14, 6:9, 7:11,15, 8:3-5, 9:13, 11:1,2,19, 12:5, 13:6,8, 14:3,17,18, 15:5-8, 16:1,7,17, 19:4, 20:4,11,12, 21:3,5,22, 22:1,3).

110 The Hebrew and Greek words for sanctuary, tabernacle, and temple are all used for the house of God but have slightly different meanings. Sanctuary simply means holy place. Tabernacle refers to a tent, and is usually used to refer to the sanctuary in the wilderness which continued to be used until the time of Solomon. He built the first temple, which means house.

of the sanctuary. Hebrews 9 indicates that Christ entered into the Holy Place after His death and resurrection, and that the entry into the "Most Holy Place" was still a future event.[111] Thus the **"open door"** signals the entrance of Jesus our High Priest into the inner sanctuary, the Most Holy Place, indicating that the heavenly events that were symbolized by the once-a-year Day of Atonement (described in Leviticus 16) would begin during the time of the Philadelphia Church. As we will see in later chapters, the Day of Atonement is one of the most prominent themes in the Book of Revelation. In chapter 4 where the **"open door"** is again mentioned we will learn more about what is happening in heaven during the Day of Atonement, but at this point we should take a brief look at an important prophecy in Daniel 8 which identifies when during the Philadelphia era the Day of Atonement began.

The Day of Atonement, 2,300 Days

On the Day of Atonement in ancient Israel there was a ceremonial "final judgment" of the sinners who had brought their sacrifices to the sanctuary throughout the year. This ceremony was a

symbolic "shadow" of the heavenly reality foretold by Daniel 8:14, the cleansing of the Heavenly Sanctuary—"For two thousand three hundred days, then the sanctuary shall be cleansed." This complex prophecy will be explained in detail in 4: *The Day of Atonement* and Appendix 5, but at this point it is only necessary to look briefly at two important concepts: when in human history does the "cleansing of the heavenly sanctuary" take place, and what is it that is cleansed?

In Daniel 8 the prophet had a vision in which he saw the history of the empires that would oppress God's people, beginning with the symbols of a ram and a goat.[112] The ram (the Persian Empire v. 20) was defeated and trampled by the goat (the Greek Empire under Alexander the Great, v. 21). After the death of Alexander the Greek Empire was divided "toward the four winds of heaven," becoming the Hellenistic kingdoms. These were superseded by a little horn "which grew exceedingly great…up to the hosts of heaven" (Daniel 8:9,10). A comparison with the visions of Daniel 2 and 7 shows that the horn symbolizes the Roman Empire as it evolved from pagan Rome into the persecuting papal power of the Middle Ages.

Daniel 8 goes on to show how the medieval Roman Catholic Church "took away" Christ's ministry of intercession in the heavenly sanctuary—"He [the horn] even exalted himself as high as the Prince of the host [Christ]; and by him the daily sacrifices were taken away, and the place of His sanctuary was cast down. Because of transgression, an army was given over to the horn to oppose the daily sacrifices; and he cast truth down to the ground" (Daniel 8:11,12).[113]

---

111 Hebrews 9: 2,3 calls the two rooms "*Agia*" (the Holy) and "*Agia ton Agion*" (the Holy of Holies). Verse 8 refers to the Holy of Holies with the shortened name "*ton Agion*," and states that the way into the Holy of Holies was not open while the first sanctuary was still standing (and the earthly sanctuary was still standing at the time the book of Hebrews was written, not being destroyed until AD 70). Moreover, vs. 11,12 (KJV) indicates that Christ entered the heavenly sanctuary and "by His own blood He entered in once into the Holy Place" (*Agia*). If Paul had wanted to indicate that Jesus had immediately entered the Holy of Holies he no doubt would have used the word "*ton Agion*" as in verse 8. It is true that a number of English versions translate "*ta agia*" in verse 12 as "the Most Holy Place" but this is not consistent with the usage in verses 2, 3 and 8. Paul was comparing the earthly shadow (both Holy Place and Most Holy Place) with the heavenly reality, and stressed that Jesus has opened the heavenly reality in all its fullness. He was not comparing an old covenant or dispensation with the "Holy Place" ministry in the first room.

112 Even the animals used to symbolize the historical empires were ones used in the sanctuary. The ram and the goat are both sacrificial animals used on the Day of Atonement. (See Leviticus 16:5).

113 In 14: *The Daily Sacrifice* there is a complete explanation of how the Papal system took away the "daily sacrifices."

This verse refers to the "army" of medieval priests, monks and theologians who created a way of "salvation" that effectively left Christ and His intercession out of the picture. An angel asked a vital question: "How long will the vision be?" (v 13). Daniel heard the answer: "For two thousand three hundred days; then the sanctuary shall be cleansed" (v. 14).

From the context of the vision, extending from the Persian empire "to the time of the end" (v. 17) it is obvious that the 2,300 days were not literal days, which would have been just a little more than six years, but are prophetic days, in which a day represents a year.[114] The angel Gabriel tried to explain the meaning, but Daniel was overwhelmed and did not understand what it meant (vs.16, 27).

Later Gabriel returned to interpret the vision, particularly the portion concerning the 2,300 "days" (Daniel 9:1, 21-23). He explained that 490 years would be designated, or "cut off" from the 2,300 years for the Jewish people in order to prepare for the Messiah. Both the 490 years and the 2,300 years would begin at the same time with the decree "to restore and build Jerusalem," which was given by the Persian king Artaxexes

in 457 BC.[115] A calculation of the 490 years starting in 457 BC reaches to the crucifixion of Jesus. A calculation of 2,300 years starting in 457 BC extends to AD 1844. At that time the "cleansing of the sanctuary" (the Day of Atonement) would begin. This important time prophecy is analyzed in much more detail in Appendix 5.

This time frame fits perfectly with the chronology of the Philadelphia period. "The sanctuary" that was to be "cleansed" (Daniel 8:14) does not refer to the earthly sanctuary, which was destroyed in AD 70 and has never been rebuilt, but rather to the heavenly sanctuary and the intercessory work of Christ. The medieval Catholic Church, symbolized by the great horn,[116] had created a system of "salvation" based upon

---

114 The day-for-a-year principle is obvious from the prophecies of Daniel. For example, the seventy weeks (490 days) of Daniel 9 were to start with "the command to restore and build Jerusalem" (which was in 457 BC) and would extend "until Messiah the Prince" (Jesus, Daniel 9:25). The prophecy of 2,300 days in chapter 8 began with "the kings of Media and Persia" (the Persian kings reigned in the 6th and 5th centuries BC) and would extend "to the time of the end" (Daniel 8:20, 17). The prophecy of "time, times and half a time" (1,260 days) in chapter 7 began at the time of the breakup of the pagan Roman Empire and extended "until the time came for the saints to possess the kingdom" (Daniel 7:22). All these prophecies began in ancient times and continued the number of *years* the prophecy specified in *days*. Other scriptural support for this principle is found in Numbers 14:34, Ezekiel 4:5,6, Job 10:5, Psalm 77:5.

115 There were actually three decrees given, the first by Cyrus (Ezra 1:1-4) which allowed for the building of "the house of the Lord God of Israel," the decree of Darius (Ezra 6:1-12) which again allowed for the building of the temple after it had been halted by opponents, and the decree of Artaxerxes (Ezra 7:11-26). However, it was only under the decree of Artaxerxes that provision was made for the building of the walls and city, as specified by the prophesy of Daniel 9:25 (See Nehemiah 2:1-9).

116 Many commentators apply the 2,300 day prophecy to the history of Antiochus Epiphanes (who ruled from 175-164 BC), the Syrian king who opposed the Jewish worship of God. He tried to impose the worship of Zeus, forcing the Jews to sacrifice swine on the altar (the so-called "transgression of desolation"). In this view, the restoration of the temple services by the Macabees was the cleansing of the sanctuary. But this event does not fit the specifications of the prophecy: 1) The "little horn" was to become "exceedingly great," "His power shall be mighty," "He shall prosper and thrive." But Antiochus Epiphanes was a relatively weak king, certainly not matching those before or after him. 2) The "little horn" king was to arise "in the latter time of their kingdom" (the Greek Seleucid kingdom). But Antiochus was only eighth in a series of 26 kings and his rule was about one hundred years before the end of the dynasty. 3) Daniel was told that "the vision refers to the time of the end" "in the latter time of the indignation; for at the appointed time the end shall be" (Daniel 8:17,19). But Daniel 11:40-12:3 makes it clear that the "time of the end" is the end of time when the great time of trouble will take place, God's people will be delivered and the dead resurrected; in other words, at the Second Coming of Christ. 4) Neither 2,300 days nor 1,150 days (2,300 evening and morning sacrifices, as some commentators interpret this period) are significant periods of time in the career of Antiochus Epiphanes (the chronology is found in 1 Macabees). 5) According to Jesus, the "abomination of desolation" was still future in His day (Matthew 24:15).

human works and human priests that obscured and desecrated Christ's intercession in the heavenly sanctuary—"the place of His sanctuary was cast down" (Daniel 8:9-11). The "rubbish" of superstition and tradition would be "cleansed" as Christ entered the final phase of His heavenly ministry, preparing the way for His Second Coming.

It is important to note that the purpose of the Old Testament Day of Atonement was not to clean the furniture in the temple—it was to provide a final cleansing of the sinners who had been confessing their sins during the year. "For on that day the priest shall make atonement for you, to cleanse you, that you may be clean from all your sins before the Lord" (Leviticus 16:30). It was a day of judgment, to determine who among all those who had brought their sacrifices to the temple during the year were continuing to trust in the salvation that had been provided for them.

3:9-13 I Am Coming Quickly

The theme of the Day of Atonement will be dealt with in more detail in chapter 4, but the point is that during the Philadelphia period Jesus, our great High Priest, began a special phase of preparation and judgment in the heavenly sanctuary, which will culminate in the sealing of His special representatives (Revelation 7). This will be followed by the "time of trouble such as never was" and the Second Coming of Christ (Daniel 12:1).

But the people of the Philadelphia period, who lived during the beginning of the great Day of Atonement, were to be spared from the rigors of the time of trouble. **"I know your works. Behold, I have set before you an open door, and no one can shut it; for you have a little strength, and have kept My word, and have not denied My name…Because you have kept the word of My patience, I will also keep you from the hour of trial, which shall come upon all the world, to**

test those that dwell on the earth." (Revelation 3:8,10). The church of the Philadelphia period zealously preached about the **"hour of trial"** and the soon coming of Christ, and those who gave the messages were often ridiculed, cast out of their churches and ostracized. As we will see in chapters 11 (the murder of the "two witnesses") and 13 (the "mark of the beast" and "death decree"), this opposition will increase until Jesus comes to rescue His people. But the final judgment that began during the Philadelphia period will vindicate God's persecuted people—**"Indeed I will make those of the synagogue of Satan, who say they are Jews and are not, but lie—indeed I will make them come and worship before your feet, and to know that I have loved you"** (Revelation 3:9).

"Behold, I come quickly; hold that fast which you have, so that no one takes your crown." Many believers during the Philadelphia era experienced a severe test of their faith when they realized that **"I am coming quickly"** did not mean what they had thought when they first studied prophecies such as the 2,300 days of Daniel 8, and that Jesus would probably not even appear in their lifetimes. Jesus, knowing in advance the disappointment and ridicule they would face, counseled them to **"persevere"** and **"hold fast"** and to take comfort in the fact that they would be kept **"from the hour of trial which shall come upon the whole world."** The underlying message here is that the final events, while brief from God's perspective, are grueling and seemingly endless for those on earth who will live through them. Satan, who has "great wrath, because he knows that he has but a short time" (Revelation 12:12) was already setting in motion his plan to defeat the people of God and **"take [their] crowns,"** using one of his most subtle tricks—wealth and materialism, the prominent features of the next (Laodicean) period.

The promise for the Philadelphia overcomers is a place in the very temple that they saw by faith through the **"open door"**—**"He that overcomes I will make a pillar in the temple of My God, and he shall go out no more, and I will write on him the name of My God, and the name of the city of My God, which is New Jerusalem, which comes down out of heaven from My God. And I will write on him My new name"** (Revelation 3:12).

Laodicea
3:14 The True Witness

"And to the angel of the church of the Laodiceans write: These things said the Amen, the Faithful and True Witness, the Beginning of the creation of God" (Revelation 3:14). With these titles Jesus emphasized His authority: He is the One who created and sustains all that we see around us (**"the Beginning of the creation of God"**), whatever He says is always true (**"the Faithful and True Witness"**), and He has the last word (**"the Amen"**). But even while the Philadelphia revivals were taking place Satan was laying the groundwork for his end-time masterpiece—to rob God of His place of authority in the lives of His children.

The Middle Ages were all about temporal authority—the authority of the church, of the popes, the bishops, the kings and emperors, of tradition, and of the ancient philosophers. The Protestant Reformation, along with the Renaissance, broke the stranglehold of the church, but in doing so it opened the way for rationalism and skepticism. Rene Descartes was one of the first modern philosophers, and his famous statement "I think, therefore I am" embodied the idea that the rational, thinking man is the starting point for all knowledge—a marked departure from the first words of scripture, "In the beginning God" (Genesis 1:1). Later philosophers built on the foundation that the human experience and reason are the basis of our understanding of the world and even of God, rather than divine revelation.

In the meantime, scientists such as Copernicus, Kepler and especially Galileo were questioning the church's understanding of the nature of the universe. The church clung to the idea that the earth was the center of the cosmos, even resorting to persecution to impose their view, and when ultimately proven wrong the church lost prestige and respect for her teaching. Isaac Newton, with his brilliant mathematical explanations of physical phenomena, transformed the view of nature into a predictable system based upon unvarying laws that did not need the immediate intervention of God in order to continue its operation. Charles Darwin developed the theory of evolution which seemed to negate the need for God as the one who directs the details and development of His creation.

The rational, skeptical attitude also invaded the field of theology. In Germany a rationalistic movement ironically known as the "enlightenment" called into question the authority and relevance of the traditional church, the existence of miracles, and the reliability of God's Word. "Higher Criticism" became prevalent, in which every detail of the scriptures was subjected to skeptical scrutiny and dissection. Intense effort was applied to the questions of which persons and events of scripture are actually historical and which verses are authentic. The natural result was widespread doubt about the authority of the scriptures. Another major movement, the "social gospel," took the emphasis away from salvation and victory over sin and placed it upon human effort to improve the plight of the poor and unfortunate.

3:15-17 Lukewarm

These philosophical, scientific and theological trends led to a tendency towards self-sufficiency and the marginalizing of religion that is unprecedented in human history. Man has always had extremely diverse spiritual beliefs and doctrines, but a belief in a supernatural spiritual power which is the greatest influence of life has been central to nearly all peoples at all times. But the Laodicean period is characterized by spiritual indifference and materialism. **"I know your works, that you are neither cold nor hot: I would that you were cold or hot. So then because you are lukewarm, and neither cold nor hot, I will spew you out of my mouth. Because you say, I am rich, and increased with goods, and have need of nothing; and do not know that you are wretched, and miserable, and poor, and blind, and naked."** (Revelation 3:15-17).

Here we see the condition of the church from the mid-nineteenth century until the present. It is a church that is comfortable and at ease—the persecutions and spiritual battles seem to be over. The fervent revivals of the Philadelphia era have lost their impact, and a great drowsiness seems to have settled over God's people, lulling them into a spiritual stupor—"men who are settled in complacency, who say in their heart, 'the Lord will not do good, nor will He do evil'" (Zephaniah 1:12). In the light of the impending disasters that are foretold in the prophecies concerning the great time of trouble as well as the dire predictions of calamity by scientists and scholars, this complacency would be incomprehensible were it not for the knowledge that the enemy of all souls is exerting superhuman effort to ensure that few are ready for the events that are about to transpire.

Most of the people in western countries would classify themselves as Christians, but Christ Himself is considered to be largely irrelevant to the problems and issues today. For the majority of people, it doesn't seem like God can help them get a better paying job, find relief from health problems, or solve problems in personal relationships. Religion means going to church and then ignoring God for the rest of the week. Paul predicted that this kind of religion would prevail—"In the last days...men will be lovers of themselves...having a form of godliness but denying its power" (2Timothy 3:5).

The church should be giving a powerful message of invitation and warning to the world, but is instead comfortably lukewarm, pandering to the desire of the people for a comfortable religion to go along with their comfortable lifestyle. There seems to be an unspoken social contract: the church will be there for baptisms, weddings, funerals and nice "religious" holidays and will preach a smooth message of love and morality ("God loves you so you should try to be good"), avoiding messages that would require true sacrifice or change. The people on their part will make sure that the church has enough money to have nice buildings, facilities, programs and salaries.

The ancient prophets foresaw this modern condition: "His watchmen are blind, they are all ignorant; they are all dumb dogs, they cannot bark; sleeping, lying down, loving to slumber. Yes, they are greedy dogs, which never have enough... They all look to their own way, every one for his own gain." "Tomorrow will be as today, and much more abundant" (Isaiah 56:10-12). "Woe to you who are at ease in Zion...woe to you who put far off the day of doom...[who] stretch out on your couches, eat lambs from the flock and calves from the midst of the stall; who sing idly to the sound of stringed instruments, and invent for yourselves musical instruments like David; who drink wine from bowls and anoint yourselves with the best ointments" (Amos 6:1-6). Here is a picture of modern Christianity, with the focus on music, entertainment and feeling good, forgetting that the church has a mission to a world held captive by the enemy, a mission that will inevitably involve conflict and suffering.

Jesus Himself predicted this danger—"But take heed to yourselves lest your hearts be weighed down with carousing, drunkenness, and the cares of this life, and that Day come on you unexpectedly. For it will come as a snare on all those who dwell on the face of the whole earth. Watch therefore, and pray always" (Luke 21:34-36).

3:18 Buy from Me—Gold

Spiritual vigilance is particularly important during the Laodicean period, which is the time when "the sanctuary [God's people] shall be cleansed" and the heavenly Day of Atonement will take place (see chapter 4). On this day God's people are commanded to "afflict your souls,"[117] prayerfully examining their lives. What specifically should the Laodiceans pray for? Jesus Himself gave the prescription: **"I counsel you to buy from Me gold tried in the fire, that you may be rich; and white raiment, that you may be clothed, and that the shame of your nakedness may not appear; and anoint your eyes with eye salve, that you may see"** (Revelation 3:18).

The spiritual poverty of the Laodiceans is summed up by the words **"wretched and miserable and poor."** Although physical poverty generally receives God's sympathy and promise of ultimate justice or blessing ("blessed are the poor"),[118] the Laodicean poverty is spiritual, caused by willful neglect of the richest spiritual blessings that have ever been available for God's people. A glut of Bibles, spiritual literature, music, media, resources, preaching, facilities and opportunities leave no excuse for the general ignorance

of God's Word and His will that is prevalent among professed Christians today.

True riches are abundantly available—**"I counsel you to buy from me."** The fact that Laodicea must buy indicates that she will have to give up something. Obviously it is the pride, self-sufficiency and love of ease and comfort that will have to be given up in exchange for that which has real value, symbolized by gold, white garments and eye salve.

"Buy from Me gold tried in the fire, that you may be rich." Gold is **"tried"** or purified in the furnace and is a symbol of the faith that results from a deep experience with God, particularly from passing through difficult trials with the Lord— "You have been grieved by various trials, that the genuineness of your faith, being much more precious than gold that perishes, though it is tested by fire, may be found" (1 Peter 1:7). "When He has tested me I shall come forth as gold" (Job 23:10).

The comfortable Laodiceans are loathe to submit themselves to the Lord and His refining work, but unless they do so they will not develop the faith they will need in order to endure the trials of the last days. "Who can endure the day of His coming? And who can stand when He appears? For He is like a refiner's fire...He will purify the sons of Levi and purge them as gold and silver, that they may offer to the Lord an offering in righteousness" (Malachi 3:2,3).

Faith is not just believing. Hebrews 11 teaches that true faith involves a response,[119] or as James expressed it, "faith without works is dead" (James 2: 17-26). An example of the development

---

117 Leviticus 23:26-32

118 Luke 6:20, See also Isaiah 58:6-8, Jeremiah 22:16, Ezekiel 16:49, Daniel 4:27, Amos 4:11,12, 8:4-7, Luke 4:18, 14:12-14, 18:22, Galatians 2:10, James 2:5,6.

119 "By faith Abel offered to God a more excellent sacrifice than Cain...By faith Noah prepared an ark...By faith Abraham went out, not knowing where he was going...By faith Abraham offered up Isaac...By faith Moses was hidden...refused to be called the son of Pharaoh's daughter... forsook Egypt...kept the Passover and the sprinkling of blood...By faith the walls of Jericho fell down after they were encircled for seven days...etc. (see Hebrews 11).

of faith is found in the story of Daniel, Shadrach, Meshach and Abednego. These young men were taken captive by the Babylonians and enrolled in the royal training school to become advisers to the king. Their first act of faith was to follow the simple dietary instructions they had received as children. Although there was considerable risk, they "purposed in [their] hearts that [they] would not defile [themselves] with the portion of the king's delicacies, nor with the wine which he drank" (Daniel 1:8). This exercise of faith had both physical and intellectual benefits. "At the end of ten days they looked healthier and better nourished than any of the young men who ate the royal food." Moreover, they were "ten times better…in all matters of wisdom and understanding" (Daniel 1:15, 20).

Their increased faith and confidence was tested by the king's demand for his advisers to interpret a dream that he could not even remember, with the threat of death if they could not. Daniel dared to tell the king that he would interpret the dream, and then he and his companions prayed earnestly and God revealed the dream to Daniel, resulting in the saving not only of their own lives but of all the other royal advisers as well.

The ultimate test came when the king made a giant image and demanded that all his citizens bow down and worship it or be thrown into a fiery furnace. Shadrach, Meshach and Abednego refused, and their answer revealed the faith that had resulted from their previous deep experiences with God: "Our God whom we serve is able to deliver us from the burning fiery furnace and He will deliver us from your hand, O king. But if not, let it be known to you, O king, that we do not serve your gods, nor will we worship the gold image which you have set up" (Daniel 3:17,18). The king in a rage had them bound and thrown into the furnace, but "the fire had no power; the hair of their head was not singed, nor were their

garments affected." Only the ropes which bound them were burned off, and "the Son of God," Jesus himself, walked with them "in the midst of the fire." As a result the king recognized and confessed the superior power of God, sending a decree to the whole nation of Babylon to worship the true God. (Daniel 3:1-30).

In this story we see that the steps of faith begin with simple obedience, which leads to powerful experiences with God. These empower even more radical obedience, which results in more profound experiences which not only build up faith but provide extraordinary witnessing opportunities. A characteristic of Laodicea is that today many Christians are afraid to take the first steps, bound by fears, sinful habits, the knowledge of their own weakness, and a desire to stay in their comfort zone. But when, acting by faith, we **"buy gold refined in the fire"** by responding to God's initiatives, the bonds which have limited us are burned off and our walk with Jesus takes on a freedom that is obvious to those around us, even if we do end up "in the furnace."

White Garments

Jesus also counsels the Laodiceans to buy **"white raiment, that you may be clothed, and that the shame of your nakedness may not appear"** (Revelation 3:18). A sense of nakedness was the first noticeable result of sin—"Then the eyes of both of them [Adam and Eve] were opened, and they knew that they were naked, and they sewed fig leaves together and made themselves coverings" (Genesis 3:7). Sinners have been "sewing fig leaves" ever since, attempting to hide or gloss over their sins. And God has been offering His garments ever since. "For Adam and his wife the Lord God made tunics of skin and clothed them." Obviously the death of an animal was required to supply the skins, and this was the first sacrificial symbol of the death of Christ, who provides His righteousness to cover the "filthy rags" of our own feeble attempts to be righteous.[120] This is what theologians call justification—the Lord declares us righteous (even though we have been and still are sinners) because of what Christ has done in living a perfect life and taking upon Himself the guilt of our sins.[121] In addition to justification God also offers sanctification, which is a change of character so that "the righteous requirements of the law might be fulfilled in us who do not walk according to the flesh but according to the Spirit" (Romans 8:4). Both justification and sanctification are gifts from God that are received through faith—we have no power to make ourselves righteous or holy.

In the Book of Revelation white garments symbolize both justification and sanctification,[122] but it is sanctification that seems to be particularly lacking during the Laodicean period. The Apostle Paul states that "In the last days perilous times will come" and then lists the sins that prevail in our modern world.[123] Tragically, he indicates that these sins are also in the church—they

are found among those who have "a form of godliness, but deny its power" (2Timothy 3:1-3).

The modern church has focused so heavily on justification that sanctification is almost considered dangerous, as if it will somehow lead to righteousness by works. But holiness is the inevitable result of true justification and is integral to salvation—"For this is the will of God: your sanctification" (1Thessalonians 4:3). "God from the beginning chose you for salvation through sanctification by the Spirit and belief in the truth" (2Thessalonians 2:13).

The key phrase in these texts is "by the Spirit." Paul asks the pointed question, "Are you so foolish? Having begun in the Spirit, are you now being made perfect by the flesh?" (Galatians 3:3). Obviously not—"For if you live according to the flesh you will die; but if by the Spirit you put to death the deeds of the body, you will live…if the Spirit of Him who raised Jesus from the dead dwells in you, He who raised Christ from the dead will also give life to your mortal bodies through the Spirit who dwells in you" (Romans 8:13, 11). According to this text, one of the most important things that the Holy Spirit does when He fills us is to enable us to "put to death the deeds of the body." This is what sanctification is all about, and this is one of the greatest needs of the Laodicean Church (see 3: 22 *Hear What the Spirit Says*).

Eye Salve

The Laodiceans are also blind, and Jesus counsels them to **"anoint your eyes with eye salve, that you may see."** Spiritual blindness is a direct result of Satan's successful attempts to misrepresent the character of God. "Our gospel is veiled…to those who are perishing, whose minds the god of this age [Satan] has blinded, who do not believe, lest the light of the gospel of the glory of God should shine on them" (2Corinthians 4:3,4). The "glory of God," according to Exodus

---

120 "But we are all like an unclean thing. And all our righteousnesses are like filthy rags" (Isaiah 64:6).

121 For example, "But to him who does not work but believes on him who justifies the ungodly, his faith is accounted for righteousness, just as David also describes the blessedness of the man to whom God imputes righteousness apart from works" (Romans 4:5,6).

122 The "great multitude" who "are before the throne…arrayed in white robes…come out of the great tribulation, and washed their robes and made them white in the blood of the Lamb" (justification, Revelation 7:13-15). During the Sardis "dead church" period there were "a few names even in Sardis who have not defiled their garments and they shall walk with Me in White…He who overcomes shall be clothed in white garments" (sanctification, Revelation 3:4,5). John saw the martyrs who "had been slain for the word of God and for the testimony which they held…then a white robe was given each of them." (sanctification, Revelation 6:11). "For the fine linen is the righteous acts of the saints." (sanctification, Revelation 19:8).

123 "Men will be lovers of themselves, lovers of money, boasters, proud, blasphemers, disobedient to parents, unthankful, unholy, unloving, unforgiving, slanderers, without self-control, brutal, despisers of good, traitors, headstrong, haughty, lovers of pleasure rather than lovers of God" (2Timothy 3:1-4).

33:18-34:7, is His name or character, and it is the basic misconceptions about the character of God that keep His children from entering into the deep relationship with him that they especially need at the end of time.

"O Righteous Father! The world has not known You" Jesus cried out,[124] diagnosing the basic spiritual problem that has plagued mankind ever since Satan convinced Eve that God was selfishly withholding something good from her. In an era when "doctrine" is a dirty word, most Christians unconsciously believe the false doctrines that misrepresent God that developed during the "dark" ages— that he arbitrarily chooses some for salvation and consigns others to an eternity of miserable separation or even torment, that natural or personal disasters are the results of His activities or neglect, that He is angry and offended and must be mollified by sacrifices, good works, or "friends in high places" (saints), that He is watching for our sins, ready to snatch away the eternal life we have been striving for, that He is blithely unconcerned about our suffering or too distant and detached to do anything about it. At every turn spiritual blindness causes people to echo the sentiments of Adam, "I heard Your voice…and I was afraid…and I hid myself" (Genesis 3:10).

These misconceptions of God are combined with fatal blindness of our own spiritual condition. The media and internet have ensured that any kind of sin that is imaginable is just the changing of a channel or the click of a mouse away. The disgusting and horrifying scenes leave most people considering themselves to be good, moral people in comparison. Self-esteem psychology avoids any reference to guilt, and post-modern political correctness accepts all lifestyles as equally valid. The modern busy lifestyle and information and image overload leave no time or opportunity for quiet reflection. As a result, the still small voice of the Spirit is drowned out and we remain blind to our own spiritual poverty.

Perhaps most damaging is our blindness to the unseen spiritual reality all around us.[125] Jesus said, "I am with you always, even to the end of the age" (Matthew 28:20), but most of us act as if God is with us only once a week or at best once a day. God is active and at work in us and all around us; are we aware of Him enough to join Him in what He is doing? Or do we forget about Him for hours or days at a time in the business of our own life? When Jesus said "seek first the kingdom of God," and "abide in Me as the branch abides in the vine,"[126] He was talking about being continually aware of and engaged with Him. When Paul wrote, "walk in the Spirit," "pray without ceasing," and "take every thought captive,"[127] he was not advising super-Christians to go live in a monastery. He was simply reminding us that a relationship with Jesus means that He is always with us through the Holy Spirit and He wants to be an active part of our everyday life.

At the same time most Christians are blind to Satan, the "prince of the power of the air," (Ephesians 2:2) and his demonic hosts. Evil spirits are continually trying to speak into our minds, take us by surprise, and launch vicious, coordinated campaigns against us. Unless our eyes are open to their activities, we will not be able to resist and rebuke them in the name of Jesus.[128]

Spiritual discernment through the indwelling presence of the Holy Spirit is the eye salve that heals spiritual blindness. We can discern the truth about God and our own sinful condition,

---

124 John 17:25.

125 Ephesians 1:15-21.

126 Matthew 6:3, John 15:4-10.

127 Galatians 5:16-18, 1Thessalonians 5:17, 2Corinthians 10:5.

128 "Submit to God. Resist the devil and he will flee from you" (James 4:7).

and we can become continuously aware of God's presence. But as with the gold of faith and the white garments of Christ's righteousness, it does not come automatically when we "pray the sinner's prayer" or attend church weekly. Jesus is longing to transform us, but He is waiting for us to open the door and let Him in.

3:19-21 I Stand at the Door

The good news is that despite the fearful rebuke, our condition is not hopeless—God still loves us, and **"As many as I love, I rebuke and chasten."** The ministry of rebuke and chastening is one of God's most precious blessings, because it shakes us out of our fatal complacency. "If you endure chastening, God deals with you as with sons; for what son is there whom a father does not chasten?…He [chastens us] for *our* profit, that *we* may be partakers of His holiness. Now no chastening seems to be joyful for the present, but painful; nevertheless, afterward it yields the peaceable fruit of righteousness to those who have been trained by it" (Hebrews 12:5-11). No one likes chastening, and for this reason Jesus urges us to learn quickly— **"be zealous therefore and repent."**

Ultimately God will never force us, and in fact His interventions in our lives are only done with our permission. **"Behold, I stand at the door, and knock. If anyone hears my voice, and opens the door, I will come in to him, and will dine with him, and he with Me"** (Revelation 3:19,20). Jesus is the one who can provide all that we need: the gold of faith, the white garments of righteousness, and the eye salve of spiritual discernment. But unlike Satan, who barges right into our lives uninvited with promises that turn out to be lies, Jesus waits for us to open the door.

Comparing this image with our own personal experience of knocking on doors, we see that Jesus is willing to endure humiliation in order to reach us (as if the humility He suffered during His life on earth and especially on the Cross was not enough to convince us of the depth of His self-sacrificing love).[129] Jesus is the one offering priceless benefits culminating in eternal life in a perfect universe, but he pictures Himself as a humble beggar standing outside waiting for the hardhearted master of the house to get around to answering his knock. The real problem is that the true master, Satan, is already inside telling lies about the "miscreant" out on the porch. But contrary to Satan's misrepresentations, what Jesus desires is the most intimate, personal love relationship: **"I will come in to him and will dine with him, and he with Me,"** and He offers it to **"anyone"** who **"opens the door"** of his heart. He provides Himself, the Bread of Life, for the meal, His blood for the drink, and fresh supplies of grace, mercy, and love.[130] He knows we could never afford to purchase these, so He offers them to us as a free gift. Why would we ever refuse Him and leave Him outside knocking?

"To him that overcomes will I grant to sit with Me on My throne, even as I also overcame, and sat down with my Father on His throne" (Revelation 3:21). Laodicea is the last of the seven churches, and this is the last message. As we will see in later chapters, Revelation has several series of seven—the seven churches, seals, trumpets and last plagues. In each case the conclusion of the message to the seventh in the series introduces the theme for the section that follows. In this case the last message to the seven churches is about God's people sitting with Him on His throne. He reminds us that he has already **"sat down with My Father on His throne"**— "He [Jesus] was received up into heaven and sat down

---

129 This is not to say that Jesus actually feels humiliation, which is a self-centered emotion. His love is totally other-centered, and the point of the illustration of Jesus standing outside knocking is to show the infinite depth of His unselfish love for sinful humans.

130 See John 6:35, 48, 54-56, Matthew 26: 26-28, Is. 55: 1,2.

at the right hand of God" (Mark 16:19).[131] Jesus wants us **"to sit with [Him] on [His] throne,"** and this is the challenge. Even if we finally "overcome," each of us has a long and sordid history of sin. Moreover, there is an enemy, "the accuser of our brethren"[132] who wanted the throne for himself and doesn't want anyone else to have a place there. The next section, the seven seals, reveals what God is doing in heaven so that we will be able to sit with Jesus on His throne.

3:22 Hear What the Spirit Says

The message to each of the seven churches ends in the same way: **"He that has an ear, let him hear what the Spirit said to the churches"** (Revelation 3:22). We notice here that these messages have a universal application. **"He** [singular] **who has an ear"**—that is, each one who has spiritual discernment, is to **"hear what the Spirit said to the churches"** (plural). We who live today do not just need the message to the Laodicean Church—we need all the messages. All Christians need to make sure they do not lose their first love, that they reject heresies such as the synagogue of Satan and Jezebel. All need to repent, hold fast what they have, and overcome. But there is only one way that God's people can possible overcome—they must **"hear what the Spirit says."** The Apostle Paul insists that being in harmony with God is only possible when we "have the Spirit of Christ" (Romans 8:1-17). Gold (faith), white garments (righteousness) and eye salve (spiritual discernment) can only become ours through the ministry of the Holy Spirit.

For a book of prophecy, Revelation has a remarkable emphasis on the Holy Spirit. Besides chapters two and three (**"hear what the Spirit says"**), the Holy spirit is emphasized in chapters four (4:5 *Seven Lamps, Seven Spirits*), five (5:6 *Seven Horns, Seven Eyes*), seven (7: *Sealing, the Law, and the Latter Rain*), and twelve (12: *Commandments of God, Testimony of Jesus*). Perhaps this is because Revelation focuses on the last days, when satanic delusions are overwhelming and impossible to discern without the guidance of the Holy Spirit.[133] Jesus contrasted those who watch and enter "in with Him to the wedding" with those who sleep and are left out.[134] The difference is the indwelling presence of the Holy Spirit.

It is critical that every Christian know how to be filled with the Holy Spirit. There is nothing obscure or mysterious about it. The first step is repentance.[135] Peter said, "Repent, and let every one of you be baptized in the name of Jesus Christ for the remission of sins; and you shall receive the gift of the Holy Spirit" (Acts 2:38). True repentance is not a "sorry, sir" apology because we have been caught sinning and may get into trouble, or miss out on heaven. It is a deep realization of what our sin has done to ourselves, to our fellow human beings, and to God. But what comes first, repentance or the Spirit? In fact, repentance can only come from the Spirit of God, which shows that God is already at work in our lives, bringing us to repentance: "I will pray the Father, and He will give you another Helper…the Spirit of truth, whom the world cannot receive, because it neither sees Him nor knows Him; but you know Him, for *He dwells with you and will be in you*" (John 14:16,17). The Holy Spirit wants to go from being an outside influence ("with you") to being a constant inner reality ("in you"). Once inside He wants to teach us to hear His voice and

---

131 See also Ephesians 1:20, Colossians 3;1, Hebrews 1:3, 8:1, 12:2.

132 Revelation 12:10

133 See Matthew 24:4,5, 11, 23-26).

134 The parable of the ten virgins, Matthew 25:1-13.

135 Long before we have made any response to God His grace has been working for our salvation—"the goodness of God leads you to repentance" (Romans 2:4).

to allow Him to show us our hidden sins and help us to repent—"Search me, O God, and know my heart; try me, and know my anxieties; and see if there is any wicked way in me, and lead me in the way everlasting" (Psalms 139:23,24).

Obedience is the second condition for receiving the Holy Spirit. Peter preached about "the Holy Spirit whom God has given to those who obey Him" (Acts 5:32). But what comes first, obedience or the Spirit? As with repentance, it is impossible to obey God without the Holy Spirit. What we need is a willingness to obey, and God will give His Spirit to enable our willingness to become a living reality. When through repentance we open ourselves to the influence of the Spirit, He begins to bring issues to our attention in the order and way that He knows to be best. "I still have many things to say to you, but you cannot bear them now. However, when He, the Spirit of truth has come, He will guide you into all truth" (John 16:12,13). Our *willingness* to obey what the Spirit brings to us opens the way for Him to fill us and to *empower* us to obey.

Finally, we receive the Holy Spirit when we desire Him enough to seek Him wholeheartedly. In Luke 11 Jesus told a story of a man who had a visitor at night and had nothing to give him to eat. Since the customs of the time demanded that a visitor be fed, he went to his neighbor even though it was night. The neighbor was in bed and refused to get up, but with persistence the man kept knocking and finally got what he wanted (Luke 11:5-8). Jesus concluded the story with the words, "how much more will your Heavenly Father give the Holy Spirit to those who ask Him!" (v.13). Seeking the Spirit is not just a one-time request. Our persistence in asking shows the seriousness of our desire. Every day we should take time to repent, confessing our willingness to obey whatever God has brought to our attention, and asking again for His Holy Spirit. "You will seek Me, and you will find Me, when you search for Me with all your heart" (Jeremiah 29:13).

In Jesus' story the man himself was satisfied at first—he had enough to be resting comfortably with his family. But then a visitor arrived who was hungry, and he realized that he didn't have anything to give him. As long as the focus is on self and our own blessings, we will not feel the kind of need that will impel us to ask persistently for the filling of the Holy Spirit. The gifts of the Spirit (for example apostleship, prophecy, teaching, gifts of miracles and healing, helps, administration, tongues, see 1Corinthians 12:28) are all for the purpose of ministry. It is when we get involved in serving the church and working for lost people that we will experience the fullness of the Spirit and hear Him speaking.

The messages to the seven churches seem to end on a note of uncertainty. The members of the Laodicean Church are so luke-warm that Jesus is about to spew them out of His mouth. But He entreats them to open the door of their hearts and let the Holy Spirit transform their lives with the true riches of gold, white garments and eye salve. It is obvious that many will heed His invitation; the next time we see the church they have "washed their robes and made them white in the blood of the lamb" and "serve Him night and day"[136] (Revelation 7:14). For this change to take place Jesus has a great work to do, and in the next chapter he invites us to "come up here" to heaven to see what He is doing there on our behalf.

---

136 Although this verse seems to portray the church in heaven, a careful reading shows that they are still on earth in the midst of the time of trouble (see 7: *In Heaven While on Earth*).

"Behold, a throne set in heaven, and One sat on the throne." Revelation 4:4
Woodcut by Matthew Merian, 1630

Chapter 4

Revelation 4:1-11

4:1 After this I looked, and, behold, a door was open in heaven. And the first voice which I heard was like a trumpet talking with me, which said, "Come up here, and I will show you things which must take place after this."

4:2 And immediately I was in the spirit; and, behold, a throne was set in heaven, and One sat on the throne.

4:3 And He that sat was in appearance like a jasper and a sardius stone; and there was a rainbow around the throne, in appearance like an emerald.

4:4 And around the throne were twenty-four thrones, and on the thrones I saw twenty-four elders sitting, clothed in white raiment; and they had on their heads crowns of gold.

4:5 And out of the throne proceeded lightning and thunder and voices; and there were seven lamps of fire burning before the throne, which are the seven Spirits of God.

4:6 And before the throne there was a sea of glass like crystal; and in the midst of the throne, and round about the throne, were four living creatures, full of eyes in front and behind.

4:7 And the first living creature was like a lion, and the second living creature was like a calf, and the third living creature had a face like a man, and the fourth living creature was like a flying eagle.

4:8 And the four living creatures had each of them six wings about him; and they were full of eyes within. And they do not rest day and night, saying, "Holy, holy, holy, Lord God Almighty, who was, and is, and is to come."

4:9 And when the living creatures give glory and honor and thanks to Him that sat on the throne, who lives forever and ever,

4:10 The twenty-four elders fall down before Him that sat on the throne, and worship Him that lives forever and ever, and cast their crowns before the throne, saying,

4:11 "You are worthy, O Lord, to receive glory and honor and power; for You have created all things, and for Your pleasure they are and were created."

4:1 A Door Open in Heaven

"**After this I looked, and, behold, a door was open in heaven. And the first voice which I heard was like a trumpet talking with me, which said, 'Come up here, and I will show you things which must take place after this.'**" (Revelation 4:1). John is invited to "**come up here**" as the action shifts from the churches on earth to events taking place in heaven. This means that on the chronological timeline there will be a break from the events on earth which have progressed through the centuries with the seven churches, so that we can catch up on what is happening meanwhile in heaven.

The first thing that John saw, which introduces the theme of the next four chapters, was "**a door...open in heaven.**" The use of the identical words in the original language indicates that this is the same open door that was "set before" the church of Philadelphia (Revelation 3:8).[137] As we saw in chapter 3, the Greek wording makes it clear that this is not a door into heaven, as if John was looking into heaven through an open door, but rather it is a door in heaven that is open, as if there was a building there with a door. The book of Hebrews tells us that there is such a building: the heavenly sanctuary (See Hebrews 8, 9). That this door is in the heavenly sanctuary is made clear by the symbolic objects that John saw there: the throne (v.2), the seven lamps of fire (v.5) and the "lamb as though it had been slain"(5:6) are all images from the ancient Hebrew sanctuary which was set up in the time of Moses.

The earthly sanctuary of the Old Testament was "a shadow of the heavenly things," "of the true tabernacle which the Lord erected" (Hebrews 8:5,2). From the "shadow" of the earthly sanctuary we can learn about the heavenly reality. An understanding of the sanctuary and its rituals is essential in order to understand chapters 4 and 5, as well as many other sections of the Book of Revelation, so before getting into the actual vision of chapter 4 we will overview some of the most important features of the sanctuary service.

The ancient sanctuary was built with a courtyard and two rooms. In the courtyard the people came and offered their sacrifices (Leviticus 4), and there was a bronze altar for burnt offerings (Exodus 27:1-8) and a large basin for washing (Exodus 30:18-21). The first room was called the "Holy Place" and in it the daily rituals were performed all year long. The Holy Place contained a table with two stacks of bread (Leviticus 24:5-8, Exodus 25:23-30), a seven-branched lampstand (Exodus 25:31-40), and a golden alter for offering incense (Exodus 30:1-10). Each of the articles symbolized an aspect of what God has done to save His people from their sins.

The inner room (the "Most Holy Place") had a box called the ark of the covenant, which contained the two stone tablets of the 10 Commandment law. On top of the ark was a "mercy seat" with two cherubim (angels) spreading their wings above it. This was the throne of God where He appeared as a glorious bright light "between the cherubim" (Exodus 25:17-22). The High Priest entered the Most Holy Place into the immediate presence of God just once a year for the yearly ritual of the Day of Atonement.

There were two doors, one into the Holy Place, and the other into the Most Holy Place (Ezekiel 41:23, 1Kings 6:31-35). Since John saw both the seven lamps (which were in the Holy Place) and the throne of God (which was in the Most Holy Place) the "**door standing open in heaven**" which John saw must be the door between the two rooms which was opened for the Day of Atonement (see Appendix 2). This will

---

137 This is clearer in the Greek, in which the exact wording for open door (*thuran ineogmenin*) is used in both verses, the only two places in scripture where this phrase is used.

become more obvious as we consider below the evidence that the scene described in Revelation 4 and 5 is the beginning of the anti-typical Day of Atonement.

Naturally we should not be too literal in our thinking of heavenly doors, rooms and rituals. The actual heavenly reality that was symbolized by these earthly figures is beyond human comprehension. But it is true that God was trying through the sanctuary and its services to teach us about the way He is relating to humanity and the sin problem, so we should try to learn all we can from them.

The earthly sanctuary had two basic types of services: the "daily" (also called the continual), and the "yearly" (the Day of Atonement). A prominent feature of the daily service was animal sacrifices. Twice a day a lamb was offered as a burnt offering, while at the same time the High Priest offered incense (Exodus 29:38—30:8). This was a sort of general offering for all the people of God. In addition, whenever an individual sinned he was to bring his own sacrifice to the sanctuary, as outlined in Leviticus 4:2-12. He would lay his hands on the animal's head, confessing his sin, and then kill the animal "before the Lord." From there the priest took over. He brought some of the blood of the animal into the sanctuary; some he sprinkled "in front of the veil" which separated the Holy from the Most Holy, some he put on the horns of the alter of incense, and some he poured out at the base of the altar of burnt offerings.

Many people have considered the Old Testament sacrifices disgusting and barbaric. It is true that the sacrifices of the surrounding heathen nations were a gross attempt to please or appease an offended or indifferent god. But when we consider that every sacrifice for sin symbolized the death of God Himself that would take place on the cross of Calvary, we see in the sacrificial system God's passionate appeal to sinners: "Your sin is killing Me, but I'm willing to die so that you can live."

The daily sacrifices are based on two vital principles that help us to understand what Jesus has done for us. Firstly, God told Moses that "the life of the flesh is in the blood" (Leviticus 17:11). The Hebrew word that has been translated "life" (*nephesh*) is the word for soul, which shows that sin, which is committed by the soul, is considered for ritual purposes to be "in the blood." Secondly, through confession sin can be transferred to an innocent substitute (Leviticus 16:21). What was happening when the sinner brought his sacrifice was that the guilt of his sin was "transferred" through confession and the laying on of hands to the "soul" of the animal, specifically to its blood since that is where the life (*nephesh*) abides.

When he killed the animal, it was as if the animal died in his place, for his sin had been transferred to it. This taught the substitutionary death of Christ for sinners: "it is the blood that makes atonement for the soul" (Leviticus 17:11). "Almost all things are purified with blood, and without shedding of blood there is no remission" (Hebrews 9:21). We are "redeemed…with the precious blood of Christ, as of a lamb without blemish and without spot" (1Peter1:18,19).

But that was not the end of the process. The sin was transferred to the blood (soul)[138] of the animal. Then the blood was poured, sprinkled and wiped on the articles of the sanctuary, thereby transferring the "sin" to the sanctuary. Thus, throughout the year the sanctuary "accumulated" the sins of the people. In other passages that have to do with the heavenly Day of Atonement[139] this concept is presented in terms of names that are entered in books of record. In computer terms, a "file" was created in the "sanctuary database" for each person who had confessed his sins and been

---

138 Animals are souls too! Genesis 9:10 "Every living creature (Hebrew *nephesh*, soul)…the birds, the cattle," (Revelation 16:3).

139 Daniel 7 and 12, Revelation 20

forgiven through the substitutionary death of the sacrificial victim.

The Day of Atonement

Once a year on the Day of Atonement the priest would "make atonement for the Holy Place, because of the uncleanness of the children of Israel and because of their transgressions, for all their sins; and so he shall do for the tabernacle of meeting which remains among them in the midst of their uncleanness" (Levitcus 16:16). Again, this "cleansing of the sanctuary" (Daniel 8:14) was accomplished with blood. Only on this day did the High priest go through the inner doors into the Most Holy Place: "Into the second part the high priest went alone once a year, not without blood, which he offered…for the people's sins committed in ignorance" (Hebrews 9:7). This, like every other sacrifice, represented the sacrifice that Jesus made on the cross.

The question naturally arises: if a sacrifice had been made when the sinner confessed his sins, why was another sacrifice needed later? Note that in Hebrews 9:7 the sacrifice of the Day of Atonement was for "the people's sins committed in ignorance." In Leviticus 16:16 it says that atonement was made on the Day of Atonement "for all their sins." Besides the specific sins the sinner had confessed when he offered his sacrifice, he also had many other sins, some which had been forgotten, sins that he committed after he brought his sacrifice, others which he did not realize were sins, and his general sinful nature.[140] These sins also required atonement, and like all

forgiveness, there must be repentance. But since these sins were "committed in ignorance," repentance of them would be determined by his general attitude toward sin on the Day of Atonement.

This attitude toward sin was indicated by his behavior on that day: the people were to "afflict [their] souls and do no work at all." "It shall be to you a Sabbath of solemn rest, and you shall afflict your souls" (Leviticus 16:29, 23:32).[141] This was crucial, because "any person who is not afflicted in soul on that same day shall be cut off from his people. And any person who does any work on that same day, that person I will destroy from among his people" (Leviticus 23:29). And so this was a day of judgment in which repentance of all sin, known and unknown, was determined by an inward attitude (afflicted in soul) and an outward symbol of obedience (keeping the "Sabbath of solemn rest").[142] It was not enough to make a profession of repentance at some point in time and expect that to cover all future behavior. The forgiven sinner had to continue in the same attitude of repentance and submission.

The Bible does not teach "once saved, always

---

140 The concept of sins of ignorance for which we are guilty is clearly taught in the Old Testament sanctuary service. For example, "If a person sins and commits any of these things which are forbidden to be done by the commandments of the Lord, though he does not know it, yet he is guilty and shall bear his iniquity…the priest shall make atonement for him regarding his ignorance in which he erred and did not know it, and it shall be forgiven him" Leviticus 5:17-19.

141 The Day of Atonement was the most solemn of all the feasts. On other feasts the people were to do "no customary work" (Leviticus 23:8,21,25,35) but on the Day of Atonement they were to do "no work whatsoever on pain of death" (Leviticus 23:30,31). In fact, the Day of Atonement is referred to in Leviticus 16:31 as the "Sabbath of Sabbaths" (literal translation).

142 The keeping of the Sabbath is not a commandment that "makes sense" like refraining from murder or the worship of idols, but is simply based on the fact that God said to keep it. As such it symbolizes willingness to obey all His commands. "How long do you refuse to keep My commandments and My laws? See! For the Lord has given you the Sabbath" (Exodus 16:28,29).

saved,"[143] but rather "eternal life to those who by patient continuance in doing good seek for glory, honor and immortality" (Romans 2:7). The Day of Atonement symbolizes the total eradication of every record of sin that has been confessed and forsaken. "When we confess our sins He is faithful and just to forgive our sins and cleanse us from unrighteousness" (1 John 1:7). These sins, being forgiven, are removed from us, "as far as the east is from the west, so far has He removed our transgressions from us" (Psalm 103:12). "You will cast all our sins into the depths of the sea" (Micah 7:19). But even in the depths of the sea there is still a record of those sins, symbolized by the pollution of the sanctuary by blood. In addition there were the "sins committed in ignorance" discussed above. During the heavenly Day of Atonement, there is a judgment made in favor of those who have continued in faith, and every record and trace of all their sins is permanently obliterated.

The Scapegoat

Two goats were offered on the Day of Atonement. "He [Aaron, the High Priest] shall take two goats and present them before the Lord at the door of the tabernacle of meeting. Then Aaron shall cast lots for the two goats: one lot for the Lord and the other lot for the scapegoat. And Aaron shall bring the goat on which the Lord's lot fell, and offer it as a sin offering. But the goat on which the lot fell to be the scapegoat shall be presented alive before the Lord...he shall bring the live goat, confess over it all the iniquities of the children of Israel, and all their transgressions, concerning all their sins, putting them on the head of the goat, and shall send it away into the wilderness by the hand of a suitable man. The goat shall bear on itself all their iniquities"[144] (Leviticus 16:7-10, 20-22).

The "Lord's goat" symbolized Christ, who took upon Himself the penalty for our sins. In the judgment He is our representative, taking the place of each sinner who has continued to repent and have faith in Him. Their sins have been transferred from their soul to His, He has died for those sins, and the sinner is judged to be perfect as if he had never sinned.

The scapegoat, on the other hand, represents Satan,[145] who, as the instigator of rebellion and sin, bears the responsibility for the death of the impenitent. Satan is the "representative" of those who have not continued in faith in the sense that these unrepentant people are under his authority and will suffer the same fate as he does.

In one sense Satan will even bear the sins

---

143 Jesus is "able to save to the uttermost those who come to God through Him, since He always lives to make intercession for them" (Hebrews 7:25). He declares, "I give them eternal life, and they shall never perish, neither shall anyone snatch them out of My hand. My Father, who has given them to Me, is greater than all; and no one is able to snatch them out of My Father's hand" (John 10:28,29). However, He never takes away our freedom of choice and we ourselves can, by continuing in sin, decide to leave His hand. The following texts make it clear that those who have accepted Christ's salvation can later leave Him and be lost. Hebrews 6:4, 10:26, 35-38, 1Timothy 1:19, 6:20,21, Matthew 18:23-35, Ezekiel 18:24, Romans 11:17-24, 1Corinthians 9:27, 15:2, Colossians 1:22,23, 1 Thessalonians 3:8, 2 Peter 1:10, 2:20,21, 3:17, 1John 5:12,13, Revelation 2:4,5. For an excellent treatment of the doctrine of perseverance see Robert Shank, *Life in the Son* , (Bloomington, MI, Bethany House, 1989).

144 The leading of the scapegoat into the wilderness represents the chaining of Satan to the uninhabited earth during the Millennium (Revelation 20:1,2).

145 The modern meaning of the term "scapegoat," someone who has been unjustly accused for the sins of others, makes it an unfortunate translation which does not really represent the meaning of the obscure Hebrew word *azazel*. The Greek Septuagint word is *apopompaio*—the one who has to leave. The scapegoat could not represent Christ because: 1) Lots were cast, "one lot for the Lord" implying that the other "lot for the scapegoat" was not for the Lord (Leviticus 16:8). 2) The blood of the scapegoat was not shed, the goat was sent alive into the wilderness (Leviticus 16:21,22)—and "all things are purified with blood, and without shedding of blood there is no remission" (Hebrews 9:22). So the scapegoat had nothing to do with purification or the remission of sins. 3) The sins placed on the scapegoat had already been atoned for by sacrifice (Leviticus 4). 4)The sins were placed on him *after* those in the sanctuary had been atoned for by the "Lord's goat" (Leviticus 16:15-19).

of the righteous. Of course, only Jesus can bear our sins in a way that provides salvation: "Surely He [Christ] has borne our griefs and carried our sorrows...the Lord has laid on Him the iniquity of us all" (Isaiah 53:3-6). But Satan will still suffer the consequences of the sins he has caused to be committed. He will spend 1000 years chained in the "bottomless pit" (Revelation 20:1-2) and will ultimately be burned in the lake of fire (Revelation 20:10, Ezekiel 28:18,19).

A Day of Judgment

The Day of Atonement was a day of judgment, in which the true spiritual condition of those who had availed themselves of God's plan of salvation was revealed,[146] and on that day their final destiny was determined. There was also, through the ritual of the scapegoat, a symbolic judgment of Satan, the originator and instigator of sin.

Some commentators have felt that because the word "judgment" does not appear in Revelation 4 and 5[147] that these chapters cannot represent the Day of Atonement, which was a day of judgment.[148] We should keep in mind, however, that the Old Testament passages that describe the

---

146 This concept will be more fully explained in chapter 5, the scroll with the 7 seals.

147 The thirteen instances of the use of the Greek words for judge and judgment are all either in the second half of the linguistic chiasm (from chapter 14 on) or refer to events which will take place at that time (6:10 and 11:18). The words are used in connection with rewards and punishments, not investigation. The two instances (14:7 and 20:4) in which the word for judgment relates to an investigative phase are followed within their context by the executive phase (14:17-20, 20:11-15).

148 Some scholars believe that this scene represents the inauguration of Christ into His priestly ministry after His resurrection and ascension. However, there are few, if any parallels in the symbolism of Revelation 4 and 5 with the Old Testament passages describing the inauguration of the high priest (Exodus 29, 40, Leviticus 9, 1Kings 8, 1Chronicles 16,17, 2Chronicles 5, 29 Ezra 6), whereas there are rich parallels with those describing the Day of Atonement. Other commentators have interpreted these passages as the coronation of Jesus to His kingly reign (see for example Ranko Stefanovic, *Revelation of Jesus Christ* (Berren Springs, MI, Andrews University Press, 2002). This theory is addressed in appendix 2.

Day of Atonement (Leviticus 16 and 23) do not have the word "judgment" either, even though the concept of judgment is very clear. But besides the "door standing open in heaven," there are other strong evidences in chapters 4 and 5 that these scenes represent the "Day of Atonement" and the judgment that took place on that day.

The importance of firmly establishing what is going on in chapters 4 and 5 cannot be emphasized too strongly. A wrong interpretation leads to erroneous conclusions about the whole first half of Revelation. For many theologians these chapters are simply an interesting picture of what heaven is like. Others set the events of these chapters in the first century, depicting the inauguration of Christ into His kingly or priestly reign. With this interpretation the following seven seals and seven trumpets have some kind of historical application, interesting but not particularly relevant to us.[149] But if these chapters are the first stage of a judgment that will escalate through the whole rest of the Book of Revelation until sin is finally eradicated, then chapters 4 and 5 are of vital importance so that we can know what is happening in the invisible spiritual realm right now.

First of all, judgment in chapters 4-7 is suggested by the corresponding section of the chiastic structure (see 1: *Chiastic Literary Structure*). The chiasm in Revelation consists of mirror image sections with related themes. For example, the church on earth is paired with the church in the kingdom and the seven trumpet plagues are paired with the seven last plagues. The section which includes chapters 4-7 is paired with Revelation 19:1-20:15, which has to do with the executive judgment, where the sentences pronounced in favor of the righteous and against

---

149 See Appendix 2 for more discussion.

sinners are carried out.[150] But the sentences that are carried out in the executive phase of judgment have already been determined before Jesus comes.[151] The two stages of judgment are familiar to anyone who has been involved in a trial, in which the evidence is examined and a sentence is pronounced by the judge or jury, and then the sentence is executed.[152] The prior determination of guilt or innocence has been termed the "investigative" or "pre-advent" judgment. We would expect that the investigative judgment would be paired in the chiasm with the executive judgment, which would mean that chapters 4-7 represent the investigative judgment that takes place during the Day of Atonement.

Moreover, the first thing John heard was a voice **"like a trumpet"** (Revelation 4:1). In the Old Testament sanctuary calender the feast of trumpets announced the Day of Atonement.[153]

The next thing John saw was a throne (v.2). Later he saw more thrones with twenty-four elders sitting on them. Of the 35 times thrones are mentioned in Revelation, 19 are in Revelation

4 and 5. The Psalmist tells us, "You sat on the throne judging in righteousness…He has prepared His throne for judgment. He shall judge the world in righteousness" (Psalms 9:4,7,8). Many other scriptures make it clear that the throne is for judgment.[154]

The prophet Daniel saw the investigative judgment in the vision of Daniel 7, and that vision has significant parallels with Revelation chapters 4 and 5. Daniel "watched till thrones were put in place…the court was seated ["the judgment was set" KJV] and the books were opened" (Daniel 7:9,10).[155] Daniel saw in this judgment scene that "a thousand thousands ministered to Him; Ten thousand times ten thousand stood before Him" (Daniel 7:10). The same number of angels is present in the judgment scene of Revelation—"I heard the voice of many angels round about the throne…and the number of them was ten thousand times ten thousand, and thousands of thousands" (Revelation 5:11).

The judgment scene in heaven described in Daniel 7 climaxed with the opening of books— "The court was seated and *the books were opened*" (Daniel 7:10). The central event of Revelation chapters 4-7 is also the opening of a book (in chapter five this will be identified as the "Lamb's Book of Life"). In Revelation 20:12 we see that the Book of Life is opened in the judgment along with other books: "Books were opened. And another book was opened, which is the Book of Life. And the dead were judged according to their works, by the things which were written in the

---

150 When Jesus comes the righteous who are alive will be caught up to be with Jesus (1 Thessalonians 4:13-17) while the unrepentant will be slain and eaten by birds (Revelation 19:21). The righteous who have died will be resurrected and will "live and reign with Christ for a thousand years" (Revelation 20:4) but the unrepentant who have died will not be resurrected "until the thousand years is finished" when they will rise to face the great white throne judgment (Revelation 20:5-15).

151 "Behold, I am coming soon! My reward is with me, and I will give to everyone according to what he has done" (Revelation 22:12 NIV).

152 Psalm 9 shows that God has a similar two-stage judgment. "The Lord…shall judge the world in righteousness, and He shall administer judgment for the peoples…The Lord is known by the judgment He executes" (Psalm 97,8,16).

153 The trumpet was used to show God's people their danger, their sin, their duty, or their reward. Once a year there was a special feast of trumpets: "In the seventh month, on the first day of the month, you shall have a holy convocation…It is a day of blowing of trumpets" (Numbers 29:1). This day occurred 10 days before the Day of Atonement (v.7) and reminded the people that this solemn day was at hand.

154 The throne is often a symbol of judgment, for example, Psalm 11:4-6, 97:2,3, Proverbs 20:8, Isaiah 16:5, Matthew 25:31-46, 1 Kings 7:7, 10:9.

155 Daniel saw the thrones being "put in place" whereas John saw the court already seated (Revelation 4:3, 4). The throne was surrounded by witnesses, angels numbering "ten thousand times ten thousand, and thousands of thousands" in both scenes (Revelation 5:11, Daniel 7:10). In Daniel 7 this court takes place before the Second Coming of Christ, while enemy powers are still warring against God's people.

Table 4.1

Revelation 4,5	Revelation 14
"A Lamb as if it had been slain…worthy is the Lamb" (Revelation 5:6,12).	"Behold, a Lamb standing on Mount Zion" (Revelation 14:1).
"Before the throne" (Revelation 4:6).	"Before the throne" (Revelation 14:3).
"I saw twenty four elders…four living creatures" (Revelation 4:4,6).	"The four living creatures and the elders" (Revelation 14:3).
"Having every one of them harps….and they sang a new song" (Revelation 5:8,9).	"Harpers harping with their harps…They sang as it were a new song" (Revelation 14:2,3).
"Receive glory…for You created all things" (Revelation 4:11).	"Give glory to Him…who made heaven and earth" (Revelation 14:7).
"Out of every tribe and tongue and people and nation" (Revelation 5:9,10).	"To every nation and tribe and tongue and people" (Revelation 14:6).

books."[156]

Besides the obvious links between this section and Daniel 7, there are also close links with Revelation 14, which clearly has to do with the investigative judgment. The central verse is Revelation 14:7— "Fear God and give glory to Him, *for the hour of His judgment has come.*" The links between the two passages are obvious (See Table 4.1).

The obvious and close connection between these two sections suggests that chapters 4 and 5 are closely related to the central theme of chapter 14—"the hour of His judgment" (v. 7).

Another prominent symbol in Revelation 4 and 5 are eyes: the lamb has seven eyes (Revelation 5:6), and the **"four living creatures"** who are **"round about the throne"** are **"full of eyes in front and behind…[and] within"** (Revelation 4:6,8). Eyes symbolize the Lord's

distinguishing judgment of those who are righteous from those who are not, for example, "A king who sits on the throne of judgment scatters all evil with his eyes" (Proverbs 20:8).[157]

The presence of the **"four living creatures"** is one of the strongest evidences that this chapter is a scene of "investigative judgment." These creatures will be explained more thoroughly later in this chapter, but briefly, they are the same creatures which figure prominently in Ezekiel chapters 1-11, which give a clear picture of the

---

156 This scene, which takes place after the 1000 year millennium, is different from chapter 4-7 which is the judging of those "who are written in the Lamb's book of life" (Revelation 21:7). This later judgment is of those "whose names have not been written in the Book of Life" (Revelation 13:8).

157 "The Lord is in His holy temple, the Lord's throne is in heaven; His *eyes behold*, His eyelids test the sons of men…For the lord is righteous, He loves righteousness; His countenance *beholds* the upright" Psalms 11:4-7. This one "judgment" passage contains three of the symbols of Revelation 4: the temple, the throne in heaven, and eyes, and has to do with distinguishing the righteous from the unrepentant, the same theme of Revelation 4-7. See also 2 Samuel 22:28, Psalms 33:13, Proverbs 5:21, 15:3, 1Kings 14:22, 15:11, 2Chronicles 12:7, Isaiah 59:15, Ezekiel 8:12, 9:9.

investigative judgment of God's people.[158]

As the scene continues into chapter five, the central drama is the Lamb taking a sealed scroll "out of the right hand of Him that sat on the throne" (Revelation 5:7). This is reminiscent of Psalms 110:5—"The Lord is at your right hand; He shall execute kings in the day of His wrath. He shall judge among the nations." Moreover, one of the titles of the Lamb is "the Root of David" (Revelation 5:5), a clear reference to Isaiah 11:1-5 where the Root of David "shall not judge by the sight of His eyes...but with righteousness He shall judge the poor, and decide with equity for the meek of the earth." Jeremiah adds, "I [God] will cause to grow up to David a Branch of righteousness. He shall execute judgment and righteousness in the earth." (Jeremiah 33:15-17, 23:5).

In summary, the language, symbols and scriptural links indicate that the scenes of Revelation 4-7 depict the investigative judgment which takes place in heaven before the Second Coming of Christ. This is the heavenly reality that was foreshadowed by the Day of Atonement in the earthly sanctuary which is described in Leviticus 16.

4:2-4 Before the Throne

"And immediately I was in the spirit; and, behold, a throne was set in heaven, and One sat on the throne. And He that sat was in appearance like a jasper and a sardius stone; and there was a rainbow around the throne, in appearance like an emerald" (Revelation 4:2,3).

As we saw above, thrones are associated with judgment, even when people sit on them. For example, "The tribes go up [to Jerusalem]... for thrones are set there for judgment" (Psalm 122:3-5). Jesus said of His followers, "I bestow upon you a kingdom...that you may eat and drink at My table in My kingdom, and sit on thrones judging the twelve tribes of Israel" (Luke 22:28-30). Jesus will sit on a throne to judge— "When the Son of Man comes in His glory... then He will sit on the throne of His glory. All the nations will be gathered before Him, and He will separate them one from another...the King will say to those on His right hand, 'Come, you blessed of My Father, inherit the kingdom'...Then he will say to those on the left hand, 'Depart from Me, you cursed, into the everlasting fire prepared for the devil and his angels" (Matthew 25:31-46).

Here in Revelation 4 it is God the Father Himself who sits on the throne of judgment, in such awesome majesty that the living creatures around the throne **do not rest day and night, saying, 'Holy, holy, holy, Lord God Almighty, who was, and is, and is to come!"** (Revelation 4:8). The **"twenty-four elders"** also sit **"around the throne on twenty-four thrones"** and **"fall down before Him that sat on the throne, and worship Him that lives forever and ever"** (Revelation 4:10,11).

From a human standpoint, there is something awesome and even frightening about judgment. We are judged in a human court when someone has accused us of some crime, and even when we are innocent there is always the fear that a perversion of justice will prevail and we will be condemned. However, with Him who is altogether righteous and holy there is no perversion, and even though in actuality we are all guilty, "God so loved [each one of us] that He gave His only Son, that *whosoever* believes in Him should not perish but have everlasting life. For God did

---

158 Representative of these chapters are the following: "Son of man, do you see what they are doing?...now turn again, you will see greater abominations...Go in and see the wicked abominations which they are doing...have you seen what the elders of the house of Israel do in the dark?...they say, 'the Lord does not see us'...therefore I also will act in fury. My eye will not spare nor will I have pity... Go through the midst of the city, put a mark on the foreheads of the men who sigh and cry over all the abominations that are done within it...utterly slay old and young...but do not come near anyone on whom is the mark." "I will judge you according to your ways, and I will repay you for all your abominations" (Ezekiel 8:5-9:6, 7:8).

not send His Son into the world to condemn the world, but that the world through Him might be saved" (John 3:16,17).

The sacrifice that Jesus made on the Cross is sufficient for all who will accept it. The Holy Spirit has given the invitation and provided His grace (the God-given ability to believe so as to be saved) to everyone who wants it. Those who accept Jesus as their Lord do not need to be afraid of the judgment. "Whoever confesses that Jesus is the Son of God, God abides in him and he in God. And we have known and believed the love that God has for us...Love has been perfected among us in this: that we may have boldness in the day of judgment...There is no fear in love, but perfect love casts out fear" (1John 4:17,18). God's mercy is emphasized by the fact that **"there was a rainbow around the throne"** (Revelation 4:3), a reminder of God's covenant of mercy (Genesis 9:9-17). God wants to declare His children innocent, not to find them guilty. And that is what the plan of salvation is all about— "that He may be just and the justifier of the one who has faith in Jesus" (Romans 3: 26).[159]

"And around the throne were twenty-four thrones, and on the thrones I saw twenty-four elders sitting, clothed in white raiment; and they had on their heads crowns of gold" (Revelation 4:4). Who are the 24 elders? They are wearing the same clothes (white raiment) as "those who overcome" (Revelation 3:5,18). They are wearing crowns, just as those who faithfully serve as elders have been promised (1Peter 5:1-4), along with all who faithfully endure trials and temptations (James 1:12, Revelation 2:10).[160] They are the same in number and clothing as the levitical elders appointed by David who led the temple music, acted as gatekeepers for the temple, and participated in the cleansing of the temple.[161] They have a special interest in the redemption of humanity.[162] Thus it is most likely that they are representatives of the human race who participate in the heavenly court.[163]

4:5 Two Kinds of Judgment

"And out of the throne proceeded lightning and thunder and voices" (Revelation 4:5). **"Lightening, thunder and voices"** proceeding from the throne of God are a recurrent theme in the book of Revelation and are based on the many Old Testament passages in which these symbols are associated with the execution of God's judgments. Lightening bolts are the "arrows" of God, which deliver His children by destroying the enemies that are oppressing them.

---

159 The prophet Daniel also reveals that the judgment has a positive outcome for those who believe: "The ancient of Days came, and a judgment was made in favor of the saints of the Most High, and the time came for the saints to possess the kingdom" (Daniel 7:22, 26,27).

160 The Greek word for crown, *stefanos* is the same word used for the crown given to the winners in the Olympic games, and symbolizes victory. This is to be distinguished from *diadema*, the crowns of authority which the dragon and beast wear in their assumed authority (Revelation 12:3, 13:1) and which Jesus wears as the true King of Kings and Lord of Lords (Revelation 19:12).

161 The 24 sons of Asaph, Heman and Jeduthan were elders/leaders who were appointed by David (along with their "sons and brethren") to take turns leading in the temple services (IChronicles 25:1-6, 9-31). They were the temple musicians and like the 24 elders were dressed in white robes (2Chronicles 5:12, 35;15, Nehemiah 12:45,46). At least some of them were also gatekeepers (1Chron.16:42), and in the days of Hezekiah they participated in the cleansing of the temple (2Chronicles 29:13-18). Thus the 24 elders of Revelation comprise another Old Testament link to the cleansing of the sanctuary that takes place during the Day of Atonement.

162 Revelation 5:8-10, 7:13-17, 11:16-18. The dominant theme of the Levitical musicians (who were the prototypes of the 24 elders) was God's mercy ("for His mercy endures forever" 2Chronicles 7:6).

163 Although the vast majority of humanity are sleeping in the grave awaiting the resurrection (1Thessalonians 4:13-18), there are some who are already in heaven: Enoch and Elijah were taken up into heaven without dying (Hebrews 11:5,6, 2Kings 2), Moses was resurrected (Jude 9), and "many" were resurrected at the crucifixion (Matthew 27:52,53, Ephesians 4:8).

Thunder is often identified as the voice of God,[164] calling forth His destructive judgments. Later in Revelation earthquakes and hail are added. All of these together coming from the temple are found in 2Samuel 22,[165] which portrays God's intervention as David calls upon the Lord to rescue him from his enemies: "I will call upon the Lord...so shall I be saved from my enemies...He heard my voice from His temple...Then *the earth shook* and trembled...because He was angry... He bowed the heavens also and came down... The Lord *thundered* from heaven and the Most High uttered His *voice, hailstones* and coals of fire. He sent out His arrows and scattered the foe, *lightnings* in abundance and He vanquished them...He delivered me from my strong enemy, from those who hated me...You have delivered me from the violent man" (2Samuel 22:1-19,49). One of the important teachings of this passage is that God's judgments are not so much to punish those who rebel as they are to protect and defend those who are being harmed (See 15:1 *The Wrath of God*).

The focus of Revelation 4-7, however, is not on God's executive judgment, but on the "investigative" judgment in which a determination is made of the status of all who have claimed to be God's people. We should keep in mind that the investigative judgment is not for God's sake, since He already knows everything that everyone has done— "For His eyes are on the ways of man, And He sees all his steps. There is no darkness nor shadow of death where the workers of iniquity may hide themselves. For He need not further consider a man, that he should go before God in judgment" (Job 34:21-23). As we will see in chapter 5, this phase of judgment is for the sake of the angels and the rest of the inhabitants

of the universe who will live eternally with the results of it.

The "investigative" judgment is followed by the "executive" judgment in which God carries out the sentences that He has pronounced against the persistently unrepentant (Revelation 8, 9, 14:17-20, 20:15). The **"lightening, thunder, and voices"** are announcements of *executive* judgment, showing that God begins to execute His judgments even during the investigative period. As each new phase of the executive judgment is announced, something new and more fearsome is added. In Revelation 8:5 "there were voices, thunder, lightning *and an earthquake*" to announce the destructive judgments of the seven trumpets. In 11:19 "lightnings, and voices, and thunders, an earthquake *and great hail*" accompany the announcement to "destroy those who destroy the earth." In 16:18-21 "There were voices, and thunders, and lightning; and there was *a great earthquake, such as had not occurred since men were on the earth, so mighty an earthquake, and so great....And huge hailstones weighing about a talent fell out of heaven on men*" accompanying the destruction of Babylon the Great. These progressively severe judgments remind us of the plagues of Egypt that increased in intensity until the persecutors of God's people were thwarted and the children of Israel were delivered (Exodus 7-12).

In general God's executive judgments are for the purpose of turning people from sin to God. It is strange but true that few people turn to God until they come face to face with their own sinfulness, helplessness and need to be saved. "Let grace be shown to the wicked, yet he will not learn righteousness" (Isaiah 26:10). But in the midst of trials and judgments sinners seek Him— "For when Your judgments are in the earth, the inhabitants of the world will learn righteousness" (Isaiah 26:9).

A wonderful thing about God is that He

---

164 See 1 Samuel 2:19, 7:10, Job 26:12-14, 37:2-5, Psalm 29, John 12:28-31, Isaiah 30:30,31, 66:6, Joel 2:10,11, 3:16.

165 See also Psalm 18, 77:13-20.

does not simply destroy us when we treat Him as an enemy—"God demonstrates His own love toward us, in that while we were still sinners, Christ died for us…for if when we were enemies we were reconciled to God through the death of His Son, much more having been reconciled, we shall be saved by His life" (Romans 5:8-10). Even in the midst of terrible judgments, announced by **"lightening, thunder and voices"** God still loves sinners and seeks to save them. "Yes, I have loved you with an everlasting love; Therefore with lovingkindness I have drawn you" (Jeremiah 31:2,3).

4:5 Seven Lamps, Seven Spirits

"**And there were seven lamps of fire burning before the throne, which are the seven Spirits of God**" (Revelation 4:5). Some commentators have concluded from this verse that the scenes of Revelation 4-7 do not represent the judgment of the Day of Atonement because in the ancient sanctuary the lamps were located in the Holy Place,[166] not the Most Holy Place where the ceremonies of the Day of Atonement took place. But it should not be surprising to find Holy Place imagery during the Day of Atonement, since the earthly Day of Atonement services described in Leviticus 16 had much of the activity taking place in the Holy Place. The services began with sacrifices "at the door of the tabernacle of meeting"(Leviticus 16:7). The priest offered a bull for himself, and took some of the blood of that sacrifice into the Most Holy Place. He then came back out and offered a goat for the congregation and took its blood into the Most Holy Place. He took burning coals from the altar in the Holy Place, put them into a censer, and went into the Most

Holy Place to offer incense "before the Lord". And finally He came back out and performed the ceremony of the scapegoat. Thus the ceremonies of the Day of Atonement took place in both the Holy Place and the Most Holy Place.

Likewise the sanctuary scene of chapters four and five shows features of both rooms of the sanctuary; the lamps were found in the Holy Place, and the throne, which is the most prominent feature of chapter 4, was found in the Most Holy Place of the ancient sanctuary.[167] Chapter 4 begins with the statement that John saw **"a door standing open in heaven,"** the door to the Most Holy Place, and with the door open John could see both the Holy and the Most Holy Place.[168]

Actually, the focus on rooms and furniture can result in a literalistic view of what is happening in heaven. But the book of Revelation is highly symbolic, and the Old Testament sanctuary imagery was God's way of conveying to finite human minds some conception of incomprehensible heavenly realities. One of these realities that the two-room scene conveys is that even while the judgment of the "Day of Atonement" is being carried out, the "daily" intercessory ministry of Jesus (the lamps, the bread and the incense) is still taking place—"He [Jesus] is also able to save to the uttermost those who come to God through Him, since He always lives to make intercession for them" (Hebrews 7:25).

The **"seven lamps of fire…are the seven Spirits of God."** Seven is the most frequently used number in the Book of Revelation (seven churches, seals, trumpets, thunders, plagues, stars, angels, etc.) and as in the rest of the Bible

---

166 The furniture in the Holy Place included the seven-branched lampstand, the table of showbread and the golden altar of incense. In the Most Holy Place was the ark of the covenant and the mercy seat. In the courtyard was the bronze altar of burnt offering and the laver for washing (Exodus 40:2-7).

167 In order to explain the presence of the throne in the Holy Place some have suggested that the table of showbread with two stacks of bread symbolized the Father and the Son. Appendix 2 discusses the problems with this view.

168 The door was not a narrow opening—it took up more than a third of the wall (Ezekiel 41:1-10), so there would be a good view of both rooms.

seven indicates fullness or completeness.[169] There is only one Holy Spirit (1Corinthinans 12:13, Ephesians 2:18) but the Spirit manifests Himself in a multitude of ways.[170]

In chapter 1 John saw seven lampstands, a very similar vision but with a much different meaning— Jesus told him that the "seven lampstands...are the seven churches" (Revelation 1:20). These two views show the close relationship between the church and the Spirit. A lampstand without a lamp gives no light at all (and the church without the Holy Spirit sheds darkness rather than light, as we saw in the tragic history of the church traced in chapters two and three). On the other hand, a lamp without a lampstand illuminates only a small part of the room. Jesus is "the true Light which gives light to every man coming into the world" (John 1:9), but now that He is in heaven He has sent the Holy Spirit to bring His light to this darkened planet. But the Spirit does not operate in a vacuum; He generates the fruits and gifts of the Spirit in the lives of believers. God's people, His church, are the receptacles of the Holy Spirit, bringing the light of Jesus to the world. This is why Jesus said "*I am the light of the world*" (John 8:12) but in Mathew 5:4 He told His disciples, "*you* are the light of the world." God's church has the essential role and privilege of lifting up Jesus to the world through the **"seven Spirits of God"** that fill and empower His followers.

4:6-8 Four Living Creatures

"And before the throne there was a sea of glass like crystal; and in the midst of the throne, and round about the throne, were four living creatures, full of eyes in front and behind. And the first living creature was like a lion, and the second living creature was like a calf, and the third living creature had a face like a man, and the fourth living creature was like a flying eagle. And the four living creatures had each of them six wings about him; and they were full of eyes within. And they do not rest day and night, saying, "Holy, holy, holy, Lord God Almighty, who was, and is, and is to come" (Revelation 4:6-8).

These living creatures are the same as the ones the prophet Ezekiel saw surrounding the mobile throne of God (Ezekiel 1:5-14).[171] The creatures accompanied the Lord as he took Ezekiel on an "investigative tour" of God's people. "He said to me, 'Son of man, do you see what they are doing?...Go in, and see'...Then He said to me, 'Son of man, have you seen what the elders of the house of Israel do...Have you seen *this*, O son of man? Turn again, you will see greater abominations than these" (Ezekiel 8:6,9,12,15). In Revelation 6 these same creatures use similar language, "Come and see," as four horses and riders come into view (Revelation 6:1,3,5,7). The fact that these creatures are "full of eyes" indicates

---

169 For example, "Then I saw another sign in heaven...seven angels having the seven last plagues, for in them the wrath of God is complete" Revelation 15:1.

170 Although the primary meaning of seven Spirits is the fullness and completeness of the Holy Spirit, the various roles of the Spirit can be delineated, eg. the Spirit of Grace (Hebrews 10:29, Romans 8:15, 26), the Spirit of Instruction, Wisdom and Truth (John 14:16,17, 15:26), the Spirit of Power (Isaiah 11:2, 2 Timothy 1:7, Ephesians 3:16), the Spirit of Judgment and Refining (Isaiah 4:3,4, 28:6, Malachi 3:1-5), the Spirit of Life (Genesis 2:7, Romans 8:2), the Spirit of Prophecy (Revelation 19:10, Ephesians 1:17), the Spirit of Comfort and Encouragement (Acts 9:31, Isaiah 40:1,2, 49:13).

---

171 In Revelation the creatures are each depicted with one face, but this emphasizes just one aspect of their role as representatives of the angels and guardians of the holiness of the universe. Ezekiel saw that each creature actually had all four of the faces, reflecting the eternal attributes of God.

that they are involved in the judgment.[172] Ezekiel identifies them as cherubim, a category of angels (Ezekiel 10:20). These living creatures appear repeatedly in the book of Revelation and the context always has to do with judgment.[173]

Jewish tradition holds that the faces of these four creatures were the same as those on the standards[174] ("flags") of the 4 leader tribes of Israel as they camped around the sanctuary in the wilderness (as recorded in Numbers 2).[175] A study of these standards and the tribes associated with them gives some interesting keys for understanding Revelation 6— the "four horsemen of the Apocalypse"—because each of the horses with their riders are introduced by one of the living creatures.

When the children of Israel were delivered from slavery in Egypt and camped in the desert, God directed that "the children of Israel shall pitch their tents, everyone by his own camp, *everyone by his own standard*, according to their armies" (Numbers1:52). The Levites camped in the middle, around the sanctuary (v. 53), while the tribes were camped around in four groups of 3 tribes apiece.[176] Each of the groups of 3 tribes had a leader tribe (Judah, Ephraim, Reuben and

Dan). Each group had a direction (north, south, east and west) from the sanctuary where they camped, and these directions have prophetic significance.[177] Each leader tribe had a standard (flag) that the group camped under, which according to tradition had one of the faces of the four living creatures. The assignment of the faces by Jewish tradition (lion-Judah, man-Reuben, ox-Ephraim, eagle-Dan) can also be deduced by comparing the tribal characteristics that are found in Genesis 49[178] and elsewhere with the symbolic characteristics of the creatures themselves. Each creature symbolizes a characteristic of God: the lion represents His power and sovereignty, the calf or ox His self-sacrificing mercy, the man symbolizes His righteousness (as seen in the humanity of Christ) and the eagle His swift justice.[179] In chapter 6 each creature with its specific characteristic introduces the judgment of people who are divided into "tribes" (categories) according to how they have responded to God.

The Four Tribes

The children of Israel camped in the wilderness in four groups around the sanctuary. "On

172 Psalms 11:4-7, 2 Samuel 22:28, 1 Kings 14:22, 15:11. The "eyes of the Lord" have two related functions: to watch and protect His children, and to discern the wickedness of His enemies. "The eyes of the Lord are in every place, keeping watch on the evil and the good" (Proverbs 15:3) "The eyes of the Lord run to and fro throughout the whole earth, to show Himself strong on behalf of those whose heart is loyal to Him" (2Chronicles 16:9). "The ways of man are before the eyes of the Lord, and He ponders all his paths. His own iniquities entrap the wicked man, and he is caught in the cords of his sin" (Proverbs 5:21,22).

173 Revelation 4:6,8,9, 5:8,11,14, 6:1-7, 7:11, 8:9, 14:3, 15:7, 19:4.

174 A standard was a banner or ensign used by the tribes of Israel and had the same function as a flag today.

175 See *The Seventh-day Adventist Bible Commentary* (Hagerstown MD, 1977) vol. 1, p. 576 commentary on Ezekiel 1:10.

176 Although there were 12 tribes, the tribe of Joseph was divided into two according to his two sons, Ephraim and Manasseh, making 13.

177 The vision of the four creatures in Ezekiel chapter one suggests that the directions associated with the creatures is the same as that of the standards in the encampment around the sanctuary in the desert. Ezekiel saw the vision coming from the north (Ezekiel 1:4). "Each had a human face in the front (south), the face of a lion on the right side (east), the face of an ox on the left side (west), and the face of an eagle at the back (north)" (Ezekiel 1:10 NLT). These are the same directions associated with the creatures on the tribal standards that are seen in Numbers chapter two.

178 The context of the descriptions of the tribes of Israel in Genesis 49 is the end of time, and specifically, what will "befall" them in the judgment, as indicated by the introductory statement, "Jacob called his sons and said, 'Gather together, that I may tell you what shall befall you in the last days" (Genesis 49:1). These are obviously spiritual rather than physical tribes as the literal tribes have been scattered and lost with the exception of the tribe of Judah (the Jews).

179 The Lion: Genesis 49:8-10, Proverbs 30:30, Hosea 11:10, Revelation 5:5. The Calf: Exodus 29:10, Leviticus 8, 9:8, Leviticus 4:3 13,14, 16:6,11, Numbers 8:8,12, Ezekiel 45:18-20. The Man: Genesis 1:26,27, Ecclesiastes 7:29, Hebrews 2:6-9. The Eagle: Deuteronomy 32:11, Exodus 19:4, Revelation 12:14

the east side, toward the rising of the sun, those of the standard of the forces with Judah shall camp" (Numbers 2:3). The east is often a Godly direction: the entrance to the temple was on the east,[180] Moses and the priests camped on the east side (Numbers 3:38) and God's glory came from the east (Ezekiel 43:2,4, Revelation 7:2).

Jacob's son Judah was an intercessor for his brothers (Genesis 37:26, 44:18-34), and the tribe of Judah was considered the kingly tribe ("the scepter shall not depart from Judah" Genesis 49:10); from Judah came the Messiah.[181] Judah was first on the list of the tribes included in the 144,000 (Revelation 7:4-8). His standard was the lion ("the Lion of the tribe of Judah"[182] Revelation 5:5, Genesis 49:9). The lion is fearless and bold, and conquers his enemies.[183] Considering this evidence, we can conclude that the first living creature who is **"like a lion"** is a mighty angel who presides over the judgment of those who are of the spiritual tribe of Judah. Chapter 6 will say more about the category of people symbolized by the tribe of Judah who are judged during the Day of Atonement.

"On the west side shall be the standard of the forces with Ephraim" (Numbers 2:18). The west was the direction of the Philistines (Isaiah 11:14) who attempted to mingle the worship of God and idols (1 Samuel 5:1,2). West was also the direction of Greece (Daniel 8:5:21), and in chapter 13 we will see that it was the influence of Greek philosophy that established false doctrine and idolatry in the church.

Ephraim was the tribe that was lavished with the richest of blessings,[184] but rather than using their blessings as spiritual leaders, they became the leaders in the idolatry of Israel. Jeroboam, an Ephraimite and the first king of the separated kingdom of Israel made two golden calves to be their gods and set one up in Bethel (a city in Ephraim) and the other in Dan (I kings 11:26, 12:25-29).

In the book of Hosea and the Psalms Ephraim is condemned again and again for their idolatry—"Because Ephraim has made many altars for sin, they have become for him altars for sinning...Ephraim exalted himself in Israel, but when he offended through Baal worship, he died. Now they sin more and more, and have made for themselves molded images...they say of them, 'let the men who sacrifice kiss the calves!' Ephraim is joined to idols, let him alone. Their drink is rebellion, they commit harlotry continually" (Hosea 8:11, 7:8-10, 13:1,2, 4:17,18). "Ephraim...did not keep the covenant of God. They refused to walk in His law, and forgot his works and His wonders that He had shown them...He [God] rejected the tent of Joseph and did not choose the tribe of Ephraim, but chose the tribe of Judah" (Psalms 78:9-11, 67,68).

Ephraim is not included on the list of the tribes that make up the 144,000.[185]

Ephraim's standard is the calf.[186] The calf or ox should symbolize strength, submission, and sacrifice, but as Ephraim departed from the Lord he was associated with calf worship in the history of Jeroboam and in the book of Hosea.[187]

---

180 Exodus 27:13-16, Ezekiel 46:1.

181 Genesis 49:8-10, Matthew 1:2,3, 2:6, Hebrews 7:14.

182 In Ezekiel's vision of the 4 living creatures the lion was on the east side, the side where Judah camped—the vision was seen "coming out of the north" and the lion was on the right, or east side.

183 Proverbs 28:1, Isaiah 31:4, Micah 5:8,9.

184 Genesis 48:8-20, 49:22-26.

185 Although 12 tribes are on the list, two tribes are missing, Ephraim and Dan. This is because Joseph is included as well as one of his sons (Manasseh). A full list with Joseph and both his sons would be 14.

186 In Ezekiel's vision the calf was on the west side, the side where Ephraim camped. Ephraim is repeatedly compared to a calf, bull or heifer (See Jeremiah 31:18, Hosea 10:11, 4:16,17)

187 Hosea 13:1,2, 10:11, 4:16,17.

He symbolizes those who claim to be Christians, but because they mix the true with the false they are actually idolaters. The second living creature, the calf, is the great angel who presides over the judgment of the category of people who are symbolized by the tribe of Ephraim.

"On the south side shall be the standard of the forces with Reuben" (Numbers 2:10). The south was considered to be the land of Egypt, where God's people went to find salvation from famine in the days of Jacob and Joseph but ended up as captive slaves (Genesis 46: 1-7, Exodus 1-13, Daniel 11.) Reuben was the firstborn, and as such should have had the birthright as the spiritual leader of God's people, but he lost his preeminence through human weakness (he slept with his father's concubine, Genesis 35:22, 49:3). Like Judah, he tried to intercede for his brother Joseph when the other brothers wanted to kill him, but his intervention was weak and ineffective (Genesis 37:22-29).[188] In his final blessing Reuben seems to represent those who "just barely" make it into the kingdom—"Let Reuben live, and not die" (Deuteronomy 33:6).

Reuben's name is on the list of the tribes included in the 144,000 (Revelation 7:4-8), although not in the first place that his birth order would ordinarily place him.[189] His standard is

the man.[190] The man should symbolize godliness (man was created in the image of God, Genesis 1:26), but under the influence of sin man became the symbol of spiritual weakness and failure— "through one man sin entered the world, and death through sin, and thus death spread to all men, because all sinned" (Romans 5:12). The third living creature, the man, is the great angel who presides over the judgment of the category of people who are symbolized by the tribe of Reuben.

"The standard of the forces with Dan shall be on the north side" (Numbers 2:25). North was the direction of the fierce enemies of God's people who conquered and scattered them— Syria, Assyria and especially Babylon.[191] In Zechariah 2 the people of God are told to "flee from the land of the north…escape [from] the daughter of Babylon" (Zechariah 2:6,7).

Dan, early in the time of the judges, separated himself from the other tribes of Israel in the far north where he turned to idol worship (Judges 18). Dan was the second tribe that hosted the calf-idols of Jeroboam, and his territory was known as a center for idolatry (1Kings 12:25-30, 2Kings 10:29). Jacob's "blessing" of the tribe of Dan showed that he was actually an enemy of God's people, even though he was one of the 12 tribes: "Dan shall judge his people as one of the tribes of Israel. Dan shall be a serpent by the way, a viper by the path that bites the horse's heels so that its rider shall fall backward" (Genesis 49:16,17).

Dan's name is not on the list of the tribes included in the 144,000 (Revelation 7:4-8). His standard is the Eagle.[192] The eagle should

---

188 Reuben's weak intercession compared to Judah's can also be seen in the brothers' attempt to guarantee Benjamin's safety to their father. Reuben said, "Kill my two sons if I do not bring [Benjamin] back to you," as if his father would be comforted by losing two grandsons in addition to his son. Judah, however, said "I myself will be surety for [Benjamin]…If I do not bring him back to you and set him before you, then let me bear the blame forever" (Genesis 42:37, 43:39).

189 In the Old Testament listings of the tribes Reuben was listed first (Genesis 49:3, Exodus 1:2, Numbers 1:5, 13:4, Deuteronomy 33:6-25, 1Chronicles 2:1). But in 1Chronicles 5:1 we see that Reuben lost his first-born privileges because of sexual sin—"Now the sons of Reuben the firstborn of Israel—he was indeed the firstborn, but because he defiled his father's bed, his birthright was given to the sons of Joseph, the son of Israel, so that the genealogy is not listed according to the birthright; yet Judah prevailed over his brothers, and from him came a ruler, although the birthright was Joseph's."

190 In Ezekiel's vision the man was on the south side, the side where Reuben camped.

191 Jeremiah 1:13-16, 25:9, Ezekiel 26:7, 38:1-39:5, Daniel 11 (the King of the North), Zephaniah 2:13.

192 In Ezekiel's vision the Eagle was on the north side, the side where Dan camped.

symbolize justice and protection, but under the influence of sin it came to represent the enemies of God's people who attack and destroy them.[193] The fourth living creature, the eagle, is the great angel who presides over the judgment of the category of people who are symbolized by the tribe of Dan.

These four tribes represent the four types of "Christians" who are evaluated in the judgment: strong, faithful Christians (the lion), false "Christians" who are actually idolaters (the calf), weak Christians (the man) and so-called Christians who are actually enemies of Christ and His people (the eagle). Only two of the four

"tribes" become members of God's eternal kingdom. This view is supported by the fact that even though Ezekiel saw the creatures (cherubim) with four faces, ("I knew they were cherubim. Each had four faces" Ezekiel 10:20,21), when cherubim were carved "throughout the temple… each cherub had [only] two faces, so that the face of a man was toward a palm tree on one side, and the face of a young lion toward a palm tree on the other side" (Ezekiel 41:18,19). The faces of the calf and the eagle were not included in the carvings that decorated the temple.[194]

Table 4.2 summarizes the living creatures and the tribes associated with them.

Table 4.2

Creature	Face	Direction	Tribe	Character
First	Lion	East	Judah	Strong
Second	Calf	West	Ephraim	False
Third	Man	South	Reuben	Weak
Fourth	Eagle	North	Dan	Enemy

193 Leviticus 11:13, Deuteronomy 28:49, Hosea 8:1, Lamentations 4:19, Habakkuk 1:6-8. There is an association between serpents (Dan is "a serpent by the way") and eagles: Satan, "that ancient serpent" is the King of Babylon (Isaiah 14:12-15). The King of Babylon is portrayed as "a great eagle" in Ezekiel 17 (see vs. 3, 12).

194 Another evidence is that when the Israelites were camped in the desert, the blowing of trumpets was to "sound the advance" and the tribes on the east and south (Judah and Reuben) were to "begin their journey" which symbolized following God (Numbers 10:5,6). There is no mention of an "advance" being sounded for the tribes of the west and north (Ephraim and Dan).

4:9-11 Praise to the Creator

"**The living creatures give glory and honor and thanks to Him that sat on the throne, who lives forever and ever**" (Revelation 4:9). Although these four angels preside over the judgment of various categories of people, including the enemies of God's chosen people, they are not *representatives* of those people. They are representatives of the angels, just as the 24 elders are representatives of the human race, and from their position **"in the midst of the throne"** they lead the universe in songs of praise and worship (Revelation 5:8,9, 7:11, 19:4). Their primary theme is the holiness of God (Revelation 4:8), which may be why they are so involved in the investigative phase of the judgment—they help to preserve the holiness and purity of the heavenly kingdom by making sure that "there shall not enter into it anything that defiles, or causes abomination or a lie, but only they which are written in the Lamb's Book of Life" (Revelation 21:27). Although their role in the investigative judgment is exceedingly important, it is a temporary addition to their eternal role as worship leaders: **"they do not rest day and night, saying, "Holy, holy, holy, Lord God Almighty, who was, and is, and is to come"** (Revelation 4:8). In the eternal kingdom their faces symbolize the attributes of God, not the perversions that the calf, man and eagle came to represent under the baleful influence of sin.

The chapter ends with a hymn of praise as **"The twenty-four elders fall down before Him that sat on the throne, and worship Him that lives forever and ever, and cast their crowns before the throne, saying, "You are worthy, O Lord, to receive glory and honor and power; for You have created all things, and for Your pleasure they are and were created"** (Revelation 4:10,11). In the midst of judgment which is necessitated by sin we are reminded that in the beginning our Holy God created everything "and indeed it was very good" (Genesis 1:31). But sin and death have reigned in this little corner of the universe from the time that Adam and Eve first listened to Satan, spoiling the beauty, harmony and love that God intended. The judgment, which begins with an investigation of those whose names have been written in the Book of Life, will culminate in "new heavens and a new earth in which righteousness dwells" (2 Peter 3:13). "And there shall be no more curse" (Revelation 22:3).

"Worthy is the Lamb who was slain to receive power and riches
and wisdom and strength and honor and glory and blessing." Rev. 5:12
Woodcut by Albrecht Durer 1498

Chapter 5

Revelation 5:1-14

5:1 And I saw in the right hand of Him who sat on the throne a book written within and on the backside, sealed with seven seals.

5:2 And I saw a strong angel proclaiming with a loud voice, "Who is worthy to open the book, and to loose the seals thereof?"

5:3 And no one in heaven, or on earth, or under the earth, was able to open the book, or to look thereon.

5:4 And I wept much, because no one was found worthy to open and to read the book, or to look thereon.

5:5 And one of the elders said to me, "Do not weep; behold, the Lion of the tribe of Judah, the Root of David, has prevailed to open the book, and to loose the seven seals thereof."

5:6 And I looked, and, behold, in the midst of the throne and of the four living creatures, and in the midst of the elders, stood a Lamb as if it had been slain, having seven horns and seven eyes, which are the seven Spirits of God sent forth into all the earth.

5:7 And He came and took the book out of the right hand of Him that sat on the throne.

5:8 And when He had taken the book, the four living creatures and twenty-four elders fell down before the Lamb, having every one of them harps, and golden vials full of incense, which are the prayers of saints.

5:9 And they sang a new song, saying, "You are worthy to take the book, and to open the seals thereof; for You were slain, and have redeemed us to God by your blood out of every tribe, and tongue, and people, and nation;

5:10 And have made us to our God kings and priests; and we shall reign on the earth."

5:11 And I beheld, and I heard the voice of many angels round about the throne and the living creatures and the elders: and the number of them was ten thousand times ten thousand, and thousands of thousands;

5:12 Saying with a loud voice, "Worthy is the Lamb that was slain to receive power, and riches, and wisdom, and strength, and honor, and glory, and blessing."

5:13 And every creature which is in heaven, and on the earth, and under the earth, and such as are in the sea, and all that are in them, I heard, saying, "Blessing, and honor, and glory, and power, be to Him that sits on the throne, and to the Lamb forever and ever."

5:14 And the four living creatures said, "Amen." And the twenty-four elders fell down and worshiped Him who lives forever and ever.

The Investigative Judgment

Chapter four introduced the theme of the "Day of Atonement," the first stage of the final judgment. This stage takes place before the Second Coming of Christ, because when Jesus comes "His reward is with Him," in other words, He has already determined the fate of everyone (Isaiah 40:10, 62:11). Revelation 5 continues this theme with the dramatic challenge to the opening of the book with seven seals. This is a serious issue, because, as we will see, it is only through the opening of this book that the judgment can proceed, and unless the judgment takes place, no one can be saved. Since the beginning of sin there has been the necessity for a judgment, which is God's way of bringing sin to an end while still saving those who believe and trust in Him. The judgment is not so that sinners can be condemned,[195] but rather so that sinners can be granted eternal life.

The scriptural pattern is for the judgment to be divided into two phases, the investigative judgment and the executive judgment. This pattern is found wherever there is a judgment, most obviously, with the original sin in the Garden of Eden, the great flood, Sodom and Gomorrah, the Babylonian captivity, and the end of time as portrayed in Daniel and Revelation. Because the two-phase judgment is such an important theme in the Book of Revelation but has not been widely recognized, a review of this concept in the scriptures will help to put Revelation 5 in perspective.

When Adam and Eve sinned "the eyes of both of them were opened, and they knew that they were naked" (Genesis 3:7). For the first time

they experienced shame and guilt, and such fear that they felt the need to hide themselves from God—"Adam and his wife hid themselves from the presence of the Lord God...'I heard your voice in the garden and I was afraid" (vs.8, 10). God came looking for them—"Then the Lord God called to Adam and said to him, 'where are you?'" (v. 9). This was the first in a series of questions: "Who told you that you were naked? Have you eaten from the tree?' And the Lord God said to the woman, 'what is this you have done?'" (vs. 11,13). Obviously God knew the answers to all of these questions, so the inquiry was not for His sake. The point is that before He pronounced and carried out his sentence (the executive judgment), He first carried out an investigative judgment.

Likewise, after Cain killed his brother Abel "the Lord said to Cain, 'where is Abel your brother?...What have you done?'" (Genesis 4:9,10). In both this case and in that of Adam and Eve, it appears that the Lord's sentence depended to some extent on their response to His inquiry. Thus the inquiry was designed to be redemptive, giving an opportunity for repentance and confession. The fact that these were not forthcoming was a clear demonstration (as we shall see, to the rest of the universe) of the deadly, corrupting influence of sin.

The most universal executive judgment of all time was the flood in the days of Noah. God, who knows all things at all times, is nevertheless portrayed as making a special inquiry—"So God looked upon the earth and indeed it was corrupt." "Then the Lord saw that the wickedness of man was great in the earth" (Genesis 6:12, 5). God pronounced sentence ("I will destroy man whom I have created" v.7), but He also set a period of

---

195 They are already condemned because "All have sinned" and "the wages of sin is death" (Romans 3:23, 6:23. See also John 3:17-21).

time in which he would strive through the Holy Spirit to bring any to salvation that He could— "My Spirit shall not strive with man forever, for he is indeed flesh; yet his days shall be one hundred and twenty years" (v. 3). The Hebrew word for "strive" means to judge.[196] This striving was done through the ministry of "Noah,…a preacher of righteousness" "by whom also He went and preached to the spirits in prison,[197] who formerly were disobedient when once the Divine longsuffering waited in the days of Noah, while the ark was being prepared" (2Peter 2:5, 1Peter 3:19,20).

After the flood the people, not trusting in God and wanting "to make a name" for themselves, began building the tower of Babel. Despite the fact that God was fully aware of what they were doing, He portrays Himself as conducting an investigation—"The Lord came down to see the city and the tower which the sons of men had built" (Genesis 11:4,5). In pronouncing His sentence, God makes it obvious that the judgment was not a unilateral act on His part; God said, "Come, let *Us* go down and there confuse their language" (v. 7). The "Us" most likely includes the angels, who are almost always involved in both investigative and executive judgments.[198]

The involvement of angels is obvious in the case of the judgment of Sodom and Gomorrah at the time of Abraham. "The Lord appeared to him [Abraham] by the terebinth trees of Mamre" (Genesis 18:1). But God was not alone: "Three men were standing by him" (v.2). Two of them turned out to be angels, and in fact by the time they got to Sodom and carried out the investigation and the execution of judgment only the angels were involved. As the Lord talked with Abraham, He informed him: "Because the outcry against Sodom and Gomorrah is great, and because their sin is very grave, I will go down now and see whether they have done altogether according to the outcry against it that has come to Me; and if not, I will know" (Genesis 18:20,21).

Actually the final period of grace began some years earlier when Abraham's nephew Lot "dwelt in the cities of the plain and pitched his tent even as far as Sodom" Genesis 13:12. Lot was "a righteous man who was distressed by the filthy lives of lawless men" (2Peter 2:7 NIV). The Sodomites themselves said of him, "this one came in to stay here, and he *keeps acting* as a judge" (Genesis 19:9), implying that his presence and witness had been a continual judgment against them. Thus just as with the flood, God gave a time of probation and a "preacher of righteousness" (Noah, Lot) so that the people received a warning before the executive judgment took place.

---

196 The Hebrew word for strive is *diyn* which means "to judge, contend, plead." Of the 24 times it is used in the Old Testament 18 are translated "judge," for example, "For the Lord shall judge [*diyn*] His people and have compassion on His servants" (Deuteronomy 32:36).

197 This was not the preaching of Jesus to souls in Hell, but the preaching of the Holy Spirit through Noah before the flood. The verses clearly state that the preaching took place "when the Divine longsuffering waited in the days of Noah, while the ark was being prepared." The "spirits in prison" (Greek *pneumasin*) were not disembodied dead people in hell, but were people who were prisoners of sin. Paul makes it clear that it is our spirit which communicates with God, not after we are dead but while we are alive (Romans 1:9, 8:16, 1Corinthians 5:3-5, 6:20, Colossians 2:5, 2Timothy 4:22). Jesus stated that it was His purpose to set free those in prison, referring to living individuals rather than people who had already died (Luke 4:18). Other texts that refer to the spirit as living individuals include Matthew 5:3, 26:41, 27:50, Mark 2:8, 8:12, 14:38, Luke 1:47, John 11:33, 13:21, Acts 17:16, 19:21, Romans 8:10,16, 1Corinthians 2:11, 5:3-5, 7:34, 2Corinthians 2:13, 7:1,13, Ephesians 4:23, Colossians 2:5, 1Thessalonians 5:23, 2Timothy 4:22, Philippians 1:25, 1Peter 3:4.

198 For example, in Daniel 7 when "the court was seated and the books were opened" (investigative judgment) the throne of judgment was surrounded by "a thousand thousands" and "ten thousand times ten thousands." Revelation 5:11 makes it clear that these are angels. Likewise, in Ezekiel 1-10 when God comes to earth to make an investigation of the sins of Israel He is accompanied by four cherubim, a class of angels (Ezekiel 10:20). When God carried out an executive judgment against Israel after David sinned by taking a census, an angel carried out the judgment (2Samuel 24:15-17). An angel also carried out the judgment against the Assyrian army that was attacking God's people (Isaiah 37:36).

There is no question that God already knew what was happening in Sodom. In the "bargaining" scene with Abraham it becomes obvious that God was seeking a way to avoid destroying the cities (Genesis 18:26-32). Ultimately the investigation did not find even ten righteous people—"the men of Sodom, both old and young, all the people from every quarter, surrounded the house" (Genesis 19:4), seeking to abuse the two angels who had come with a final offer of salvation. In the executive phase of judgment those who were true to God (Lot and his two daughters) were rescued from the fires that destroyed the unrepentant.

The ultimate example of executive judgment in the history of the Jewish people was the destruction of Jerusalem by the Babylonians and the taking into captivity of the children of Israel in 586 BC. Five years earlier Ezekiel, a priest who had been taken to Babylon in the second deportation,[199] had a vision which is recorded in Ezekiel 1-11. The prophet saw a number of the elements found in Revelation chapters 4-6, most notably the four living creatures and the Lord on his "mobile" throne. This pre-executive-judgment visit by the Lord was an *investigative* judgment in which the Lord Himself,[200] who already knew about the abominable sins of the children of Israel, revealed them to Ezekiel both to show him why executive judgment was necessary and to give a final opportunity for repentance.

The prophet was carried to the inner court in Jerusalem to see the "image of jealousy" (Ezekiel 8:5). Next he was instructed to excavate a door to an inner room where the "elders of the house of Israel" were worshiping "every sort of creeping thing, abominable beast, and all the idols of the house of Israel," arrogantly asserting that "The Lord does not see us" (vs. 6-12). Next he was shown women weeping for Tammuz (v.14), the counterfeit messiah of the Babylonian religion. Finally he was taken to the inner court of the temple to see twenty-five men "with their backs toward the temple of the Lord and their faces toward the east, and they were worshiping the sun" (v.16). This part of the investigation offered proof that even at the highest levels of the Jewish religious establishment the executive judgment was justified.

But the investigative judgment was not simply to identify the evil among God's so-called people. God also identified His true people (the "remnant"). In Ezekiel chapter nine God gave a vision of the destruction of Jerusalem and His apostate people by "those who have charge of the city [angels]…each with a deadly weapon in his hand" (Ezekiel 9:1). But before they were allowed to commence their work of destruction, another man "clothed with linen" with "a writers inkhorn at his side" was told to "go through the midst of the city…and put a mark on the foreheads of the men who sigh and cry over all the abominations that are done within it" (vs. 2,4).

The pattern is consistent. Before God pronounces and executes judgment, He conducts an investigative judgment. He gives a period of grace and sends a strong message to repent. Even though He already knows all the facts, He conducts an investigation for the sake of the angels who are also involved. During the investigative judgment God seeks to provide a last chance for repentance, and to identify and save His faithful ones. The "wicked" (those who have refused to respond to God's offer of mercy), on the other hand, are oblivious to the judgment that is taking place until the executive phase of judgment

---

199 Daniel was taken captive in the first deportation in 606 BC (2Kings 23:36-24:2, Daniel 1:1-6) and Ezekiel in the second which occurred with the revolt of Jehoichin in 597 BC (2Chronicles 36:9,10, Ezekiel 1:2).

200 A comparison of his description in Ezekiel 8:2 with that in 1:27,28 (in which the glowing man was identified as the Lord) shows that it was the Lord Himself who took Ezekiel on this investigative tour.

bursts upon them: "The wicked boasts of his heart's desire…in his proud countenance he does not seek God; God is in none of his thoughts… *Your judgments are far above, out of his sight…*but You have seen, for you observe trouble and grief, to repay it by Your hand" (Psalm 10:3-5,14).[201]

Judgment in the Book of Daniel

It is significant that the judgment, and particularly the investigative phase, is the central focus of the visions in the book of Daniel, the book of the Bible that is most like the Book of Revelation. The visions of Daniel predict the history of God's people from the time of Daniel until they are delivered at the Second Coming of Christ, with each vision adding more detail. In the first vision of the multi-metal image in chapter 2, there is a review of the world empires that oppressed God's people, from Babylon through Persia, Greece, Rome and Papal Rome. But the climax of the vision is the final judgment, represented by a stone from heaven that destroys the oppressive kingdoms and sets up God's eternal kingdom.

More detail is added to this skeleton outline in chapter 7, where the same world empires are represented by four wild animals and a "little horn" which blasphemes God and persecutes 'the saints." Again the real focus is the final judgment when "the court was seated and the books were opened" (Daniel 7:10). This judgment takes place in heaven with an examination of books of record (vs. 9,10), in other words it is an *investigative*

judgment.[202] The main purpose is not to establish the guilt of those who reject God, but to save the saints and establish them in His kingdom—"a judgment was made in favor of the saints of the Most High, and the time came for the saints to possess the kingdom" (v. 22, see also vs. 26,27).

In the next vision found in chapter 8 the persecuting kingdoms are represented by a ram, a goat and a "little horn which grew exceedingly." This vision shows that the anti-God system represented by the horn does not just affect God's people on earth but has an effect on the whole universe—"it grew up to the host of heaven, and it cast down some of the host and some of the stars to the ground, and trampled them. He even exalted himself as high as the Prince of the hosts; and by him the daily sacrifices were taken away, and the place of His sanctuary was cast down" (Daniel 8:10,11). Once again the climax of the vision is God's solution to the problem—"For two thousand three hundred days; then the sanctuary shall be cleansed" (v. 14). This important verse is explained in detail in 14:7 *The Hour of His Judgment*, showing that the cleansing of the sanctuary is the investigative judgment, as symbolized by the Day of Atonement.

Daniel "was astonished by the vision but no one understood it" and was "sick for days" (v.27) because of his misunderstanding of the 2,300 days and the cleansing of the sanctuary. In Daniel 9 the angel returned to clear up Daniel's misconception and to reveal the time when the investigative judgment would begin (see 14: *When in History?* and Appendix 5 for more details).

---

201 The stages of judgment can be seen in Jesus' parable of the sheep and the goats (Matthew 25:31-46). 1) The Lord sits on the throne of judgment with the angels around him (v. 31). 2) All nations are gathered before Him and they are separated into two groups (vs. 32,33). This is not a literal gathering, as the separation is determined before the Second Coming. 3) The sentence is pronounced for both groups (vs. 34-45). 4) The rewards and punishments are meted out (v. 46).

202 Daniel 7 is not showing the executive judgment which takes place at the Second Coming of Christ when Jesus comes "on the clouds of heaven" to this earth (Matthew 26:64), but rather Jesus is seen "coming with the clouds of heaven to the Ancient of Days" (Daniel 7:13). The progression of events is that the horn is making war against the saints, then a judgment is made in favor of the saints and the "Son of Man" is given a kingdom, and finally the time comes for the saints to possess the kingdom (Daniel 7:21,22,13,14).

In the eleventh and twelfth chapters of Daniel God gave the prophet a detailed outline of the great war that has been raging on for centuries between the King of the North and the King of the South (see 9: *Kings of the North and South*). As in the previous visions, that which is of primary importance is not the revelation of world history, but the judgment at the end of time when "Michael shall stand up…there shall be a time of trouble such as never was…and at that time your people shall be delivered, *everyone who is found written in the book*" (Daniel 12:1).

This overview shows that the investigative judgment, which involves investigation of "the books" and the deliverance of God's followers from their oppressors, is the central theme of Daniel. Therefore we would expect that the investigative judgment would also be a central theme in the Book of Revelation. In fact, many of the same elements are present, particularly the opening of the books of heaven before the throne of God with the participation of the myriads of angels.

It may seem to some readers that there has been an inordinate emphasis on the investigative judgment. But as we will see later in this chapter, this is a judgment that is taking place right now. The next great event is the beginning of the executive judgment, which will culminate in the Second Coming of Christ. We are no longer looking at vague and indefinite periods of time that will continue until we finally come to the last days. We are right in the midst of the last days, and most of the world is totally unaware that human history as we have known it is about to come to an end.

5:1 The Sealed Book

"And I saw in the right hand of Him who sat on the throne a book written within and on the backside, sealed with seven seals" (Revelation 5:1). There has been a great deal of speculation about the sealed book,[203] much of it involving comparisons with books or scrolls used in Roman times such as books of covenant deeds or wills and testaments. However, we would expect that a book so important that a whole chapter is devoted to the controversy surrounding its opening would be mentioned elsewhere in Revelation.

Besides the sealed book of Revelation 5 there are three other books mentioned in Revelation. In Revelation 1:11 John was directed to write in a book the things which he saw in vision and send it to the 7 churches, which resulted in the Book of Revelation. In Revelation 22 this same book is called the "book of this prophecy" and is mentioned five times. John is specifically warned, "do not seal the words of the prophecy of this book" (v. 10). This literal book which was to be read by the churches on earth could not be the same one John saw in heaven sealed with seven seals.

The second "book" is the "little book" of chapter 10. There are no links between the themes and language of chapter five and chapter 10; even the Greek word for book is different.[204]

The third book is the Book of Life. This book is mentioned 7 times,[205] and like the book in Revelation 5, is closely linked to Jesus in His role as the sacrificial lamb (it is given to the lamb in Revelation 5 and in Revelation 21:27 it is called the "Lamb's Book of Life"). It is closely linked to judgment: "And another book was opened, which is the Book of Life. And the dead were judged out of those things which were written in the books, according to their works." "And whoever was not

---

203 It has been argued by some commentators that the ceremony depicted in Revelation 5 is the coronation of Christ as King of the universe, and the sealed book is the equivalent of the book of the law which the newly coronated kings of Israel were to receive (Deuteronomy 17:18-20). This view is examined in appendix 2.

204 The Greek word for "little book" in chapter 10 is *biblaridion*, whereas the word for "book" in chapter 5 is *biblion*.

205 Revelation 3:5. 13:8, 17:8, 20:12, 15, 21:27, 22:19.

found written in the Book of Life was cast into the lake of fire" (Revelation 20:12,15). As we saw in chapter 4, the whole scene of Revelation 4-7 has to do with the "investigative judgment" and the Day of Atonement. Just as the judgment of the Old Testament Day of Atonement determined who ultimately would be included among the people of God (Leviticus 23:27-30), so the Book of Life is the means used to determine who will ultimately be saved into the eternal kingdom (Revelation 20:15). God's enemies who follow the beast are not written in the Book of Life (Revelation 13:8, 17:8). God's people are exhorted to live in such a way that their names will not be blotted out of the Book of Life (Revelation 3:5, 22:19).

Thus the Book of Life is concerned with eternal, life-and-death issues. This makes it easy to understand John's strong reaction—**"And I wept much, because no one was found worthy to open and to read the book, or to look thereon"** (Revelation 5:4). Without the opening of the Book of Life no one could be judged, which would mean that no one could be saved—"there shall by no means enter [the Holy City] anything that defiles, or causes an abomination or a lie, but *only those who are written in the Lamb's Book of Life*" (Revelation 21:27).

A little "catechism" helps identify the sealed scroll.

Q. After the One "who sat on the throne" gave the book to the Lamb, whose book was it?

A. The Lamb's book.

Q. Is there any book in Revelation that is called "the Lamb's book?"

A. Yes, "the Lamb's Book of Life" (Revelation 21:27).

Q. Why did the Lamb take the book?

A. So that He could open it (Revelation 5:5).

Q. Is there any book that is opened in Revelation?

A. Yes, "another book was opened, which is the Book of Life" (Revelation 20:12).

Q. If the Book of Life was not opened, would it be cause for John to cry?

A. Yes, "Anyone not found written in the Book of Life [will be] cast into the lake of fire" (Revelation 20:15).

The names in the Book of Life appear with their social, circumstantial, and historical context. People are judged with consideration of the light they have received and the circumstances of their lives: "I will make mention of Rahab [Egypt] and Babylon to those who know Me: Behold O Philistia and Tyre, with Ethiopia: 'This one was born there.' And of Zion it will be said, 'This one and that one were born in her'...The Lord will record, when He registers the peoples: 'This one was born there" (Psalm 87:5,6). The trials we encounter (Psalm 56:8), our attempts to improve our spiritual condition (Malachi 3:16), and in fact all that we have said and done (Revelation 20:13) are considered.

The Book of Life is not the only book that is opened in the judgment: "The court was seated and the *books* were opened" (Daniel 7:10). These include the book of God's law (Galatians 3:10, Deuteronomy 28:58,61), the book of the covenants God has made with His people (2Chronicles 34:30,31), and the book with God's plans for each of our lives (Psalms 139:16). That which is written in the Book of Life is "compared" with what is in the other books.

Naturally God does not need to open any books in order to know what His judgments will be, and in fact the whole concept of "books" (records) that could include information about the whole human family makes more sense today in the digital age when mass information can be stored and manipulated. The reality of heavenly "technology" will be incredible. But the point is that the books are not opened for God, but for the **"ten thousand times ten thousand and thousands of thousands"** who are gathered around the throne. Because they will be eternal neighbors of those who are redeemed, the angels have a vested interest in making sure that no one will enter the eternal kingdom who would reactivate sin and grief.

Who Is Written in The Book?

The Bible does not say categorically whose names are registered in the Book of Life. Certainly faithful Christians are written in, especially those who have sacrificed to share the Gospel with others—Paul referred to "Clement also, and the rest of my fellow workers, whose names are in the Book of Life" (Philippians 4:3). The faithful in Old Testament times were also included—Moses pleaded for his people after their idolatry with the golden calf, "Yet now, if You will forgive their sin—but if not, I pray, blot me out of Your book which You have written" (Exodus 32:32). Abraham is a representative of those who may not know the name of Jesus but they have known *Him* through the Holy Spirit—he is "the father of all those who believe, though they are uncircumcised, that righteousness might be imputed to them also" (Romans 4:11).

Many are in spiritual darkness, but under the influence of the Holy Spirit they "seek the Lord, in the hope that they might grope for Him and find Him" (Acts 17:27). God reveals Himself to them through His creation: "His invisible attributes are clearly seen, being understood by the things that are made, even His eternal power and Godhead," so that "the Gentiles, who do not have the law, by nature do the things in the Law…who show the work of the law written in their hearts" (Romans 2:14,15). No doubt these also are written in the Book of Life.

It appears that those who at one time or another have responded to the Holy Spirit have had their names (along with the historical context of their lives and their individual circumstances) written in the Book of Life. On the other hand, those who resist or refuse the promptings of the Spirit do not have their names written in. The beast of Revelation 13 is given authority over "all…whose names *have not been written* in the Book of Life" (Revelation 13:7,8).

Furthermore, names that have been written can later be removed. At the end of Revelation there is a solemn warning: "If anyone shall take away from the words of the book of this prophecy, God shall take away his part out of the Book of Life" (Revelation 22:19). Jesus told the church of Sardis, "He that overcomes, the same shall be clothed in white raiment; and I will not blot out his name out of the Book of Life, but I will confess his name before My Father, and before His angels" (Revelation 3:5). This verse refers to the very scene recorded in Revelation 4-7, where the Book of Life is opened by the **"Lamb as though it had been slain."** In this judgment the names of those who have not "overcome" are "blotted out" or removed.[206]

To summarize, the investigative judgment of Revelation 4-7 is analogous to the "Day of Atonement" of the Old Testament sanctuary service. It is a time when all trace of sin will be "blotted out" (Acts 3:19) from the "records" of those who have continued to trust in the Lord. It is also a time when the names of those who have not held "the beginning of [their] confidence steadfast to the end" will be blotted out of the Book of Life (Hebrews 3:6).

Many people shudder at the thought of being judged, aware of and condemned by the sin they know exists in their own hearts. But we should always remember that it is God the Father, the One who "so loved the world that He gave His only begotten Son," who is giving the Book of Life to Jesus. And Jesus, the **"Lamb that was**

---

206 Overcoming is not a matter of "being good" through personal effort, but is through the grace of God: "They overcame him by the blood of the Lamb and by the word of their testimony" (Revelation 12:11, See chapter 12:11,12 *They Overcame by the Blood*).

slain," who gave His life to save us, is the One who will open the scroll. God carries out a judgment because He wants us to be saved!

Daniel saw that the purpose of the judgment is to rescue those who love God (the "saints") from this world of sin so they can live forever in His glorious kingdom: "The court was seated and the books were opened…Judgment was made in favor of the saints of the most High, and the time came for the saints to possess the kingdom…then the kingdom and dominion and the greatness of the kingdoms under the whole heaven shall be given to the people, the saints of the Most High. His kingdom is an everlasting kingdom" (Daniel 7:10, 22, 26,27). The investigative judgment is good news! Although the reign of sin seems endless and sometimes the pressures of this world seem overwhelming, Jesus promised that He is able to keep those who want to be kept by Him. "My sheep hear My voice, and I know them, and they follow Me. And I give them eternal life, and they shall never perish; neither shall anyone snatch them out of My hand. My Father, who has given them to Me is greater than all, and no one is able to snatch them out of My Father's hand" (John 10:27-29).

5:2-4 Who Is Worthy?

"And I saw a strong angel proclaiming with a loud voice, 'Who is worthy to open the book, and to loose the seals thereof?' And no one in heaven, or on earth, or under the earth, was able to open the book, or to look thereon. And I wept much, because no one was found worthy to open and to read the book, or to look thereon" (Revelation 5:2-4).

The Book of Life contains the names of "[God's] people" who "shall be delivered, every one who is found written in the book" (Daniel 12:1). There is only one "strong angel" who would want to challenge the right to open the book that makes possible the deliverance of God's people—"the angel of the bottomless pit,"[207] Satan. "The whole world lies under the sway of the wicked one" (1John 5:19), trapped in "the snare of the devil, having been taken captive by him to do his will" (2Timothy 2:26). As the "accuser of our brethren" (Revelation 12:10) he reminds the universe that "all have sinned" and "the wages of sin is death" (Romans 3:23, 6:23). Nor is there anyone **in heaven or on the earth or under the earth** who is able to provide a ransom: "No man can redeem the life of another, or give to God a ransom for him—the ransom for a life is costly, no payment is ever enough—that he should live on forever" (Psalm 49:7-9 NIV). It is no wonder that John **"wept much"**—he felt like Jeremiah who said, "My eyes will weep bitterly and run down with tears, because the Lord's flock has been taken captive" (Jeremiah 13:17).[208]

Unless the accusations about the sins of those written in Book of Life could be met, no one could be saved. With his accurate accusations Satan claims that every single person who has ever lived (with the exception of Jesus Christ) has joined him in his sin and rebellion and thus belongs on his side. The devil even contended over Moses, one of the holiest people who ever lived, a man with whom "the Lord spoke…face to face, as a man speaks to his friend" (Jude 9, Exodus 33:11). The evidence of faith that meets these accusations is found in the Book of Life,[209] but it was sealed up and no one could open it. But that which no one could do, God Himself did, establishing the right to save sinners through the sacrifice of His own life as Jesus, the Lamb of God.

---

207 Revelation 9: 1,11.

208 Some commentators have seen the scroll with its seven seals as an unfolding of the history of the world in the Christian era, or as a revelation of what the future holds. But it is unlikely that John would "weep much" because a history book could not be opened. History is in the Book of Life because the historical context of each person is included.

209 Revelation 20:12-15, 21: 27.

5:5-7 The Lion, the Root and the Lamb

"And one of the elders said to me, 'Do not weep; behold, the Lion of the tribe of Judah, the Root of David, has prevailed to open the book, and to loose the seven seals thereof.' And I looked, and behold, in the midst of the throne and of the four living creatures, and in the midst of the elders, stood a Lamb as if it had been slain, having seven horns and seven eyes, which are the seven Spirits of God sent forth into all the earth. And He came and took the book out of the right hand of Him that sat on the throne" (Revelation 5;5-7). Here is introduced the real hero of the story. Jesus is depicted with three different symbols, each of which emphasizes a different aspect of His identity.

Jesus is the **"Lion of the tribe of Judah."** This phrase refers to Genesis 49, where Jacob blessed Judah and his brothers, the progenitors of the twelve tribes of Israel. "Judah is a lion's whelp... he lies down as a lion; and as a lion, who shall rouse him? The scepter shall not depart from Judah, nor a lawgiver from between his feet, until Shiloh comes; And to Him shall be the obedience of the people" (Genesis 49:9,10). Here the fearless strength of the Lion, which conquers every foe, is used to symbolize the tribe God chose to rule His people—"The scepter shall not depart from Judah." This verse also foretells the coming of "Shiloh"[210] (Christ), who was of the tribe of Judah. He is the one to whom "shall be the obedience of the people." The day will come when every person who has ever lived will "stand before the judgment seat of Christ" and even His enemies will acknowledge His right to rule—"Every knee

shall bow to Me and every tongue shall confess to God" (Romans 14:10,11). As the mighty victor who conquers all His enemies, Jesus is the **"Lion of the tribe of Judah,"** and this gives Him the power to open the sealed Book of Life.

He also has the authority to open the book because He is **"the Root of David."** The Jews, in expectation of the Messiah, repeatedly called Jesus "the Son of David." Jesus is the Son of David according to His human genealogy (Matthew 1:1), but He is much more; in Revelation 22:16 Jesus says, "I am the Root *and* the Offspring of David." As the *Root* of David Jesus is the very foundation of the throne that David sat on. David's right to rule was not because of his tribe or family, but rather "the Lord has sought for a man after His own heart, and the Lord has commanded him to be commander over His people" (1 Samuel 13:14). Jesus was the true man after God's own heart. He fully took upon himself human nature, identifying with the human race—"In all things He had to be made like His brethren, that He might be a merciful and faithful High Priest." "Inasmuch then as the children have partaken of flesh and blood, He Himself likewise shared in the same" (Hebrews 2:17,14). Jesus did not come with the nature of an angel or as some kind of superhuman who could neither provide us an example nor be our substitute. He came as the **"Root of David,"** the man after God's own heart, with our very nature but without sin. As the "new Adam,"[211] the perfect man, Jesus has the authority to open the Book of Life.

But if He was *only* a lion, with infinite power, it would not be enough. Power alone cannot answer the accusations of Satan against those whose names are written in the Book of Life. If He was *only* the Root of David, the perfect man after God's own heart, it would not be enough.

---

210 The Hebrew word *Shiloh* means peace, but in this passage it is used as a name (the peaceful one) which correlates well with Christ's title "the Prince of Peace" (Isaiah 9: 6).

211 Romans 5:12-21.

Perfect identity with humanity only goes so far—He can "sympathize with our weaknesses" because He has experienced our nature, but He "was in all points tempted as we are, yet without sin" (Hebrews 4:15) and here is where the identity ends. "All have sinned" (Romans 3:23), and as sinners we are all subject to "the wages of sin…death" (Romans 6:23). Because all of humanity is condemned to die, when Jesus actually takes the scroll, it is as **"a Lamb that was slain."**

The Sacrificial Lamb

The sacrificial lamb is the most important and prominent symbol in the Bible, from the first book to the last and all through the Old and the New Testament. Jesus is "the Lamb slain from the foundation of the world" (Revelation 13:8). This important verse shows that God did not have different plans, different "dispensations" for saving mankind from the condemnation of sin—the plan has always been the same. God created the world with perfect creatures (humans) that had free will, but this very freedom made sin a possibility. Because of the potential for sin, God made provision before He created the world. Before sin ever appeared, Jesus "laid down His life for us" (1John 3:16).

When Adam and Eve sinned, God took the initiative; He searched for them, calling to Adam, "Where are you?" (Genesis 3:8,9). He confronted them with their sin and announced they would have to die. But all was not hopeless—God promised a redeemer who would defeat their enemy the serpent (Satan), the initiator of sin (Genesis 3:15). Then God provided the first symbol of the sacrifice Jesus would make thousands of years later for their sins—"For Adam and his wife the Lord God made tunics of skin and clothed them" (Genesis 3:21). The skins represented His perfect righteousness which He credits to us as a gift—"He has covered me with the robe of righteousness" (Isaiah 61:10). Obviously an animal had to die in order to provide the skins, and this was the first symbolic sacrifice for sin.

"Abel [Adam and Eve's son] brought the firstborn of his flock" (Genesis 4:4) and God accepted this sacrifice, which represented Christ. But He did not accept Cain's offering of garden produce, a symbol of his own efforts. The details are not given in Genesis but it is obvious that God taught Cain and Abel the plan of salvation, because "by *faith* Abel offered to God a more excellent sacrifice" and "faith comes by hearing, and hearing by the word of God" (Hebrews 11:4, Romans 10:17). Apparently the knowledge of the symbolic sacrifice was retained by the "sons of God" down to the time of Noah, because the first thing Noah did after disembarking from the ark after the world-wide flood was to offer sacrifices to the Lord. (Genesis 8:20,21).

God chose Abraham to be the father of the faithful, and everywhere he went he built an altar to offer sacrifices to God. (Genesis 12:7,8, 13:18). His ultimate act of faith was to offer his own son Isaac (Genesis 22), a picture of what God would do nearly 2,000 years later—"God so loved the world that He gave His only begotten Son" (John 3:16). God provided a ram as a substitute for Isaac, symbolic of how God would offer himself in the person of Jesus, the Lamb of God, as our substitute, dying the death that we deserve.

The descendents of Abraham went down to Egypt and ended up slaves. Pharaoh was determine keep them in bondage forever, despite the devastating plagues which fell upon the Egyptians; He was only willing to let them go when the firstborn were killed by the destroying angel. The firstborn of Israel were also included in the sentence of death, but through the sacrifice of a lamb as their substitute they were saved.[212] Through the blood of the lamb that was slain their lives were spared and they were freed from slavery, just as we are by "the precious blood of Christ, as of a lamb without blemish and without spot" (1Peter 1:19).

After freeing them from slavery God gave the children of Israel the law at Mt. Sinai, and they promised to keep it: "All that the Lord has spoken we will do" (Exodus 19:8). But the law could not save—"If there had been a law given which could have given life," there would not have ever needed to be another sacrifice (Galatians 3:21). God knew their sinful nature—"there is not a just man on earth who does good and does not sin" (Ecclesiastics 7:20)—and so as soon as he gave the law, he also gave them instructions to build a sanctuary where they offered sacrifices (Exodus 20:22-26).

Almost all heathen nations also offered sacrifices, but there was an essential difference: The sacrifices of the nations were designed to appease their offended gods, but the sacrifices of Israel were a symbol of the self-sacrifice God would make for His offended and separated children. The lambs and other animals that were sacrificed were "shadows" of the one perfect sacrifice that was still in the future. "The law [of sacrifices] is a shadow of the good things to come," "but the substance is of Christ" (Hebrews 10:1, Colossians 2:16,17). For the next 1,500 years millions of lambs and other animals were offered in the sanctuary,[213] each one a "shadow" of Jesus on the Cross. The average Israelite did not recognize the significance, thinking that the shadow was the reality, and so they misunderstood the message of John the Baptist who announced "Behold! The Lamb of God who takes away the sin of the world!" (John 1:29).

God's chosen people sacrificed the Son of God,[214] as any other nation would have done if they had been in their place.[215] As Jesus poured out His life He prayed, "Father, forgive them, for they do not know what they do" (Luke 23:34). "And Jesus cried out with a loud voice, and breathed His last. Then the veil of the temple was torn in two from top to bottom" (Mark 15:37,38). With the tearing of the veil the mystery of the earthly sanctuary was over; no longer would the sacrifice of animals have meaning, because the reality that they had pointed to had come. "The Lamb slain from the foundation of the world" was no longer a shadow, but a historical fact. Christ's sacrifice as the Lamb of God is the heart of the Gospel, the object of our faith and our only hope. "I declare to you the gospel...by which you are saved... that Christ died for our sins" (1Corinthians 15:1-3). "Christ also has loved us and given Himself for us, an offering and a sacrifice to God"

---

212 "Every man shall take for himself a lamb...then the whole assembly of the congregation of Israel shall kill it at twilight. And they shall take some of the blood and put it on the two doorposts... for I will pass through the land of Egypt on that night, and will strike all the firstborn in the land of Egypt...Now the blood shall be a sign for you on the houses where you are. And when I see the blood, I will pass over you; and the plague shall not be on you to destroy you" (Exodus 12:4-13).

213 The regular morning and evening sacrifices by themselves for the approximately 1,400 years that the sanctuary was operating would amount to more than one million sacrifices. In addition there were the personal and special sacrifices that were offered, as well as special occasions such as the inauguration of the temple when Solomon offered 22,000 bulls and 120,000 sheep (see 1 Kings 8:63).

214 See John 11: 47-53, the story of the Jewish leader's decision "that one man should die for the people."

215 The Jews, as God's chosen people, had the privilege of "hosting" Jesus during His 33 years on this earth, but their response in murdering Him was the same as what any other race or people would have done. Those who believe that they as a people or even as individuals would not have done the same simply do not understand the evil animosity against God that lurks in the unconverted human heart and the susceptibility of the weak human will to the sophistry of Satan.

(Ephesians 5:2). "He has appeared to put away sin by the sacrifice of Himself" (Hebrews 9:26).

Who Is the Lamb?

As the texts quoted above show, **"The Lamb that was slain"** is Jesus. All Christian and many non-Christian religions "believe in Jesus."[216] But from the very beginning of the church there has been fierce controversy about just who Jesus is. Although there are many issues about the nature of Christ that can never be resolved because of our limited capacity to comprehend, there is one critical aspect that is very clear: Jesus is fully God, He is not a created being.

The prophets of the Old Testament and the writers of the New Testament clearly witnessed to the divinity of Christ. "For to us a child is born, to us a son is given, and the government will be on his shoulders. And he will be called Wonderful Counselor, *Mighty God, Everlasting Father,* Prince of Peace" (Isaiah 9:6). "In the beginning was the Word and the Word was with God, and *the Word was God*" John 1:1.[217] "But *to the Son* He says: '*Your throne, O God*, is forever and ever'" (Hebrews 1:8). Paul and John identified Him as the Creator: "All things were made through Him, and without Him nothing was made that was made," "For by Him all things were created that

are in heaven and that are on earth, visible and invisible" (John 1:3, Colossians 1:16). Thus Jesus, called the Word of God before His incarnation, is the God of creation:[218] "In the beginning *God created* the heavens and the earth" (Genesis 1:1).

Jesus allowed people to worship Him,[219] even though He Himself had said "You shall worship the Lord your God, and Him only you shall serve" (Matthew 4:10). To the contrary, neither the apostle Peter nor the angels allowed anyone to worship them.[220] Jesus did not rebuke Thomas when he exclaimed, "My Lord and my God" (John 20:28). Indeed, "All the angels of God worship Him" (Hebrews 1:6) and "at the name of Jesus every knee should bow...every tongue should confess that Jesus Christ is Lord" (Philippians 2:10,11).

Jesus also forgave sins,[221] which no other person in the Bible ever did, and even the Pharisees recognized that this was a claim to be God, exclaiming,"Who can forgive sins but God alone?"[222] Jesus expressed His identity with the Father, saying, "He who has seen Me has seen the Father," and "I and My Father are one" (John 14:9, 10:30). One of His names, Immanuel, means "God with us" (Matthew 1:23). Jesus also applied the divine name to Himself. He declared Himself to be the "I AM" who appeared to Moses in the burning bush in Exodus 3. A careful reading of the whole passage shows that "I AM" is God

---

216 Three of many examples that could be given are Islam, which teaches that Jesus was a great prophet, the Jehovah's Witnesses who teach that He was the greatest (created) man who ever lived, and Unity which teaches that He was a great moral teacher and a divine idea.

217 The Jehovah's Witnesses claim that because there is no article (the equivalent of "the") in the original Greek text, it can be translated "and the word was a god," expressing the idea that He was divine but not God Himself. However, there are several instances in which the word for God (*Theos*) is used to refer to God Himself without the article (*o*). See for example Mark 12:27, Luke 20:38, John 8:54, Romans 8:33, 9:5, 1Corinthians 8:4, 2Corinthians 1:21, 5:15, 19, Galatians 2:6, 6:7, 1Thessalonians 2:5, 2Thessalonians 2:4, 1Timothy 3:16, Titus 1:2, Hebrews 3:4, Revelation 21:7. Ancient Greek uses another word (*theios*) to express the idea of divine (see Acts 17:29, 2Peter 1:3,4).

218 God in Genesis 1 is *Elohim*, a plural word which shows that God the Father, Son, and Holy Spirit were all involved in creation.

219 Matthew 8:2, 9:18, 14:33, 15:25, 28:9, 17, Mark 5:6, Luke 24:52, John 9:38, Hebrews 1:6.

220 Acts 10:25, Revelation 19:10, 22:8,9 In contrast, Satan, the beast and evil angels seek worship (see Matthew 4:9, Luke 4:7, Acts 7:42, 17:23, 19:27, Revelation 13:8, 12).

221 Matthew 9:2, Mark 3:5, Luke 5:20, 24, 7: 47, 48.

222 Mark 2:7, Luke 5:21.

(Elohim) and the Lord (Yahweh).[223]

The divinity of Christ is not simply a theme for theologians to argue over. It is of vital importance for having a correct understanding of the character of God. God created the angels, including Lucifer and the third of the angels who eventually sinned. He created human beings who also fell into sin. That sin requires death—"sin, when it is full grown, brings forth death" (James 1:15). God wanted to save sinners, which meant that someone else would have to pay "the wages of sin [which] is death" (Romans 6:23). But God did not create a substitute and then let him suffer the consequences of humanity's sin; this would have been a very ugly picture of a God who did not take responsibility for His own creation. Instead God Himself took upon Himself the full burden of the sins of the whole world, and died the death that we should die so that we could live. When God "gave His only begotten Son" (John 3:16) He was giving Himself. Expressing this truth in the words of Isaiah, "Surely He [God] has borne our griefs and carried our sorrows... He [God] was wounded for our transgressions, He [God] was bruised for our iniquities; the chastisement

for our peace was upon Him [God], and by His [God's] stripes we are healed... and the Lord has laid on Him [on Himself] the iniquity of us all" (Isaiah 53:3-6).

Why Was the Lamb Slain?

Although nearly all Christians understand that Jesus died for sinners, many do not understand why He had to die. And for non-Christians the death of the "so-called god of the Christians" is incomprehensible and ridiculous. This is of course to be expected—Paul said, "the message of the cross is foolishness to those who are perishing" (1Corinthians 1:18). But even those who believe that they are saved because of Christ's sacrifice often do not really know why. Many, if they were asked, would reply that Jesus simply had the misfortune of falling into the hands of wicked sinners.

But Jesus is "the Lamb slain from the foundation of the world" (Revelation 13:8). Before sin ever entered the world God had ordained the plan of salvation which involved the sacrifice of Jesus. In their efforts to understand the fullness of why Jesus had to die, Christians have disagreed, even to the point of violence. But as in everything that God does, He accomplishes many things simultaneously with his acts, and this is particularly true of His sacrificial death.

1. Jesus' sacrifice satisfied justice. It is no arbitrary law that demands the death of those who sin. As Ezekiel put it, "the soul who sins shall die" (Ezekiel 18:4). But for reasons we cannot fully understand, Jesus could be a substitute for sinners, dying the death that they should die so that they could live—"Christ died for our sins" (1Corinthians 15:3).

2. Jesus identified with our humanity so that we can be identified with His divinity. Jesus did not cease to be fully divine when He became fully human. This point has been the source of innumerable heresies and foolish disputes, because

---

223 In Exodus 3 "the Angel of the Lord appeared to [Moses] in a flame of fire from the midst of a bush" (v. 2). It turns out that the "Angel of the Lord" was God Himself: "God called to him from the midst of the bush" (v. 4, see also verses 6, 11, 13, 14, 15,16). The Hebrew word for God is *Elohim*, the same God who "in the beginning...created the heavens and the earth." This God, *Elohim*, was also *Yahweh* (Jehovah): "So when the Lord [*Yahweh*] saw that he turned aside to look, God [*Elohim*] called to him from the midst of the bush. (v. 4, see also verses 7, 15, 16, 18, 4:2, 4, 5, 6, 10, 11, 14). This God was the God of the Bible Patriarchs: "Go and gather the elders of Israel together, and say to them, 'the Lord [*Yahweh*] God [*Elohim*] of your fathers, the God [*Elohim*] of Abraham, of Isaac, and of Jacob, appeared to me" (v. 16). This same God told Moses that He had another name: I AM (*Hayah*). "Moses said...'what is His name?' And God said to Moses, 'I AM WHO I AM'. And He said, 'Thus you shall say to the children of Israel, 'I AM has sent me to you" (vs. 13, 14). Jesus applied the divine name "I AM" to Himself: "Jesus said to them, 'Most assuredly, I say to you, before Abraham was, I AM" (John 8:58). The Pharisees understood that He was claiming to be God and attempted to stone Him (v. 59).

it is incomprehensible to our finite minds, but regardless of the fact that we cannot understand it, we can still believe by faith that it is true. Jesus became fully human and then made us one with Him (John 17: 21-23) so that we could be "partakers of the divine nature" (2 Peter 1:4). "If we have been united together in the likeness of His death, certainly we also shall be in the likeness of His resurrection" (Romans 6:5).

3. Jesus died as a demonstration of the love of God. As we saw in the previous section, Jesus is fully God, and God died for us after taking upon Himself the full burden of our sins so that we could realize the extent of His love and how far He was willing to go to save us. "God demonstrates His own love toward us, in that while we were still sinners, Christ died for us" (Romans 5: 8).

4. Jesus lived and died as an example to us. He fully took upon Himself the same humanity that we have, lived a perfect, sinless life and died a perfect death to show us how to live and die. "Inasmuch then as the children have partaken of flesh and blood, He Himself likewise shared in the same, that through death He might destroy him who had the power of death, that is the devil…therefore, in all things He had to be made like His brethren" (Hebrews 2: 14, 17). "For to this you were called, because Christ also suffered for us, leaving us an example, that you should follow His steps: Who committed no sin, nor was deceit found in His mouth" (1 Peter 2:21, 22).

Although the church has disputed as to which is the "real" reason Jesus died, the reality is that these are all true, and the death of Christ encompasses much more as well. No doubt for all of eternity we will continue to marvel at the depth of love expressed in the sacrifice of the **"Lamb that was slain."** The fact that God the Lamb was slain answers the question, **"Who is worthy to open the book, and to loose the seals thereof?"**

5:6 Seven Horns, Seven Eyes

"A Lamb as if it had been slain, having seven horns and seven eyes, which are the seven Spirits of God sent forth into all the earth" (Revelation 5:6). Horns in scripture symbolize the power that is wielded by the head that controls them. For example, in Revelation 17 John saw a scarlet beast with seven heads and ten horns. "The ten horns which you saw are ten kings…they will give their *power and authority* to the beast. These will make war with the Lamb" (Revelation 17:12-14). In these verses the ten horns are ten kings that the beast uses to make war.

In Revelation 5:8-10, just after the Lamb has been shown with His seven horns, the saints (represented by the 24 elders) sing a new song to the Lamb, **"saying, You…have made us kings and priests to our God."** God's people are kings, and as such they are the horns of Jesus. Empowered by His Spirit they invade the territory of the enemy, "pulling down strongholds, casting down arguments and every high thing that exalts itself against the knowledge of God" (2Corinthians 10:4,5).

In chapter four the seven lamps of fire were identified as "the seven Spirits of God." We saw in 4:5 *Seven Lamps, Seven Spirits* that the seven lamps symbolize the fullness of God's Spirit shining in and through His people, illuminating the darkness of the world around them. Here the **"seven eyes"** of the lamb are also identified as **"the seven Spirits of God"** with the further specification that they are **"sent out into all the earth."** Again, it is the disciples of Christ who have been commanded to "go into all the world" (Mark 16:15). The Spirit does not operate in a vacuum; He fills men, women and children who take Him into the world, and both the seven lamps and the seven eyes symbolize the fullness of the Spirit operating in believers.

Jesus pictures Himself as a Lamb with **"seven horns and seven eyes"** because He has empowered His church to take Him **"into all the world."** His Spirit (eyes, lamps) enables His people to see the needs and opportunities around them and His power (horns) enables them to respond effectively. "For the eyes of the Lord run to and fro throughout the whole earth, to show Himself strong on behalf of those whose heart is loyal to Him" (2Chronicles 16:9).[224] Jesus announced this to be His own ministry through the Holy Spirit— "The Spirit of the Lord is upon Me, because He has anointed Me to preach the gospel to the poor; He has sent Me to heal the brokenhearted, to proclaim liberty to the captives and recovery of sight to the blind, to set at liberty those who are oppressed; to proclaim the acceptable year of the Lord" (Luke 4:18,19).

God has "anointed" each of His children to enter into this same work. That is what the gifts and fruit of the Spirit are all about—He empowers those who are born again and then sends them out to "make disciples of all nations" (Matthew 28:19). The early church had this experience—"when they had prayed, the place where they were assembled together was shaken; and they were all filled with the Holy Spirit, and they spoke the word of God with boldness" (Acts 4:31). God wants nothing less for His children today. The infilling of the Holy Spirit is not so that we can have impressive experiences, but so that we can minister to those who are "oppressed by the devil" (Acts. 10:38).

Thus the **"seven horns and seven eyes"** of the Lamb refer to Christ's ministry here in the world, which He carries out through His people. Jesus, presenting His qualification for opening the Book of Life, also presents the Holy Spirit ministering through the church! When we believe,

God gives us new life and unites us with His body (the church), and then through the church the Holy Spirit reaches out to lost sinners all over the world. The result is that when He opens the Book of Life there will be multitudes of people whose names have been written in because they accepted the gospel invitation that was given to them by Spirit-filled believers, and they will be citizens of the Kingdom of God, our eternal friends and neighbors!

5:7,8 "Then He Came"—When?

"And He came and took the book out of the right hand of Him that sat on the throne. And when He had taken the book, the four living creatures and twenty-four elders fell down before the Lamb, having every one of them harps, and golden vials full of incense, which are the prayers of saints" (Revelation 5:8).

When in the stream of time does all of this happen? In order to answer this question we must first understand that there is a vast difference between time as we know it and eternity. We are tied to temporal time, and the "threescore and ten" years of our lifetime[225] sometimes seem to be endless, but the years can also slip away before we know what has happened. God, however, is "the High and Lofty One who inhabits eternity" (Isaiah 57:15) and Peter tells us that "with the Lord one day is as a thousand years and a thousand years as one day" (2Peter 3:8). God does not see things in terms of the past and the future as we do, because for him the end is known from the beginning (Isaiah 46:10).

"Grace was given us in Christ Jesus before the beginning of time" (2Timothy 1:9). The redemption of mankind was ensured before the creation, when the Trinity "made the decision"

---

224 See also Psalms 11:4, 34:15, Proverbs 5:21, 15:3.

225 Psalm 90:12 indicates that the years of life are 70 (threescore and 10) or 80 (fourscore) "if we have strength." Even now 3,000 years later this is still the average lifespan.

that God the Eternal Word would provide "the atoning sacrifice...for the sins of the whole world" (1John 2:2). However, in terms of human history, Jesus, the Lamb of God was slain in AD 31, a date that would appear to be arbitrary, but which was predicted with astonishing accuracy in Daniel chapter nine with the prophecy of 70 weeks (see Appendix 4). The point is that eternal, heavenly reality breaks into human history at unexpected times and in unexpected ways. The ultimate example will be the Second Coming of Christ, which will take place "at an hour you do not expect" (Matthew 24:44).

The challenge to the opening of the book was answered with the crucifixion, when Jesus established His right to forgive sinners and give eternal life to "whosoever believes in Him." But the crucifixion was the sacrifice of the Lamb, and from God's perspective Jesus was "the Lamb slain from the foundation of the world" (Revelation 13:8). Thus the opening of the book was assured with God's decision "from the foundation of the world," a decision that became a human reality when Jesus died on the Cross in AD 31. The heavenly drama portrayed in Revelation 5 could have taken place at any time after the Cross, and was probably the "first order of business" after Jesus rose from the dead and returned to heaven. No doubt this drama was closely related to Satan's being irrevocably cast out of heaven, in light of Jesus' statement in John 12:31, "Now (with the crucifixion and resurrection about to take place) is the judgment of this world; now the ruler of this

world will be cast out" (see 12: *War in Heaven*).[226] The *right to open* the Book of Life was established when Jesus returned to heaven, in the ceremony of taking the sealed book depicted in Revelation 5. But the actual *opening* of the book (the beginning of the investigative judgment) would break into human history at the seemingly arbitrary time that God had chosen and predicted in prophecy.

As we saw in 3: *The Day of Atonement, 2,300 Days*, the vision of the Day of Atonement in Revelation chapter four begins with a view of the "door open in heaven" which is linked with the Philadelphia period (Revelation 3:8, 4:1). According to the Revelation timeline, this was the period of the great revivals from the mid-eighteenth through the mid-nineteenth centuries.

We also saw that the book of Daniel refers to the Day of Atonement with the longest of all time prophecies, "And he said to me, for two thousand three hundred days; then the sanctuary shall be cleansed" (Daniel 8:14). Appendix 5 goes into quite a bit of detail on certain aspects of this prophecy, showing first of all that in many prophecies, including this one, a day in prophecy is often a literal year in human history. Appendix 5 also examines the relationship between the 2,300 days (years) and the 70 weeks (490 years)

---

226 It is interesting to compare Revelation 5 with Revelation 12. The sequence there is that the pure woman gives birth to a male child (Christ) which Satan the dragon tries to destroy, but the Child was caught up to God and His throne (vs. 4,5). This is a thumbnail sketch of the birth, death, resurrection and ascension of Christ. Then there is war in heaven between Michael (Christ) and Satan (v.7). The issue seems to involve the accusing of the brethren (v. 10), but Satan is defeated, cast out of heaven, and there is no longer any place for him (vs. 8,9). This results in rejoicing in heaven (v. 12). If Satan is the "strong angel" who challenges the opening of the scroll, chapter 5 probably represents the same scene. After the death, resurrection and ascension of Christ, His first order of business would have been to deal with the "accuser of the brethren" who was challenging His right to save sinful human beings (symbolized by the sealed Book of Life). He answered the challenge by presenting His sacrifice (the lamb that was slain), and Satan had nothing more to say or any place in the heavenly courts. This resulted in the great outpouring of praise and rejoicing recorded in Revelation 5:9-14.

of Daniel 9:24, showing that the "Seventy weeks are determined" (literally, cut off) from the 2,300 years, and that the 70 weeks (490 years) as well as the 2,300 years that they were cut off from began with "the command to restore and build Jerusalem" (Daniel 9:25), which took place in 457 BC. Some simple arithmetic shows that the 70 weeks prophecy ended with the crucifixion of Christ, and the 2,300 day prophecy ended in AD 1844. According to the prophecy, "then the sanctuary shall be cleansed."

Thus, in terms of human history and experience, the investigative judgment began in 1844 as Jesus, along with the angels of heaven, began a final phase of their ministry to save humanity and bring sin to an end. Although at first glance 1844 seems like an arbitrary, unlikely date, it is no more arbitrary than AD 27 when Jesus was baptized or AD 31 when He was crucified. This date marks the beginning of a prophetic period called "the time of the end"[227] or "the last days."[228] To summarize, the right to judge was verified in AD 31 when Jesus returned to heaven after his resurrection and answered the challenge posed by Satan to the opening of the Book of Life (Revelation 5:1-7). The actual investigative judgment began in 1844 and is depicted in the opening of the seven seals in Revelation 6 and 7. The investigative judgment will continue through the seven trumpets until the "end of probation," followed by the seven last plagues and the Second Coming of Christ.

5:9-14 Worthy Is the Lamb

The powerful enemy challenged, **"Who is worthy to open the book, and to loose the seals thereof?"** "The Lamb that was slain" took the Book of Life with the eternal destiny of those He died to save sealed up inside. Only He had the right to open the book, "to proclaim liberty to the captives" (Luke 4:18). We do not fully understand all that this will mean, but somehow it involves the eternal happiness of the entire universe. "For we know that the whole creation groans and labors with birth pangs together until now…For the earnest expectation of the creation eagerly waits for the revealing of the sons of God… because the creation itself also will be delivered from the bondage of corruption into the glorious liberty of the children of God" (Romans 8:19-22).

The opening of the seals is cause for celebration! **"And they sang a new song, saying, 'You are worthy to take the book, and to open the seals thereof; for You were slain, and have redeemed us to God by your blood out of every tribe, and tongue, and people, and nation; and have made us to our God kings and priests; and we shall reign on the earth"** (Revelation 5:9,10).

The angels and the creatures in heaven, as well as those humans who have already been translated or resurrected began to sing this **"new song"** as they welcomed Jesus back to heaven from his mission to earth where He thoroughly defeated Satan and ensured the deliverance of the universe "from the bondage of corruption." But the rest of us will have to wait until the seals have all been opened, the trumpets have all been blown, the plagues have all been poured out, until we finally hear "the trumpet of God. And the dead in Christ will rise first. Then we who are alive and remain shall be caught up together in the clouds to meet the Lord in the air. And thus we shall always be with the Lord" (1 Thessalonians 4:16,17).

Then we will join our voices with **"the voice of many angels round about the throne and the living creatures and the elders: and the number of them was ten thousand times ten thousand, and thousands of thousands; saying with a loud voice, 'Worthy is the Lamb that was slain to receive power, and riches, and wisdom, and**

---

227 Daniel 8:17, 11:35, 40, 12:4,9.

228 Genesis 49:1, Acts 2:17, 2 Timothy 3:1, James 5:3, 2 Peter 3:3.

strength, and honor, and glory, and blessing" (Revelation 5:11,12). Then the whole universe will will be in complete harmony and unity of praise for our Creator and for our Redeemer. **"And every creature which is in heaven, and on the earth, and under the earth, and such as are in the sea, and all that are in them, I heard, saying, "Blessing, and honor, and glory, and power, be to Him that sits on the throne, and to the Lamb forever and ever."** (Revelation 5:13).

"I saw under the altar the souls of those who had been slain
for the word of God and for the testimony which they held." Rev. 6:9
Woodcut by Lukas Cranach 1522

Chapter 6

Revelation 6:1-17

6:1 And I saw when the Lamb opened one of the seals, and I heard one of the four living creatures saying as the voice of thunder, "Come and see."

6:2 And I looked, and behold a white horse; and he that sat on him had a bow, and a crown was given to him, and he went forth conquering, and to conquer.

6:3 And when He opened the second seal, I heard the second living creature say, "Come and see."

6:4 And there went out another horse that was red; and power was given to him that sat thereon to take peace from the earth, and that they should kill one another; and there was given to him a great sword.

6:5 And when He opened the third seal, I heard the third living creature say, "Come and see." And I looked, and behold a black horse; and he that sat on him had a pair of balances in his hand.

6:6 And I heard a voice in the midst of the four living creatures say, "A measure of wheat for a denarius, and three measures of barley for a denarius; and do not hurt the oil and the wine."

6:7 And when He opened the fourth seal, I heard the voice of the fourth living creature say, "Come and see."

6:8 And I looked, and behold a pale horse; and his name that sat on him was Death, and Hades followed with him. And power was given to them over the fourth part of the earth, to kill with sword, and with hunger, and with death, and with the beasts of the earth.

6:9 And when He opened the fifth seal, I saw under the altar the souls of them that were slain for the word of God, and for the testimony which they held.

6:10 And they cried with a loud voice, saying, "How long, O Lord, holy and true, will You not judge and avenge our blood on those that dwell on the earth?"

6:11 And white robes were given to every one of them; and it was said to them, that they should rest yet for a little season, until both their fellow servants and their brethren, that should be killed as they were, should be fulfilled.

6:12 And I looked when He opened the sixth seal, and, behold, there was a great earthquake; and the sun became black as sackcloth of hair, and the moon became as blood;

6:13 And the stars of heaven fell to the earth, even as a fig tree casts its untimely figs, when it is shaken by a mighty wind.

6:14 And the sky departed as a scroll when it is rolled together; and every mountain and island were moved out of their places.

6:15 And the kings of the earth, and the great men, and the rich men, and the chief captains, and the mighty men, and every slave, and every free man, hid themselves in the dens and in the rocks of the mountains;

6:16 And said to the mountains and rocks, "Fall on us, and hide us from the face of Him that sits on the throne, and from the wrath of the Lamb.

6:17 For the great day of His wrath has come; and who shall be able to stand?"

6:1,2 The First Horseman

Chapter six is one of the most intriguing portions of Revelation, with the appearance of the mysterious "four horsemen of the Apocalypse." Some have seen them as symbolic of the parade of human or church history,[229] others as a portent of fearsome events to come, and some believe they are demonic wraiths that haunt the scenes of war and violence. By allowing the Bible to interpret its own symbols we can get a clearer picture of what is being communicated. But just a word of caution is in order: the opening of the

seven seals in chapter six is a continuation of the heavenly courtroom scene in chapters four and five. Those chapters clarify the context and issues involved, and if you have not yet read them you may find this presentation of the opening of the seven seals to be confusing and implausible.

To review briefly, chapters four and five departs from the "on earth" timeline in order to set the stage for the beginning of the the judgment of humanity. In chapter four there is a portrayal of the heavenly courtroom, the same scene that Daniel saw in Daniel 7:9,10 in which "the court was seated and the books were opened." In chapter five there is what could be considered a "flashback" to the heavenly drama that took place when Jesus returned to heaven after His resurrection and presented Himself to the heavenly hosts as the "Lamb as though it had been slain" (Revelation 5:6). His sacrifice established His right to open the sealed Book of Life. The Book of Life has inside the names, circumstances, decisions and deeds of the people who at one time or another have responded to the Holy Spirit. When the seals are broken and the Book of Life is opened, these people are "investigated" by the angels. This is what is portrayed in chapter six, where the people in the Book of Life are judged and separated into categories. In human history the actual opening of the books takes place during the Day of Atonement, which began

---

229 In attempting to give a historical interpretation to the seals and trumpets some commentators have tried to follow the pattern of Daniel, in which each successive prophecy builds on the previous, filling in more details. But there are at least five problems with this approach: 1) In Daniel every detail of the prophecies can be clearly correlated with historical facts, but the historical interpretations of the seals and trumpets of Revelation either ignore and gloss over many of the prophetic details, or assign fantastic, "far-out" interpretations in which the symbols seem to be strained to fit with the historical facts. 2) The repeating prophecies of Daniel correlate well one with the other, but the historical interpretations of Revelation do not seem to be able to correlate the seven churches with the seven seals or with the seven trumpets. 3) The historical interpretation destroys the order and continuity of the various passages, requiring an aimless jumping from one theme and time period to another. 4) Daniel's repetitive visions each began with Daniel giving his own personal context (eg. "In the third year of the reign of King Belshazzzar a vision appeared to me—to me, Daniel...I was in Shushan, the citadel...Daniel 8:1,2). But this type of personal context is only given once in Revelation (Revelation 1:9,10), indicating a continuous rather than repetitive vision. 5) The visions of Daniel were interspersed with stories of Daniel's experiences in Babylon, and these kinds of stories do not appear in Revelation.

in 1844 according to the prophecy of Daniel 8:14, "for two thousand three hundred days, then the sanctuary shall be cleansed" (see 5:7,8 *Then He Came—When?*).

"And I saw when the Lamb opened one of the seals, and I heard one of the four living creatures saying as the voice of thunder, 'Come and see.' And I looked, and behold a white horse; and he that sat on him had a bow, and a crown was given to him, and he went forth conquering, and to conquer" (Revelation 6:1,2).

Each of the "horsemen" is actually composed of several elements. Each is announced by one of the four living creatures that were introduced in Chapters 4 with the words **"come and see."** Each has a horse of a different color: white, red, black and pale. Each horse has a rider, and each rider has something with him: the first, a bow and a crown, the second a great sword, the third a pair of scales, and the fourth, Hades. And each rider has an activity: the first, to conquer, the second, to take peace from the earth and cause people to kill each other, the third, to weigh in the balance and protect "oil and wine," and the fourth, to kill with sword, hunger, "death" and beasts.

The first horse is announced by the first living creature.[230] In 4: *Four Living Creatures* we saw that in Jewish tradition these creatures were said to have the same faces that were found on the standards ("flags") of the four leader tribes when the tribes of Israel camped around the tabernacle in the desert. The first (a lion) was associated with the tribe of Judah, the second (a calf) with the tribe of Ephraim, the third (a man) was associated with the tribe of Reuben and the fourth (an eagle) with the tribe of Dan.

With this in mind the white horse could be said to be under the standard of the Lion of the tribe of Judah.[231] Lions are bold, fearless, and victorious in battle. They well characterize the tribe of Judah, the royal or kingly tribe with its line of kings starting with David and Solomon down to Christ, the King of kings. Apparently the first living creature presides over the judgment of those those who are faithful and true to Christ, boldly conquering the kingdom of Satan in their own lives and in the world. The lion bids us to **"come and see"** these faithful and true Christians, who are symbolized by a **"white horse."**

"I looked, and behold a white horse." Horses are used in scripture to symbolize groups or tribes of people (in this case the horses represent the categories of people who are being judged). For example, in Isaiah 63:11-14 the children of Israel, being led by Moses through the wilderness, are compared with horses—"[God] led them by the right hand of Moses...who led them through the deep, as a horse in the wilderness." In the book of Zechariah, which, like Revelation, uses various colored horses as a prominent symbol,[232] the tribe of Judah is specifically declared to be the Lord's horse: "The Lord of hosts will visit His flock, the house of Judah, and will make them as His royal horse in the battle" (Zecheriah 10:3). The first horse is white, which is the color of godliness and purity.[233]

Horses have riders who direct them; in other words, a horse is subservient to its rider. In the case of the white horse, the rider is obviously

---

230 Verse 1 says "one of the living creatures" but in the subsequent horsemen they are called "the second...the third...the fourth living creature," so obviously the first is the first living creature described in Revelation 4:6-8.

231 This does not mean that the first living creature *represents* the first horse—the creatures are great angels who lead worship in heaven. But apparently a part of their role in the Day of Atonement is to preside over the judgment of the various categories of people written in the Book of Life.

232 See Zechariah 1:8-15, 6:1-8.

233 White is associated with purity and godliness (eg. "Though your sins are as scarlet, they shall be as white as snow" Isaiah 1:18). In Revelation God sits on a white throne, Christ rides a white horse and the saints wear white clothes made white in the blood of the Lamb (see Revelation 7:14, 19:11,14, 20:11).

Christ Himself. The parallels with Revelation 19:11-16 which depicts the Second Coming of Christ are too marked to be coincidental. There too is a rider with crowns who is also conquering, riding on a white horse. "He was clothed with a robe dipped in blood and His name is called The Word of God"—in other words, the rider is Jesus Christ (Revelation 19:13).

The rider holds in his hand a bow, one of the primary weapons of warfare.[234] Again, this is associated in the book of Zechariah with the tribe of Judah: "the Lord of hosts will visit His flock, the house of Judah...From him comes the cornerstone, from him the tent peg, *from him the battle bow.*" "For I have bent *Judah, my bow*" (Zechariah 10:3,4, 9:13). Here we see that as Jesus rides into the world **"conquering and to conquer,"** His faithful people are His principle weapons.

Of themselves God's people can do nothing, but with "Jesus in the saddle," God's "lions" have been advancing His kingdom from the days of the apostles right down to the present. Peter, Paul and John were white horses, as were Photios, John Huss, Martin Luther and other fearless reformers. But most of the white horses are simple and faithful Christians whose lives and words have been a consistent witness for their faith. They have allowed the Holy Spirit to "destroy the works of the Devil"[235] in their own lives, and with their faithful words and godly behavior they have penetrated the enemy's kingdom and led people who have been in spiritual darkness into the light of the Lord. The apostle Paul described the life and witness of the white-horse Christians: "For though we walk in the flesh, we do not war according to the flesh. For the weapons of our warfare are not carnal, but mighty in God for pulling down strongholds"

(2Corinthians. 10:3,4).

6:3,4 The Second Horseman

"And when He opened the second seal, I heard the second living creature say, 'Come and see.' And there went out another horse that was red; and power was given to him that sat thereon to take peace from the earth, and that they should kill one another; and there was given to him a great sword" (Revelation 6:3,4).

The second living creature who announces the red horse is like a calf. Calves are a symbol of sacrifice, but under the baleful influence of sin the calf becomes a symbol of idolatry[236] and is associated with the tribe of Ephraim. Despite the fact that Ephraim was blessed with the richest blessings of all the tribes, he was one of the two tribes that were leaders in idolatry. Jeroboam, the first king of divided Israel and an Ephraimite, set up golden calf-idols in Bethel, a city in the territory of Ephraim. His idolatry set the pattern for the godless rebellion of future kings.[237]

At the second creature's bidding to **"come and see,"** a fiery red horse **"went out."** Red is often used as a symbol of sin,[238] just the opposite of white: "though your sins be like scarlet, they shall be as white as snow; though they are red like crimson, they shall be as wool" (Isaiah 1:18). This horse represents people who, even though they are written in the Book of Life, are characterized by living in sin, especially idolatry, and as

---

234 2Samuel 22:35, Psalms 7:11-13, Jeremiah 50:14, 29.

235 1John 3:8.

236 See Leviticus 9:7,8, Deuteronomy 9:16, and 4: 6-8: *Four Living Creatures.*

237 For example, "Jehu did not turn away from the sins of Jeroboam the son of Nebat, who had made Israel sin, that is, from the golden calves that were at Bethel and Dan" (2Kings 10:29).

238 In the Book of Revelation red is a symbol of Satan and his agents: John saw "a great, fiery red dragon...the Devil and Satan" (Revelation 12:3,9). In Chapter 17 "the great harlot...was arrayed in purple and scarlet" and was "sitting on a scarlet beast which was full of names of blasphemy" (Revelation 17:1-5).

such their names will be blotted out.[239]

It is significant that all of the other three horses simply appeared (**"behold, a white horse,"** **"behold, a black horse,"** **"behold a pale horse"**) whereas the red horse **"went out."** The Greek word used here (*eksilthe*) is the same word that is used in 1 John 2, speaking of the "many antichrists [which] have come." "They [the antichrists] *went out* from us, but they were not of us…they *went out* that they might be made manifest, that none of them were of us" (1 John 2:18,19). These verses describe people who make strong claims about their Christian identity, but instead they are antichrist.[240] Likewise the red horse group claim to be Christians, but their lives show them to be false Christians. Naturally their rider is Satan, which can be seen by his activity: he **"takes peace from the earth"** and causes people to **"kill one another."**

These are the tares among the wheat that Jesus warned against (Matthew 13:24-30). Judas was a red horse, as were Ananias and Sapphira (Acts 5:1-11). The theologians and religious leaders who persuaded church councils to allow the worship of images, relics and saints were red horses, as are the television evangelists who preach a twisted gospel or who are caught practicing immorality or corruption. But much more common are the church members who sleep through the church service and then wreak havoc at the church board meeting, who turn prayer meeting into a gossip session and have adulterous affairs while presenting themselves as being faithful believers.

In modern "Christian" society there are millions of red horses who are indifferent to God and have set up idols of wealth, possessions, appearance, power, and reputation that are much more precious to them than Jesus and His kingdom. Although they consider themselves Christians, they have chosen to ignore Jesus and thus they forfeit the eternal life that could have been theirs. But much more tragic are the spiritual deaths that have resulted when red horses actively take the name of Christ and misrepresent Him through false doctrines, unchristian behavior and spiritual hypocrisy, turning honest seekers away from God. According to Ephesians 6:17 the "sword of the Spirit" is "the word of God." The false, perverted word is a **"great sword"** in the hand of the devil that he uses through unconverted "Christians" to **"take peace from the earth."**

6:5,6 The Third Horseman

"And when He opened the third seal, I heard the third living creature say, "Come and see." And I looked, and behold a black horse; and he that sat on him had a pair of balances in his hand. And I heard a voice in the midst of the four living creatures say, "A measure of wheat for a denarius, and three measures of barley for a denarius; and do not hurt the oil and the wine" (Revelation 6:5,6).

The third horse is announced by the third living creature, who is like a man and is associated with the tribe of Reuben. Man was created in the image of God,[241] but because of sin man and Reuben are appropriate symbols of the weak and degenerate human nature; Reuben lost his birthright when he succumbed to the temptation to sleep with his father's concubine (Genesis 35:22, 49:3,4). Yet in spite of his mortal sin, his final blessing was "Let Reuben live, and not die, nor let his men be few" (Deuteronomy 33:6).

The horse is black, which is a symbol of

---

239 See Exodus 32:32,33, Psalms 9:5, 69:28, 109:13, Revelation 3:5.

240 Antichrist in the original Greek can mean either against Christ or instead of Christ.

241 Genesis 1:26,27, Ecclesiastes 7:29.

spiritual darkness.[242] However, the rider is apparently Jesus, holding a scales or balance in His hand—"Honest weights and scales are the Lord's" (Proverbs 16:11). He is the one who weighs in the balance (Daniel 5:27) in order to demonstrate the righteousness of those who have been accused of unrighteousness. Job, being accused by his friends and even feeling like God was accusing him, cried out "let me be weighed on honest scales, that God may know my integrity" (Job. 31:6).

Thus the black horse represents people who are in spiritual darkness, but when "weighed in the balance" they are found to have Jesus as their rider. How can this be? A **"voice which is in the midst of the four living creatures"** declares their true spiritual condition: **"A measure of wheat for a denarius, and three measures of barley for a denarius; and do not hurt the oil and the wine."**

Wheat and barley were the grains from which bread was made, and these prices[243] would indicate a famine for bread. Bread is the symbol of several things: It represents Jesus ("I am the bread of life" John 6:35), in which case the black horses would represent people who do not know much about Jesus. Bread also represents Christ's body, the church ("The bread which we break, is it not the communion of the body of Christ? For we, though many, are one bread and one body" 1Corinthians 10:16,17), in which case these would be people who have not had much contact or communion with the church of God. Bread

can also represent the true teaching of God's word (Matthew 4:4, 16:5-12), in which case these would be people who have not had adequate or true teaching from the Bible. Probably all of these may be lacking to one degree or another, and to outward appearances these people may not appear to be candidates for eternal life. But He who holds the balance sees that there has been no harm to the oil and the wine: they have been taught by the Holy Spirit (the oil)[244] and because by faith they have responded to the Spirit, Jesus has applied his blood (the wine)[245] for the forgiveness of their sins.[246]

There are black horses in remote jungles and deserts, in teeming cities of the world where there is no witness for Christ, and in fact they have been sprinkled all over the world all through human history. They are also found in "Christian" churches where they are taught to be "righteous" by selling books or burning candles or paying penance; but in the quiet place of their hearts they hear the voice of the Spirit telling them to love God and their neighbors.

Paul describes this group as those who "by nature do the things in the law...although not having the law...who show the work of the law written in their hearts, their conscience also bearing witness" (Romans 2:14,15). "They...seek the Lord, in the hope that they might grope for Him and find Him" and although they are in darkness "these times of ignorance God overlooked" (Acts 17:27-30). Because of God's great heart of love and mercy they have a future in His

---

242 Surprisingly, the word for black (the root word, *melas*, refers to ink) is rarely used in the Bible and not in a particularly negative way. In Revelation 6:12, just before Jesus comes, "the sun became black as sackcloth of hair, and the moon became like blood." The parallel passage in Matthew 24:29 says "the sun will be darkened, and the moon will not give its light." Black and darkness are synonymous, and black is associated with a lack of light (ignorance) rather than evil. Jesus declared, "I have come as a light into the world, that whoever believes in Me should not abide in darkness" (John 12:46).

243 A **"denarius"** was a day's wage and a **"measure"** was about a quart or liter.

244 Zechariah 4:2-6, 1Samuel 16:13.

245 Matthew 26:27-29.

246 While it is true that "there is no other name under heaven given among men by which we must be saved" (Acts 4:12), this does not mean that it necessary to know the name of Jesus in order to be saved by Him. In fact, the parade of the faithful in Hebrews 11 who will be "made perfect" together with the faithful Christians (v.40) are all people who never heard the name Jesus, but they knew Jesus through the ministry of the Holy Spirit.

kingdom: "The people who walked in darkness have seen a great light." "For behold, the darkness shall cover the earth, and deep darkness the people; But the Lord will arise over you, and His glory will be seen upon you" (Isaiah 9:2, 60:2).

6: 7,8 The Fourth Horseman

"And when He opened the fourth seal, I heard the voice of the fourth living creature say, 'Come and see.' And I looked, and behold a pale horse; and his name that sat on him was Death, and Hades followed with him. And power was given to them over the fourth part of the earth, to kill with sword, and with hunger, and with death, and with the beasts of the earth" (Revelation 6:7,8).

The fourth living creature has the face of an eagle, and is associated with the tribe of Dan. The eagle is a symbol of justice, but under the influence of sin it represents the fierce enemies of God's people who attack them and tear them to pieces.[247] Dan was a tribe which very early separated itself from Israel in the far north, and was one of the two tribes that led in the idolatry of the northern 10 tribes.[248] His birthright "blessing" shows that he is actually an enemy of God's people: Dan "bites the horses heels so that its rider shall fall backward" (Genesis 49:16,17).

The fourth horse is described as pale in English versions, although the actual color in the original Greek is green. This is the ghastly green color of "leprous" mold,[249] the color of death. The pale horse represents those who have somehow at some time been written in the Book of Life, but

unlike the deceptive "red horse" false Christians, these have actually become persecuting enemies of Christ's followers.[250]

The rider is **"Death, and Hades followed with him."** Obviously this refers to "him who had the power of death, that is, the devil" (Hebrews 2:14). His activity is to destroy with **"sword, and with hunger, and with death, and with the beasts of the earth."** These are the same four destructive judgments that are promised against God's people if they are unfaithful to Him. For example, through Ezekiel God promised that if His people "sin against me by persistent unfaithfulness, I will stretch out My hand" sending "My four severe judgments on Jerusalem—the sword and famine and wild beasts and pestilence—to cut off man and beast from it" (Ezekiel 14:13-21).[251] But these judgments have a redemptive purpose—"there shall be left in it a remnant who will be brought out…and you will see their ways and their doings. Then you will be comforted concerning the disaster that I have brought upon Jerusalem' says the Lord God" (vs. 14:22,23). God is constantly trying to bring to repentance those who have strayed from Him, even if it involves painful judgments that He allows their enemies to inflict.[252]

Thus it is with the pale horse enemies of God.

---

247 Leviticus 11:13, Deuteronomy 28:49, Hosea 8:1, Lamentations 4:19, Habakkuk 1:6-8.

248 Judges 18, 1Kings 12:25-29.

249 Leviticus 13:49, 14:37. The Greek Septuagint shows this to be the same root word for green as the "pale" horse. The presence of this green "leprosy" was a sign to burn the garment or tear down the house in which it was present.

250 The malicious enemy of God's people in the book of Revelation is Babylon, and as we will see in chapters 14-18 where the theme of Babylon is developed, Babylon is a false religious system that claims to be the true body of Christ, all the while persecuting God's people who are known as the "remnant." Especially in chapter 17 it becomes obvious that Babylon has two aspects—deceptive false religion, represented by the harlot (these are the "red horse" false Christians) and the oppressive political system, represented by the seven-headed beast (these are the "pale horse" enemies of Christ).

251 These four judgments are a repeating theme, see for example Leviticus 26:14-25. These judgments have a redemptive purpose: to get God's apostate children to "confess their iniquity…with which they were unfaithful to Me" (v. 40).

252 An example of God using His enemies to punish His unfaithful children in an effort to win them back is found in the history of the kingdom of Judah and the Babylonian captivity (see Jeremiah 25, 32:27-44).

They are allowed to carry out judgments against those who are unfaithful—**"power was given to them over the fourth part of the earth, to kill with sword, and with hunger, and with death, and with the beasts of the earth."** This no doubt refers to the deadly wars and genocides that have been carried out by "Christian" nations since the time that Christianity became a state religion supported by armies and violence. Pale horses include the priests and church leaders who were in charge of the Inquisition and crusades during the Dark Ages. Even today "pale horse" church officials plot to oppose and persecute those who would spread the gospel in "their" territories. Here also are people who had some kind of an experience with the Lord when they were young, but turned away and plunged deeper than ever into sin, crime, and violence. Many of the atheists who use the courts and political influence to damage the church once had a tender moment when their names were written into the Book of Life, but rejecting the Holy Spirit they became the worst enemies of God's people. However, there is a limit to what God will allow; Hades is close on the heels of the pale horse and his rider. Unless they repent they will find their place in "the everlasting fire prepared for the devil and his angels" (Matthew 25:41).

When the seals are finally and fully opened, those who have been written in the Lamb's Book of Life will be found to be one of the four horses with one of the two riders. Then it will be too late to change. But "now is [still] the day of salvation" (2Corinthians 6:2); no one has to remain in the red or pale horse camp. God sends His Spirit to plead with each of us, "choose for yourselves this day whom you will serve" (Joshua 24:15), hoping that "they may come to their senses and escape the snare of the devil, having been taken captive by him to do his will" (2Timothy 2:26). Everyone has the right to choose who will be his rider, and Jesus is constantly working to turn every person into a white horse. "Today if you will hear His voice, do not harden your hearts…but exhort one another daily while it is called 'today,' lest any of you be hardened through the deceitfulness of sin" (Hebrews 3:7-14).

Table 6.1 summarizes the categories of people who have been written in the Book of Life, who will be judged during the investigative judgment.

Table 6.1

Horse	Announcer	Tribe	Rider	Article	Activity	Category
1st White	Lion	Judah	Christ	Bow	Conquer	Strong Faithful
2nd Red	Calf	Ephraim	Satan	Sword	Take peace	Apostate
3rd Black	Man	Reuben	Christ	Scales	Judge, protect	Weak Faithful
4th Pale	Eagle	Dan	Satan	Hades	Kill	Enemies

6:9,10 Souls Under the Altar

"And when He opened the fifth seal, I saw under the altar the souls of them that were slain for the word of God, and for the testimony which they held. And they cried with a loud voice, saying, 'How long, O Lord, holy and true, will You not judge and avenge our blood on those that dwell on the earth?" (Revelation 6:9,10).

Those who have been martyrs for God have a special category in the judgment. Not only have they been faithful, but they have been "faithful unto death" (Revelation 2:10), suffering "mockings and scourgings, yes, and of chains and imprisonment. They were stoned, they were sawn in two, were tempted, were slain with the sword… destitute, afflicted, tormented—of whom the world was not worthy" (Hebrews 11:27,28). Following the example of the "Captain of their salvation" who was made "perfect through sufferings,"[253] "they did not love their lives to the death," sharing in "the fellowship of His sufferings, being conformed to His death" (Hebrews 2:10, Revelation 12:11, Philippians 3:10). This fellowship in the sufferings of Christ is symbolized by their position **"under the alter."** The alter represents the atoning death of Christ on the Cross; thus these martyrs are as close as it is possible to

be to Jesus as He pours out His love and grace.[254]

"Under the alter" does not at first glance seem to be a particularly desirable place for the **"souls"** to wait for the vengeance of God, and in fact there are many problems with trying to make a literal application of this passage. The brief study of the soul that follows shows that the soul is a combination of the dust of the earth (the body) and the breath of life from God (the spirit). Souls are not immortal; they sleep after death and will be resurrected, either to live eternally or to face judgment and destruction.

One of the first references to the soul is in Genesis 2:7, "And the Lord God formed man of the dust of the ground, and breathed into his nostrils the breath of life; and man became a living soul." This verse, quoted by the apostle Paul in 1Corinthians 15:45, identifies the 3 "components" of man listed in 1Thessalonians 5:23: "spirit, soul, and body." However, note that Adam *became* a living soul by the combination of dust (body) and the breath of life (spirit). There is no suggestion that Adam *had* a soul—he *was* a soul.

The concept of the soul as a unity, the whole person, fills the Old Testament. Typical of many examples are the uses of the Hebrew word for soul, *nephesh*, in Leviticus 5: "If a person [*nephesh*] touches any unclean thing, whether it is the carcass of an unclean beast" (v.2); "Or if a person [*nephesh*] swears, speaking thoughtlessly with his lips" (v.4); "If a person [*nephesh*] sins, and commits any of these things which are forbidden" (v.17). Here we see souls touching (physical), speaking thoughtlessly (mental), and sinning (spiritual). A study of the hundreds of

---

253 Jesus was "made perfect," not in the sense of becoming perfectly holy (He was always perfectly holy—He "was in all points tempted as we are, yet without sin") but in the sense of becoming a perfect sacrifice, identifying perfectly with the human race which suffers the effects of sin—"He had to be made like His brethren, that He might be a merciful and faithful High Priest in things pertaining to God, to make propitiation for the sins of the people. For in that He Himself has suffered, being tempted, He is able to aid those who are tempted" (Hebrews 2:17,18).

---

254 In the ancient sanctuary service the sinner brought a lamb and confessed his sins with his hands on its head, transferring his sin to the victim. The lamb was slain and its blood was collected in a bowl. This blood was the life or "soul" of the animal ("the life [*nephesh*] is in the blood" Leviticus 17:11). Some of the blood was put "on the horns of the alter," but "the remaining blood was poured "at the base of the alter." Thus the "soul" ended up under the alter.

verses in both the Old and New Testaments that mention the soul invariably show the meaning to be the person, self, life, heart, being.[255]

Therefore the souls under the alter are not some component of the martyrs that are waiting for their bodies, but symbolize the martyrs themselves. They are not conscious entities ("the dead know nothing" Ecclesiastic 9:5,[256] see 20: *The Soul Sleeps*),[257] but rather they cry out in the same sense that the "soul"[258] of the first martyr cried out: "The Lord said to Cain, 'Where is Abel your brother?…The voice of your brother's blood cries out to Me from the ground" (Genesis 4:9,10).

The souls are depicted crying out for vengeance—**"How long, O Lord, holy and true, will You not judge and avenge our blood on those that dwell on the earth?"** (Revelation 6:10). Here is more evidence that this passage should not be taken literally. Those who believe that the souls of the righteous go straight to heaven at death also believe that the souls of the wicked go straight to hell when they die. According to a literal interpretation of this verse, the martyrs are not satisfied seeing the souls of their enemies in hell, but want further vengeance. But these martyrs are not bloodthirsty and vindictive; to the contrary, they have been the ones closest to the heart of God, and as such they loved their enemies (Matthew 5:44-46). This passage is not trying to reveal the thoughts and desires of the martyrs, who, after all, are resting in the grave (they are even told in verse 11 that **"they should rest yet for a little season,"** a reference to their unconscious condition).

The point of this passage is that God's justice is to be delayed. **"And white robes were given to every one of them; and it was said to them, that they should rest yet for a little season, until both their fellow servants and their brethren, that should be killed as they were, should be fulfilled"** (Revelation 6: 11). Some have concluded from this text that God has a quota of martyrs and that history cannot be completed until they have all been killed. But the Greek word, *plihroo*, does not mean "number," but rather fulfillment or completion. In other passages of scripture where this word for fulfillment is used it refers to the completion of an unfortunate but unavoidable requirement in the plan of God.[259]

These requirements are necessary because of the presence of sin and the challenges to God's character and government that have been made by the enemy. Because of the great controversy it is necessary for history to continue, and Satan will always make sure that there will be martyrs. These martyrs provide the ultimate witness, to both humans and to the observing universe, of the value of Jesus and His kingdom: it is worth dying for. "God has displayed us, the apostles, last,

---

255 Jesus made this point clear in His parallel passages, Mark 8:36 "For what will it profit a man if he gains the whole world, and loses his own soul?" and Luke 9:25, "For what profit is it to a man if he gains the whole world, and is himself destroyed or lost?"

256 See also Psalms 6:5, Psalms 115:17, Psalms 146:4, Job 14:12.

257 The unconscious state of believers who have died (including the martyrs) is made clear in Paul's description of the Second Coming in 1Thessalonians 4. Paul did not want his brethren "to be ignorant…concerning those who have fallen asleep" (v. 13). Here we see the unconscious condition of the dead—they are asleep. There is no concept of the body sleeping while the soul lives in Paradise. "For if we believe that Jesus died and rose again, even so God will bring with Him those who sleep in Jesus" (v.14). Paul is not talking about bringing souls (who supposedly have been living with Him in Heaven) to be reunited with their bodies. It is "those who sleep," in other words, the souls of the righteous dead, that he "will bring with Him" from earth back to heaven. "For the Lord Himself will descend from heaven with a shout, with the voice of an archangel, and with the trumpet of God. And the dead ("those who are asleep," v.15) in Christ will rise first. Then we who are alive and remain shall be caught up together with them in the clouds to meet the Lord in the air" (vs.16,17).

258 Leviticus 17:11 states that "the life [soul—*nephesh*] of the flesh is in the blood." Thus, when the blood of Abel cried out from the ground, his "soul" could be said to have cried out.

259 For example, "Jerusalem will be trampled by Gentiles until the times of the Gentiles are *fulfilled*" (Luke 21:24. See also Matthew 26:54,56, Mark 14:49).

as men condemned to death; for we have been made a spectacle to the world, both to angels and to men" (1Corinthians 4:9). But when "all is fulfilled" (Matthew 5:18) the great controversy will come to an end and the prayers of the martyrs will become reality.

Those who suffer persecution and face a martyr's death often feel alone and abandoned, even by God. But the message of the fifth seal teaches that God has a special place of honor in the judgment for those who make the ultimate sacrifice. It also teaches that far from being meaningless, every martyr's death is a powerful witness on earth and to the angels of heaven that "love is as strong as death" (Song of Solomon 8:7,6).

6: 12-17 Rocks, Fall on Us

"And I looked when He opened the sixth seal, and, behold, there was a great earthquake; and the sun became black as sackcloth of hair, and the moon became as blood; And the stars of heaven fell to the earth, even as a fig tree casts its untimely figs, when it is shaken by a mighty wind. And the sky departed as a scroll when it is rolled together; and every mountain and island were moved out of their places. And the kings of the earth, and the great men, and the rich men, and the chief captains, and the mighty men, and every slave, and every free man, hid themselves in the dens and in the rocks of the mountains; And said to the mountains and rocks, 'Fall on us, and hide us from the face of Him that sits on the throne, and from the wrath of the Lamb. For the great day of His wrath has come; and who shall be able to stand?" (Revelation 6: 12-17).

Since the preceding five seals represent categories of people whose names have been written in the Book of Life and who will be considered in the investigative judgment, it follows that the sixth seal would also be a category of people. The context is a great earthquake, signs in the sun

and moon, falling stars, and the shaking of the powers of heaven and earth. These are the same signs that are listed in Matthew 24 and Luke 21 as immediately preceding the Second Coming of Christ.[260] Besides the heavenly signs, Matthew and Luke also mention the fear and distress of those who see these signs ("all the tribes of the earth will mourn," "distress of nations with perplexity," "men's hearts failing them from fear"),[261] which is a direct parallel to the distress of the **"kings of the earth, and the great men"** who call on **"the mountains and rocks"** to **"fall on us and hide us from the face of Him who sits on the throne and from the wrath of the Lamb."**

The only sign in this passage that is not mentioned in Matthew 24 is the great earthquake,[262] and within the Book of Revelation itself this earthquake is identified: it is the tremendous earthquake of Revelation 16:18 which throws down the great city of Babylon, and which, like the earthquake of chapter 6, also destroys the islands and mountains (Revelation 16:20). This earthquake occurs during the seventh of the seven last plagues, just before the Second Coming of Christ. The obvious conclusion is that all of these signs, as well as their counterparts in Matthew 24 and Luke 21, take place immediately before the

---

260 "Immediately after the tribulation of those days the sun will be darkened, and the moon will not give its light; the stars will fall from heaven, and the powers of the heavens will be shaken. Then the sign of the Son of Man will appear in heaven, and then all the tribes of the earth will mourn, and they will see the Son of Man coming with power and great glory" (Matthew 24:29-31). "And there will be signs in the sun, in the moon, and in the stars; and on the earth distress of nations with perplexity, the sea and the waves roaring; men's hearts failing them from fear and the expectation of those things which are coming on the earth, for the powers of the heavens will be shaken. Then they will see the Son of man coming in a cloud with power and great glory" (Luke 21:25-27).

261 Matthew 24:30, Luke 21:25,26.

262 "Earthquakes in various places" are mentioned in Matthew 24:7 and Luke 21:11, but these are general signs, the "beginnings of sorrows" (Matthew 24:8), but "the end is not yet" (v.6). The earthquake mentioned in Revelation 6:12 is a specific super-destructive earthquake.

Second Coming.[263] This implies that the portion of the sixth seal that is depicted in chapter 6 is the investigative judgment of one of the two classes of people who will be alive when Christ comes (the other class is portrayed in chapter 7).

It is clear that the people mentioned in Revelation 6:15-17 are not God's faithful people who have been eagerly waiting for Him to come and redeem them; rather, they are those who have realized that they are Christ's enemies. In Revelation 19:11-21 this same group (see v. 18) is portrayed as being "killed by the sword which proceeded from the mouth of Him who sat on the horse" (v.21). This is a symbolic picture of Jesus at his Second Coming, and those who have resisted Jesus and persecuted His followers will die and their bodies will become food for the birds who "gather for the supper of the great God" (v. 17). The great deceptions of the last days will be so subtle that multitudes will believe that they have been loving and serving God, but as we will see in chapter 13, they will actually be worshiping "the beast." In the investigative judgment their names will be blotted out of the Book of Life.[264]

In Jesus' description of the investigative judgment (the separating of the sheep from the goats in Matthew 25:31-46), it is apparent that many who believe that they are meeting all of God's requirements are actually refusing to serve Him in the person of His needy children, and as such they will forfeit their right to eternal life—"inasmuch as you did not do it to one of the least of these [help the hungry, thirsty, naked, sick or those in prison], you did not do it to me… depart from Me, you cursed" (Matthew 25:45, 41). He also made it clear that many who seem to be filled with the Spirit and blessed with great spiritual gifts actually do not know Jesus—"Many will say to Me in that day, 'Lord Lord, have we not prophesied in Your name, cast out demons in Your name, and done many wonders in Your name?' And then I will declare to them, 'I never knew you; depart from Me, you who practice lawlessness!'" (Matthew 7:21-23).

Jesus warned that in the very last days "many will come in My name, saying 'I am the Christ' and will deceive many" and "many false prophets will rise up and deceive many" (Matthew 24:5,11). The ultimate deception will be by the "beast and the false prophet" mentioned in chapters 13 and 19 who work signs and false miracles through

---

263 There are some scholars who believe that these signs, as well as those in Matthew 24, were fulfilled in the past, with events such as the Lisbon earthquake of 1755, the dark day in New England in 1780 and the extensive Leonid meteor shower of 1833. However, it is obvious from Revelation 16:18-20 that at least the earthquake was within the context of the seven last plagues (the earthquake resulted in the destruction of the islands and mountains, which is also the final result of the signs of 6:12-14), which calls into question applying these earlier events as the primary fulfillment of the signs in the sun, moon and falling stars. In addition, these signs as they are listed in Matthew 24 come "immediately after the tribulation of those days." The tribulation of the medieval period ended in 1798 with the arrest of the pope (see 13:3 *The Deadly Wound*) but the Lisbon earthquake and the dark day took place before the end of the tribulation, not immediately after. The tribulation itself is a reference back to v. 21 "Then there will be great tribulation, such as has not been since the beginning of the world until this time, no, nor ever shall be." It is apparent from the language that this is the same time period referred to by Daniel 12:1, "And there shall be a time of trouble (the same Greek word that is used for tribulation in Matthew 24:21), such as never was since there was a nation, even to that time." In Daniel it is obvious that this time of trouble happens at the very end when Michael stands up. Both tribulations are said to be the greatest that would ever happen, suggesting that they are the same event. Therefore the signs that follow: the earthquake, darkening of sun and moon, falling of the stars, the rolling up of the sky, and the disappearance of the mountains and islands, all happen at about the same time—just as Christ is ready to come. It is actually incredible to think that the signs of Christ's immediate coming would be spread over more than 250 years. While the earlier signs were notable, it is probable that these events were important in drawing the attention of the people of that time to the momentous heavenly event of 1844, the beginning of the Day of Atonement. In that sense they were a fulfillment, but not the primary fulfillment, of the prophecies, just as the fall of Jerusalem in AD 70 was a fulfillment but not the primary one of these same prophecies, and the Day of Pentecost was a fulfillment, but not the primary one, of the prophecies of Joel (see Acts 2:16-23, Joel 2:28-30).

264 "all that dwell on the earth shall worship him [the beast], whose names are not written in the Book of Life of the Lamb slain from the foundation of the world" (Revelation 13:8).

which they "deceived those who received the mark of the beast" (Revelation 19:20). In Revelation 13:13-17 it is apparent that the Babylon religion of the last days will even incite those who are deceived to persecute and kill those who are true to God, just as Jesus predicted—"the time is coming that whoever kills you will think that he offers God service" (John 16:2).

The difference between those who are deceived and those who are not does not have to do with their understanding of prophecy, but rather with their willingness to love and obey God and know Him through His Holy Spirit. "The coming of the lawless one is according to the working of Satan, with all power, signs and lying wonders, and with all unrighteous deception among those who perish, *because they did not receive the love of the truth* that they might be saved. And for this reason God will send them strong delusion, that they should believe the lie, *that they all may be condemned who did not believe the truth but had pleasure in unrighteousness*" (2 Thessalonians 2:9-12).

This passage shows that it is the love of sin that brings people to the point that they participate in the persecution of God's children, believing that they are serving Him by doing so! But during the tremendous upheavals of nature just preceding Christ's Second Coming they will suddenly realize that they have never really known Jesus. As they see Him coming they will try to hide themselves **"in the dens and in the rocks of the mountains,"** seeking any possible way to flee **"from the face of Him that sits on the throne, and from the wrath of the Lamb."**

"Wrath" and **"Lamb"** seem to be a contradiction, the lamb being a symbol of God's mercy. However, God's wrath is not like man's anger, but is an expression of His glory and his character of love (see 15: *Wrath of God*). The raw, blinding energy of love that radiates from God will be life and joy to the righteous, but will provoke an overwhelming sense of guilt and condemnation in those who love and cherish sin. In the day when His glory fills the whole earth, He will not force anyone to live in His glorious presence if they have formed a character that would make His presence a continual torment. And that is what it would be for this sixth-seal sub-group, as is proven by their final cry, **"the great day of His wrath has come, and who is able to stand?"** (Revelation 6:17). This cry brings us to the real focus of the sixth seal and the subject of chapter 7: those who *are* able to stand.

"I saw four angels standing at the four corners of the earth, holding the four winds of the earth…saying, 'do not harm the earth, the sea or the trees till we have sealed the servants of our God on their foreheads.'" Rev. 7:1,3

Woodcut by Albrecht Durer

136

Chapter 7

Revelation 7:1-17

7:1 And after these things I saw four angels standing on the four corners of the earth, holding the four winds of the earth, that the wind should not blow on the earth, nor on the sea, nor on any tree.

7:2 And I saw another angel ascending from the east, having the seal of the living God; and he cried with a loud voice to the four angels, to whom it was given to hurt the earth and the sea,

7:3 Saying, "Hurt not the earth, neither the sea, nor the trees, until we have sealed the servants of our God in their foreheads."

7:4 And I heard the number of those which were sealed: and there were sealed 144,000 of all the tribes of the children of Israel.

7:5 Of the tribe of Judah were sealed 12,000. Of the tribe of Reuben were sealed 12,000. Of the tribe of Gad were sealed 12,000.

7:6 Of the tribe of Asher were sealed 12,000. Of the tribe of Nephthali were sealed twelve thousand. Of the tribe of Manasseh were sealed 12,000.

7:7 Of the tribe of Simeon were sealed 12,000. Of the tribe of Levi were sealed 12,000. Of the tribe of Issachar were sealed 12,000.

7:8 Of the tribe of Zebulun were sealed 12,000. Of the tribe of Joseph were sealed 12,000. Of the tribe of Benjamin were sealed 12,000.

7:9 After this I looked, and, behold a great multitude, which no one could number, of all nations, and tribes, and peoples, and tongues, stood before the throne and before the Lamb, clothed with white robes, and palm branches in their hands.

7:10 And they cried with a loud voice, saying, "Salvation to our God who sits on the throne, and to the Lamb."

7:11 And all the angels stood around the throne, and the elders and the four living creatures, and fell before the throne on their faces, and worshiped God,

7:12 Saying, "Amen. Blessing, and glory, and wisdom, and thanksgiving, and honor, and power, and might, be to our God forever and ever. Amen."

7:13 And one of the elders answered, saying to me, "These which are arrayed in white robes, who are they and from where did they come?"

7:14 And I said to him, "Sir, you know." And he said to me, "These are the ones coming out of the great tribulation, and they washed their robes, and made them white in the blood of the Lamb.

7:15 Therefore they are before the throne of God, and serve him day and night in his temple; and He that sits on the throne shall dwell among them.

7:16 They shall hunger no more, neither thirst any more; neither shall the sun beat on them, nor any heat.

7:17 For the Lamb which is in the midst of the throne shall feed them, and shall lead them to living fountains of waters; and God shall wipe away all tears from their eyes."

7:1 The Four Winds

"And after these things I saw four angels standing on the four corners of the earth, holding the four winds of the earth, that the wind should not blow on the earth, nor on the sea, nor on any tree" (Revelation 7:1). Chapter seven is a continuation of the last portion of chapter 6, which introduces the investigative judgment of those who are alive at the time of the Second Coming of Christ. In Revelation 6:12-17 the people who do not know Jesus cry out for the rocks to fall on them and hide them from the face of the Lamb. They ask a significant question: "the great day of His wrath has come; *and who shall be able to stand?*" (Revelation 6:17). In answer to this question, two groups are brought to view in chapter 7: The 144,000 (v. 4) and the great multitude (v. 9). As we will see in this chapter, these two groups comprise the people who will be alive and who will be saved (they are "able to stand") at the Second Coming of Christ.

What is involved in "the great day of [God's] wrath?" John was first shown **four angels standing at the four corners of the earth holding the four winds of the earth.**" This language is similar to that found elsewhere in Revelation, in Daniel and in other prophecies. For example, in Revelation 20:7,8 we learn that after the 1000 years "Satan will be released from his prison and will go out to deceive the nations *which are in the four corners of the earth.*" In this passage

the four corners of the earth are linked with the releasing of Satan from "his prison," enabling him to "deceive the nations" into attacking "the saints and their beloved city" (v. 9). In Daniel 7:2 "*The four winds* of heaven were stirring up Great Sea. And four great beasts came up from the sea." The four beasts represented the great world empires, Babylon, Persia, Greece and Rome, which attacked and conquered the people of God. The four winds represented the strife, tumult and warfare that brought these empires into power. In other passages the four winds represent the wars and strife that have scattered God's people to every corner of the earth.[265]

Comparing these verses, we see that the four angels holding the winds represent the supernatural forces that bring on the affliction, chaos and warfare that Satan uses to persecute and scatter

---

265 Ezekiel 5:10,12, Zechariah 2:6, Jeremiah 49:32-36, Matthew 24:31.

God's people.[266] These forces are restrained, but when they are released Satan will be allowed to use the nations of the earth to bring about the great tribulation that is the central drama of the Book of Revelation.

7:2,3 The Seal of God

"And I saw another angel ascending from the east, having the seal of the living God; and he cried with a loud voice to the four angels, to whom it was given to hurt the earth and the sea, saying, 'Hurt not the earth, neither the sea, nor the trees, until we have sealed the servants of our God in their foreheads" (Revelation 7:2,3). The Greek word for angel, *aggelos*, means messenger and in Revelation is used both for messengers from God and for agents of Satan. The **"angel ascending from the east"** is obviously from God, having His seal. This angel restrains the four angels that have been **"given to hurt"** the earth. The **"four angels,"** on the other hand, do not seem to be messengers from God. First of all, they **"harm the earth"** and in chapter 11 a curse is pronounced against those who "destroy the earth." Moreover, four angels who will be released are mentioned again in chapter 9. They are bound at the river Euphrates (the headquarters of Satan's "Babylon" kingdom) and they will kill a third of mankind. They are also closely associated with "the angel of the bottomless pit,"[267] Satan (see chapter 9). It is likely that within the context of the great controversy Satan has been given a limited period of time in which he will be allowed to carry out his destructive plans without the restraining influence of God's Spirit. But he will not be "released" (permitted to create affliction) until God's servants are **"sealed…in their foreheads."**

A seal in its most common Biblical application has to do with documents, such as the book of chapter 5 that was "sealed with seven seals." Seals in the Bible served three main purposes. The seal *proved the authenticity* of what was written in the document.[268] It also *protected* the document from those who did not have the right of access to it.[269] Finally, it *secured* the document from being changed.[270] John **heard the number of those who were sealed, one hundred and forty-four thousand."** God's seal on His 144,000 is like the seals on documents—it *proves the authenticity* of His saints, *protects* them in the time of trouble and *secures* their place in His kingdom. Because the sealing and the ministry of the 144,000 are the central theme of the next 8 chapters we will examine these three aspects of the sealing in more detail.

God's seal proves the authenticity of His saints. The servants of God are sealed in their foreheads. Obviously this is not some kind of tattoo or visible mark, but rather refers to what God does in their minds and hearts. In the parallel passage, Revelation 14:1-5, instead of a seal it says that the 144,000 have the "Father's name written in their

---

266 It is not clear from Revelation 7:2 whether the four angels are angels of God who are restraining the destruction of the "four winds of the earth" or are angels of Satan who are given permission to use the four winds to cause chaos and destruction. The language of verse two suggests the latter: "He [clearly an angel of God "ascending from the east"] cried with a loud voice to the four angels *to whom it was granted to harm the earth and the sea.*" The Greek word for "granted" (*edothi*) is used in the trumpets and elsewhere in Revelation to indicate permission given to Satan and his agents to cause destruction. See for example Revelation 6:4,8, 9:1,3,5, 13:5,7,14,15. We see later in the trumpets four destructive angels that are clearly Satan's agents (Revelation 9:14,15). This commentary takes the position that the seven trumpets are Satan's activity that he is allowed to carry out during the time of trouble, and both sets of four angels (7:1-3, 9:14-19) are Satan's angels of destruction.

267 Revelation 9:11.

268 See 1Kings 21:8, Jeremiah 32:9-14.

269 "Who is worthy to open the scroll and to loose its seals?" Revelation 5:2, see also Daniel 12:9.

270 "The king sealed it with his own signet ring…that the purpose concerning Daniel might not be changed" (Daniel 6:17, see also Esther 8:8).

foreheads" (v.1).[271] The Father's name refers to His character.[272] This righteous and holy character is both imputed (declared to be theirs) and imparted (made a reality in their lives) to His children. This is what it means to have His name written on their foreheads,[273] and this is what proves that they are the children of God.

Jesus, through His death on the cross, frees us from the condemnation of the law by declaring us "not guilty" (imputed righteousness). Then He sends the Holy Spirit to write (seal) the law of love in our minds and hearts, transforming our lives and making us new creatures: "You were sealed with the Holy Spirit of promise…therefore…do not grieve the Holy Spirit of God, by whom you were sealed for the day of redemption. Let all bitterness, wrath, anger, clamor and evil speaking be put away from you, with all malice. And be kind to one another, tenderhearted, forgiving one another, even as Christ forgave you. Therefore be imitators of God" (Ephesians 1:13, 4:25-5:1).

Being an imitator of God does not mean trying hard to be good. There is no amount of trying or effort that can make us kind and forgiving or take away bitterness, anger and evil habits. The only effort that can transform the life is the effort to know God and be filled with the Holy Spirit. God through His Spirit can create new hearts and minds that are open to Him when we accept the

sacrifice Jesus made for us. The Holy Spirit then carries on a work of healing and repentance in our lives—healing us from the injuries the enemy has inflicted, and bringing us to repentance for the destructive ways we have responded to those wounds in futile attempts to relieve the pain they were causing us. As we grow in the grace and knowledge of God the Holy Spirit empowers us to become the holy people that God declared us to be when He forgave us of our sins.

"Holiness to the Lord" was written on the foreheads of the priests of the ancient sanctuary (Exodus 28:36-38). Likewise, God's name, His holy character, is written in the foreheads of the 144,000. Their holy character proves their authenticity to the rest of the universe (the angels, etc.) who are looking on to see what humans are like when they come into harmony with God.[274]

The Seal Protects and Secures the 144,000

God's seal protects His people. Just as documents were protected by the seals that were placed upon them, so God's people will be protected by the seal of God. God's people have always been sealed (Ephesians 1:13), but the urgency and danger of the time just before the coming of Christ requires a special sealing, described as being **"sealed…in their forehead."** A special protective mark is not a new concept. As God was delivering the Children of Israel out of slavery in Egypt through a series of plagues, He instructed them to put a mark on their doorposts, the blood of a lamb that was slain. The special mark protected them from the final plague, the slaying of the first-born children.

During the final crisis, God's people will again

---

271 See also Revelation 3:12 and 22:4.

272 God told Moses, "I will *proclaim the name* of the Lord before you." When God proclaimed His name, He proclaimed His character: "The Lord, the Lord God, merciful and gracious, longsuffering and abounding in goodness and truth, keeping mercy for thousands, forgiving iniquity and transgression and sin, by no means clearing the guilty" (Exodus 33:18-34:7).

273 Note the clear parallel of Revelation 22:4 and 1John 3:2: *"They shall see His face,* and His name shall be in their foreheads" "We know that we shall be like Him, for *we shall see Him* as He is." When we see Him as He is, He can give us His name (His character) and we become like Him. This becomes obvious in Revelation 14:1-5 where the holy character of the 144,000 is described.

---

274 "We have been made a spectacle to the world, both to angels and to men" (1Corinthians 4:9). "The creation waits in eager expectation for the sons of God to be revealed" (Romans 8:19).

need protection. The locusts of the fifth trumpet were "commanded…that they should not hurt the grass of the earth, nor any green thing, nor any tree; but only those men who do not have the seal of God in their foreheads" (Revelation 9:4). In chapters 8 and 9 we will see that this seal will protect them from Satan's attempts to destroy them through chaos and warfare. They will also be protected from the destructive judgments of the seven last plagues, in contrast to those who receive the mark of the beast (Revelation 14:9-12).

The protective sealing is a perfect parallel of Ezekiel 9, where the destroyers are also restrained while God's servants are being marked. The prophet Ezekiel heard the announcement, "Let those who have charge over the city draw near, each with a deadly weapon in his hand" (v.1). He saw six "men" (apparently angels) with battle axes in their hands, and among them was a "man" who was "clothed with linen and had a writers inkhorn at his side" (v.2). The man in linen was told, "Go through the midst of the city…and put a mark on the foreheads of the men who sigh and cry over all the abominations that are done within it" (v.4). The angels with their deadly weapons were commanded, "Go after him through the city and kill, do not let your eye spare nor have any pity…but do not come near anyone on whom is the mark" (v. 5,6). Likewise the 144,000 will be protected by **"the seal of the living God…in their foreheads."**

God's seal secures His people's place in His kingdom. The investigative judgment allows the unfallen inhabitants of the universe to join in the determination of who will finally be admitted into God's eternal kingdom. For the believers of all ages who have died, this determination is made while they sleep in the grave during the investigative judgment when "the court is seated and the books are opened" (Daniel 7:10). They will rise in the resurrection to meet Jesus at His Second Coming. However, those who are still alive when Jesus comes will have already had their names considered in the investigative judgment. Jesus said "Behold I am coming quickly, and My reward is with Me, to give to every one according to his work" (Revelation 22:12, see also Isaiah 40:10, 62:11). When Jesus comes the righteous "shall be caught up…to meet the Lord in the air" (1 Thessalonians 4:17), while the unrighteous "shall be punished with everlasting destruction… when He comes" (2 Thessalonians 1:9,10).

These verses show that the final determination will have already been made by the time Jesus comes. This means that those who are sealed will be guaranteed to be secure as citizens of the heavenly kingdom while they are still living on earth during the chaos of the time of trouble. Apparently, as a part of the great controversy Jesus will present the 144,000 to the universe and will seal them, guaranteeing that they will remain faithful until the end. In this respect they are like Job. Satan challenged that the earth was all his, but God pointed to Job as one who was and who would remain faithful, even when Satan demanded and received permission to try him to the uttermost (see Appendix 8).

Sealing, the Law and the Latter Rain

God's seal is closely linked with His law: "*Seal the law* among my disciples" (Isaiah 8:16).[275] The essence of the law is not a list of rules, but is summarized in the two great commandments, "You shall love the Lord your God with all your heart, with all your soul, with all your strength, and with all your mind, and your neighbor as yourself" (Luke 10:27, see also Matthew 22:36-40).

---

275 The law summarizes God's character and the character He wants to develop in His children. The negatives "Thou shalt not" (Exodus 20:1-17) reveal that sin has no part in His character. The positive summary "Thou shalt love" (Matthew 22:37-40) shows that His kind of self-sacrificing love reaches out and embraces His creatures in order to help and save them.

Thus the law is a reflection of God's character of love, and it is sealed in the minds and hearts of those who enter into the new covenant experience—"I will make a new covenant...I will put My laws in their mind and write them on their hearts; and I will be their God, and they shall be My people" (Hebrews 8:8-10).

Revelation 14, which describes the 144,000 and their ministry, shows that they have God's law sealed in them: "Here is the patience of the saints; here are those that keep the commandments of God, and the faith of Jesus" (Revelation 14:12). This verse makes it clear that the keeping of God's commandments is integrally related to "the faith of Jesus." Righteousness by faith does not simply result in a new status (saved), but in a new life of loving obedience to God's will.

The parallel passage in Revelation 12:17 emphasizes that it is the Holy Spirit, received by "the faith of Jesus," which empowers the 144,000 to "keep the commandments."[276] Receiving the fullness of the Holy Spirit is what it means to be sealed. "God...has sealed us and given us the Spirit in our hearts as a deposit" (2Corinthians 1:22). "You were sealed by the Holy Spirit of promise (Ephesians 1:13, 4:30). People have been receiving the Holy Spirit since the beginning of the church (and even in Old Testament times).[277] But the sealing of the 144,000 will be a mass outpouring of the Holy Spirit, similar (but on a much greater scale) to what happened on the Day of Pentecost. "When the Day of Pentecost had fully come, they were all with one accord in one place. And suddenly there came a sound from heaven, as of a rushing mighty wind...and they were all filled with the Holy Spirit" (Acts 2:1-4).

The experiences of the Day of Pentecost and the similar but greater outpouring at the end of time are the fulfillment of the Old Testament prophecies concerning the former and the latter rain. "For He has given you the former rain faithfully, and He will cause the rain to come down for you—the former rain, and the latter rain" (Joel 2:23). In Palestine the "former rain" came in October and allowed the newly planted seeds to sprout and take root. They would grow slowly through the winter despite setbacks from storms and frost, but in March the "latter rain" would come, drenching the earth and giving the moisture needed to bring the plants to maturity for the harvest. The former rain represents the outpouring of the Holy Spirit at the Day of Pentecost that established the Christian Church. Throughout the long "winter" of church history the church has continued to grow and extend despite the "storms" that have beset her.

But in the "latter days" God will send the "latter rain"—an unprecedented outpouring of the Holy Spirit that will bring the church to maturity.[278] Empowered by the Holy Spirit the church will preach the gospel and demonstrate the love of Jesus to a world that is starving and desperate,

---

276 God's sealed people are called "the remnant of her seed, which keep the commandments of God and the testimony of Jesus Christ." The "testimony of Jesus" is defined in Revelation 19: 10 as "the Spirit of prophecy." Having the "Spirit of Prophecy" (the Holy Spirit) is thus integrally connected with keeping the commandments. As long as the law is external, on tables of stone, it serves only to condemn the sinner, reminding him of the death he deserves; it is "the ministry of death, written and engraved on stones" (2Corinthians 3:7). But "what the law could not do...God did by sending His own Son...that the righteous requirements of the law might be fulfilled in us who do not walk according to the flesh but according to the Spirit" (Romans 8:4).

277 See for example Exodus 31:3, Numbers 11:25, Judges 6:34, 1Samuel 10:10, 16:13, 2Chronicles 15;1, 20:14, 24:20, Psalms 51:11, Isaiah 63:11, Daniel 5:11.

278 In Ephesians 4 Paul lists the gifts of the Spirit that are given "for the equipping of the saints for the work of ministry, for the edifying of the body of Christ, till we all come to the unity of the faith and of the knowledge of the Son of God, to a perfect man, to the measure of the stature of the fullness of Christ; that we should no longer be children, tossed to and fro and carried about with every wind of doctrine," that we "may grow up in all things into Him who is the head—Christ" (Ephesians 4:12-14). The division and disunity that still exists within the Christian Church shows that this is a promise that still awaits its fulfillment in the future.

battered and abused by the enemy. This is God's most fervent desire. He wants nothing more than to save as many as can be saved and bring sin to an end. So why doesn't God send the latter rain now?

The Holy Spirit is given "for the equipping of the saints for the work of ministry" (Ephesians 4:12), in other words, to empower God's people to effectively share the good news that they have received with others who do not know God. But God is not interested in giving spiritual gifts and power to people who only know Him superficially at best. The outpouring of the Holy Spirit in the former rain is the model for the latter rain. The disciples walked with Jesus for three years, but by the time of His sacrifice they still had not received the fullness of the Holy Spirit.[279] And no wonder; their "gospel" was, "Jesus is going to help us get rid of the Romans and I will be the greatest in the kingdom." Even after Jesus had risen from the dead, walked with them for forty more days and was ready to return to heaven they were still asking, "Lord, will You at this time restore the kingdom to Israel?" (Acts 1:6). It was not until they "continued" 10 days "with one accord in prayer and supplication…in one place" that they were "filled with the Holy Spirit" and powerfully proclaimed "the wonderful works of God" (Acts 1:14, 2:1-11).

God characterizes the church today as Laodicea, bankrupt without the gold of faith, naked without the white garments of Christ's righteousness, blind without the eye salve of Spirit-empowered discernment. The lukewarm Laodicean church will never receive the latter rain because God will not empower their "gospel" of self-centered complacency. The latter rain does not transform our priorities; it empowers our priorities which have been "transformed by the renewing of [our] minds"(Romans 12:2).

The latter rain will come when God's people realize their spiritual poverty and seek His Spirit and power with the same determination that the disciples did before the Day of Pentecost: "I [the Lord] will return again to My place till they acknowledge their offense. Then they will seek My face; in their affliction they will earnestly seek Me. 'Come, and let us return to the Lord…Let us pursue the knowledge of the Lord. His going forth is established as the morning; He will come to us like the rain, like the latter and former rain to the earth" (Hosea 5:15-6:3).

Now, at the end of the age, it is time for God's people to come together in prayer, learning to love one another and the lost people around them, and pleading for His power. Then the 144,000 will be **"sealed in their foreheads"** and go out to give the last message to the world. "Ask the Lord for rain in the time of the latter rain. The Lord will make flashing clouds; He will give them showers of rain" "Break up your fallow ground, for it is time to seek the Lord, till He comes and rains righteousness on you" (Zechariah 10:1, Hosea 10:12).

7:13-17 In Heaven While on Earth

The sealed 144,000 are so connected to God's kingdom that it is as if they are in heaven even while still on earth during the time of trouble. This dual state of being secure citizens of heaven while still on earth is indicated by the language used in chapter seven. **"And one of the elders answered, saying to me, "These which are arrayed in white robes, who are they and from where did they come?" And I said to him, "Sir, you know." And he said to me, "These are the ones coming out of the great tribulation, and**

---

279 He who believes in Me, as the Scripture has said, out of his heart will flow rivers of living water. But this He spoke concerning the Spirit, whom those believing in Him would receive; for the Holy Spirit was not yet given (John 7: 38,39).

they washed their robes, and made them white in the blood of the Lamb. Therefore they are before the throne of God, and serve him day and night in his temple; and He that sits on the throne shall dwell among them. They shall hunger no more, neither thirst any more; neither shall the sun beat on them, nor any heat." (Revelation 7:13-16).

They are pictured as standing **"before the throne and before the Lamb, clothed with white robes"** (Revelation 7:9) with **"all the angels…and the elders and the four living creatures"** (v.11), in other words, they are portrayed as if they are in heaven. But paradoxically, they still seem to be on earth in the midst of the time of trouble. When John dialogues with the angel about who these people are, he is told, **"These are the ones coming out of the great tribulation"** (v. 14). The Greek present participle verb for **"coming out"** (*erhomeni*) [280] has the definite sense that while they are standing before the throne they are still in the process of coming out of the tribulation! Moreover, verse 15 says that **"they *are* before the throne of God,"** using the present tense. But in the next verse it says that **"They *shall* hunger no more, neither thirst any more; neither *shall* the sun beat on them…and God *shall* wipe away all tears from their eyes"** (vs. 16,17). The future tenses that are used in the original Greek imply that at the time they are before the throne, relief from hunger, thirst and the heat of the sun is still in the future, along with having their tears wiped away. But despite the fact that they are still

experiencing severe trials of their faith, the seal in their forehead is a sign to the universe that they are so absolutely secure in the Kingdom that they are essentially already there.

This passage also specifies that **"They…*serve Him day and night in His temple"*** (v. 15), which cannot refer to the future heavenly kingdom or the new earth. First of all, there is no night in the future kingdom (see Revelation 22:5). Moreover, when John saw the vision of heaven he "saw no temple therein, for the Lord God Almighty and the Lamb are its temple" (Revelation 21:22). The temple ministry will cease with the eradication of sin, so the service **"day and night in His temple"** refers to the ministry of God's faithful servants on earth[281] before the Second Coming of Christ.[282] As we will see in chapter 14, this passage describes the ministry of the 144,000, which takes place during "the hour of His judgment" (Revelation 14;7) as they call the captives in "Babylon" to "come out of her my people" (Revelation 18:4). Their present service on earth is contrasted with their future when "They *shall* see His face" (Revelation 22:4) and **"He that sits on the throne *shall* dwell among them"** (v. 15).

In chapter 14, which is a parallel of chapter 7, the 144,000 are again shown both in heaven and on earth. In verses 1-5 they are "on mount Zion," "before the throne of God" with "the four living creatures and the elders," singing "a new song." But in verses 6-13 they are on earth, preaching "to those who dwell on earth" (v.6), patiently enduring the persecution of the beast (v.12) and

---

280 The Greek word *"erhomeni"* is translated in the New King James version "the ones who come out," which gives the sense of something they do repeatedly or habitually. This is closer to the meaning than the King James version "they which came out," or New International version "they who have come out," both of which give the sense of a completed action. The difficult-to-translate present participle of the passive verb is perhaps best translated as in The New Living Translation, "these are the ones coming out," which shows that the coming out is still in process at the time they are standing before the throne.

281 The New Testament makes it clear that the temple is the body of believers. The ministry of the 144,000 is to bring people into the temple, in other words, to unite them with other believers in the church. See 1Corinthians 3:16,17, 6:19, 2Corinthians 6:16, Ephesians 2:21, 1Peter 2:5.

282 This position is supported by the statement of Paul in Acts 26:7, "To this promise our twelve tribes, earnestly serving God night and day, hope to attain." Obviously Paul was referring to service on earth (the same verb as in Revelation 7:15, *latreuo* is used), not future service in the eternal kingdom.

even suffering martyrdom (v.13).

Again in chapter 15 the same group is pictured "on the sea of glass," "having harps of God," singing the victory "song of Moses."[283] In verse 2 they are called "those that have the victory over the beast." Again the present participle is used ("those having the victory"), indicating that this is a victory that is still in progress. In the very next scene we see seven angels coming out of the temple to pour out the seven last plagues. The sealed saints are spiritually in heaven on the sea of glass, and at the same time they are on earth, victorious over the beast while all around them the most fearsome plagues in human history are falling! This incredible experience is unique in all human history[284] and will be an eternal blessing to those who live through it, as evidenced by the new song that they sing, "and no one could learn that song except the hundred and forty-four thousand who were redeemed from the earth" (Revelation 14:3).

7:4-8 The Tribes of Israel

"And I heard the number of those which were sealed: and there were sealed 144,000 of all the tribes of the children of Israel. Of the tribe of Judah were sealed 12,000. Of the tribe of Reuben were sealed 12,000. Of the tribe of Gad were sealed 12,000. Of the tribe of Asher were sealed 12,000. Of the tribe of Nephthali were sealed twelve thousand. Of the tribe of Manasseh were sealed 12,000. Of the tribe of Simeon were sealed 12,000. Of the tribe of Levi were sealed 12,000. Of the tribe of Issachar were sealed 12,000. Of the tribe of Zebulun were sealed 12,000. Of the tribe of Joseph were

sealed 12,000. Of the tribe of Benjamin were sealed 12,000" (Revelation 7:4-8).

Who are the 144,000? So far we have seen that they are people who are alive at the time of the Second Coming of Christ. They are sealed, which means that 1) the Holy Spirit has developed the character of Jesus in them, thus proving them genuine, 2) they are under God's protection during the great tribulation, and 3) they are secure in God's kingdom even though they are still facing the trials and tribulations of the time of trouble.

Verse 4 reveals that they are sealed out of **"all the tribes of the children of Israel,"** followed by a list of the tribes. A comparison of this list with the lists of the twelve tribes given in the Old Testament shows that it is significantly different from all other lists,[285] suggesting that there is a symbolic meaning. Since the Jews lost their right to be the true Israel of God[286] and the literal tribes have long since lost their identity, Israel here must refer to the spiritual Israel identified by the Apostle Paul: "They are not all Israel who are of Israel, nor are they all children because they are the seed of Abraham (Romans 9:6,7). "For he is not a Jew who is one outwardly…but he is a Jew who is one inwardly, and circumcision is that of the heart, in the Spirit" (Romans 2:28, 29). "For you are all sons of God through faith in Christ Jesus…There is neither Jew nor Greek… for you

---

283 The victory song of Moses is found in Exodus 15 where the children of Israel celebrated God's victory over the Egyptians.

284 There have been a few, such as Enoch, who have "walked with God" while on earth (Genesis 5: 22-24, Hebrews 11:5), but the 144,000 will have this experience during the great time of trouble.

285 Typical lists of the tribes are found in Numbers 2 and Ezekiel 48. Levi is not listed, since he was the tribe associated with the temple and did not have an inheritance. His place was taken by dividing Joseph into two tribes, Ephraim and Manasseh. However, the list in Revelation 7 includes Levi, includes Joseph and one of his sons, Manasseh, but does not include Ephraim. Dan, who is included in every list in the Old Testament, is also left out.

286 In Daniel 9 the Jews were given 490 years of probation, but when they crucified Jesus and persecuted His followers they failed to carry out the conditions that would allow them to continue to be the chosen people (see a detailed explanation in Appendix 4: *The Secret Rapture*). Jesus, in the parable of the wicked vinedressers, clearly taught that "the kingdom of God will be taken from you and given to a nation bearing the fruits of it" (Matthew 21:33-43).

are all one in Christ Jesus. And if you are Christ's then you are Abraham's seed, and heirs according to the promise" (Galatians 3:26-29). These and other texts[287] show that the New Testament designation "Israel" refers to those who are declared righteous because of their faith in Jesus rather than according to physical lineage.[288]

The listing of the names of the tribes does not refer to a physical genealogy, but rather to the *spiritual characteristics* of those who are sealed as the 144,000.[289] The characteristics of the tribes are given in Genesis 49, where Jacob said, "Gather together that I may tell you what shall befall you *in the Last Days*" (Genesis 49:1). The twelve tribes that make up the 144,000 are quite a diverse lot. There are likely candidates such as Judah with his kingly scepter (v.10) and Joseph, the fruitful bough (v.22). There are unlikely candidates such as Reuben, "unstable as water" (v.3,4), Simeon and Levi with their cursed anger and cruelty (vs.5-7) and Benjamin, who is like a ravenous wolf (v.27). A full study of the characteristics of the tribes of Israel could be a whole chapter by itself.

The point is that God can make almost any kind of character suitable for an exalted position among the 144,000. But a careful comparison with the tribes mentioned in Genesis 49 shows that there is one tribe missing: Dan is not included among the 144,000 listed in Revelation 7. In chapter 4: *The Four Tribes* we saw that this is explained by considering his character: he judges his people, and he is a serpent, biting at the horse's heels causing its rider to fall backwards (Genesis 49:16,17). The history of his tribe, as recorded in Judges 18, shows that Dan was the first tribe to separate itself from Israel and to get involved in worshiping idols, and the territory of Dan was later known as a center of idolatry.[290]

Dan's place on the list of the 144,000 is taken by Joseph's son Manasseh. In several of the Old Testament lists of tribes Joseph's two sons, Ephraim and Manasseh, are listed, so that there are actually 13 tribes.[291] However, even though Ephraim would be expected to be on the list (since his brother Manasseh is included), he is omitted along with Dan. As we saw in Chapter 4, Ephraim was the leader in the idolatry that eventually resulted in the dispersion of the 10 northern tribes of Israel. In the book of Hosea Ephraim's idolatry is repeatedly condemned (eg. "Ephraim is joined to idols. Let him alone" Hosea 4:17).

The picture that emerges is that God can use

---

287 For example, James addresses his epistle to "the twelve tribes who are scattered abroad" (James 1:1) but there is nothing in the letter that would indicate that it is not to the whole church, both Jews and Gentiles. Paul refers to gentile believers in Galatia as "the Israel of God" (Galatians 6:16). Paul referred to literal Jews as "my brethren, my countrymen according to the flesh, who are Israelites" (Romans 9:3.4), and it is within this same context that he refers to them as "Israel" without specifying if he is talking about spiritual or physical (for example Romans 10:1). This shows that it is from the context that we determine the physical or spiritual meaning of "Israel," and in the case of the 144,000 the context of chapter 7 clearly indicates a spiritual meaning.

288 This does not mean that the New Testament does not recognize the physical lineage. In Romans 9:11 Paul is concerned about "my brethren, my countrymen according to the flesh, who are Israelites" (Romans 9:2,3). In this passage Paul shows that the Jews are beloved because of "the fathers," that they can be saved in the same way that anyone else can be saved and are not totally rejected just because they rejected Jesus as a people. He also shows that God will do a special work for their salvation, and that they along with the "fullness of the Gentiles" will constitute the people of God who will inherit eternal life—"And so all Israel will be saved" (Romans 11:26).

289 In Revelation 21:12,24,25 we see that New Jerusalem has "twelve gates...and names written on them, which are the names of the twelve tribes of the children of Israel...and the nations of those who are saved shall...bring their glory and honor into it. Its gate shall not be shut." Here we can see that New Jerusalem has gates designated for the tribes of Israel, but all the saved of every "nation" shall enter in. Thus the names are symbolic and include people from every literal physical tribe.

290 1Kings 12:29,30, 2Kings 10:29.

291 For example, in Numbers 2 the twelve tribes (Ephraim and Manasseh taking the place of Joseph) camp around the tabernacle, with Levi in the middle. Similarly, in Ezekiel 48 there are six tribes on each side of the temple, with Levi as the 13th in the middle.

all kinds of people with a variety of character faults for the vital mission of the 144,000, but He cannot use those who have not been loyal to Him. Even though the 144,000 have human weaknesses and failings, they are totally devoted to Christ. "These are the ones who follow the Lamb wherever He goes" (Revelation 14:4). This does not mean that idolaters cannot be saved. Throughout history, the majority of those saved have been former idolaters. But the 144,000 have a special role in the last days, and those who have committed spiritual adultery are disqualified for this special work.

Sealing the 144,000

An **"angel ascending from the east, having the seal of the living God"** commanded the angels who hold the four winds to wait for the sealing of the 144,000. The Greek word for **"the east"** (*anatolis ilio*) means the rising of the sun. This is in contrast to other angels of Revelation who came down from heaven to make their announcements or carry out their missions.[292] The sealing angel does not burst upon the scene, but does his work gradually, as the rising sun gradually enlightens the earth. Apparently the sealing of the 144,000 is a gradual work, starting with just a few until all have been sealed. When the sealing is completed, the **"four angels standing on the four corners of the earth"** will release **"the four winds"** which will harm **"the earth, the sea and the trees"** (Revelation 7:1-3).

Is 144,000 a literal or symbolic number? Since the Bible does not say, all opinions are a matter of conjecture. On the one hand, it seems to have symbolic elements, being the multiple of 12 times 12 times 1000. This brings to mind the twelve tribes whose names are written on the twelve gates of the New Jerusalem and the twelve apostles whose names are written on the twelve foundations of its walls (Revelation 21:12,13).

On the other hand, it is possible that God could have made a "deal" with Satan that he could prepare 144,000 people who had such godly characters that they could be sealed and remain faithful, without compromise, even through the trials and temptations of the great tribulation. This would be reminiscent of the deal God made with Satan concerning Job in the first two chapters of the book of Job.[293] Whether literal or symbolic, we should note that the 144,000 are not the only ones who are saved. They are a special group who live in the last moments of earth's history, and as the discussion below will indicate, there is **"a great multitude"** of others who will also be saved at that time.

Character of the 144,000

A key characteristic of the 144,000 is found in Revelation 14:4: "These [the 144,000] are they which were not defiled with women; for they are virgins." Women in prophecy symbolize God's people (or those who claim to be God's people, see 12:1,2 *The Woman*). They may be either pure and virtuous as in Revelation 12:1-6[294] or

---

292 Angels were seen flying in the midst of heaven (8:13, 14:6), coming down from heaven (10:1, 14:7, 18:1, 20:1), coming out of the temple (14:7) and standing in the sun (19:17) but nowhere else are they shown coming from the rising of the sun. When Revelation makes reference to the direction east the word *anatolis* (rising) is used by itself, without *ilio* (sun), as in Revelation 21:13 "three gates on the east (*anatolis*). The only other verse in Revelation where *anatolis ilio* is used is Revelation 16:12 "Then the sixth angel poured out his bowl on the great river Euphrates, and its water was dried up, so that the way of the kings from the east might be prepared." This refers to the coming of Christ with the hosts of heaven (see 16:12 *The Kings from the East*). According to Matthew 24:30, this also is a process rather than an immediate event, starting first with the appearance of the sign of the Son of Man, then the mourning of the nations, then the coming of Christ on the clouds.

293 See appendix 8 for a discussion of the great controversy in the book of Job.

294 Other examples include Jeremiah 6:2, Isaiah 54:1-6, Ephesians 5:22-33.

immoral harlots as in Revelation 17.[295] A virgin has not committed fornication or adultery, and the highly symbolic context of Revelation 14 shows that it is spiritual adultery that the 144,000 have not committed.

There are two important passages in Revelation that refer to spiritual immorality. In Revelation 2:20 the church of Thyatira is condemned because they "allow that woman Jezebel, who calls herself a prophetess, to teach and to seduce My servants to commit fornication, and to eat things sacrificed to idols." Jezebel symbolized the great apostasy of the medieval papal church (see 2:18-20 *You Tolerate Jezebel*). This passage emphasizes the false teachings and doctrines that seduce people to worship a false god in the name of worshiping the true God.

In Revelation 17 spiritual adultery at the very end of time is depicted under the symbolism of the "great harlot that sits on many waters" (v.1). Like the 144,000 she also has a name written on her forehead, but it is the blasphemous name, "Mystery, Babylon the Great, the Mother of Harlots and Abominations of the Earth" (v.5). This woman is obviously Rome,[296] but Rome is not the only harlot: one of the woman's names is "The Mother of Harlots," so obviously she has daughters as well. The angel explained to John, "Come, I will show you the judgment of the great harlot...with whom the kings of the earth committed fornication" (Revelation 17: 1,2). This verse emphasizes the illicit political relationships that characterize the apostate church.

From these two passages we can see that spiritual adultery is to believe the teachings and participate in the ceremonies of a false god and to be a part of a false religious system that exploits political powers ("the kings of the earth") to accomplish her purposes. This is seen in the beast/Babylon system of Revelation 13, which uses false teaching and political alliances to deceive the world into persecuting God's true people. The false doctrines and political power are very seductive and addictive—they are called "a golden cup in her hand full of abominations and filthiness of her fornication" and "the inhabitants of the earth have been made drunk with the wine of her fornication" (Revelation 17:4,2).

The 144,000 have not been involved in this kind of spiritual immorality—they are "virgins," which means that they have not been a part of Babylon. In fact, in chapter 14 they are the ones who announce Babylon's fallen condition[297] and warn the world not to commit fornication with her—"Babylon is fallen, is fallen, that great city, because she has made all nations drink of the wine of the wrath of her fornication" (Revelation14:8). Their message is repeated in chapter 18 with even more power, where they are depicted as an "angel come down from heaven, having great power; and the earth was lightened with his glory. And he cried mightily with a strong voice, saying, "Babylon the great is fallen, is fallen, and has become the habitation of devils"

---

295 Other examples include Ezekiel 23 and Hosea 3:1-5.

296 "The woman whom you saw is that great city which reigns over the kings of the earth" (Revelation 17:18). Rome is the only city which is also a church (symbolized by the harlot), and during the Middle Ages she did reign over the kings of the earth, and according to the prophecy of Revelation 17 she will do so again. Moreover, "The seven heads [of the beast which the woman rides] are seven hills on which the woman sits" (v. 9 NIV). Since ancient times Rome has been known as the city built on seven hills. Finally, the beast that the woman rides is nearly identical to the sea beast of Revelation 13, which is obviously the Roman Catholic Church of the Middle Ages (see 13:1,2 *The Beast from the Sea*).

297 In chapter 14 the Lamb with the 144,000 are presented. After describing their character (vs. 1-5) God's final message to the world is presented (the "three angels' messages of vs. 6-12). The juxtaposition of the 144,000 with the message suggests that the 144,000 are the ones who give the message.

(Revelation 18:1,2).[298] This is God's final plea for His people to escape from Babylon. "And I heard another voice from heaven, saying, "Come out of her, my people, that you do not partake of her sins, and that you do not receive of her plagues" (v.4).

Incredible as it may seem, there are many people who are a part of Babylon but who are called God's people ("come out of her My people"). These are people who love God, who want to serve him, but who have been deceived or "seduced" (Revelation 2:20) into worshiping idols in the name of God. The Lord's 144,000 messengers will call them to come out of Babylon. Even the Greek word "come out" can have the sense of ending a sexual relationship.[299] The message is for those who have "come in to" the harlot to "come out of her." So compelling is the appeal of the 144,000 that **"a Great Multitude"** will come out of Babylon.

7:9,10 The Great Multitude

"After this I looked, and, behold a great multitude, which no one could number, of all nations, and tribes, and peoples, and tongues, stood before the throne and before the Lamb, clothed with white robes, and palm branches in their hands. And they cried with a loud voice, saying, 'Salvation to our God who sits on the throne, and to the Lamb'" (Revelation 7:9,10).

Who are the great multitude? Some commentators have identified them as the saved of all ages. However, in verse 14 the angel specifically says that **"These are the ones coming out of the great tribulation."** In the original Greek it reads "the tribulation the great," in other words, a specific great tribulation, not the general tribulation that has plagued this planet during the entire reign of sin. The great tribulation that is mentioned specifically in the Bible is described in Daniel 12:1: "There shall be a time of trouble[300] such as never was since there was a nation, even to that time. And at that time your people shall be delivered." This is the tribulation that occurs just before Jesus comes, the same tribulation that the great multitude comes out of.

Other commentators have considered the great multitude to be the same as the 144,000,[301] with John first hearing a symbolic number (v.4) and then seeing the literal people (v.9).[302] However, from the verses in Chapters 14 and 18 that were considered above, it is obvious that there are two sub-groups of God's people at the very end: God's people who are in Babylon, who have committed spiritual adultery with her but

---

298 The message of Revelation 18 is the same as that of Revelation 14, which is given by the 144,000. This suggests that the 144,000 give both messages. This theme will be developed in more detail in chapters 11 and 14.

299 The Greek word is *exelthate*, which is from two roots, *erhome*, come, and *ex*, out. The Greek Septuagint word for sexual relations is *eiserhome*, with the same root *erhome*, come, and *eis*, into. For example, "Now Samson went to Gaza and saw a harlot there, and went in to her" (Judges 16:1).

300 The same Greek word, *thlipsis*, is used in both Revelation 7:14 (great *tribulation*), Daniel 12:1 (time of *trouble*), and Matthew 24:21 (great *tribulation*).

301 See for example, Stefanovic, Ranko *Revelation of Jesus Christ*, 2002 (Berrien Springs, MI Andrews University Press) pp. 264-271 "They are not a select group of God's people separated from the larger body and granted special privileges…in God's kingdom there are no clans, cliques, or ranks." This misses the point that within the church of God the various members have a variety of roles, some with various spiritual gifts, others with positions of responsibility such as elders and deacons. The 144,000 are not a heavenly clique, but a group with a special role during the time of trouble. However, once the great multitude has come out of Babylon there will no longer be any differentiation between them and the 144,000. In the resurrection the only special mention is for "those who had been beheaded for their witness" (Revelation 20:4).

302 There are a few instances in which John uses this literary device of introducing something orally and then displaying it visually, most notably in Revelation 1:10-13, 5:5,6, 21:9,10. However, in the majority of cases John either hears something and sees nothing or sees something unrelated. Sometimes he sees first and then hears. The pattern does not seem to be so clear or consistent that it could provide a basis for interpretation (See for example Revelation 4:1, 5:11,13, 8:13, 9:13, 10:4,8, 11:12, 12:10, 14:1,2,13,14, 16:1,5,7, 18:1,4, 19:1,6, 21:2,3, 22:8).

are called to come out of her (18:1-4), and the 144,000 who are virgins, having never been in Babylon, who are calling the great multitude to come out of Babylon. The Greek wording used to show their origins[303] also suggests the distinction between the two groups—the 144,000 are sealed from **"all the tribes of the children of Israel"** (7:4) while the great multitude are **"of all nations, and tribes, and peoples, and tongues"** (7:9).

Although there is a distinction between the two groups at the time the 144,000 give the great appeal to come out of Babylon, this distinction is not permanent. The great multitude will come out of Babylon and will join the 144,000, and together they will stand by faith on the sea of glass before the throne, waiting for the final plagues to finish and for Jesus to come (See Revelation 15:2-7).

The chapter ends with a reference to the glorious eternal inheritance of those **"who come out of the great tribulation, and washed their robes and made them white in the blood of the lamb"** (Revelation 7:14 NKJV). They have suffered hunger, thirst, and the scorching heat of the sun (Revelation 7:16). They have gained "the victory over the beast, over his image and over his mark and over the number of his name" (Revelation 15:2), and they finally see Him coming whom they have waited for. Just as the multitudes welcomed Jesus with palm branches at His triumphant entrance into Jerusalem (John 12:13), so also the great multitude have **"palm branches in their hands"** and cry out in triumph, **"salvation to our God who sits on the throne, and to the Lamb"** as they welcome Jesus at His Second Coming. "For the Lord Himself will descend from heaven with a shout, with the voice of an archangel, and with the trumpet of God...Then we who are alive and remain shall be caught up together with them in the clouds to meet the Lord in the air. And thus we shall always be with the Lord" (I Thessalonians 4:16,17). And then **"the Lamb which is in the midst of the throne shall feed them, and shall lead them to living fountains of waters; and God shall wipe away all tears from their eyes"** (Revelation 7:17).

---

303 In both verse 4 and 9 the Greek uses the word *ek* (out of) and *pas* (all), but the 144,000 are out of all the tribes of Israel and the great multitude are out of all nations, tribes, peoples and tongues. In other words, the origin of the 144,000 emphasizes limitation (from the tribes of Israel, and not even from all of the tribes) while the origin of the great multitude emphasizes universality.

"The seven angels who had the seven trumpets prepared themselves to sound…
and hail and fire followed, mingled with blood…and a great mountain burning with fire
was thrown into the sea…and a great star fell from heaven." Rev. 8:6,7,8,10
Woodcut by Albrecht Durer 1498

Chapter 8

Revelation 8:1-13

8:1 And when he opened the seventh seal, there was silence in heaven for about half an hour.

8:2 And I saw the seven angels which stood before God; and to them were given seven trumpets.

8:3 And another angel came and stood at the altar, having a golden censer; and there was given to him much incense, that he should offer it with the prayers of all the saints on the golden altar which was before the throne.

8:4 And the smoke of the incense, with the prayers of the saints, ascended up before God out of the angel's hand.

8:5 And the angel took the censer, and filled it with fire of the altar, and cast it to the earth; and there were voices, and thunder, and lightning, and an earthquake.

8:6 And the seven angels which had the seven trumpets prepared themselves to sound.

8:7 The first angel sounded, and there followed hail and fire mingled with blood, and they were cast on the earth. And a third of the trees were burned up, and all green grass was burned up.

8:8 And the second angel sounded, and something like a great mountain burning with fire was cast into the sea; and a third of the sea became blood;

8:9 And a third of the creatures which were in the sea and had life, died; and a third of the ships were destroyed.

8:10 And the third angel sounded, and there fell a great star from heaven, burning like a lamp, and it fell upon a third of the rivers, and upon the springs of waters.

8:11 And the name of the star is called Wormwood; and a third of the waters became wormwood, and many men died of the waters, because they were made bitter.

8:12 And the fourth angel sounded, and a third of the sun was smitten, and a third of the moon, and a third of the stars, so a third of them was darkened; and the day did not shine for a third of it, and the night likewise.

8:13 And I beheld, and heard an angel flying in the midst of heaven, saying with a loud voice, "Woe, woe, woe, to the inhabitants of the earth because of the remaining voices of the trumpet of the three angels, which are yet to sound!"

8:1 Silence in Heaven

"And when he opened the seventh seal, there was silence in heaven for about half an hour" (Revelation 8:1). One of the striking patterns of the Book of Revelation is the repeating series of seven—the seven churches, seals, trumpets, thunders, and last plagues. In each case the seventh of the series introduces a theme that is expanded in the chapters that follow. For example, the seventh plague (Revelation 16:17-21) announces the judgment of "great Babylon," and introduces the next three chapters which give details of the judgment of Babylon.[304]

The seventh seal mentions **"silence in heaven for about half an hour."** According to the pattern, this should be an introduction to what follows in the next few chapters, which is the seven trumpets. In other words, there is some sense in which the seven trumpets take place in a symbolic **"half an hour,"** during which there is **"silence in heaven."**

The seven trumpets are a series of severe disasters that fall upon nature and people, often destroying a third of what is stricken. In the chiasm outline they are mirrored by the seven last plagues, and in fact the trumpet plagues seem to

be a limited version of the seven last plagues.[305] By correlating texts that have to do with disastrous plagues or judgments, silence in heaven, and hours (**"half an hour"**), a pattern begins to emerge.

Plague judgments in the Book of Revelation are portrayed symbolically as taking place in one hour. For example, the judgments on Babylon take place in one hour ("Alas, alas that great city Babylon, that mighty city! For in *one hour* has your judgment come" Revelation 18:10, see also vs. 17 and 19). The final judgment takes place in a symbolic "hour" ("the *hour* of His judgment has come" Revelation 14:7). Most relevant to the seventh seal is "the hour of trial, which shall come upon all the world, to test those that dwell on the earth" (Revelation 3:10).

This "hour of trial" is called the "time of trouble" in Job 38:23. The Greek Septuagint version calls this the "hour" of trouble, using the same root word (*ora*) which is used for *"hour of trial"* in Revelation 3:10 and *"half an hour"* in Revelation 8:1.

The time of trouble or "hour of trial" seems to be divided into two parts. The seventh seal mentions **"half an hour,"** and is followed by the seven-trumpet plagues. During this period heaven is silent—**"there was silence in heaven for about half an hour."** Apparently this is a period when God does not intervene, because in scripture, when God intervenes he no longer keeps silent. "Our God shall come, and *shall not keep silent*; A fire shall devour before Him... He shall call to the heavens from above, and to the earth, that He may judge His people...But to the wicked God says:...These things you have

---

304 The seventh church ends with the statement, "To him who overcomes I will grant to sit with Me on My throne, as I also overcame and sat down with My Father on His throne." The following chapters show the Father on His throne and the judgment drama that allows humanity to sit with Him on His throne. Likewise, the seventh trumpet (Revelation 11:15-19) introduces the theme of the final executive judgment ("the nations were angry, and your wrath has come, and the time of the dead, that they should be judged, and to give the reward to your servants the prophets, and to the saints, and to those who fear your name, small and great; and to destroy those who destroy the earth" v. 18). This is followed by chapters 12-20 which explain in detail how, why and upon whom these judgments will be meted out.

305 For example, the second trumpet involves a mountain thrown into the sea turning a third of the sea to blood, while the second plague is poured on the sea and it all becomes blood. The third trumpet falls on a third of the rivers and waters and makes them blood while the third plague is poured on all the rivers and springs and they became blood, etc.

done and *I kept silent*;...But I will rebuke you... Now consider this, you who forget God, lest I tear you in pieces, and there be none to deliver" (Psalms 50:3,4,16,21,22). "Behold, it is written before Me: *I will not keep silence*, but will repay—even repay into their bosom—your iniquities and the iniquities of your fathers together" (Isaiah 65:6,7).

In these verses we see a period of silence ("I kept silent") in which God does not intervene, but during this time He gives the ungodly an opportunity to "consider this, you who forget God, lest I tear you in pieces." In other words, God sends a powerful warning and a call to repentance before he sends His judgments. This time of silence correlates with the **"half an hour"** in which the trumpet plagues take place. This is followed by the remainder of the "hour of trial" in which God "shall not keep silence, but will repay...your iniquities"— in other words, the time for repentance is over and God sends His judgments. This correlates with the Seven Last Plagues.

Diagram 8.1 illustrates the two parts of the "hour of trial" (also called the time of trouble and the great tribulation).

The Trumpets

If God is keeping silent (not intervening) during the seven-trumpet plagues, then who is bringing on the plagues? A number of features of the plagues make it obvious that the trumpets are Satan's activity, a counterfeit of the seven last plagues.

First of all, the trumpet plagues affect a third—a third of the sea, a third of the living creatures, a third of the ships, a third of the rivers and springs of water, a third of the sun, moon and stars, killing a third of mankind (Revelation 8:8-12, 9:15,18). In Revelation 12:4 we see that it is the fiery red dragon, Satan, who "drew a third of the stars of heaven, and cast them to the earth." Damaging a third indicates satanic activity.

God, being love, must by His very nature share and give; even the Godhead itself is a Trinity, in which the outgoing principle of love is expressed among the three members. One-third is the anti-trinity, reflecting Satan's desire to have all the glory himself, sharing with no one. Thus one-third is a Satanic number, and the trumpets with their destruction of **"a third"** show the results of his activity.

In chapter 7 we saw an "angel ascending from the east having the seal of the living God" restraining "four angels, standing at the four corners of the earth holding the four winds of the earth." We saw that the four angels are agents of Satan who will be "granted" permission to harm the earth, sea and trees (see 7:1 *The Four Winds*). The seven trumpets begin with disasters that harm the earth, sea and trees, showing that they are a result of the activity of Satan's "four angels."

Moreover, the "king" in charge of the fifth plague is specifically identified as "the angel of the bottomless pit," Satan (Revelation 9:11). The sixth trumpet plague involves the release of "the

Diagram 8.1

Hour Of Trial (Time Of Trouble)

Silence for Half an Hour	Shall Not Keep Silent
Seven Trumpets	Seven Last Plagues

four angels who are bound at the great river Euphrates" (Revelation 9:14). The Euphrates runs through the center of Satan's Babylon kingdom, and when God acts in the seven last plagues, He dries up the waters of the Euphrates.[306]

The last three trumpets are called "woes" (Revelation 8:13, 9:12, 11:14). The only other use of the word "woe" in the Book of Revelation shows that the source is the activity of Satan— "Woe to the inhabitants of the earth and sea! For the devil has come down to you, having great wrath, because he knows that he has but a short time" (Revelation 12:12).

Finally, one of the main purposes of trumpets in scripture is to warn God's people of the approach of their enemies.[307] **"And I saw the seven angels which stood before God; and to them were given seven trumpets"** (Revelation 8:2). Angels are blowing trumpets, warning God's people that Satan, who has to a certain extent been bound or restrained (as pictured by the "four angels standing at the four corners of the earth, holding the four winds" Revelation 7:1) is now going to be loosed and allowed to bring destruction. The fact that God does not restrain Satan is called **"silence in heaven."** It is analogous on a world scale to what happened in the book of Job—Satan challenged God, and so God gave him "permission" to try to prove his point by attacking Job ("Behold, he is in your power" Job 1:10-12).[308] With the trumpets Satan will use

an expanded strategy: instead of simply attacking God's people, as Satan did with Job, he will also create general chaos and destruction which will be attributed to God's faithful children, in an attempt make them targets for persecution so as to destroy their faith (see 11:7-10 *The Two Witnesses Killed*).[309]

8:3 The Golden Censer

The interpretation that God's protection is suspended during the trumpets is supported by the next scene—the casting down of the censer. **"And another angel came and stood at the altar, having a golden censer; and there was given to him much incense, that he should offer it with the prayers of all the saints on the golden altar which was before the throne. And the smoke of the incense, with the prayers of the saints, ascended up before God out of the angel's hand"** (Revelation 8:3).

A censer is a small metal container suspended by cords or chains full of burning incense which produces a cloud of aromatic smoke. The censer was used by the priests in the Old Testament temple service.[310] On the Day of Atonement the high priest took a censer of incense with him into the Most Holy Place. It gave off a cloud of smoke, veiling him from the direct glory of God, "lest he die" (Leviticus 16:12,13). The censer was thus an instrument of mediation and protection.

In the story of the rebellion of Korah, Dathan and Abiram at the time of Moses in the wilderness (Numbers 16) it is obvious that the censer

---

306 Revelation 16:12.

307 "They have blown the trumpet and made everyone ready" (Ezekiel 714). See also Nehemiah 4:18-20, Jeremiah 4:5,6,19-21, 6:1, Ezekiel 33:1-6, Joel 2:1-12.

308 See Appendix 8 for a discussion of the great controversy in the book of Job. Even when God allowed Satan access to Job, he still limited his destructive activities ("all that he has is in your power, only do not lay a hand on his person... Behold, he is in your hand, but spare his life" (Job 1:12, 2:6). Likewise, in the time of trouble, Satan will be released, but will still have limits (for example, in the fifth trumpet he can only harm "those men who do not have the seal of God in their foreheads" Revelation 9:4).

309 God accepts responsibility for the destruction he allows Satan to bring about. It was Satan who "went out from the presence of the Lord" and destroyed Job's property and his children, and yet when he returned to again accuse Job, God told him "you incited Me against him, to destroy him without cause" (Job 2:3). The ultimate example of God taking responsibility for the sins of His creatures is Jesus taking upon himself the sins of the world and dying the second death in the place of sinful humans.

310 2Chronicles 26:18,19, Hebrews 9:4.

represents intercession and protection from destruction. These leaders, along with 250 others, challenged Moses saying that they also should be able to officiate as priests since "all the congregation is holy, every one of them" (Numbers 16:3). God showed His rejection of their rebellious premise by opening the earth and swallowing up the leaders and bringing fire down from heaven which burned up the rebel followers.

Despite the obvious action of God, "on the next day all the congregation of the children of Israel complained against Moses and Aaron, saying, 'You have killed the people of the Lord.' And the Lord spoke to Moses, saying 'Get away from among this congregation that I may consume them in a moment'...So Moses said to Aaron, '*Take a censer* and put fire in it from the altar, put incense on it, and take it quickly to the congregation *and make atonement for them*; for wrath has gone out from the Lord. The plague has begun.' Then Aaron took it as Moses commanded, and ran into the midst of the assembly...So he put in the incense and made atonement for the people. *And he stood between the dead and the living; so the plague was stopped*" (vs. 44-48).

The censer represented the intervention or mediation that protected the people from the destructive judgments they deserved. Those who have refused God's offer of grace and have continued in sin deserve to be in the hands of Satan, the leader they have chosen, who wants nothing more than to destroy them. Jesus, in His great love and mercy, intercedes for sinners, represented here by the angel with a golden censer. But the issues involved in the great controversy between God and Satan necessitate that someday that intervention and protection will be suspended for a brief period of time.[311] When the censer is thrown down God's protection will be withdrawn (**"silence in heaven"**) and the seven-trumpet plagues will begin.

Are the Trumpets Past or Future?

One of the important considerations concerning the trumpets is their chronology—have they already taken place in history, or are they still in the future, and if they are future, how do they relate to the time of trouble, the close of probation, the rapture of the church, and the Second Coming? Since the trumpets comprise nearly twenty percent of the Book of Revelation, it is important to get the context correct.

Some commentators teach that the trumpets give a review of some aspects of history, comparing the pattern in the book of Daniel in which there are a series of visions that review the historical progression of world empires, with each consecutive vision covering the same history and adding more details. However, there are a number of problems with applying this pattern to the trumpet plagues.

First of all, the book of Daniel is a series of visions, interspersed with stories from Daniel's life in Babylon. The Book of Revelation, in contrast, presents itself as one continuous vision with a number of scenes, more like one of the visions

---

311 See chapter 12 for an analysis of the issues and details of the great controversy between Satan and God. Satan's whole point in tempting and harassing God's followers is to get them to misrepresent God and thus prove that God is not worthy of worship and allegiance.

of Daniel than the book of Daniel.[312] Moreover, the elements of the repetitive visions of Daniel have obvious correlations with each other, but this is not the case in the series of seven churches, seals and trumpets in Revelation.[313] The chiastic structure organizes the Book of Revelation and aids in its understanding rather than the repetition-of-history structure that is used in the book of Daniel.

The internal context of the trumpets does not allow them to be placed in the distant historical past. In chapter 7 the angel from the rising sun told the four angels to hold "the four winds of the earth that the wind should not blow on the earth, nor on the sea, nor on any tree'...saying, 'hurt not the earth, neither the sea, nor the trees, until we have sealed the servants of our God in their foreheads" (Revelation 7:1-3). In the next verses this sealing is shown to be that of the 144,000—"And I heard the number of those which were sealed: and there were sealed 144,000 of all the tribes of the children of Israel" (v. 4). The sealing of the 144,000 is clearly an end time event, as discussed in chapters seven and fourteen. As the trumpets begin, the destruction falls on the earth, sea and trees, the very things that were to be spared until after the sealing of the 144,000; thus these trumpets must be last day events as well.

Furthermore, the locusts of the fifth trumpet were "commanded...that they should not hurt the grass of the earth, nor any green thing, nor any tree; but only those men who do not have the seal of God in their foreheads" (Revelation 9:4). Although there are a number of seals spoken of in the scriptures,[314] this text refers to a specific seal, "the seal of God in their foreheads." This is identified in Revelation 7:3,4 as the sealing of the 144,000, so the fifth trumpet takes place after the sealing of the 144,000 rather than in the historical past.

The locust army itself (Revelation 9:3-12) is the same army mentioned in the book of Joel (see 9:3 *The Locust Army*). The context is the "day of the Lord" (Joel 1:15), when "the sun and moon grow dark" (2:10). The battle of the locust army in turn correlates with the final battle between the King of the North and the King of the South, which takes place "at the time of the end" (Daniel 11:40, see 9: *Kings of the North and South*).

Finally, attempts to find an application of the seven trumpets in history have resulted in fantastic, speculative interpretations of the

---

312 The book of Daniel does have repetitions of history. However, each repetition is part of an obviously distinct vision in which the prophet tells the date of the vision, often the location where it took place and his own personal situation. For example, the vision in chapter 8 of the ram, the goat and the "little horn" begins "in the third year of the reign of King Belshazzar...I was in Shushan, the citadel, which is in the province of Elam, and I saw in the vision that I was by the river Ulai" (Daniel 8:1,2. See also Daniel 2:1, 7:1, 9:1, 10:1,4). The Book of Revelation does not have these kinds of obvious divisions; John only gives the setting of the vision once at the beginning (Revelation 1:9,10).

Moreover, the historical portion of each of the visions of Daniel starts at the time of the vision rather than some years earlier or later. In contrast, most of the historical interpretations of the seven churches, seals and trumpets begin not at the time of John's exile on Patmos (usually thought to be about AD 95) but at an earlier or later date.

313 The details of the various visions of Daniel can be correlated with each other. For example, the iron legs and ten toes of the fourth kingdom of Daniel 2 correlate with the iron teeth and ten horns of the fourth empire of chapter 7. Likewise the four heads of the third empire of chapter 7 correlate with the four horns which came up toward the four winds of heaven of chapter 8, and also correlate with the "kingdom...divided toward the four winds of heaven" of chapter 11.

In contrast, the symbols and details of the trumpets cannot be correlated with the other "historical" passages (the seven churches and seven seals, according to those who hold this theory). For example, the elements of the first trumpet are hail, fire, blood, trees, green grass and burning up. These do not correlate with the elements of the first church (seven stars, golden lampstands, false apostles) or with the elements of the first seal (the first living creature, a voice like thunder, a white horse, a bow, crowns, conquering activity). Likewise the other trumpets do not correlate with their "corresponding" seals or churches.

314 These include the sealing of the Holy Spirit (Ephesians 1:13, 4:30, 2Corinthians 1:22), the seal of circumcision (Romans 4:11) and the seal of apostleship (1Corinthians 9:2).

symbols, the assigning of historical importance to obscure events which do not even appear in a standard encyclopedia, and the ignoring of some of the details of the prophecies which, if they are actually a part of history, should be readily identifiable.[315]

Other scholars have concluded that the trumpets take place after the "close of probation," that the throwing down of the censer shows that Jesus no longer mediates in the heavenly sanctuary, so forgiveness of sins is no longer possible after this point. It is true that during the sixth trumpet "the rest of the men who were not killed by these plagues did not repent" (Revelation 9:21). However, John was told that he "must prophesy again" (Revelation 10:11), and after the ministry of the "two witnesses" (Revelation 11:1-13) "the remnant were afraid, and gave glory to the God of heaven" (vs.11, 13). This is an obvious response to the great appeal of Revelation 14:7, "Fear God and give glory to Him," an appeal that takes place before the close of probation (see 15:5-8, *The Close of Probation.*)

Moreover, when the seventh trumpet sounds "the temple of God was opened in heaven, and there was seen in His temple the ark of his covenant" (Revelation 11:19), implying that the door of mercy is still open. It is not until the seven last plagues are about to fall that "the temple was filled with smoke from the glory of God and from His power, and no one was able to enter the temple" (Revelation 15:8). This is the end of probation, not the throwing down of the censer.

Finally, many evangelical commentators have placed the trumpets after the rapture of the church, in other words, after the faithful Christians have been taken to heaven before the time of trouble. This theory does not have scriptural support (see 9: *The Rapture— When?* and Appendix 4). This commentary takes the position that the seven trumpets take place during the time of trouble, after the sealing of the 144,000 and before the close of probation, and that during the time of the seven trumpets God makes a final, powerful appeal for repentance to those who are in "Babylon."

Are the Trumpets Literal or Symbolic?

Another important consideration is whether the figures used in the trumpets should be considered to be fairly literal, or instead are highly symbolic or metaphorical. Obviously, much of Revelation is highly symbolic, but the extensive use of simile[316] in the first six trumpets (chapters eight and nine) suggests a fairly literal interpretation. John saw "something *like* a great mountain burning with fire…the appearance of the locusts was *like* horses prepared for battle…their faces were *as* the faces of men" etc. The words for *like* and *as* (Greek *hos, omios*) are used to indicate a similarity between two things that are compared rather than a metaphorical or symbolic usage.

This understanding is supported by the chiastic pairing of the trumpets with the seven last plagues (see 1: *Chiastic Literary Structure*). One of the helpful features of the chiastic organization is that it allows a comparison of the analogous

---

315 In the historicist interpretation of Daniel, every beast, metal, and horn can be identified in the well-known facts of history. This is in contrast, for example, to the locusts of Revelation 9:7-10 with their hair like women's hair, teeth like lions' teeth, breastplates of iron, wings with a sound like chariots and tails like scorpions. Most commentators who support a historical interpretation do not even attempt to make an application of these details.

316 Simile is "a figure of speech in which two distinct things are compared by using "like" or "as," as in "she is like a rose." Compare metaphor, which is the application of a word or phrase to an object or concept it does not literally denote…(a) symbol" *Random House Webster's College Dictionary*, (New York, NY, Random House, 1997)

sections to see if the corresponding section uses images and figures in a literal or a highly symbolic way. The section analogous to the seven trumpets is the seven last plagues/judgment of Babylon. The seven last plagues themselves use figures which seem to be fairly literal. For example, the first plague causes "a terrible and grievous sore...on the men who had the mark of the beast" (Revelation 16:2). There is nothing to indicate that this is not a literal sore, especially since later "they blasphemed the God of heaven because of their pains and their sores" (v.11). The sea and water becoming like blood (vs.3,4), the sun scorching men with great heat (v.8,9), the great earthquake (v.18) and great hail from heaven (v. 21) all seem to be literal.[317]

This is followed by the judgment of Babylon, which uses highly symbolic language, with beasts, horns, a woman, hills—and in this section there are explanations for a number of the symbols that are used.[318]

From this pattern we would expect that the seven trumpets would also have two sections, one relatively literal and the other more symbolic.[319] This seems to be the case, with a relatively literal section from Revelation 8:7 through 9:21 (the first six trumpets) followed by a symbolic section in chapters 10 and 11 (the seven thunders, the eating of the little book and the two witnesses).

8:5,6 Throwing Down the Censer

"And the angel took the censer, and filled it with fire of the altar, and cast it to the earth; and there were voices, and thunder, and lightning, and an earthquake. And the seven angels which had the seven trumpets prepared themselves to sound" (Revelation 8:5,6). At the beginning of chapter four the focus shifted from events on earth (the history of the church, as portrayed by the messages to the seven churches) to events in heaven ("come up here and I will show you things which must take place" Revelation 4:1). Heavenly events included the seating of the court (chapter 4), the challenge to the opening of the Book of Life (chapter 5) and the investigative judgment of the dead and the living (chapters 6 and 7). With the throwing down of the censer the attention and timeline is shifted back to events taking place on earth.[320]

The last view of God's people on earth was the Laodicean Church (Revelation 3:14-22). This church is comfortable and at ease, "in need of nothing." Jesus is seeking to enter into intimate fellowship ("I stand at the door and knock"). Apparently many will heed the invitation—while the "four angels" are restrained from releasing the winds of strife, God seals His special servants, the 144,000 (Revelation 7:1-4).

Obviously the 144,000 would have been a part of Laodicea, since she is the church of the end times. This part is called "the remnant" (see 12:17, *The Remnant*). But the complacency of the remainder of the people in Laodicea who are not sealed, as well as the rest of the people of the world

---

317 There are some symbols in this section such as the River Euphrates (v. 12) and the unclean spirits like frogs (v. 13). But even verse 13 uses simile rather than metaphor ("like frogs"), and is a reference to the plague of frogs in Egypt. As we will see in 16:13 *The Unholy Trinity*, the purpose of this figure is to show that the evil spirits "like frogs" will be everywhere.

318 For example, "the ten horns are ten kings...the waters which you saw, where the harlot sits, are peoples, multitudes, nations and tongues" (Revelation 17: 12, 15).

319 This phenomenon is also found in the seals (chapters 4 thorough 7) which are highly symbolic. Their analogous section, the executive judgment found in chapters 19 and 20, is also highly symbolic.

---

320 The language of chapter 8 emphasizes the shift from heaven to earth: "the angel took the censer...and cast it to the earth" (Revelation 8:5); "hail and fire...were cast on the earth" (verse 7); "a great mountain...was cast into the sea" (verse 8); "there fell a great star from heaven" (verse10); "Woe, woe, woe to the inhabitants of the earth because of...the trumpet[s]" (verse 13).

who are not part of the church, will be suddenly shattered by the throwing down of the golden censer and the releasing of the four winds. This should not be considered to be the end of Jesus' mediation to provide forgiveness for repenting sinners, nor is it the cutting off of the help of the Holy Spirit or of angels for His children who cry out to Him. It is the end of Jesus' intervention to protect the world from the destruction that they deserve and which Satan wants to inflict.

This is no doubt what the Apostle Paul referred to in 1 Thessalonians 5:3, "for when they say, 'peace and safety!' then sudden destruction comes upon them, as labor pains upon a pregnant woman. And they shall not escape." Just as labor pains are progressively more intense, there is an escalation in the severity of the destructive judgments through the seven trumpet plagues and into the seven last plagues, culminating in the seventh plague when God announces, "It is done!" and His "people shall be delivered" (Revelation 16:17, Daniel 12:1). But Paul emphasizes the "sudden destruction" which initiates the time of trouble. This sudden destruction begins with the first trumpet.

What is Satan trying to accomplish in bringing destruction upon the world? One purpose is to bring pain and grief to God by harming His children. Satan also seeks to misrepresent God, promoting the idea that God brings about the evil that in fact Satan himself causes, trying in this way to convince people that God is not worthy of their love and devotion. In the specific case of the seven trumpets, this destruction takes place after the sealing of the 144,000 (see below), and this group is a special demonstration to the universe of God's ability to sanctify a people who are steadfast in their love and loyalty to Him, even in the face of severe trials. Satan wants desperately to cause the 144,000 to lose their faith and turn their backs on God, and within the chaos and afflictions of the seven trumpet plagues he will seek opportunities to discourage or destroy the 144,000 and to keep people from responding to their message.

8:7-11 The First Three Trumpets

"The first angel sounded, and there followed hail and fire mingled with blood, and they were cast on the earth. And a third of the trees were burned up, and all green grass was burned up.

And the second angel sounded, and something like a great mountain burning with fire was cast into the sea; and a third of the sea became blood; And a third of the creatures which were in the sea, and had life, died; and a third of the ships were destroyed.

And the third angel sounded, and there fell a great star from heaven, burning like a lamp, and it fell on a third of the rivers, and on the fountains of waters. And the name of the star is called Wormwood; and a third of the waters became wormwood, and many men died of the waters, because they were made bitter" (Revelation 8:7-11).

The first three trumpets are fairly similar—hail and fire mingled with blood falling on the earth, a mountain burning with fire thrown into the sea turning it into blood, and a star burning like a torch making the waters bitter. Since these represent disasters which Satan will bring about in the future, it is largely a matter of conjecture as to what they will actually be. Jesus said "I tell you before it comes that when it does come to pass, you may believe" (John 13:19), and this principle applies here—God's followers will through the Holy Spirit recognize these disasters as the fulfillment of prophecy, and this will help them to know where they are in the stream of time.

That being said, there are a couple of fairly obvious candidates. One would be a collision of the earth with a comet or asteroid. A few years ago the comet Shoemaker-Levy 9 struck the planet Jupiter. As it approached the planet gravity tore it into pieces and it made a series of strikes, some large "chunks" (**"mountain burning"?**) and others smaller (**"hail and fire"?**). Whether the "dirty ice" of a comet could cause the type of fiery and poisonous destruction described in this passage is a question that science cannot yet answer. Many scientists believe that a strike by a huge asteroid caused enough destruction to wipe out the dinosaurs and many other forms of life. Regardless of whether this actually happened, computer models show that a collision with a large asteroid would cause massive destruction and climate change.

A more likely candidate would be a nuclear attack with multiple warheads. Besides the resulting fires which could destroy trees, grass and ships, the poisonous radiation would be like **"wormwood,"** contaminating water (making it "bitter") so that it would kill those who drank it. Since the trumpets are brought about by Satan's activity, it seems more likely that they would represent warfare which he could easily incite rather than a collision with a heavenly body like an asteroid or comet which he presumably does not control.[321] And in fact, the language of the rest of the trumpets points to a terrible armed conflict. For example, in the fifth trumpet John saw an army of "locusts" whose appearance was "like horses prepared for battle" and whose sound was "like the sound of chariots with many horses running into battle" (Revelation 9:7,9). As we will see in chapter 9, this is the same army and war that Joel and Daniel were shown. The sixth trumpet also involves a huge army—"the number of the army of the horsemen was two hundred million" who kill "a third of mankind...by the fire

and the smoke and the brimstone which came out of their mouths" (Revelation 9:16-18). The language and images all point to a global conflict incited and directed by Satan himself—"and they had as king over them the angel of the bottomless pit" (Revelation 9: 11).

8:12 The Fourth Trumpet

"And the fourth angel sounded, and a third of the sun was smitten, and a third of the moon, and a third of the stars, so a third of them was darkened; and the day did not shine for a third of it, and the night likewise" (Revelation 8:12). The fourth trumpet may simply be the atmospheric results of the first three trumpets. Whether a comet, an asteroid, nuclear bombs or something else, the kind of explosive destruction and fires described in the first three trumpets would cause dust and smoke to billow up into the atmosphere, causing darkness and severe weather disturbances. Little "ice ages" and summerless years have been geologically correlated with major volcanic eruptions, and computer models show that volcanoes, large asteroid strikes or extensive nuclear warfare with resulting dust and smoke could result in the partial obscuring of the sun. The emphasis that the plagues destroy "a third" may not be an attempt to quantify the extent of the destruction[322] as much as to identify its source—Satan, the "angel of the bottomless pit"

---

321 See Job 9:5-10.

322 This book takes the view that the first six trumpets describe a world war that primarily takes place in the Middle East (see 9:3 *The Locust Army*) but has a worldwide impact on humanity. Some commentators have assumed a much larger scope of the disaster, noting that a third of the sea turns to blood (v. 8) and envisioning a third of the oceans affected. But there are no references to the ocean in the Bible and the Greek word for sea that is used in Revelation (*Thalassa*) can refer to a lake (Sea of Galilee, Dead Sea) and most generally, to the Mediterranean Sea. Daniel, describing this war, points out that the King of the North (the Locust Army of Revelation 9) "shall plant his palace between the seas" (the Dead Sea and the Mediterranean Sea) (Daniel 11:45) and his army shall also be destroyed between the two seas (Joel 2:20), indicating a limited geographical scope of the seven-trumpets war.

who is introduced in the fifth trumpet, and who began his career of destruction by dragging down "a third of the stars of heaven" (Revelation 12:4).

"**And I beheld, and heard an angel flying in the midst of heaven, saying with a loud voice, 'Woe, woe, woe, to the inhabitants of the earth because of the remaining blasts of the trumpet of the three angels, which are yet to sound!'**" (Revelation 8:13). The chaos that results from the first four trumpet plagues set the stage for the three "woes" that follow. These will bring about the most extensive and intense period of suffering the world has known up to that time, and they will arrest the attention of every person living upon the earth. They will also prepare the way for the most powerful proclamation of the gospel that has ever taken place.

"The four angels who had been prepared for the hour and day and month and year, were released to kill a third of mankind." Rev. 9:15
Woodcut by Albrecht Durer 1498

Chapter 9

Revelation 9:1-21

9:1 And the fifth angel sounded, and I saw a star fallen from heaven to the earth; and to him was given the key of the bottomless pit.

9:2 And he opened the bottomless pit, and there arose smoke out of the pit, as the smoke of a great furnace; and the sun and the air were darkened because of the smoke of the pit.

9:3 And there came out of the smoke locusts on the earth; and to them was given power, as the scorpions of the earth have power.

9:4 And it was commanded them that they should not hurt the grass of the earth, nor any green thing, nor any tree; but only those men who do not have the seal of God in their foreheads.

9:5 And to them it was given that they should not kill them, but that they should be tormented five months; and their torment was as the torment of a scorpion, when it strikes a man.

9:6 And in those days men shall seek death, and shall not find it; and shall desire to die, and death shall flee from them.

9:7 And the appearance of the locusts was like horses prepared for battle; and on their heads were as it were crowns like gold, and their faces were as the faces of men.

9:8 And they had hair as the hair of women, and their teeth were like the teeth of lions.

9:9 And they had breastplates like breastplates of iron; and the sound of their wings was as the sound of chariots, of many horses running to battle.

9:10 And they had tails like scorpions, and there were stings in their tails; and their power was to hurt men five months.

9:11 And they had a king over them, the angel of the bottomless pit, whose name in Hebrew is Abaddon, but in the Greek language he has the name Apollyon.

9:12 One woe is past; and, behold, two woes are yet to come after these things.

9:13 And the sixth angel sounded, and I heard a voice from the four horns of the golden altar which is before God,

9:14 Saying to the sixth angel which had the trumpet, "Release the four angels which are bound at the great river Euphrates."

9:15 And the four angels were released, those prepared for the hour, and day, and month, and year, to slay a third of men.

9:16 And the number of the army of the horsemen was two hundred million: and I heard the number of them.

9:17 And thus I saw the horses in the vision, and those that sat on them, having breastplates of fire, and of hyacinth, and sulfur; and the heads of the horses were as the heads of lions; and out of their mouths issued fire and smoke and brimstone.

9:18 By these three a third of men were killed, by the fire, and by the smoke, and by the brimstone, which issued out of their mouths.

9:19 For their power is in their mouth, and in their tails, which were like serpents, having heads, and with them they do harm.

9:20 And the rest of the men who were not killed by these plagues did not repent of the works of their hands, that they should not worship demons, and idols of gold, and silver, and brass, and stone, and of wood, which can neither see, nor hear, nor walk.

9:21 Neither did they repent of their murders, nor of their sorceries, nor of their fornication, nor of their thefts.

9:1,2 The Bottomless Pit

"And the fifth angel sounded, and I saw a star fallen from heaven to the earth; and to him was given the key of the bottomless pit. And he opened the bottomless pit, and there arose smoke out of the pit, as the smoke of a great furnace; and the sun and the air were darkened because of the smoke of the pit" (Revelation 9:1,2).

The first two verses describing the fifth trumpet seem to be a review of the third and fourth trumpets. In the third trumpet "a great star fell from heaven."[323] The fourth trumpet shows the darkening of the sun, moon, stars, day, and night which results from the falling of the star. The fifth trumpet shows the specific cause of the darkness: **"the sun and air were darkened because of the smoke of the [bottomless] pit."** Apparently the **"star fallen from heaven"** of the fifth trumpet is not a new star,[324] but instead is referring to the same destructive "great star" that was portrayed in the third trumpet.[325] It causes the same darkness that was seen in the fourth trumpet. What is new in the fifth trumpet is the opening of **"the bottomless pit"** and the destructive forces that emerge from it.

The Greek word for bottomless pit, *abussos* (often translated abyss), is the same word that the Greek Septuagint uses to depict the watery, chaotic conditions of the earth before the first day

---

323 In the third trumpet the verb form for the word "fell" ("a great star fell from heaven," Revelation 8:10) is the simple past, pointing to the moment when the star fell. In the fifth trumpet John "saw a star fallen from heaven" (Revelation 9:1). The perfect participle of the verb, "fallen," is used to emphasize the aftermath and results of the falling.

324 There is the possibility that the "star fallen from heaven" who had "the key to the bottomless pit" is the same being as "the angel of the bottomless pit" (Revelation 9:11). It is true that stars are sometimes used as symbols for angels, but this usage seems less likely because 1) chapter 9 is not highly symbolic (see 8: *Trumpets: Literal or Symbolic?*). 2) It seems inconsistent that in verse 1 this entity would be called a star and in verse 9 an angel.

325 The translation of pronouns describing the two stars causes some confusion. In the third trumpet "a great star fell from heaven… and *it* fell on a third of the rivers" (Revelation 8:12). In the fifth trumpet John "saw a star fallen from heaven to the earth. To *him* was given the key to the bottomless pit" (Revelation 9:1). The implication is that the first star is a neuter "it" and the second is a personal "he." The Greek word for star, *astir*, is masculine in both passages. In the third trumpet there actually is no pronoun in the Greek, but if one were used in translation to English it should be "he" to be consistent with the gender of the word "star" and the pronoun usage in 9:1.

of creation[326] ("darkness was over the face of the *deep*" Genesis 1:2). *Abussos* is also used for the reservoirs of water that burst forth to destroy the earth at the time of the flood—"the fountains of the great *deep* were broken up" (Genesis 7:11). Demons begged Jesus not to send them to the abyss (Luke 8:31). The beast of Revelation 17, who is a manifestation of Satan himself, comes from the bottomless pit, (Revelation 17:8) and Satan will be chained in it for 1000 years (Revelation 20:1-3). Apparently the bottomless pit symbolizes both the earth in chaos and the dark, chaotic realm of Satan and the source of his destructive activity. As we will see later in this chapter, he is the **"angel"** and **"king"** of **"the bottomless pit"** under the name **"Abaddon"** or **"Apollyon,"** names which mean destroyer in Hebrew and Greek respectively (Revelation 9:11). The physical, social and spiritual chaos that results from the first four trumpets gives him a **"key"** or opportunity to bring about his "woes."

9:3, 7-9 The Locust Army

"And there came out of the smoke locusts on the earth; and to them was given power, as the scorpions of the earth have power...And the appearance of the locusts was like horses prepared for battle; and on their heads were as it were crowns like gold, and their faces were as the faces of men. And they had hair as the hair of women, and their teeth were like the teeth of lions. And they had breastplates like breastplates of iron; and the sound of their wings was as the sound of chariots, of many horses running to battle" (Revelation 9:3, 7-9).

---

326 The first day of creation in Genesis 1 was not the beginning of matter. Obviously the earth existed (covered with water—see Genesis 1:2) and in fact there was even life in other parts of the universe (Job 38:4-7). It is interesting to note that before God began his creative work the world was a "bottomless pit" and at the end of time when He withdraws His protection the world returns to that condition.

Notice that John uses the comparative words "like" and "as" to describe the locusts— **"like horses prepared for battle...hair *as* the hair of women...their teeth were *like* lion's teeth... the sound of their wings was *as* the sound of chariots."** The use of simile is also found in the description of the horses in verse 17. This contrasts with scenes in other chapters, for example, the "woman clothed with the sun, with the moon under her feet, and on her head a garland of twelve stars" (Revelation 12:1), which are obviously symbols. The use of the comparative in chapter 9 shows that John was not using symbols, but instead he was trying to describe something literal, and having never seen anything like it before he had to use simile. This, along with the chiastic pairing of the trumpet plagues with the literal seven last plagues of chapter 16 show that this chapter is depicting real events rather than highly symbolic metaphors (see 8: *Are The Trumpets Literal or Symbolic?*).

But real does not mean familiar. The fact that the locusts come out of the bottomless pit suggests that there is something demonic about them since the bottomless pit is not just chaotic conditions of the earth, but is also the prison of demons. Both Peter and Jude reveal that "the angels who did not keep their proper domain, but left their own abode, He has reserved in everlasting chains under darkness for the judgment of the great day" (Jude 6, 2Peter 2:4). Apparently during the seven trumpets the demons will be released from their chains (come out of the bottomless pit) and will add their maddening influence to the horrors of the trumpet war. The demons who possessed the two demoniacs from Gadarenes begged Jesus not to send them into the abyss. When He allowed them to enter a herd of swine their maddening influence caused the swine to plunge over a cliff to their death (Luke 8: 26-33). This kind of influence will affect the locust army as they are goaded on by the demons that will be released from the bottomless pit. As we will see below, the locust army is a real army, but there is a demonic element and intensity involved in their attack on **"those men who do not have the seal of God in their foreheads"** (Revelation 9:4).

The war that is described is the most extensive and the most destructive of all time. As we will see in the sixth trumpet, it will involve 200 million soldiers and a third of mankind will be killed. We would expect that a war of this magnitude which takes place during the last days would be mentioned in other prophecies, and this is the case. Daniel tells the story of a war that lasts for 2,500 years.[327] The last battle takes place during "the time of the end" when "the King of the South shall attack [the King of the North], and the King of the North shall come against him like a whirlwind, with chariots, horsemen and with many ships, and he shall enter the countries, overwhelm them, and pass through" (Daniel 11:40).

The prophet Joel also describes a war that takes place in the last days, the invasion of a locust army. A careful comparison shows that the army of the final King of the North, the locust army in the book of Joel, and the locust army of the fifth trumpet are the same. First of all, the locust army that John saw in Revelation 9 and the locust army in the book of Joel are one and the same. (See Table 9.1)

Table 9.1

Locust Army of Revelation 9:3-11	Locust Army of Joel
The fifth angel sounded [his trumpet] (v.1).	Blow the trumpet in Zion (2:15).
There came out of the smoke locusts (v.3).	The swarming locust…My great army (2:25).
The appearance of the locusts was like horses (v.7).	Their appearance is like the appearance of horses (2:4).
Their teeth were like lions' teeth (v. 8).	His teeth are the teeth of a lion (1:6).
The sound of their wings was as the sound of chariots, of many horses (v 9).	Like swift steeds, so they run, with a noise like chariots (2:5).
Their power was to hurt men…their torment was as the torment of a scorpion when it strikes a man (vs. 10, 5)	Before them the people writhe in pain (2:6).

---

327 The vision of Daniel 11 begins with the "kings of Persia" (Daniel 11:2). The kings mentioned (Cambyses, Darius Hystaspis, Xerxes) reigned from 525 BC through 465 BC. The struggle between the King of the North and the King of the South began after the death of Alexander the Great (324 BC) with the feud between the Hellenistic kingdoms in Syria (north) and Egypt (south). The war continues until "the time of the end" and the "time of trouble" (Daniel 11:40, 12:1).

From the description in Joel it is obvious that these are not literal locusts, but rather an army which the prophet saw but could not adequately describe with the vocabulary of the time.[328]

"For a *nation* has come up against my land" (Joel 1:6).

"A people come, great and strong" (2:2).

"The locust…. my great army, which I sent among you" (2:25).[329]

"Over mountaintops they leap, with a noise of a flaming fire that devours the stubble, like a strong people set in battle array…They run like mighty men, they climb the wall like men of war; every one marches in formation, and they do not break ranks. They do not push one another; every one marches in his own column. Though they lunge between the weapons, they are not cut down…the earth quakes before them, the heavens tremble (Joel 2:5-10).

9:4-6 A Real War

Since the locust army of Revelation nine is the same as that described in Joel, its activity would also represent some kind of military equipment and operation. One artist has rendered a compelling comparison of literal locusts and attack helicopters.[330] The weaponry of the locusts seems to be somewhat unconventional, causing severe pain but not death—perhaps chemical, biological or radiation. **"And it was commanded them that they should not hurt the grass of the earth, nor any green thing, nor any tree; but only those men who do not have the seal of God in their foreheads. And to them it was given that they should not kill them, but that they should be tormented five months; and their torment was as the torment of a scorpion, when it strikes a man. And in those days men shall seek death, and shall not find it; and shall desire to die, and death shall flee from them"** (Revelation 9:4-6).

The picture that emerges is that out of the chaos which results from what seems to be a catastrophic military attack, perhaps nuclear (the first four trumpets), comes a major military operation that causes intense suffering. God's people, protected by the **"seal of God in their foreheads,"** are shielded, even as the children of Israel in Egypt were protected from the plagues which fell upon the Egyptians.[331] Since wars involve at least two sides, it is reasonable to think that the first four trumpets represent a preemptive attack, and the fifth trumpet is a retaliation. A careful comparison of the prophecies of Revelation 9, Joel, and Daniel 11 gives some intriguing clues as to the identity of the antagonists.

Joel indicates that the locust army will be defeated. "But I will remove far from you the northern army, and will drive him away into a barren and desolate land, with his face toward the eastern sea and his back toward the western sea. His stench will come up, and his foul odor will rise, because he has done monstrous things" (Joel 2:20). There are four points of particular interest in this passage: 1) This army is called the northern army (the ancient Hebrew and Greek read "the northern one" or "the from the north"). 2) The northern army will come to its end. 3) Defeat will take place between the two seas of Palestine, the eastern sea (the Dead Sea) and the western sea (the Mediterranean). 4) This will take place during "the Day of the Lord" when "the sun and moon grow dark" (Joel 2: 1, 10), in other words, the time of the end.

---

328 Locusts are used elsewhere to symbolize armies, see for example Jeremiah 51:17,22.

329 God calls them His army, even though they are agents of Satan, just as he did the Babylonians who, though controlled by Satan, accomplished God's purpose of chastening His people who had fallen into idolatry (Jeremiah 25:9, 51:7).

330 Joe Maniscalco, slide program "Revelation 9 and the Neutron Bomb."

331 Genesis 8:22,23, 9:4, 26, 10:23, 11:5-7.

Kings of the North and South

The same identifying points that Joel used to describe the end of the "northern army" are also found in Daniel 11:40-45 describing the fate of the "King of the North."[332] At the "time of the end" (Daniel 11:40) he will invade "the Glorious Land" (Palestine, v. 41) and he will "plant the tents of his palace between the seas (the Dead Sea and the Mediterranean). But he "shall come to his end, and no one will help him" (v. 45). Comparing these developments with the description of the defeat of the northern locust army of Joel described in the previous section, we see that the final King of the North is the same as Joel's northern locust army (which is the same as the locust army of the fifth trumpet of Revelation 9).

Apparently the first five trumpets represent the beginning of the last battle in a fierce contest that has been ongoing for nearly 2,500 years: the war between the Kings of the North and the Kings of the South. The details of this war are presented in the vision of Daniel 11, which is analyzed in Appendix 3. Although it is written in a style that is difficult to understand, there are a number of "landmarks" which make it possible to identify who these antagonists are through the progression of history and at the end of time.[333] Keep in mind while reading the brief analysis of Daniel 11 given here or the fairly extensive analysis in Appendix 3 that the previous discussion showed that the last army of the King of the North is the same as Joel's locust army, which is the same as the locust army of Revelation 9. Thus the last battle of the King of the North and the King of the South is the same war that is described in the seven trumpets.

The vision of Daniel 11 begins with the kings of Persia and shows their defeat by Alexander the Great (vs. 1-3). His Hellenistic (Greek) Empire was divided after his death and two of the divisions were the King of the North (the Seleucid Empire in Syria), and the King of the South (the Ptolemaic Empire in Egypt, vs. 4-15). Both of these Hellenistic kingdoms were defeated by Rome, which became the new King of the North, first under the Caesars and then ruled by the Papacy (vs. 15-24). The King of the South, who is not mentioned during the pagan Roman era, reappears in the Middle Ages as the Islamic Ottoman Empire and the war resumes with the Crusades (vs. 25-30).

Consistent with the parallel visions in Daniel 7 and 8 there is a major focus on the doctrinal compromises of the medieval Papacy (taking away the daily sacrifices) and the persecution of

---

332 "At the time of the end the King of the South shall attack him; and the King of the North shall come against him like a whirlwind, with chariots, horsemen, and with many ships; and he shall enter the countries, overwhelm them, and pass through. He shall also enter the Glorious land [Palestine]." Here we see an initial attack by the "king of the South" against the "king of the North" (the first four trumpets?). The "northern army" of the king of the North makes a fierce "whirlwind" counterattack with "chariots, horsemen, and with many ships" (the fifth-trumpet counterattack of the locust army?). "But tidings out of the east and the north shall trouble him [the king of the North]; therefore he shall go out with great fury to destroy and annihilate many. And he shall plant the tents of his palace *between the seas* [between the Dead Sea and the Mediterranean] in the glorious holy mountain [Palestine]; yet he shall *come to his end*, and no one will help him" (Daniel 11:44, 45).

333 For example, in Daniel 11:3,4 there is a "mighty king" whose kingdom "shall be divided toward the four winds of heaven." A comparison with the vision of chapter 8 shows that this is Alexander the Great and the division of his kingdom to form the Hellenistic kingdoms. This shows that the kings of the North and South begin as the Hellenistic kingdoms. Verse 22 mentions "the prince of the covenant," Jesus, showing that the King of the North has evolved into the Roman Empire. Verse 31 mentions the attack upon the daily sacrifices and setting up of the abomination of desolation. A comparison with Daniel 8:10,11 shows that this attack is by the medieval Papacy, which has become the King of the North. A review of history shows that the antagonist from the south (the King of the South of the Middle Ages) was the Ottoman Empire and the battles were the crusades. Finally, verse 40 is set in "the time of the end." With this skeleton outline the details in between can be deduced from the major facts of history.

God's faithful remnant (the abomination of desolation). During this time the King of the South disappears again, consistent with the long decline of the Ottoman Empire (31-39).

The major focus of Daniel 11 (vs. 23-39) on the King of the North as the medieval papacy is consistent with the focus of the visions of Daniel chapter 7 (the "little" horn which "shall speak pompous words against the most high" and "shall persecute the saints"),[334] of chapter 8 (the "little" horn which "cast down some of the host," takes away "the daily sacrifice" and sets up "the transgression of desolation")[335] and of Revelation 13 (the beast which rose out of the sea and "opened his mouth in blasphemy against God" and "made war with the saints").[336] All of these refer to the persecuting papal power of the Middle Ages. A comparison of the four visions show that they have many elements in common, confirming their identity and filling out details not found in any one vision by itself. (See Table 9.2)

Table 9.2

Daniel 7 Little Horn	Daniel 8 Little Horn	Daniel 11 King of the North	Revelation 13 First Beast
Another horn, a little one …whose appearance was greater than his fellows (vs.8,20).	A little horn which grew exceedingly great (v. 8).	He shall come up and become strong with a small number of people (v. 23).	I saw a beast rising up (v. 1).
He shall speak pompous words against the Most High (v. 25).	He even exalted himself as high as the Prince of the host (v. 11).	He…shall speak blasphemies against the God of gods (v. 36).	He opened his mouth in blasphemy against God (v. 6).
He shall persecute the saints of the Most High (v. 25).	It cast down some of the host and some of the stars to the ground, and trampled them (v. 10).	They shall fall by sword and flame, by captivity and plundering (v. 33).	It was granted to him to make war with the saints and to overcome them (v. 7).
He shall persecute… for a time, times and half a time (v. 25).	It refers to many days in the future (v. 26).	For many days they shall fall by the sword (v. 33).	He was given authority to continue for forty-two months (v. 5).
He shall intend to change times and law (v. 25).	By him the daily sacrifices were taken away, and the place of His sanctuary was cast down (v. 11).	Shall defile the sanctuary fortress; then they shall take away the daily sacrifices (v. 31).	To blaspheme…His tabernacle (v. 6).
The same horn was making war against the saints, and prevailing (v. 21).	An army was given over to the horn…He did all this and prospered (v. 12).	The king shall do according to his own will…and shall prosper (v. 36).	All the world marveled …saying, 'Who is like the beast? Who is able to make war with him?' (vs. 3,4).

---

334 Daniel 7:25.

335 Daniel 8:9-14.

336 Revelation 13:1-10.

The point of these comparisons is that since these four powers are obviously the same, it is possible to learn details about one from the activity of the others. You may have wondered why the visions of Daniel and Revelation 13 seem to spend such an inordinate amount of attention on the medieval Papacy. The reason is because it is from Daniel and Revelation 13 that we learn the characteristics and strategies of the end-time persecuting power. In particular, in Revelation 13 we see that "the beast rising out of the sea" recovers from a "deadly wound" and forms an alliance with the "beast coming up out of the earth" which sets up the image, mark and number of the beast. In chapters 13 and 17 we will see that this alliance consists of the United States of America with oppressive religious leadership, acting as the military arm of a "reborn" Roman Catholic Papacy with "the beast from the bottomless pit" at its head and supported by an international alliance of "10 kings." This alliance is also the last King of the North, Joel's "northern" locust army, and the locust army of Revelation chapter nine.

At the "time of the end" the King of the South will reappear ("the King of the South shall attack him"), and it will be this offensive which provokes the extreme reaction of the King of the North who "shall come against him like a whirlwind" (Daniel 11:40). Since the last-days King of the North is an evolution of the medieval papal King of the North, it is most likely that the last-days King of the South will be an evolution of the Islamic powers that fought against Europe during the Middle Ages.[337] With this in mind, this verse seems to predict the resurgence of militant Islam (the King of the South) with a powerful, coordinated end-time attack against the King of the North (the United States, Europe and other allies) that ushers in the time of trouble.[338]

This is the attack that is described in the first four trumpets and the retaliation that is described in the fifth trumpet. As Daniel puts it, their armies "with chariots, horsemen and with many ships shall enter the countries, overwhelm them, and pass through" (Daniel 11:40). The part of the world where this takes place is specified—"Edom, Moab, and...Ammon" (present-day Jordan, v. 41), and Egypt, Libya and Ethiopia are mentioned (vs. 42, 43). A crushing defeat will take place "between the seas and the glorious holy mountain" (in Palestine, v. 45). Apparently this is World War III, fought in the Middle East, and it will be the beginning of a period of inconceivable suffering—"At that time Michael [Jesus][339] shall stand up, the great prince who stands watch over the sons of your people; and there shall be a time of trouble such as never was since there was a nation, even to that time" (Daniel 12:1). But God will save his people—"at that time your people shall be delivered, every one who is found written in the book."

---

337 This is supported by the geographical location of the final battle—Israel ("the glorious land"), Egypt, Libya and Jordan ("Edom, Moab and...Ammon") are specifically mentioned (Daniel 11:41).

338 In chapter eight it was pointed out that the great time of trouble has two parts—the seven trumpets (chapters 8-11), which are Satan's attempt to defeat God's people, and the seven last plagues (chapters 15-19), which are God's rescue of His people.

339 See 12: 7-9 *Michael Casts Satan Out* for the evidence that Michael is the title used for Jesus when He confronts Satan. Jesus sitting refers to His ministry of mediation— "We have such a High Priest, who is seated at the right hand of the throne of the Majesty in the heavens...He is also able to save to the uttermost those who come to God through Him, since He always lives to make intercession for them" (Hebrews 8: 1, 7:25). His standing up means the end of His mediation, in other words, the end of probation (see 15: 5-8 *The Close of Probation*").

This scenario for the "trumpet war" has mentioned elements from a number of prophecies. To summarize:

- The seven trumpets describe a war during the first portion of the time of trouble.
- One of the main combatants is described in the fifth trumpet as an army of locusts.
- This locust army is the same as the locust army of Joel 2.
- The Locust army of Joel 2 is the same as the last-days manifestation of the King of the North of Daniel 11.
- The King of the North changes identity through history, but from the Middle Ages is the same as the "little horn" of Daniel 7, the "great horn" of Daniel 8 and the "beast from the sea" of Revelation 13.
- The "beast from the sea" of Revelation 13 is the papacy, supported during the time of trouble by the United States of America (the beast from the earth) and "10 kings."
- The King of the South of Daniel 11 who fights against the King of the North also changes identity through history, but from the Middle Ages is militant Islam.
- Thus the major combatants in the war described in the seven trumpets are papal Europe and the United States with their allies, opposed by militant Islam.

The fact that the United States is the sole world superpower and radical Islam is extremely antagonistic toward both the US and Europe indicates that the stage is now set and the trumpet war could start at any time. It will apparently begin with a series of attacks, probably with nuclear weapons, by Islamic militants against Europe or the United States.

9:4 Protected by the Seal

"And it was commanded them that they should not hurt the grass of the earth, nor any green thing, nor any tree; but only those men who do not have the seal of God in their foreheads" (Revelation 9:4). There is only one other verse in the Bible that mentions the seal of God in the forehead: "And I saw another angel ascending from the east, having the seal of the living God; and he cried with a loud voice…saying, 'Hurt not the earth, neither the sea, nor the trees, until we have sealed the servants of our God in their foreheads.' And I heard the number of those which were sealed: and there were sealed 144,000 of all the tribes of the children of Israel" (Revelation 7:2-4). In the first three trumpets the very things that were not to be harmed until the 144,000 are sealed (the earth, the sea, and the trees) are then harmed. This makes it clear that the group with **"the seal of God in their foreheads"** who are not harmed by the locusts of the fifth trumpet are the 144,000.

A mark that protects them from the destructive plagues that fall upon those around them is reminiscent of the experience of the children of Israel during the plagues of Egypt. God intended to bring His people out of the slavery of Egypt to the Promised Land, and He could have done so by simply wiping out the Egyptians. God said to Pharaoh through Moses, "Now if I had stretched out My hand and struck you and your people with pestilence, then you would have been cut off from the earth" (Exodus 9:15).

But God wanted to accomplish more than just free His people. He wanted the Egyptians to know about Him—"that you [Pharaoh and the Egyptians] may know that I am the Lord in the midst of the land" (Exodus 8:22). He wanted them to know that He was above their nature gods—"that you may know that the earth is the Lord's" (Exodus 9:29). He wanted the rest of the world to know about Him—"that I may show My power in you, and that My name may be declared in all the earth" (Exodus 9:16). He accomplished this by protecting His people in the midst of the plagues—"I will set apart the land of Goshen… that you may know that I am the Lord." "There was thick darkness in all the land of Egypt…but all the children of Israel had light in their dwellings." "All the firstborn in the land of Egypt shall die, from the firstborn of Pharaoh who sits on his throne, even to the firstborn of the female servant who is behind the handmill, and all the firstborn of the animals…but against none of the children of Israel shall a dog move its tongue, against man or beast, *that you may know that the Lord does make a difference between the Egyptians and Israel*" (Exodus 8:22, 10:22,23, 11:5-7).

The children of Israel were protected from the last plague (the death of the firstborn children) by putting a mark on their doorposts.[340] The result of the protection of God's people in the midst of the destruction of Egypt was that the whole world did hear about the God of Israel. Moreover, when the children of Israel went out of Egypt a multitude of Egyptians went out with them—"And the Lord had given the people favor in the sight of the Egyptians…then the children of Israel journeyed…a mixed multitude went up with them also" (Exodus 12:36-38).

Because of the seal in their foreheads God's followers will be protected from the plagues. This protection is not simply to spare God's people from pain, but it is designed to be a witness to the people of the whole world, a part of God's last great effort to bring them to repentance. As it was in Egypt, the result will be the deliverance of a great multitude.

Witness of the 144,000

One of the major themes of the Book of Revelation is that the world has been deceived by the false religious system known as Babylon, and that God is calling people out of Babylon to be a part of His kingdom. The most powerful call to come out of Babylon will be given by 144,000 "angels" (messengers) during the chaos of the seven trumpets. In chapter 14 the 144,000 are portrayed (verses 1-5), followed by a picture of three angels giving a powerful call to worship the Creator and escape from "fallen" Babylon (verses 6-12). Chapter 18 repeats the same language of chapter 14, with a powerful angel giving more details of the danger of Babylon and an even clearer appeal to escape: "Babylon the great is fallen, is fallen, and has become a habitation of devils…Come out of her, my people, that you do not partake of her sins, and that you do not receive of her plagues" (Revelation 18:1-4). In chapter 7 the 144,000 are also portrayed, being sealed out of "all the tribes of the children of Israel." Immediately after this John saw "a great multitude which no one could number, of all nations, tribes, peoples and tongues…clothed with white robes" (Revelation 7:9). John heard the question, "Who are these arrayed in white robes, and where did they come from?" (v. 13). The answer was, "These are the ones coming out of the great tribulation, and they washed their robes, and made them white in the blood of the Lamb" (v. 14). To summarize the important points of these three passages:

- In chapter 7 the 144,000 are described, and then a great multitude are seen "coming out of the great tribulation."

---

340 "For I will pass through the land of Egypt on that night, and will strike all the firstborn in the land of Egypt, both man and beast; and against all the gods of Egypt I will execute judgment…Now the blood shall be a sign for you on the houses where you are. And when I see the blood, I will pass over you, and the plague shall not be on you to destroy you" (Exodus 12:12,13).

- In chapter 14 the 144,000 are again portrayed, and then they (as symbolized by three angels) give their message, which includes "Babylon is fallen."
- In Chapter 18 "another angel" gives the same powerful message, "Babylon is fallen...come out of her my people."

Comparing these passages, it is obvious that it is the 144,000 who will call the great multitude out of Babylon during the great tribulation (see 7: 9,10, *The Great Multitude* and 11:3-6, *Who Are the Two Witnesses?*). A multitude came out of Egypt with the children of Israel, convinced and convicted by the distinction they saw between the children of Israel (who were protected by God) and the Egyptians (who arrogantly rejected Him). Likewise, in the time of trouble a multitude will be convinced and convicted to come out of Babylon when they see not only the protection of the 144,000, but also when they hear their powerful message and see Christ's character reflected in their lives (the seal in their foreheads). That story is told in chapter 11.

The Rapture—When?

God will allow His most faithful people, the 144,000, to be His witnesses on Earth during the great tribulation. God's people will be protected from the full force of the plagues by the seal of God, but they will still suffer to a certain extent; some will even face martyrdom.[341] This being the case, they obviously cannot have been "raptured" (taken to heaven) before the time of trouble.

Many Evangelical Christians today believe that the present "dispensation" (phase of God's activity) is the "time of the gentiles."[342] They teach that those who are faithful Christians now will be secretly "raptured"—that God will take them to heaven before the great tribulation. This is supposed to be followed by the seven-year time of trouble which is God's dispensation for the conversion of the Jews and those "gentiles" who were not converted and raptured before the time of trouble.[343] This theme has been popularized by books and movies such as the "Left Behind" series which portray a sudden disappearance of Christians, snatched away from the driver's seat of cars, from airplanes, out of their beds. The sealing of the 144,000 is, according to this theory, the conversion of Jews, who then become witnesses during the time of trouble. Those who were true

---

341 See 14:13, *Martyrs During the Time of Trouble.*

342 Dispensationalists point to texts such as Luke 21:24, "And Jerusalem will be trampled by Gentiles until the times of the Gentiles are fulfilled" as evidence that God has different plans for saving the Gentiles and the Jews. According to this theory, God's plan for the Jews during the Old Testament was that they would be saved because they were obedient in keeping the law, that during the time of the Gentiles people could be saved by grace through faith, and that the Jews would have another chance to be saved during the time of trouble after the "rapture" of the church. The converted Jews would then preach the gospel to the other people who had been "left behind."

343 It should be kept in mind that the 144,000, who are sealed in their foreheads and protected in the midst of the trumpet plagues (Revelation 9:4) are not Jews who have rejected Jesus but will be converted during the time of trouble. 1) They are sealed before the plagues begin (Revelation 7:1-8) whereas the rapture theorists contend that the Jews will be converted during the great tribulation. 2) They "were not defiled with women, for they are virgins" (Revelation 14:4), which indicates that they have not been involved in false religious systems (see chapter 14:1-5). 3) They are sealed out "of all the tribes of the children of Israel" (Revelation7:4), whereas the Jews are descendents of the tribes of Judah, Benjamin and Levi (1Kings 12, esp. vs.19-24, 2Kings 17, esp. v. 18). In chapter 7 it was pointed out that Israel is now spiritual Israel, and includes all who are true "children of Abraham," having the faith of Abraham (Romans 4:9-16). Paul makes it clear that many Jews will be saved (Romans 11), along with "the fullness of the Gentiles...and so all [spiritual] Israel will be saved" (Romans 11:25,26). But there is nothing in scripture to indicate that the Jews will ever again be God's chosen people. 4) There are no earlier texts (or later ones either) in Revelation that can be pointed to as being the rapture event. Revelation 4:1 is sometimes cited, but it is clear that it is John who is taken to heaven in vision, not the church.

and faithful Christians will have been raptured and will look on from the safety of heaven.

While this is a nice theory, and most Christians would love to escape the time of trouble, the Bible does not teach this anywhere. Instead of a clear teaching from the Bible, the doctrine of the secret rapture is presented and then texts are given which supposedly support it. Many of these texts actually teach the exact opposite of the secret rapture. This theory is analyzed in Appendix 4: *The Secret Rapture*. The important point is that God's witnesses, the 144,000, are from spiritual Israel, not literal, and will be sealed before the great tribulation. They will not be raptured away, but will be on earth, protected by **"the seal of God on their foreheads."** Even though protected, it will be a fearsome time, as portrayed in Psalm 91: "He who dwells in the secret place of the Most High shall abide under the shadow of the Almighty...Surely He shall deliver you from the snare of the fowler and from the perilous pestilence...A thousand may fall at your side, and ten thousand at your right hand; But it shall not come near you, only with your eyes shall you look and see the reward of the wicked...No evil shall befall you, nor shall any plague come near your dwelling; for he shall give His angels charge over you" (Psalm 91).

The danger of believing in the secret rapture is that when the time of trouble strikes, those who have expected to be carried away beforehand will be plunged into doubt concerning their own spiritual condition. No doubt Satan will make it appear that some have been raptured away, and those who believed in the rapture will think that they were left behind. The thought that their faith was insufficient to be among God's raptured people will be used by Satan to tempt them to give up on God.

But even the Apostle Paul expected to be on earth until the resurrection if Jesus had returned in his lifetime. "We who are alive and remain[344] until the coming of the Lord will by no means precede those who are asleep [those who have died]. For the Lord Himself will descend from heaven...and the dead in Christ will rise first. Then we who are alive and remain shall be caught up together with them in the clouds in the air" (1 Thessalonians 4:15,16). We will be raptured, but it will happen at the Second Coming, when the dead will be resurrected. During the time of trouble God's people will be on earth, threatened by enemies but safe in Him.

9:4,5,10 Five Months— Literal or Prophetic Time?

"And it was commanded them that they should not hurt the grass of the earth, nor any green thing, nor any tree; but only those men who do not have the seal of God in their foreheads. And to them it was given that they should not kill them, but that they should be tormented five months; and their torment was as the torment of a scorpion, when it strikes a man...And they had tails like scorpions, and there were stings in their tails; and their power was to hurt men five months" (Revelation 9:4,5,10).

What is the significance of five months? In many prophecies a day is equal to a year. For example, in the 70 weeks prophecy of Daniel 9 there were to be 70 weeks that would extend from the decree to rebuild Jerusalem in 457 BC until the Messiah (see Appendix 4). Obviously this could not take place in seventy literal *weeks*, but was fulfilled exactly by seventy *weeks of years* (490 years). Likewise in Daniel chapter eight, the vision beginning with "the kings of Media and

---

344 The Greek word is *perileipomenoi* which means those left behind, the survivors. So Paul expected himself to be among those left behind!

Persia" (Daniel 8:20) and extending "to the time of the end" (v.17) could not be fulfilled in 2,300 literal *days* (v. 14), but could be in 2,300 *years* (see Appendix 5). The Papal supremacy and persecution of the saints during the Dark Ages which was prophesied in Daniel 7 and Revelation 12 and 13 obviously continued for more than "a time and times and half a time" (Daniel 7:25), "forty-two months" (Revelation13:5) or "One thousand two hundred and sixty days" (Revelation 12:6).[345] But papal supremacy did continue for 1,260 *years*, from the early fifth century until the eighteenth century.

The "day-for-a-year principle" obviously applies to the long time prophecies which extend from the time of the prophet to the time of the end, and this understanding is supported by texts such as Ezekiel 4:6 ("I have laid on you a day for each year") and Numbers 14:34 ("for each day you shall bear your guilt one year"). But does this apply to time prophecies which take place *during* the time of the end, such as the **"five months"** of the fifth trumpet?

There is evidence in Daniel 12 that prophecies within the time of the end use literal time. Daniel 12 is the final portion of the long vision concerning the Kings of the North and South that was summarized above. After focusing on the damage done by the medieval Papacy, the vision proceeds to the same end-of-time war that is described in Revelation 9. "At the time of the end…the King of the North shall come against him [the King of the South] like a whirlwind… yet he shall come to his end, and no one will help him. At that time Michael shall stand up…and there shall be a time of trouble, such as never was since there was a nation, even to that time, and at that time your people shall be delivered, every one who is found written in the book. And many

of those who sleep in the dust of the earth shall awake, some to everlasting life, some to shame and everlasting contempt. Those who are wise shall shine" (Daniel 11:40-12:2).

After the long narrative concerning the war, two angels talked about the vision and one of them mentioned in Daniel 12:7 that the papal oppression (which is a central focus of all of Daniel's visions) would continue "for a time, times, and half a time" (1,260 years). But Daniel did not understand what the angel meant, and furthermore he was not as interested in the events of the Middle Ages as he was in the amazing announcements he had heard at the end of the vision: that "Michael [would] stand up," that Daniel's "people shall be delivered," about the resurrection when "many of those who sleep in the dust of the earth shall awake," and about the glorification of the redeemed who "shall shine" (Daniel 12:1-3). "Although I [Daniel] heard, I did not understand. Then I said, 'My Lord, what shall be the end of these things?" (v. 8).

The Hebrew word translated "the end" (*achariyth*) can be translated "after part," "latter part," or "latter time." Thus we see that Daniel was most interested in the final portion of the prophecy, when his "people shall be delivered." After telling him that the words "are sealed till the time of the end" (v. 9) the angel informed him, "from the time that the daily sacrifice is taken away, and the abomination of desolation is set up, there shall be one thousand two hundred and ninety days. But blessed is he who waits, and comes to the one thousand three hundred and thirty-five days" (v 11,12).

These time prophecies are given in the context of the "time of the end," just before "many of those who sleep in the dust of the earth shall awake" (Daniel 12:2), in other words, the time leading up to the Second Coming of Christ. Although they could have a secondary application to the papal period, there is evidence within

---

345 These periods are all the same—see 12: *One Thousand Two Hundred and Sixty Days*

the prophecies themselves and in Matthew 24 that they apply primarily to the time of trouble, so they must refer to literal time in order to fit into that relatively short period. See Appendix 10 for a detailed examination of these important prophecies.

We see from this example that it is from the context of the prophecy that we can tell if a time period is literal time or prophetic time, and that literal time is used in at least some time prophecies during the "time of the end." This is no doubt the case with the "five months" of torment in Revelation nine, which would be 300 years of prophetic time. This would put them into a historical context, and we have already seen that the seven trumpets are end-time events that have not yet taken place (see chapter 8: *Trumpets: Past or Future*).

The five literal months of torment from the locust army is called the first of three woes: **"One woe is past; and, behold, two woes are yet to come after these things"** (Revelation 9:12). During the first woe Satan and his agents **"were not given authority to kill"** (v. 5 NKJV). But Satan's evil angels are released more fully during the second woe,[346] resulting in the most massive slaughter in human history.

9:13,14 Sixth Trumpet, Second Woe

"And the sixth angel sounded, and I heard a voice from the four horns of the golden altar which is before God, saying to the sixth angel which had the trumpet, "Release the four angels which are bound at the great river Euphrates" (Revelation 9:13,14).

"The golden altar which is before God" is a reference to the altar of incense that was in the first room of the sanctuary (the "Holy Place"), just in front of the veil that separated it from the Most Holy Place. Every day the fragrant smoke from this altar, mingled with prayers of intercession, drifted into the Most Holy Place where the throne and the visible presence of God were located. On the Day of Atonement the high priest took coals from this altar in his censer into the Most Holy Place before the very presence of God. When the blood of the sacrifices was brought into the sanctuary "the priest…put some of the blood on the horns of the altar of sweet incense before the Lord" (Leviticus 4:7) as a part of the forgiveness process. Thus the **"golden altar"** had the closest and most intimate connection with God of any part of the sanctuary outside of the Most Holy Place, and was associated with intercession, protection and forgiveness.

Ironically, from this place of intercession, covered by the blood of countless sacrifices, comes the cry to **"release the four angels which are bound at the great river Euphrates,"** a release that results in even greater destruction than the previous five trumpets. The message may be the same as in the throwing down of the censer in chapter 8 (which took place before the same altar)—that Jesus' intercession that has protected this world from many of the destructive consequences of sin is no longer being offered. God's purpose in the trumpets is to allow Satan to "have his way" and cause the havoc that is the inevitable result of his malevolent nature.[347] God does this by releasing Satan in a series of stages of increasing intensity.

The first stage is introduced in chapter seven. As the 144,000 are about to be sealed, John "saw four angels standing at the four corners of the earth, holding the four winds of the earth that

---

346 Revelation 9:13-15.

347 Satan has already revealed his name or character in this chapter as Abaddon (Hebrew) or Apollyon (Greek), both of which mean "destroyer" (Revelation 9:11).

the wind should not blow on the earth, on the sea, or on any tree" (Revelation 7:1). But when the 144,000 had been sealed, the angel with the golden censer "threw it to the earth" and the four winds were released. The earth, sea and trees that had been protected were now destroyed in the first three trumpets.

With the fifth trumpet God makes a further release—the **"star fallen from heaven to the earth...was given the key to the bottomless pit"** (Revelation 9:1), and the locust army came forth to torture (but not kill) men for five months. Finally, with the sixth trumpet **"the four angels which are bound at the great river Euphrates"** are released **"to slay a third of men."** Satan's ulterior motive is revealed in chapters 11 and 13—to defeat the sealed 144,000. But when it becomes obvious to the whole universe that Satan's purpose is to provoke those under his control to destroy God's people,[348] God Himself will directly intervene. He will send "out of the temple...seven angels having the seven last plagues" (Revelation 15:6,1) which will thwart Satan's evil plans.

9:15-21 A Third of Mankind Killed

"Release the four angels which are bound at the great river Euphrates.' And the four angels were released, those prepared for the hour, and day, and month, and year, to slay a third of men. And the number of the army of the horsemen was two hundred million: and I heard the number of them" (Revelation 9:15,16).

The **"great river Euphrates"** is the same as

the "many waters" of Babylon. Babylon is itself the kingdom of the enemies of God's people (Jeremiah 51:13), and the end time symbol of spiritual wickedness. The waters of Babylon are identified in Revelation 17 as "peoples, multitudes, nations and tongues." This shows that the support system of end-time Babylon includes multitudes of people from all over the world. The war described in the seven trumpets is much more than a regional conflict in Iraq (where ancient Babylon was located). Babylon is the whole system described in Revelation 13 and 17, with "the beast" controlling the nations of Europe, the United States, and those countries subject to its influence. Therefore these verses seem to indicate that there will be a multi-national army, and with two hundred million soldiers it will be the largest army ever assembled.

Since Babylon corresponds in Daniel 11 with the "King of the North," this may represent a continuation of the final battle between the King of the North and the King of the South—"At the time of the end the King of the South shall attack him; and the King of the North shall come against him like a whirlwind, with chariots, horsemen, and with many ships...he shall go out with great fury to destroy and annihilate many" (Daniel 11:40,44). It appears that Europe, the United States and their allies (the end time King of the North) will unleash their formidable military machine against the "King of the South."

Perhaps there will be a two-stage response to the attack by the King of the South. The first (the fifth trumpet) could consist of some kind of chemical, biological or radiation warfare that continues for five months. The second (the sixth trumpet) seems to involve two hundred million soldiers and results in the death of a third of mankind. The second stage seems to be conventional warfare, and considering that at the time John wrote there was not even such a thing as gunpowder, his description is remarkably accurate

---

348 Chapter 11 presents the murder of the two witnesses. We will see that this is Satan's attempt to destroy the 144,000. The same attempt is shown in chapter 13, expanding the details to show how Satan will use the beast from the sea and the beast from the earth to persecute God's people through the image, mark and number of the beast and the death decree against "as many as would not worship the image of the beast" (Revelation 13:15).

in its graphic depiction of the cannons, tanks and firearms of conventional warfare. **"And thus I saw the horses in the vision, and those that sat on them, having breastplates of fire, and of hyacinth, and sulfur; and the heads of the horses were as the heads of lions; and out of their mouths issued fire and smoke and brimstone. By these three a third of men were killed, by the fire, and by the smoke, and by the brimstone, which issued out of their mouths. For their power is in their mouth, and in their tails, which were like serpents, having heads, and with them they do harm"** (Revelation 9:17-19).

The fact that these attacks kill **"a third of men"** again shows their origin: they are inspired by Satan, **"the angel of the bottomless pit."** But Satan is only able to carry out this carnage because God allows him to do so. Naturally the question arises: why would a God of love allow Satan to destroy His creation? Why would the voice releasing the destructive malice of the enemy come from the alter of intercession?

It is important to remember that God does not want any of this to happen. He "is longsuffering toward us, not willing that any should perish" (2Peter 3:9). "Why should you die?" He pleads, "For I have no pleasure in the death of one who dies…turn and live!" (Ezekiel 18:31,32). He calls the destruction of the unrepentant "His strange act" (Isaiah 28:21) because "He does not afflict willingly, nor grieve the children of men" (Lamentations 3:33). God intends to preserve human freedom of choice (even the choice of sin and death), but to also bring sin to an end, and to do so in a way that will forever demonstrate to the universe that Satan's ways are the ways of death. Therefore He finally allows Satan a short period

of unrestrained activity. The final result will be that the whole universe will be fully convinced of the falsehood of Satan's principles, and will forever remain free from a second experiment with sin—"He will make an utter end of it. Affliction will not rise up a second time" (Nahum 1:9).

But in the midst of bringing an end to sin, God still tries to save as many as He can. At this point (the sixth trumpet) the door of mercy is still open. The affliction the world suffers in these plagues, combined with a powerful call to repentance, is the last opportunity that sinners will have to turn away from sin. In fact, the disasters shake up their complacency and bring them face to face with their need for God. "Let grace be shown to the wicked, yet he will not learn righteousness…when Your judgments are in the earth, the inhabitants of the world will learn righteousness" (Isaiah 26:9,10).

Judgments by themselves are not enough to turn people from their sins, and this is definitely the case with the disasters Satan brings through the seven trumpets. **"And the rest of the men who were not killed by these plagues did not repent of the works of their hands, that they should not worship demons, and idols of gold, and silver, and brass, and stone, and of wood, which can neither see, nor hear, nor walk. Neither did they repent of their murders, nor of their sorceries, nor of their fornication, nor of their thefts"** (Revelation 9:20,21). Satan's destructive attacks will not bring anyone to repentance, but the ministry of the "little book" and the "two witnesses" will take place even while the trumpet war is raging (presented in the next two chapters), and will finally convince the "great multitude" to accept God's mercy and come out of Babylon.

"Then I took the little book out of the angel's hand and ate it." Rev. 10:10.
Woodcut by Albrecht Durer 1498

Chapter 10

Revelation 10:1-11

10:1 And I saw another mighty angel coming down from heaven, clothed with a cloud, and a rainbow was on his head, and his face was like the sun, and his feet as pillars of fire.

10:2 And he had in his hand a little book open, and he set his right foot on the sea, and his left foot on the earth,

10:3 And cried out with a loud voice, as when a lion roars. And when he had cried out, seven thunders uttered their voices.

10:4 And when the seven thunders uttered their voices, I was about to write; and I heard a voice from heaven saying to me, "Seal up those things which the seven thunders uttered, and do not write them."

10:5 And the angel whom I saw standing on the sea and on the earth lifted up his hand to heaven,

10:6 And swore by Him who lives forever and ever, who created heaven, and the things which are therein, and the earth, and the things which are therein, and the sea, and the things which are therein, that there should be time no longer.

10:7 But in the days of the voice of the seventh angel, when he is about to sound, the mystery of God should be finished, as He has declared to His servants the prophets.

10:8 And the voice which I heard from heaven spoke to me again, and said, "Go and take the little book which is open in the hand of the angel which stands on the sea and on the earth."

10:9 And I went to the angel, and said to him, "Give me the little book." And he said to me, "Take it, and eat it; and it will make your belly bitter, but it shall be in your mouth sweet as honey."

10:10 And I took the little book out of the angel's hand, and ate it; and it was in my mouth sweet as honey; and as soon as I had eaten it, my belly was bitter.

10:11 And he said to me, "You must prophesy again before many peoples, and nations, and tongues, and kings."

10:1-7 The Seven Thunders

"And I saw another mighty angel coming down from heaven, clothed with a cloud, and a rainbow was on his head, and his face was like the sun, and his feet as pillars of fire. And he had in his hand a little book open, and he set his right foot on the sea, and his left foot on the earth, And cried out with a loud voice, as when a lion roars. And when he had cried out, seven thunders uttered their voices. And when the seven thunders uttered their voices, I was about to write; and I heard a voice from heaven saying to me, 'Seal up those things which the seven thunders uttered, and do not write them" (Revelation 10:1-4).

Chapters 8 and 9 were fairly literal descriptions of a devastating war at the end of time. Chapter 10 makes a major shift. Although still a part of the seven trumpets, the focus now is upon what God and His people are doing during the Satan-inspired war, and this is presented using highly symbolic language.[349]

John saw **"another angel"** who came down from heaven, holding a little book in his hand. When he spoke it sounded like a lion roaring, and at the same time **"seven thunders uttered their voices."** The messages of the seven thunders seem at first glance to be frustrating. Although they are so important that they were delivered in great glory and majesty, thundered with the voice of God from heaven, John was told, **"seal up those things which the seven thunders uttered, and do not write them,"** so we do not have the opportunity to know what the thunders said, let alone the meaning of their messages.

Actually, this very fact gives a clue to their content. Sealed messages are generally prophetic. For example, Daniel was told to "seal up the vision" of the 2,300 days "for it refers to many days in the future" (Daniel 8:26). Later, when he was given a vision including information about the "time of trouble" when "your people shall be delivered" and "many of those who sleep in the dust of the earth shall awake," he was told, "shut up the words and seal the book until the time of the end" (Daniel 12:1-4). The angel gave Daniel time periods for the last day events ("a time, times and half a time," "one thousand two hundred and ninety days…one thousand three hundred and thirty-five days" Daniel 12:7,11,12) but he did not explain their significance. Daniel kept asking about these end-time prophecies and the angel finally told him, "Go your way, Daniel, for the words are closed up and sealed till the time of the end" (Daniel 12:9).[350]

Jesus also made it clear that the people of His day were not to know the details of the end of time. When He was about to ascend to heaven the last thing his disciples wanted to know was when he would establish His kingdom. "And he said to them, 'It is not for you to know times or seasons which the Father has put in His own authority" (Acts 1:7).

Jesus insisted that no one knows the day and hour of His coming, only the Father (Matthew 24:36, Mark 13:32). But at the same time He gave a list of signs as well as time prophecies so that His followers could know when the time was near. We can conclude that the sealed messages of the seven thunders have to do with the timing, the events, the signs and the judgments leading up to the return of Christ.

This interpretation is supported by the fact that the mighty angel **"cried with a loud voice, as when a lion roars."** The prophet Amos links

---

349 The chiastic counterpart of the seven trumpets are the seven last plagues, which also consist of the fairly literal plagues (chapter 16) followed by the highly symbolic portrayal of the judgment of Babylon (chapters 17 and 18).

350 See also Isaiah 29:11,12.

prophecies that reveal the future with the roaring of a lion—"Surely the Lord God does nothing, unless He reveals His secret to His servants the prophets. A lion has roared! Who will not fear? The Lord God has spoken! Who can but prophesy?" (Amos 3:7,8). Moreover, these messages are called **"seven thunders."** Seven refers to fullness and completeness. "Thundering" in Revelation is associated with the pouring out of executive judgments (see 4: *Two Kinds of Judgments*). This would suggest that the message of the seven thunders contain information about the fullness of the judgments to come, culminating with the return of Christ.

But the most conclusive evidence that the messages of the seven thunders have to do with the end-time prophecies comes from the parallel passage in Daniel, which shows that information about the events of the last days was to be sealed, but would be revealed and understood at the end of time.

Clues in Daniel

"And the angel whom I saw standing on the sea and on the earth lifted up his hand to heaven, and swore by Him who lives forever and ever, who created heaven, and the things which are therein, and the earth, and the things which are therein, and the sea, and the things which are therein, that there should be time no longer. But in the days of the voice of the seventh angel, when he is about to sound, the mystery of God should be finished, as He has declared to His servants the prophets" (Revelation 10:5-7).

The prophet Daniel gave a parallel message in Daniel chapters 10-12, apparently delivered by the same mighty angel. John and Daniel used slightly different language, expressing what they saw in their own words, but it is obvious that they were seeing the same vision (See Table 10.1).

Table 10.1

Daniel 10-12	Revelation 10
"A certain man clothed in linen" (10:5).	"Another angel…clothed with a cloud" (v. 1).
"His face like the appearance of lightning" (10:6).	"His face was like the sun " (v. 1).
"His arms and feet like burnished bronze in color" (10:6).	"His feet as pillars of fire" (v. 1).
"The man…was above the waters" (12:6)	"He set his right foot on the sea and his left foot on the earth" (v. 2).
"He held up his right hand and his left hand to heaven" (12:7).	"Lifted up his hand to heaven" (v.5).
"Swore by Him who lives forever" (12:7).	"Swore by Him who lives forever and ever" (v. 6).
"The words are closed up and sealed till the time of the end" (12:9).	"Seal up those things which the seven thunders uttered" (v. 4).

It is obvious that both Daniel and John saw the same messenger, and the message must also be closely related. It is from Daniel that we learn what the message was about. In vision Daniel had seen terrible things happening to his people during the long war between the "King of the North and the King of the South" (Daniel 10:19-11:45). But the angel had assured him that there would be a good ending—"Michael shall stand up...your people shall be delivered...many who sleep in the dust of the earth shall awake...those who are wise shall shine like the brightness of the firmament, and those who turn many to righteousness like the stars forever and ever. But you, Daniel, shut up the words and *seal the book, until the time of the end*. Many shall run to and fro, and *knowledge shall increase.*" (Daniel 12:1-3).

As Daniel looked on in wonder he heard someone ask, "How long shall the fulfillment of these wonders be?" The answer was, "It shall be for *a time, times and half a time*; and *when the power of the holy people has been completely shattered*, all these things shall be finished" (Daniel 12:7). Daniel still did not understand and asked for clarification—"Then I said, 'My Lord, what shall be *the end of these things?*" Daniel was told, "The words are closed up and sealed till *the time of the end*...none of the wicked shall understand, but *the wise shall understand*. And from the time that the daily sacrifice is taken away and *the abomination of desolation* is set up, there shall be *one thousand two hundred and ninety days*. Blessed is he who waits and comes to the *one thousand three hundred and thirty-five days*" (Daniel 12:8-13).

This message is packed with information about prophetic events and time periods—the shattering of the power of the holy people, the abomination of desolation, time, times, and half a time, 1,290 days and 1,335 days. The "words" concerning them were to be sealed at the time they were given "till the time of the end" when

"knowledge shall increase." This implies that at the time of the end they would be unsealed, and "the wise shall understand."

In Revelation 10, the same angel Daniel saw appeared, holding **"a little book open in his hand."** Apparently this is the same book whose "words [were] closed up and sealed till the time of the end" in Daniel 12. Sealed in the book is the revelation of the meaning of the end-time prophetic periods and associated events, information that is vital for God's people at the end of time. Daniel was told to "seal the book until the time of the end; many shall run to and fro, and knowledge shall increase" (Daniel 12:4). This verse does not refer to the rapid advances in communication, transportation and technology, impressive as these are. The context[351] shows that it is knowledge of the sealed prophecies that will increase. Much of this "knowledge" is found in the books of Daniel and Revelation. Significant insight is also found in Jesus' discourse about the last days in Matthew 24 (and its parallel passages Mark 13 and Luke 21).

Matthew 24 has important links to Daniel 12 and to Revelation 10. According to Daniel 12:11, a key to understanding the final events and time periods would be "the time that...the abomination of desolation is set up" (Daniel 12:11). Jesus in Matthew 24 also urged his followers to understand and respond to the "abomination of desolation spoken of by the prophet Daniel" (Matthew 24:15).

Moreover, the **"mighty angel"** with the **"little book open in his hand...swore by Him who**

---

351 The context of Daniel 12 is the events and time periods of the last period of earth's history when there will be "a time of trouble such as never was" and when God's people "shall be delivered." There is nothing in the chapter, and particularly in Daniel's questions, that would be answered by a delineation of last-day advances in technology and transportation. Moreover, the Hebrew for "knowledge" uses the article ("the knowledge"), showing that it is specific, not general knowledge, and the specific knowledge that has been mentioned is the understanding of the prophecies.

lives forever and ever, who created heaven, and the things which are therein, and the earth, and the things which are therein, and the sea, and the things which are therein" (Revelation 10:6). This is a clear reference to Exodus 20:11, the Sabbath commandment: "In six days the Lord made the heavens and the earth, the sea and all that is in them, and rested the seventh day." Matthew 24 also mentions the Sabbath in the context of the emergency brought on by the abomination of desolation,[352] and we will see in chapter 13 that the Sabbath will be an exceedingly important issue during the time of trouble. Because of these links (the abomination of desolation and the Sabbath) as well as a need for understanding all of the end-time prophecies in order to "unseal" the messages of the seven thunders, a study of Matthew 24 will now be presented.

Clues in Matthew 24

In Mathew 24 Jesus gave a brief but remarkably comprehensive outline of the future until His coming. The setting for Jesus' prophesy was two days before the Passover feast when Jesus would be crucified. The scribes, Pharisees and Sadducees had tried unsuccessfully to trap Him with clever arguments and He in turn had fully unmasked their hypocrisy. He ended weeping for His city and His people: "O Jerusalem, Jerusalem, the one who kills the prophets and stones those who are sent to her...See! Your house is left to you desolate" (Matthew 23:37,38).

The disciples were shocked to hear this. The temple was one of the wonders of the world at that time, the pride of the nation, and the thought that it would be "left...desolate" was inconceivable.

But in answer to their suggestions that the massive stone buildings were impregnable, Jesus gave an even more shocking reply. "Then Jesus went out and departed from the temple, and His disciples came up to show Him the buildings of the temple. And Jesus said to them, "Do you not see all these things? Assuredly, I say to you, not one stone shall be left here upon another, that shall not be thrown down" (Matthew 24:1,2).

For something this momentous to happen the disciples assumed that Jesus must be talking about the end of the world when He would come to establish His kingdom. Wanting to understand what He meant, "His disciples came to Him privately, saying, 'tell us, when will these things be? And what will be the sign of Your coming, and of the end of the age?" (v.3). Although they didn't know it, the disciples were actually asking three questions, about three events that they mistakenly assumed would happen at about the same time.

1. "When will these things be?" "These things" referred to what He had been talking about: the destruction of the temple and Jerusalem in AD 70 by the Roman army under Titus.

2. "What will be the sign of your coming?" Here the disciples were asking for signs of the Second Coming of Christ.

3. "[What will be the sign of] the end of the age?" In other passages Jesus used the phrase "the end of the age" to refer to that last period of time when the angels would judge and separate the

---

352 "When you see the abomination of desolation...flee to the mountains...and pray that your flight may not be...on the Sabbath" (Matthew 24:15-20). Even those who believe that Matthew 24 refers only to the destruction of Jerusalem in AD 70 must admit that Jesus expected the Sabbath to be important to Christians long after His crucifixion and resurrection.

righteous from the unrepentant.[353] The prophet Daniel called this period "the time of the end" (Daniel 8:17), and he was shown that "the time of the end" would begin at the end of the 2,300 prophetic days (years) prophesied in Daniel 8:14 when "the sanctuary shall be cleansed." This is the Day of Atonement which began in AD 1844.[354]

We see that the disciples were asking three questions concerning three separate events, which happen at three separate times. Jesus did not clarify their thinking at this time, and in fact they were psychologically and spiritually unprepared for a full revelation of the future.[355] Instead He gave a skillfully blended reply which answered all three questions at once.[356]

Jesus introduced His prophecy by warning His followers that understanding the last events would not be easy. *"And Jesus answered and said to them: 'Take heed that no one deceives you. For many will come in my name, saying 'I am the Christ' and will deceive many"* (Matthew 24:4). The purpose of His discourse was not to give a point-by-point revelation of future events, but rather to help those who would live through these events so that they would not be deceived. Three times He emphasizes the deceptions that would surround the destruction of Jerusalem, the approach of "the end of the age" and His Second Coming.

Jesus also cautioned against interpreting or finding application of prophecy from the current headline news. *"And you will hear of wars and rumors of wars. See that you are not troubled; for all these things must come to pass, but the end is not yet. For nation will rise against nation, and kingdom against kingdom. And there will be famines, pestilences and earthquakes in various places. All these are the beginning of sorrows"* (Matthew 24:6-8). Every time there is a war, a major earthquake or disastrous weather conditions people begin to speculate about the end of

---

353 In the parable of the wheat and the tares, given in Matthew 13:24-43, Jesus said that "the kingdom of heaven is like a man who sowed good seed in his field, but while men slept, his enemy came and sowed tares among the wheat" (vs. 24, 25). They were to be left to grow together until the harvest—"at the time of harvest I will say to the reapers, first gather together the tares and bind them in bundles to burn them, but gather the wheat into my barn" (v. 30). This shows a process of separating, gathering and bundling before the final burning of the tares. In His interpretation Jesus said "the harvest is the end of the age ." The Greek is "*suntelia aeonos*" which means end of the ages. Jesus goes on to explain: "the reapers are the angels. Therefore as the tares are gathered and burned in the fire, so it will be at the end of this age. The Son of Man will send out His angels, and they will gather out of His kingdom all things that offend, and those who practice lawlessness, and will cast them into the furnace of fire" (vs. 39-42). Here we see the two phases of judgment: separation (the investigative judgment) and reward and punishment (executive judgment). This is even more clear in the parable of the dragnet in Matthew 13: 47-51. "The kingdom of heaven is like a dragnet that was cast into the sea and gathered some of every kind, which, when it was full, they drew to shore; and they sat down and gathered the good into vessels but threw the bad away. So it will be at *the end of the age*. The angels will come forth, separate the wicked from among the just, and cast them into the furnace of fire." Here Jesus makes it clear that "the end of the age" is the time when the unrepentant and the righteous are distinguished and separated, resulting in the unrepentant being burned and the righteous inheriting the kingdom. This corresponds to the final Day of Atonement, also known as the investigative judgment, which began in AD 1844, followed by the executive judgment which takes place in two stages: at the Second Coming and after the Millennium.

354 See sections 3:8, 4:1, 5:7,8, 14:7 and Appendix 5 for further explanation of the Day of Atonement and the calculation of the 2,300 days.

355 At this time the disciples did not even have a clear conception of what His kingdom was, let alone how it would come about. "I still have many things to say to you, but you cannot bear them now" (John 16:12).

356 The use of a blended prophecy with multiple applications finds its model in Isaiah 13, a judgment against Babylon which was directed both toward ancient Babylon ("I will stir up the Medes against them" v. 17) and last-days Babylon ("the day of the Lord comes…the sun will be darkened in its going forth and the moon will not cause its light to shine. I will punish the world for its evil" vs. 9-11). Likewise the prophecy of Joel 2:28-32 was applied by Peter to the day of Pentecost ("I will pour out My Spirit on all flesh" v. 28) but the context shows the primary application to be the last days ("The sun shall be turned into darkness and the moon into blood before the coming of the great and awesome day of the Lord" v. 31).

the world. Certainly events such as the two world wars of the twentieth century and recent destructive earthquakes, storms, and famines captured everyone's attention, but Jesus said not to be troubled; we are to look elsewhere for the signs of His coming.

The Abomination of Desolation

One of the keys to understanding these prophecies is found in verse 15: *"Therefore when you see the abomination of desolation spoken of by Daniel the prophet, standing in the holy place (whoever reads let him understand)"* (Matthew 24:15). Jesus links an understanding of His prophecies with the understanding of the "abomination of desolation" which was "spoken of by Daniel." The "abomination of desolation" is actually mentioned in three places in Daniel, each with a different context, corresponding to the three events Jesus was addressing in Matthew 24:

1. The abomination of desolation is mentioned within the context of the 70 weeks (490 years) of probation that was given to the Jewish nation—"Seventy weeks are determined for your people and for your holy city" (Daniel 9:24). This probationary period ended with the "Messiah, the Prince" (Jesus) who was to be "cut off, but not for Himself" (on the cross He was "cut off" for sinful humanity). "He [the Messiah] shall confirm a covenant with many for one week;[357] But in the middle of the week He shall bring an end to sacrifice and offering" (through His sacrifice

Jesus brought the sacrificial system to an end). "And the troops of the prince who is to come [the Romans] shall destroy the city and the sanctuary...and in their place shall be an abomination that desolates" (Daniel 9:26,27).[358] In these verses the abomination of desolation is linked to the destructive judgments which the Jews suffered after their rejection of Christ, particularly the destruction of the temple and Jerusalem by the Romans in AD 70 (see Appendix 10 and Appendix 4 for more information).

2. The second reference to the abomination of desolation is within the detailed outline of the history of the great war between the "King of the North" and the "King of the South" in Daniel 11 (see 9: *Kings of the North and South* and Appendix 3 for details). Briefly, the Kings of the North and South are two opposing forces, both enemies of the people of God. They appeared after the division of the Greek Empire established by Alexander the Great (Daniel 11:3,4), with the northern Seleucid kingdom (in present-day Syria and Turkey) and the southern Ptolemy kingdom in Egypt. As the prophecy progresses, the King of the North evolves into the Roman Empire and later the Holy Roman Empire under the control of the Papacy, opposed by the southern Muslim empires during the time of the crusades. God's true followers, first in Palestine and later primarily in Europe, were caught between these opposing forces. As the stream of history reaches the Middle Ages the angel explains, "And forces shall be mustered by him [the King of the North, the medieval Papacy], and they shall defile the sanctuary fortress; then they shall take away the daily sacrifices, and *place there the abomination of desolation*" (Daniel 11:31). The abomination of desolation mentioned here is the persecution

---

357 This "week" (seven years in prophetic time) included the 3 ½ years of Christ's ministry plus the 3 ½ years up to the stoning of Stephen, during which the gospel was offered exclusively to the Jews. At the end of their probationary period "a great persecution arose against the church...and those who were scattered went everywhere preaching the word" (Acts 8:1-4). The Jews had sealed their rejection of the Messiah and lost their chance to be God's chosen people. For further explanation of the 70 week prophecy see appendix 4.

358 New Revised Standard Version.

of true Christians who would not accept the papal system, culminating in the Inquisition (see Appendix 10).

3. The third reference is in Daniel 12. In response to the final attacks of the King of the North (Daniel 11:40-45), Michael (Christ)[359] "stands up" (finishes his work of mediation) which ushers in "a time of trouble such as never was since there was a nation" (Daniel 12:1). At that time God's "people shall be delivered" and "many of those who sleep in the dust of the earth shall awake" (the Second Coming and resurrection, v. 2). Daniel "heard," but "did not understand" and asked the angel, "My lord, what shall be the end of these things?" (v. 8). The angel informed him that "from the time that the daily sacrifice is taken away, and the abomination of desolation is set up, there shall be one thousand two hundred and ninety days." (v. 11,12). The context here is the end of time when "many of those who sleep in the dust of the earth shall awake" (v. 2), in other words the time just before the Second Coming of Christ.[360]

Thus "the abomination of desolation spoken of by Daniel the prophet" (Matthew 24:15) actually has three contexts of time, but in all three cases it was a demand to submit or die (to the Romans in 70 AD, to the medieval Papacy during the Inquisition, or to persecuting "Babylon" during the time of trouble). The three applications conform perfectly to the three questions the disciples asked: when will the temple be destroyed, what signs will mark the approach of the end of the age, and what signs will accompany the Second Coming of Christ. As we will see below, Jesus' answer to the disciples' question was amazingly blended so that he answered the three questions together.

Warnings

Jesus continued, giving warnings and predictions that applied to the destruction of Jerusalem, the beginning of the time of the end, and the Second Coming of Christ.

"Then they will deliver you up to tribulation and kill you, and you will be hated by all nations for my name's sake" (Matthew 24:9). This was fulfilled in the first century with the persecutions of Christians by the Jews, as well as with the brief but vicious persecution by the Romans under Nero, which took place in AD 64. It was also fulfilled in the Middle Ages by the Inquisition which continued until the time of the end (late 18th-early 19th century). And it will be fulfilled again at the end of time when the "great harlot" will be "drunk with the blood of the saints and with the blood of the martyrs of Jesus" (Revelation 17:6).[361]

"For many will come in My name, saying, 'I am the Christ' and will deceive many" (Matthew 24:5). *"Then many false prophets will rise up and deceive many"* (v. 11). *"For false christs and false prophets will rise, and show great signs and wonders to deceive, if possible, even the elect"* (v.24). Jesus warned three times of the appearance of false prophets and false christs (antichrists). This was fulfilled during the apostolic period. John wrote that in his day "many antichrists have come" (1 John 2:18). Even the Apostle Paul was mistaken for a false Egyptian prophet who had deceived 4000 people (Acts 21:37,38). Also,

---

359 See 12: 7-9 *Michael Casts Satan Out.*

360 Some scholars have assumed that the "days" here are prophetic days, or years. However, the context of Daniel 12 is after Michael stands up, and Daniel's question in verse 8 has to do with the last part of the vision (again, after Michael stands up). Moreover, the fact that individuals could "wait and come to" the end of these time periods rules out hundreds of years. See Appendix 10 for a more complete explanation.

---

361 This is not the persecution of the Middle Ages because "Babylon the Great" is now "The Mother of Harlots" which indicates that the church has divided into the mother church and her daughters. The Roman Catholic "mother church" did not gain "daughters" until after the Middle Ages with the Protestant reformation.

around the beginning of the "time of the end" there was a flurry of those who came with "special messages" from God, such as Joseph Smith who founded the Mormon Church in the 1830's and the Fox sisters who started the modern spiritualist movement in 1848. The ultimate example will be just before the Second Coming of Christ when "the lawless one [the final Antichrist] will be revealed with all power, signs and lying wonders" (2 Thessalonians 2:8,9).

"And this gospel of the kingdom will be preached in all the world as a witness to all the nations and then the end will come" (Matthew 24:14). Paul declared that in his day "the gospel... was preached to every creature under heaven" (Colossians 1:23), testifying to the power of Spirit-filled men and women who spread the good news of Jesus Christ by word of mouth to the whole known world. In the 18th century William Carey launched the modern missionary movement, which by the mid 1800's had sent Protestant missionaries to nearly every country. But the ultimate fulfillment will not take place until Jesus' disciples "preach the gospel to every creature" "and then the end will come" (Mark 16:15, Matthew 24:14).

"Therefore when you see the abomination of desolation spoken of by Daniel the prophet standing in the holy place...then let those who are in Judea flee to the mountains" (Matthew 24:15,16). The parallel passage in Luke gives the application at the time of the destruction of Jerusalem:[362] "When you see Jerusalem surrounded by armies, then know that its desolation is near. Then let those who are in Judea flee to the mountains" (Luke 21:20,21). After years of rebellion and

resistance to Roman rule, the Roman army under Cestius Gallus surrounded Jerusalem in A.D. 66, threatening the Jews that they must submit to Rome or perish. According to the historian Josephus, the Romans were on the verge of victory but inexplicably withdrew. The Christians who lived in Jerusalem, remembering the words of Jesus, fled and escaped the slaughter that occurred when the army of Rome under Titus returned and destroyed the city and the temple in A.D. 70.[363] The abomination of desolation was the presence of pagan soldiers in the Holy City, demanding that the Jews surrender or perish.

In the Middle Ages the Roman Catholic Church set up the "abomination of desolation," this time with the papacy persecuting those accused of heresy (see Appendix 10). The Inquisition formalized the laws and court procedures that were applied against those who refused to submit to the laws of the church, and set up the system of interrogation with torture by the church followed by sentencing and punishment by the government. Faithful Christians such as the Waldenses found refuge in the mountains of Piedmont, and many of the followers of the Protestant Reformation during the 16th century had to "flee to the mountains" of Germany and Switzerland where they found refuge and safety.[364] Again the demand was to submit or perish.

The ultimate fulfillment will take place at the very end of time with the mark and number of the beast.[365] Laws will be passed, first making it

---

362 It is possible that this applies to all three applications. Jerusalem was surrounded by armies (the Crusades) at the time the inquisition was set up. And Jerusalem will again be surrounded by armies during the final battle of the war between the King of the North and the King of the South (see 9: *Kings of the North and South*)

363 For a description of this tragedy see Mervyn Maxwell, *God Cares 2* (Nampa, ID Pacific Press, 1985) p. 24

364 Martin Luther was hidden in the mountain fortress of Wartburg when condemned by Charles V after the diet of Worms. John Calvin, William Farel and John Knox are among the many who fled from France and England and found refuge in mountainous Switzerland. See E.G. White, *The Great Controversy* (Nampa, ID. Pacific Press).

365 See 13:15 *The Image of the Beast* through the end of chapter 13 for complete information about the image, mark and number of the beast and the religio-political entities that will be involved.

impossible to buy or sell without the mark, and finally a death decree will be imposed against those who refuse to submit. At that time it will be essential that true Christians recognize the final "abomination of desolation" so that they can "flee to the mountains" (See 13:15 *The Image of the Beast* and Appendix 10).

"For then there will be great tribulation, such as has not been since the beginning of the world until this time, no, nor ever shall be. And unless those days were shortened, no flesh would be saved; but for the elect's sake those days will be shortened" (Matthew 24:21,22). The siege of Jerusalem with the unbelievable suffering and loss of life rates as one of the greatest human disasters of all times, with the result that the Jews permanently lost their temple. With Jerusalem destroyed, this was the end of the prophecy's application to the Jews and Jerusalem.

The tribulation of the Middle Ages was the greatest in the sense that it continued for hundreds of years with massive loss of life. The crusades, religious wars and persecutions of the Middle Ages were a bloodbath—some historians estimate that 50 million people were slaughtered.

But there never was and never will be anything that can compare with the "time of trouble such as never was since there was a nation, even to that time" (Daniel 12:1). This will take place when the "four winds of the earth" are released (the seven trumpets) and "Michael shall stand up" (the seven last plagues). Jesus said, "Unless those days were shortened, no flesh would be saved" (Matthew 24:22).

Signs

Since the application of Jesus' prophecy to the temple in Jerusalem was completely fulfilled with its destruction in AD 70, the rest of the prophecy applies only to the beginning of the time of the end and the Second Coming of Christ.

"Immediately after the tribulation of those days the sun will be darkened, and the moon will not give its light, the stars will fall from heaven, and the powers of the heavens will be shaken" (Matthew 24:29). The period of papal supremacy ended in the late 1700's. Around that time there was a day when the sun was darkened, May 19, 1780. A strange and extensive darkness covered much of New England, which people at the time interpreted as a sign of the end of the age. A few years later on Nov. 13, 1833 one of the most spectacular meteor showers in history occurred, with up to 60,000 meteorites per hour. These celestial signs arrested the attention of those Christians who were aware of Jesus' prophecy and that of Revelation 6:12,13.[366] They were interpreted as signs of the imminent coming of Christ, and served their purpose of directing attention to the beginning of the "time of the end" in 1844.

The primary fulfillment of these celestial signs will take place "immediately after the tribulation of those days" at the end of the seven last plagues (see Appendix 10 footnote). In the Gospel of Luke Jesus describes these as "signs in the sun, in the moon, and in the stars; and on earth distress of nations with perplexity, the sea and the waves roaring...for the powers of the heavens will be shaken. Then they will see the son of Man coming in a cloud with power and great glory" (Luke 21:25-27). John mentions these same signs in the context of "the great day of His wrath" (Revelation 6:17) with the additional detail of the devastating earthquake that will destroy "great Babylon"— "there was a great earthquake; and the sun became black as sackcloth of hair, and the moon became as blood; and the stars of heaven fell to the earth, even as a fig

---

366 The prophecy of Revelation 6:12 also mentions "a great earthquake", and again around this time, on Nov. 1, 1755, the Lisbon earthquake, which was one of the most extensive and destructive in history, was seen as a fulfillment of this prophecy.

tree casts its untimely figs, when it is shaken by a mighty wind. And the sky departed as a scroll when it is rolled together; and every mountain and island were moved out of their places" (Revelation 6:12-14). The "great earthquake" that moves every "mountain and island" takes place during the seventh plague, just before the Second Coming (Revelation 16:17-20).[367]

"Then the sign of the Son of Man will appear in heaven and then all the tribes of the earth will mourn" (Matthew 24:30). It is no wonder that the ungodly will mourn as they witness the world as they have known it crumbling around them. At this time "the kings of the earth, and the great men, and the rich men, and the chief captains, and the mighty men, and every slave, and every free man, hid themselves in the dens and in the rocks of the mountains; and said to the mountains and rocks, 'Fall on us, and hide us from the face of Him that sits on the throne, and from the wrath of the Lamb!'" (Revelation 6:16). They are afraid of the One who loves them and longed to be their Savior, because they did not know Him.

But for those who have known Him this will be the day they have been waiting for, when they will meet their Savior face to face: *"They will see the Son of Man coming on the clouds of heaven with power and great glory. And He will send His angels with a great sound of a trumpet, and they will gather together His elect from the four winds, from one end of heaven to the other"* (Matthew 25:30,31). "And it will be said in that day; 'Behold, this is our God; we have waited for Him and He will save us…We will be glad and rejoice in His salvation" (Isaiah 25:9). "For the Lord Himself will descend from heaven with a shout, with the voice of an archangel, and with the trumpet of God. And the dead in Christ shall

rise first. Then we who are alive and remain shall be caught up together with them in the clouds to meet the Lord in the air. And thus we shall always be with the Lord" (1 Thessalonians 4:16,17).

With the threefold application of His prophecy of Matthew 24 Jesus has given those who will be living during the final time of trouble an outline of what to expect, with examples from the historical applications so that we can recognize the final events by comparing them with the previous ones. He also gave links to other prophecies such as the abomination of desolation and the final signs. In the book of Revelation He has given the details of the trumpet plagues, including the final war, the appearance of the angel from the bottomless pit, the mission and experience of the two witnesses, as well as the events described in Revelation 13:11-18 (the mark of the beast, etc.), chapter 14 (the three angels' messages), and the seven last plagues, including the judgment of Babylon (chapters 15-19). In other words, God through the prophecies has given us a treasure of information about what will happen during the time of trouble. We should become very familiar with these prophecies now, even though we do not fully understand what they mean, trusting that the meaning of these prophecies will become obvious as they unfold.

Most Christians will go into the time of trouble not really knowing what is happening, why God is allowing it, and how long this most fearsome time will continue. The message of the seven thunders is the revelation of all this. It has been sealed but will be revealed as the knowledge becomes essential. "See, I have told you beforehand." "Now I tell you before it comes, that when it does come to pass, you may believe" (Matthew 24:25, John 13:19). God's people may never know the "day nor the hour in which the Son of Man is coming," but they will know many details in advance. This will be a witness to "the great multitude" of God's people who are

---

367 An additional detail of the final devastation is the "great hail from heaven" with "each hailstone about the weight of a talent" (about 75 pounds!).

in "Babylon." God's messengers will be able to predict and explain the awesome events that are taking place, and this will give hope and courage.

10:7 The Mystery of God

"But in the days of the voice of the seventh angel, when he is about to sound, the mystery of God should be finished, as He has declared to His servants the prophets" (Revelation 10:7). Chapter seven showed that there will be two groups of people who will be saved (besides those who are resurrected) when Jesus comes. The first group is the 144,000 "of all the tribes of the children of Israel" (Revelation 7:4). The angel commanded that the winds of the earth should not be released until they were sealed in their foreheads (vs. 1-3). After their sealing the winds will be released, resulting in the first six trumpet plagues. The sealed 144,000 will be protected from at least some of the damage of the plagues (see 9:4 *Protected by the Seal*).

But there is a second group: a "great multitude" from "all nations, tribes, peoples, and tongues," who "come out of the great tribulation" (Revelation 7:9,13,14). One of the major themes of the Book of Revelation is that many of God's people are in "Babylon," the false religious system. God, at the very end, will reveal the truth about Babylon ("Babylon the great is fallen, is fallen, and has become the habitation of devils" Revelation 18:2) and will call His people out of Babylon ("Come out of her my people" v. 4). Their coming out takes place sometime during the time of trouble, because they "come out of the great tribulation." When the great multitude are delivered from Babylon, **"The mystery of God will be finished."**

First of all, the mystery will be finished **"in the days of the sounding of the seventh angel."** The seventh trumpet takes place in Revelation 11:15 when "the kingdoms of this world…become the kingdoms of our Lord and of His Christ." This

verse suggests that a massive change of allegiance will take place,[368] which is what would have to happen for a great multitude to "come out of [Babylon]."

But the verse also emphasizes the importance of the period **"when he [the seventh angel] is about to sound,"** in other words, the period just before the seventh trumpet. This time is described in Revelation 11:3-13, and involves the ministry of the "two witnesses." Their ministry will be presented in detail in chapter eleven, but briefly, the two witnesses symbolize those who give the last powerful testimony to the world. They are overcome and symbolically "killed" by "the beast that ascends out of the bottomless pit." God raises them up again in the sight of "their enemies," and "in the same hour there was a great earthquake…seven thousand people were killed [this section is highly symbolic] and the rest were afraid and gave glory to the God of heaven" (Revelation 11:13). As we will see, "the rest" are the great multitude, and it is their acceptance of the last message that is indicated by the phrase "the kingdoms of this world have become the kingdoms of our Lord and of his Christ." This is the essence of **"The mystery."**

The **"mystery"** was **"declared to His servants the prophets."** This is the same language that is found in Ephesians 3:3-10, "The *mystery of Christ…as it has now been revealed by the Spirit to His holy apostles and prophets: that the Gentiles should be fellow heirs, of the same body, and partakers of His promise in Christ through the gospel…*to make all see what is the fellowship

---

368 Actually the kingdoms of this world can become the kingdoms of Christ in two ways. One is for the people to repent and change their allegiance, which is what happens with the great multitude. The other way is for them to be overcome and destroyed by Christ, which is what will happen to those who follow the beast at the Second Coming. This verse shows that we will no longer have the situation in which Satan is "the ruler of this world" and his evil kingdom co-exists with God's kingdom.

of the *mystery*…to the intent *that now the manifold wisdom of God might be made known by the church to the principalities and powers in the heavenly places.*"

Paul states in these verses that the mystery, which was revealed to the apostles and prophets, was that through the gospel the Gentiles (those not of "Israel") will become a part of God's body of believers, and this will reveal God's wisdom to the rest of the universe. Writing to the Gentiles in the city of Colossae, Paul expounds on "the mystery which has been hidden from ages and from generations, but now has been revealed to His saints…the riches of the glory of this mystery among the Gentiles: which is Christ in you, the hope of glory"(Colossians 1:26, 27).

We see in this passage that God made known a mystery to the "saints" (those who were the "chosen people"). The mystery was "among the Gentiles." The "saints" have never considered it to be mysterious that they themselves could be saved. After all, they were "Israelites, to whom pertain the adoption, the glory, the covenants, the giving of the law, the service of God, and the promises; of whom are the fathers and from whom, according to the flesh, Christ came" (Romans 9:4,5). But the idea that Christ could actually save Gentiles who had been "aliens from the commonwealth of Israel and strangers from the covenants of promise, having no hope and without God in the world" (Ephesians 2: 12) was an incomprehensible mystery.

Peter had to see a vision of unclean animals three times and then see the Holy Spirit fall upon Cornelius and his Gentile servants before he could believe that salvation was for the Gentiles too (Acts 10). "Those of the circumcision who believed were astonished, as many as came with Peter, because the gift of the Holy Spirit had been poured out on the Gentiles also" (Acts 10:45).

Later when "the apostles and brethren who were in Judea" heard about all that had happened, "they became silent; and they glorified God, saying, 'Then God has also granted to the Gentiles repentance to life" (Acts 11:1-18). As Paul put it, "in Christ Jesus you who once were far off have been brought near by the blood of Christ" (Ephesians 2: 13).

Today we still have those who grew up with the Bible, the gospel, the law and the prophets, and to them it is a great mystery how God will ever reach the billions of people who are lost in "the world." But according to Revelation 7:9, before it is all over God will win "a great multitude which no man could number" of men, women and children who have been Gentiles "of all nations, tribes, peoples and tongues." Although they were born and raised outside of the knowledge of God, He will "clothe [them] in white robes" which were "made…white in the blood of the Lamb," give them a place "before the throne" and then present them as His holy church, a demonstration to the universe. Seeing this, "all the angels… fell on their faces before the throne and worshiped God" (v.11). Satan has used this world of sin to call into question God's very character, but when **"the mystery of God [is] finished"** there will be no more questions about His goodness, love and wisdom.

The Shattering of the Power of the Holy People

Revelation 10, which includes the **"seven thunders"** and the finishing of **"the mystery of God,"** is paralleled by Daniel 12, as outlined at the beginning of this chapter. (See Table 10.2)

The verse which corresponds to Revelation **10:7 ("the mystery of God should be finished")**

Table 10.2

Revelation 10	Daniel 12
"The angel…lifted up his hand to heaven" (v. 5).	"The man…held up his right hand and his left hand to heaven" (v. 7).
[He] "swore by Him who lives forever and ever" (v. 6).	[he] "swore by Him who lives forever" (v. 7).
"In the days of the voice of the seventh angel, when he is about to sound" (v. 7).	"When the power of the holy people has been completely shattered" (v. 7).
"the mystery of God should be finished" (v. 7).	"All these things shall be finished" (v. 7).

is Daniel 12:7 ("all these things shall be finished"). The dialogue between two angels began with the question, "How long shall the fulfillment of these wonders be?" In both Daniel and Revelation the angel raised his hand to heaven and swore by him who lives forever. In Revelation the angel said, **"In the days of the sounding of the seventh angel, when he is about to sound, the mystery of God would be finished."** In Daniel he said, *"when the power of the holy people has been completely shattered*, all these things shall be finished" (Daniel 12:7).

As we saw in the previous section, the finishing of the mystery of God is the winning of the great multitude out of Babylon, in other words, when "the kingdoms of this world have become the kingdom of our Lord" (Revelation 11:15). According to Daniel 12:7, this will happen "when the power of the holy people has been completely shattered." The corresponding verse, Revelation 10:7, shows that "the power of the holy people" will be "completely shattered" "in the days of the voice of the seventh angel, when he is about to sound."[369]

Who are the "holy people?" In the Old Testament, the "holy people" are the children of Israel, in contrast to the Gentiles around them (Deuteronomy 7:6, Isaiah 63: 17,18). The book of Deuteronomy shows that a particular identifying mark of the "holy people" is that they keep all of God's commandments.[370] The "holy people" are also identified in Isaiah as those who proclaim the coming of the Lord to the ends of the earth.[371] The corresponding "holy people" in the book of Revelation are the 144,000. They also are "of the children of Israel" (Revelation 7:4), they "keep the commandments of God" (Revelation 14:12) and have "the everlasting gospel to preach to those who dwell on the earth—to every nation, tribe, tongue and people" (Revelation 14:6).

According to Daniel 12:7, the "holy people," known in Revelation as the 144,000 or the

---

369 The time when the "seventh angel…is about to sound" is the time of the ministry of the "two witnesses" as outlined in chapter 11. The "shattering of the power of the holy people" is analogous to the killing of the two witnesses (see 11:7-10 *The Two Witnesses Killed*).

370 "The Lord has proclaimed you to be His special people…that you should *keep all His commandments…and that you may be a holy people to the Lord your God*" (Deuteronomy 26:18,19, 7:6, 14:2, 28:9).

371 "Prepare the way for the people; build up, build up the highway! Take out the stones, lift up a banner for the peoples! The Lord has proclaimed to the end of the world:…Surely your salvation is coming; behold, His reward is with Him…*and they shall call them The Holy People*, the redeemed of the Lord; And you shall be called Sought Out" (Isaiah 62:10-12). The fact that they are called "Sought Out" is another clue to their end-time identity. In the last days the "nations" will seek God's true people, recognizing their real relationship with God—"In those days ten men from every language of the nations shall grasp the sleeve of a Jewish man, saying, 'Let us go with you, for we have heard that God is with you'" (Zechariah 8:23).

"two witnesses," will have an experience during the time of trouble that will shatter their power. Revelation 11 shows that this will take place after they have given their testimony to the world. "When they [the two witnesses] have finished their testimony, the beast that ascends out of the bottomless pit will make war against them, and shall overcome them, and kill them…And they that dwell on the earth shall rejoice over them" (Revelation 11:7-10).[372] The wrath of the whole world will be focused upon them, they will be blamed for the time of trouble, and the majority will reject their message and follow the beast. But when they feel like they have reached the end of their endurance, God Himself will intervene. "The Lord will judge His people and have compassion on His servants, *when He sees that their power is gone*" (Deuteronomy 32:36).[373]

The Christian life, from start to finish, is a continual dying to self. The irony is that there is always more to die; self has a way of hiding or being resurrected so that sin still has a stronghold in the soul. But in the final experience of the 144,000 self will die completely so that only Jesus will be seen in His resurrection power, and this will be a powerful witness to the world. "Those from the peoples, tribes, tongues and nations will see their dead bodies three-and-a-half days… now after the three-and-a-half days the breath of life from God entered them, and they stood on their feet, and great fear fell on those who saw them…and the rest were afraid, and gave glory to the God of heaven" (Revelation 11:9-13). This

story will be explained more fully in 11:7-10, *The Two Witnesses Killed*.

10:8-11 Eating the Little Book

God's special messengers will be "shattered" by all that is involved in giving the last message to the world. This experience of suffering while ministering for the sake of the captives in Babylon is symbolized by eating a little book that was sweet at first but then became bitter. **"And the voice which I heard from heaven spoke to me again, and said, 'Go and take the little book which is open in the hand of the angel which stands on the sea and on the earth.' And I went to the angel, and said to him, 'Give me the little book.' And he said to me, 'Take it, and eat it; and it will make your belly bitter, but it shall be in your mouth sweet as honey.' And I took the little book out of the angel's hand, and ate it; and it was in my mouth sweet as honey; and as soon as I had eaten it, my belly was bitter. And he said to me, 'You must prophesy again before many peoples, and nations, and tongues, and kings'"** (Revelation 10:8-11).

The fact that the angel told John **"You must prophesy again"** implies that the prophetic messages of the little book will be given more than once. Although no previous prophesying has been mentioned in chapter 10, an obvious candidate is mentioned just three verses later in Revelation 11:3: "And I will give power to my two witnesses, and *they shall prophesy 1,260 days, clothed in sackcloth*." John is a symbolic representative of the "two witnesses" who bring God's messages to the world. These texts show that the two witnesses will "prophesy" for 1,260 "days." After the 1,260 days are over they will eat the bitter-sweet book, and then they will **"prophesy again."**

The "two witnesses" did "prophesy in sackcloth" during the 1,260 years of the Dark Ages. God's underground "remnant" shared the light

---

372 This episode is found in Revelation 11: 11-13, just before the sounding of the seventh trumpet (Revelation 11:15). Thus it fits the specifications of Revelation 10:7, that the "mystery of God will be finished" "in the days of the voice of the seventh angel, when he is about to sound."

373 This refers to the experience of God's people as they face the "image of the beast" which will "cause that as many as would not worship the image of the beast should be killed" and "to receive a mark on their right hand or on their foreheads, that no one may buy or sell except he that had the mark" (Revelation 13:15-17).

of the Old and New Testament, resulting in the Protestant Reformation. As this period was finishing, the understanding of end time prophesies began to increase as the contents of the **"little book"** began to be revealed. In 10:1-7 *The Seven Thunders* we saw that the **"little book"** contains information about the meaning of prophetic events including the prophetic time periods found in the book of Daniel. "The words [were] closed up and sealed till the time of the end" but at that time "the wise shall understand" (Daniel 12:9,10). In the symbolic words of Revelation 10, diligent students of the scriptures **"took the little book out of the angel's hand, and ate it."**

In concrete terms, what happened was that an understanding of the great prophetic periods developed during the Philadelphia era, which began in the late 18th century. This time frame coincided with the end of the 1,260 years of papal persecution (see 12:12-14 *The Woman in the Wilderness*) and the beginning of the "time of the end" (see 3:8 *The Open Door*). At that time Bible students who led out in the Millerite movement searched out the meaning of the cleansing of the sanctuary (the 2,300 day prophecy of Daniel 8), the 490 years of probation given to the Jewish nation (the "seventy weeks" of Daniel 9) and the 1,260 years of papal oppression (the "time, times and half a time" of Daniel 7).[374] As they taught about these important prophecies and their relationship (as they understood it) to the Second Coming of Christ, a tremendous spiritual interest and excitement was generated (the book **"was in my mouth sweet as honey"**). Much of the interest was because they confused the Second Coming of Christ with the cleansing of the sanctuary (which was to take place in 1844 according to the 2,300 day prophecy).[375]

The message itself was much more comprehensive than simply finding some dates for the prophecies. The Day of Atonement was brought into focus, calling for a radically different relationship with God and deep searching of heart. But when Jesus did not come as expected and they were faced with ridicule and rejection, they were bitterly disappointed (**"it will make your belly bitter"**).

But God had not finished His revelation to the world. Even though there had been a great disappointment, God's faithful messengers **"must prophesy again before many peoples, and nations, and tongues, and kings."** In other words, there was to be a similar prophetic movement but with a much more extensive, worldwide audience. The experience of the earlier messengers was a "type"[376] of the experience the 144,000 will have during the time of trouble. Again they will have a message based on prophecy. It will be the comprehensive message that has been sealed in the **"Seven Thunders."** Besides the earlier understanding of the great time prophecies of Daniel, there will be a focus on "the everlasting gospel" (Revelation 14:6), Jesus' comprehensive end-time prophecy in Matthew 24 including the abomination of desolation, the mysterious

---

374 See chapters 3:8 "The Day of Atonement" and 12:12-14.

375 See appendix 5 for details about the 2,300 day prophecy. Briefly, the prophecy is in Daniel 8:14, "for two thousand three hundred days: then the sanctuary shall be cleansed." From the prophecy of seventy weeks in Daniel 9 it was clear that these were prophetic days (a day for a year) and the starting point for both prophecies could be determined "from the going forth of the command to restore and build Jerusalem" which took place in 457 BC. Two thousand three hundred years extended to 1844, and the date Oct. 22 was fixed upon as it was the date of the Jewish Day of Atonement that year. The Millerites assumed that the cleansing of the sanctuary referred to the cleansing of the earth by fire at the Second Coming of Christ. The passing of the date was termed "the great disappointment."

376 A type is "a symbol of something in the future, as an Old Testament event prefiguring a New Testament event…to represent prophetically, foreshadow, prefigure" *Random House Webster's Dictionary*, (New York, NY, Random House, 1997).

time prophecies of Daniel 12, the mark, number, name and image of the beast of Revelation 13, the "three angels' messages" of Revelation 14, and the great harlot/scarlet beast vision of Revelation 17. The understanding and sharing of these messages will be **"sweet as honey"** as the faithful messengers experience the joy of witnessing for the Lord with the latter-rain power of the Holy Spirit making their witness compelling and effective. But the deadly reaction of "the beast" and his followers, as outlined in chapters 11 and 13, will **"make [their] belly bitter."**

In spite of the opposition of the beast, they **"must prophesy...before many peoples, and nations, and tongues and kings."** They will give the message of Revelation 18 with "great authority," exposing the Babylon politico-religious system ("Babylon the great is fallen, is fallen and has become a dwelling place of demons") and calling the people of the world to "Come out of her, my people, that you do not partake of her sins, and that you do not receive of her plagues" (Revelation 18:1-4). In the face of deadly opposition it will seem to them that they are risking their lives in vain, but in the end their witness will accomplish its purpose—a "great multitude" will "come out."

This experience finds its parallel in Ezekiel 2 and 3. In those chapters the prophet was given a message that was directed to God's people who had been captured and taken to Babylon.[377] The captives were hopeless and hardened by their experiences in Babylon, just as God's weak followers in end-time "Babylon" will be hopeless and hardened by Satan's fierce attacks during the trumpet plagues. God told Ezekiel, "I am sending you to the children of Israel, to a rebellious nation...for they are impudent and stubborn children...and you shall say to them, 'Thus says the Lord God'...You shall speak My words to them whether they hear or whether they refuse" (Ezekiel 2:3-7, 3:8,9).

Just like the message in Revelation 10, the message given to Ezekiel was depicted as words he would eat which would initially be sweet. "Now when I looked, there was a hand stretched out to me; and behold, a scroll of a book was in it...Moreover He said to me, 'Son of man, eat what you find; eat this scroll, and go speak to the house of Israel'...So I ate, and it was in my mouth like honey in sweetness...Moreover He said to me: 'Son of man, receive into your heart all My words that I speak to you, and hear with your ears. And go, get to the captives, to the children of your people, and speak to them and tell them, 'Thus says the Lord God,' whether they hear, or whether they refuse" (Ezekiel 2:9,10, 3:1-3, 10,11).

Ezekiel's ministry in Babylon prefigured the experience the 144,000 will have as they "go...to the captives." Chapter 11 tells more about their awesome experience as they deliver God's final appeal to the world to repent and be saved.

---

377 See Ezekiel 3:15, 11:24,25.

"The beast that ascends out of the bottomless pit will make war against them, overcome them, and kill them. And their dead bodies will lie in the street of the great city" Rev. 11:7,8

Matthew Merian 1630

Chapter 11

Revelation 11:1-19

11:1 And there was given me a reed like a staff, and the angel stood, saying, "Rise, and measure the temple of God, and the altar, and those who worship therein.

11:2 But leave out the court which is outside the temple, and do not measure it; for it is given to the Gentiles, and they will trample the holy city for forty-two months.

11:3 And I will give power to my two witnesses, and they shall prophesy 1,260 days, clothed in sackcloth."

11:4 These are the two olive trees, and the two lampstands standing before the God of the earth.

11:5 And if anyone wants to harm them, fire proceeds out of their mouth, and devours their enemies; and if anyone wants to harm them, he must in this manner be killed.

11:6 These have power to shut heaven, that rain will not fall in the days of their prophecy. And they have power over the waters to turn them to blood, and to strike the earth with every plague, as often as they want.

11:7 And when they have finished their testimony, the beast that ascends out of the bottomless pit will make war against them, and shall overcome them, and kill them.

11:8 And their dead bodies will lie in the street of the great city, which spiritually is called Sodom and Egypt, where also our Lord was crucified.

11:9 And they of the peoples and tribes and tongues and nations will gaze at their dead bodies three and a half days, and will not allow their dead bodies to be put in graves.

11:10 And they that dwell on the earth shall rejoice over them, and make merry, and shall send gifts one to another; because these two prophets tormented those that dwell on the earth.

11:11 And after three and a half days the Spirit of life from God entered into them, and they stood upon their feet; and great fear fell upon those who saw them.

11:12 And they heard a great voice from heaven saying to them, "Come up here." And they ascended up to heaven in a cloud; and their enemies beheld them.

11:13 And the same hour there was a great earthquake, and a tenth of the city fell, and in the earthquake were slain of men seven thousand; and the remnant were afraid, and gave glory to the God of heaven.

11:14 The second woe is past, and, behold, the third woe comes quickly.

11:15 And the seventh angel sounded, and there were great voices in heaven, saying, "The kingdoms of this world have become the kingdom of our Lord, and of His Christ; and He shall reign forever and ever."

11:16 And the twenty-four elders, sitting before God on their thrones, fell on their faces and worshiped God,

11:17 Saying, "We give You thanks, O Lord God Almighty, who is, and who was, and who is to come; because You have taken your great power, and reigned.

11:18 And the nations were angry, and your wrath has come, and the time of the dead, that they should be judged, and to give the reward to your servants the prophets, and to the saints, and to those who fear your name, small and great; and to destroy those who destroy the earth."

11:19 And the temple of God was opened in heaven, and there was seen in His temple the ark of his covenant. And there were lightnings, and voices, and thunders, and an earthquake, and great hail.

11:1,2 Measuring the Temple

"And there was given me a reed like a staff, and the angel stood, saying, 'Rise, and measure the temple of God, and the altar, and those who worship therein'" (Revelation 11:1,2). What temple was John to measure, and what is the significance of measuring it? As usual in the Book of Revelation, we cannot understand the meaning without understanding the underlying reference passages in the Old Testament.

The parallel Old Testament passage is Ezekiel 40-48 where there is also a man with "a measuring reed[378] in his hand" (Ezekiel 40:3), who measured a temple and its surroundings. The prophet was told, "Declare to the house of Israel everything you see" (v.4). What follows is a highly detailed description, complete with dimensions, of a temple that has never existed on earth.

The key verses are in Ezekiel 43. "And He said to me, 'Son of man, this is the place of My throne and the place of the soles of My feet, where I will dwell in the midst of the children of Israel forever. No more shall the house of Israel defile My holy name…Son of man, describe the temple to the house of Israel, that they may be ashamed of their iniquities" (Ezekiel 43:7,10). God wanted to "dwell in the midst of the children of Israel forever" and in order for this to happen they must "be ashamed of their iniquities" and "no more… defile My holy name." Measuring the temple was not simply giving them dimensions of a building. Somehow this measuring would help them to become the kind of people they needed to be so that God could dwell in their midst.

This message was given to the children of Israel when they were captives in Babylon because of their sins.[379] With the idolatry of Babylon all around them, they themselves were committing "harlotry" and "abominations." But through the prophet they were given the "heavenly standards" and a call to repentance—"and if they are ashamed of all that they have done, make known to them the design of the temple and its arrangements…that they may keep its whole design and all its ordinances and perform

---

378 The Greek Septuagint version uses the same word, *kalamos*, for rod in Ezekiel that is used for reed in Revelation.

379 "The Spirit took me…into Chaldea, to those in captivity…so I spoke to those in captivity of all the things the Lord had shown me" Ezekiel 12:24,25.

them" (Ezekiel 43:11).

The temple was the building in which sacrificial ceremonies were carried out, a "shadow" of the heavenly reality. When Ezekiel was told to measure the temple, there was no temple on earth to measure, because it had been destroyed by the Babylonians. Nor did his measurement match the temple that was rebuilt by the Jews. He measured the heavenly temple, which is the original and model for all of the earthly temples,[380] a symbolic picture of God's plan of salvation.[381]

By the time John wrote Revelation there was again no physical temple—it had been destroyed by the Romans in AD 70. Paul and Peter made it clear that the church, "the body of Christ" (1Corinthians 12:27), is the New Testament temple.[382] But just as Ezekiel was not to measure the earthly temple but the heavenly, so John was not to measure the imperfect earthly church, but the perfect heavenly Body, Christ Himself.[383] The measuring of the temple is a "Revelation of Jesus Christ."

In order to understand what this passage is saying we need to keep in mind the context. Chapter 11 is a continuation of chapter 10, which began by presenting the seven thunders, prophetic messages that were sealed until the last days. At the end of time they will be unsealed— God's final messengers will understand them and share them with the world. In 10:7 *The Mystery of God* we saw that the final messages will be given to the "Gentiles," people who have been deeply deceived by false concepts about God. As a result a great "mystery" will be accomplished—Gentiles,

who have not known God and have been slaves of sin, will through God's grace become His holy people, and their transformation will be a witness to the whole universe.

In 10:8-11 *Eating the Little Book* John was given a little book to eat. Comparing with Ezekiel chapters 2 and 3 and Daniel 12, we saw that God's final messengers will understand the prophecies that expose the lies of "Babylon," reveal the true character of God and show what will happen during the time of the end. This understanding is "sweet as honey" but when the messengers and their message is rejected "it will make [their] stomach bitter." However, despite the bitter experience "you must prophesy again" (Revelation 10:11)—God's messengers must persevere in bringing God's message to the "captives in Babylon," even though they face opposition and persecution.

The same context continues in chapter 11. The angel told John to **measure the temple of God, and the altar, and those who worship therein.**" As we saw above, the **"temple of God"** refers to the heavenly temple and measuring it is a revelation of the character of God Himself. In Revelation 21 where the New Jerusalem is likewise measured with a reed, John says "I saw no temple in it, for *the Lord God Almighty and the Lamb are its temple*" (Revelation 21:22). The psalmist wrote, "Walk about Zion [the temple mount][384] and go all around her, count her towers, mark well her bulwarks, consider her palaces that you may tell it to the generation following, *for this is God*" (Psalm 48:12). In the earthly temple, all of the features were portrayals of some aspect of God. The seven-branched lamp

---

380 See Hebrews 8:1-5, 9:11, 24.

381 See Hebrews 9: 1-28.

382 2 Corinthians 6:16, Ephesians 2:21, 1Peter 2:4,5.

383 Jesus insisted that His body was the temple of God, both before and after the resurrection ("destroy this temple and in three days I will raise it up" John 2:29). His insistence that He was the temple was one of the main accusations against Him at His trial (Matthew 26:1, Mark 14:58).

384 "David brought the ark to Zion, and the hill henceforth became sacred (2 Samuel 6:1-12). When Solomon later removed the ark to the temple on nearby Mount Moriah, the name Zion was extended to take in the temple" (Isaiah 8:18, 18:7, 24:23, Joel 3:17, Micah 4:7). *Pictorial Bible Dictionary*, (Grand Rapids, MI Zondervan 1973), p. 914. Use by permission.

represented the fullness of the Holy Spirit which enlightens the darkness. The table of showbread represented Jesus feeding His children the Bread of Life through His Word. The altar of incense represented Christ's intercession for sinners, and the ark of the covenant covered by the mercy seat represented the justice, mercy and glory of God. Unfortunately, every aspect of God has been tragically misrepresented by the Babylonian false religion that claims to represent Christ.

The great need of the world is to know God as He really is. "Behold, God is great, and we do not know Him" (Job 36:26).[385] This is particularly true of those who are Christ's but are caught in the confusion of Babylon. Millions believe that God would torture people forever for not believing in Him, or arbitrarily choose some for salvation and others for destruction, or give a law that cannot be kept and then condemn people for not keeping it, or exclude people from heaven because they didn't happen to have exposure to the Christian message—and these are just a few of the many misconceptions about God. Measuring the temple will reveal the love, mercy, righteousness and justice of God, clearing up all the "contradictions" and misconceptions.

The Altar and Those Who Worship There

John was also to measure **"the altar."** There were two altars in the ancient sanctuary, the bronze altar of sacrifice and the golden altar of incense. Both have to do with the ministry of Jesus—the former with His sacrifice and the latter with His ongoing mediation.[386] Both of these aspects of Jesus' ministry are greatly

misrepresented by the Babylonian "Christian" Church.

The bronze altar symbolized the sacrifice of Jesus on the Cross. Many see the death of Jesus as physical torture which Jesus endured because He fell into the hands of wicked sinners,[387] or as punishment which Jesus endured on our behalf for "the original sin of Adam" which God arbitrarily imputed to us, or as a sacrifice by the loving Jesus to appease the wrath of the "angry and offended Father." But Jesus did not die of torture; He died of a broken heart, experiencing the separation from God that is the natural result of the sin of mankind, which He took upon Himself. And Jesus did not do this in order to appease an angry God. At the Cross God the Father, Son and Holy Spirit were together reaching out with inexpressible love to sinful men, women, and children, pleading with them to be reconciled to God and to be free of the guilt and separation that is destroying them. "God was in Christ reconciling the world to Himself." "For God so loved the world that He gave His only begotten Son" (2Corinthians 5:19, John 3:16).

Besides the bronze altar of sacrifice the sanctuary also had the golden altar of incense, which portrays Christ's ongoing mediation.[388] Jesus did not finish the work of salvation and then go to sit around in heaven waiting for God to finally decide that it was time for Him to return to earth. His cry on the Cross, "it is finished," referred to the perfect sacrifice that He offered which made salvation possible, but it did not signify the end of His work for our salvation. As essential as

---

385 The Hebrew word for "know" is *yada*, the same word used in Genesis 4:1 "Adam knew his wife and she conceived," referring to the most intimate relationship possible.

386 Exodus 37: 25- 38: 7, Exodus 20:24, Revelation 8:3.

387 The Jews who killed Jesus were no more (or less) wicked than any other race—they were simply the representatives of humanity who, being sinners, did what any race of sinners would have done.

388 "He was given much incense that he should offer it with the prayers of all the saints upon the golden altar which was before the throne. And the smoke of the incense with the prayers of the saints, ascended before God from the angel's hand" (Revelation 7:3,4. See also Hebrews 4:14-16, 7:25).

Christ's death and resurrection were, so essential is His ministry of mediation in the heavenly sanctuary—"Seeing that we have a great High Priest who has passed through the heavens, Jesus the Son of God,…let us therefore come boldly to the throne of grace, that we may obtain mercy and find grace to help in time of need…He is able to save to the uttermost those who come to God through Him, since He always lives to make intercession for them" (Hebrews 4:14-16, 7:25).

It is not the human priest who is our mediator—"For there is one God and one Mediator between God and men, the Man Christ Jesus" (1Timothy 2:5). It is not necessary for us to confess to the priest, nor do we receive pardon from him. We do not need to pray to the saints so that they can "more effectively" present our petitions to God. The measuring of the altar will show God's people in Babylon that we have direct access to God through Jesus Christ, and we have no need to be afraid to come to Him.

John was also commanded to measure **"Those who worship therein"** which refers to His faithful covenant people. In chapter seven John saw those "coming out[389] of the great tribulation, and they washed their robes and made them white in the blood of the Lamb. Therefore they are before the throne of God, *and serve Him day and night in his temple*" (Revelation 7:14,15). What does a person who has truly washed his robes in Jesus' blood look like in real life? How does serving Jesus "day and night" translate into human interactions in the real world? The measuring of God's true church includes the revelation of what it really means to be a Christian.

This threefold revelation of the character of God, the ministry of Jesus and the true children of God will stand in stark contrast to the false

picture of God, of Jesus and of the worshipers of the false Babylon church. When this contrast is revealed to the world it will enrage the followers of Babylon against God's faithful servants. But as we will see, the true revelation will also win the hearts of a "great multitude" of God's people who are "captives" in Babylon.

11:2 Leave Out the Court

"But leave out the court which is outside the temple, and do not measure it; for it is given to the Gentiles, and they will trample the holy city for forty-two months" (Revelation 11:2). In the temple Ezekiel described, the outer court was the part of the temple where the common people gathered.[390] In Revelation 11:2 the common people who are found in the outer court are called **"the Gentiles."** In God's covenant arrangement all of God's people were to be priests, ministering to the nations around them (the "Gentiles" in the "outer court") in order to bring them into God's family.

But unfortunately, instead of the church invading the world to bring them the gospel, unconverted **"Gentiles"** invaded and took over the church, resulting in the tragic history that we saw in the messages to the seven churches in chapters 2 and 3. "When you brought in foreigners, uncircumcised in heart and uncircumcised in flesh, to be in My sanctuary to defile it—My house…then they broke My covenant because of all your abominations" (Ezekiel 44:7). The church became corrupt, and was no longer representative of God. The corrupt Christian church as it has been in history is not to be the "standard" for the end-time people of God—**"leave out [do**

---

389 The Greek could be translated, "the coming out ones," implying that they are still in the process of coming out, but not yet in heaven. See 7: *In Heaven While On Earth.*

390 The priests would come there to "sanctify the people" but before they came they would change their clothes from the holy garments they wore when they prepared the sacrifices and grain offerings, which were offered in the inner court. This emphasized the marked distinction between the priests and the common people (Ezekiel 42:14, 44: 9, 46:20-24).

not measure] **the court which is outside the temple…for it is given to the Gentiles."**

The fact is that the historical church has often been the greatest enemy of God's true followers. This is indicated by the fact that **"they will trample the holy city for forty-two months."** This period of time will be explained in further detail in chapters 12 and 13, but briefly, it is the same period[391] as the "time, times and half a time," when the "little horn" of Daniel seven "persecuted the saints of the Most High" (Daniel 7:25). It is also the same as the "one thousand two hundred and sixty days" when the true church "fled into the wilderness" and was "in sackcloth" (Revelation 12:6, 11:3). These periods all refer to the long centuries of papal supremacy which lasted from just after the breakup of the western Roman Empire until after the Protestant Reformation, when the papal church was the oppressor of God's faithful people. The true church of God must reject the model given by this "gentile" church of history.

But just as we saw in chapter 10 that Jesus' discourse in Matt. 24 had an application to both the papal period and the final time of trouble (see 10: *Clues in Matthew 24*), so it is here. During the time of trouble God's **"two witness…will prophesy one thousand two hundred and sixty days, clothed in sackcloth"** and at the same time **"the Gentiles…will tread the holy city underfoot for forty-two months"** (see Appendix 10). It is this end-time application that is the primary focus of both the measuring of the temple and the ministry of the two witnesses.[392]

11:3-6 Who Are the Two Witnesses?

"And I will give power to my two witnesses, and they shall prophesy 1,260 days, clothed in sackcloth. These are the two olive trees, and the two lampstands standing before the God of the earth. And if anyone wants to harm them, fire proceeds out of their mouth, and devours their enemies; and if anyone wants to harm them, he must in this manner be killed. These have power to shut heaven, that rain will not fall in the days of their prophecy. And they have power over the waters to turn them to blood, and to strike the earth with every plague, as often as they want" (Revelation 11:3-6).

The Greek word for witness is *marturos*,

---

391 The three periods coincide historically but focus on different aspects of this period. The 42 months (Revelation 11:2, 13:5) deal exclusively with desecration and persecution by God's enemies. The 1,260 days (Revelation 11:3, 12:6) refer exclusively to the experiences of God's people. A time, times and half a time (Daniel 7:25,12:7, Revelation 12:14) refer to the interaction between the persecuting enemies and the persecuted saints.

392 It is evident that the ministry of the two witnesses is primarily end time because this section is within the context of the sixth trumpet, also known as the second woe. Immediately after the victory of the two witnesses in 11:13 comes the statement that "the second woe is past. Behold, the third woe is coming quickly" (Revelation 11:14), which is followed directly by the statement that "The nations were angry, and Your wrath has come, and the time of the dead that they should be judged, and that You should reward Your servants the prophets and the saints…and destroy those who destroy the earth" (Revelation 11:17,18). This is a clear reference to the seven last plagues and the Second Coming, which means that the trumpets, including the trampling by the Gentiles and the ministry of the two witnesses, are a part of the final events which culminate in Christ's coming.

The fact that the two witnesses "have power over the waters to turn them to blood, and to strike the earth with every plague, as often as they want" (11:6) points to either the seven trumpet plagues or the seven last plagues. Both of these series of plagues are last-day events (see 8: *Trumpets: Past or Future?*)

Moreover, "when they finish their [1,260 day] testimony, the beast that ascends out of the bottomless pit will make war against them, overcome them, and kill them" (Revelation 11:7). As we will see later in this chapter and in chapter 17: 6-8, "the beast…ascends out of the bottomless pit" during the time of trouble. Furthermore, as a result of the ministry, death and resurrection of the two witnesses "the rest were afraid and gave glory to the God of heaven" (Revelation 11: 13). This is a clear response to the first angel's message ("fear God and give glory to Him" Revelation 14: 7), which is given during the last days.

which is defined as one who declares facts directly known to himself from firsthand knowledge, or from firsthand experience, who tells what he believes, even though it results in his being killed for it. Peter and the other disciples who had been with Jesus declared, "We are His witnesses," and many of them ended up in prison or were killed because of their witness.[393]

Jesus' final commandment to His disciples was that they were to be witnesses to the whole world—"You shall receive power when the Holy Spirit has come upon you and you shall be witnesses to Me in Jerusalem, and in all Judea and Samaria, and to the end of the earth" (Acts 1:8). Peter, John, and the rest of the Apostles were direct witnesses.[394] During their lifetimes they told thousands of people about Jesus. But fortunately for us who live two thousand years later, they wrote down what they had experienced, just as the Old Testament prophets had done before them. At the most basic level, the two witnesses are their testimony, found in the Old Testament (which presents God and His plan of salvation in types and shadows), and the New Testament (which portrays the living reality in Jesus Christ). Through the ages the church has misunderstood and even twisted the witness of the scriptures, but they have stood as an anchor, bringing God's people back to a true knowledge of Him.

But the two witnesses are more than a book. Billions of people have died having never heard an effective witness of Jesus, even though the Bible has been in constant existence. Effective witness only takes place when the Word of God has become a living reality in the lives of men, women and children who love God with all their hearts and who then heed the command of Jesus to "Go into all the world and preach the gospel to every creature."[395] The two witnesses are the people who bring the light of God's Word to those who are in darkness.

"They shall prophesy 1,260 days, clothed in sackcloth."[396] God's fearless servants faithfully proclaimed the word of God during the 1,260 years of papal idolatry. During the Dark Ages it seemed like the whole world was against the few who were true to God. The Bible was chained in convent cells and those who dared to stand for the truth faced the Inquisition, torture and death. False witnesses abounded, perverting the Word of God. But the faithful martyrs and reformers "did not love their lives to the death" (Revelation 12:11) and were bright lights shining in the darkness.

Both the Old and the New Testament teach that a message, in order to be valid and accepted, must be confirmed by "the testimony of two witnesses."[397] The ministry of the two witnesses began even when Jesus was still here on earth— "The Lord appointed seventy others also, and

---

393 "We are witnesses of all things which He did...Him God raised up on the third day, and showed Him openly, not to all the people, but to witnesses chosen before by God, even to us, who ate and drank with Him after He arose from the dead...to Him all the prophets witness" (Acts 10:39-43). "We [Peter and the other apostles] are His witnesses to these things, and so also is the Holy Spirit whom God has given to those who obey him.' When they [the high priest and the Sadducees, v.17] heard this, they were furious and plotted to kill them." "Then he [Herod] killed James the brother of John with the sword...he proceeded further to seize Peter also...he put him in prison" (Acts 5:32,33, 12: 1-4).

394 They were direct witnesses in the sense that they had first-hand knowledge—"That which we have heard, which we have seen with our eyes, which we have looked upon, and our hands have handled...we declare to you" (1John 1:1-3).

395 Mark 16:15.

396 Sackcloth is a symbol of mourning, repentance, affliction of soul, hopeless consternation and humble entreaty in the face of overwhelming, seemingly hopeless adversity. See Psalms 30:11, Amos 8:10, Nehemiah 9:1, Daniel 9:3,4, Isaiah 58:5, 2Kings 6:24-30, 2Kings 18:17-19:2.

397 Deuteronomy 17:6, 19:15, John 8:17, Hebrews 10:28.

sent them *two by two* before His face *into every city and place where He Himself was about to go*" (Luke 10:1). Now, at the end of the age, Jesus is "about to go" to every corner of the world—He is coming again and "every eye will see Him" (Revelation 1:7). As we will see in chapter 14, the 144,000 are the ones who, during the time of the end, have the special task of preparing people for that event as they scatter "two by two" to bring the truth of the God's Word to every nation, city, village and neighborhood. The medieval time of trouble was a type of the "time of trouble such as never was" (Daniel 12:1), when the crushing weight of the beast system, with its image, mark and number will bear down on the 144,000 who "keep the commandments of God and the faith of Jesus" (Revelation 14:12). The sweet "little book" that they have eaten will be bitter in their stomach, but they will heed the command, "You must prophesy again before many peoples, nations, tongues and kings" (Revelation 10:9-11). This final witness to the world by the 144,000 during the time of trouble is the primary application of the prophecy of the two witnesses.

Old Testament Types of the Two Witnesses

The description of the two witnesses is extremely rich in scriptural imagery, painting a composite picture from the various references.

"**These** [the Two Witnesses] **are the two olive trees and the two lampstands standing before the God of the earth**" (Revelation 11:4). The two witnesses are portrayed as "**olive trees**" and "**lampstands**"—images which are taken from Zechariah chapter 4.

The prophet Zechariah saw "a lampstand of solid gold with a bowl on top of it, and on the stand seven lamps…Two olive trees are by it, one at the right of the bowl and the other at its left…that drip into the receptacles of the two

gold pipes from which the golden oil drains" (Zechariah 4:2,3,12). An angel explained that the lampstands with the olive trees feeding them with oil represented the Spirit-empowered ministry of Zerubbabel, the leader who led the children of Israel back to Jerusalem from Babylon to rebuild the temple:[398] "This is the word of the Lord to Zerubbabel: Not by might, nor by power, but by my spirit, says the Lord of hosts. Who are you, O great mountain? Before Zerubbabel you shall become a plain!…The hands of Zerubbabel have laid the foundation of this temple; His hands shall also finish it" (Zechariah 4:6-10). Zerubbabel, who led literal Israel back to Jerusalem from their Babylonian captivity, was a type of the 144,000 who will bring a "great multitude" of last-day captives out of spiritual Babylon.

"**And if anyone wants to harm them, fire proceeds out of their mouth, and devours their enemies; and if anyone wants to harm them, he must in this manner be killed**" (Revelation 11:5). The fire in the mouths of the two witnesses is the word of God. "Thus says the Lord, the God of hosts: Because they have spoken this word, I am now making *My words in your mouth a fire*, and this people wood, and *the fire shall devour them*" (Jeremiah 5:3,14).

God's word is a consuming fire to sin. Those who submit themselves to God will be refined by His word, and it will burn away the impurities leaving the pure gold (Malachi 3:2,3). But those "who do wickedly will be stubble and the day which is coming shall burn them up" (Malachi 4:1-3).[399] During the time of trouble when the image, mark and number of the beast are in force, it will appear that the enemies of God have the upper hand. But this scripture shows that their final end is destruction, and this is what is meant by the

---

398 Ezra 2:1,2, 3:8, 5:2 Nehemiah 7:6,7, Haggai 1,2.

399 See also Isaiah 33:14-16.

phrase, **"if anyone wants to harm them** [God's faithful messengers] **he must...be killed."**

"These have power to shut heaven, that rain will not fall in the days of their prophecy" (Revelation11:6). This passage compares the ministry of the two witnesses to that of Elijah, who declared to the apostate king of Israel, "There shall not be dew nor rain these years, except at my word" (1Kings 17:1). Interestingly, the period of time of the drought was three years and six months,[400] the same length of time (1,260 days) that the two witnesses are to **"prophesy"** (Revelation 11:3).

During this period Jezebel killed the prophets of God and led Israel deeper into the worship of Baal (1Kings 18:4,13,19). Elijah gathered Israel and challenged them to choose who they would serve (1Kings 18:21). Elijah proposed a test (bringing fire down from heaven) to prove if God or Baal had true spiritual power. When the prophets of Baal had totally failed, Elijah offered a simple prayer of faith. "Then the fire of the Lord fell and consumed the burnt sacrifice, and the wood and the stones and the dust, and it licked up the water that was in the trench. Now when all the people saw it, they fell on their faces; and they said, 'The Lord, He is God!'"[401]

Elijah, as God's spokesman, had **"power to shut heaven, that rain will not fall"** and this was a part of the demonstration of the power of God that won the people from false worship to the true God. The book of Malachi predicts that Elijah will come again—"Behold, I will send you Elijah the prophet before the coming of the great and dreadful day of the Lord" (Malachi 4:5). The two witnesses will have an "Elijah message" that will be accompanied by the power of God, which will be so compelling that the whole world will

be brought to a decision for or against the Lord.

"And they have power over the waters to turn them to blood, and to strike the earth with every plague, as often as they want" (Revelation 11:6). This verse compares the ministry of the two witnesses to Moses and the plagues of Egypt. God had, through Joseph,[402] brought His chosen people to Egypt to save them and nurture them while He waited for conditions to be right to establish them in the Promised Land (Genesis 15:13-16).[403] The enemy sought to thwart God's plan, using "a new king over Egypt, who did not know Joseph" (Exodus 1:8). He first subjected them to cruel slavery, and eventually began to practice genocide, murdering the male babies.[404] At the time of God's choosing He revealed Himself to Moses in a burning bush and commanded him to go "to Pharaoh that you may bring My people, the children of Israel, out of Egypt" (Exodus 3:10). Pharaoh refused with the arrogant statement, "Who is the Lord that I should obey His voice to let Israel go? I do not know the Lord, nor will I let Israel go" (Exodus 5:2). God, through Moses, turned all the water of Egypt into blood, the first of a series of ten plagues that broke the will of Pharaoh, and he finally allowed Israel to go free out of Egypt and slavery (Exodus 7:14-25).

Moses, as a prophet of God, announced the plagues that would fall upon those who stubbornly resisted God. In the last days God's two witnesses, knowing from prophecy what will take place, will also be able to announce the plagues that will fall upon the world. In fact, several of the plagues have to do with water and blood. The first trumpet plague rains fire and blood upon

---

400 James 5:17.

401 1Kings 18:20-40.

402 Genesis 37-47.

403 God showed here his fairness and patience; although it was his will that the children of Abraham inherit the land of Canaan, he did not disenfranchise the Amorites who lived there until they, by their gross idolatry, immorality and violence filled up the cup of their iniquity (Genesis 15:16).

404 Exodus 1:9-22.

the earth, with the second trumpet plague the sea becomes blood, with the third the waters become bitter, and during the seven last plagues the sea and waters become blood. The two witnesses' foreknowledge and prediction of these plagues is their **"power over the waters to turn them to blood, and to strike the earth with every plague,"** and this will so enrage the followers of "the beast" that they **"make war against them, and shall overcome them, and kill them"** (Revelation 11:7).

Why Is This Important?

A summary of the Old Testament references in Revelation 10 and 11 confirms and clarifies the role of the two witnesses. Eating the little book refers to the message Ezekiel was to give to the people of God who were captives in Babylon. Measuring the temple refers to the measuring of Ezekiel's "new temple" which showed the standards required of those who would return from Babylon. The two olive trees and two lampstands refer to the ministry of Zerubbabel, who brought God's people back to Israel from Babylon to rebuild the temple. The power of the two witnesses to shut heaven so that no rain falls refers to Elijah and his ministry to bring the people of God who were in idolatry to repentance and back to the true God. Turning water to blood and striking with plagues refers to the ministry of Moses, who announced the plagues that God used to bring His people out of captivity in Egypt. All of these references have a consistent theme: the faithful witness brought a message to God's people who were in captivity, leading them out of physical and spiritual slavery and back to God (See Table 11.1).

Table 11.1

Two Witnesses—God's Last-Day Messengers to the Captives in Babylon		
Verses in Revelation	**Old Testament Parallel**	**Summary of Old Testament Passages**
Revelation 10: 8-11	Ezekiel 2, 3	Ezekiel ate a little book, then gave its message to the captives in Babylon.
Revelation 11: 1,2	Ezekiel 40-48	The temple was measured, giving the captives in Babylon the standards that were expected of them.
Revelation 11: 4	Zechariah 4: 6-10	Two olive trees and two lampstands represented the Spirit-filled ministry of Zerubabbel, who led Israel back from Babylon.
Revelation 11: 6	1 Kings 17, 18	Elijah announced a drought, followed by miracles that convinced God's people to abandon idolatry.
Revelation 11: 6	Exodus 7-12	Moses turned water to blood, and then announced a series of plagues which resulted in deliverance for God's people.

What is the significance of this for us, who live before the time of trouble? Today most of the people of the world do not consider themselves to be Christians; they are Hindus, Buddhists, Muslims, animists, atheists and many other mixtures. However, one thing they all have in common is that they have never heard the gospel presented effectively. The Christian church, which should be bringing them the gospel, is a confusing and confused assortment of various denominations who are characterized in Revelation as Laodicea, the church of wealth and spiritual apathy. Lukewarm Laodicea will never do an effective job of taking "the gospel to every creature" (Mark 16:15), and for this reason God is now putting together an evangelistic "team," known in the book of Revelation as the remnant, the two witnesses and the 144,000.[405] Satan is also assembling his team, presented symbolically in chapters 13 and 16 as the followers of the beast and the false prophet, who will use false miracles along with the mark and the number of the beast to deceive and coerce the world to worship the image of the beast (see chapter 13).

The time of trouble will begin suddenly with the trumpet plagues. As the world descends into chaos all the people of the world will be frantically trying to find out how to get God's help. Satan will make every effort to destroy as many as possible before they can make a decision for God—Revelation 9:15 indicates that he will manage "to slay a third of men." Those who are not killed will suffer such agony and torment that they "will seek death and will not find it; they will desire to die and death will flee from them" (Revelation 9:6).

Their misery will be in contrast to those who have been sealed by God. Although they will be persecuted and in distress, they will be protected by God's unseen providence (See 9:4 *Protected by the Seal*). They will not rely on their own talents and abilities; when they are "sealed in the forehead" they will receive the long-awaited "latter rain" and will experience the joy of ministering in the power of the Holy Spirit (See 7: *Sealing, the Law and the Latter Rain*).

According to Revelation 7, the 144,000 will be sealed before the time of trouble begins. Now God is calling his luke-warm Laodicean people to throw off their apathy and become His special witnesses. Jesus says, "I stand at the door and knock" (Revelation 3:20). He offers us "gold tried in the fire that you may be rich, and white raiment, that you may be clothed…and eye salve, that you may see" (Revelation 3:18). He is ready to pour out the "latter rain," the fullness of the Holy Spirit. This is an experience that no one should miss. If you are a Christian and you are reading this, now is the time to seek God with all your heart, to make sure your sins are forgiven and forsaken, to learn to hear His voice and through His power to obey Him.

Can you put this off and still be saved? It is true that a great multitude will be saved in the midst of the time of trouble. But there is no guarantee that you will be among them. The truth is that if you are wavering in your commitment to Christ you will be among the primary targets of Satan, either to be wiped out with the multitudes that will perish or to fall under the overwhelming deceptions of that time. Jesus is pleading with you, "*Today*, if you hear His voice, do not harden your hearts" (Hebrews 3:7,8).

---

405 These titles all refer to God's faithful messengers, but each has a slightly different emphasis. The remnant (Revelation 2:24, 12:17) is a characterization found frequently in the Old and New Testament to describe those who are faithful in the face of apostasy and persecution. The two witnesses are the witnesses to the world. The 144,000 are the same group but their witness is to the entire universe within the context of the great controversy.

11:7-10 The Two Witnesses Killed

"And when they have finished their testimony, the beast that ascends out of the bottomless pit will make war against them, and shall overcome them, and kill them. And their dead bodies will lie in the street of the great city, which spiritually is called Sodom and Egypt, where also our Lord was crucified. And they of the peoples and tribes and tongues and nations will gaze at their dead bodies three and a half days, and will not allow their dead bodies to be put in graves. And they that dwell on the earth shall rejoice over them, and make merry, and shall send gifts one to another; because these two prophets tormented those that dwell on the earth" (Revelation 11:7-10).

In chapter 10 the explanation of Matthew 24 showed that prophecy can have both a historical and a last-day application, the historical events giving a foretaste of what will happen at the end of time. The historical application of the killing of the two witnesses took place after the 1,260 years of **"prophecy in sackcloth,"** which constituted the period of papal supremacy from the mid sixth century until the end of the eighteenth century (see chapter 13). At the end of that period a new power arose—militant atheism, in the form of the French Revolution, a revolution that had a far-reaching influence on the violent revolutionary movements that followed, including atheistic communism. These movements made war on the Word of God, and in the case of communism, on the "witnesses" who dared to proclaim it.

The primary fulfillment, however, will take place during the time of trouble. Just as Jesus sent His disciples "two by two before His face into every city and place where He Himself was about to go" (Luke 10:1), so God's **"two witnesses,"** the 144,000, will be present in every part of the world, sharing the truth from God's word. Wherever

they are they will be attacked and persecuted. Jesus predicted this experience in Mark 13:13, "You will be hated by all for My sake. But he who endures to the end shall be saved."

Two factors show that this is primarily an end-time event.[406] First of all, the dead bodies of the two witnesses will be seen by "those from the peoples, tribes, tongues, and nations." This phrase, which is found seven times in the book of Revelation, is used within the context of the universal movements of the last days.[407] This is not referring to a local, historical event.

The second factor that shows that the ministry and death of the two witnesses happens at the very end of time is the fact that **"the beast that ascends out of the bottomless pit will make war against them, and shall overcome them and kill them."** As we will see below, a comparison of **"the beast that ascends out of the bottomless pit"** with the end-time antichrist described by Paul in 2 Thessalonians 2 shows that they are one and the same.

---

406 These factors are in addition to those already given in footnote 392 in section 11:2 *Leave out the Court.*

407 Variations on this phrase are found seven times in the book of Revelation (Revelation 5:9, 7:9, 10:11, 11:9, 13:7, 14:6, 17:15) and each time the context is the universality of either the persecuting activity of Babylon or of the gospel message and its results, which are only complete at the very end of time. The last sign before Jesus comes is the gospel going to the whole world. "And this gospel of the kingdom will be preached in all the world as a witness to all the nations, and then the end will come" (Matthew 24:14). "You shall be witnesses to Me in Jerusalem, and in all Judea and Samaria, and to the end of the earth" (Acts 1:8). This command of Jesus is finally fulfilled by the last judgment-hour message—"And I saw another angel flying in the midst of heaven, *having the everlasting gospel to preach to those that dwell on the earth, and to every nation, and tribe, and tongue, and people,* saying with a loud voice, 'Fear God, and give glory to Him, for the hour of His judgment has come; and worship Him that made heaven, and earth, and the sea, and the fountains of waters" (Revelation 14:6,7). This is the "first angel's message" and it is given along with the second and third angels' messages, which expose and condemn Babylon. These messages will be given by the 144,000 and they will enrage "those who dwell on the earth" and cause them to "rejoice,…make merry, and send gifts to one another" when these witnesses who "tormented them" with their straight, cutting testimony are "killed" (Revelation 11:9,10).

Satan's Impersonation of Christ

The end-time antichrist who plays such an important role during the time of trouble is identified in 2Thessalonians 2 as "the man of sin," "the son of perdition," and "the lawless one." "Concerning the coming of our Lord Jesus Christ… let no one deceive you by any means; for that day will not come unless the falling away comes first and *the man of sin is revealed, the son of perdition who opposes and exalts himself above all that is called* God or that is worshiped, so that he sits as God in the temple of God, showing himself that he is God" (2Thessonians 2:1-4). Here we see that before the Second Coming of Christ the "man of sin," also called "the son of perdition" will appear. The Greek word for "perdition" is *apoleias*, which means destruction, and we will see that this word is one of the keys to his identity. The "man of sin…exalts himself above all that is called God," just like Satan, who wanted to "exalt [his] throne above the stars of God" and "be like the Most High" (Isaiah 14:13,14).

"And now you know what is restraining that he may be revealed in his own time. For the mystery of lawlessness is already at work; only *He who now restrains* will do so until He is taken out of the way. And *then the lawless one will be revealed*, whom the Lord will consume with the breath of His mouth and destroy with the brightness of His coming" (2Thessalonians 2:6-8). Here we see that there is some restraining power that will hold "the lawless one" in check until the restraint is removed.[408] The setting is the very end of time,

because this lawless one will be destroyed "with the brightness of His coming." In fact, the context of this entire passage is "concerning the coming of our Lord Jesus Christ."

"The coming of the lawless one is according to the working of Satan, *with all power, signs and lying wonders*, and with *all unrighteous deception* among those who perish, because *they did not receive the love of the truth* that they might be saved" (2Thessalonians 2:9,10). In these verses we see that Satan will be intimately involved, producing false miracles to deceive the people of the world who have not accepted "the love of the truth."[409]

To summarize, these verses in 2Thessalonians 2 show that just before the Second Coming of Christ God will remove some restraining influence, which will allow Satan to manifest himself as a personality, the "man of sin." He will use miracles to deceive the people of the world who have not accepted the love of the truth. But the man of sin will be destroyed at the Second Coming by "the breath of His [Jesus'] mouth and the brightness of His coming."

Such a crucial personality and important activity, appearing at around the time of the Second Coming of Christ, would certainly be included in the Book of Revelation. Revelation 19 is the chapter that presents the Second Coming. Jesus appears as a rider on a white horse who "judges and makes war," having a sharp sword coming out of His mouth with which He strikes the nations and kills those who oppose Him

---

408 Those who believe in the "rapture" theory claim that it is the church that restrains the antichrist with its holy presence and prayers, and that with the rapture the church will be taken "out of the way," allowing the antichrist to appear and act. But the Greek word for "He who now restrains" (*o katexon arti*) is masculine, while "the church" (*h ekklisia*) is feminine. This shows that Paul is not referring to the church.

409 A "love of the truth" is simply a love of Jesus and His teachings (He is "the way, the truth and the life," John 14:16).

(Revelation 19:11-15, 21).[410] Furthermore, there is an individual in Revelation 19 who opposes Jesus. He is called "the beast" and he is the leader of "the kings of the earth and their armies" and together they "make war against Him who sat on the horse" (v. 19). He uses miracles by which "he deceived those who had received the mark of the beast," but he is destroyed by Jesus at His coming—"the beast was captured" and "cast alive into a lake of fire" (v. 20).

Both "the beast" of Revelation 19 and the "man of sin" of 2 Thessalonians 2 are present at the Second Coming. Both are warring against Christ. Both use miracles to deceive the unbelievers, and both are destroyed at Christ's coming. From these comparisons it is obvious that "the beast" and "the man of sin" are the same individual—the last day antichrist.

In Revelation 19 the beast is shown leading "the kings of the earth" in the last great battle against Jesus. In chapter 16 the same beast is shown organizing the battle, sending out evil spirits to the same "kings of the earth…to gather them to the battle of that great day of God almighty" (Revelation 16:13,14). In chapter 17 an angel comes to explain more about the beast. John sees a vision of a seven-headed scarlet beast ridden by a harlot. This will be explained in more detail in chapter 17, but briefly, the scarlet beast is a global political entity which is controlled by an apostate religious entity (the harlot). But as the explanation proceeds, the angel who is explaining

the vision focuses attention on the seven heads of the scarlet beast. These heads are a series of seven kings, followed by an eighth king who is also called "the beast." This beast "will ascend out of the bottomless pit and go to perdition" (v. 8). Here we see that "the beast" is both a political entity (the scarlet beast) and an individual (the eighth king), the same individual who organizes and then leads the final battle when Jesus comes. We also see another connection: the "man of sin… [is] the *son of perdition*" (2 Thessalonians 2) and "the Beast…shall ascend out of the bottomless pit and *go into perdition*" (Revelation 17).

The Greek words for "perdition" and "the bottomless pit" are also key links showing that "the beast" is the same individual as "the angel of the bottomless pit" of Revelation 9. That chapter describes a locust army that "had a king over them, the angel of the bottomless pit, whose name in Hebrew is Abaddon, but in the Greek language he has the name Apollyon" (v. 11).[411] The name "Apollyon" is from the same Greek root that means "perdition."[412] This suggests that the "angel of the bottomless pit"[413] whose name means "perdition" is the same as "the beast… who shall ascend from the bottomless pit and go to perdition" (Revelation 17:8), the same beast who will organize the Battle of Armageddon in chapter 16 and who will be thrown into the lake of fire in chapter 19.

---

410 Ephesians 6 mentions "the sword of the Spirit" using the Greek word *"pnevma"* which means both spirit and breath. Thus there is a link between the sword from the mouth of the horseman (Jesus) which kills His enemies in Revelation 19 and the "breath of [Jesus'] mouth" which kills the antichrist in 2 Thessalonians 2.

411 These names mean "destroyer" and refer to Satan, the fallen angel whose great work is "to steal, and to kill, and to destroy" (John 10:10). Isaiah 14, describing the fall of Satan, refers to him as a destroyer. "Is this the man who made the earth tremble, who shook kingdoms, who made the world as a wilderness and destroyed its cities, who did not open the house of the prisoners…you have destroyed your land and slain your people" (Isaiah 14:16-20).

412 John makes an interesting play on words. "Apollyon," the destroyer, will go to perdition, which is from the same Greek root and means to be totally destroyed. This is his final fate—"The beast was…cast alive into the lake of fire burning with brimstone" (Revelation 19:20). The destroyer will be totally destroyed!

413 The fact that he is an angel is even more suggestive that he is actually a manifestation of Satan, the leader of the fallen angels.

When Will the Beast Appear?

With this understanding, the time of the appearance of the antichrist (the beast) can be ascertained. "The beast...will ascend from the bottomless pit" (Revelation 17:8) and the bottomless pit is "opened" during the fifth trumpet (Revelation 9:1,2). Moreover, the locusts who come out of the bottomless pit during the fifth trumpet "had as king over them the angel of the bottomless pit" (Revelation 9:11). The fifth trumpet takes place "at the time of the end" during the last phase of the long war between the King of the North and the King of the South (see 9:3 *The Locust Army*).

In the introduction to the trumpets we can see what it is that has been the restraining influence preventing the appearance of "the man of sin." In Revelation 7:1 four angels are shown "holding the four winds of the earth...until we have sealed the servants of our God in their foreheads." This restraining is shown again in Revelation 8:3-5 as an angel with a censer, offering up prayers and incense. As we saw in 8:3 *The Golden Censer*, the censer is a symbol of God's merciful protection of sinners from the disasters that they deserve. The casting down of the censer symbolizes the end of this protection, allowing Satan to instigate the trumpet plagues with the chaos and suffering he has long wanted to bring on this earth. Satan will not be released until the 144,000 are sealed.

The chaotic conditions that are brought about by the first four trumpets (fiery hail, a burning mountain and a burning poisonous star which causes smoke that blots out the light of the sun, moon and stars) are called the opening of the bottomless pit (see 9:1,2 *The Bottomless Pit*). It is out of the bottomless pit that the beast ascends to make his attack on the two witnesses. It is God and his angels who are restraining Satan, but after the 144,000 have been "sealed in their foreheads" the censer will be cast down, the four angels will be allowed to release the four winds, the bottomless pit will open, and the beast will appear.

Thus the ministry of the two witnesses takes place at the same time that **"the beast...ascends out of the bottomless pit."** This is the end-time, worldwide and universal appearance of the antichrist. He is the one who **"will make war against them, and shall overcome them, and kill them. And their dead bodies will lie in the street of the great city, which spiritually is called Sodom and Egypt, where also our Lord was crucified"** (Revelation 11:7,8). This is not a particular city, but represents every city of the world, where licentious immorality (**"Sodom"**), godlessness (**"Egypt"**) and hostility to Christ (**"where also our Lord was crucified"**) reign supreme.[414]

The details of the last furious effort to destroy God's people, carried out by the enraged followers of the beast, are found in chapters 13 and 17—the image, mark and number of the beast and the battle of the beast and the ten kings against the Lamb. The harlot (the false church) which "sits on" (controls) the scarlet beast (alliance of nations) in chapter 17 is "drunk with the blood of the saints and with the blood of the martyrs of Jesus" (Revelation 17:6). This confirms the fact that some last day witnesses may become martyrs, at least during the time before the close of probation when there will be "silence in heaven."[415]

However, the chiastic structure indicates that this section is highly symbolic (see 8:3, *Trumpets: Literal or Symbolic?*). Some of the **"two witnesses"** may end up being actual martyrs, but all will die a spiritual death. This is the overwhelming death

---

414 God's people were called out of both Sodom (Lot and his family) and Egypt (the Children of Israel). This is another confirmation that this section is dealing with the last great message of repentance, "Babylon is fallen...come out of her my people" Revelation 18: 1-4.

415 See section 8:1 *Silence in Heaven* for an explanation of the meaning of this phrase. See 14:13 *Martyrs During the Time of Trouble* for more information about the possibility of martyrs.

to self that is described in 10:7 *The Shattering of the Power of the Holy People*. It will come about as the faithful witnesses face great disappointment ("It will make your stomach bitter" Revelation 10:9) that their message seems to be rejected ("the rest of mankind…did not repent" Revelation 9:20). Instead of a positive response they will see that their witness has brought about persecution and threat of death to themselves and those they love most (Revelation 13:15). The followers of the beast will believe that God's people are responsible for the plagues they have been suffering, and they will rejoice at their grief and apparent defeat—**"they that dwell on the earth shall rejoice over them, and make merry, and shall send gifts one to another; because these two prophets tormented those that dwell on the earth"** (Revelation 11:10). But the "resurrection" of the two witnesses will be a compelling witness that will finally convince a great multitude to abandon Babylon and take their place with God's remnant.

11:11-13 Resurrection of the Two Witnesses

"And after three and a half days the Spirit of life from God entered into them, and they stood upon their feet; and great fear fell upon those who saw them. And they heard a great voice from heaven saying to them, "Come up here." And they ascended up to heaven in a cloud; and their enemies beheld them. And the same hour there was a great earthquake, and a tenth of the city fell, and in the earthquake were slain of men seven thousand; and the remnant were afraid, and gave glory to the God of heaven" (Revelation 11: 11-13).

The **"breath of life"** that **"entered into them"** is God's Spirit, which causes lifeless things to come to life. In the Garden of Eden the breath of life caused dirt to live. "And the Lord God formed man of the dust of the ground, and breathed into his nostrils *the breath of life*; and man became a living being." (Genesis 2:7). "The Spirit of God has made me, and the breath of the Almighty gives me life" (Job 33:4).

The two witnesses will be thoroughly traumatized and shattered by their experience, but they will not let go of their hold on God until **"the breath of life from God [enters] them."** In this respect they are like Jacob who "struggled with God and with men and…prevailed," and in fact Jeremiah brings this experience to view, calling it the "time of Jacob's trouble"—"Alas! For *that day is great*, so that none is like it; and it is *the time of Jacob's trouble*, but he shall be saved out of it" (Jeremiah 30:7). The "day [that] is great, so that none is like it" is the "time of trouble, such as never was" (Daniel 12:1), and Jeremiah tells us that during that time God's people will have an experience like the "time of Jacob's trouble." Jacob had a "time of trouble" when he was faced with the death and destruction of all that was precious to him.

The story of Jacob and his brother Esau is found in Genesis 25-33. Jacob had lied to his father and twice cheated his brother. Fleeing from his angry brother, he spent the next twenty-one years being exploited by his conniving uncle Laban and learned how wrong it is to lie and cheat. But it was when his brother and 300 armed men approached him, apparently to take his life and the lives of his loved ones, that Jacob felt the deep remorse for his sin that was symbolized by his wrestling all night with an Angel. When the night was almost over the Angel (who was actually God, Genesis 32:30) touched his hip, permanently crippling him, but he did not let go. He cried out, "I will not let you go unless you bless me!" (Genesis 32:26). Because he held on in the face of despair his name was changed from Jacob (supplanter) to Israel (God prevails).

This will be the experience of the two witnesses who will be totally crushed by the apparent failure of their mission. Their "stubborn" refusal to worship the beast will imperil not only their own lives but the lives of their families and loved ones. In their despair they will, as Jesus promised, drink the cup that Jesus drank (Matthew 20:22,23), which is the sense of separation from God.[416] But they will not let go, and at the end of the "night" God will touch them and give them a "new name" ("to him that overcomes I will give…a new name" Revelation 2:17). They will **"ascend into heaven"**—they will by faith stand "before the throne of God," even while the plagues are falling around them (see 7: I*n Heaven While On Earth*).[417]

The "two witnesses" are not the only ones who will be shaken. By withdrawing His protecting mediation during the trumpet plagues, God will shake the foundations of human society. This is symbolized by a great earthquake (**"there was a great earthquake, and a tenth of the city fell"**).[418] These trials will fully harden the stubbornly unrepentant, symbolized by **"seven thousand people [who] were killed."** They will be "sealed" in their unbelief (see 15:5-8 *The Close of Probation*) and will redouble their efforts to destroy the remnant.

In contrast, **"the remnant"**—the great multitude who have accepted the call to come out of Babylon—will stand in awe as they see the radiant glory of the transformed witnesses. **"The remnant were afraid and gave glory to the God of heaven."** This is a direct response to the final appeal of Revelation 14, "fear God and give glory to Him, for the hour of His judgment has come," again confirming the last hour context of this section. It is significant that those who respond are called **"the remnant"** (Greek *loipos*). This identifies them with "the remnant [*loipos*] of her seed who keep the commandments of God and have the testimony of Jesus Christ" (Revelation 12:17). These are the ones who refuse to submit to the beast, and they join the 144,000 "before the throne and before the lamb…and serve Him day and night in His temple" (Revelation 7:9,15).

11:14,15 The Kingdoms of Our Lord

"The second woe is past, and, behold, the third woe comes quickly. And the seventh angel sounded, and there were great voices in heaven, saying, "The kingdoms of this world have become the kingdom of our Lord, and of His Christ; and He shall reign forever and ever!" (Revelation 11:14,15).

To summarize what has been presented so far, the **"second woe"** is the sixth trumpet, which is the most fearful destruction to ever fall upon mankind up until this time, involving a war with a two-hundred-million man army in which a third of mankind is killed.[419] Satan, the "angel of the bottomless pit" will bring about this destruction with the aim of destroying "the two witnesses" and silencing their message to God's people who are in Babylon. Despite Satan's opposition, the

---

416 Jesus told His disciples, "You will indeed drink my cup" (Matthew 20:23). When He was about to be sacrificed He said, "Shall I not drink the cup which My Father has given Me?" (John 18:11). The essence of the cup was not the physical torture He endured, but the sense of separation from God, expressed in His cry from the Cross, "My God, My God, why have You forsaken Me?" (Matthew 27:46).

417 In this sense they will be like Jesus, who spoke of Himself as being in heaven even as He was facing the trials of His earthly life (John 3:13).

418 Chapters 10 and 11 are highly symbolic. The "great city" is based on 3 literal cities (v. 8), showing that it is symbolic of all the cities of the world, and "seven thousand" is a highly symbolic number. A literal earthquake that killed 7,000 people would not be "great" considering that earthquakes in history have killed hundreds of thousands of people. This points to a symbolic earthquake with spiritual results.

419 Revelation 9:15,16.

two witnesses will give the final appeal calling the world to repentance,[420] and the message will be totally effective—Satan's efforts to hold onto this world as his kingdom will utterly fail. This is reflected in the announcement, **"The kingdoms of this world have become the kingdoms of our Lord and of His Christ."** Through His faithful witnesses Jesus will convince a "great multitude" out of "every nation, tribe, tongue and people" that He is worthy of their love and allegiance.

The end of the **"second woe"** marks the last chance for repentance before the "close of probation."[421] Considering that "the wages of sin is death," every sinner should have been destroyed the moment he first sinned. "Probation" refers to the time when sinners are allowed to live, with the hope that they will recognize God's love for them as expressed in Jesus' sacrifice, repent of their sins and accept the forgiveness that has already been provided for them, and receive the free gift of eternal life. Up until the end of the second woe the close of probation has been the death of each individual—"it is appointed for men to die once, but after this the judgment" (Hebrews 9:27). But at the very end of time "this gospel of the kingdom will be preached in all the world as a witness to all the nations, and then the end will come" (Matthew 24:14). The final message will be so powerful and compelling, coming as it does within the context of the time of trouble, that everyone on earth will make a conscious decision to either accept or reject the invitation.

When everyone has made his or her decision, then "Michael shall stand up" (Daniel 12:1),

which indicates the end of Christ's mediation for sinners. This is marked by the fearsome declaration "He who is unjust, let him be unjust still; he who is filthy, let him be filthy still, he who is righteous, let him be righteous still; he who is holy, let him be holy still. And behold I am coming quickly...to give to every one according to his work" (Revelation 22:11,12). Those who have accepted the gospel invitation will be sealed for eternal life. Those who have refused the invitation of salvation will face eternal death.

11:16-18 Announcement of the Judgment

"And the twenty-four elders, sitting before God on their thrones, fell on their faces and worshiped God, saying, 'We give You thanks, O Lord God Almighty, who is, and who was, and who is to come; because You have taken your great power, and reigned. And the nations were angry, and your wrath has come, and the time of the dead, that they should be judged, and to give the reward to your servants the prophets, and to the saints, and to those who fear your name, small and great; and to destroy those who destroy the earth" (Revelation 11:16-18).

This pivotal passage is crucial for the understanding of the rest of the Book of Revelation. First of all, it announces a change in God's activity—**"You have taken Your great power and reigned."** God has never lacked in power, but this verse shows that up until this point He has not **"taken"** His great power, but instead has allowed another to reign. Clearly that other is the evil usurper, Satan, whom Jesus called "the ruler of this world."[422] Satan, in claiming this world as his own in the book of Job, pointed to the faults and failings of God's people as evidence that he

---

420 The details of the last messages are elaborated in Revelation 14:6-13 (the three angels' messages) and Revelation 18:1-5 (the mighty angel's message to come out of Babylon).

421 Chapter 11 ends with the announcement of the opening of the temple. Chapters 12-14 leave the timeline in an elaboration of the issues and players in the great controversy, and then in chapter 15 the narrative returns to the opening of the temple and the close of probation (see 15:5-8 *The Close of Probation*).

---

422 John 12:31, 14:30, 16:11.

had every right to "walk back and forth" and "go to and fro on the earth"[423] that he had stolen from Adam. God has allowed Satan to rule, not because he had any right to, but because mankind chose Satan to be their ruler.

God has always placed the highest honor on the free choice of humanity, even if it has meant having to endure watching His beloved children suffer in the hands of their chosen ruler. But the choice of the great multitude to abandon Babylon will settle the issue and bring the great controversy to an end. God will no longer be silent—**"Your wrath has come."** He will end the destruction that Satan and his followers have been carrying out (He will **"destroy those who destroy the earth"**),[424] and He will **"reward"** those who have been faithfully waiting for Him.

This theme of the great controversy is expanded and elaborated in the next three chapters of Revelation. There will be an exposition of **"the nations"** that **"were angry,"** of God's enemies **"who destroy the earth,"** of those **"who fear [His] name, small and great,"** and of what it means to **"be judged."** In these chapters Revelation makes an extensive digression from the linear timeline, going back in history to the very beginning of the controversy when the "great, fiery red dragon" "drew a third of the stars of heaven and cast them to the earth" (Revelation 12:3,4).

11:19 The Ark of the Covenant

"And the temple of God was opened in heaven, and there was seen in His temple the ark of His covenant. And there were lightnings, and voices, and thunders, and an earthquake, and great hail" (Revelation 11:19).

---

423 Job 1:6-12, 2:1-6 See Appendix 8 for a discussion of the great controversy in the book of Job.

424 This passage is not specifying ecological destruction but rather the whole corruption of God's creation caused by sin. The Greek word (*dievtheiro*) is used for example in 1Timothy 6:5, "men of *corrupt* minds."

God told Moses to have the children of Israel "make Me a sanctuary [temple], that I may dwell among them. According to all that I show you, that is, the pattern of the tabernacle and the pattern of all its furnishings, just so you shall make it" (Exodus 25:8,9). When God told Him to make it "according to the pattern" He was not simply giving Him a design. The pattern for the tabernacle and its furnishings, including the ark of the covenant, was a heavenly reality, which John saw when **"the temple of God was opened in heaven."** Although the full reality of the **"ark of His covenant"** and the **"temple of God"** in heaven are incomprehensible to sinful humanity, we can understand them to a certain extent by studying the issues surrounding the earthly **"ark of His covenant."**

The ark was a box approximately four feet long, two feet wide and two feet high, made of Acacia wood covered inside and out with gold. The ark contained the two tables of stone with the Ten Commandments written on them—"the ark of the covenant overlaid on all sides with gold, in which were…the tablets of the covenant" (Hebrews 9:4). It was called the ark of the covenant because the Ten Commandments are a central part of God's covenant with His people—"He declared to you His covenant which He commanded you to perform, the Ten Commandments; and He wrote them on two tablets of stone" (Deuteronomy 4:13).

Some Bible students have concluded from this and similar passages that the law of God was the "old covenant," a way of "salvation" given to the Jews in which they could be saved by faithfully obeying the commandments. The fact that commandment keeping could not have been God's covenant of salvation is evident since no one (except Jesus) has ever kept God's law (Romans 3:23, 1John 3:4). This means that God would have given the Jews an ineffective means of salvation. Furthermore, in the new covenant period (even down to the end of time, as seen in this passage of Revelation) the ark in heaven (which presumably has some kind of original of the law of God) is still called **"the ark of His covenant."**

Actually, God's commandments are just one of the four elements of each of the covenants He made with humanity. These elements are 1) God's *promise* to bless humanity through His chosen people. 2) His *requirements* (commandments). 3) His *provision* to save those who violate His requirements (the plan of salvation). 4) The sign of His covenant. These elements can be seen most clearly in the covenant God made with Noah after the flood, in His covenant with Abraham, in the "old covenant" God made with Moses and the Children of Israel, and in the new covenant with the Christian Church. Significantly, all of these covenants are called an "everlasting covenant," showing that the essence of God's covenants does not change.

These elements are analyzed in each of the covenants in Appendix 9. Their manifestation in the new covenant is central in the climax of the great controversy, which is presented in chapters 12-14. The *promise* of the new covenant is that the Christian church will reveal God to the world—"You are a chosen generation, a royal priesthood, a holy nation, His own special people, that you may proclaim the praises of Him who called you out of darkness into His marvelous light" (1Peter 2:9,10). The *requirement* of the new covenant is God's law, written by the Spirit in the heart—"This is the covenant that I will make with the house of Israel after those days,' says the Lord, 'I will put my laws in their mind and write

them on their hearts" (Hebrews 8:10). The *provision* of the new covenant is the sacrifice of Christ on the Cross, received by faith—"He [Christ] is the Mediator of the new covenant, by means of death, for the redemption of the transgressions" (Hebrews 9:15). The sign of the new covenant is the Sabbath, the symbol of creation and redemption (see Appendix 9).

The everlasting covenant is brought into focus when **"the temple of God was opened in heaven, and there was seen in His temple the ark of His covenant."** In the book of Daniel, Satan's enmity against the covenant is manifested through the activity of his earthly agent, the "King of the North" who "shall be moved *against the holy covenant*; so he shall do damage…and [he shall] show regard for those who *forsake the holy covenant*…he shall corrupt with flattery those who do *wickedly against the covenant*" (Daniel 11:28, 30, 32). The "King of the North" who wars against the covenant turns out to be none other than "the beast from the sea" whose destructive activity is featured in Revelation chapter 13.

The next three chapters are the climax of the great controversy theme of Revelation, beginning with "war in heaven." We will see that the four elements of the covenant are the great issues of the final struggle, with each coming under fierce attack by the dragon, "that serpent of old." Satan hates Christ's people and the message they have for the world, and he also hates God's law, His sacrifice, and the sign of His covenant. But the opening of the temple in heaven and the revealing of **"the ark of His covenant"** is God's announcement of Satan's utter defeat.

"Michael and his angels fought with the dragon…so the great dragon was cast out,
that serpent of old, called the Devil and Satan" Rev. 12:7,9
Woodcut by Albrecht Durer 1498

Chapter 12

Revelation 12:1-17

12:1 And a great sign appeared in heaven: a woman clothed with the sun, and the moon under her feet, and on her head a crown of twelve stars.

12:2 And she, being with child, cried out, travailing in birth and in pain to be delivered.

12:3 And there appeared another sign in heaven, and behold, a great red dragon, having seven heads and ten horns, and seven crowns on his heads.

12:4 And his tail drew a third of the stars of heaven, and cast them to the earth. And the dragon stood before the woman who was ready to be delivered, in order to devour her child as soon as it was born.

12:5 And she brought forth a male child, who was to rule all nations with a rod of iron; and her child was caught up to God, and to his throne.

12:6 And the woman fled into the wilderness, where she has a place prepared by God, so that there she would be nourished for 1,260 days.

12:7 And there was war in heaven: Michael and his angels fought against the dragon, and the dragon fought and his angels;

12:8 And they did not prevail, neither was their place found in heaven any longer.

12:9 And the great dragon was cast out, that old serpent, called the Devil, and Satan, who deceives the whole world; he was cast to the earth, and his angels were cast out with him.

12:10 And I heard a loud voice saying in heaven, "Now have come salvation, and strength, and the kingdom of our God, and the power of his Christ; for the accuser of our brethren has been cast down, who accused them before our God day and night.

12:11 And they overcame him by the blood of the Lamb, and by the word of their testimony; and they loved not their lives to the death.

12:12 Therefore rejoice, you heavens, and you that dwell in them. Woe to the inhabitants of the earth and of the sea! For the devil has come down to you, having great wrath, because he knows that he has but a short time."

12:13 And when the dragon saw that he was cast to the earth, he persecuted the woman who brought forth the man child.

12:14 And to the woman were given two wings of a great eagle, that she might fly into the wilderness to her place, where she is nourished for a time, and times, and half a time, from the face of the serpent.

12:15 And the serpent cast water out of his mouth like a flood after the woman, that he might cause her to be carried away by the flood.

12:16 But the earth helped the woman, and the earth opened its mouth, and swallowed up the flood which the dragon cast out of his mouth.

12:17 And the dragon was enraged with the woman, and went to make war with the remnant of her seed, who keep the commandments of God, and have the testimony of Jesus Christ.

12:1,2 The Woman

"And a great sign appeared in heaven: a woman clothed with the sun, and the moon under her feet, and on her head a crown of twelve stars. And she, being with child, cried out, travailing in birth and in pain to be delivered." (Revelation 12:1,2). In the previous verses (Chapter 11:18) the 24 elders announced an awesome and fearsome development: the time has come for the wrath of God, for the dead to be judged, and for the servants of God to be rewarded. These final developments will manifest themselves in the second half of Revelation as the seven last plagues, the Second Coming of Christ, the Millennium, the "white throne" (executive) judgment, and the creation of the new heavens and new earth.

The 24 elders also mentioned a number of categories of people: "the dead" who "should be judged," God's "servants, the prophets and the saints," whom He "should reward," those "small and great" who "fear [God's] name," and those "who destroy the earth" (Revelation 11:18). Before describing the actual final events, chapters 12-14 present an impressive drama which identifies the characters involved in the great controversy, shows their roles in the final events and makes it clear why they receive their reward or punishment.

John saw **"a great sign...in heaven: a woman."** Women in the Bible are often symbols of God's chosen people (Israel in the Old Testament, the church in the New Testament),

and may be either pure and holy[425] or corrupt and wicked.[426] This particular woman is seen with the sun, the moon and twelve stars. The only other Bible passage in which the sun, the moon, and twelve stars are mentioned is in Genesis 37. There, Joseph told his father and brothers about his dream of the sun, moon, and stars, in which the sun represented his father Jacob, the moon his mother Rebekah, and the twelve stars the twelve sons of Jacob. These individuals, along with Abraham and Isaac, were the patriarchs and forefathers of the nation of Israel.[427] Thus the woman with the sun, moon and twelve stars represents the Hebrew nation, consisting of the twelve tribes of Israel. The woman is depicted as pregnant, about to give birth. God's purpose in setting apart a unique, chosen people for Himself

---

425 For example, "I have likened the daughter of Zion [God's people] to a lovely and delicate woman" (Jeremiah 6:2). In Isaiah 54, referring to His people as a barren woman who will yet bear offspring, God says "Sing, O barren, you who have not borne!...For more are the children of the desolate than the children of the married woman. For you will forget the shame of your youth, and will not remember the reproach of your widowhood anymore. For your Maker is your husband...for the Lord has called you like a woman forsaken...like a youthful wife when you were refused. (Isaiah 54:1-6). See also Ephesians 5:22-33.

426 "There were two women...they committed harlotry...Their names, Oholah and Oholibah...Samaria is Oholah, and Jerusalem is Oholibah" (Ezekiel 23). Here the prophet is obviously referring to the corrupt chosen people of the northern kingdom of Israel and the southern kingdom of Judah. Another example is from Revelation: "The woman which you saw is that great city [spiritual Babylon] which reigns over the kings of the earth" (Revelation 17:18). See also Hosea 1-3.

427 Acts 7:8.

is about to be fulfilled—Israel would "give birth" to the Messiah.[428]

12:3,4 The Dragon

"**And there appeared another sign in heaven, and behold, a great red dragon, having seven heads and ten horns, and seven crowns on his heads. And his tail drew a third of the stars of heaven, and cast them to the earth**" (Revelation 12:3,4). Here we see the adversary of God and the bane of the universe. In verse 9 the dragon is identified as "**that ancient serpent, called the Devil, and Satan, who deceives the whole world**" (Revelation 12:9).

One of the most perplexing puzzles is the existence of Satan and evil. Portrayed as he often is as a caricature with horns and a pitchfork, the devil is often considered to be a vestige of the Dark Ages. However, a misunderstanding of Satan and his involvement in the origin and existence of evil has been the source of the most slanderous challenges to God's character of love. Millions have the attitude that since there is evil, God cannot be both loving and all-powerful. They reason that if He was loving, He would not want evil, and if He was all-powerful He wouldn't allow it. So either He is not powerful enough to get rid of evil, or He is not really loving and is willing to tolerate evil. A correct understanding of the origin of sin in heaven answers these serious charges.

Under the figures of "the King of Tyre" and "the King of Babylon"[429] in Isaiah 14 and Ezekiel 28 the history of "Lucifer, son of the morning"[430] is traced. Lucifer was an angel, created to be "the anointed cherub who covers,"[431] a position which put him closest to the throne of God "on the holy mountain of God" where he "walked back and forth in the midst of the fiery stones"[432] (Ezekiel 28:13,14). He was incredibly intelligent and beautiful, "the seal of perfection, full of wisdom and perfect in beauty," clothed with glory that resembled precious stones, and apparently a skilled musician[433] (vs.12,13). It is a gross

428 God promised this when He made Abraham the father of His chosen people: "In your seed all the nations of the earth shall be blessed" (Genesis 22:18). The Apostle Paul makes it clear that the Seed is Christ (Galations 3:8,16).

429 In Ezekiel 28:1-10 the prophet writes about the "prince of Tyre," the context showing that he is talking about the actual earthly monarch who ruled the Phoenician kingdom of Tyre. However, starting in verse 11 he speaks about the "king of Tyre," showing that behind the earthly "prince" was the real ruler, Satan. Since the "king of Tyre" was "in Eden, the garden of God" and was "the anointed cherub who covers," it is obvious that this is not referring to the earthly ruler, but to Satan. In Isaiah 14 the "king of Babylon" is called Lucifer. His ambition to "exalt [his] throne above the stars of God… [to] be like the Most High" shows that this refers to Satan. Actually, Tyre and Babylon are fitting symbols for Satan's kingdom. Babylon was the source and center of spiritual corruption, and the people of Tyre were the chief traders of the world (Satan was corrupted "by the abundance of [his] trading"), symbolizing the evangelical zeal with which Satan spreads his lies everywhere.

430 Isaiah 14:12.

431 In the earthly sanctuary the ark of the covenant, the throne of God, was a box containing the Ten Commandments with the "mercy seat" above. Two angels (cherubim) "cover the mercy seat with their wings." "There I will meet with you and I will speak with you from above the mercy seat, from between the two cherubim" Exodus 25:10-22.

432 "Walking back and forth" indicates having a rightful position. In heaven, Lucifer, through God's appointment, had a right to his place "walking back and forth in the midst of fiery stones." Thus, with his statement in Job 1:7 in the heavenly assembly that he had come "from going to and fro on the earth, and from walking back and forth on it" (Job 1:7), Satan was asserting his right to ownership of the earth, having stolen it from Adam. His mindset that he is the "ruler of this world" is obvious in his statement to Christ. After showing Him "all the kingdoms of the world and their glory" he said "all these things I will give You if You will fall down and worship me" (Matthew 4:8,9).

433 His musical instruments, "timbrels [tambourine] and pipes [flutes]" were "prepared for [him] on the day [he was] created" (Ezekiel 28:13). This shows that a part of Lucifer's original purpose was to create music.

misrepresentation to accuse God of "creating the devil" because God Himself said to Lucifer "You were perfect in your ways from the day you were created, till iniquity was found in you" (v. 15).

Origin of Satan and Sin

How could evil arise in a perfect being? Most of God's creation, the rocks, the plants, and even most animals do not have true freedom to choose, but simply exist and behave as they are "programmed." But at least two classes of beings, humans and angels, have been created with true freedom of choice, including the freedom to choose evil.

We should not assume that God created both evil and good to choose from. Everything that God created was good, including angels and humans, with their ability to think creatively and to make choices. But creative beings can creatively choose to take good things God has created and combine them in ways that were never intended. When something good is used in an incomplete or unintended manner, evil can be the result—even in paradise God declared one aspect of His creation "not good" until it was completed. When Adam had been created but Eve was still in the future, God said, "It is *not good* that man should be alone" (Genesis 2:18). God designed that man would be in unity with woman, and until that unity was accomplished with the creation of Eve the situation was "not good," even though the man was good. Finally, when everything was complete God declared His creation "very good" (Genesis 1:31).

Creative humans and angels with their free wills have the ability to "undo" the completeness of God's creation, creating for themselves a "not good" condition of incompleteness, and this can result in evil. For example, sexual intimacy within the context of a permanent, exclusive relationship (marriage) was designed by God and is good. But the sexual organs can be used in very

incomplete, destructive ways, as is evidenced by the tragedies of rape, abuse and gross immorality. "God is Love," and His "very good" creation was totally in harmony with the law of love. But when angels or humans choose attitudes and behaviors that have elements of good but which do not include the complete principles of love, evil is the result.

In practice, choosing evil means disregarding God's law ("sin is the transgression of the law," 1John 3:4). For example, worship is good, but if the object of worship is anything or anyone besides God it is a transgression of the first and second commandments, not because God selfishly covets worship only for Himself, but because worship of anyone but God leads to grief. Desiring, using and enjoying things is good, but not if they belong to someone else—then it is coveting and stealing, transgression of the 10th and 8th commandments. When sin is finally eradicated, we will understand the wisdom of God in creating both humans and angels with true freedom, including the freedom to transgress His law. But until then we suffer from the results of the activities of Satan, the first sinner, who, although created "perfect in [his] ways," was "found" to have "iniquity in [him]" (Ezekiel 28:15).

How did Satan fall? In Ezekiel 28:16 the Lord says to "the king of Tyre," "By the abundance of your *trading* you became filled with violence within and you sinned."[434] The essence of trading is that I evaluate what I have, compare it with what you have, and try to convince you of the value of mine in comparison with yours—in other words, a focus on self in comparison with others. Trading involves intercommunication, interactions and transactions. All of these take place on a "horizontal" level of peers, not in vertical

---

434 Tyre was a fitting symbol because the Phoenicians of Tyre were the world's foremost traders, traveling even as far as Africa and all through the known world of the Mediterranean.

relationships. Masters do not trade with their servants; people on the same level trade with one another.[435] Apparently Lucifer, rather than focusing on the vertical relationship with his Creator, began to excessively focus on comparative relationships with his fellow angels, and this led to pride: "Your heart was lifted up because of your beauty; you corrupted your wisdom for the sake of your splendor" (v.17).

This pride actually led Lucifer to aspire to the position of his Creator. "How you are fallen from heaven, O Lucifer, son of the morning!…For you have said in your heart: I will ascend into heaven, I will exalt my throne above the stars of God…I will ascend above the heights of the clouds, I will be like the Most High" (Isaiah 14:12-14).

The idea of being like God while not being subject to Him is the same theme that Satan used to tempt Eve in the Garden of Eden. In His instructions to Adam and Eve, God had emphasized His lavish liberality, saying, "Of *every* tree of the garden you may freely eat," while still emphasizing that they were beings with freedom of choice: "But of the tree of the knowledge of good and evil you shall not eat" (Genesis 2:16,17). Satan slyly twisted God's words: "Has God indeed said, 'You shall *not* eat of every tree of the garden?" This confusing question did not make it clear if the serpent was implying that they were not allowed to eat of any tree or of every tree, but what it did do was to change the focus from God's liberal allowance to His restriction, thus totally misrepresenting His character. When Eve repeated God's warning, that if she ate of the tree of knowledge she would die, Satan essentially called God

a liar: "You will not surely die." He held out the promise of a more exalted state—"your eyes will be opened…knowing good and evil." Finally, he zealously tried to convert Eve to his own sinful ambition: "You will be like God" (Genesis 3:1-5).

Here we see the issues of the great controversy between God and one of the brightest of His created beings. Satan claims that God is restrictive, that He is a liar, that He has a high position that he wants to selfishly retain exclusively for Himself, and that He does not have the best interests of His creatures at heart. He asserts that we don't need God to tell us what is good, but can judge for ourselves. He claims that we can have a better life independent from God, that being wise is more important than being righteous (obedient), and that through disobedience God's creatures can elevate themselves to the exalted position of being "like the Most High."[436]

War in Heaven

Satan was apparently able "through the abundance of [his] trading" to persuade many of His fellow angels to side with him—**"his tail drew a third of the stars of heaven and cast them to the earth."** This was the first of two falls.[437] After

---

435 Satan's shrewd trading abilities are revealed in his interaction with Jesus in the Wilderness. The world and everything in it belong to Christ, since "all things were created through Him and for Him" (Colossians 1:16). God gave its stewardship to Adam (Genesis 1:28), but through deceit Satan stole it from him and then had the audacity to try to trade it back to Jesus if He would worship him! (Matthew 4:9).

436 We can understand other issues in the great controversy from Jesus' encounter with Satan in the wilderness (Matthew 4:1-11). Satan said, "Command that these stones become bread" (v. 3)—in other words, exercise personal spiritual power independent of the Creator. "Throw yourself down, for…He [God] shall give His angels charge over you" (v.6)—manipulate the Creator rather than obeying Him. "The devil said…'fall down and worship me'" (v.9)—this is the ultimate desire of Satan, to have worship directed to himself. All of these characteristics are seen in the false religions of the world.

437 Jesus said in Luke 10:18 "I saw Satan fall like lightning from heaven," showing that during His ministry Satan had already fallen. However, as Jesus prepared for His sacrifice on the Cross, he said, "Now is the judgment of this world; now the ruler of this world will be cast out" (John 12:31). This second casting out is the one described in Revelation 12:7-9.

the first fall Satan still had access to heaven,[438] where he asserted his accusations against God and against God's loyal creatures. But with the self-sacrifice of Christ on the cross, Satan was totally banished from heaven: **"And there was war in heaven: Michael and his angels fought against the dragon, and the dragon fought and his angels; and they did not prevail, neither was their place found in heaven any longer"** (Revelation 12:7,8). We should not imagine that this was physical warfare; it was a war of words, of arguments, of loyalties,[439] and with Satan's ruthless instigating of the murder of the Son of God, he was fully unmasked and could no longer find a listening ear or a place in the hearts of the inhabitants of heaven—**"neither was their place found in heaven any longer"** (Revelation 12:8).

That which Satan was not able to accomplish in heaven, the establishment of his throne, rule, and authority, he now tries to accomplish on earth among humans. **"Therefore rejoice, you heavens, and you that dwell in them. Woe to the inhabitants of the earth and of the sea! For the devil has come down to you, having great wrath, because he knows that he has but a short time"** (v. 12). In God's frame of reference in which "one day is as a thousand years and a thousand years as one day," the 2,000 years that

Satan has been exclusively confined to earth is just **"a short time."** But for **"the inhabitants of the earth,"** suffering from the activities of Satan and the effects of sin, this terrible time of **"woe"** seems interminable and unbearable. This brings up the difficult question that has led millions to reject faith in God: why does God allow Satan, sin, and suffering to continue?

The Eradication of Sin

The Book of Revelation clearly teaches that in the end sin and Satan will cease to exist. When it is all over "there shall be no more curse," "there shall be no more death, neither sorrow, nor crying, neither shall there be any more pain; for the former things have passed away" (Revelation 22:3, 21:4). Satan and his followers will be "cast into the lake of fire and brimstone" which "shall burn them up," leaving them "neither root nor branch," and Satan "shall be no more forever" (Revelation 20:10, Malachi 4:1, Ezekiel 28:19. See also 20: *Eternal Fire*).

However, eradicating sin once it has come into existence is not a simple matter. Some have argued that God never should have created beings with the possibility of sin in the first place. But there is far too much that is unknown and incomprehensible for a finite creature to make that kind of judgment. The infinite price of redemption makes it clear that God, who hates sin with its pain and death more than any human possibly can, still considers His creation to be worth all the pain.

If we believe by faith that God was loving, righteous and wise when He created beings with free wills who ultimately sinned, we are led to the painful conclusion that even God cannot stop atrocities and tragedies without taking away the very freedom that He died on the Cross to

---

438 Job 1:6 depicts "a day when the sons of God [from the context it is obvious that these were not human beings—no doubt angels or other created beings] came to present themselves before the Lord and Satan also came among them." In this heavenly gathering Satan claimed territory (he said he had been "walking back and forth" on the earth v.7), disputed God's wisdom and judgment ("does Job fear God for nothing?" v.9) and accused Job of superficial loyalty to God ("touch all that he has, he will surely curse You to Your face!" v.11). In Zechariah 3:1-5, another scene in heaven, Joshua the high priest is pictured "standing before the Angel of the Lord, and Satan standing at his right hand to oppose him." These two passages show that before the Cross Satan had access to the heavenly courts.

439 Paul says that "the weapons of our warfare are not carnal but mighty in God for pulling down strongholds, casting down arguments and every high thing that exalts itself against the knowledge of God, bringing every thought into captivity to the obedience of Christ" (2Corinthians 10:4,5).

preserve.[440] Instead God endures the pain of seeing His creation suffer, while offering Himself as the remedy to those who will choose to accept Him, all the while working toward the time when sin can effectively be brought to a permanent end.

God has at least two reasons for His temporary toleration of sin. First, He wants to save as many of His children as He can so that they can live with Him forever.[441] And second, He wants to so thoroughly demonstrate the contrast between His principles and the principles of Satan that sin will never rise up again. God "could have"[442] destroyed Satan when he first rebelled, but this would have left his slanderous charges and accusations unanswered. Satan was not alone in his rebellion: **"his tail drew a third of the stars** [myriads of angels] **of heaven,"** and besides the angels who overtly rebelled, no doubt many others had questions in their minds about Satan's accusations. Even if Satan and all his followers were destroyed, another "Satan" would have arisen, and then another and another, with God destroying them but never proving that they were wrong.

Satan's every-man-a-law-to-himself sin

principle can only be purged by allowing it to fully demonstrate itself. To stop sin prematurely would mean exercising arbitrary, coercive control on Satan and sinners, the very beings God created to have free choice. Since "all have sinned" and "the wages of sin is death," God would have to kill all people and rebellious angels in order to put a stop to the pain and suffering that go along with sin. Although He does not do this, He does restrain evil and limit suffering—"Because of the Lord's great love we are not consumed, for His compassions never fail" (Lamentations 3:22 NIV).

At the end of time, in order to allow the ultimate demonstration of the sin principle, God will briefly withdraw his restraint of the murderous passions and the disasters that are the natural results of sin, ushering in "a time of trouble such as never was since there was a nation" (Revelation 7:1, Daniel 12:1). But in all fairness to the human race God wants everyone on earth to have a chance to be prepared for that catastrophic experience. This is why Jesus said "this gospel of the Kingdom will be preached in all the world as a witness to all the nations, and then the end will come" (Matthew 24:14). By then God will have developed a full demonstration of His kingdom principles. Through the ministry and the gifts of the Holy Spirit, God's special messengers will have "come to the unity of the faith and of the knowledge of the Son of God, to a perfect man, to the measure of the stature of the fullness of Christ" (Ephesians 4:7-16).

The contrast between those led by the Spirit and those controlled by sin will be such that there will be an eternal witness to the whole universe of the righteousness of God and the malignity of sin—"to the intent that now the manifold wisdom of God might be made known by the church to the principalities and powers in the heavenly

---

440 For example, at what point in the chain of events would God interfere to stop someone who had decided to drink until intoxicated and then drive recklessly, with the very real possibility of causing a terrible tragedy? Would he manipulate the person's mind so that he wouldn't want to drink, or paralyze his arm so he couldn't, or change the nature of the alcohol so it wouldn't have an intoxicating effect, or move cars out of the way of the inebriated driver? Obviously there would be no real freedom of choice in such a world.

441 "The heavens and the earth…are reserved for fire until the day of judgment and perdition of ungodly men" because "the Lord…is longsuffering toward us, not willing that any should perish but that all should come to repentance" (2Peter 3:3-9).

442 It is actually illogical to talk about what God "could have" done. God can only act in harmony with His own character of love, and in this sense His sinful creatures can do things that He cannot. For example, "It is impossible for God to lie" (Hebrews 6:18), but sinners can lie, as well as break all of God's laws. Obviously God cannot break His own law since it is a reflection of His character.

places" (Ephesians 3:10). Sin will come to a permanent end: "The Lord is slow to anger and great in power, and will not at all acquit the wicked… The Lord is good, a stronghold in the day of trouble, and He knows those who trust in Him…The mountains quake before Him, the hills melt and the earth heaves at His presence…He will make an utter end of it. Affliction will not rise up a second time" (Nahum 1:1-9).

12: 4,5 The Male Child

"**And the dragon stood before the woman who was ready to be delivered, in order to devour her child as soon as it was born. And she brought forth a male child, who was to rule all nations with a rod of iron; and her child was caught up to God, and to his throne**" (Revelation 12:4,5). The "**male Child**" who "**rules…with a rod of iron**" is a reference to Psalm 2 in which Christ is portrayed, not as "meek and lowly in heart" or "a man of sorrows, acquainted with grief,"[443] but as Ruler of the nations. "Why do the nations rage?…The kings of the earth set themselves, and the rulers take counsel together, against the Lord and against His Anointed…. *You shall break them with a rod of iron*; You shall dash them to pieces like a potter's vessel" (Psalm 2:1-9). This passage helps us to keep in perspective the next two chapters of Revelation, which show the success of the nations under Satan's leadership in persecuting God's people.

This theme is picked up again in Revelation 19. John saw "heaven opened" and a rider on a white horse, obviously Jesus, "clothed with a robe dipped in blood, and His name is called The Word of God." He has "a sharp sword, that with it He should smite the nations; and He shall rule them with a rod of iron. And He treads the wine press of the fierceness and wrath of Almighty God" (Revelation 19:11-16). This shows us that even though in Revelation 12 Jesus is pictured as a child who was caught up to heaven out of reach of the dragon, He will ultimately triumph over evil and "**rule all nations with a rod of iron**"— sin and those who cling to sin will be destroyed.

As we saw above, "**the woman who was ready to be delivered**" symbolizes Israel, God's chosen people, represented by Mary the mother of Jesus.[444] "When the fullness of the time had come, God sent forth His Son, born of a woman, born under the law, to redeem those who were under the law, that we might receive the adoption as sons" (Galatians 4:4,5). Satan the dragon, represented by the wicked king Herod, was indeed there "**before the woman who was ready to be delivered, in order to devour her child as soon as it was born.**" In the killing of "all the male children who were in Bethlehem and in all its districts, from two years old and under" (Matthew 2:16), Satan showed the fiendish and desperate lengths he is willing to go to in order to prevent the destruction of his kingdom. But God preserved His Son, and after living a perfect life and making a perfect sacrifice Jesus "**was caught up to God and to His throne.**" As Paul expressed it in Hebrews, "Jesus, the author and finisher of our faith, endured the Cross, despising the shame, and has sat down at the right hand of the throne of God" (Hebrews 12:2).[445]

---

443 Matthew 11:29, Isaiah 53:3.

444 Mary was the human agent but she was simply a representative of Israel, God's chosen "bride." That the woman is not primarily a symbol of the virgin Mary is seen by the fact that after the birth the dragon pursues the woman for "one thousand two hundred and sixty days" (Revelation 12:6). As we will see later in this chapter, this represents the centuries during which God's people (the woman) were persecuted. This shows that the woman represents all of God's covenant people, not just a particular person.

445 See also Hebrews 1:13, 8:1, 10:12,13, 1Peter 3:22.

12:7-9 Michael Casts Satan Out

"And there was war in heaven: Michael and his angels fought against the dragon, and the dragon fought and his angels; and they did not prevail, neither was their place found in heaven any longer. And the great dragon was cast out, that ancient serpent, called the Devil, and Satan, who deceives the whole world; he was cast to the earth, and his angels were cast out with him" (Revelation 12:7-9).

Just before He went to the Cross Jesus said, "Now is the judgment of this world; now the ruler of this world will be cast out" (John 12:31). The implication of this verse, compared with Revelation 12:7-9, is that after the resurrection and ascension one of Christ's first actions was to cast Satan out of heaven.

Michael is the leader of the angelic hosts that cast out **the dragon and his angels."** The Hebrew word "Michael" means "who is like God?," a challenge to Satan's contention "I will be like the most high" (Isaiah 14: 14). A careful comparison of the other scriptures that mention Michael show that he is Jesus in His role as the One who contends with Satan.[446] Jesus presents Himself in a variety of roles, each with a different name: He is "the Lion of the tribe of Judah, the Root of David" (Revelation 5:5), "a Lamb as though it had been slain" (Revelation 5:6), the "King of kings and Lord of lords" (Revelation 19:16), Immanuel (God with us), the Son of man (Matthew 1:23, 9:6) and many more. When he contends with Satan He is called Michael.

This is an important point. The view that Michael is simply one of the powerful angels

---

446 Michael is called "the archangel" in Jude 9, a title which can mean leader of the angels. This title is never used in the Bible for any other angel; only church tradition has assigned it to Gabriel and other angels. At the Second Coming of Christ "the Lord Himself will descend from heaven with a shout, with *the voice of the Archangel...* and the dead in Christ will rise first" (1 Thessalonians 4:16). Jesus made it clear that it is His voice that will bring the dead out of their graves, thus He is "the Archangel" (John 5:26-29).

In Jude 9 "Michael the Archangel, in contending with the devil over the body of Moses...said, 'The Lord rebuke you.'" In Zechariah 3 (the only other place in the Bible where this phrase is used), "The Lord (Yahweh) said to Satan, 'The Lord rebuke you Satan!'" (Zechariah 3:2). This shows that it is the Lord Himself who rebukes the devil, which implies that Michael the Archangel is "the Lord."

Some have thought it strange that Jesus would be called an angel, but a number of Old Testament texts show that one of God's titles was "the Angel of the Lord." In Exodus 3 God who spoke from the burning bush is first identified as "the Angel of the Lord" (v.2), then as God (Elohim, vs. 4, 6, 11, 13, 14, 15, 16, 4:5), and the Lord (Yahweh, vs. 4, 7, 15, 16, 4:2, 4, 6). He also identified Himself as "I AM" (Exodus 3:14), a name Jesus applied to Himself (John 8:58). Also compare Judges 6:11 with vs. 14, 16, 22 and 23, compare Judges 13:3, 9, 15 and 16 with vs. 22 and 23, and compare Acts 8:30-35, 38 with Exodus 19:3,11,19, 20:20-22.

In Daniel 10-12 Michael is called "one of the chief princes" (10:13), "your Prince" (10:21) and "the Great Prince that stands for the children of your people" (12:1). He is depicted doing battle with the powers of spiritual wickedness and contending with earthly authorities for the benefit of His people (Daniel 10:13, 20,21). In chapter 8 He is called "The Prince [Hebrew *sars*] of the host." This exact Hebrew phrase is also found in Joshua 5:14 where a "Man stood opposite him [Joshua]" and said, "as Captain [*sars*] of the host of the Lord I have come." He allowed Joshua to fall on his face and worship Him and told him to "take your sandal off your foot, for the place where you stand is holy" (prerogatives of God only). The passage continues, "And the Lord [Yahweh] said to Joshua" (Joshua 6:2). These verses in Daniel and Joshua show that Michael, "the Prince of the host," is "the Lord." And in fact, it is hard to imagine a lesser being contending over the body of Moses or casting Satan out of heaven.

would mean that the **"war in heaven"** is an angelic battle, with God curiously absent, "minding His own business" while angelic factions struggle for supremacy. But a correct view shows that God is intimately and personally involved in the struggles and battles of the great controversy, deeply concerned about everything that affects His creatures. Obviously, God versus Satan is no contest in terms of raw power; God has omnipotence on His side. This shows again that the **"war in heaven"** is a battle of ideas, loyalties and affections. Satan on the one hand can use what God cannot—lies, sophistry, flattery, accusations, threats, and persecution. God uses love and self-sacrifice to demonstrate His beautiful character.

This controversy is not some kind of heavenly "theological society" arguing about fine points of doctrine. The battles play out in a very real way on earth. For example, in Daniel 10 a mighty angel contended with "the prince of the kingdom of Persia" (a strong demonic angel), and called on Michael for assistance as he sought to influence "the kings of Persia" (Daniel 10:13). The result of the invisible but very real spiritual victory was that Cyrus, the king of Persia, allowed God's people to return from Babylonian captivity. The angel informed Daniel (verse 20) that he had to "return to fight with the prince of Persia" (some of the struggles are recounted in the books of Ezra and Esther), and that waiting in the wings was another powerful demon, "the prince of Greece" (Greece ruled over God's people after Alexander the Great defeated the Persians). The greatest and most important battle of all is the one described in Revelation 12 when **"Michael and His angels fought against the dragon...and his angels"** and Satan was cast out of heaven.

12:10 Accuser of the Brethren

"And I heard a loud voice saying in heaven, 'Now have come salvation, and strength, and the kingdom of our God, and the power of his Christ; for the accuser of our brethren has been cast down, who accused them before our God day and night" (Revelation 12:10).

Revelation 12:10 shows that one of Satan's main activities is that of accusing **"the brethren,"** the followers of God. We see this activity manifested in the story of Job—in the heavenly council he accused, "Does Job fear God for nothing? Have You not made a hedge around him?... You have blessed the work of his hands...but now stretch out Your hand and touch all that he has, and he will surely curse You to your face!" (Job 1:9-11).[447] In Zechariah 3 we also have a chance to look behind the scenes. "Joshua the high priest" who was one of the leaders in the re-establishment of the temple worship after the Babylonian captivity[448] is pictured "standing before the Angel of the Lord," apparently in the judgment,[449] with "Satan standing at his right hand to oppose him" (v.1). Satan was able to point to the inconsistencies and impure motives even in Joshua's service to God—"Joshua was clothed with filthy garments"(v.3).[450]

What does Satan have to gain in his

---

447 See appendix 8 for a discussion of the great controversy in the book of Job.

448 In the book of Haggai, Zerubbabel and Joshua were instrumental in encouraging that which Satan hates the most: the sanctuary service, which dramatically portrays the sacrifice and priestly ministry of Jesus.

449 2Corinthians 5:10 tells us that "we must all appear before the judgment seat of Christ." However, from these passages in Job and Zechariah we see that we may be unaware that we are being judged.

450 In Isaiah 64:6 filthy garments (rags) are a symbol of our own attempts to be righteous: "all our righteousnesses are like filthy rags." This contrasts with the righteousness of Christ which covers our uncleanness: "God has clothed me with the garments of salvation, He has covered me with the robe of righteousness" (Isaiah 61:10). After the angel rebukes Satan, He commands, "Take away the filthy garments from him...see, I have removed your iniquity from you, and I will clothe you with rich robes" (Zechariah 3:4). This is a beautiful picture of the righteousness God credits to our account when we believe in Jesus and allow God "to give repentance to [us] and forgiveness of sins" (Acts 5:31).

accusations against the people of God? It is possible that these accusations are part of his strategy to prolong his own survival. Satan is well aware of the character of God and seeks to play two of God's primary characteristics, His justice and His mercy, against one another. "Righteousness and justice are the foundation of Your throne"[451] (Psalms 89:14). The justice of God demands the destruction of the unrighteous: "The unrighteous will not inherit the kingdom of God" (1Corinthians 6:9). "All the wicked He will destroy" (Psalm 145:20). Satan, as the instigator and leader of the "spiritual hosts of wickedness in the heavenly places" (Ephesians 6:12) would be first on the list for destruction. All who pursue wickedness deserve wrath and destruction,[452] but Satan, unlike many who sin in ignorance, is fully aware of God's decree that "the wages of sin is death" (Romans 6:23). For this reason he tries to capitalize on another of God's chief attributes: His mercy.

"Righteousness and justice are the foundation of Your throne: Mercy and truth go before Your face" (Psalm 89:14). As basic as justice is, mercy is closer to God's mind and heart.[453] With his accusations Satan seeks to prove that all are guilty, just as he is. Satan knows very well God's great heart of love,[454] and so he tries to prove that there is no real difference between those who call themselves God's people and himself. If God in His great mercy forgives anyone and allows them to live, he argues, then He will have to allow Satan to live as well.

Along with arguments such as these, Satan offered the irrefutable proof of his accusations that "there is none righteous, no not one...they have all turned aside...there is none who does good, no, not one" (Romans 3:10-12). But God met Satan's challenge in Jesus. He became a man, taking upon Himself human nature: "Inasmuch then as the children have partaken of flesh and blood, He Himself likewise shared in the same." He led a perfect life, being "in all points tempted as we are, yet without sin," and then died for us "that through death He might destroy him who had the power of death, that is, the devil" (Hebrews 2:14, 4:15). "He has borne our griefs and carried our sorrows...and the Lord has laid on Him the iniquity of us all" (Isaiah 53:4-6).

The good news of the gospel is that through Jesus and His sacrifice God can be both "just and the justifier of the one who has faith in Jesus" (Romans 3:26). When we believe in Him, His perfect obedience is credited to our account as if it was our own righteousness (Romans 4:1-12). His death is credited to us as if it was our own death for our sins (Romans 5:6-8). This is where

---

451 In the earthly sanctuary, the throne of God (the "mercy seat") sat upon the "foundation" of the ark of the covenant, which contained the Ten Commandments (Exodus 25:10-22, Hebrews 9:4,5).

452 "The expectation of the wicked is wrath...so he who pursues evil pursues it to his own death...Though they join forces, the wicked will not go unpunished" (Proverbs 11:19-23).

453 When God declared His name to Moses, He emphasized first His mercy and then His justice: "The Lord God, merciful and gracious, longsuffering and abounding in goodness and truth, keeping mercy for thousands, forgiving iniquity and transgression and sin, yet by no means clearing the guilty" (Exodus 34:6,7).

454 A poignant example of God's mercy is found in God's treatment of Ephraim in the book of Hosea. God repeatedly points out Ephraim's sin. "Ephraim is joined to his idols" "For now, O Ephraim, you commit harlotry" "Ephraim has mixed himself among the peoples...they do not return to the Lord their God nor seek Him" "Because Ephraim has made many altars for sin, they have become for him altars for sinning." (Hosea 4:17, 5:3,4,11, 6:4, 7:8,9, 8:11). Yet despite all of Ephraim's sin, God at an emotional level could not bring Himself to give them up. "I taught Ephraim to walk, taking them by their arms; but they did not know that I healed them. I drew them with gentle cords, with bands of love. How can I give you up, Ephraim?...My heart churns within Me; My sympathy is stirred. I will not execute the fierceness of My anger; I will not again destroy Ephraim. For I am God and not man" (Hosea 11:3,4,8,9).

Satan's accusations fail: eternal life is a provision for those who believe that they are guilty sinners and that Jesus took their place on the Cross. Satan does not believe this; he continues to believe that God is wrong and he is right. But Michael (Jesus) said to Satan, "The Lord rebuke you!" (Jude 9), and Satan, having been cast out, can no longer appear in heaven to accuse us. Now we who believe and trust in Jesus can have the courage to "come boldly to the throne of grace, that we may obtain mercy and find grace to help in time of need" (Hebrews 4:16).

12: 11,12 They Overcame by the Blood

"And they overcame him by the blood of the Lamb, and by the word of their testimony; and they loved not their lives to the death. Therefore rejoice, you heavens, and you that dwell in them. Woe to the inhabitants of the earth and of the sea! For the devil has come down to you, having great wrath, because he knows that he has but a short time" (Revelation 12:11,12).

The devil has **"great wrath"** because he has been cast out of heaven, knowing that it is just a matter of time now until he will meet his doom. More than ever before he wants to tempt people to sin and abandon the Lord and thus prolong the controversy. But God has not abandoned us. He said, "I am with you always" (Matthew 28:20), and He gives us counsel as to how we may overcome the enemy: all who believe can overcome Satan **"by the blood of the Lamb and by the word of [our] testimony."** This is one of the most vital themes of the Book of Revelation, because it is the key to receiving the promises that are offered.

Each of the seven churches are promised rich blessings—"to eat from the tree of life" (2:7), to "not be hurt by the second death" (2:11), "some of the hidden manna,…a white stone,…a new

name" (2:17), "power over the nations…the morning star" (2:26,28), "white garments" (3:5), to be "a pillar in the temple" (3:12), the right "to sit with [Jesus Christ] on [His] throne" (3:21). These wonderful gifts are promised "to him who overcomes." The last two chapters of Revelation portray the beauty of New Jerusalem and the blessed inheritance of those who live there, but it is clear that this is not for everyone—"He who overcomes shall inherit all things, and I will be his God, and he shall be My son" (Revelation 21:7).

What must we overcome in order to "inherit all things?" "Do not be overcome by evil, but *overcome evil* with good" (Romans 12;21). "The word of God abides in you, and you have *overcome the wicked one*" (1 John 2:14). "For this is the love of God, that we keep His commandments. And His commandments are not burdensome. For whatever is born of God *overcomes the world*. And this is the victory that has overcome the world – our faith" (1John 5:3,4). God commands us to overcome evil, the wicked one (Satan) and the world. Revelation 12:11 shows that two crucial factors that allow us to overcome sin and Satan are **"the blood of the lamb"** and **"the word of [our] testimony."**

Satan **"accused them before our God day and night."** We cannot answer his accusations on the basis of moral behavior or good works, but only on the basis of the sacrifice of Christ—**"they overcame him by the blood of the Lamb."** His perfect life and His death for our sins, credited to our account, is the effectual answer to the accusations of the devil. This is the good news of the gospel. Jesus does not grant us forgiveness through His blood and then leave us to struggle with sin and temptation on our own. "He who has begun a good work in you will complete it until the day of Jesus Christ" (Philippians 1:6). Through **"the blood"** we overcome, not just in the judgment but also as we face the trials and temptations of this life.

Many Christians fail on this very point. When they have sinned they focus on their guilt and feel that they are too wicked to come to God. Some give up, and plunge more deeply into sin. Others try to be good until the hot shame has worn off a bit and then come to God for forgiveness. Still others go to a priest, receive penance (good works to perform) and never do come directly to Christ. The answer to all of this is Christ's sacrifice on the Cross—**"the blood of the Lamb."** There we see how God really feels about us. Even those who condemned Him to death and pounded the nails were included in the mercy that He extended there—Jesus prayed, "Father, forgive them, for they do not know what they do," even as they hung Him on the Cross. (Luke 23:34). In the sacrifice on the Cross, we see the depth of God's love for us, and it is this that causes us to love Him in return—"We love Him because He first loved us" (1 John 4:19). It is love for Him that breaks our hearts and causes us to hate the sin that nailed Him there.

Unfortunately, all too often the main motivation to overcome sin is the fear that it might jeopardize my entrance into heaven, or that by sinning I might expose myself to the wrath of God, or forfeit God's protection from the devil. In other words, I don't want to sin because I might get into trouble or lose out. If we have these attitudes it shows that we haven't really grasped the deeper meaning of Christ's sacrifice.[455] It was not just to pay a penalty, but to demonstrate the fullness of God's love that Jesus suffered and died.

As I look to the Cross and see the torture and the horror of guilt Jesus endured for my sins and realize that it was love for me that caused Jesus to suffer, it causes me to hate the sin I once loved, and to turn to Him for the power to overcome. Overcoming **"by the blood of the Lamb"** means that I focus my mind and heart on the sacrifice of Christ, recognizing my part in His death, and with a broken heart I repent of my sins while seeking His forgiveness and grace for victory over sin.

And by Their Testimony

God's people also overcome by **"the word of their testimony."** The consecration of our lives to God is not a private matter. We overcome when we "confess with [our] mouth the Lord Jesus and believe in [our] heart that God has raised Him from the dead...for with the heart one believes unto righteousness [**"the blood of the Lamb"**] and with the mouth confession is made unto salvation" [**"the word of their testimony"**] (Romans 10:9,10).

In the face of persecution and even death, thousands have refused to renounce their Savior. They have testified that Jesus is Lord of their lives and have renounced every opposing allegiance, even if it meant martyrdom—**"they did not love their lives to the death."** It is actually the testimony that they hear themselves saying that gives them the courage to face ridicule, opposition and even **"death."** Not everyone is called to be a martyr, but God calls each of his followers to "die daily" to sin, (1Corinthians 15:31) "to lay down our lives for the brethren" (1 John 3:16), to "present our bodies a living sacrifice, holy, acceptable to God" (Romans 12:1).

In the context of Satan's deadly last-days attempt to defeat the people of God, Jesus promises that "they will lay their hands on you and persecute you, delivering you up to the synagogues and prisons. You will be brought before kings and rulers for My name's sake. But it will

---

455 Although Jesus only died once in a sacrifice that paid for the sin of the whole world, in some sense when we continue to sin we torment Him as if He was on the cross again. Those who "have tasted the good word of God and the powers of the age to come, if they fall away...crucify again for themselves the Son of God and put Him to an open shame" (Hebrews 6: 5,6). By holding on to sinful habits I "trample the Son of God underfoot, count the blood of the covenant by which [I] was sanctified a common thing, and insult the Spirit of grace" (Hebrews 10: 29).

turn out for you as *an occasion for testimony.* Therefore settle it in your hearts not to meditate beforehand on what you will answer." "For it will be given to you in that hour what you should speak; for it is not you who speak, but the Spirit of your Father who speaks in you" (Luke 21:12-15, Matthew 10:19-22).

Those who live in "Christian" countries where most people are lukewarm and indifferent about their faith cannot imagine how anything like this could possibly happen. However, the anxiety and stress of the time of trouble and especially the appearance of the antichrist will bring about tremendous polarization and fanaticism. Now is the time for us to learn to speak up for the Lord, as a preparation for that time when our failure to give our testimony will put us into the enemy's camp.

Most people never say anything about the Lord; they feel that their relationship with Him is a private matter that should not be discussed. It is true that that many people do not want to hear what we have to say about God. However, God commands his people not to be silent. He compares us to watchmen on the walls who see danger coming—"I have set watchmen on your walls, O Jerusalem; They shall never hold their peace day or night. You who make mention of the Lord, do not keep silent" (Isaiah 62:6). The simple fact that you are reading this book means that you have crucial information that most of the world is completely unaware of. They need to know what you know; they need to hear **"the word of [your] testimony."**

Our faith is proven by our willingness to speak—"We believe, and therefore speak" (2Corinthians 4:13). "Therefore whoever confesses Me before men, him I will also confess before My Father who is in heaven. But whoever denies Me before men, him I will also deny before My Father who is in heaven" (Matthew 10:32,33). Many Christians believe that since they are not trained theologians they have nothing to say.

However, many of the most powerful witnesses in the Bible were not theologians, priests or professional clergymen, but were simple people who deeply loved the Lord. People facing the pressures of modern life today do not so much need theology as a living, experiential knowledge of a real God who works in real ways in the lives of real people.

"The word of their testimony" is the job description Jesus has given to his followers. It is so vital that in all four books of the gospel and the book of Acts, the last thing Jesus said before He left his disciples and went to Heaven was to go out into the world and tell people about Him.[456]

Jesus is active and at work in every dark corner of this world, and He is inviting us to join Him in one of those corners, maybe in our own families, in our neighborhoods, or in some distant mission field. Before Jesus left His disciples He promised, "I go to prepare a place for you…that where I am, there you may be also" (John 14:2,3). As surely as Jesus has prepared a place for us in heaven, He has prepared a place for each one of us with Him here on this earth. **"The word of [our] testimony"** may entail scorn, abuse, or even death. But in giving our testimony, we open the door for the Holy Spirit to fill us, and as the Spirit energizes our testimony we do not just convince others, we convince ourselves as well!

---

456 In the book of Matthew, the last thing Jesus said was, "Go therefore and make disciples of all nations, baptizing them in the name of the Father and of the Son and of the Holy Spirit, teaching them to observe all things that I have commanded you" (Matthew 28:19,20). In the book of Mark, the last thing He said was, "Go into all the world and preach the gospel to every creature" (Mark 16:15). In the book of Luke, the last thing Jesus said was, "Repentance and remission of sins should be preached in [My] name to all nations, beginning at Jerusalem, and you are witnesses of these things" (Luke 24:47,48). In the book of John, the last message of Jesus to all his disciples was, "Peace to you! As the Father has sent Me, I also send you" (John 20:21). And in the book of Acts, as Jesus was just about to ascend into Heaven, the last thing He told his disciples was, "You shall receive power when the Holy Spirit has come upon you; and you shall be witnesses to Me in Jerusalem, and in all Judea and Samaria, and to the end of the earth" (Acts 1:8).

The gifts of the Holy Spirit are given to empower our witness; when we speak in favor of Jesus the Spirit gives our words supernatural force, because He wants to convince the one we are speaking to. But when our testimony is accompanied by the power of the Spirit, we are the ones who are most in awe, because we know how weak and helpless we really are, and we know that the words we have spoken have a source much greater than ourselves. And ultimately it is the power of the Holy Spirit that enables us to overcome sin; this is why **"the word of [our] testimony"** empowers us. "If you live according to the flesh you will die; but if by the Spirit you put to death the deeds of the body, you will live…So then, those who are in the flesh cannot please God. But you are not in the flesh but in the Spirit, if indeed the Spirit of God dwells in you…If the Spirit of Him who raised Jesus from the dead dwells in you, He who raised Christ from the dead will also give life to your mortal bodies through His Spirit who dwells in you" (Romans 8:13, 8-11).

For many Christians, overcoming sin, the devil and the world means trying harder to be good. But Revelation 12:11 shows us the key: **"They overcame him by the blood of the Lamb and by the word of their testimony."** There are many things we can focus on in our religious life. Many who are reading this book have focused on prophecy, others on doctrinal understanding, on spiritual gifts, on personal devotions and disciplines, on the glories of the future heavenly kingdom, on the history of the church and of the saints, on proper Christian behavior, on the needs of people in the world, or on the church and its programs, rituals and requirements. These themes all deserve our attention, but if we find that we are being defeated by sin, Satan and sinful society, it should be a signal to us that our focus has drifted away from the essential core:

the sacrifice of Christ for our sins (**"the blood of the Lamb"**) and the privilege we have of telling others about it (**"the word of their testimony"**).

12:12-14 The Woman in the Wilderness

"And her child was caught up to God, and to his throne. And the woman fled into the wilderness, where she has a place prepared by God, so that there she would be nourished for 1,260 days" (Revelation 12:5,6).

"Woe to the inhabitants of the earth and of the sea! For the devil has come down to you, having great wrath, because he knows that he has but a short time.' And when the dragon saw that he was cast to the earth, he persecuted the woman who brought forth the male child. And to the woman were given two wings of a great eagle, that she might fly into the wilderness to her place, where she is nourished for a time, and times, and half a time, from the face of the serpent" (Revelation 12:12-14).

Both of these passages refer to the same thing: the fleeing of the woman from the persecutions of Satan to a place in the wilderness which God had prepared. The woman who gave birth to the male child represented the chosen people of God of the Old Testament period, the Jewish nation. However, Jesus made it clear that He was transferring the title, privileges and responsibilities from the Jews to the church[457]—"God placed all things under His [Christ's] feet and appointed Him to be head over everything for the church, which is His body, the fullness of Him who fills everything in every way" (Ephesians 1:22). This means that after **"her child [Jesus] was caught up to God and His throne"** (the resurrection and ascension) the woman now represented the church of God, "whoever believes in Him" from "every nation, tribe tongue, and people."[458]

A quick reading of Revelation 12:1-6 makes it appear that immediately after the resurrection of Christ the church **"fled into the wilderness"** for **"one thousand two hundred and sixty days."** However, this passage is a brief outline, with the details being filled out in verses 7-17. Particularly, in verses 13 and 14 it becomes obvious that there are a number of stages. First, the dragon saw that he had been **"cast to the earth"** (he no longer had access to the angels in heaven). Then he **"persecuted the woman"** and finally the woman **"was given two wings of a great eagle that she might fly into the wilderness."** Being given **"two wings of a great eagle"** is a reference to the deliverance of the children of Israel from Egypt. They suffered increasing persecution until God, through miracles and plagues, finally brought them out of Egypt to the wilderness where they experienced

His providence and refining for forty years. "You have seen what I did to the Egyptians, and how *I bore you on eagles' wings* and brought you to Myself" (Exodus 19:4). This experience foreshadowed the experience of the church.

Satan, knowing **"that he has but a short time,"** tried various strategies to defeat the church. The first persecutions were by the Jews following the stoning of Stephen, but this plan totally backfired: "At that time a great persecution arose against the church which was at Jerusalem, and they were all scattered throughout the regions of Judea and Samaria...therefore those who were scattered went everywhere preaching the word" (Acts 8:1,4). The Romans also persecuted the Christians starting with Nero in AD 64, but again these persecutions tended to strengthen the believers and the faith spread rapidly. Finally Satan hit upon a more successful plan: corrupting the church from the inside.[459] With the "conversion" of emperor Constantine in AD 312 the stage was set for the persecution of the Christian church *by* the "Christian" church.

"The woman fled into the wilderness" (v. 6). The wilderness was a place of protection for the people of God.[460] Stephen referred to the fledgling congregation that left Egypt under the leadership of Moses as "the church in the wilderness" (Acts 7:38),[461] and this wilderness church of the exodus was brought to a place of safety "on eagles'

---

457 In the parable of the vine dressers Jesus described with cutting accuracy the response of the Jews to God's initiatives, culminating in the killing of the son. In response to this He said, "Therefore the kingdom of God will be taken from you and given to a nation bearing the fruits of it" (Matthew 21:43). Then in Matthew 23, after outlining the hypocrisy of the Jewish leaders and their rejection of those God had sent to them, Jesus lamented, "O, Jerusalem, Jerusalem, the one who kills the prophets and stones those who are sent to her!...See! Your house is left to you desolate" (Matthew 23:36-38). Now God's plan is that "whoever believes in Him should not perish but have eternal life" (John 3:16). "You are all sons of God through faith in Christ Jesus...There is neither Jew nor Greek, there is neither slave nor free, there is neither male nor female; for you are all one in Christ Jesus" (Galatians 3:26-28), "that now the manifold wisdom of God might be made known through the church" (Ephesians 3:10).

458 John 3:16, Revelation 14:6.

459 The corruption of the church began during the lifetime of the Apostles and intensified after they died. "The mystery of lawlessness is already at work" (2 Thessalonians 2:7). "As you have heard that the antichrist is coming, even now many antichrists have come (1 John 2:18). "For I know this, that after my departure, savage wolves will come in among you, not sparing the flock. Also from among yourselves men will rise up, speaking perverse things, to draw away the disciples after themselves" (Acts 20:29,30).

460 "David stayed in strongholds in the wilderness...Saul sought him every day, but God did not deliver him into his hand" (1 Samuel 23:14).

461 The Greek word that is translated "assembly" or "congregation" in many versions is *ekklisia*, the same word that is used for "church" in the New Testament.

wings." In the same way the remnant underground church of the Middle Ages was protected from annihilation—**"To the woman were given the two wings of a great eagle"** (Revelation 12:14). Thus eagles' wings symbolize divine protection.[462] This protection does not mean that God's people are totally free from danger. Since Satan is "the ruler of this world,"[463] he makes sure that even in the wilderness God's people are pursued (**"the serpent cast water out of his mouth like a flood after the woman,"** see next section). But God did preserve a remnant during the **"1,260 days"** who kept the knowledge of the Lord alive.

One Thousand Two Hundred and Sixty Days

"She has a place prepared by God, that they should feed her there 1,260 days" (Revelation 12:6). This specific period of time is repeated several times in different ways in the books of Daniel and Revelation. In Revelation 12:14 the period is called **"a time** [1 year], **times** [2 years] **and half a time,"** (total 3½ years)[464] that the woman was **"nourished"** in the wilderness. In Revelation 13:5 the same period is referred to as "forty-two months"[465] in which "the beast" spoke "great things and blasphemies" and made "war with the saints," having "authority…over every tribe, tongue and nation" (v. 5-7). In Daniel 7

the "little horn" "speaks pompous words against the Most High" and "Shall persecute the saints of the Most High, and shall intend to change times and law…for *a time and times and half a time*" (Daniel 7:24,25). The same period is also mentioned in Daniel 12:7 and Revelation 11:2,3.

With so many references in such crucial sections of the most important last-day prophecies, it is obvious that this is a critical period for the people of God, and a correct understanding is essential. In chapter 12 **"the dragon"** (Satan) is portrayed as the one who persecutes **"the woman."** However, this chapter is highly symbolic. Just as the woman represents real men, women and children who are a part of God's church on earth, so the dragon has his agents on earth who carry out the actual persecutions. In Chapter 13 the identity of the persecutors is revealed under the symbol of "a beast rising out of the sea."

The 1,260 days, the time, times and half a time, and the 42 months, if taken literally, are a fairly short period of time. However, the context of Revelation 13 and Daniel 7 indicates that a much longer period of time is indicated. Numbers 14:34 and Ezekiel 4:5,6, as well as the prophecy of seventy weeks in Daniel 9 (which are explained in appendixes 4 and 5) show that in many time prophecies a day represents a year. [466]

Thus the period of time when **"the dragon… persecuted the woman"** who **"fled into the wilderness…[for] 1,260 days"** (Revelation 12:13,6) refers to the 1,260 years of papal supremacy

---

462 See also Deuteronomy 32:10-12, Isaiah 40:28-31.

463 John 12:31, 14:30, 16:11.

464 The Greek word here is *kairos*, which can refer to an indefinite period of time or a set or proper time. However, in this instance it is obvious that it refers to the usage of Daniel 7:25, "The saints shall be given into his hand for a time and times and half a time," the Hebrew word being *iddan*, which means a set time, technically a year.

465 The Bible month is considered to be 30 days. Thus in Genesis 7 and 8, the 5 months that the flood continued (7:11, 8:4) amounted to 150 days (7:24, 8:3,4). A year was 12 months (with an extra month every 3 years as a leap year). Thus 42 months and 3 ½ years are both equal to 1,260 days.

466 In Numbers 14:34, referring to the spying out of the land of Canaan and the refusal to enter in, God said "According to the number of the days in which you spied out the land, forty days, for each day you shall bear your guilt one year, namely forty years." Again in Ezekiel 4 the prophet was instructed to be a human symbol for the punishment that would fall upon Israel and Judah: "I have laid on you the years of their iniquity, according to the number of the days, three hundred and ninety days, so you shall bear the iniquity of the house of Israel…Then you shall bear the iniquity of the house of Judah forty days. I have laid on you a day for each year" (Ezekiel 4:5,6).

during the Middle Ages, as detailed in chapter 2 (the church of Thyatira). It was the medieval Christian church which became the deadly persecutor of "heretics," culminating in the Inquisition in which thousands were tortured and killed. Persecution continued during the Protestant Reformation, including the martyrdom of reformers such as Huss and Jerome, the slaughter of the Huguenots and others who dared to follow the Bible and the dictates of their conscience.

Although these persecutions waxed and waned through the centuries, it could be argued that the 1,260 years began in AD 538. In that year the last of the opposing Arian tribes were driven from Rome. This allowed the edict of Emperor Justinian of AD 533 to become a reality, in which the Pope, the Bishop of Rome was declared the head of all churches and *the corrector of heretics*. With this mandate the Papacy was able to become the effective power of the Western Roman Empire. Although the Papacy gathered its power gradually with major setbacks at times, by the 1200's the church had gained such control that Pope Innocent III could claim, "Ecclesiastical liberty is nowhere better preserved than where the Roman Church has full power in temporal as well as spiritual matters."[467]

This power, however, waned rapidly toward the end of the 18th century, as the church lost much of its influence and its Papal States during the French and Italian Revolutions. In 1798, exactly 1,260 years after the liberation of Rome in 538, the French armies of Napoleon under General Berthier took Pope Pius VI prisoner, symbolic of the end of the church's period of military supremacy. However, during the 1,260 years the medieval church was indeed "making war against the saints, and prevailing against them" and did "wear out the saints of the Most High"

(Daniel 7:21,25). **"The woman fled into the wilderness."** True believers hid in the mountains, or fled to areas of Germany or Switzerland where religious freedom was tolerated.

12:15,16 A Flood After the Woman

"And the serpent cast water out of his mouth like a flood after the woman, that he might cause her to be carried away by the flood" (Revelation 12:15). The flood of water that Satan spewed forth to destroy the church symbolizes a flood of hostile people. In Revelation 17:15, an angel explained to John that "the waters which you saw…are peoples, multitudes, nations, and tongues."

Satan has conflicting goals; on the one hand, by destroying people through wars and epidemics of disease he can snuff out people's lives before they have a chance to repent, or at least cause grief to God by destroying His creation. This seems to have been his primary plan through most of human history.[468] On the other hand, he can effectively use populations that are under his control to persecute a minority that is trying to remain faithful to God, and in such cases, the more subjects he has, the better. As the Protestant Reformation gathered momentum and spread in Europe there also began the most dramatic increase of human population in history.[469] This put pressure on God's true followers, making it more and more difficult for them to find "wilderness" places where they could avoid being the targets of persecution.

"But the earth helped the woman, and

---

467 Contributors, *Your Dictionary*, http://biography.yourdictionary.com/innocent-iii, accessed 12-09-2014.

468 For example, in the 14th century the bubonic plaque killed more than 25% of the European population.

469 The world population increased very slowly for most of human history, but it doubled between 1650 and 1850, and the doubling time has been decreasing ever since.

the earth opened its mouth, and swallowed up the flood which the dragon cast out of his mouth" (Revelation 12:16). Wars and persecution threatened to exterminate those who resisted the papal authority, but with the discovery of the New World there was a mass movement of population, including those seeking religious freedom. The American principles of separation of church and state and religious liberty had a strong influence on the European countries as well, and by the end of the 1,260 years (late 18th century) most of the persecution of Christians by the "Christian" church had come to an end.

12:17 The Remnant

"And the dragon was enraged with the woman, and went to make war with the remnant of her seed, who keep the commandments of God, and have the testimony of Jesus Christ" (Revelation 12:17). This text identifies the particular targets of Satan's wrath—they are a small percentage of those who call themselves Christians. The King James translation, "the remnant of her seed" (loipon tou spermatos) is the literal translation of the original Greek text, and links this group with the many references to the "remnant" in both the Old and New Testament.

In the Old Testament the remnant was the small number of God's people who remained after destructive judgments had come upon them because of their unfaithfulness. "Thus says the Lord God: 'How much more it shall be when I send My four severe judgments on Jerusalem—the sword and famine and wild beasts and pestilence—to cut off man and beast from it? Yet behold there shall be left in it a remnant who will be brought out" (Ezekiel 14:21,22).[470] The remnant refuse to compromise with the enemy, depending wholly on the Lord: "The remnant

of Israel…will never again depend on him who defeated them, but will depend on the Lord… The remnant will return to the Mighty God. (Isaiah 10:20-22).

The apostle Paul called those of Israel who accepted the Messiah a remnant: "Though the number of the children of Israel be as the sand of the sea, the remnant will be saved" (Romans 9:27). Joel prophesied that there would be a remnant at the end of time: "And it shall come to pass afterward that I will pour out My Spirit on all flesh… and I will show wonders in the heavens and in the earth…there shall be deliverance, as the Lord has said, among the remnant whom the Lord calls" (Joel 2:28-32).

In the history of the church as portrayed in the messages to the seven churches a remnant appears during the darkest chapter (Thyatira, the church of the Middle Ages). The message to Thyatira rebukes the majority who have compromised—"I have a few things against you, because you allow that woman Jezebel, who calls herself a prophetess, to teach and seduce My servants" (Revelation 2:20). But there is a remnant: "To the rest [Greek loipois, meaning remnant] in Thyatira, as many as do not have this doctrine, who have not known the depths of Satan…hold fast what you have till I come" (Revelation 2:20-25). Satan had corrupted the majority of the church, but he was not satisfied as long as there was a remnant that could threaten his kingdom. This is why "the dragon was enraged" and began to lay plans to defeat the final remnant, "who keep the commandments of God and have the testimony of Jesus Christ" (Revelation 12:17).

Commandments of God, Testimony of Jesus

The remnant "keep the commandments of God," not as a means of salvation, but as a demonstration of their love for their Savior. Jesus

---

470 See also Ezra 9:14,15, Jeremiah 42:2.

said, "If you love me, keep My commandments" (John 14:15). Our love for others, expressed in the keeping of God's commandments, proves our love for God: "By this we know that we love the children of God, when we love God and keep His commandments. For this is the love of God, that we keep His commandments. And His commandments are not burdensome" (1John 5:2,3).

Satan has a particular hatred of God's law because it condemns his aspirations. The first commandment, "You shall have no other gods before me" (Exodus 20:3) directly opposes his expressed goal, "I will be like the Most High" (Isaiah 14:13,14). The second commandment forbids the worship of idols, the chief means that he uses to trick people into worshiping him. The fourth (Sabbath) commandment is based on the fact that "in six days the Lord made the heavens and the earth, the sea and all that is in them" (Exodus 20:11), a claim that Satan cannot make. The commandments not to murder and lie condemn his primary means of achieving his goals. The tenth commandment not to covet strikes at the heart of what he wants most: a position that he has not been appointed to ("I will exalt my throne above the stars of God," Isaiah 14:13).

Satan does everything he can to get rid of the law, because "sin is lawlessness (the transgression of the law, KJV)" and "the devil has sinned from the beginning" (1John 3:4,8).[471] He even brings the doctrine of lawlessness into the church with "new covenant" theology that claims that the law of God was "nailed to the cross"[472] But Jesus himself said, "Do not think that I came to destroy the law…but to fulfill. For assuredly I say to you, till heaven and earth pass away, one jot or one tittle will by no means pass from the law till all is

---

471 Although legalism (the attempt to be saved by keeping the law) is incompatible with saving faith, the answer to legalism is not to throw out the law. God sent "His own Son in the likeness of sinful flesh, on account of sin; He condemned sin in the flesh, that the righteous requirements of the law might be fulfilled in us" (Romans 8:3,4). Paul asked, "Do we then make void the law through faith? Certainly not! On the contrary, we establish the law" (Rom 3:31). Why? Because "by the law is the knowledge of sin" (Rom 3:20) and "the law was our tutor to bring us to Christ, that we might be justified by faith" (Galatians 3:24). The law has never been a means of salvation, but it does reveal our sinful condition, showing us our need for Christ, and thus bringing us to Jesus that he might save us.

472 The text quoted is from Colossians 2:14 and reads, "Having wiped out the handwriting of requirements that was against us, which was contrary to us, and He has taken it out of the way, having nailed it to the cross." This cannot refer to the Ten Commandment law because "handwriting" shows the human element in its production, whereas the Ten Commandments were "written and engraved on stones" by the finger of God. In addition, these "requirements" are "against us" and "contrary to us" whereas "the law is holy, and the commandment holy and just and good" (Romans 7:12). The law that is against us is "the law of sin and death" (Romans 8:2) which says, "the soul that sins shall die" (Ezekiel 18:4). This law was delineated in "the covenant which the Lord commanded Moses to make with the children of Israel in the land of Moab, *besides the covenant which He made with them in Horeb*" (Deuteronomy, 29:1). This "second" covenant meets the specifications of Colossians 2:14. It was handwritten: "You shall set up for yourselves large stones and whitewash them with lime…and you shall write very plainly on the stones all the words of this law" (Deuteronomy 27:2,8). It had many requirements: "Cursed is the one who makes a carved or molded image…Cursed is the one who moves his neighbors landmark… Cursed is the one who takes a bribe" etc. (vs. 11-28). It promised punishment: "If you do not obey…all His commandments and His statutes which I command you today, all these curses will come upon you" (28:15). It was "against us": "When Moses had completed writing the words of this law in a book…Moses commanded,…'take this book of the law, and put it beside the ark of the covenant of the Lord your God, *that it may be there as a witness against you*" (Deuteronomy 31:24-26). The curses associated with this law were nailed to the cross with Jesus: "Christ has redeemed us from the curse of the law, having become a curse for us" (Galatians 3:13).

fulfilled" (Matthew 5:17).[473]

The remnant are also a threat to Satan and "his property" (the world that he holds in captivity) because they **"have the testimony of Jesus Christ."** The **"testimony of Jesus"** is defined as "the Spirit of prophecy" (Revelation 19:10). "Prophecy" does not just mean telling the future— "He who prophesies speaks edification and exhortation and comfort" (1Corinthians 14:3). The prophet has a specific message from God for individuals or for the church. "If all prophesy, and an unbeliever or an uninformed person comes in, he is convinced by all, he is convicted by all. And thus the secrets of his heart are revealed: and so falling down on his face, he will worship God and report that God is truly among you" (vs. 24,25). Through prophecy people can become aware of the strongholds of Satan in their lives and escape from them.

According to Ephesians 4:11-15, the gift of prophecy will be present in the church until sin, division, and misunderstanding of God have ceased—in other words, until Christ returns. The apostle Paul exhorted that we should "earnestly desire the best gifts...Desire spiritual gifts, but especially that you may prophesy...I wish...even more that you prophesied...Desire earnestly to prophesy" (I Corinthians 12:31, 14:1,5, 39).

These verses show us that the gift of prophecy is a specific spiritual gift that Paul tells us to "desire." He makes it clear that not all Christians

will be prophets,[474] but a clear mark of God's church is that the spirit of prophecy is active in it.[475] However, even if many Christians are not prophets themselves, the "spirit of prophecy," in other words, the Spirit that filled the prophets, should be present in every born-again believer. Having special messages from God should not be the exclusive domain of a few "super Christians," but should be a characteristic of all of God's people as they learn to hear His voice and share what He says.

Some Christians have comforted themselves with the thought that they are members of the "Remnant Church" that **"keep the commandments of God and have the testimony of Jesus Christ."** But we should be clear that belonging to a church that teaches the keeping of God's commandments does not make one a part of the remnant.[476] It is the remnant *people* who **"keep the commandments of God."** Belonging to a church that has prophets, or having a bookshelf full of books by prophets does not make one a part of the remnant.[477] It is God's Spirit, the same Spirit that filled the prophets, that empowers each

473 In contrast to many modern theologians, Jesus and the New Testament writers continually emphasized keeping the commandments. See Matthew 5:17-19, 7:12, 15:3-6, 22:36-40, 23:23, Mark 7:8,9, 10:17-19, Luke 10:26-28, 16:17, 23:56, John 14:15,21, 15:9-14, Romans 2:12-14, 3:20,31, 7:7,12-14, 8:3,4, 13:9, Galatians 3:24, Ephesians 6:2,3, 1Timothy 1:8,9, James 1:25, 2:8-12, 2Peter 2:20-22, 1John 2:3,4,7, 3:22-24, 5:2,3, 2John 1:4-6, Revelation 12:17, 14:12, 22:14.

474 In 1Corinthians 12 Paul makes it clear that there are a variety of spiritual gifts (vs. 8-12), that the Spirit decides who will receive a specific gift (v.7,11), that each gift is essential for the whole body of believers (vs. 14-25) and that they are for corporate rather than individual benefit (v. 7).The gift of prophecy may be emphasized in the last-day remnant because at that time special messages from God will be more essential than ever and there will be many deceptive messages supposedly from God (Matthew 24:5,11,23-26).

475 A careful comparison of Revelation 19:10 and Revelation 22:9 shows that the "spirit of prophecy" is the gift of prophecy. The remnant has the "testimony of Jesus" ("the spirit of prophecy," Revelation 12:17 19:10), and this means that they have people among them with the gift of prophecy (Revelation 22:9).

476 The Greek word for remnant (*loipon*) is plural, showing that Paul is referring to people rather than a single organization.

477 Many denominations have institutionalized the rejection of some of God's commandments, such as the second which forbids idolatry and the fourth which requires the keeping of the seventh-day Sabbath. Other denominations reject the idea that there could be prophets in the church today. Believers will need to come out of these churches in order to be a part of the remnant.

person who is a part of God's remnant to obey the messages of the prophets, in other words, to **"keep the commandments"** and to share **"the testimony of Jesus."** As we will see in the next chapter, Satan has a well-laid plan to force the remnant to break God's commandments and to silence their testimony.

"And I saw a beast rising up out of the sea, having seven heads and ten horns…then I saw another beast coming up out of the earth, and he had two horns like a lamb and spoke like a dragon" Rev. 13:1,11
Woodcut by Albrecht Durer

Chapter 13

Revelation 13:1-18

13:1 13:1 And I stood on the sand of the sea, and saw a beast rise up out of the sea, having seven heads and ten horns, and on his horns ten crowns, and on his heads a blasphemous name.

13:2 And the beast which I saw was like a leopard, and his feet were like the feet of a bear, and his mouth like the mouth of a lion; and the dragon gave him his power, and his throne, and great authority.

13:3 And I saw one of his heads as if it was wounded to death, and his deadly wound was healed; and all the world marveled after the beast.

13:4 And they worshiped the dragon which gave power to the beast, and they worshiped the beast, saying, "Who is like to the beast? Who is able to make war with him?"

13:5 And there was given to him a mouth speaking great things and blasphemies; and power was given to him to continue for forty two months.

13:6 And he opened his mouth in blasphemy against God, to blaspheme his name, and his tabernacle, and those that dwell in heaven.

13:7 And it was given to him to make war with the saints, and to overcome them. And power was given him over all tribes, and tongues, and nations.

13:8 And all that dwell on the earth shall worship him, whose names are not written in the Book of Life of the Lamb slain from the foundation of the world.

13:9 If anyone has an ear, let him hear.

13:10 He that leads into captivity shall go into captivity; he that kills with the sword must be killed with the sword. Here is the patience and the faith of the saints.

13:11 And I beheld another beast coming up out of the earth; and he had two horns like a lamb, and he spoke like a dragon.

13:12 And he exercises all the power of the first beast before him, and causes the earth and those who dwell therein to worship the first beast, whose deadly wound was healed.

13:13 And he does great wonders, so that he makes fire come down from heaven on the earth in the sight of men,

13:14 And deceives them that dwell on the earth by the means of those miracles which he had power to do in the sight of the beast; saying to them that dwell on the earth, to make an image to the beast, which had the wound by a sword, and lived.

13:15 And he had power to give life to the image of the beast, that the image of the beast should both speak, and cause that as many as would not worship the image of the beast should be killed.

13:16 And he causes all, both small and great, rich and poor, free and bond, to receive a mark on their right hand, or on their foreheads;

13:17 And that no one could buy or sell, except he that had the mark, or the name of the beast, or the number of his name.

13:18 Here is wisdom. Let him that has understanding count the number of the beast, for it is the number of a man; and his number is 666.

13: 1,2 The Beast from the Sea

"**And I stood on the sand of the sea, and saw a beast rise up out of the sea, having seven heads and ten horns, and on his horns ten crowns, and on his heads a blasphemous name. And the beast which I saw was like a leopard, and his feet were like the feet of a bear, and his mouth like the mouth of a lion; and the dragon gave him his power, and his throne, and great authority**" (Revelation 13:1,2).

Chapter 12 ended with the dragon (Satan) frustrated and enraged that his attack on the woman had been thwarted. He "went to make war with the remnant of her seed." In the next scene we see John[478] standing on the sand of the sea, and a beast that looks a lot like the dragon is rising out of the sea. "**The sand of the sea**" is a symbol of multitudes of people, either the people of God ("The number of the children of Israel shall be as the sand of the sea, which cannot be measured or numbered" Hosea 1:10) or the multitudes of the ungodly ("the nations which are in the four quarters of the earth, Gog, and Magog…the number of whom is as the sand of the sea" Revelation 20:8). The sea itself is a symbol of "peoples, multitudes, nations and tongues" (Revelation 17:15), so the emphasis is upon the multitudes of nations and people that give rise

to the beast.

The beast closely resembles the dragon of chapter 12, which also had seven heads and ten horns. The main difference is that the dragon had crowns,[479] the sign of authority, on its heads, but the beast from the sea has crowns on its horns. The head symbolizes ruling, planning and directing,[480] showing that the dragon (Satan) is in charge and exercises authority by formulating and and directing plans. Horns are a symbol of executive or military powers,[481] personified by kings,[482] which carry out the plans of the head. Thus the power and authority of the beast from the sea, as represented by the crowns on its horns, is its political and military power which it uses to carry out the plans of Satan who "**gave him his power, and his throne, and great authority.**"

The beast from the sea is a terrifying composite of three ferocious predators: a leopard, a

---

478 Some of the ancient texts (and English versions based on them) say that it was the dragon who stood on the sand of the sea.

479 The Greek word for crown used here is *diadima*, not the more commonly used *stefanos* crown of victory. It is the word used in 1Macabees 12:39 "Then Trypho attempted to become king in Asia and put on the crown [*diadima*] and to raise his hand against King Antiochus." The *diadima* crown indicates a claim to power and authority, (in this case, a rebellious claim). Satan likewise claims authority in rebellion to Christ, who has all true authority, as indicated by the many crowns (*diadima*) that he wears (Revelation 19:12).

480 For example, Daniel 2:38 : "He [God]…has made you ruler over them all—you *are* this head of gold."

481 1Kings 22:11, Zechariah 1:18-21.

482 Daniel 7:24, 8:20,21.

bear, and a lion, and it has ten horns. These are the same animals which "came up from the sea" in the vision of Daniel 7. This implies that this beast somehow embodies a combination of the characteristics of the wild animals of Daniel 7. The following section will give a very brief overview of the vision of Daniel 7. For a more detailed exposition see Appendix 11.

The Sea Beast and the Wild Animals of Daniel 7

The vision of the wild animals in Daniel 7 builds on the vision of Daniel 2, which was of a huge multi-metal image of a man. The different metals represented the world empires that dominated and oppressed God's chosen people from the time of Daniel until the time of the end. The image had a head of gold that symbolized the Babylonian empire, a chest of silver that represented the Medo-Persian empire, a belly of brass that represented the Greek Hellenistic empire, iron thighs that symbolized the pagan Roman empire, and legs of iron mixed with clay that represented the powers of Europe bound together by the Roman Catholic papacy.

The vision of Daniel 7 presents the same picture but fills in more details about the empires that persecuted God's people. The prophet saw four wild animals rising from the "Great Sea." The first was like a lion, again representing Babylon. The second, like a bear, symbolized the Medo-Persian empire which defeated Babylon. The third animal was a four-headed leopard that represented the divided Greek Hellenistic kingdoms that succeeded Medo-Persia. The fourth animal was a monster unlike anything Daniel had ever seen before, with "huge iron teeth; it was breaking in pieces, and trampling the residue with its feet" (Daniel 7:7). This fierce monster represented the Roman Empire that conquered the Greek kingdoms. Out of this dreadful beast 10 horns arose, and then "there was another horn, a little one, coming up among them…He shall be different from the first ones…He shall speak pompous words against the Most High, shall persecute the saints of the Most High, and shall intend to change times and law" (Daniel 7:8,24,25). The "little horn" that arose from the Roman Empire represented the medieval papacy that dominated the European powers, represented by the ten horns. Table 13.1 summarizes the image of Daniel 2 and the animals of Daniel 7.

Table 13.1

Image of Daniel 2	Animals of Daniel 7	Empire Represented
Head of Gold	Lion	Babylonian Empire
Breast of Silver	Bear	Medo-Persian Empire
Belly of Brass	Leopard	Greek Hellenistic Empire
Legs of Iron	Terrible Beast	Pagan Roman Empire
Feet of Iron and Clay	Ten Horns and Little Horn	Papal Roman Empire

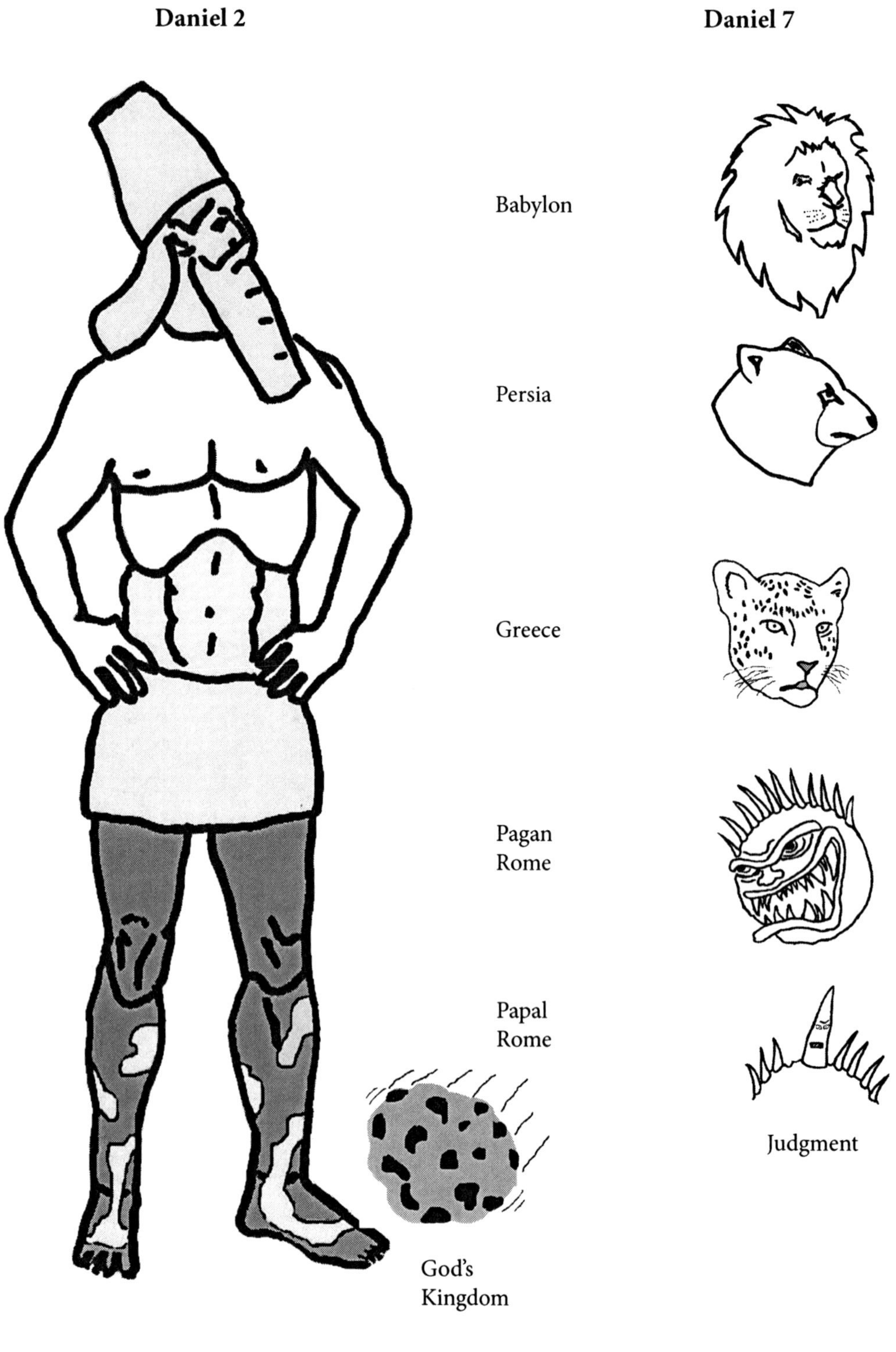

Daniel 2   **Daniel 7**

Babylon

Persia

Greece

Pagan
Rome

Papal
Rome

God's
Kingdom

Judgment

The wild animals of Daniel 7 had a total of seven heads and ten horns and were the same animals that comprised the beast that rose out of the sea in Revelation 13. This implies that the seven heads of the sea beast symbolize seven major characteristics that derive from the ancient empires represented by the animals. John said that the sea beast was **"like a leopard"** (Revelation 13:2), in other words, it most resembled the characteristics of the leopard of Daniel 7, which symbolized the Greek Empire. The leopard had 4 heads, representing four major characteristics of the Greek Empire: the pantheon of Greek gods, highly advanced Greek philosophy, the pervasive Hellenic culture, and the unity of church and state. The sea beast had the **"feet of a bear."** Feet (paws) symbolize executive power, and the Persian Empire, represented by the bear, was known for its effective executive system, with a highly organized hierarchical government and unchangeable laws. **"His** [the sea beast's] **mouth [was] like the mouth of a lion."** The lion symbolized Babylon, and the "mouth" of Babylon was the Chaldean priesthood with their ritual magic. The sea beast had **"ten horns"** like the vicious Roman monster of Daniel 7, and these horns symbolize overwhelming military might.

Appendix 11 provides a detailed analysis of the characteristics of these ancient empires, and shows how they are also the basic characteristics of the medieval Papacy. This is not surprising, because the visions of Daniel found in chapters two, seven, eight, and eleven all focus on the papal Roman Catholic Church. The Catholic Church of the Middle Ages had the characteristics of the ancient empires: a pantheon of "gods" (the saints), a theology based on Greek philosophy, a pervasive Catholic culture, the union of church and state, a hierarchy with the pope at the top creating infallible laws, a system of priests performing "magic" rituals, and the powerful military forces of the European nations at its disposal.

Why is there such a focus on the medieval Papacy in both Daniel and Revelation? This identification is important because the papacy of the Middle Ages is the prototype for the final persecuting power of the last days. We will see later in this chapter and in chapter 17 that it is very similar to the beast that John saw rising out of the sea. The final enemy of God's faithful followers will not be communism, secular humanism, atheism or neo-paganism. It will be legalistic "christianity," which, like the medieval Papacy, will use coercive force to impose its version of "God's will."

The Little Horn and the Sea Beast

In Daniel 7 the papacy is symbolized by the "little horn" (see 3: *Thyatira* and Appendix 11). Comparing the little horn of Daniel 7 with the sea beast of Revelation 13, we find confirmation that the beast from the sea represents the medieval Roman Catholic Church. The little horn had "a mouth speaking…pompous words against the Most High" (Daniel 7:8,25). Likewise, the sea beast **"was given a mouth speaking great things and blasphemies…and he opened his mouth in blasphemy against God, to blaspheme His name, His tabernacle and those who dwell in heaven"** (Revelation 13:6). This description fits the medieval Papacy, which has a long history of blasphemous claims, such as that of pope Leo XIII who, in his pastoral letter "The Reunion of Christendom" of June 20, 1894, asserted that "we [the popes] hold on this earth the place of God Almighty."[483]

The little horn "was making war against the saints and prevailing against them" and "shall persecute the saints of the Most High" (Daniel 7:21,25). Likewise, the sea beast was allowed **"to make war with the saints and to overcome them. And authority was given him over every tribe, tongue and nation"** (Revelation 13:7). Again the Papacy of the Middle Ages fits the specifications, having carried out the Inquisition, the Crusades, and the persecution and execution of reformers such as John Huss, as well as a series of vicious wars against "heretics" such as the Waldenses, the Huguenots and the Reformed Churches of northern Europe.

The little horn would prevail "for a time, times and half a time" (Daniel 7:25). The sea beast **"was given authority to continue for forty-two months"** (Revelation 13:5). In chapter 12 we saw that the "1,260 days," "time, times, and half a time," and "42 months" refer to the same period: the 1,260 years of papal political supremacy. These close parallels between the little horn of Daniel 7 and the sea beast leave no question as to its identity: the beast from the sea represents the papal Roman Catholic Church of the Middle Ages. (See Table 13.2)

Table 13.2

"Little" Horn of Daniel Seven	Sea Beast of Revelation 13
"a mouth speaking…pompous words against the Most High" (Daniel 7:8,25).	"a mouth speaking great things and blasphemy… against God" (Revelation 13:5,6).
"was making war against the saints and prevailing against them" (Daniel 7:21,25).	allowed "to make war with the saints and to overcome them" (Revelation 13:7).
would prevail for "a time, times and half a time" (Daniel 7:25).	"was given authority to continue for forty-two months" (Revelation 13:5).

---

483   Papal Encyclicals Online http://www.papalencyclicals.net/
Leo13/l13praec.htm accessed 12-10-2014.

The Beast's Agenda—to Change God's Law

The fact that the sea beast is the same as the little horn makes it possible to learn its agenda—it "shall intend to change times and law" (Daniel 7:25). Obviously this does not refer to human or political laws since all governments change their laws continually. This power makes an attempt to change God's law, and specifically the first four of the Ten Commandments that have to do with man's relationship with God.

The first commandment, "You shall have no other gods before me" (Exodus 20:3) forbids the worship of anything except the true God who "made heaven and earth, the sea and all that is in them" (v.11). But in verse 3 we learn that **"all the world marveled after the beast. And they worshiped the dragon which gave power to the beast, and they worshiped the beast"** (Revelation 13:3,4). This worship is not based on love for God, but rather it is based on power, fear and threats: **"Who is like the beast? Who is able to make war with him?...He...causes** [makes, forces] **the earth and those dwell therein to worship"** (vs. 4, 12).

The second commandment forbids the creation and worship of any image. But the second beast of Revelation 13 deceives and forces **"them that dwell on the earth, to make an image to the beast, which had the wound by a sword, and lived** [the sea beast]. **And he had power to give life to the image of the beast, that the image of the beast should both speak, and cause that as many as would not worship the image of the beast should be killed"** (Revelation 13:14,15).

The third commandment states that "You shall not take the name of the Lord your God in vain" (Exodus 20:7). The sea beast, in blatant defiance, **"opened his mouth in blasphemy against God, to blaspheme his name, and his**

tabernacle, and those that dwell in heaven" (Revelation 13:6).

The "little horn" (the sea beast) "shall intend to change times and law." The law that has to do with time is the fourth, the Sabbath commandment. We will see later in this chapter that the fourth commandment is a particular target of the beast because it identifies God's authority as Creator and Redeemer.

Since the sea beast is the agent of Satan, it is not surprising that it attacks God's law. The law of God exposes and condemns Satan's ambition to set himself in the place of God. For this reason the apostle Paul calls the antichrist "the lawless one:" "The lawless one will be revealed, whom the Lord will consume with the breath of His mouth and destroy with the brightness of His coming. The coming of the lawless one is according to the working of Satan, with all power, signs, and lying wonders" (2 Thessalonians 2:8,9). The Greek word for lawless is *anomos*, "as *having no law, not subject to law.*" The lawlessness of the sea beast is a reflection of Satan's ambition to destroy the law of God: "whoever commits sin also commits lawlessness, and sin is lawlessness...He who sins is of the devil, for the devil has sinned from the beginning" (1 John 3:4,8).

13:3 The Deadly Wound

"And I saw one of his heads as if it was wounded to death, and his deadly wound was healed; and all the world marveled after the beast. And they worshiped the dragon which gave power to the beast, and they worshiped the beast, saying, **"Who is like to the beast? Who is able to make war with him?"** (Revelation 13:3,4). As we saw above, the sea beast had seven heads, each a basic characteristic of the medieval Roman Catholic Church. It was the political/military "head" of the Papacy that was severely wounded toward the end of the Middle Ages. The military and political capabilities developed slowly over many centuries. The Church of Rome began as a persecuted church—first by Nero in AD 64 and later in the general persecution of the Jews. As Christians began to distinguish themselves from the Jews, they were persecuted because of their "atheistic" refusal to worship the old Roman gods and their "anarchic" refusal to give homage to the emperor.

After becoming the official Roman religion under Constantine in the fourth century, the Church of Rome enjoyed official protection. But by the fifth century the western empire was disintegrating, and the eastern capital at Constantinople was too far away to provide effective protection from the barbarian tribes who followed the teachings of Arius.[484] In AD 476 the last Roman emperor fell and Odoacer, an Arian "heretic," ruled Rome. This severely restricted the political influence of the Roman church. However, in AD 496 Clovis, the king of the Franks, was converted to the Roman Catholic faith and the Franks became the military champions of the church. The Arian Visigoths, Ostrogoths, Vandals, Burgundians and Lombards were driven back and were eventually either destroyed or they abandoned their Arian faith.

Essential aid also came from the the eastern empire which, after of period of decline, was reasserting its military power under the brilliant emperor Justinian. His armies came to the aid of the Roman church, driving the Ostrogoths from Rome in AD 538.[485] The Catholic Church was now free to expand, and by the eighth century

dominated essentially all of Europe. The church reached the peak of its power in the 13th century, and the establishment of the religious court (the Inquisition) in 1231 made it possible to effectively stamp out resistance.

The "mortal wound" was not a single decisive event, but rather a series of setbacks for the Papacy. Church corruption along with the sale of indulgences used to finance the building of St. Peter's Cathedral in Rome caused great disillusionment and set the stage for the Protestant Reformation. The Reformation made it clear that the Roman Catholic Church would not be the only church in Europe. Much of northern Europe was torn out of the hands of the Papacy, but not without the bloodbath of the Thirty Years' War,[486] which proved that the Catholic Church could not totally dominate militarily. But perhaps the greatest blow was the French Revolution, when the champion of the Papacy became its worst enemy.

The French Revolution

The Protestants in France, known as the Huguenots, were severely persecuted by a series of kings who were urged on by the Roman Catholic clergy. The Massacre of St. Bartholomew's Day was just one of many atrocities which resulted in the flight from France of hundreds of thousands of Protestants. The common people who remained carried the burden of supporting the luxurious lifestyle of both the nobility and the clergy, who were exempt from taxation. Centuries of anger and frustration boiled over in

---

484 Arius (AD 250-336) taught that Christ was in some sense a created being.

485 Wikipedia contributors, "Siege of Rome (537–38)," *Wikipedia, The Free Encyclopedia*, http://en.wikipedia.org/w/index.php?title=Siege_of_Rome_(537%E2%80%9338)&oldid=637180995 (accessed December 13, 2014).

486 The peace of Westphalia, which ended the war in 1648, declared that the people of each state must follow the religion of their ruler. This principle greatly weakened the Holy Roman Empire. It also ended the medieval idea of a Christian commonwealth of nations harmoniously directed by the supreme authority of pope and emperor.

the French Revolution, when the people turned on their oppressors, slaughtering thousands of aristocrats and priests.[487] Churches were desecrated and the "Goddess of Reason and Liberty" became the religion of the revolution.[488]

In the meantime France under the generalship of Napoleon Bonaparte was at war with most of Europe; the Roman Catholic Church, with its Papal States in Italy and France, became an object for conquest. By the spring of 1797 all of northern Italy, including the Papal States, had been conquered. The "Directory," the committee which was ruling France, sent Napoleon his instructions: "The Roman religion will always be the irreconcilable enemy of the Republic…do all that you deem possible, without rekindling the torch of fanaticism, to destroy the papal government."[489]

The opportunity came the next year. "The French General Duphot was shot and killed, whereupon the French took Rome on February 10, 1798 and proclaimed the Roman Republic. Because the pope [Pius VI] refused to submit,

he was forcibly taken from Rome."[490] Though seriously ill, he was hurried from one city to another and finally died in Valence, France in 1799, dramatically fulfilling the prophecy of Revelation 13:10, **"He that leads into captivity shall go into captivity"** (Revelation 13:10). The arrest and deportation of the pope in 1798 was neither the first nor the last of a series of blows to the Roman Catholic Church,[491] but the dramatic removal of the head of the church symbolizes the "deadly wound" prophesied in Revelation 13. It also came exactly 1,260 years after AD 538, the year in which the Arian "heretics" were driven from Rome, and is thus a remarkable fulfillment of prophecy.

The Deadly Wound Healed

"And I saw one of his heads as if it was wounded to death, and his deadly wound was healed; and all the world marveled after the

---

487 In 1789 the revolutionary assembly voted that the possessions of the clergy be placed at the disposal of the nation. The next year the religious orders were suppressed. All citizens, even Protestants or Jews, were given the right to hold church offices, and "the first obligation of the priests was to take an oath of fidelity to the constitution, which denied to the Pope any effective power over the church" Georges Goyau, "French Revolution," *The Catholic Encylopedia*, www.newadvent.org/cathen/13009a.htm (Accessed August 15,2014). Any priest who would not take the oath, was deported to Guinea, West Africa. In 1793 "missionary representatives" were sent to the provinces to close churches, hunt down citizens suspected of religious practices, to constrain priests to marry and threaten with deportation those priests who refused to abandon their posts.

488 Wikipedia contributors, "Dechristianisation of France during the French Revolution," *Wikipedia, The Free Encyclopedia,* http://en.wikipedia.org/w/index.php?title=Dechristianisation_of_France_during_the_French_Revolution&oldid=635540666 (accessed December 10, 2014).

489 Georges Goyau, "Napoleon I (Bonaparte)" *The Catholic Encylopedia*, www.newadvent.org/cathen/10687a.htm (Accessed August 15, 2014).

490 *Ibid*

491 In 1804 Napoleon crowned himself Emperor of France, and he continued his war against the Papacy. A new pope, Pius VII, had been elected. At first there was an uneasy peace but as the pope refused to co-operate in Napoleon's grandiose empire-building, he ordered the pope arrested in July, 1809. When the pope attempted to continue his political and religious directives from prison, "the conditions of the pope's captivity were made more severe, all his correspondence had to pass through Paris, to be inspected by the Government, he could no longer receive visits without the presence of witnesses, a gendarme demanded of him the ring of St. Peter, which Pius VII surrendered after breaking it in two" Georges Goyau, "Napoleon I (Bonaparte)" The Catholic Encyclopedia, www.newadvent.org/cathen/10687a.htm (Accessed August 15, 2014). "The Church suffered enormous losses as a result of the French Revolution. For example, the great abbeys of Europe disappeared, and with them the influence of the monastic orders as the papacy's most effective instrument of government. The Papal States were gradually absorbed by secular states. In 1870, the Papacy gave up all claim to the Papal States…The French government passed anti-church laws in 1880. These laws expelled religious orders from France, banned religious education in the schools, and excluded the church from several other areas of French life. In Italy, hostility came from the people as well as the government. This hostility led to anti-papal—and anti-Christian—laws and demonstrations" "Roman Catholic Church," World Book Encyclopedia (Chicago, World Book) 1986.

beast ." (Revelation 13:3). **"He** [the second beast] **causes the earth and those who dwell therein to worship the first beast, whose deadly wound was healed"** (Revelation 13:12). **"He** [the second beast] **deceives them that dwell on the earth... saying to them...to make an image to the beast which had the wound by a sword, and lived"** (Revelation 13:14).

The political and military head of the Roman Catholic Church was severely damaged during the revolutionary movements of the 18th and 19th centuries. Significantly, this coincided with the high point of God's true church (the Philadelphia era, see chapter 3). However, the **"deadly wound was healed"**—the Catholic Church would regain its political and military power. This began even as the blows were still falling. "Even during those years when Napoleon was ill-treating Pius VII and keeping him prisoner, Catholicism in France was reviving and expanding day by day. Numerous religious congregations came to life again and expanded rapidly."[492] A major turning point took place in 1929 when Benito Mussolini, the dictator of Italy, signed a concordat which granted the pope full authority over the State of Vatican City. The Catholic Church was now legally an international political entity, a status it had lost in 1870 when the Papal Territories were absorbed by Italy and the Pope became a "prisoner of the Vatican." During the twentieth century the influence and reputation of the Papacy grew rapidly, helped by the Second Vatican Council (1962-1965). This influence was recognized when President Ronald Reagan appointed an ambassador to Vatican City in 1984.

One of the most stunning proofs that the deadly wound of the Papacy has been healed is shown by the collapse of communism through the influence of Pope John Paul II. In 1978 Cardinal Wojtyla was elected pope as John Paul II, the first non-Italian pope in 455 years, and at age 58, one of the youngest. Within a year of his election he made a dramatic visit to his homeland Poland. A student, describing its impact, said "We saw each other for the first time after decades of communism. We saw we were united. There were millions like us. We discovered community, solidarity and power." The trip was the beginning of the Solidarity Movement. John Paul now had a world stage on which to do battle and the Vatican became "a beehive of anti-Communist sedition."[493]

The Solidarity Movement was facing a military crackdown in Poland in June, 1982 when Pope John Paul II had a secret meeting with President Ronald Reagan at the Vatican. They were convinced that a free, non-communist Poland would be a dagger to the heart of the Soviet Empire; and if Poland became democratic, other East European states would follow. Tons of equipment were smuggled into Poland via channels established by priests and American agents. Money for the banned union came from CIA funds, secret accounts in the Vatican and Western trade unions.[494] "The informal secret alliance between the Holy See and the administration of President Ronald Reagan hastened the most profound political change of the age. Both CIA director Casey and Ronald Reagan believed that there was a potential third superpower in the world—the twenty-block-square Vatican city-state—and that its monarch, Pope John Paul II, had at his command a remarkable arsenal of unconventional weaponry that might

---

492 Georges Goyau, "France," *The Catholic Encylopedia*, http://www.newadvent.org/cathen/06166a.htm. (Accessed August 27, 2014).

493 Jonathan Kwitny, *Man of the Century: The Life and Times of Pope John Paul II* (Henry Holt &Co.) 1997.

494 Carl Bernstein, Time Magazine article *The Holy Alliance* February 24, 1992 http://content.time.com/time/magazine/article/0,9171,974931,00.html accessed August 16, 2014.

tip the balance in the cold war…the Pope would thereafter receive virtually every relevant scrap of information the CIA possessed, not only on Poland, but on other matters of importance to Wojtyla and the Holy See."[495] The result of this "Holy Alliance" was the fall of communism in Poland, and from there the other nations of the Soviet Empire fell like dominoes.

This example has been given a fair bit of attention because the healing of the deadly wound paves the way for the development of the final persecuting power, Babylon, which is described in chapters 16-19. Babylon will exercise universal authority, like the medieval Papacy, but will not be limited to the nations of Europe, or to a single organizational entity. **"And it was given to him to make war with the saints, and to overcome them. And power was given him over all tribes, and tongues, and nations. And all that dwell on the earth shall worship him, whose names are not written in the Book of Life of the Lamb slain from the foundation of the world"** (Revelation 13:7,8).

In this future manifestation the beast will have a powerful ally to promote and enforce its program, one who was clearly prophesied nearly two thousand years ago under the symbol of a beast from the earth with two horns like a lamb.

13:11,12 The Beast from the Earth

"And I beheld another beast coming up out of the earth; and he had two horns like a lamb, and he spoke like a dragon. And he exercises all the power of the first beast before him, and causes the earth and those who dwell therein to worship the first beast, whose deadly wound was healed" (Revelation 13:11,12). Here a new power comes into view which has not been mentioned in Daniel's prophecies. As it is coming up it looks quite innocent and even Christ-like, with its two lamb-like horns, but when it speaks it is obvious that the heart of Satan the dragon is in it.[496]

Unlike the first beast, which rose out of the sea ("peoples, multitudes, nations and tongues" Revelation 17:15), this beast rises out of the earth. In chapter 12 we saw that when the dragon was pursuing the woman (the true church) during the 1,260 years of papal domination, "the earth helped the woman, and the earth opened its mouth, and swallowed up the flood which the dragon cast out of his mouth" (Revelation 12:16). During the Middle Ages there was for the first time in history a sudden and dramatic increase in human population ("the serpent cast water out of his mouth like a flood after the woman" v. 15), but with the discovery of the western hemisphere, God's people could flee for safety ("the earth… swallowed up the flood"). The earth represented the sparsely populated American continents that were a refuge for the religiously persecuted.

Thus it appears that this new beast with lamb-like horns arises from the relatively unpopulated Western Hemisphere. It comes into power after the forty-two months of authority of the first beast and the receiving of the deadly wound, which occurred at the end of the 18th century. Obviously the United States of America is the country which arose in the western hemisphere and started to become a powerful nation after the 18th century, and in fact it came into its greatest power during the twentieth century when the healing of the deadly wound was taking place. The phrase **"he exercises all the authority of the first beast in his presence"** (Revelation 13:12 NKJV)

---

495 *Ibid*

496 Jesus said, "Brood of vipers! How can you, being evil, speak good things? For out of the abundance of the heart the mouth speaks" (Matthew 12:34).

shows that the two powers exist at the same time rather than one succeeding the other, as was the case with the animals/empires of Daniel 7.

13:11 A Lamb or a Dragon?

"He had two horns like a lamb and he spoke like a dragon" (Revelation 13:11). In both Daniel and Revelation horns represent power and authority, although not always in exactly the same form. In Daniel 7 the "dreadful" beast (the pagan Roman Empire) had ten horns, which represented barbarian tribes that took over the empire (vs.7,8,19,20). A "little horn" came up in their midst, which represented the oppressive Roman Catholic Church of the Middle Ages (vs. 8, 20-25). In Daniel 8 a ram had two horns, which represented "the kings of Media and Persia" (v. 20). The "large horn" on a shaggy goat represented "the first king" of Greece, Alexander the Great (v. 21). Four horns came up in its place, representing the divisions of the Greek Empire (v. 8), but "out of one of them" came "a little horn which grew exceedingly great," representing the progression from pagan to papal Roman authority (vs. 9-12). In Revelation 17 the scarlet beast has ten horns, which are identified as "ten kings who have received no kingdom as yet" (v. 12). In these examples horns represent empires, kingdoms, kings and oppressive churches. In other words, horns often represent the power centers of those political and religious entities that oppress God's people.

The **"beast coming up out of the earth,"** (the future oppressive United States of America) has **"two horns like a lamb,"** in other words, the horns appear to be innocent and harmless. As we saw above, horns can represent kings and political churches. The "king" of the United States is the democratically elected president, and the "national church" is a fractured multitude of mostly Protestant denominations that are constitutionally forbidden to wield political power

by the separation of church and state. These certainly seem as harmless as a lamb. However, this prophecy shows that these two horns (democratically elected political leadership and the independent, diverse "Church of America"), despite their harmless appearance, will become the power and authority of a system with a satanic heart that **"[speaks] like a dragon."**

In chapter 12, the story of the dragon, there was a description of how the dragon speaks—he is "the accuser of our brethren…who accused them before our God day and night" (Revelation 12:10). The beast with the lamb-like horns is a nation, and nations speak through their legislative or lawmaking bodies. Thus the prophecy predicts that at a legislative level the United States will bring accusations against God's true people. And it is not hard to guess the subject of these accusations since this beast is causing (forcing) **"the earth and those who dwell therein to worship the first beast, whose deadly wound was healed."** (Revelation 13:12). We have already seen that the agenda of the first (sea) beast is "to change times and law." In the following sections we will see that the beast from the earth, the United States, will try to force the world to obey the altered "times and law" that were established by the medieval papal church, and will accuse and persecute those Christians who refuse.

13:13,14 Fire from Heaven

"And he does great wonders, so that he makes fire come down from heaven on the earth in the sight of men, and deceives them that dwell on the earth by the means of those miracles which he had power to do in the sight of the beast; saying to them that dwell on the earth, to make an image to the beast, which had the wound by a sword, and lived" (Revelation 13:13, 14).

The beast from the earth has two horns that work together, its political and its religious system. Is the fire that comes down from heaven from the political or from the religious side, and is it literal or symbolic fire? From a political or military point of view the United States, with its military might, could make fire (such as conventional and nuclear bombs or laser weapons) **"come down from heaven."** However, the manifestation of military power serves to frighten people into subjection rather than deceive them, as this passage specifies.

Jesus made it clear that in the last days deception would be from false prophets coming in His name (Matthew 24:11). As we will see later, another name for the beast from the earth is "the false prophet" (see 16:13 *The Unholy Trinity*). We should also remember that the purpose of the deceptive signs is to get those **"that dwell on the earth, to make an image to the beast, which had the wound by a sword, and lived."** The image is a religious object of worship (the world will be forced to **"worship the image of the beast"**). The **"beast, which had the wound by a sword"** represents the apostate Roman Catholic Church. Everything in this passage points to deceptive religious activity by a church that claims to be Christian, which tells people that they must make **"an image to the beast"** and convinces them by making **"fire come down from heaven."**

Fire from heaven is reminiscent of what happened in the time of Elijah, as recorded in 1Kings 18. King Ahab, spurred on by his wicked wife Jezebel, had led the people of Israel to abandon the worship of God and to worship Baal. Elijah called the people to Mt. Carmel and challenged them, "How long will you falter between two opinions? If the Lord is God, follow Him; but if Baal follow him." But the people were so spiritually confused that they didn't know what to decide (1Kings 18:21). Elijah arranged a test: there would be two alters, two sacrifices, and the God who answered by fire would be their God.

The priests of Baal tried first, using all of their magic and rituals, but could not bring down fire.[497] Elijah offered a simple prayer "that the people may know that you are God" (v. 37), "then the fire of the Lord fell and consumed the burnt sacrifice and the wood and the stones and the dust, and it licked up the water that was in the trench. And when all the people saw it they fell on their faces; and they said, 'The Lord, He is God! The Lord, He is God!'" (vs. 38,39). Fire falling from heaven was a powerful miracle from God which convinced the people to worship Him.

In several other passages miraculous fire was a sign that confirmed God's acceptance or blessing.[498] Even today the "miracle of the holy fire" which appears every Easter at the Church of the Holy Sepulcher in Jerusalem[499] is considered proof of God's presence and blessing. But God through Moses made it clear that His people were not to be led astray by miracles that were accompanied by false teaching.[500]

In the last moments of history people will still be convinced by miracles, but God will not be the only one working them.[501] "The coming of the lawless one is according to the working of Satan, with all power, *signs and lying wonders, and with all unrighteous deception* among those who perish, because they did not receive the love of the truth, that they might be saved...but had pleasure in unrighteousness" (2Thessalonians 2:9-12).

---

497 Since Satan is able to bring fire down from heaven (as he did in Job 1:16) he obviously would have liked to have answered the priests of Baal, thus locking the nation of Israel more tightly into heathenism.

498 Leviticus 9:24, Judges 6:21, 2 Kings 1:12, 1Chronicles 21:26, 2 Chronicles 7:1.

499 For contrasting views on this miracle see www.holyfire.org and www.greatlie.com.

500 "If there arises among you a prophet or a dreamer of dreams, and he gives you a sign or a wonder, and the sign or the wonder comes to pass, of which he spoke to you saying, 'Let us go after other gods'—which you have not known—'and let us serve them,' you shall not listen to the words of that prophet or that dreamer of dreams" (Deuteronomy 13: 1-3).

501 Job 1:6-12, 16 shows that Satan also can make "the fire of God" fall from heaven.

Jesus warned repeatedly in Matthew 24, "Take heed that no one deceives you...*For false christs and false prophets will rise and show great signs and wonders to deceive*, if possible, even the elect" (Matthew 24:4, 24). In chapters 16 and 19 we will again encounter the beast from the earth, there known as "the false prophet." He is one member of the unholy trinity which is the source of "spirits of demons, performing signs" (Revelation 16:14), and he will "work signs...by which he [will] deceive those who received the mark of the beast and those who worshiped his image" (Revelation 19:20).

All of these passages use the word "signs" (Greek *simeion*) which, surprisingly, is the same word that is used to describe the miracles that Christians filled with the Holy Spirit will perform—"and these signs (*simeion*) will follow those who believe: In My name they will cast out demons, they will speak with new tongues...they will lay hands on the sick, and they will recover" (Mark 16:17,18).[502] The American "false prophet" will employ miraculous signs which will be almost impossible to distinguish from the signs and miracles from the Holy Spirit, making **"fire come down from heaven"** to **"deceive them that dwell on the earth by the means of those miracles which he had power to do in the sight of the beast"** (Revelation 13:14).

13:15 The Image of the Beast

What is the goal of the beast from the earth in this deception? It convinces **"them that dwell on the earth by the means of those miracles which he had power to do in the sight of the beast; saying to them that dwell on the earth, to make an image to the beast, which had the wound by a sword, and lived. And he had power to give life to the image of the beast, that the image of the beast should both speak, and cause that as many as would not worship the image of the beast should be killed"** (Revelation 13:14,15). An image is a likeness or resemblance, so the image of the beast, which will be set up by the beast from the earth (the United States of America), will resemble the characteristics of the beast from the sea (the medieval Roman Catholic Church).

First of all, the sea beast was a religious power, involved in worship. **"They worshiped the beast...all who dwell on the earth will worship him"** (Revelation 13:4,8). Likewise, the "image of the beast" is involved in worship—**"[it] causes the earth and those who dwell therein to worship the first beast."** (Revelation 13:12). Although the United States has had a wall of separation between church and state, this prophecy shows that the wall will be broken down, and the U.S. government, prodded by the church, will legislate and enforce religious behavior.

Secondly, the sea beast was an international political power—**"power was given him over all tribes, and tongues, and nations"** (Revelation 13:7). At the height of its power in the Middle Ages the Roman Church ruled the world through its European subjects. The beast from the earth with its image also operates in the international political sphere—**"He exercises all the power of the first beast"** (Revelation 13:12), and has control of commerce—**"no one could buy or sell, except he that had the mark, or the name of the beast, or the number of his name"** (Revelation 13:17). The United States could certainly set up an international image; since the fall of communism the U.S. has been the sole international military superpower, having authority and influence all over the world.

The sea beast used military might to impose its agenda on the world—**"all the world marveled after the beast...saying, 'Who is like**

---

502 See also Mark 16:20, John 4:48,54, 6;2,14,26, 12:18, Acts 2:43, 4:9,16,22, 5:12,15,16, 8:6,7,13, 1Corinthians 14:22, 2Corinthians 12:12, Hebrews 2:4, Revelation 16:14, 19:20.

to the beast? **Who is able to make war with him?**" (Revelation 13:4). The beast from the earth does not have its own agenda, but uses its superpower status and **"causes [forces] the earth and those who dwell therein to worship the first beast, whose deadly wound was healed"** (Revelation 13:12). In other words, the United States will be the end time military instrument of the Babylon/beast system, and having the most powerful military forces ever assembled, is in a unique position to impose the religious agenda of the beast on the rest of the world.

The sea beast was a blasphemous power—**"there was given to him a mouth speaking great things and blasphemies"** (Revelation 13:5). Blasphemy involves ascribing to humans the attributes and prerogatives that belong to God only,[503] mocking God's word and power,[504] and knowing God's law but publicly breaking it.[505] A prominent example is the blasphemous attempt to change God's law described in Daniel 7 (See 13: *The Beast's Agenda*). In making an image of the beast the United States will continue the blasphemous attempts to take God's prerogatives and will mock His word by legislating and enforcing changes in God's law (this point will be explained further under 13:16: *The Mark of the Beast*).

The most prominent characteristic of the sea beast is its persecution of the saints. **"it was given to him to make war with the saints, and to overcome them"** (Revelation 13:7). The war against the saints during the Middle Ages is the

dominant feature of the 1,260 year prophecies of Daniel 7 and Revelation 12—"the same horn was making war against the saints and prevailing against them…then the saints [were] given into his hand for a time and times and half a time" (Daniel 7:21,25).[506] Likewise, the image will be a persecuting power—**"the image of the beast should both speak, and cause that as many as would not worship the image of the beast should be killed"** (Revelation 13:15). This prophecy shows that in the last days the United States will be like the Roman Catholic Church of the Middle Ages, persecuting the true believers in Christ.

Revelation 17:1-6 shows that the sea beast is a church which controls a powerful political entity that persecutes God's people. The image of the beast will also be a union of church and state. Since it is set up by the second beast **"out of the earth,"** the image will be a persecuting union of church and state set up by the United States of America. It will demand conformity to the Roman Catholic religious agenda under threat of death (**"causes the earth and those who dwell in it to worship the first beast whose deadly wound was healed"** Revelation 13:12). Throughout its history the United States has not been officially involved in religious issues, but this prophecy shows that this will change and America will become a persecutor of God's remnant people. And in fact the seeds of this can already be seen.

Many American Christians today long to "take back our nation for God," to create a Christian society. The Book of Revelation teaches that they will get their wish! But what they do not realize is that a society with legislated morality based on a national religion was the essence of the medieval Catholic Church and is the model

---

503 The Pharisees charged Jesus with blasphemy because he called himself the Son of God (John 10:30-33, 8:58,59, Matthew 26:64,65) and claimed to have the power to forgive sins (Mark 2:5-7).

504 On the cross the Pharisees mocked Christ's claim that he would rebuild the temple (of His body) that they were tearing down in three days (Mark 15:29) and the irreverent thief mocked Him as being unable to save Himself (Luke 23:39). These insults were both termed blasphemy.

505 "You who make your boast in the law, do you dishonor God through breaking the law? For the name of God is blasphemed among the Gentiles because of you" (Romans 2:22,23).

506 See also Daniel 11:35, Revelation 12:13-17.

of future Babylon. The United States will create an **"image to the beast,"** in which Christian values and even worship will be imposed through government mandate. But the end result will be the mark of the beast, 666 and the death decree.

13:16,17 The Mark of the Beast

"And he causes all, both small and great, rich and poor, free and bond, to receive a mark on their right hand, or on their foreheads; and that no one could buy or sell, except he that had the mark, or the name of the beast, or the number of his name" (Revelation 13:16,17). For nearly 2,000 years there has been intense curiosity and imaginative speculation about the mark of the beast. Brands or tattoos have been suggested, and in recent years attention has focused on an imbedded microchip. While any of these could happen (and Satan certainly could arrange for a counterfeit to draw attention from the real issues), the scriptures give significant clues as to the true nature of the mark of the beast

A correct understanding is not simply a matter of satisfying idle curiosity. The most fearful warning in all of scripture is given against receiving the mark of the beast: "If any one worships the beast and his image, and receives his mark on his forehead, or on his hand, he also shall drink of the wine of the wrath of God, which is poured out without mixture into the cup of His indignation; and he shall be tormented with fire and brimstone in the presence of the holy angels, and in the presence of the Lamb" (Revelation 14:9,10).

One important characteristic is that it is **"on their right hand or on their foreheads."** The first century Christian readers of Revelation would have certainly remembered that Moses told the children of Israel, "Obey my commandments which I command you today…You shall lay up these words of mine in your heart and in your soul, *and bind them as a sign on your hand, and they shall be as frontlets between your eyes*"

(Deuteronomy 11:13, 18, 6:8). In these verses we see that it is God's "commandments" that were to be a "sign," bound to their hand or forehead. Although ultra-orthodox Jews have taken this commandment literally and made little boxes with a copy of the law inside and fastened them to their wrists and on their foreheads, the real issue is "in your heart and in your soul."

In the new covenant God promises, "I will put My laws in their mind and write them on their hearts" (Hebrews 8:10). From the heart proceed thoughts (symbolized by the forehead) and actions (symbolized by the hand). From this text in Deuteronomy we can assume that the beast will try to replace God's laws with *his* laws, and his antichrist laws will be reflected in the minds and hearts (forehead), or at least in the actions (hand) of those who submit to the beast.

The mention of the hand and forehead is also found in Exodus 13, and gives another clue as to the specific nature of the mark. Moses reviewed with the people their experience when they "went out of Egypt, out of the house of bondage" (v. 3), and he told them to keep the Feast of Unleavened Bread as a memorial of their deliverance. "Seven days you shall eat unleavened bread and *on the seventh day there shall be a feast to the Lord…And you shall tell your son in that day, saying, 'This is done [keeping the feast] because of what the Lord did for me when I came up from Egypt. It shall be as a sign to you on your hand and as a memorial between your eyes, that the Lord's law may be in your mouth…You shall therefore keep this ordinance in its season"* (vs. 8-10). Again the law of God is mentioned, and the symbolic meaning is obvious—the keeping of the religious memorial feast "in its season" is the "sign in your hand and…memorial between your eyes." This verse suggests that the mark of the beast could be a religious memorial celebration, supposedly a part of God's law but actually a false one, which honors Satan's kingdom.

Putting these two verses together with the fact that Satan always tries to counterfeit what God does, an obvious possibility would be a counterfeit of the Sabbath, which is a part of the law of God and a memorial of creation and redemption. A change of the Sabbath would be expected since the agenda of the beast, as presented in Daniel 7, is "to change *times and laws*" (Daniel 7:25). The Sabbath is the only part of God's Ten Commandment law that has to do with time. By changing God's law Satan tries to prove that he has greater authority than God who gave the law, and this is his ultimate goal—"the man of sin…opposes and exalts himself above all that is called God or that is worshiped, so that he sits as God in the temple of God, showing himself that he is God" (2 Thessalonians 2:3,4).

God's law is eternal and unchangeable, so the beast can only "think" to change it. But with the change of the Sabbath to Sunday, a change without scriptural support, he has managed to deceive the vast majority of the Christian world. This, of course, is not what it means to receive the mark of the beast. People who keep Sunday because of custom or because they have been taught that it is the "Lord's Day" have not had a clear teaching about the fourth commandment, and God does not consider people guilty of breaking laws that they do not know about.[507] At any rate, it is the image of the beast which **"causes all…to receive the mark of the beast,"** and the image of the beast has not yet been set up. However, when the Sabbath becomes an international issue and the false Sabbath is effectively exposed as unscriptural, those people who still choose to obey the beast rather than the Bible in order to escape punishment and sanctions (**"no one may buy or sell"**) will receive the mark of the beast.

The pressure to conform will not be from economic sanctions alone. **"He…[will] cause that as many as would not worship the image of the beast should be killed"** (Revelation 13:15). This death decree is the final manifestation of the "abomination of desolation" (see 10: *The Abomination of Desolation*), and according to Jesus, it is a signal for believers to "flee to the mountains" (Matthew 24:15,16).

Of Man's Devising

The Greek word used for **"mark"** is *haragma*, which is defined as a mark or stamp, made by engraving, etching, imprinting, branding; likeness, handiwork, the thing formed.[508] This word only appears eight times in the Bible, and seven of them are in the book of Revelation, referring to the "mark of the beast." The other occurrence is in Acts chapter 17.

Paul was in Athens and "his spirit was provoked within him when he saw that the city was given over to idols" (Acts 17:16). He preached to the philosophers who gathered in the market concerning the "unknown God" that they were "groping after" during "these times of ignorance." "He is not far from each one of us, for in Him we live and move and have our being…for we are also His offspring. Therefore, since we are the offspring of God, we ought not to think that the Divine Nature is like gold or silver or stone, *something shaped [haragma] by art and man's devising*" Acts 17:27-29. The *haragma* or mark in this verse is the creation of man, "something…[of] man's devising." The story of Jeroboam in 1 Kings shows that the altering of God's appointed memorial days is this kind of "something of man's devising," and is an abomination to God.

Jeroboam, rebelliously seeking to establish

---

507 "Sin is not imputed when there is no law" (Romans 5:13).

508 See any Greek Lexicon such as Thayer, Friberg, Liddel-Scott, etc. for the definition.

his own religious authority,[509] "*ordained a feast on the fifteenth day of the eighth month, like the feast that was in Judah,* and offered sacrifices on the altar…he installed the priests of *the high places which he had made.* So he made offerings on *the altar which he had made* at Bethel on the fifteenth day of the eighth month, *in the month which he had devised in his own heart.* And he ordained a feast for the children of Israel." (1Kings 12:26-33).

Just as the *haragma* that Paul saw in Athens was "something of man's devising," so Jeroboam's change of the feast was something "which he had devised in his own heart." All through the Old Testament the wicked kings of Israel are condemned because they "did not depart from the sins of Jeroboam, who had made Israel sin." (2Kings 10:31 *et al*). The sinful, natural man, seeking independent self-exaltation, always tries to replace the perfect work of God with his own human effort. Salvation by human effort is the basis of every false religion.

True Christianity, by contrast, is based on resting in God's completed work. This is symbolized by the Sabbath, and for this reason Satan wars against it and tries to replace it with something "of his own devising." The issue is not about worshiping on the wrong day. It is about an attitude of trusting in the act of creation that God has already accomplished for us, in contrast to trying to make ourselves righteous through our own efforts. The false Sabbath "of man's devising" symbolizes man's efforts to save himself by his own works.

The Roman Catholic Church in her catechisms proudly admits that she changed the Sabbath to Sunday, "devising" a new day of rest and worship. One of many examples which could be given is *The Catechism Simply Explained* which presents these questions and answers:

"What is the third commandment?"

"The third commandment is, 'Remember that thou keep holy the Sabbath day.'"

"What are we commanded by the third commandment?"

"By the third commandment we are commanded to keep Sunday holy."

"The Jews' Sabbath Day was the Saturday; we Christians keep Sunday holy. The church, by the power our Lord gave her, changed the observance of the Saturday to the Sunday."[510]

This same admission is found in the Catholic encyclopedia. "The Ten Commandments…are found twice recorded in the Pentateuch, in Exodus 20 and Deuteronomy 5, but *are given in an abridged form in the catechisms*…The church, after changing the day of rest from the Jewish Sabbath, or seventh day of the week, to the first, made the Third Commandment refer to Sunday as the day to be kept holy as the Lord's Day."[511]

Satan did not pick the Sabbath randomly

---

509 Solomon, through his marriages with pagan women, led the nation of Israel into idolatry. For this reason God, through the prophet Ahijah, told Jeroboam (an official in Solomon's service) that He would tear ten of the twelve tribes of Israel away from Solomon's son and give them to Jeroboam (1 Kings 11: 26-40). This happened when Solomon's son Rehoboam foolishly heeded the harsh council of his young advisers (1Kings 12:1-19). But Jeroboam understood that this was not to be a permanent arrangement (God had told him "You shall be king over Israel…but not forever" 1Kings 11:37,39). In rebellion against God, he sought to ensure that the ten tribes would not return to David's descendents because of contact with the temple worship in Jerusalem. "And Jeroboam said in his heart, 'Now the kingdom may return to the house of David; if these people go up to offer sacrifices in the house of the Lord at Jerusalem, then the heart of this people will turn back to their lord, Rehoboam king of Judah, and they will kill me.' Therefore the king made two calves of gold, and said to the people, 'It is too much for you to go up to Jerusalem. Here are your gods, O Israel, which brought you up from the land of Egypt'…Jeroboam ordained a feast on the fifteenth day of the eighth month, like the feast that was in Judah, and offered sacrifices on the altar…in the month which he had devised in his own heart." (1Kings 12:26-33).

510 H. Canon Cafferata, *The Catechism Simply Explained*, quoted in Uriah Smith, *Daniel and the Revelation* (Hagerstown, MD, Review and Herald), 1972 p. 611.

511 John Stapelton, "The Ten Commandments," *The Catholic Encyclopedia*, <http://www.newadvent.org/cathen/04153a.htm, Accessed August 22, 2014.

as the point of God's law for special attack. For one thing, it is the one commandment that tells us who God is. The Sabbath identifies "the Lord [who] made the heavens and the earth, the sea, and all that is in them, and rested the seventh day" (Exodus 20:11). It is the Creator God, and not just the God of any creation story, but the God revealed in Genesis, who ends His creation work with the Sabbath rest. All religions claim to worship "God," and some, like Islam, claim to worship the "God of Abraham." But by rejecting the Sabbath they have broken the connecting link to the Creator of the heavens and the earth.[512]

In the second giving of the law in Deuteronomy the Sabbath is presented as a memorial of redemption: "Observe the Sabbath day…remember you were a slave in the land of Egypt, and the Lord your God brought you out from there by a mighty hand" (Deuteronomy 5:15). By reminding us of God's mighty acts, the Sabbath points us to the God who is revealed in the Bible, not the gods that are portrayed in other "scriptures" or philosophical systems.

It is significant that the apostles "with one accord" quoted the Sabbath commandment (Exodus 20:11) to identify the Lord "who made heaven and earth and the sea and all that is in them" as they petitioned Him to give them boldness and power to face the threats of the Jewish religious authorities (Acts 4:23-31). The threats they faced prefigured the experience God's people will have during the persecutions of the time of trouble.

---

512 Most who do not accept the Sabbath have not rejected it; they have never considered it. But at some point in history their religion rejected the seventh-day Sabbath, and this has been an entry point for Satan's influence. At the end of time the Sabbath will become such an issue that all will either accept it (along with Jesus, the "Lord of the Sabbath" Mark 2:28) or will reject it and come under the authority of the beast.

Attack on the Everlasting Covenant

A fundamental reason for Satan's attack on the Sabbath is that it is the sign of the everlasting covenant. In 11:19 *The New Covenant* and in Appendix 9 we saw that the new covenant has four elements, and these are all under attack by Satan and his agent, the beast. The first element is God's promise to make His people a blessing to the world, a "holy priesthood." But in the beast system the priesthood of every believer is replaced by a professional priesthood and the believer becomes a passive spectator. The Sabbath in particular is the day God designated for His people to minister to the world, and Jesus demonstrated this by performing the majority of His miracles of healing on the Sabbath. By changing the Sabbath into an hour of spectator worship on Sunday rather than a day of worship and service on the seventh day which God blessed, the beast religion has nullified the primary provision in time that God created for His people to be the blessing to the world that His covenant intended them to be.

The second element of the new covenant is God's requirement, His law—"This is the covenant I will make…I will put my laws in their mind and write them on their hearts" (Hebrews 8:10). A direct attack by Satan on God's law would be counterproductive, since most of the commandments, such as honoring parents and refraining from stealing or murder, are obviously in the public interest. But by changing the fourth commandment from God's appointed seventh day to the first day of the week, the beast religion shows its contempt for all of God's law—"for whoever shall keep the whole law, and yet stumble in one point, he is guilty of all" (James 2:10). The Sabbath commandment in particular is like the tree in the midst of the Garden of Eden—the only reason someone would know to keep it is because "God said so." Thus it is a fitting sign of our willingness to obey, not simply the dictates of reason and social order, but the naked word of God. This point is vital at the end of time when the international "image of the beast" will be set up and will command the world to break God's law under threat of death.

The third element of the covenant is the provision for the salvation of those who have broken the commandments—the sacrifice of Jesus. The Sabbath is the symbol of salvation that is found in the heart of the law of God. "Observe the Sabbath day…remember that *you were a slave* in the land of Egypt, and *the Lord your God brought you out* from there by a mighty hand and by an outstretched arm; *therefore the Lord your God commanded you to keep the Sabbath day*" (Deuteronomy 5:12-15). Slavery in Egypt is a symbol of slavery to sin. Deliverance from slavery so they could rest from making bricks epitomized the salvation of the children of Israel, and likewise the Sabbath rest is a memorial that we have been rescued from the slavery of sin.

God not only ransoms us from slavery but He makes us a new creation, and this is also symbolized by the Sabbath. "Remember the Sabbath day…for in six days the Lord made the heavens and the earth, the sea and all that is in them, and rested the seventh day. Therefore the Lord blessed the Sabbath day and hallowed it" (Exodus 20:8-11). God deserves more praise and honor than we can ever express for His original creation. But the Sabbath also symbolizes the new creation that we become as a result of Jesus' sacrifice on our behalf. "[Jesus] died for them and rose again…Therefore, if anyone is in Christ, *he is a new creation*; old things have passed away, behold all things have become new" (2Corinthians 5:15-17).

The Sabbath rest is symbolic of the fact that God accomplished our salvation, not with the help or merit of our good works or obedience,

but by His grace alone. "For He has spoken of the seventh day in this way: 'And God rested on the seventh day from all His works'…There remains therefore a rest [*sabbatismos*, the keeping of the Sabbath] for the people of God. For he who has entered His rest has himself also ceased from his works as God did from His" (Hebrews 4:4-10).[513] The Sabbath is the symbol that God has done everything necessary for our salvation, and we can rest in His finished work.

The forth element of the eternal covenant is the sign, and with the Sabbath's central role and symbolism in every aspect of the new covenant, it is no wonder that it is the sign of the new covenant. Nor is it any surprise that Satan, the master counterfeiter, would hijack the Sabbath, "think to change" it to "a day of his own choosing," and make the false sabbath the mark of his own beast kingdom.

13:18 The Name and Number of the Beast

"Here is wisdom. Let him that has understanding count the number of the beast, for it is the number of a man; and his number is 666" (Revelation 13:18). The mark of the beast, the number of the beast and the name of the beast are all closely related. The mark of the beast is called **"the mark or name of the beast"** and "the mark of his *name*" (Revelation 13:17, 14:11). The number of the beast is also called **"the number of his name"** (Revelation 13:17). Those "who keep the commandments of God and the faith of

---

513 The book of Hebrews was written to Jewish Christians. Many of the central aspects of their traditional religion ended with with the life, death and resurrection of Christ. The priesthood, Levites, sacrifices, festivals, circumcision and the temple were obsolete because they were shadows of the life and sacrifice that Jesus offered. But the fourth chapter of Hebrews tells us that the rest of trusting in God's finished work still remains for each person to enter by faith. For this reason the keeping of the Sabbath (*Sabbatismos*) is still relevant, pointing us to the necessity of entering into God's rest.

Jesus" will "have the victory over the beast, over his image and over his mark, and over the number of his name" (Revelation 14:12, 15:2).

The beast from the sea has been shown to be the Roman Catholic Church of the Middle Ages. However, as we will see in chapters 16 and 17, the final manifestation of the beast will be both a religio-political entity and a person, the final antichrist, and it is his name that is linked to the mark and the number of the beast. "The beast that you saw was, and is not, and will ascend out of the bottomless pit and go to perdition…the beast… is himself also the eighth [of a series of kings]" (Revelation 17:8,11). The last-days appearance of the antichrist beast will be explained in detail in 17:6-8, but he is mentioned in a number of passages in Revelation. He is a part of the unholy trinity in chapter 16. In chapter 11 "the beast that ascends out of the bottomless pit will make war against them [the two witnesses], overcome them, and kill them" (Revelation 11:7).

The first mention of this beast in chapter 9 reveals his name. "And they had as king over them the angel of the bottomless pit, whose name in Hebrew is Abaddon, but in Greek he has the name Apollyon" (Revelation 9:11). This is Satan, the fallen angel who was cast out of heaven, who will appear on earth at the end of time as "the beast." His name in this role is Abaddon in Hebrew and Apollyon in Greek. Both of these names mean "destroyer."[514] There are several names for Satan that are used in the Bible, such as the accuser, the serpent, the devil, father of lies and the dragon, but as the final antichrist his name is "Destroyer." As such he is the exact opposite of the true God who is the "Creator." This is the link between the name, mark and number of the beast. God is the Creator, and He is identified by the Sabbath—"In six days the Lord made the heavens and the earth, the sea and all that is in them, and rested the seventh day" (Exodus 20: 11). The beast, on the other hand, can never claim to be the creator, and in fact he is the destroyer. His mark and number have to do with the anti-sabbath.

The close relationship between the mark, the name and the number of the beast shows that the meaning of **"the number of the beast"** must be closely related to the meaning of **"the mark or the name of the beast."** When we are commanded to **"count the number of the beast"** we must keep in mind the mark, which was shown to be the false sabbath of the papal system, and the name, Destroyer, which shows hostility towards the Creator.

There have been numerous attempts to find numbers associated with the names of particular people or institutions that add up to 666. For example, the application of the numerical values of the letters of various names in Greek, Latin or Hebrew (Nero, Napoleon, various popes or papal titles such as *VICARIUS FILII DEI* and many others)[515] can be made to add up to 666. More recently interest has focused on the universal bar code that is electronically scanned for purchases, with the idea being that this could be used to determine if people could **"buy or sell."** These suggestions are based on speculation rather than on a study of God's word. Whatever the number of the beast is, it would have to be comprehensible to the Christians of the first century to whom Revelation was originally written, as they were admonished to **"count [calculate, determine] the**

---

514 The Hebrew word Abaddon is found in Job 26:6, 28:22, Psalms 88:11 and Proverbs 15;11, 27:20. It is translated destruction and is associated with death and the grave. The Greek name Apollyon is only found in this passage but the root verb is used many times, for example Matthew 2:13, 10:28, 12:14, 22:7.

515 The context of the mark and number of the beast is the end of time, which rules out specific individuals from the past. Moreover, true believers will "have the victory over the beast, over his image and over his mark, and over the number of his name" (Revelation 15:2). This indicates that the number (along with the mark) will be some kind of a trial or temptation that must be overcome, not a title.

number."[516]

There may be confusion concerning the phrase **"for it is the number of a man."** Several English versions insert the article "a" ("the number of *a* man"), which is not in the original Greek. This makes it seem as if it refers to a particular man. However, Greek often uses the singular "man" to refer to mankind[517] (the NIV translates **"for it is man's number"**). Man was created to be a dependent unity of the human and the divine, but with sin man declares his rebellious independence, rejecting the submission, dependence and unity with God he was designed for; 666 symbolizes man as he became after sin.

Going back to the creation story in Genesis 1, man was created on the sixth day, and although he was declared "very good," it was not until the seventh day that creation was complete. Adam and Eve spent their first full day, the seventh day, resting with their Creator, having done nothing themselves to add to the creative process; they did not even see the creation taking place. The rest they experienced still remains: "There remains therefore a rest[518] for the people of God" (Hebrews 4:9). This is the rest of faith, believing that God has completed the work of creation ("Remember the Sabbath day...for in six days the Lord made the heavens and the earth")[519] and that He has completed the work of redemption ("You were a slave in the land of Egypt, and the Lord your God brought you out from there by a mighty hand")[520] The Sabbath symbolizes our faith and total dependence on God to do what we cannot do—to create and to redeem. But sinful man wants to remain in the sixth day, not entering into the seventh-day experience of acknowledging his Creator and his need for a Redeemer. In order to be whole he must enter into the Sabbath rest on the seventh day that God blessed. By refusing man says "NO!" to the Father, Son and Holy Spirit; perhaps this is why the triple repetition of 6 is the number of the beast.

"The Sabbath was made for man" (Mark 2:27). This means that without the seventh-day Sabbath, man is lacking something that was designed for him. That something is the personal Father-child relationship between man and his Creator which the Sabbath is designed to symbolize and safeguard. "If you keep your feet from breaking the Sabbath and from doing as you please on My holy day, if you call the Sabbath a delight and the Lord's holy day honorable, and if you honor it by not going your own way and not doing as you please or speaking idle words, then you will find your joy in the Lord, and I will cause you to ride on the heights of the land and to feast on the inheritance of your father Jacob" (Isaiah 58:13,14 NIV). But the unconverted man, rather than finding his "joy in the Lord," wants to go his "own way," to do "as [he] pleases." This includes "breaking the Sabbath...My holy day."

When man rejects the Sabbath he asserts his independence, siding with Satan who not only declared himself independent but actually sought to take God's place ("I will be like the Most High" Isaiah 14:14). The number 666 gives

---

516 The Greek word for calculate, *psifizi*, does not have the primary meaning of performing mathematical calculations, but most commonly in other Greek literature refers to making a decision by voting.

517 Examples of this usage include John 2:25, 5:34, Hebrews 2:6, 1Peter 1:24.

518 The Greek word for rest is *Sabbatismos*, which means the keeping of the Sabbath day of rest.

519 Exodus 20:8-11.

---

520 Deuteronomy 5:12-15. The Sabbath command is the only one which has a significant change in the second recitation of the Ten Commandments. The change is the reason given for the Sabbath—in Exodus 20 the Sabbath symbolizes God's creation, in Deuteronomy 5 it symbolizes his redemption. This shows the broadness of the meaning of the Sabbath and its appropriateness as an eternal demonstration of faith.

triple emphasis to what it is not—it is not seven,[521] God's number of completeness. It symbolizes man as he is without his Creator and Redeemer—incomplete and therefore evil, a hopeless sinner who lives as an enemy of God and His people.[522] As such it is **"man's number,"** and represents the religion of the beast that wars against God and His people.

666, The Number of Disobedience

The only other appearance of the number 666 in the Bible confirms it as the number of rebellious disobedience. King Solomon was considered one of the greatest kings of Israel, but actually his disobedience to God's commandments laid the foundation for Israel's ruin. In Deuteronomy 17 God predicted that the people would say, "I will set a king over me like all the nations that are around me" (v. 14). This was not God's will, but recognizing that this would happen, he gave just three commandments for the king, all of which Solomon broke. "He shall not multiply horses for himself, nor cause the people to return to Egypt to multiply horses…neither shall he multiply wives for himself, lest his heart turn away; nor shall he greatly multiply silver and gold for himself" (vs. 16, 17). Ignoring these commandments, "Solomon gathered one thousand four hundred chariots and twelve thousand horsemen…horses imported from Egypt" (1Kings10:26,28). "King Solomon loved many foreign women…from the nations of whom the Lord had said, 'You shall not intermarry with them…He had seven hundred

wives…For it was so, when Solomon was old, that his wives turned his heart after other gods" (1Kings 11:1-4).

But perhaps even more than his infatuation with horses and women was his love of gold. King Solomon made an alliance with Hiram, the idolatrous king of Tyre.[523] Solomon built a fleet of ships, and Hiram supplied the seamen to help in Solomon's project of accumulating wealth.[524] "The weight of gold that came to Solomon yearly was *six hundred and sixty six* talents[525] of gold" (1Kings 10:14). No doubt there was some yearly variation, but the Bible writer used the specific number 666 as a measure of Solomon's vast yearly accumulation of gold. However, unlike the gold which his father David had gathered to prepare for the building of the temple of the Lord, Solomon used his gold to build up his own defense and glory—to make shields, a fabulous throne, to make drinking vessels, to buy horses and chariots.[526] "So, King Solomon surpassed all the kings of the earth in riches and wisdom. Now all the earth sought the presence of Solomon" (1Kings 10:23,24). The 666 talents of gold Solomon accumulated every year symbolizes and epitomizes his pride and self-exaltation, and most of all his disobedience to the explicit commandments God had specifically given for the kings of Israel to follow.

Thus **"The number of the beast,"** 666, is a symbol of willful disobedience, a declaration that "I'm going to do things my way, regardless of what God says." It is **"the number of man,"** man's "declaration of independence," which is manifested by his rejection of the seventh-day Sabbath. It represents man's attempt to establish his own

---

521 The number seven is the most frequent number in the book of Revelation, used 51 times. This compares with four, (19 times), twelve (14 times), ten (11 times) three (9 times), twenty-four (7 times) and six (2 times).

522 "Once you were alienated from God and were enemies in your minds because of your evil behavior" (Colossians 1:21). See also Romans 5:10, Matthew 10:36.

---

523 It is interesting to note that the real king of Tyre is Satan himself (Ezekiel 28:13-19).

524 1Kings 9:11, 26-28.

525 666 talents is about 23 metric tons!

526 1Kings 10:16-29.

honor and glory, to do what he wants, even if it means breaking the clear commandments of God. This symbol of rebellious independence is the epitome of Satan's plans, purposes and kingdom, and goes hand in hand with the mark of the beast. **"The mark of the beast"** is the acceptance and honoring of Sunday, the false sabbath. **"The number of the beast,"** 666, is the rejection of the seventh day, the true Sabbath. One is the flip side of the other, and both symbolize submission to the beast rather than to God. With economic sanctions and finally with the threat of death, the worship of the image of the beast will be enforced. This will be the climax of Satan's efforts to impose his worship, and it is the climax of the first half of the book of Revelation.

The climax of the second half is found in chapter 14, which presents "the Lamb…and with Him one hundred and forty four thousand" who, refusing to bow to the threats and pressure of the beast, "keep the commandments of God and the faith of Jesus" (Revelation 14:1,12).

"He who sat on the cloud thrust in His sickle on the earth, and the earth was reaped" Rev. 14:16
Woodcut by Lukas Cranach 1522

Chapter 14

Revelation 14:1-20

14:1 And I looked, and, behold, a Lamb standing on mount Zion, and with him 144,000, having His Father's name written in their foreheads.

14:2 And I heard a voice from heaven, as the voice of many waters, and as the voice of great thunder. And I heard the voice of harpers harping with their harps;

14:3 And they sang as it were a new song before the throne, and before the four living creatures, and the elders: and no one could learn that song but the 144,000, who were redeemed from the earth.

14:4 These are they which were not defiled with women; for they are virgins. These are they which follow the Lamb wherever he goes. These were redeemed from among men, being the first fruits to God and to the Lamb.

14:5 And in their mouth was found no guile; for they are without fault before the throne of God.

14:6 And I saw another angel flying in the midst of heaven, having the everlasting gospel to preach to those that dwell on the earth, and to every nation, and tribe, and tongue, and people,

14:7 Saying with a loud voice, "Fear God, and give glory to Him; for the hour of His judgment has come; and worship Him that made heaven, and earth, and the sea, and the fountains of waters."

14:8 And there followed another angel, saying, "Babylon is fallen, is fallen, that great city, because she made all nations drink of the wine of the wrath of her fornication."

14:9 And the third angel followed them, saying with a loud voice, "If any one worships the beast and his image, and receives his mark on his forehead, or on his hand,

14:10 He also shall drink of the wine of the wrath of God, which is poured out without mixture into the cup of His indignation; and he shall be tormented with fire and brimstone in the presence of the holy angels, and in the presence of the Lamb.

14:11 And the smoke of their torment ascends up forever and ever; and they have no rest day or night, who worship the beast and his image, and whoever receives the mark of his name.

14:12 Here is the patience of the saints; here are those that keep the commandments of God, and the faith of Jesus."

14:13 And I heard a voice from heaven saying to me, "Write, blessed are the dead who die in the Lord from now on. Yes, said the Spirit, that they may rest from their labors; and their works do follow them."

14:14 And I looked, and behold a white cloud, and on the cloud sat One like the Son of Man, having on His head a golden crown, and in His hand a sharp sickle.

14:15 And another angel came out of the temple, crying with a loud voice to Him that sat on the cloud, "Thrust in your sickle, and reap; for the time has come for You to reap; for the harvest of the earth is ripe."

14:16 And He that sat on the cloud thrust in his sickle on the earth; and the earth was reaped.

14:17 And another angel came out of the temple which is in heaven, he also having a sharp sickle.

14:18 And another angel came out from the altar, who had power over fire; and cried with a loud cry to him that had the sharp sickle, saying, "Thrust in your sharp sickle, and gather the clusters of the vine of the earth; for her grapes are fully ripe."

14:19 And the angel thrust in his sickle into the earth, and gathered the vine of the earth, and cast it into the great wine press of the wrath of God.

14:20 And the wine press was trodden outside the city, and blood came out of the wine press, up to the horses' bridles, for 1,600 stadia.

14:1 Climax: the Lamb with the 144,000

The remarkable chiastic organization shows that the Book of Revelation has two climaxes, one for the first half of the book and the other for the second half (see 1:*Chiastic Literary Structure*). The first climax was reached at the end of chapter 13 with the image, mark and number of the beast. This shows that the first half of the book has to do with Satan's efforts to defeat God's kingdom. The fruits of these efforts can be seen in the progressive corruption of the church as outlined in the messages to the seven churches, Satan's challenge to the opening of the Book of Life in chapter 5, the destructive satanic plagues of the seven trumpets, the murder of the two witnesses in chapter 11, the pursuit of the "woman" and the "remnant" in chapter 12, and the fierce attacks of the beast from the sea and the beast from the earth in chapter 13. At the climax of the first half of the book we see the full development of the character of Satan, who is represented by a miracle-working, deceptive and coercive politico-religious system which demands and enforces compliance with "religious" requirements, using economic pressure and finally the threat of death.

The corresponding climax of the second half of the book is found in chapter 14, which begins by presenting **"a Lamb standing on mount Zion, and with him 144,000, having His Father's name written in their foreheads"** (Revelation 14:1). God Himself is the central figure, and although God could be depicted in innumerable ways, He presents Himself at the peak of the great controversy as Jesus, the Lamb of God. In striking contrast to the deceptive, oppressive character of Satan, God presents Himself as the self-sacrificing Savior who gave Himself for sinful humanity.

Just as the character and purpose of Satan is demonstrated by his followers in the beast system, so the Lamb is portrayed along with His representatives—the **"144,000, having His Father's name written in their foreheads."** This group was first introduced in chapter 7, where they were sealed in their foreheads out of "all the tribes of the children of Israel" (7:4). In chapter 11 the 144,000 appear again as the two witnesses, giving a powerful testimony to God's people who are in Babylon (see chapter 11: 3-6 *Who Are the Two Witnesses?*). They appear again in 15:2-4 on the sea of glass,[527] rejoicing in their victory over the beast even as the seven last plagues are about to be poured out. They appear one last time in chapter 18, symbolized by "an angel come down from heaven" who cries "mightily with a strong voice" to God's people who are in Babylon, "come out of her my people" (18:1-4)[528].

With so many important references it should not be surprising to find the 144,000 on center stage at the climax of the book. But it is important to remember that people are not the heroes of Revelation—**"a Lamb standing on Mount Zion"** and **"His Father"** are the central focus. The 144,000 were hopeless sinners like everyone else, and only God's grace led them to repentance, gave them victory over sin and enabled them to persevere in the face of the overwhelming pressure of the time of trouble.[529] Through His grace they reveal Jesus as He truly is, exposing all the lies and misconceptions Satan has foisted on the world.

The Father's Name on Their Foreheads

"**And I looked, and, behold, a Lamb standing on mount Zion, and with him 144,000, having His Father's name written in their foreheads**" (Revelation 14:1). Having the Father's name written in our foreheads is much more than having our names written in the books of a church. First of all, God's name is inseparable from His character;[530] to have the Father's name written in their forehead means that the 144,000 reflect His character. God's name also means His presence; from the Old Testament temple worship we learn that wherever God's name is, His presence is there.[531] The earthly temples are long gone, but now God's people are the temple of God: "Do you not know that you are the temple of God, and that the Spirit of God dwells in you?" "Your body is the temple of the Holy Spirit who is in you, whom you have from God" (1Corinthians 3:16, 6:19). The Father's name written in the foreheads of the 144,000 means that He, through the Holy Spirit, is living in them and shining out of them.

God's name in the forehead has a purpose: to reveal Him to those who do not know Him.

---

527 The description of the 144,000 in chapter 14 and of the victors in chapter 15 both mention harps. The 144,000 are standing "before the throne." The sea of glass, where the victors are standing, is also before the throne (Revelation 4:6 7:9, 14:3). The 144,000 give the third angel's message to overcome "the beast and his image, and...his mark" Revelation 14:9. Those on the sea of glass have had the victory "over the beast, over his image and over his mark" (Revelation 15:2). The victors include both the messengers (the 144,000) and those who responded to it (the great multitude).

528 The message of this mighty angel is the same (come out of Babylon) as that of the 144,000 (Revelation 14:8).

529 See Romans 2:4, 1Corinthians 15:57, Revelation 14:12.

530 Moses heard God proclaim His own name. "The Lord...proclaimed the name of the Lord: 'The Lord God, merciful and gracious, longsuffering and abounding in goodness and truth, keeping mercy for thousands, forgiving iniquity and transgression and sin, by no means clearing the guilty" (Exodus 34:6,7). His name is synonymous with His glory, holiness, strength, even His "jealous" desire for an exclusive love relationship with His bride. See Deuteronomy 32:3,4, Isaiah 59:19, 57:15, Psalms 54:1, Exodus 34:14.

531 King Jehosaphat said to the children of Israel, "[We] have built you a sanctuary in it *for your name...*We will stand before this temple and *in Your presence (for Your name is in this temple)...* (2Chronicles20:7-9). God told Moses, "You shall seek the place where the Lord your God chooses, out of all your tribes, *to put His name for His dwelling place,* and there you shall go" (Deuteronomy 12:5,11, 14:23, 16:2). Solomon declared, "I have built a temple *for the name of the Lord God of Israel*" and God replied, "I have consecrated this house which you have built to put My name there forever, and *My eyes and My heart will be there perpetually*" (1Kings 8:18-20, 9:3. See also 1Kings 11:36, Jeremiah 3:17).

By redeeming the 144,000 as **"firstfruits"** God declares Himself to the world. This is why His name is **"in their foreheads,"** the most visible part of of the body. God's people define His name to those around them: "You are great, O Lord God. For there is none like You…and who is like Your people, like Israel, the one nation on the earth whom God went to redeem for Himself as a people, *to make for Himself a name*…For you have made Your people Israel Your very own people forever…*So let Your name be magnified forever*" (2Samuel 7:22-26).

In Ezekiel 36 God promised a new heart and a new spirit to those who had previously profaned His name, so that through their new character His name would be glorified. "And I will *sanctify My great name*, which has been profaned among the nations, which you have profaned in their midst; and the nations shall know that I am the Lord' says the Lord God, *'when I am hallowed in you* before their eyes…I will cleanse you from all your filthiness, and from all your idols. I will give you a new heart and put a new spirit within you; I will take the heart of stone out of your flesh and give you a heart of flesh. I will put My spirit within you and cause you to walk in My statutes, and you will keep My judgments and do them…*Then the nations which are left all around you shall know* that I, the Lord, have rebuilt the ruined places and planted what was desolate" (Ezekiel 36:21-36). In other words, God, by making His people pure and holy, "makes for himself a name" which is "magnified" and "sanctified" in the eyes of "the nations" all around. This is what He does in and through the 144,000 at the end of time, symbolized by **"having His Father's name written in their foreheads."**

14:2-5 Representatives of the Lamb

To summarize the above, the 144,000 have the character of God, they are filled with His presence, and their purpose is to magnify and sanctify God's holy name. This is the culmination of God's plan to perfect for Himself a people who will be His witnesses during the **"hour of His judgment"**—"Love has been perfected among us in this: that we may have boldness in the day of judgment; because as He is, so are we in this world" (1John 4:17).

"And I heard a voice from heaven, as the voice of many waters, and as the voice of great thunder. And I heard the voice of harpers harping with their harps; and they sang as it were a new song before the throne, and before the four living creatures, and the elders: and no one could learn that song but the 144,000, who were redeemed from the earth. These are they which were not defiled with women; for they are virgins. These are they which follow the Lamb wherever he goes. These were redeemed from among men, being the firstfruits to God and to the Lamb. And in their mouth was found no guile; for they are without fault before the throne of God. (Revelation 14:2-5).

Although overall the 144,000 are **"without fault,"** some particular traits are emphasized. First of all, they **"were not defiled with women, for they are virgins."** In chapter 12 we saw that women in prophecy represent the church, either pure as in Revelation 12:1 (the woman clothed with the sun, moon and stars), or corrupt as in chapter 17 (the great harlot). To be **"defiled with women"** means uniting at a heart level with a corrupt church—the harlot or her daughters (Revelation 17:5). These churches are a part of "Babylon," and although a great multitude will be called out of Babylon, the 144,000 who will do the calling have not been stained by the corrupting influence of her idolatry.

They also **"follow the Lamb wherever He goes."** These are people who are so in harmony with the Holy Spirit that they hear His voice telling them where to go, what to do and what to say. God is always at work all around us, seeking to open people's hearts. When someone responds to the Holy Spirit's prompting, God needs one of His human representatives to help them progress from having an impression in their heart to being a disciple of Jesus. Abraham, Moses and Elijah are just three of many Biblical examples of people who had such a well-developed relationship with God that they understood His directions and were willing to respond.[532] The 144,000 will have this kind of relationship with God, and they will need it in order to deliver the powerful final messages during the treacherous conditions created by the image to the beast.

They are **"redeemed from among men, being the firstfruits to God and to the Lamb."** The firstfruits were a sample of the first and best produce of the land, a promise of a rich harvest to come.[533] Jesus, through His death and resurrection, became the "firstfruits of those who have fallen asleep" (1Corinthians 15:20-23), a guarantee that there will be a great harvest of resurrected saints. The 144,000 are the firstfruits of those who will live until Jesus comes, a guarantee of an abundant harvest (the great multitude) of other men, women and children who will also have the righteous character of Christ.

Twice in this passage the 144,000 are said to be **"before the throne"** (vs.3, 5) and at first glance it would appear that the vision has moved forward to the time after the Second Coming of Christ when God's people will be in heaven. However,

in Revelation 7:15 they were also pictured as being "before the throne," and there we saw that they will have the awesome experience of being physically on earth in the midst of the plagues, but spiritually in heaven before the throne (See 7: *In Heaven While On Earth*). This passage (14:1-5) is sandwiched between the final attack of the beast (the mark, number and name) and the final message of God (the three angels' messages), and thus has the same context—God's representatives are still on earth just before His Second Coming. In this sense they are like Jesus, who said, "*Now I am no longer in the world*" (John 17:11), even though He still had three days of suffering, crucifixion and the grave ahead of Him. He told Nicodemus, "No one has ascended to heaven but He who came down from heaven, that is, the son of Man *who is in heaven*" (John 3:13). Even though He had come down from heaven, He was still spiritually in heaven with His Father.

Stephen had this experience as he was about to be stoned—"He, being full of the Holy Spirit, gazed into heaven and saw the glory of God, and Jesus standing at the right hand of God, and said 'Look! I see the heavens opened and the Son of Man standing at the right hand of God!" (Acts 7:55,56). Paul said, "God raised us up with Christ and *seated us with him in the heavenly realms* in Christ Jesus" (Ephesians 2:6), using the past tense which shows that spiritually and by faith we are already sitting with Christ on His throne. He invites us to "come boldly to the throne of grace" (Hebrews 4:16), even though His throne is in heaven and we are on earth.

These are faith experiences which we can taste now, but the unique experiences God's people will have during the time of trouble will take them to a new level. On the one hand, the 144,000 will be facing the threats that go along with the image, mark, and number of the beast, and on the other hand, they will be receiving the outpouring of the Holy Spirit in latter-rain power.

---

532 For example, Genesis 12:1-4, Exodus 3,4, 1Kings 17,18.

533 Exodus 23:17, 34:23, Deuteronomy 16:16, Numbers 18:3,4, Deuteronomy 26:1-10.

In this context the heavenly realm will become such a reality that they will already be **"before the throne."** This experience will inspire the **"new song"** that they will sing. The reason that **"no one could learn that song except the hundred and forty-four thousand"** is because they will have an experience unique in human history, as they proclaim the three angels' messages to the world during the time of trouble.

14:6 The First Angel

"And I saw another angel flying in the midst of heaven, having the everlasting gospel to preach to those that dwell on the earth, and to every nation, and tribe, and tongue, and people" (Revelation 14:6). This verse introduces the first of three of the most powerful messages ever given to humanity. The fact that the messages are portrayed as being given by angels **"flying in the midst of heaven"** does not mean that angels will fly around in the sky, shouting to the people on earth. The Greek word for angel simply means one sent to bring a message, and elsewhere in Revelation angels symbolize human messengers.[534] The three angels symbolize the people who will deliver these last-hour messages. The messages are given immediately after the description of the 144,000, which suggests that they are the ones who will proclaim the messages. The fact that they are given **"in the midst of heaven"**[535] indicates that they will be so widespread and conspicuous that they will be impossible to ignore. The universality of the messages is underscored by the fact that they are directed **"to every nation, tribe, tongue and people."**

The foundation of the three messages is **"the everlasting gospel."** The Greek word for gospel simply means good news, and there are many kinds of good news in the Bible. In the New Testament the word "gospel" refers to specific good news, best summarized by Paul in 1Corinthians 15. *"I declare to you the gospel...in which you stand, by which also you are saved... that Christ died for our sins according to the Scriptures"* (1Corinthians 15:1-3). The fact that "Christ died for our sins" is absolutely essential for our salvation because "all have sinned" and "the wages of sin is death" (Romans 3:23, 6:23). We were "dead in trespasses and sin" "having no hope and without God in the world," but God "made us alive together with Christ...In Him we have redemption through His blood, the forgiveness of sins" (Ephesians 2:1, 12,5, 1:7). Jesus "loved us and washed us from our sins in His own blood" (Revelation 1:5), taking away the enmity that separated us from Him.

Moreover, *"He was buried, and...rose again the third day." "Now Christ is risen from the dead and has become the firstfruits of those who have fallen asleep* [died]*"* (1Corinthians 15:4,20). Our hope goes beyond this life. The resurrection of Jesus ensures life beyond the grave for those who accept His sacrifice on their behalf, and a place in His glorious kingdom which he has "prepared for those who love Him" (1Corinthians 2:9).

But the good news did not end with the resurrection of Christ. Jesus returned to heaven where *"He must reign till He has put all enemies under His feet"* (1Corinthians 15:25). This refers to His work of mediation in the heavenly sanctuary. "We do have such a high priest [Christ]... who serves in the sanctuary, the true tabernacle set up by the Lord, not by man." "He is also able to save to the uttermost those who come to God through Him, since He always lives to make intercession for them" (Hebrews 8:1,2, 7:25).

"Then comes the end, when He delivers the

---

534 In chapters 2 and 3 the messages to the 7 churches were sent "to the angel of the church of (Ephesus, Smyrna, etc.)." Obviously the messages were to the leaders of the churches, not to heavenly angels. See also Revelation 21:7.

535 There are three heavens: the atmosphere, the heaven of the stars and the heaven where the angels dwell. According to Revelation 19:17 the "midst of heaven" is the atmosphere where the birds fly.

kingdom to God the Father, when He puts an end to all rule and all authority and power" (1 Corinthians 15:24). Jesus is coming again! "I will not leave you orphans. I will come to you" (John 14:18). "So Christ, having been offered once to bear the sins of many, will appear a second time…to save those who are eagerly waiting for him" (Hebrews 9:28 NRS). *"The last enemy that will be destroyed is death" (1 Corinthians 15:26).* Perhaps the best news of all is that "there shall be no more death, neither sorrow, nor crying, neither shall there be any more pain; for the former things have passed away" (Revelation 21:4). If eternal life was like this life but continuing forever, it wouldn't be good news. But He promises, "Behold, I make all things new" (v. 5).

The gospel is called **"everlasting"** because it was not an afterthought or an emergency plan devised in response to the appearance of sin. Jesus is "the Lamb slain from the foundation of the world" (Revelation 13:8). When God the Father, Son and Holy Spirit created man with free will and the possibility of choosing evil, He also made the provision that the Father would give "His only begotten Son" so that sinners who deserved death could instead receive life. The gospel was first announced when God told Satan, the serpent, "[I will] put enmity between you and the woman, and between your seed and her Seed" (Genesis 3:15). This was the gospel that was symbolized by all the Old Testament sacrifices. The gospel tells us what God has done, is doing and will do to save us, and we are saved from eternal death by believing the gospel.

The Daily Sacrifice

The final message begins by emphasizing **"the everlasting gospel"** because the context is an international final effort by Satan, the "dragon," to impose his religious system on the world through the beast from the sea whose "deadly wound was healed," supported by the beast from the earth (Revelation 13:3,11,12). These are the final manifestations of the system that ruled the world for 1,260 years during the Middle Ages (see 12:12-17). The persecution of the saints was a prominent feature of this rule, and in chapter 13 we saw that there was also a fierce attack on God's law and on the everlasting covenant. But the most subtle and dangerous of the dragon's attacks is on the everlasting gospel.

The messages to the seven churches (chapters 2 and 3) is the story of Satan's steady infiltration and corruption of the church. His purpose in this was to pervert the gospel. In the book of Daniel this is presented as an attack on "the daily sacrifices." "Because of transgression, an army was given over to the horn [the Papacy] *to oppose the daily sacrifices*; and he cast truth down to the ground." "And forces shall be mustered by him…then *they shall take away the daily sacrifice*" (Daniel 8:12, 11:31).

The Hebrew word *"tamid."* translated "daily sacrifices" in the book of Daniel, means daily or continual—the whole round of services that were performed every day in the ancient Hebrew sanctuary. These services graphically symbolized the gospel. They included the morning and evening sacrifice of a lamb (Exodus 29:38,39), the continuous presence of the bread (Exodus 25:30, Leviticus 24:5-9), the trimming and continuous burning of the lamps (Exodus 27:20,21, Leviticus 24:1-8), the burning of incense every morning and evening (Exodus 30:1-9) and the continual burnt offering (Leviticus 6:9-13). The papal system of theology that was developed in the Middle Ages "takes away" every phase of the daily:

1) The daily sacrifice of the lambs symbolized the once-for-all sacrifice of Christ on the Cross (1 Peter 1:18,19). This was "taken away" by the mass, in which the priest supposedly "creates" the body and blood of Christ in a "renewed

sacrifice"[536] and gives it to the worshipers to eat for their salvation.

2) The continual presence of the bread represented Jesus as He is found in the Word of God that His people are to continually feed upon.[537] But God's Word was superseded by the "holy tradition" and writings of the "fathers."

3) The ever-burning lamps represented the Holy Spirit working in every born-again believer, giving him gifts to bless the church.[538] But the gifts of the Spirit became the propriety of the professional clergy, and set liturgies were introduced, which ruled out the moving of the Spirit and the active participation of the worshipers.

4) The daily offering of incense represented Christ's mediation, mingling His prayers with ours and interceding for us.[539] But this was obscured by the mediation of the priests, the saints and the Virgin Mary.

5) The continuous burnt offering represented the transforming, refining, sanctifying work of God in the life of the believer, purging him of his sinfulness as he repents and confesses his sins to God.[540] But this was replaced by confession to the priest and works of penance to "atone" for sins, by ritualized prayers such as the rosary, by pilgrimages and the lighting of candles, and with

purgatory after death if penance was inadequate.[541]

These doctrines and practices did not pop up overnight as the result of an assault by evil schemers. They were infused gradually by Satan himself as he inspired and prompted decisions that seemed good and honorable at the time, but which struck at the heart of the gospel. The powerful messages of the three angels begin by clarifying this most basic and crucial teaching—**"the everlasting gospel."** We are saved, not because of what we do or what the priest does or what the "saints" do. Jesus Himself is the good news, because salvation is 100% of Christ. Even the faith that believes the gospel is a gift from Him.

14:7 Fear God and Give Glory to Him

"Saying with a loud voice, 'Fear God, and give glory to Him; for the hour of His judgment has come; and worship Him that made heaven, and earth, and the sea, and the fountains of waters" (Revelation 14:7). At first glance it seems incongruous that the "good news" begins with the statement, **"Fear God."** Perhaps this is because a command to fear any other person would mean to be afraid of him. But the story of the beginning of sin shows that fear of God does not mean being afraid of Him.

Before Adam and Eve sinned, "the man and his wife were both naked, and they felt no shame" (Genesis 2:25). It was only after they disobeyed that they began to feel the negative emotions of shame, guilt and fear—"Adam and

536   Joseph Pohle, "The Sacrifice of the Mass," *The Catholic Encylopedia*,   http://www.newadvent.org/cathen/10006a.htm, accessed August 30, 2014.

537   Isaiah 54:10,11, Matthew 4:4, Amos 8:4, John 6:33,41.

538   Revelation 4:5, 1Corinthians 12:7-11, 14:26-31.

539   Revelation 5:8, 8:3,4.

540   1John 1:9, Malachi 3:2,3, 1Peter 1:6,7.

541   The Roman Catholic doctrine of purgatory teaches that the temporal penalty for sins committed after baptism must be paid through acts of penance. If these have not been adequate, purgatory, a "middle state" of torment between heaven and hell, exists where these debts will be settled. Prayers for the departed or indulgences granted by the pope can help the suffering soul finish his penance more quickly and move on to heaven. See Edward Hanna, "Purgatory," *The Catholic Encyclopedia*, http://www.newadvent.org/cathen/12575a.htm. Accessed August 30,2014

His wife hid themselves from the presence of the Lord God…Then the Lord God called to Adam and said to him, 'Where are you?' So he said, 'I heard Your voice in the garden and I was afraid" (Genesis 3:8-10). From this passage we see that being afraid of God is a result of the guilt that accompanies sin, but that God seeks out those who are hiding in fear. We also see that something in the way God related to Adam after his sin made him feel like he could answer and come out of hiding and resume interaction with God. That something is God's love that "is not willing that any should perish, but that all should come to repentance" (2 Peter 3:9).

All through the scriptures we find the seemingly contradictory messages, "fear God" and "do not fear." For example, in Luke 12:5 Jesus said, "I will show you whom you should fear: fear Him [God] who, after He has killed, has power to cast into hell; I say to you, fear Him!" But then a few verses later He said, "Do not fear, little flock, for it is your Father's good pleasure to give you the kingdom" (v. 32).

This apparent contradiction highlights the fact that there are two kinds of "fear of the Lord" described in the Bible. Unbelievers and those who are disobedient should fear God because of the judgments they are bringing upon themselves. God's abhorrence of sin and its results (pain, suffering and death) is such that He cannot let sin continue to exist, even though its destruction means judgment and death for the beloved sinners who refuse to let go of it.[542] We should not think that God has picked out some behaviors

he doesn't happen to like (sin) and lashes out to punish those who dare to disobey Him. Death is inherent in sin. God, in love for all who suffer together from the results of sin, will eliminate sin and everything connected to it. This is what the judgment is about, and this is why Jesus said, "Fear Him who is able to destroy both body and soul in hell" (Matthew 10:28). God will destroy sin, and because of this unrepentant sinners should be afraid to continue in it.

Those who believe the Gospel do not have to be afraid of the judgment. Jesus said, "He who hears My word and believes in Him who sent Me has everlasting life, and shall not come into judgment, but has passed from death into life" (John 5:24). This is what the apostle John meant when he said, "By this, love is perfected with us, that we may have confidence in the day of judgment. There is no fear in love; but perfect love casts out fear, because fear involves punishment." (1 John 4:17,18). God depicts Himself as a loving father welcoming us with open arms. The prodigal son returned home from his life of dissipation, and his father, who represents God, "saw him and had compassion, and ran and fell on his neck and kissed him" (Luke 15:20). We do not need to be afraid of God. However, even if we love God and believe in Him we need to have the "fear of the Lord."

This is the fear that recognizes that I am a sinner, and but for God's grace I would be just as hopelessly lost as any murderer, rapist or thief on earth—"If You, Lord, should mark iniquities, O Lord, who could stand? But there is forgiveness with You, *that You may be feared*" (Psalms 130:3,4). It is the fear that recognizes that I am totally dependent upon Him for my very existence—"*Let us fear the Lord our God*, who gives autumn and spring rains in season, who assures us of the regular weeks of harvest" (v. 24). The fear of the Lord is to share His hatred of sin, which has blighted our lives and destroyed the

---

542 This is clearly taught in Psalms 34—"Come you children, listen to me; *I will teach you the fear of the Lord*…Depart from evil and do good; seek peace and pursue it. The eyes of the Lord are on the righteous, and His ears are open to their cry. The face of the Lord is against those who do evil, to cut off the remembrance of them from the earth…Many are the afflictions of the righteous, but the Lord delivers him out of them all…Evil shall slay the wicked, and those who hate the righteous shall be condemned" (Psalms 34:11-22).

lives of those we love—"*The fear of the Lord* is to hate evil: Pride and arrogance and the evil way" (Proverbs 8:13).

Most of all, the fear of the Lord is the knowledge that I am a simple decision away from leaving the Lord's "narrow way" and embarking on the "broad way"[543] of pain, sorrow and death that the devil would like to lure me onto— "*I will put My fear in their hearts* so that they will not depart from Me" (Jeremiah 32:40). We should fear doing anything that would result in our ending up with Satan as our lord.

The result of fearing the Lord is obedience, and this is what it means to **"give glory to Him."** Jesus said, "By this My Father is glorified, that you bear much fruit...If you keep My commandments, you will abide in My love, just as I have kept My Father's commandments and abide in His love" (John 15:8-10).[544] This is the final result of the three angels' messages: **"Here are those who keep the commandments of God and the faith of Jesus"** (Revelation 14:12).

The Hour of His Judgment

"Fear God, and give glory to Him; for the hour of His judgment has come; and worship Him that made heaven, and earth, and the sea, and the fountains of waters" (Revelation 14:7). The people of the world who have been ignoring God or worshiping Him in vain are now called to attention, to give God the respect, awe and glory that He deserves, and to understand that the time for the judgment has arrived.

The last-day judgment consists of several phases of both investigative and executive judgment. The first phase of the investigative judgment (which was presented in chapters four through seven) is the pre-advent judgment (pre-advent means before the Second Coming of Christ). It is "a judgment made in favor of the saints of the most high" which enables them "to possess the kingdom" (Daniel 7:22). It is obvious that this judgment takes place before the Second Coming of Christ, because when He comes "His reward is with Him," showing that a determination has already been made.[545]

A second investigative phase takes place during the thousand year reign with Christ, described in Revelation 20:4-6, in which the resurrected and translated saints will judge those who were not a part of the first resurrection, as well as the fallen angels. This phase is mentioned by the apostle Paul: "Do you not know that the saints will judge the world?...Do you not know that we shall judge angels?" (1 Corinthians 6:2,3).

The executive judgment, in which the sentences pronounced in the investigative judgment are carried out, has three phases. The first phase involves the pouring out of the seven last plagues and the destruction of Babylon, as described in Revelation 15-18. The second phase is at the Second Coming of Christ, when the beast and the false prophet are thrown into the lake of fire, and "the rest [those who opposed Christ] were slain with the sword of Him that sat on the horse [Christ], which proceeded out of His mouth (Revelation 19:11-21). The final phase of the executive judgment takes place "When the thousand years are over." John saw all "the dead, small and great, standing before God and books were opened...and the dead were judged according to their works...anyone not found written in the Book of Life was cast into the lake of fire" (Revelation 20:7,11-15).

The **"hour of His judgment"** referred to in Revelation 14:7 applies to the first phase of

---

543 See Matthew 7:13,14.

544 See also 1 Peter 2:12, 2 Corinthians 9:13.

545 "Behold, I am coming quickly, and my reward is with me, to give every one according as his work shall be" Revelation 22:12. See also Isaiah 40:10, 62:11, Matthew 16:27.

the investigative judgment. This can be seen by the fact that it is given in the context of the final appeal **"to those who dwell on the earth"** to **"fear God and give glory to Him"**—in other words, the last call to repentance. Repentance is only possible during the first phase of the investigative judgment; the other phases of the judgment take place after the close of probation (see 5: *The Investigative Judgment* and 15:5-8 *The Close of Probation*).

In chapter four we saw that the investigative judgment was foreshadowed by the Day of Atonement in the sanctuary service of the Old Testament. It was a day when the people who had come to the sanctuary throughout the year to confess their sins and make sacrifices were to "afflict their souls." On that day "the priest shall make atonement for you, to cleanse you, that you may be clean from all your sins before the Lord" (Leviticus 16:30, 16). This final atonement and cleansing of the sanctuary was a symbol of the investigative judgment that takes place in the heavenly sanctuary, when the angels verify that those who have been written in the Book of Life have remained faithful. In Daniel 7 this judgment is identified by the statement "The court was seated and the books were opened… and a judgment was made in favor of the saints" (Daniel 7:10,22). In Daniel 8:14 this same time is identified with the statement "for two thousand three hundred days; then the sanctuary shall be cleansed." A study of these prophecies allows us to pinpoint the time (**"the hour"**) that the heavenly judgment begins.

When in History?

The pronouncement, **"the hour of His judgment has come"** emphasizes the arrival of a specific historical **"hour"** that will determine the eternal destiny of mankind. When in human history does this **"hour of His judgment"** take place? This message does not specify, but the

fulfillment of other prophecies enables those who live in the time of the judgment to know that they have arrived at that critical time.

In chapter four this same judgment was introduced with the words, "Behold, a door standing open in heaven" (Revelation 4:1). There we saw that the open door refers to the door into the Holy of Holies in the heavenly sanctuary which Jesus, our great High Priest, enters on the Day of Atonement. The only other place in the Bible where this exact Greek phrase for open door is used is in the message to the Philadelphia Church ("I have set before you an open door" Revelation 3:8). This links the beginning of the Day of Atonement (the judgment) to the Philadelphia period of history which started in the late 18th century and continued through much of the 19th century.[546]

This same judgment was the focus of the vision of Daniel 7, "The court was seated and the books were opened" (Daniel 7:10). Daniel saw four beasts arising from the sea, representing the world empires that would oppress God's people through history (See 13: *The Wild Animals of Daniel 7*). Out of the fourth beast came a "little horn" that became large and aggressive and persecuted God's people. Daniel described this oppressive reign: "He [the little horn] shall speak pompous words against the Most High, shall persecute the saints of the Most High, and shall intend to change times and law. Then the saints shall be given into his hand for *a time and times and half a time*" [547] (Daniel 7:25). In previous

---

546 See 3: *Philadelphia* and specifically 3: *The Open Door* for more information.

547 This time period is the same as the "one thousand two hundred and sixty days" of Revelation 13:6 and the "forty two months" of Revelation 11:2. A time is a year, times is two years and half a time is half a year. The Hebrew year was 360 days, so this equaled 1,260 prophetic days, with one day representing a year.

chapters[548] we have seen that this represents the 1,260 years of papal oppression during the Middle Ages that began in the early 6th century and lasted until the end of the 18th century. But after this period *"the court shall be seated*, and they shall take away his dominion, to consume and destroy it forever, then the kingdom and dominion...shall be given to the people, the saints of the Most High"* (Daniel 7:27). In other words, the investigative judgment would begin in the 19th century after the 1,260 years of papal oppression were over. Again the time frame of the Philadelphia era is indicated.

An even more specific date can be calculated from the prophecy of the 2,300 days of Daniel 8. The vision of Daniel 8 is parallel to that of Daniel 7, showing the succession of empires that subjugated God's people, but focusing on the oppressive papal reign of the Middle Ages. Daniel saw a ram that symbolized the Persian Empire, which was attacked by a male goat, representing the Greek Empire that began under Alexander the Great. Out of the goat came a horn, which represented first pagan and then papal Rome.[549] This horn started small but "grew up to the host of heaven... He even exalted himself as high as the Prince of the host [Jesus] and by him the daily sacrifices were taken away, and the place of His sanctuary was cast down" (Daniel 8:10,11). This vision focuses on the attack on the sanctuary and the gospel that was described earlier in this chapter. Daniel heard a heavenly being ask the question, "How long will the vision be?" The answer came, "For two thousand three hundred days; *then the sanctuary shall be cleansed*" (Daniel 8:13,14). This final statement refers to the investigative

judgment. The interpretation of this vision, given by the angel Gabriel, is somewhat complex, and is described in detail in Appendix 5: *The 2,300 Days of Daniel 8*. To briefly summarize:

The context of chapter 8 is the rise and fall of empires from Daniel's day until the time of the end. This shows that the 2,300 days are prophetic days, each of which stands for a year. [550] But in chapter 8 no starting point was given for the 2,300 years. The angel Gabriel came to explain the vision in chapter 8, but Daniel was so overwhelmed that he could not understand all of it. Specifically, he did not understand the significance of the 2,300 days. Gabriel returned in chapter 9 to finish his explanation. He did so by stating that 70 prophetic weeks (490 years) were "cut off" or designated for Daniel's people, the Jews. The 490 years were cut off from the longer 2,300-year period. This period of "probation" for the Jews would end with the Messiah (Jesus).[551]

The beginning of both the 490 years and the 2,300 years would be "the command to restore and build Jerusalem" (Daniel 9:25) which was given by Artaxerxes in 457 BC.[552] Some simple arithmetic shows that the 2,300 years ended in AD 1844. In 1844 Jesus began a new phase of His ministry during which "the sanctuary shall

---

548 See 12: *One Thousand Two Hundred and Sixty Days* and 13: *The Little Horn and the Sea Beast*.

549 Many commentators interpret the little horn as Antiochus Epiphanes, a Syrian king who ruled from 175-164 BC. See 3: *The Day of Atonement, 2300 Days*, footnote 116 for an analysis of the Antiochus theory.

550 The day-for-a-year principle is obvious from the prophecies of Daniel. For example, the seventy weeks (490 days) of Daniel 9 was to start with "the command to restore and build Jerusalem" (which was in 457 BC) and would extend "until Messiah the Prince" (Jesus) (Daniel 9:25). The prophecy of 2,300 days in chapter 8 began with "the kings of Media and Persia" (the Persian kings reigned in the 6th and 5th centuries BC) and would extend "to the time of the end" (Daniel 8:20, 17). The prophecy of "time, times and half a time" (1,260 days) in chapter 7 began at the time of the breakup of the pagan Roman Empire and extended "until the time came for the saints to possess the kingdom" (Daniel 7:22). All these prophecies started in ancient times and continued the number of *years* the prophecy specified in *days*. Other scriptural support for this principle is found in Numbers 14:34, Ezekiel 4:5,6, Job 10:5, Psalm 77:5.

551 For an explanation of the 70 weeks prophecy of Daniel 9 see Appendix 4: *The Secret Rapture*.

552 For a discussion of the decree to rebuild Jerusalem see Appendix 4 footnote 831.

be cleansed." This phase was foreshadowed by the Day of Atonement, in which the high priest entered the Most Holy Place "to make atonement for you before the Lord your God" (Leviticus 23:28). The announcement **"the hour of His judgment has come"** refers to this specific period of time, which began in 1844.

The following illustrations show the relationship between the prophecies of Daniel 7 and Daniel 8 and between the 70 Weeks of Daniel 9 and the 2,300 days of Daniel 8.

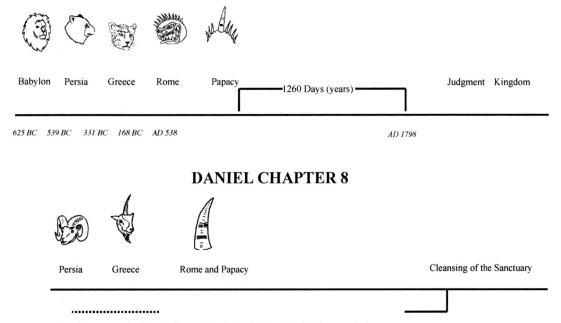

DANIEL CHAPTER 7

| Babylon | Persia | Greece | Rome | Papacy | 1260 Days (years) | | Judgment | Kingdom |

625 BC   539 BC   331 BC   168 BC   AD 538   AD 1798

DANIEL CHAPTER 8

Persia   Greece   Rome and Papacy   Cleansing of the Sanctuary

*No date or event is given in chapter 8 for the beginning of the 2300 year period

Seventy Weeks (490 Years) Of Daniel 9

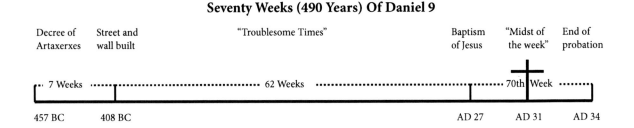

2300 Days Of Daniel 8 And 9

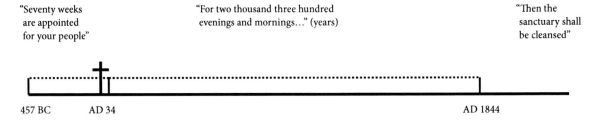

Who Is Being Judged, and Why?

Many people have a concept of the judgment as a time when God finds out if we have been good enough for heaven, making a list of the good things we have done and comparing it with our sins that are written in "the books." However, God doesn't have any "finding out" that He has to do, and being good is not the criteria. Every person who has ever lived is a sinner, and the wages of sin is death. But those who in faith have trusted in Christ's atoning death on the Cross "have passed from death into life" (John 5:24).

The investigative judgment was symbolized by the Day of Atonement, in which the priest made a final atonement for the people who had confessed their sins when they brought their sacrifices to the sanctuary. The obvious question is,

why would any additional atonement be needed for Christians, since Christ has forgiven the sins that we have confessed and "cast all our sins into the depths of the sea" (Micah 7:19)?

As we saw in chapter 4, during the earthly service the priests dealt daily with the sins that the Israelites committed and which they confessed upon the head of the sacrificial animal. But besides these sins there were many other sins they committed; some that they were ignorant of, some which did not seem important enough to bring to the sanctuary, some which were forgotten, as well as the sinfulness that was a part of their general sinful human nature. These also needed to be atoned for, and "on that day [the Day of Atonement] the priest shall make atonement for you, to cleanse you, that you may be clean from *all* your sins before the Lord" (Leviticus 16:30).

This brings up an even more fundamental issue. God already knows all that is in our hearts, whether our repentance was genuine or simply an attempt to avoid getting in trouble. He knows whether we have continued to believe, or if we just believed at some time in the past and then went back to a worldly life of sin. Obviously the investigative judgment is not so that God can gather more information with which to make a decision concerning our eternal fate. "For His eyes are on the ways of man, and He sees all his steps. There is no darkness nor shadow of death where the workers of iniquity may hide themselves. *For He need not further consider a man, that he should go before God in judgment...Therefore He knows their works*" (Job 34:21-25). When Daniel saw in vision that "the court was seated and the books were opened...and a judgment was made" (Daniel 7:10, 22), and when John heard that **"the hour of His judgment has come,"** they were not learning about a process that God needs in order to make a decision.

Perhaps the key to understanding this is the fact that although we are saved by faith, we will be judged by our works ("And they were judged, every man according to their works" Revelation 20:13).[553] God sees the heart, so he can save us according to the faith that He sees. But the rest of the universe is integrally involved in the judgment, and they cannot see the heart, they can only see the works that are evidence of the faith we profess. The courtroom scenes of Daniel and Revelation emphasize the myriads of heavenly creatures that are present.[554] The Old Testament examples of investigative judgment were for the sake of men

and angels, not for God.[555] The apostle Paul said "we have been made a spectacle to the world, both *to angels and to men* (1Corinthians 4:9). "His [God's] intent was that now, through the church, the manifold wisdom of God should be made known *to the rulers and authorities in the heavenly realms*" (Ephesians 3:10). Judgment is for the sake of the rest of the universe, not for God.

The fact that the intelligent universe will be convinced of God's wisdom in the judgment brings up a crucial point: God, more than anyone else, has been accused and slandered. In a sense, the investigative judgment is also a time in which God Himself is judged—**"the hour of *His* judgment has come."** This incredible thought is captured in Romans 3:4, "Indeed, let God be true, but every man a liar. As it is written: 'That *You* [God] *may be justified in Your words, and may overcome when You are judged.*" God has submitted Himself to the judgment of His creation! God has been maliciously accused of being selfish, unloving and a liar, with restrictive laws that limit the happiness of His creatures. Rather than defending Himself, God answers these charges with exhibit A—**"those who keep the commandments of God and the faith of Jesus"** (Revelation 14:12). The joy and "beauty of holiness"[556] of these overcomers is a rebuke to the "accuser of the brethren" and vindicates God's law, His government, His wisdom in creating man and His plan of salvation.

---

553 See also Revelation 2:23, Ecclesiastes 12:14, Matthew 12:36,37, 16:27, 25:31-46, 2Corinthians 5:10.

554 Daniel 7:9,10, Revelation 4:4, 5:11.

555 For example, "The Lord" and two angels came to Abraham and announced that they were going down to Sodom and Gomorrah to "see whether they have done altogether according to the outcry against it that has come to Me: and if not, I will know." But the Lord Himself did not go down, only the two angels (Genesis 18:16-19:15). Likewise, in Ezekiel 8 and 9 there was an investigative judgment but it was "the Lord" showing Ezekiel the abominations of the people and directing angels to go find and mark those "who sigh and cry over all the abominations."

556 1Chronicles16:29, Psalms 29:2, 96:9.

Worship the Creator

"Worship Him that made heaven, and earth, and the sea, and the fountains of waters." (Revelation 14:7). Here a neglected aspect of God is presented—the fact that He is the Creator of the universe. As much as the redemption of man makes God worthy of honor and worship, redemption and salvation bring man back to the original perfection that existed before sin. Without the perfect creation that was marred by sin there would be nothing to redeem. "The heavens declare the glory of God and the firmament shows His handiwork" (Psalms 19:1). Even our bodies, degenerated by sin, are "fearfully and wonderfully made" (Psalms 139:14). The tremendous advances in modern science give awe-inspiring proof of the infinite intelligence, creativity and artistry of our Creator. Paradoxically, most of the people of the world believe scientists who claim that there was no Creator, that the universe came into being with an undirected "big bang," and life evolved out of non-living elements. The first angel's message denies this world view and challenges humanity to remember their Creator.

Revelation 14:7 is a direct reference to the fourth commandment: "Remember the Sabbath day, to keep it holy,…For in six days the Lord *made the heavens and the earth, the sea, and all that is in them*, and rested on the seventh day. Therefore the Lord blessed the Sabbath day and hallowed it." (Exodus 20:8-11). The fourth commandment identifies the true God out of all the myriad of gods which clamor for recognition, and in particular it distinguishes the genuine Father, Son and Holy Spirit of the Bible from the counterfeits who are masquerading by the same name within the Babylon religion.

When God points to the Sabbath as an identifying mark of His authority it is the antithesis of the spurious first-day "sabbath," which was shown in chapter 13 to be the mark of the beast.

Since the fourth commandment is highlighted in the universal end-time message of the first angel, we can see that the number of the beast (666, the refusal to honor the seventh-day Sabbath) will be an issue that will agitate the whole world, and God through His messengers will make the issues very clear. Their lives will be a witness to the truth: **"Here is the patience of the saints; here are those that keep the commandments of God, and the faith of Jesus"** (Revelation 14:12). They will keep God's commandments, including the fourth (Sabbath) commandment despite the pressure and persecution of the beast.

The faithful remnant will face economic threats and finally a death decree for those who refuse to honor the beast's first-day "sabbath." But keep in mind that the issue is much larger than which day is the right day to worship. The alternate days are symbols of loyalty, one to Jesus and His gospel, law and faith, and the other to the false Jesus and the spurious "gospel" of human works. Both sides will claim to be followers of Jesus and will point to the Bible as the basis of their faith. Jesus warned, "Take heed that no one deceives you, for many will come in My name" (Matthew 24:4,5).

Did Jesus Establish Sunday?

The mark and number of the beast are the culmination of the attack Satan has made on the Sabbath from the beginning of creation.[557] He has constantly tried to change it, eliminate it, pervert it, cause it to be a burden or curse, associate it with the "old covenant" or "the Jews who rejected Jesus" and transform it from the symbol of faith and redemption into a symbol of bondage. These attacks are a part of his war against the

---

557 A careful reading of the New Testament shows that the animosity of the Jewish leaders against Jesus had to do with His restoration of the true meaning of the Sabbath. See Matthew 12:1-15, Luke 13:10-17, 14:1-6, John 5:1-19, 7:19-24, 9:1-41, Acts 13:27,28.

everlasting covenant and the law of God, which Satan hates because they condemn his sin, aspirations and kingdom principles. In an absence of scriptural support some of the arguments against the Sabbath are very creative. These are briefly touched upon here and examined fully in Appendix 6.

It is claimed that Jesus abolished the Sabbath and established Sunday as the day of worship by meeting with His disciples on the first day of the week. Some even assert that every time Jesus met with His disciples after the resurrection was on a Sunday. However, a careful analysis shows that several meetings were definitely not on Sunday, and those meetings that were on the first day were not worship services and there was no sharing of the Lord's supper.[558] Instead, these meetings were an opportunity for Jesus to prove to His doubting disciples that He had risen from the dead, and to give them their commission to take the gospel to the world.

This is consistent with the symbolism in Genesis chapter one of the first day as the day to start working, and of the Sabbath as a symbol of resting in the work God has already done. In other words, Sabbath is a symbol of faith, a day to worship and serve those in need. Sunday is a symbol of work and is a day, like every other working day, to prove to unbelievers that Jesus is alive. The resurrection is not a historical event to celebrate with a memorial service on Sunday; it is an experience of the power of the resurrected Jesus, which the Christian lives out every day.

There are no Biblical examples of Sunday being a special day of worship (see Appendix 6). In fact, if examples were to be followed, they should be that of Jesus who "went to the synagogue on the Sabbath day, as was His custom" (Luke 4:16 NRSV), or Paul who, "as his custom

was, went in to them, and for three Sabbaths reasoned with them from the Scriptures...He reasoned in the synagogue every Sabbath" (Acts 17:2, 18:4). Jesus consistently upheld the law of God and condemned those who would try to minimize its claims.[559]

It is obvious that neither Jesus nor the apostles changed the Sabbath because there is no Biblical record of a Sabbath controversy. When God made changes in the ceremonial law, such as abolishing animal sacrifices, circumcision and the Levitical priesthood, He made it perfectly clear in the New Testament that He was doing so, but this is not the case with the Sabbath.[560] Neither did a "new covenant" make the Sabbath, along with the rest of God's law, obsolete.[561] Keeping the Sabbath is not evidence that one is "under the law" any more than honoring parents or refraining from idolatry or adultery puts one "under the law." In reality, one must be "under grace" in order to keep any part of God's law (including the Sabbath) because "the carnal mind is enmity against God; for it is not subject to the law of God, nor indeed can be" (Romans 8:7).

In summary, the first angel's message,

---

558 The only "Lord's Supper" Jesus shared with His disciples was Thursday evening before His crucifixion.

559 "Do not think that I came to destroy the Law or the Prophets. I did not come to destroy but to fulfill. For assuredly, I say to you, till heaven and earth pass away, one jot or one tittle will by no means pass from the law till all is fulfilled" (Matthew 5:17,18). It is sometimes argued that "all [was] fulfilled" on the Cross, therefore the law could pass away. But all has not been fulfilled, because sin is still very much with us, both in and out of the church. Therefore the law is still needed to condemn sin. Moreover, "heaven and earth" have not "passed away" as the verse specifies.

560 See Appendix 6.

561 Jesus, referring to the last-day trials of the time of trouble, urged His followers to "pray that your flight may not be in winter or on the Sabbath" (Matthew 24:20). This does not make any sense if the Sabbath was to be done away with. Even in the "new heavens and new earth...all flesh shall come to worship before Me...from one Sabbath to another" (Isaiah 66:22,23). One of the main provisions of the new covenant was that "I will put my laws in their mind and write them on their hearts" (Hebrews 8:10). That this is not some new, watered down "law of love" is shown by the fact that Paul quotes from Jeremiah 31:33, an Old Testament passage that would not refer to any law except the law given on Mt. Sinai.

announcing **"the hour of his judgment has come,"** is an urgent call to every person from **"every nation, tribe, tongue and people"** to reject the human works-oriented beast religion and by faith accept the **"everlasting gospel."** The command, **"Worship Him who made heaven and earth, the sea and springs of water"** is a compelling imperative to honor our Creator and Redeemer by resting on the seventh-day Sabbath.

14:8 The Second Angel's Message

"And there followed another angel, saying, "Babylon is fallen, is fallen, that great city, because she made all nations drink of the wine of the wrath of her fornication" (Revelation 14:8). This is the first verse in Revelation that mentions Babylon by name. She is called "that great city" both here and in Revelation 16:19 as well as in Revelation 18:10,21. Revelation 17:18 adds that she is "that great city which reigns over the kings of the earth," showing the international political power that she wields. Revelation 17 portrays her as a harlot riding on a scarlet beast that is nearly identical to the beast from the sea, which in chapter 13 was identified as the papacy of the Middle Ages. The great harlot sits on seven mountains (Revelation 17:9) and this in itself confirms the identity: Rome is the city which from ancient times was known to sit on seven hills or mountains, and as the capital of first the Roman Empire and then of Roman Catholic Europe she has indeed reigned over the kings of the earth. The fact that she is called a harlot shows that it is the Roman Church rather than the pagan Roman Empire that is the model for last-day Babylon.[562]

The context of chapter 14 is **"the hour of His judgment"** so Babylon refers to the end-time manifestation of the Roman Catholic Church together with her "daughter" churches,[563] after the "deadly wound [has been] healed" (Revelation 13:3,12,14). She is allied with the "beast coming out of the earth," the United States of America, which creates an image to her and causes the earth and those who dwell in it to worship her under threat of death (Revelation 13:12,15). This is, in fact, a "one world government," symbolized by "ten kings who…receive authority for one hour as kings with the beast" (Revelation 17:12). This will be explained in more detail in chapters 17 and 18.

The second angel's message, **"Babylon is fallen,"** does not mean that she has been defeated or destroyed. We will see in the third angel's message that she is still very active, imposing the mark of the beast. This message exposes the fallen, corrupting religious system of Babylon. The long story of her fall has already been told in the messages to the seven churches and will be summarized here.

The first stage of her fall was during the "Ephesus" period of the second century—"I have this against you, that you have left your first love" (Revelation 2:4). Persecution by the Jews made it easy for Christians to lose their love for the Jewish people, and this hatred had a corrupting influence on the church. The theology of hatred for the "Jesus-killing Jews" led to the first major doctrinal compromise: rejection of the "Jewish" seventh-day Sabbath (see 2:1-5 *First Love*).

During the "Smyrna" period (the second and third centuries) the church battled against the Gnostic heresy, and although gnosticism was rejected, its influence led to the development of

---

562 A woman in scripture refers to a "church" (either pure or corrupt), not an empire. See 12:1,2 *The Woman.*

563 Revelation 17:5 refers to the end-time Babylon as a harlot and "the mother of harlots," showing that churches that have accepted the false Roman Catholic doctrines and political entanglements share her harlot status.

the "synagogue of Satan" (see 2:8,9 *Synagogue of Satan*). The apostolic church, which had focused on knowing Jesus through the Holy Spirit, evolved into a "secret society" possessing "life-giving" mysteries, liturgies and relics of the martyrs, all administered by a rigid hierarchy of priests.

During the "Pergamos" period of the fourth and fifth centuries the "throne of Satan" was set up (see 2:12,13 *Throne of Satan*). This was the union of church and state as manifested in the era of the great church councils. Despite the protest of the faithful "Antipas" Christians, idolatry came into the church with the worship of the saints and the "mother of God" (See 2: *Antipas*). The "doctrine of Balaam" (See 2:14 *Doctrine of Balaam*) saw corrupt priests and monks exploiting the superstitions of the masses, amassing wealth by "selling" access to relics, rituals, holy days and places "hallowed" by the saints. The Nicolaitan heresy (See 2:15 *Nicolaitans*) split the church into the spiritually elite (the "celibate" priests and monks in remote monasteries), and the immoral masses. This system in turn led to the development of the system of penance, indulgences and purgatory to "propitiate" for a continuing life of sin.

During the "Thyatira" era of the Middle Ages Babylon was full blown as the persecuting "Jezebel" (See 2:18-20 *You Tolerate Jezebel*). The Crusades, the Inquisition, millions of martyrs and bloody religious wars were the result. The Protestant reformation brought life back into the church, but even this was spoiled during the "Sardis" post-reformation period with dead formalism, intolerance, false doctrine and state religion (see 3:1,2 *The Dead Church*). Finally the modern "Laodicean" period left all these errors doctrinally intact, while glossing over differences through the numbing influence of spiritual apathy and materialism (See 3: 15-17 *Lukewarm*).

The message **"Babylon is fallen"** was first proclaimed by the Protestant reformers, and intensified during the great reforms of the "Philadelphia" period. It will reach a mighty climax when the mark of the beast is formed, as portrayed in the loud cry of Revelation 18: "Babylon the great is fallen, is fallen, and has become the habitation of devils, and the hold of every foul spirit, and a cage of every unclean and hateful bird!...Come out of her, my people, that you do not partake of her sins, and that you do not receive of her plagues" (Revelation 18:2-4).

14:9-11 The Third Angel's Message

"And the third angel followed them, saying with a loud voice, 'If any one worships the beast and his image, and receives his mark on his forehead, or on his hand, he also shall drink of the wine of the wrath of God, which is poured out without mixture into the cup of His indignation; and he shall be tormented with fire and brimstone in the presence of the holy angels, and in the presence of the Lamb. And the smoke of their torment ascends up forever and ever; and they have no rest day or night, who worship the beast and his image, and whoever receives the mark of his name" (Revelation 14:9-11).

Coming out of Babylon is not simply a matter of religious preference. It is literally a life and death decision, made all the more critical by the fact that the beast will threaten death to those who dare to withhold their worship. (See 13:15 *The Image of the Beast*).

This passage contains the most fearsome warning in all of scripture—"the wrath of God, **which is poured out without mixture," "tormented with fire and brimstone," "no rest day or night,"** all of this for those who **worship the beast and his image, and...receive his mark."** If someone had only these verses, he would be hard pressed to find evidence that "God is love"

(1John 4:8). But there are some important points to keep in mind. First of all, this outpouring of wrath is provoked by the worship of the beast. The agenda of the beast is to destroy God's children, and those who participate in the beast system of religion and politics are aiding and abetting if not actually participating in the plot to annihilate God's children. God's purpose is to protect His people rather than to lash out in rage at His enemies.

Secondly, the wrath of God is not like the wrath of man (see 15:1 *The Wrath of God*). We should not assume that God is offended and furious because someone did not do what He wanted. He is desperately anxious that those who hear this message will take it to heart, repent of their sins and accept the eternal life He is offering along with His fearsome warning.

Moreover, we should not read into this text something that is not there. The fact that they are **"tormented with fire and brimstone,"** that the **"smoke of their torment ascends forever and ever,"** and **"they have no rest day or night"** has led some readers to conclude that God is threatening sinners with eternal torture. The fact that impenitent sinners shall be **"tormented with fire and brimstone"** is in harmony with Revelation 20:15: "anyone not found written in the Book of Life was cast into the lake of fire." This is simply the fire that destroys sinners for eternity, even as Jesus said in Matthew 10:28, "Fear Him who is able to destroy both soul and body in Hell" (see 20: 11-15 *The White Throne Judgment*). The only thing that is eternal in this passage is the **"smoke of their torment"** which **"ascends forever and ever,"** an eternal memorial to the deadly malignancy of sin. This phrase also appears in Isaiah 34:10, referring to the destruction of the earth by fire at the last day.[564] After the fire consumes

all that can be consumed God will create a "new heaven and a new earth"[565] which obviously will not be burning. This shows that eternally rising smoke does not equate with eternal burning.[566]

It is true that **"they have no rest day or night, who worship the beast and his image."** The Greek use of the present active verb participle *proskunountas* (translated "worship") shows that the time when they have no rest is when they worship the beast.[567] Since the number of the beast is refusal to honor God's Sabbath rest, it is no wonder that they have no rest since they are actively opposing Him who said, "Come unto me…and I will give you rest." (Matthew 11:28).

God is not making savage threats in order to coerce behavior, as the beast does with his death decree and economic sanctions. He is simply informing the world of reality as it is. Those who continue to participate in the beast system after it has been shown to be in opposition to God disqualify themselves for eternal life, and God wants everyone in the world to know this so that they can flee to Him and be saved. That is why the three angels' messages are given.

14:12 Commandments of God, Faith of Jesus

Even though God warns against being on the side of the beast, this does not mean that it will be easy to be on God's side. The followers of the beast will do everything they can to make life hell for God's people, and when the death decree goes into effect and God's people have to "flee to the

---

564 Compare with the description of the Second Coming in Revelation 6:14. See also 2Peter 3:10-13.

565 2 Peter 3:13. The description in Isaiah 35 follows the destruction of chapter 34.

566 The smoke of the "harlot" who has been utterly destroyed also "rises up forever and ever" (Revelation 19:3). But obviously she is not being eternally tortured—"she will be utterly burned with fire" and she "shall not be found anymore" Revelation 18:8,21.

567 A more accurate but awkward translation might be "they have no rest day or night worshiping the beast."

mountains" (Matthew 24:16) there will be anxiety, distress and hardship.

"**Here is the patience of the saints; here are those that keep the commandments of God, and the faith of Jesus**" (Revelation 14:12). The Greek word for "**patience**," *ipomoni*, is defined as "steadfast adherence to a deliberate purpose and course of action, loyalty to faith and piety in spite of the greatest trials and sufferings, *perseverance, endurance, fortitude*."[568] It will take tremendous endurance and fortitude to continue to "**keep the commandments of God**" when the law of the land commands the breaking of at least the fourth commandment, and in fact, this kind of patience is the fruit of "**the faith of Jesus**." The form of the Greek word for faith in this phrase, as related to Jesus, is unique in scripture, and a number of translations, including the King James, render it "the faith of Jesus" rather than "faith in Jesus" as found in a few versions. The implication is that it is not our faith in Him that will get us through this trying time; rather, it is His faith, that he imparts to us.

Jesus had faith in God's word, "This is My beloved Son,"[569] which sustained Him through forty days of fasting followed by the subtle suggestions of the devil, "If you are the son of God…" He had faith that the handful of followers "whom You [the Father] have given me,"[570] who were still squabbling about who would be the greatest and who abandoned Him in His hour of trial, would establish His church and take the gospel to the whole world. He had faith that the world would "see the Son of Man sitting at the right hand of the Power and coming on the clouds of heaven,"[571] even when the weight of the sins of the whole world was bearing down on Him, shutting out His view of the Father and a future beyond the grave. In other words, His faith was fully in the word of God, despite all the evidences of his circumstances or feelings. Only this kind of faith, which is a gift of God's grace, will sustain God's people in the time of trouble. The fact that keeping the commandments of God is integrally linked to the faith of Jesus shows that there is no contradiction between obedience and faith. True obedience is the fruit of faith, is impossible without faith, and if lacking proves that the so-called faith is not genuine.[572]

This is the great test that confirms the identity of those who claim to come in the name of the Lord. "He who says 'I know Him' and does not keep His commandments is a liar, and the truth is not in him" (1John 2:4). "To the law and to the testimony! If they do not speak according to this word, it is because there is no light in them" (Isaiah 8:20). The test of obedience to God's word will enable God's people to see through the false miracles and deceptive sophistry of "the beast and the false prophet" (Revelation 19:20). Although they will talk of faith and work marvelous miracles, their teaching and example will be against "**the commandments of God.**"

14:13 Martyrs During the Time of Trouble?

"**And I heard a voice from heaven saying to me, 'Write, blessed are the dead who die in the Lord from now on. Yes, said the Spirit, that they may rest from their labors; and their works do follow them**" (Revelation 14:13).

Will there be martyrs during the time of trouble? This text seems to indicate that there will be, a conclusion strengthened by the fact

---

568 See any comprehensive Greek lexicon such as Friberg, Thayer, Louw-Nida, etc.

569 Matthew 3:17.

570 John 17:6.

571 Matthew 26:64.

572 See James 2:14-26.

that the harlot of Revelation 17, the final manifestation of Babylon, is "drunk with the blood of the saints and with the blood of the martyrs of Jesus" (Revelation 17:6). Moreover, those who suffer from the seven last plagues (which are the final phase of the time of trouble) "have shed the blood of saints and prophets" (Revelation 16:6).

The Greek word for martyr means one who gives witness. The peace and joy of those who die for their faith has always been a powerful witness to unbelievers. One of the most influential moments in the transition from the persecutor Saul to the apostle Paul came when Saul witnessed the stoning of Stephen (Acts 7:55-60).

The context of this verse is the worldwide proclamation of the three angels' messages. This is a powerful call to repentance, and repentance only takes place before death or before the close of probation (the time when all will have made their irrevocable decisions for or against Christ). Probation does not close until Christ's heavenly ministry is finished, just before the pouring out of the seven last plagues (See 15:5-8 *The Close of Probation*). During that fearsome time there would be no purpose for martyrs, as the time for witnessing and repentance will be over, and in fact there is no mention of martyrdom occurring after the close of probation.[573] But during the first half of the time of trouble when "the nations [are] angry" (Revelation 11:18) there may be many who will lose their lives for Jesus.

Although few people want to become a martyr, this verse shows that if it happens there are some positive prospects. They are **"blessed,"** a Greek word which, when used in a non-religious context means happy, fortunate, or lucky. Those **"who die in the Lord…may rest from their labors,"** which underlines the stress and anxiety that all people, including those who are faithful to God, will experience during the time of trouble. The common attitude is that death is the ultimate misfortune, but for the Christian who knows that the next thing he will see is Jesus coming in the clouds, death can be a happy moment, especially when it brings relief from trials and persecution.

"And their works do follow them." No one ever has been or ever will be saved by his works. On the other hand, Jesus promised, "For the Son of Man will come in the glory of His Father, with His angels, and then He will reward each according to his works" (Matthew 16:27). Our work for the Lord here on earth will have an eternal reward in the kingdom of God. The greatest reward will be the joy of seeing men, women and children who have found Jesus and salvation as a result of our witness. The apostle Paul said, concerning people he had led to Christ, "For what is our hope, or joy, or crown of rejoicing? Is it not even you in the presence of our Lord Jesus Christ at His coming?" (1 Thessalonians 2:19).

14:14-20 The Great Harvest

"And I looked, and behold a white cloud, and on the cloud sat One like the Son of Man, having on His head a golden crown, and in His hand a sharp sickle. And another angel came out of the temple, crying with a loud voice to Him that sat on the cloud, 'Thrust in your sickle, and reap; for the time has come for You to reap; for the harvest of the earth is ripe.' And He that sat on the cloud thrust in his sickle on the earth; and the earth was reaped" (Revelation 14:14-16).

Chapters 12-14 digress from the linear timeline of the Revelation narrative in order to portray the history and the outcome of the great controversy. Satan has claimed that God is a selfish

---

573 Martyrs are mentioned in Revelation 17:6 ("the woman, drunk with the blood of…the martyrs of Jesus") but this section is an elaboration of the judgment of Babylon, which departs from the chronological timeline (see 1:*Chronological Organization*). Martyrs are also mentioned in chapter 20, showing that they will rise in the first resurrection and will live and reign with Christ for a thousand years (Revelation 20:4-6).

liar and that His law is restrictive, preventing us from reaching our full potential (see 12: *Origin of Satan*). God answers these charges by displaying the 144,000 who **"keep the commandments of God and the faith of Jesus."** They give the three angels' messages, which call the great multitude to come out of Babylon. The witness is so powerful and universal that the whole world is brought to a decision. The final results are the two harvests. God's children are compared to grain that is gathered in the harvest. Believers are often compared with wheat, and it is a fitting symbol of the church, whose ministry "feeds" the world with spiritual nourishment.[574]

The ungodly, on the other hand, are compared to grapes, which are gathered and trampled into bloody wine. **"And another angel came out of the temple which is in heaven, he also having a sharp sickle. And another angel came out from the altar, who had power over fire; and cried with a loud cry to him that had the sharp sickle, saying, 'Thrust in your sharp sickle, and gather the clusters of the vine of the earth; for her grapes are fully ripe"** (Revelation 14:17,18). The fate of the unrepentant is portrayed here as a part of the demonstration of the final outcome of the great controversy, but chronologically, the harvest of the grapes takes place both at the Second Coming of Christ when the living unrepentant will be slain,[575] and at the end of the thousand years when the resurrected but still-rebellious

"nations" are judged and cast into the lake of fire (see 20:7-10 *Satan Released*).

Grapes and wine have mixed symbolism in the Bible. On the one hand, the closest relationship that God's children can have with Jesus is compared to grape branches that are connected to the vine ("I am the vine and you are the branches" John 15:1-8). Jesus designated the "fruit of the vine" to be the symbol of His blood in the communion service (Matthew 26:27-29, 1Corinthians 11:25,26). On the other hand, in Revelation 17:2 the great harlot has a cup with which she makes the nations "drunk with the wine of her fornication." Those who took the Nazirite vow of consecration to God were "not [to] eat anything that comes from the vine, nor… drink wine or similar drink" (Judges 13:14).

Perhaps wine is one of the most fitting symbols of sinful humanity. New, fresh wine (grape juice) is delightfully sweet, and the fact that billions of dollars are spent on sweetened drinks today shows how enjoyable it must have been when it was one of the only sweet drinks available. This is expressed in scriptures such as Psalm 104:14,15, "[God] makes…plants for man to cultivate—bringing forth food from the earth: wine that gladdens the heart of man, oil to make

---

574 "He will thoroughly clean His threshing floor, and gather His wheat into the barn." "The harvest is the end of the age, and the reapers are the angels…I will say to the reapers,…'Gather the wheat into my barn" (Matthew 3:12, 13:39, 30). Jesus compared himself to a kernel of wheat that falls to the ground, dies, and then comes to life, producing a rich harvest (John 12:24).

575 Treading the winepress and slaying the unrepentant at the Second Coming are linked in Revelation 19—"the rest were slain with the sword of Him that sat on the horse, which proceeded out of His mouth." "And out of His mouth goes a sharp sword, that with it He should smite the nations…And He treads the wine press of the fierceness and wrath of Almighty God" (Revelation 19:21, 15).

his face shine, and bread that sustains his heart."[576]

But, as anyone who has made grape juice knows, it almost immediately begins to spoil, producing first alcohol and finally vinegar. There are many negative statements about wine, such as Proverbs 20:1 ("Wine is a mocker...and whoever is led astray by it is not wise") and Proverbs 23:29-32 ("Who has woe,...sorrow,... contentions,...complaints,...wounds without cause? Those who linger long at the wine...Do not look on the wine when it is red, when it sparkles in the cup, when it swirls around smoothly; at the last it bites like a serpent"). These verses refer to the evil influence that results when delightful "new wine" becomes intoxicating "old wine."[577] Likewise, every baby is born delightfully

innocent with a clean slate,[578] but almost immediately, contact with sin begins to spoil the childish innocence so that unless he is born again he inevitably becomes hopelessly corrupt, unfit for eternal life.

"And the angel thrust in his sickle into the earth, and gathered the vine of the earth, and cast it into the great wine press of the wrath of God. And the wine press was trodden outside the city, and blood came out of the wine press, up to the horses' bridles, for 1,600 stadia" (Revelation 14:19,20).

The comparison of treading out grapes with the destruction of the unrepentant is a common theme in Old Testament texts such as Isaiah 63:1-6 ("I [the Lord] have trodden the winepress alone...I have trodden down the peoples in My anger") and Joel 3:12,13 ("I will sit to judge all the surrounding nations...the winepress is full, the vats overflow—for their wickedness is great"). These are not simply threats by the stern God of the Old Testament. The loving Jesus pictures Himself as treading the winepress at His Second Coming: "And I saw heaven opened, and behold a white horse; and He that sat on him was called Faithful and True, and in righteousness He judges and makes war...and His name is called The Word of God...and He shall rule them [the nations] with a rod of iron. And *He treads the wine press of the fierceness and wrath of Almighty God*" (Revelation 19:11,13,15).

The imagery of trampling grapes, and words such as "fierceness" and "wrath" have caused many to wonder what the phrase "God is love" really means. The next chapter will show how the wrath of God and His destruction of the

---

576 There are two main words for wine in the Old Testament. *Tiyrowsh* is often translated "new wine" and is the unfermented fresh juice of grapes. It consistently refers to what God provides for His people, for the priests, and as tithe (Genesis 27:37, Numbers 18:12, Deuteronomy 7:13, 11:14, 12:17, 14:23, 18;14, 33:28, 2Chronicles 31:5, Nehemiah 10:37, 13:5, Psalms 4:7, Proverbs 3:10, Is. 62:8, Jeremiah 31:12, Hosea 2:8,9,22, Joel 2:19,24). New wine cheers the heart of man and makes him thrive. (Judges 9:13, Zechariah 9:17). The other main word for wine is *Yayin*. It can mean new wine (Isaiah 16:10, 65:8, Jeremiah 40:12, 8:33), it is used as the sin offering (Leviticus 23:13, Numbers 15:5), and it can be an acceptable part of the diet which God neither condemns nor approves (2Samuel 16:1, 1Chronicles 12:40, Ecclesiastes 9:7, 10:19, Jeremiah 40:10). But in many cases it has a negative connotation, associated with drunkenness, foolishness, personal distress and disaster, fatal mistakes, pagan feasts and reveling, and is used to symbolize God's wrath (Genesis 9:21, 19:32, 27:25, Leviticus 10:9, Numbers 6:3, Deuteronomy 32:33, Judges 13:4, 1Samuel 1:14, 2Samuel 13:28, Esther 1:7, Job 1:13, Psalms 60:3, 75:8, Proverbs 4:17, 20:1, 21:1,7, 23:30,31, 31:4,6, Ecclesiastes 2:31, Isaiah 5:11,12,22, 22:13, 28:17, 56:12, Jeremiah 13:12-14, 23:9, 25:15, 51:7, Ezekiel 44:21, Daniel 1:5, 5:1, Hosea 7:5, Joel 3:3, Amos 2:8, 6:6, Micah 2:11, Habakkuk 2:5).

577 Some have maintained that Paul advocated or at least allowed fermented wine in his advice to Timothy, "No longer drink only water, but use a little wine for your stomach's sake and your frequent infirmities." (1Timothy 5:23). But this text shows that Timothy's previous practice did not include drinking wine, only water, and he changed because he needed a medicine, not a different beverage. Many harmful substances are used in small amounts as medicines but should not be used except in cases of illness.

578 Contrary to the claims of those who believe in "original sin," babies are not born into the world having inherited guilt from Adam that must be atoned for. Ezekiel made this clear in chapter 18, which is summarized in verse 20, "The soul who sins shall die. The son shall not bear the guilt of the father."

unrepentant are acts of love. Chapter 15 will also return to the Revelation timeline with the close of probation and the pouring out of the seven last plagues.

"I saw something like a sea of glass mingled with fire, and those who have the victory over the beast, over his image and over his mark and over the number of his name, standing on the sea of glass" Rev. 15:2
Woodcut by Albrecht Durer, 1498

Chapter 15

Revelation 15:1-8

15:1 And I saw another sign in heaven, great and marvelous, seven angels having the seven last plagues; for in them is filled up the wrath of God.

15:2 And I saw as it were a sea of glass mingled with fire, and those that have the victory over the beast, and over his image, and over his mark, and over the number of his name, standing on the sea of glass, having the harps of God.

15:3 And they sing the song of Moses the servant of God, and the song of the Lamb, saying, "Great and marvelous are Your works, Lord God Almighty; just and true are Your ways, King of saints.

15:4 Who will not fear You, O Lord, and glorify Your name? For You only are holy; for all nations shall come and worship before You, for Your judgments have been revealed."

15:5 And after that I looked, and, behold, the temple of the tabernacle of the testimony in heaven was opened.

15:6 And the seven angels came out of the temple, having the seven plagues, clothed in pure and white linen, and having their chests girded with golden sashes.

15:7 And one of the four living creatures gave to the seven angels seven golden bowls full of the wrath of God, who lives forever and ever.

15:8 And the temple was filled with smoke from the glory of God, and from His power; and no one was able to enter into the temple, until the seven plagues of the seven angels were fulfilled.

15:1 The Double Inclusio

"And I saw another sign in heaven, great and marvelous, seven angels having the seven last plagues; for in them is filled up the wrath of God" (Revelation 15:1). Chapters twelve through fourteen are unique in their critical importance in the book of Revelation. They constitute the two climaxes of the chiastic structure, thus giving the clearest focus on the overall theme of Revelation: the great controversy between good and evil. They also focus on the most difficult and critical decision of all history, which everyone who is living at the very end of time will have to make: to accept the seal of God or the mark of the beast.

These chapters are also unique in that they leave the linear time line of the rest of the book to give a broad historical overview of Satan's war against heaven and God's people. The uniqueness of this section is demonstrated by two sets of literary "brackets." Chapter twelve begins by stating that "a great *sign appeared in heaven*" (Revelation 12:1,3). Thus begins the story of the "war in heaven" which, when Satan was cast to the earth, became a war against "the woman and… the rest of her offspring" (Revelation 12:17). The culmination of his attacks are the image, mark and number of the beast, but the surety of his defeat is demonstrated with the vision of the 144,000 worshiping "before the throne," then giving the three angels' messages, and finally the ultimate outcome, the two harvests.

This section ends just as it began, with the words **"I saw another sign in heaven."** Although many heavenly visions are seen in Revelation, these are the only two places where the phrase **"sign in heaven"** is used. This phrase brackets Revelation 12-14, showing its critical importance. As if to give even further emphasis, this section also begins and ends with a vision of the temple of God opened in heaven (Revelation 11:19, 15:5). These kinds of brackets highlighting a particular passage are called a literary inclusio,[579] and they emphasize the importance of the material contained within them. Chapters 12-14 are bracketed by a double inclusio which looks like this:

of Revelation. These themes include the war in heaven, the beasts from the sea and the earth, the image, name, mark and number of the beast, the everlasting gospel, the hour of God's judgment, the law, the Sabbath, the 144,000, the three angels' messages, and the "harvest" of both the saved and the lost. These are themes that every Christian needs to understand, especially as we approach the time of trouble when they will become life-and-death issues.

The chiasm with the double inclusio could be diagrammed like this:

$$\{\{E\text{-}1\ E\text{-}2\}\}$$
$$D\text{-}1 \qquad D\text{-}2$$
$$C\text{-}1 \qquad\quad C\text{-}2$$
$$B\text{-}1 \qquad\qquad B\text{-}2$$
$$A\text{-}1 \qquad\qquad\quad A\text{-}2$$

At the beginning of the double inclusio chapters 12-14 departed from the chronological timeline to give an extensive elaboration of the great controversy. Now in chapter 15 the narrative returns to the timeline with the next great event: **"the seven last plagues"** through which **"the wrath of God…is filled up."**

{Temple opened {sign in heaven—**CHAPTERS 12-14**—sign in heaven} Temple opened}

Chapters 12-14 have already been highlighted as the climax of the chiastic structure. It is as if God inspired John to use every means possible to super-emphasize the themes that are found in these three chapters that are the heart

The Wrath of God

"The seven last plagues, for in them is filled up the wrath of God" (Revelation 15:1). The wrath of God is mentioned several times in Revelation. It is part of the "third woe," it is poured out upon those who worship the beast, it is compared to a harvest of grapes which are trampled, it is manifested in the seven last plagues and it destroys Babylon, the beast and his followers at the Second Coming of Christ (Revelation 11:14-18, 14:10,19, 15:7, 16:1,19,

---

579 "In literature, inclusio is a literary device based on a concentric principle, also known as bracketing, which consists of creating a frame by placing similar material at the beginning and end of a section…Many instances can be found in the Bible." Wikipedia contributors, "Inclusio," *Wikipedia, The Free Encyclopedia*, http://en.wikipedia.org/w/index.php?title=Inclusio&oldid=612946496 (accessed September 7, 2014).

19:15-21). A distorted view of God's wrath has been used for centuries to try to terrify sinners into repenting.[580] But whatever God's wrath is, it must be consistent with love. "God is love" (1John 4:8,16),[581] which means that all He does is an expression of love. God does not hate His enemies when he pours the seven last plagues upon them, but somehow love demands that He do this.

Throughout the scriptures "the wrath of God" is a phrase used to describe the destructive actions which God must take against human beings. For example, in response to the sin of the children of Israel God warned them, "My wrath will become hot, and I will kill you with the sword; your wives shall be widows and your children fatherless" (Exodus 22:24). We should not assume from this that God is interested in having widows and orphans, or that He somehow loses control of His temper. It simply says that because

of certain types of behavior (in this case the previous verses mention sorcery, bestiality, sacrifices to idols, and oppression of strangers, widows and orphans) God will "kill you with the sword." Since God himself does not wield a physical sword, the practical outworking is that someone will intend to kill them, and God will either not protect them or perhaps will even facilitate their death.

Another example from the wilderness wandering of the children of Israel is found in Numbers 11. God had miraculously delivered them from slavery in Egypt and performed a miracle every day providing food for them (manna), but they were not satisfied, complaining, "Who will give us meat to eat?...Our whole being is dried up; there is nothing at all except this manna before our eyes" (Numbers 11:4-6). Their complaints were such a burden to Moses that he was ready to die (vs. 14,15). God provided meat for the people, bringing in a huge flock of quail, "but while the meat was still between their teeth, before it was chewed, the wrath of the Lord was aroused against the people, and the Lord struck the people with a very great plague...There they buried the people who had yielded to craving" (vs. 33,34).

These kinds of stories have led many to conclude that the God of the Old Testament is somehow different, more stern and vindictive than Jesus or the Father in the New Testament. However, God is "the same yesterday, today and forever" (Hebrews 13:8). The "wrath of the Lamb [Jesus]" includes the fearsome seven last plagues. A few basic observations will help to put God's wrath into perspective.

First of all, for God to allow or even cause death should not seem so unusual in a world of sin where everyone dies. In certain circumstances most people consider death to be a blessing, such as a terminal illness with terribly suffering. And there is no illness more terminal than sin, which causes pain and suffering both to the victim and

---

580 For example, the Great Awakening of the 18th century was largely a result of preaching such as that of Jonathan Edwards, who said in his sermon, "Sinners in the Hands of an Angry God," "All you that were never born again...are in the hands of an angry God... his wrath towards you burns like fire; he looks upon you as worthy of nothing else, but to be cast into the fire; he is of purer eyes than to bear to have you in his sight... God is dreadfully provoked, his anger is as great towards [you] as to those that are actually suffering the executions of the fierceness of his wrath in hell...He will inflict wrath without any pity. When God beholds the ineffable extremity of your case, and sees your torment to be so vastly disproportionate to your strength, and sees how your poor soul is crushed, and sinks down, as it were, into an infinite gloom; he will have no compassion upon you, he will not forbear the executions of his wrath, or in the least lighten his hand; there shall be no moderation or mercy...Now God stands ready to pity you; this is a day of mercy; you may cry now with some encouragement of obtaining mercy. But when once the day of mercy is past, your most lamentable and dolorous cries and shrieks will be in vain; you will be wholly lost and thrown away of God. Therefore, let every one that is out of Christ, now awake and fly from the wrath to come." This famous and influential sermon can be found in its entirety on many sites online.

581 Love is not just one among the many attributes of God, it is His very essence. The attributes (God is just, merciful, kind, etc.) are all adjectives, in other words, descriptive words, but in the phrase "God is love" (not "God is loving"), love is a noun, which shows that this is a definition of God's essence rather than a description of His character.

to those around him. Considering that sinners increase their measure of guilt, condemnation, and judgment the longer they continue living in sin, the best thing for those who will never repent is to die as soon as possible. Jesus Himself taught this in Luke 17:1,2: "It is impossible that no offenses should come, but woe to him through whom they do come! It would be better for him if a millstone were hung around his neck, and he were thrown into the sea, than that he should offend one of these little ones." These verses teach that it would be "better" for God to put incorrigible sinners out of their misery, but in general God does not do that. He bears patiently with sinners, giving them every opportunity to repent, and considering how those who reject Him provoke, mock and misrepresent Him, the many scriptures that emphasize His longsuffering (patience)[582] are the ultimate understatement. When God finally does pour out His wrath, He has good reasons.

Why Wrath?

One of the reasons for God's wrath is to protect His children from their enemies. The Psalmist pleaded, "Pour out Your wrath on the nations that do not know You...For they have devoured Jacob and laid waste his dwelling place" (Psalms 79:6,7,10). David, hunted by Saul, wrote, "Deliver me from my enemies, O my God...for look, they lie in wait for my life...Consume them in wrath, consume them, that they may not be" (Psalms 59:1,2,13).[583] Because only God can get the right mixture of love for both His children and their enemies, He tells His children to let Him defend them—"Do not avenge yourselves, but rather give place to wrath; for it is written,

'Vengeance is Mine, I will repay' says the Lord."[584]

God may be forced to pour out His wrath on His own children who have given Him permission to intervene in their lives. This can happen if their sin threatens their relationship with Him, in which case He sometimes allows trouble to chasten them and bring them to repentance. Hezekiah warned the people of Judah to learn from the mistakes of their forefathers: "Our fathers have trespassed and done evil in the eyes of the Lord our God; they have forsaken Him, have turned their faces away from the dwelling place of the Lord, and turned their backs on Him...*therefore the wrath of the Lord fell upon Judah and Jerusalem*, and he has given them up to trouble" (2Chronicles 29:6,8,9). The Babylonian captivity was the ultimate example of redemptive wrath: "Because our fathers provoked the God of heaven to wrath, He gave them into the hand of Nebuchadnezzar king of Babylon, who destroyed this temple and carried the people away to Babylon." (Ezra 5:12).[585]

This does not mean that God will continue to inflict redemptive wrath upon those who determinedly reject his chastening. He always respects our free will, and those who reject Him will ultimately be left to the choices they have made. Elihu expressed this reality to Job: "Man is chastened with pain on his bed, and with strong pain in many of his bones, so that his life abhors bread, and his soul succulent food...his soul draws near the Pit, and his life to the executioners...Behold, *God works all these things, twice, in fact, three times* with a man, to bring back his soul from the Pit, that he may be enlightened with the light of

---

582 For example, Numbers 14:18, Psalms 86:15, Romans 2:4, 9:22, 1Peter 3:20, 2Peter 3:9,15.

583 See also Job 34:24-28.

584 Apparently our taking revenge ourselves may actually interfere with the punishment God planned for our enemy—"Do not rejoice when your enemy falls, and do not let your heart be glad when he stumbles; Lest the Lord see it and it displease Him, and He turn away His wrath from Him" (Proverbs 24:17,18).

585 See also Job 19:29, Isaiah 54:8, 60:10, Jeremiah 32:37, Zechariah 7:12-14.

life" (Job 33:19-22, 29,30).

At times God must hide Himself from His people for reasons that they do not understand, and although they may react to this as an expression of His wrath, it is not true wrath because God is neither trying to destroy them nor is He chastening them. The psalmist expressed the separation from God that Jesus experienced when He took the sins of the world upon Himself and felt the sense of the wrath of God: "My soul is full of troubles and my life draws near to the grave…*Your wrath lies heavy upon me* and You have afflicted me with all Your waves…I am shut up and I cannot get out…Lord, why do You hide Your face from me?…I suffer Your terrors; I am distraught. *Your fierce wrath has gone over me*" (Psalms 88:3,7,8,14-16). David, Jeremiah and other prophets experienced the sense of separation from God as wrath as they faced rejection and persecution in response to their acts of faith.[586]

Wrath Brings Sin to an End

God's wrath may protect and chasten His children, but the main end-time purpose of His wrath is to bring an end to sin. "The Lord is the true God…At His wrath the earth will tremble…The gods that have not made the heavens and the earth shall perish from the earth and from under these heavens" (Jeremiah 10:10,11). "Your hand will find all Your enemies, Your right hand will find those who hate You. You shall make them as a fiery oven in the time of Your anger; the Lord shall swallow them up in His wrath and the fire shall devour them" (Psalms 21:8,9).[587]

Since God must bring sin to an end but "is not willing that any should perish, but that all should come to repentance" (2Peter 3:9), His wrath is always the last resort after every effort to bring about repentance has failed. The history of the Israelites when they went into exile is a case in point—"The Lord God of their fathers sent warnings to them by His messengers, rising up early and sending them, because He had compassion on His people and on His dwelling place. But they mocked the messengers of God, despised His words, and scoffed at His prophets, *until the wrath of the Lord arose against His people, till there was no remedy*" (2Chronicles 36:15,16). In fact, God seeks for people to intercede on behalf of sinners so that He will not have to pour out His wrath. "So *I sought for a man* among them who would make a wall, and stand in the gap before Me on behalf of the land, that I should not destroy it, *but I found no one. Therefore I have consumed them with the fire of My wrath*" (Ezekiel 22:30,31).[588]

God calls the destruction of sin and sinners His "strange act" (Isaiah 28:21), strange because He is the source of life and it is His nature to bless. "I have no pleasure in the death of one who dies' says the Lord" (Ezekiel 18:32). To the contrary, "there is joy in the presence of the angels of God over one sinner who repents" because the repentant sinner "has passed from death to life" (Luke 15:10, 1John 3:14). God's plea has always been, "Yield yourselves to the Lord…and serve the Lord your God, that the fierceness of His wrath may turn away from you" (2Chronicles 30:8). "Cast away from you all the transgressions which you have committed, and get yourselves a new heart and a new spirit. For why should you die?" (Ezekiel 18:31).

The Bible definitely does not teach that God's wrath is a way of "getting back at" or "getting even with" those who have displeased him. The

---

586 See also Psalms 89:38-51, 102, Isaiah 60:10, Lamentations 3.

587 See also Deuteronomy 9:8, 29:23, 2Chronicles 19:2, Nahum 1, Zephaniah 1:14-18, John 3:36, Romans 1:18, 2:5-10,12, 4:15, 5:9, Ephesians 5:5,6, Colossians 3:5,6.

588 See also Exodus 32:10, Leviticus 10:6, Numbers 1:53, 16:46, 18:5, 2Chronicles 30:8, Job 42:7,8, Psalms 2:12, 106:23,40.

idea that God would torment people for eternity as a punishment for a life of misbehavior or for rejecting and insulting Him is a complete misrepresentation of God's character. It is true that words such as punishment, vengeance and retribution are used, but a careful study shows that these words are simply an attempt to describe in human terms the indescribable attitude of God when he is forced to bring sin and sinners to an end.

"God keeps covenant and mercy for a thousand generations with those who love Him and keep His commandments; and He repays those who hate Him to their face, to destroy them" (Deuteronomy 7:9,10). God destroys "those who hate Him" because they could never be eternally happy living in a universe without sin; in fact they would spoil the sinless universe with their sin addiction. Thus Paul says, "The Lord Jesus [will be] revealed from heaven with His mighty angels, in flaming fire taking vengeance on those who do not know God, and on those who do not obey the gospel of our Lord Jesus Christ. These shall be punished with everlasting destruction from the presence of the Lord and from the glory of His power when He comes in that Day" (2 Thessalonians 1:6-9). The phrase "everlasting destruction" does not mean everlasting torment, but rather destruction that lasts forever. Jeremiah put it this way: "For the Lord is the God of recompense, He will surely repay… they shall sleep a perpetual sleep, and not awake" (Jeremiah 51:56,57). See 20:11-15 *The White Throne Judgment* for more details.

The seven last plagues in which **"the wrath of God…is filled up"** only come after the gospel has gone to the whole world (Matthew 24:14) and everyone has had a chance to repent. Those destroyed by God's wrath will have stubbornly refused the offers of grace, and God's wrath, rather than bringing repentance, will protect His children who are threatened with death.

15:2-4 The Song of Victory

"And I saw as it were a sea of glass mingled with fire, and those that have the victory over the beast, and over his image, and over his mark, and over the number of his name, standing on the sea of glass, having the harps of God. And they sing the song of Moses the servant of God, and the song of the Lamb, saying, 'Great and marvelous are Your works, Lord God Almighty; just and true are Your ways, King of saints. Who will not fear You, O Lord, and glorify Your name? For You only are holy; for all nations shall come and worship before You, for Your judgments have been revealed" (Revelation 15:2-4).

The victorious ones, who have been facing the death decree in connection with the mark of the beast, are pictured standing before the throne on a sea of glass just as the plagues are about to be poured out. This does not mean that they have been raptured to heaven and will watch the time of trouble[589] from a safe vantage point out of harms way. As in Revelation 7:14, the use of the present participle (Greek *nikontas*, having the victory) suggests that they are still in the process of having victory over the beast (See 7: *In Heaven while on Earth*). By faith they are before the throne, while the plagues are falling all around them. Although their lives seem to be in jeopardy, their attention is totally focused on God rather than themselves: **"Great and marvelous are Your works, Lord God Almighty! Just and true are Your ways, King of saints! Who will not fear You, O Lord, and glorify Your name? For You only are holy."**

Their question, **"Who shall not fear You, O Lord, and glorify Your name?"** suggests that this group includes those who have responded to

---

589 Daniel 12:1, Matthew 24:21.

the three angels' messages which began with the admonition, "Fear God and give glory to Him" (Revelation 14:7). They are singing **"the song of Moses, the servant of God, and the song of the Lamb."** Moses led the children of Israel from Egyptian slavery in the midst of plagues that were similar to the seven last plagues,[590] and they also were pursued (by the Egyptian army). God fought for the them during the crossing of the Red Sea, just as He will fight for His people in the Battle of Armageddon (See 16:16 *The Battle of Armageddon*). When they were safe on the other side Moses led them in a song of victory recorded in Exodus 15:1-21. It was a song of praise for the greatness and excellence of the Lord, declaring His mighty attributes: "I will sing to the Lord, for He has triumphed gloriously…Your right hand, O Lord, has become glorious in power…and in the greatness of Your excellence You have overthrown those who rose against you…Who is like You, O Lord, among the gods? Glorious in holiness, fearful in praises, doing wonders?"

The **"song of the Lamb"** that they sing along with the **"song of Moses"** probably refers to the songs recorded in Revelation 5: 9-13: "They sang a new song, saying: 'You are worthy…for You were slain, and have redeemed us to God by Your blood…Worthy is the Lamb that was slain to receive power, and riches, and wisdom, and strength, and honor, and glory, and blessing!" The great multitude singing the **"song of Moses… and the song of the Lamb,"** which include the declaration, **"All nations shall come and worship before You,"** are prime examples and emphasize of one of the most important themes in the Book of Revelation: worship.

What Is False Worship?

The heart of Revelation (chapters 13 and 14) shows that worship is a dominant issue in the great controversy. The Greek word for worship used in the Book of Revelation is *proskuneo* which means to bow down before one who is superior. Satan, in his effort to elevate himself above God, seeks the worship that only God deserves by making images that reflect his principles and character and imposing them through deceit or coercion. God, in contrast, is worthy of worship because of His infinite knowledge, power, creativity, and character of love; He only prohibits worship of others because it leads to grief and destruction.

On the "devil's side" of the great controversy in Revelation is false, blasphemous worship—"All the world marveled after the beast. So they worshiped the dragon…and they worshiped the beast." "And he…causes the earth and those who dwell therein to worship the first beast, whose deadly wound was healed…he had power to give life to the image of the beast…and cause that as many as would not worship the image of the beast should be killed." (Revelation 13:3,4,12,15). Meanwhile, on God's side the 144,000 are shown worshiping "before the throne," and then giving the three angels' messages which include the command, "Fear God and give glory to Him… and *worship Him* who made heaven and earth." They also give the fearful warning, "If anyone worships the beast…He also shall drink of the wine of the wrath of God" (Revelation 14:7,9,10). Thus the issue of true and false worship is literally a life and death matter.

The beast from the earth will set up an image and try to force all people to worship it. This is reminiscent of the image king Nebuchadnezzar set up in ancient Babylon, and a review of that story in Daniel chapter three reveals some of the elements of false worship.

First of all, Nebuchadnezzar's new religion

---

590 Both the Egyptian and the seven last plagues mention water turning to blood, darkness, sores and frogs .

required the worship of a created god rather than God the Creator: "Nebuchadnezzar the king made an image of gold" (Daniel 3:1). The Ten Commandments strictly forbid the worship of anything created. The first commandment ("You shall have no other gods before me," Exodus 20:3) forbids the worship of any "god" created by the true God, including the sun or other heavenly bodies, animals, plants, bodies of water, geographical features or intelligent beings such as angels or people. The second commandment ("You shall not make for yourself a carved image—any likeness of anything…you shall not bow down to them nor serve them," Exodus 20:4,5), forbids the worship of anything made by man, whether the worship is of the object itself or of something or someone (including God) represented by the object.[591]

Nebuchadnezzar's image was set up in rebellion against God. God had revealed to Nebuchadnezzar in a dream an image made of four metals that informed him that there would be a succession of kingdoms, which would ultimately be destroyed by the true God of heaven. Nebuchadnezzar, refusing to accept the fact that his kingdom would ever pass away, created his image all of gold. He said nothing about the true God, even though he had previously acknowledged that He is "the God of gods and the Lord of kings" (Daniel 2:47). Thus a second element of false worship is that it involves disobedience to God and to His Word.[592]

The important officials who were called to worship the image had no personal relationship with the god/image. "King Nebuchadnezzar sent word to gather together the satraps, the administrators, the governors, the counselors, the treasurers, the judges, the magistrates, and all the officials of the province, to come to the dedication of the image" (Daniel 3:2). This was the first time they had ever seen the god, but they still bowed down and worshiped it during the ceremony. This is a third element of false worship—it is not dependent on a personal relationship with God that includes the daily prayers, Bible study and fellowship that true Christians have. Instead it has its basis in the worship experience or ceremony itself.[593]

A fourth element of false worship is that music or other sensory input is used to create an emotional atmosphere and experience. "At the time you hear the sound of the horn, flute, harp, lyre and psaltery, in symphony with all kinds of music, you shall fall down and worship the gold image" (Daniel 3:4,5). The emotions of reverence, gratitude and love which should come about from the presence of the Holy Spirit are brought about by music and spectacle.[594]

A fifth characteristic is the absence of teaching. The true worship of the children of Israel included instruction about God and His plan of salvation through the sacrifices and symbols of the sanctuary that foreshadowed the sacrifice of Christ. At the dedication of Nebuchadnezzar's image there was no teaching about the new god, his character, his deeds or his plans for mankind—the only instruction had to do with the

---

591 Paul emphasized this in Romans 1. "The wrath of God is revealed from heaven against all ungodliness and unrighteousness of men, who suppress the truth in unrighteousness…although they knew God, they did not glorify Him…[they] worshiped and served the creature rather than the Creator" (Romans 1:18-25).

592 Rebellious worship is the heart of Satan's desire. He was willing to give up the whole world if only Jesus would bow down and worship him—"If you will worship before me all will be yours" (Luke 4:5-8).

593 Eternal life is based upon a personal relationship with Jesus— "This is eternal life, that they may know You, the only God, and Jesus Christ whom You have sent" (John 17:3). In the judgment many who claimed to be filled with the power of God will be rejected because they did not know God (Matthew 7:22,23).

594 This kind of emotional worship was characteristic of the worship of the golden calf (Exodus 31:1-6, 17-19) and of the priests of Baal (1 Kings 18:26-29).

required worship behavior of the people. True Christian worship always involves teaching and revelation that edifies the worshipers. "Whenever you come together each of you has a psalm, has a teaching, has a tongue, has a revelation, has an interpretation. Let all things be done for edification" (1Corinthians 14:26). The sermons of Peter and Paul acknowledged the hopelessly sinful nature of man, the offer of salvation through the life, sacrifice, resurrection and mediation of Christ, and the necessity of holiness through faith. False worship avoids the subject of sin and repentance,[595] and even if there is a focus on the Cross of Christ, it is a general or emotional appeal that does not touch the pet sins of the worshipers.

A particularly repugnant element of false worship is that it involves threats. "And whoever does not fall down and worship shall be cast immediately into the midst of a burning fiery furnace" (Daniel 3:6). Much worship today includes the underlying threat that God is ready to throw those who do not please Him into ever-burning fire. Preachers vividly portray the terrors of the time of trouble, which can supposedly be avoided by being ready for the "rapture" now. And of course the death decree will be the dominant feature of the worship of the image of the beast.

In summary, false worship is directed toward the creation rather than the Creator, allows or includes disobedience to God's Word, does not require a personal relationship with God, is primarily an emotional experience enhanced by sensory input such as music and spectacle, avoids the subject of personal sin, and includes an overt or implied threat of punishment or death for those who do not worship in the prescribed manner. Unfortunately, it is not just pagans who

offer false worship; these characteristics can even come to dominate "Christian" worship.

What True Worship Is and Is Not

True worship, the kind offered by the faithful in Revelation 14 and 15, is just the opposite of the false worship offered in Babylon. First of all, true worship is directed to God the Father, Son and Holy Spirit and to Him alone. Although this would seem to be so obvious that it wouldn't need mentioning, in actuality it is easy for creature worship to creep into what is intended to be worship of God. We see this in the adoration given to people who seem to be filled with the Spirit and power of God, whether they be living individuals who perform miracles and works of healing, or of holy individuals (saints) who have supposedly passed on to a higher realm where they can answer petitions and prayers. Worship of the creature can also take place when honor and adoration are given to symbols or art that represent God; the object itself can be transformed in the minds of the worshipers from a representation into a power object that is itself sought as a source of benefit or healing. This kind of worship is seen in the multitudes who flock to a shrine where a particular piece of art or a relic has supposed miracle working power. But true worship does not focus on a representation of God or of a great man of God—it focuses on God.

True worship has its basis in faith and obedience to God—"Here are those that keep the commandments of God and the faith of Jesus" (Revelation 14:12). While true worshipers may stumble and fall, they will not cherish known sin in their hearts. "He who says, 'I know Him' and does not keep His commandments is a liar, and the truth is not in him" (1John 2:4). This does not mean that sinners should avoid God until they can get their sin problems straightened out. We

---

595 Jeremiah wrote, for example, "Your prophets have seen for you false and deceptive visions; they have not uncovered your iniquity" (Lamentations 2:14).

should come to God, especially when we have sinned, not to gloss over our sin with a feel-good religious experience, but to confess our sins and receive forgiveness, cleansing and power to overcome. This is the heart of worship as we recognize our own sinfulness and need, and God's goodness and mercy.

Besides individual sin, we must be certain that our worship does not involve institutional sin that is an integral part of our church. In chapter 13 we saw that a major area of disobedience in the last days will be the substitution of a false day of worship for the Sabbath of the fourth commandment. We have also considered the idolatry that is an integral part of many Christian denominations.

True worship springs from an intimate relationship with God—"These are they who follow the Lamb wherever He goes" (Revelation 14:4). True worshipers do not ignore God all week and then come to a service to get "pumped up." The psalmist said "I will bless the Lord *at all times*, His praise shall *continually* be in my mouth" (Psalms 34:1). Corporate worship is not a substitute for personal worship, and likewise personal worship does not negate the need for worshiping and having fellowship with the Body of Christ.

Regarding music in worship, from the examples in Revelation it is obvious that music is a vital part of true worship. The worshipers of chapter 15 **"sing the song of Moses…and the song of the Lamb,"** and songs of worship and praise fill the Psalms and the Book of Revelation. True worship is not characterized by tired, stale music, but is fresh and touches the emotions ("They sang as it were a new song before the throne" Revelation 14:3). On the other hand, it should not be a noisy cacophony that relies on powerful instruments and driving rhythm to artificially ignite the emotions—this was characteristic of the false worship of Babylon with "the horn, the flute, harp, lyre, and psaltery, in symphony with all kinds of music" (Daniel 3:5).

True worship is characterized by clear Bible teaching that focuses on the sacrifice of Jesus for the guilty sinner. The evil and pervasive nature of evil is exposed and contrasted to the holiness of God. There is preaching and teaching from the Word of God that exposes popular sins and cuts the sinner to the heart, causing him to fall down in repentance and be covered by the cleansing blood of Jesus. True worship encourages the worshipers to "wash their robes and make them white in the blood of the Lamb" (Revelation 7:14). And it teaches the truth about God's character and kingdom principles and exposes the errors and lies that Satan seeks to propagate.

Finally, God does not use threats to force anyone to worship Him. Instead of threatening, He warns of the consequences of worshiping false gods, and appeals to all to "worship Him who made heaven and earth, the sea and the springs of water" (Revelation 14:7).[596]

Other common features of worship are practiced in many churches but are not characteristic of true worship. As mentioned already, true worship does not include bowing before any man, creature or object. John, overwhelmed by the visions the angel had presented, "fell at his [the angel's] feet to worship him, but he said…'See that you do not do that! I am your fellow servant, and of your brethren who have the testimony of Jesus. Worship God!" (Revelation 19:10).[597] The apostle Peter (who according to Catholic theology

---

596 It is true that Revelation 14:9-11 gives a severe warning against those who engage in false worship, but there are no threats against those who do not engage in true worship. This represents the difference between a threat to force obedience and warnings of inevitable consequences.

597 This is in striking contrast to the practice in the Catholic and Orthodox churches where the worshipers bow before statues or icons of the saints who are believed to be as angels in heaven, waiting to intercede for us. This theme of not worshiping angels was so important that it was repeated again in Revelation 22:8,9.

was the first pope) refused to allow Cornelius to bow down to him—"Cornelius met him and fell down at his feet and worshiped him. But Peter lifted him up, saying, 'Stand up; I myself am also a man.'"[598]

Although many of the great men of faith who are now worshiped as saints had already died by the time the Bible was written,[599] there is no instance of anyone in the New Testament worshiping or praying to any saint. Aaron in the wilderness made a golden calf, which was supposed to be a visible representation or symbol of the Lord,[600] but God rejected this and every instance of trying to represent Him with a visible object of worship (Exodus 32). Indeed, the second commandment states clearly, "You shall not make for yourself a carved image—any likeness of anything that is in heaven above, or that is in the earth beneath, or that is in the water under the earth; you shall not bow down to them" (Exodus 20:4,5). Bowing down before people, "holy relics" or works of religious art is not a part of true worship.

The focus on someone other than God can even become the dominant theme of prayers and hymns. For example, in the Catholic Church one of the most important private prayers is the "Hail Mary," which says, "Hail Mary, full of grace, the Lord is with you. Blessed are you among women, and blessed is the fruit of your womb, Jesus. Holy Mary, mother of God, pray for us sinners now and at the hour of our death. Amen." This prayer is repeated over and over by supplicants desiring a worship experience or offering penance for sins. But nearly all of the prayer focuses on "the mother of God" and "us sinners" rather than God. The repetition of the prayer itself is a focus on self, my sin and my need for mercy, in effect denying the fact that mercy has already been granted at the Cross and is applied as soon as we ask—not after hundreds or thousands of repetitions.[601]

True worship is not a social hour in which the "worshipers" focus on each other. Although there should be a time for social interaction among Christians, it should not take the place of worship which is focused on God. Certainly a worship service that is so dry and predictable that the "spectators" feel free to use it as a time to catch up on the latest gossip is not worship at all.

Worship Like They Have in Heaven

The Book of Revelation shows that the true worship that is offered by the angels and heavenly creatures is totally directed toward God, thanking Him, praising Him, acknowledging the attributes of His character and nature. For example, in chapter 4 the living creatures and twenty-four elders worship, saying, "You are worthy, O Lord, to receive glory and honor and power; for You have created all things, and for Your pleasure they are and were created" (Revelation 4:11). Any mention of the creature who has received benefit is secondary, with the primary focus on the One who saved them—"You were slain, and have redeemed us to God by your blood out of every tribe, and tongue, and people, and nation; and

---

598 The apostle Paul also refused to allow obeisance. See Acts 14:8-18.

599 For example, in the Orthodox and Catholic churches, John the Baptist, Stephen and James are considered saints, but in the New Testament, which was written after their deaths, there is no mention of anyone directing prayers, petitions or worship toward them.

600 Aaron made the calf, but did not proclaim a feast to a new god, but rather "made a proclamation and said, 'Tomorrow is a feast to the Lord'" (Exodus 32:5).

601 The repetition of "Lord have mercy on me" could be considered a violation of the third commandment ("You shall not take the name of the Lord your God in vain") because the very repetition shows a lack of faith in God to grant what He has promised. Jesus warned, "When you pray, do not use vain repetitions as the heathen do, for they think that they will be heard for their many words" (Matthew 6:7).

have made us to our God kings and priests; and we shall reign on the earth" (Revelation 5:9,10). But even as they mention the exalted role God has prepared for them (kings and priests!), their the focus quickly shifts back to God—"Worthy is the Lamb that was slain to receive power, and riches, and wisdom, and strength, and honor, and glory, and blessing!" (v. 12) Worship in heaven is a continual anthem of praise.

Some of the attributes of God that are themes of praise in the Book of Revelation are His love, holiness, worthiness, power, creativity, riches, wisdom, strength, honor, glory, might, eternal existence, justice, truth, righteousness, salvation, omnipotence, sovereignty, tenderness, purity, brightness, and grace. These attributes should not be lists to rattle off in prayer; instead, each is a theme of contemplation and praise.

In general, Christians are much more proficient at offering confession, thanksgiving and petition than at offering praise, yet praise is the type of worship that is being offered continually in Heaven![602] Satan, "the ruler of this world," makes every effort to distract us from praising our Creator so that he can continue to sit on the throne of our hearts and affections.[603] But through praise God's people evict the usurper so that God can sit on His rightful throne—"You are holy, enthroned in the praises of Israel" (Psalms 22:3).[604]

When we come to God in worship, we expect to receive a blessing. But one of the most astounding teachings of the book of Psalms (in numerous verses) is that when we praise God we are actually a blessing to Him! For example, the psalmist begins Psalm 104 with the words, "Bless the Lord, O my Soul!" Then he goes on to praise the wonderful things about the Lord: His creation, His love and care of His creatures, His plan to bring an end to sin, ending again with "Bless the Lord, O my soul! Praise the Lord!" When we consider that most of what God gets from humanity is insults, misrepresentations, blame for bad situations and requests for favors, it is no wonder that it is a blessing for God to hear someone say something nice about Him. And this is what true worship is all about: acknowledging the truth about God's goodness and love.

Jesus said, "The true worshipers will worship the Father in spirit and truth; for the Father is seeking such to worship Him. God is Spirit, and those who worship Him must worship in spirit and truth" (John 4:23,24). Those who are not filled with the Holy Spirit cannot really worship God. They may go through the motions, and with the right combinations of music, prayers and preaching there may be a level of emotional experience. However, without the Holy Spirit there will not be a true encounter with God.[605]

Jesus emphasized that we must worship in both "Spirit *and* truth," and the truth about God is expressed in doctrines. Today many Christians say that they do not want to talk about doctrine, just about Jesus. But the question is, what Jesus? There are plenty of evil spirits that seek worship for themselves in the name of Jesus. Doctrine is simply a statement of what we believe about God, and without it each person has his own private version of who God is and what He is like. The

---

602 With thanksgiving we enter the door of the heavenly sanctuary, but it is praise that brings us into His presence—"Enter into His gates with thanksgiving, and into His courts with praise" (Psalm 100:4).

603 John 12:31, 14:30, 16:11.

604 God places such a high value on human free will that He only sits on the throne of the church and the individual by invitation. This characteristic of God was illustrated by David, the "man after [God's] own heart." Although anointed king of Israel, he refused to try to oust King Saul. Even after his death David did not take the throne until Israel invited him to (2 Samuel 5:1-5). Later, when his son Absalom claimed the throne, David simply left town and did not return until the people asked him to (2Samuel 19:9-14).

---

605 Chapter 3:22 elaborates on how to be filled with the Holy Spirit.

trinity, for example, is a doctrine that says that Jesus really is God, not just a good man who lived two thousand years ago. Many false doctrines give such a negative picture of God that it is nearly impossible to worship Him in love and adoration. For example, the teaching that God will torment forever those who do not please Him makes it very difficult to love Him. It is no wonder that millions of Christians prefer to worship the mother of Christ, hoping that she will be more sympathetic and will be able to entreat mercy from her Son, who will in turn intercede with the Father. The more we understand the "truth as it is in Jesus" (Ephesians 4:21), the more we will be able to break through the cloud of religiosity and enter the presence of God.

Through worship and praise our hearts can be lifted up from the earth and its problems to the heavenly realm. This is the meaning of the invitation, "Come boldly to the throne of grace" (Hebrews 4:16). One author[606] has given the example of a small child with his father in a crowded elevator. From his perspective the world consists of knees, purses and backsides, and he is getting bumped, squished and stepped on. But when he looks up and cries, "Daddy, lift me up," he opens the way for a new perspective. This is what worship does—through songs and prayers of thanksgiving and praise we can enter emotionally and by faith into the heavenly realms before the throne of God, and from that perspective we can see that our earthly concerns are not as significant as they seemed. This is the experience of **"those that have the victory over the beast, and over his image, and over his mark, and over the number of his name"** who are seen **"standing on the sea of glass, having the harps of God. And they sing the song of Moses the servant of God, and the song of the Lamb, saying, 'Great** and marvelous are Your works, Lord God Almighty; just and true are Your ways, King of saints. Who will not fear You, O Lord, and glorify Your name? For You only are holy; for all nations shall come and worship before You, for Your judgments have been revealed .'"** (Revelation 15:1,2).

15:5 The Tabernacle of the Testimony

"And after that I looked, and, behold, the temple of the tabernacle of the testimony in heaven was opened" Revelation 15:5. This verse refers to the Old Testament "tabernacle of the testimony"[607] which was the original tabernacle set up by Moses. It was called the tabernacle of the *testimony* because it contained the "ark of the testimony"[608] (the "ark of the covenant")[609] which had the "testimony" inside. The testimony was the law of God on two tablets of stone, the Ten Commandments.[610] As we saw at the beginning of this chapter, this verse, which focuses on the law of God, is one end of the "inclusio" that highlights chapters 12-14. The other end is Revelation 11:19, "the temple of God was opened in heaven, and the ark of His covenant was seen in the temple," again highlighting the ark with the Ten Commandments inside.

Thus both ends of the inclusio emphasize the law of God. Moreover, the chiastic structure shows that the three chapters highlighted by this inclusio are the climax of Revelation. Within the climax passage (chapters 12-14) God's people are twice characterized as keepers of the law—"Here are those who keep the commandments of God"

---

606 Tommy Tenney, *God's Eye View* (Nashville, TN, Thomas Nelson) 2002

607 See Exodus 38:21, Numbers 1:53, 10:11.

608 Exodus 25:22, 26:33,34, 30:6, 26, et.al.

609 Numbers 10:33, 14:44, 10:8, Deuteronomy 31:9, 25, 26 et. al.

610 Exodus 25: 16, 21, 31: 18, 32: 15, 34: 29, 40: 20.

(Revelation 12:17, 14:12). The mark and the number of the beast were shown in chapter 13 to be integrally related to God's law, specifically the Sabbath command, and the fourth commandment was quoted in Revelation 14:7. The Sabbath will be a major end-time issue, not because God is "picky" about a day, but because it is the "seal" in the midst of the law—it gives God's name ("the Lord your God"), the extent of His dominion (the heavens and the earth, the sea and all that is in them") and the basis of His authority as the Creator and source of the law. The Book of Revelation ends with the promise, "Blessed are *they that do His commandments*, that they may have the right to the tree of life, and may enter in through the gates into the city" (Revelation 22:14).

This commentary has emphasized the law of God because of the obvious emphasis in the Book of Revelation. Most modern Christian books focus on faith, love and the grace of God, and this book has had much to say about those themes as well. But few modern books focus on the law or the wrath of God, and no doubt some readers have concluded that this book has a legalistic orientation. But an emphasis on the law of God is not necessarily legalistic.

Why Emphasize the Law?

The Book of Revelation has such a focus on the law because the theme of Revelation is the great controversy between God and Satan. A main point of Satan's original challenge was that the law of God is unnecessary and restrictive.[611] This is why he is called "the lawless one"[612] and this is why he has worked fiendishly from the beginning of time to get people to break God's law. But hypocrite that he is, his true aim is to set up his own law—the beast, carrying out Satan's

agenda, seeks to change God's law, and makes his law a legal requirement to obey or be killed. Satan's goal from the beginning was to take God's place and receive the worship and obedience that only God deserves.

There is no question that the law can never save anyone, nor can it change us, make us holy or make us acceptable to God. Those who attempt to gain favor with God by keeping the commandments have not understood the gospel and are legalists, not Christians. The apostle Paul said, "Walk in the Spirit, and you shall not fulfill the lusts of the flesh…If you are led by the Spirit, you are not under the law" (Galatians 5:16, 18). But it is equally clear that the law must be included with the gospel. Sinners are sinners because they have broken the law of God. The sacrifice of Christ is necessary because we have not obeyed God's law. The dramatic and sickening increase of sin both in the world and in the church shows that Satan's lawless agenda has conquered the world. Paul said, "We know that the law is good if one uses it lawfully, knowing this, that the law is not made for a righteous person, but for the lawless" (1 Timothy 1:9).

Unfortunately, even in the church there are lawless, unconverted people, as well as people who have been tempted and fallen into sin and others who have unconsciously wandered away from Jesus. For this reason the law is essential, even for Christians. "By the law is the knowledge of sin" (Romans 3:20). "The law was our tutor, to bring us to Christ that we might be justified by faith" (Galatians 3:24). As long as there is sin in the world and in the church and there are people who wander away from Christ, the law must be presented along with grace, faith and the gospel. One of the great deceptions of the last days is that the law has been done away with. In the new covenant the Spirit writes the law in our hearts, and in carrying out the will of God we are simply carrying out our own desires.

---

611 The first temptation in the Garden of Eden basically said that it was not necessary or even desirable to obey God's law.

612 2 Thessalonians 2: 3-12, 1 John 3: 4-8.

In the very heart of the Book of Revelation God confronts this deception: "Here are they who keep the commandments of God and the faith of Jesus" (Revelation 14:11). This message is needed now more than ever before—"It is time for you to act, O Lord, for they have regarded your law as void" (Psalms 119:126). The open **"temple of the tabernacle of the testimony in heaven"** directs attention to the neglected commandments of God.

15:5-8 The Close of Probation

In Revelation 11:14 the pivotal announcement was made, "the second woe is past. Behold, the third woe is coming quickly." The first two woes are the anger and strife of nations, while the third is the wrath of God—"The nations were angry, and Your wrath has come…that you should reward Your servants…and should destroy those who destroy the earth." The wrath of God, announced in Revelation 11:18, is declared in Revelation 15:1 to be **"The seven last plagues, for in them is filled up the wrath of God."**

The first announcement of the wrath of God was accompanied by the statement, "the temple of God was opened in heaven, and there was seen in His temple the ark of His covenant" (Revelation 11:19). Then followed chapters 12-14 which elaborated on the players and events of the great controversy. John returns to the chronological timeline in the same way he left it, with the announcement, **"The temple of the tabernacle of the testimony in heaven was opened."** But the temple is not opened to provide access to God's mercy; it is opened so that the seven angels with **"seven golden bowls full of the wrath of God"** can come out to "pour out the bowls of the wrath of God on the earth" (Revelation 15:7, 16:1). As soon as the angels have come out, the temple is closed to access—**"And the temple was filled with smoke from the glory of God, and from His power; and no one was able to enter into the temple, until the seven plagues of the seven angels were fulfilled"** (Revelation 15:8). In order to understand what is happening here we need to study the three Old Testament passages that refer to a cloud filling the temple so that no one could enter.

Nearly 25% of the book of Exodus is concerned with the building of the wilderness tabernacle. "When Moses finished the work, then the cloud covered the tabernacle of meeting, and the glory of the Lord filled the tabernacle, and Moses was not able to enter the tabernacle of meeting because…the glory of the Lord filled the tabernacle" (Exodus 40:33,34). The cloud filled the tabernacle when the work of building it was completed. Now the church is God's temple;[613] God is building His people as "living stones" into a "spiritual house" through the ministry of the Holy Spirit (1Peter 2:5). The temple is "finished" when God's people reach the "unity of the faith" and "the fullness of Christ" (Ephesians 4:9-13).[614] Applying this to Revelation 15:8, when Christ has "finished the work" of perfecting the church, the cloud of glory will fill the heavenly tabernacle and no one will be **"able to enter the temple till the seven plagues…[are] fulfilled."**

The same theme is found in the inauguration of Solomon's temple, with the emphasis specifically on the unity of God's people. "When the trumpeters and singers were as one, to make one sound to be heard in praising and thanking the Lord…the house of the Lord, was filled with a cloud, so that the priests could not continue

---

613 "You are the temple of the living God. As God has said, 'I will dwell in them and walk among them. I will be their God, and they shall be My people" 2Corinthians 6:16. See also 1Corinthians 3:16, Ephesians 2:19-22.

614 "To each one of us grace was given…for the equipping of the saints for the work of ministry, for the edifying of the body of Christ, till we all come to the unity of the faith and of the knowledge of the Son of God, to a perfect man, to the measure of the stature of the fullness of Christ" (Ephesians 4:9-13).

ministering because of the cloud; for the glory of the Lord filled the house of God" (2Chronicles 5:13,14). The cessation of the temple ministry by the priests was associated with unity and perfect worship by the "trumpeters and singers" who were "as one…in praising and thanking the Lord." If we apply this passage to Revelation 15:8, when God's people reach the unity of worship and praise that characterized the early church, the temple of God in heaven will be **"filled with… the glory of God."** Then the seven last plagues will be poured out, which will protect God's people from their enemies and prepare the way for the Second Coming of Christ.

The same event is recorded in 1Kings 8. There it says that the priests took the ark of the covenant into the Most Holy Place, "and it came to pass, when the priests came out of the Holy Place, that the cloud filled the house of the Lord, so that the priests could not continue ministering because of the cloud" (1Kings 8:10,11). In all three passages, when the cloud filled the temple, the ministry in the temple came to an end, and this passage emphasizes that this happened when the priests came out of the Most Holy Place.[615] Jesus is our great high priest in the heavenly sanctuary (Hebrews 8:1,2), and he is constantly mediating for sinners, applying the merits of His sacrifice on behalf of those who repent of their sins (Hebrews 7:25). He will continue to do so until everyone on earth who ever will repent has repented. Then He will "stand up" (Daniel 12:1) and leave the Most Holy Place, ending His ministry of mediation to bring sinners to repentance.

Considering these three passages together and applying them to the end of time, when God's church has reached the perfection of unity and worship, then Jesus, our high priest, will end His ministry of intercession and will leave the Most Holy Place of the heavenly sanctuary. By this time the ministry of the two witnesses (the 144,000 who will proclaim the three angels' messages[616]), will have done its work. Everyone on earth will have made their choice, as reflected in the solemn announcement, "He that is unjust, let him be unjust still; and he that is filthy, let him be filthy still; and he that is righteous, let him be righteous still; and he that is holy, let him be holy still. And, behold, I am coming quickly, and my reward is with me, to give every one according as his work shall be" (Revelation 22:11,12). This has been called the "close of probation," when the Lord's work of intercession is finished.

Isaiah 26:21,22 shows that when "the Lord comes out of His place" (finishes His ministry of mediation) it initiates a brief final period when the work of God's people for sinners will have ended. They will "hide themselves" in the safety of Jesus' protection, and God Himself will punish Satan and bring iniquity to an end. "Come, my people, enter your chambers, and shut your doors behind you; hide yourself, as it were, for a little moment, until the indignation is past. For behold, *the Lord comes out of His place*[617] to punish the inhabitants of the earth for their iniquity; the earth will also disclose her blood, and will no more cover her slain. In that day the Lord with His severe sword, great and strong, will punish Leviathan the fleeing serpent [Satan]" (Isaiah 26:20-27:1). The rest

---

615 This is consistent with the ceremonies on the Day of Atonement: when the high priest came out of the Most Holy Place, he was finished making atonement for the people and from then he made atonement for the temple itself and assigned punishment to the scapegoat, who represented Satan, the instigator of sin (See Leviticus 16:17-22 and 4: *The Day of Atonement*).

616 These are different aspects of the same end-time work of calling the great multitude out of spiritual Babylon.

617 The Hebrew word for place, *maqown*, is used to designate the place for the Ark of the Covenant (2Samuel 6:17, 1Kings 8:6,7,21, 1Chronicles 15:1, 3). 2Chronicles 5:7 makes it clear that this is the Most Holy Place of the Sanctuary: "Then the priests brought in the ark of the covenant of the Lord to its place (*maqowm*), into the inner sanctuary of the temple, to the Most Holy Place, under the wings of the cherubim.

of the book of Revelation deals with the events
after probation has closed, when the impenitent,
spurred on by the devil, will try to annihilate
God's people, who will be protected by the wrath
of God and the Second Coming of Christ.

"Then I heard a loud voice from the temple saying to the seven angels,
'go and pour out the bowls of the wrath of God on the earth" Rev. 16:1
Woodcut by Lukas Cranach 1522

Chapter 16

Revelation 16:1-21

16:1 And I heard a loud voice out of the temple saying to the seven angels, "Go, and pour out the bowls of the wrath of God on the earth."

16:2 And the first went, and poured out his bowl on the earth; and a terrible and grievous sore came on the men who had the mark of the beast, and on those who worshiped his image.

16:3 And the second angel poured out his bowl on the sea; and it became as the blood of a dead man, and every living creature in the sea died.

16:4 And the third angel poured out his bowl on the rivers and springs of waters; and they became blood.

16:5 And I heard the angel of the waters say, "You are righteous, O Lord, who are, and who were, O Holy One, because You have judged these things.

16:6 For they have shed the blood of saints and prophets, and You have given them blood to drink; for they are deserving."

16:7 And I heard another out of the altar saying, "Even so, Lord God Almighty, true and righteous are your judgments."

16:8 And the fourth angel poured out his bowl on the sun; and power was given to him to scorch men with fire.

16:9 And men were scorched with great heat, and blasphemed the name of God, who has power over these plagues; and they did not repent to give him glory.

16:10 And the fifth angel poured out his bowl on the throne of the beast; and his kingdom was full of darkness, and they gnawed their tongues because of the pain,

16:11 And blasphemed the God of heaven because of their pains and their sores, and did not repent of their deeds.

16:12 And the sixth angel poured out his bowl on the great river Euphrates; and its water was dried up, that the way of the kings of the east might be prepared.

16:13 And I saw three unclean spirits like frogs come out of the mouth of the dragon, and out of the mouth of the beast, and out of the mouth of the false prophet.

16:14 For they are the spirits of devils, working miracles, which go forth to the kings of the earth and of the whole world, to gather them to the battle of that great day of God Almighty.

16:15 "Behold, I come as a thief. Blessed is he that watches, and keeps his garments, lest he walk naked, and they see his shame."

16:16 And he gathered them together to the place that in Hebrew is called Armageddon.

16:17 And the seventh angel poured out his bowl into the air; and there came a great voice out of the temple of heaven, from the throne, saying, "It is done."

16:18 And there were voices, and thunders, and lightning; and there was a great earthquake, such as had not occurred since men were on the earth, so mighty an earthquake, and so great.

16:19 And the great city was divided into three parts, and the cities of the nations fell. And Babylon the Great was remembered before God, to give to her the cup of the wine of the fierceness of His wrath.

16:20 And every island fled away, and the mountains were not found.

16:21 And huge hailstones weighing about a talent fell out of heaven on men; and men blasphemed God because of the plague of the hail, because that plague was exceedingly great.

16:1-7 The First Three Plagues

"And I heard a loud voice out of the temple saying to the seven angels, 'Go, and pour out the bowls of the wrath of God on the earth.' And the first went, and poured out his bowl on the earth; and a terrible and grievous sore came on the men who had the mark of the beast, and on those who worshiped his image. And the second angel poured out his bowl on the sea; and it became as the blood of a dead man, and every living creature in the sea died. And the third angel poured out his bowl on the rivers and springs of waters; and they became blood" (Revelation 16:1-4).

In chapter 8 we saw the similarities between the trumpet plagues and the seven last plagues. However, although there are striking similarities, the obvious differences show that they are not the same events. Although the first trumpet and the first plague are both poured out on the earth, the second are both poured on the sea and the third are both poured on the rivers and springs of water, the nature of the trumpet plagues and the seven last plagues themselves are very different.

The first three trumpets had a lot in common—burning fire, either in the form of hail, a mountain, or a star, falling and contaminating (turning to blood) a third of the environment that they fell on. The first of the seven last plagues, however, has its affect on "men who had the mark of the beast and on those who worshiped his image," causing a "grievous sore" (Revelation 16:2). This points out one important difference: the first plague takes place after the image and mark of the beast are in place, whereas the first trumpet occurs after the sealing of the 144,000 (Revelation 7:1-8), but before the image and mark of the beast.

Moreover, there is no clear indication that the trumpet plagues cause direct damage to people[618] until the fifth trumpet (the first "woe"). In contrast, the very first of the seven last plagues directly affects those with the mark of the beast, causing "a terrible and grievous sore." These sores

---

618 The fiery hail, burning mountain and poisonous star of the first three plagues damage trees, grass, water and ships. Many people died from drinking the poisonous water, but this was indirect rather than direct damage. There may have been people killed who were in the forests, fields or ships but it is not mentioned.

will apparently be so painful (causing those who have them to **"gnaw their tongues because of the pain"** v. 10) that they will effectively divert the attention of the beast followers away from their goal of persecuting the true worshipers of God. In 15: *The Wrath of God* we saw that one of the main purposes of God's wrath is to protect God's people from their enemies, and the progressive nature and increasing intensity of the seven last plagues seems designed to disrupt the plan of the beast kingdom, which is to "cause that as many as would not worship the image of the beast should be killed." (Revelation 13:15).

Another important difference is that the trumpet plagues are of limited scope: "A third of the sea became blood,…a third of the living creatures in the sea died,…a third of the waters became wormwood,…a third of the [sun, moon and stars] were darkened" and so on (Revelation 8:7-12). The seven last plagues, on the other hand, seem to be universal in scope. The whole sea **"became as the blood of a dead man; and every living creature in the sea died"** (Revelation 16:3) and all **"the rivers and springs of water…became blood"** (Revelation 16:4) and the whole **"kingdom…of the beast…was full of darkness"** (Revelation 16:10)

Moreover, the fact that "a third" is prominently emphasized in the trumpets is an indication that they are the activity of Satan, which God allows (See 8: *The Trumpets*). The angels sound the trumpets to warn of the trumpet plagues, whereas in chapter 16 the angels actually pour out the seven last plagues, showing that **"God… has power over these plagues"** (Revelation 16:9) and they constitute His wrath (See 15:1).

The Purpose of the Plagues

The trumpet plagues are allowed by God to bring sinners to repentance and, together with the ministry of the two witnesses, ultimately result in the salvation of a great multitude (See chapter 11). In contrast, the seven last plagues take place after the close of probation and do not result in repentance. To the contrary, they **"blasphemed the God of heaven because of their pains and their sores, and did not repent of their deeds."** (Revelation 16:9,11,21).

Although the primary purpose of the seven last plagues is to protect God's people, those who are affected fully deserve the terrible conditions they experience in the plagues—**"And I heard the angel of the waters say, 'You are righteous, O Lord, who are, and who were, O Holy One, because You have judged these things. For they have shed the blood of saints and prophets, and You have given them blood to drink; for they are deserving.' And I heard another from the altar saying, 'Even so, Lord God Almighty, true and righteous are your judgments"** (Revelation 16:5-7).

This does not mean that God is finally giving sinners all that they deserve. One of the primary characteristics of God is that He *does not* give us what we deserve, and as fearful as the seven last plagues are, they are but a fraction of the punishment these persecutors of God's people would receive if they really reaped the fullness of what they have sown. This will not be fully revealed until after "the thousand years are finished." Then they will stand before the "great white throne" and "the books [will be] opened" (Revelation 20:5,11,12). When the records are revealed, no one will ever be able to accuse God of giving them more punishment than **"they are deserving."**

The remarkable similarity of the seven last plagues with the plagues of Egypt during the time of Moses shows their purpose: the deliverance of God's people. (See Table 16.1)

Table 16.1

Seven Last Plagues	Plagues of Egypt
"a terrible and grievous sore" (Revelation 16:2).	"Boils that break out in sores" (Exodus 9:9).
"Water…became blood" (Revelation 16:3,4).	"All the waters that were in the river were turned to blood" (Exodus 7:14-24).
"His kingdom was full of darkness" (Revelation 16:10).	"There was thick darkness in all the land of Egypt" (Exodus 10:21-29).
"Three unclean spirits like frogs" (Revelation 16:13).	"Frogs shall come up on you" (Exodus 8:1-14).
"Huge hailstones…fell out of heaven upon men" (Revelation 16:21).	"The Lord rained hail on the land of Egypt" (Exodus 9:13-36).

God's blessing upon the children of Israel caused them to prosper and multiply in the land of Egypt, but a "new Pharaoh" who, by his own admission did not know the Lord,[619] considered them to be a menace to his kingdom. They went from being a favored people to being slaves until finally they were threatened with annihilation.[620] But when the situation appeared hopeless, God intervened in a miraculous way with the plagues, which led to the deliverance of His people and the destruction of their enemies who had risen up against them.[621]

Likewise, the beast coalition will seek to coerce God's people into worshiping the image of the beast through economic sanctions ("no one may buy or sell" Revelation 13:17) and will ultimately seek to exterminate them ("As many as would not worship the image of the beast [would] be killed" v. 15). As we saw in chapter 9, Satan will exploit the trumpet plagues that he has brought about, convincing the followers of the beast that it is God's people who are responsible for their

suffering because of their stubborn refusal to "worship the image of the beast." With the death decree in force, it will appear that all of God's people are about to become martyrs. But God, through the seven last plagues, will thwart the plans of **the dragon,…the beast, and…the false prophet,** and bring about a miraculous deliverance of His people.

16:8-11 The Fourth and Fifth Plagues

"And the fourth angel poured out his bowl on the sun; and power was given to him to scorch men with fire. And men were scorched with great heat, and blasphemed the name of God, who has power over these plagues; and they did not repent to give him glory. And the fifth angel poured out his bowl on the throne of the beast; and his kingdom was full of darkness, and they gnawed their tongues because of the pain, and blasphemed the God of heaven because of their pains and their sores, and did not repent of their deeds" (Revelation 16:8-11).

As we saw in 8: *Trumpets: Literal or Symbolic?*, there is no reason to believe that the seven last plagues are not essentially literal. Real sores will

---

619 Exodus 5:2.

620 Exodus 1:8-22.

621 The kingdom of Egypt was destroyed by the plagues, and the army which pursued the children of Israel was drowned in the Red Sea. See Exodus 14.

cause real pain, the literal sun[622] will radiate scorching heat and there will be literal darkness. This is not to say that there are no symbolic elements (such as the great river Euphrates, kings from the east and unclean spirits like frogs in verses 12 and 13), but in general chapter 16 does not use the highly symbolic language of, for example, chapter 17 with its beasts and horns.

The fourth and fifth plagues affect the sun; first it is too powerful, causing scorching heat, and then it is blotted out, causing the beast kingdom to be in darkness. The Babylon form of worship of the beast kingdom is a continuation of the sun worship that has been one of the primary forms of false worship all through the ages. In chapter 13 we saw that one of the main issues, the mark of the beast, involves Sunday worship, and the plagues will be poured out **"upon the men who [have] the mark of the beast,"** in other words, on those who obey the Sunday law instituted by the image of the beast. The first Sunday law, instituted by the Emperor Constantine, referred to "the venerable day of the sun," and in fact the beast religious system is a direct descendent of the Mithraic sun worship which was prominent in pagan Rome during the first centuries of the Christian era.[623] During the plagues of Egypt, God used multitudes of frogs and water becoming blood to expose the powerlessness of the Nile River god which was worshiped by the Egyptians. Likewise the plagues involving the sun demonstrate the futility of modern sun worship.

This is not to say that there are cults of

modern people who bow down to the rising sun. The essence of sun worship is the worship of that which is created rather than the Creator, and in the thousands of cultures which exist in the world there are that many variations of how people offer the best of their time, talents and energies on the altar of that which is created. In western societies today this manifests itself in the relentless quest to earn and spend money on consumer items such as houses, cars, expensive toys and hobbies. These things will all be swept away during the time of trouble, but that will not be the end of "sun worship." With the traumatic and supernatural events that will commence with the trumpet plagues, the whole world will become religious fanatics, desperately seeking for the right combination to make the painful chaos go away. Unfortunately, the majority will opt for creature worship, finding their answers in rituals, ceremonies, sacrifices, and painful, humiliating or difficult service, all held together by the glue of false doctrine that has its roots clear back to Babylonian sun worship. Before the close of probation a great multitude will come out of this false system, but those who remain will fully demonstrate their hopeless incorrigibility; they will **not repent and give Him glory** but rather will **"blaspheme the God of heaven because of their pains and their sores"** (Revelation 16:9,11).

16:12 The Kings from the East

"And the sixth angel poured out his bowl on the great river Euphrates; and its water was dried up, that the way of the kings of the east might be prepared" (Revelation 16:12). The Euphrates was the river that ran through ancient Babylon, providing the water it needed to exist. It was dried up when Cyrus, emperor of the Persian Empire, diverted the river so that his troops could enter and conquer Babylon through the dry riverbed. Thus the drying up of the river Euphrates points to the downfall of Babylon.

---

622 The King James and New King James versions use the pronoun "he" for the sun, as if it were a person rather than an inanimate object. However, the Greek word for sun (*ilio*) is masculine so the pronoun (*autos*) is also masculine. Most other versions recognize this and use "it" rather than "he," for example, "The fourth angel poured his bowl on the sun, and it was allowed to scorch them with fire" (New Revised Standard).

623 See Bacchiocchi, "From Sabbath to Sunday" (Biblical Perspectives, Berrien Springs, MI. 1977) chapter 8.

Babylon at the time of the seven last plagues is the international religious system led by the "beast," which, through the sophistry of Satan, manages to "deceive the whole world" (Revelation 12:9). Waters in Revelation represent "peoples, multitudes, nations and tongues,"[624] so the drying up of the river Euphrates would represent the time when the people of the world will suddenly wake up and realize that they have been deceived and will withdraw their support from the Babylon religious system.

The previous (fifth) plague was poured **"on the throne of the beast and his kingdom was full of darkness"** (v.10), striking right at the heart of the beast system. Just as the plague of darkness in Egypt only affected the Egyptians while the people of God "had light in their dwellings" (Exodus 10:21-24), so this darkness will only affect **"the beast and his kingdom."** The deceived masses will finally begin to understand that they have been on the wrong side, that the "god" they have been serving has no power to protect them, and that instead God is protecting the saints who are being attacked by their politico-religious system. This is elaborated on in chapter 17, where the great harlot (the false church) is shown riding or controlling the "scarlet beast" (the political system). But the final manifestation of the scarlet beast, symbolized by ten horns, will in the end turn against the harlot—"the ten horns… shall hate the harlot, and shall make her desolate and naked, and shall eat her flesh, and burn her with fire" (Revelation 17:16). This quantum shift in thinking will prepare the way for **"the kings from the east."**

There has been much speculation as to the players in the drama of Revelation 16, especially those connected with the Battle of Armageddon such as **"the kings from the east,"** with most of the attention focused on China. Although this commentary has correlated the seven trumpets with the last great war between the King of the North and the King of the South, which apparently takes place in the Middle East,[625] and it is possible that China could be involved, the Battle of Armageddon will be much more universal in nature. It is Satan's last attempt to exterminate God's people wherever they may be found. The evidence indicates that **"the kings from the east"** are not the armies of earthly superpowers; they represent the "armies of heaven" (Revelation 19:14), coming to earth on a rescue mission.

The phrase **"from the east"** is found in only one other place in the Book of Revelation: "And I saw another angel ascending *from the east*, having the seal of the living God" (Revelation 7:2). It is clear in this verse that it is a messenger from God's kingdom who comes from the east. Moses, Aaron and his sons, and the faithful tribe of Judah all camped on the east side of the tabernacle (Numbers 2:3, 3:38), and the children of Israel entered the Promised Land from the east (See Joshua 4:19). "The glory of the God of Israel came from the way of the east…and the glory of the Lord came into the temple by way of the gate which faces toward the east" (Ezekiel 43:2,4). All of these verses indicate that it is God's kingdom that comes from the east.

The "King of kings," Jesus, is the One **"from the east"** and this verse refers to the Second Coming of Christ.[626] In some sense His coming is **"prepared"** by the drying up of **"the great river Euphrates."** The multitudes of the world (**"the great river Euphrates"**) will realize that they have been deceived by Babylon. In a flash

---

624 Revelation 17:15.

625 See 9:3 *The Locust Army.*

626 Jesus Himself said, "For as the lightning comes from the east and flashes to the west, so also will the coming of the Son of Man be." Matthew 24:27

of insight they will see that they have been fighting against their Creator, and they will cry "to the mountains and rocks, 'fall on us and hide us from the face of Him who sits on the throne and from the wrath of the Lamb!" (Revelation 6:16). The use of the plural (***kings* of the east**") shows that Jesus does not come alone. Christ comes with "the armies of heaven" who "followed him on white horses" (Revelation 19:14) These armies no doubt include kings such as the 24 elders who "sang a new song, saying, 'You…have made us kings and priest to our God; and we shall reign on the earth" (Revelation 5:9,10).

16:13 The Unholy Trinity

"**And I saw three unclean spirits like frogs come out of the mouth of the dragon, and out of the mouth of the beast, and out of the mouth of the false prophet**" (Revelation 16:13). This verse reveals the unholy trinity of the very end of time, Satan's counterfeit of the Holy Trinity. This trinity is the mastermind as well as the visible leadership of end-time Babylon in the final attempt to defeat God's people.

"**The dragon**" is clearly Satan, "the great dragon…that ancient serpent, called the Devil, and Satan, who deceives the whole world" (Revelation 20:2, 12:9). "The whole world" includes every people and every religion, so this is the "god" of the heathen, who uses the countless forms of spirit manifestations which pervade Buddhism, Hinduism, Islam, animism, secular superstition and New Age, taking in the majority of the world's teeming multitudes.

"The beast" will be more clearly identified in chapter 17, which depicts the final manifestation of the Babylon system. He is "the beast that…was, and is not, and will ascend out of the bottomless pit and go to perdition…the beast is himself also the eighth" of a series of last day "kings" (Revelation 17:8,11). John "saw the beast, and the kings of the earth, and their armies, gathered together to make war against Him that sat on the horse [Jesus], and against His army. And the beast was captured, and…cast alive into a lake of fire burning with brimstone" (Revelation 19:19,20). Chapter 19 will more clearly describe the Second Coming of Christ as "King of kings and Lord of lords" and shows how Jesus will destroy the forces that oppose Him, which will be led by an actual person, called "the beast."

This same personage is seen in 2 Thessalonians 2:3-10—"The man of sin…[who] sits as God in the temple of God, showing himself that he is God…The lawless one will be revealed, whom the Lord will consume with the breath of His mouth and destroy with the brightness of His coming. The coming of the lawless one is according to the working of Satan, with all power, signs, and lying wonders, and with all unrighteous deception among those who perish." This is Satan's counterfeit of Christ, the final antichrist who will deceive the whole world, with the exception of those who have received the seal of God and have refused the mark of the beast.

"**The false prophet**" is closely identified with the beast from the earth with the two horns like a lamb but who spoke like a dragon (Revelation 13:11-16). (See Table 16.2)

This beast/false prophet was identified in 13:11,12 *The Beast from the Earth* as an American union of church and state which will deceive the masses of the world and impose the worship of the papal "beast." But he is more than just a political system. During the time of trouble there will be both the beast religio-political system and "the beast" (antichrist) who is a personification of the system. It is therefore likely that the false prophet will also be a person, a powerful, miracle-working religious leader of apostate American Protestantism. He will probably be elected president because the image of the beast is the union of church and state, and is modeled

Table 16.2

Beast from the Earth	False Prophet
"He exercises all the authority of the first beast in his presence" (Revelation 13:12).	"The false prophet who worked signs in his [the beast's] presence" (Revelation 19:20).
"He performs great signs…and he deceives" (vs. 13,14).	"Worked signs…by which he deceived" (v. 20).
"He causes all…to receive…the mark or the name of the beast" (vs. 16,17).	"He deceived those who received the mark of the beast" (v. 20).
"He was granted power to give breath to the image of the beast" (v. 15).	"He deceived those…who worshiped his [the beast's] image" (v. 20).

after the papacy where the pope is both political and religious leader.

Thus the unholy trinity will consist of:

- Satan the dragon in his invisible, pervasive form, "the prince of the power of the air" (Ephesians 2:2), revealing himself with spiritualistic manifestations.
- The beast who will arise out of the Roman Catholic wing of the Babylon system and will be the visible leader of the anti-Christ coalition.
- The false prophet with his American (Protestant) miracle-working religion and military might, who enforces the worship of the beast.

Whatever earthly manifestations there may be, there is a demonic element that will give diabolical intensity and effectiveness to the plans of the satanic trinity. **"And I saw three unclean spirits like frogs come out of the mouth of the dragon, and out of the mouth of the beast, and out of the mouth of the false prophet."** There is only one other place in scripture that mentions

frogs:[627] the second plague of Egypt. Moses had shown Pharaoh miracles to convince him to let God's people go free from their slavery. Pharaoh refused, and so God through Moses told him, "The river shall bring forth frogs abundantly, which shall go up and come into your house, into your bedroom, on your bed, into the houses of your servants, on your people, into your ovens, and into your kneading bowls. And the frogs shall come up on you, on your people, and on all your servants" (Exodus 8:3,4).

The emphasis is on the ubiquity of the frogs. They were everywhere and there was no getting away from them. In Satan's last demonic attack he will throw everything he has at God's people, both earthly and demonic resources. From 2 Peter 2:4 we learn that many of the fallen angels have been kept in "chains of darkness" in "hell" (Greek *tartarus*[628]), which no doubt corresponds to the abyss or "bottomless pit" that the legion of demons begged Jesus not to send them into (Luke 8:30,31). But during the time of trouble

---

627 The story is in Exodus 8:1-15 and is referred to in Psalms 78:45, 105:30.

628 This word for the hell that imprisons the fallen angels is unique to this scripture.

God allows the bottomless pit to be opened,[629] releasing the demons who have been imprisoned there, so that Satan will have his full forces at his disposal, hell-bent on deceiving the impenitent and destroying the righteous. Just like the frogs of Egypt, the demonic forces and manifestations will be everywhere.

The plague of frogs was also the last miracle that the Egyptian magicians were able to counterfeit. By imitating through tricks and the power of Satan the miracles of Moses (turning his rod into a serpent, turning water into blood and bringing frogs out of water, Exodus 7:11,22, 8:7), the magicians hardened Pharaoh's heart in disbelief. But with the next plague (turning the dust of Egypt into lice), "the magicians so worked with their enchantments to bring forth lice, but they could not...Then the magicians said to Pharaoh, 'this is the finger of God'" (Exodus 8:16-19). Thus frogs represent Satan's last successful effort to deceive. The whole web of trickery and occult power perfected through the centuries will still be highly effective through the "unclean spirits like frogs," but it is on the verge of unraveling in total defeat.

16:14 Demons Performing Signs

"For they are the spirits of devils, working miracles, which go forth to the kings of the earth and of the whole world, to gather them to the battle of that great day of God Almighty" (Revelation 16:14). Many of the great religions of the world have pointed to signs and miracles as proof of their validity. Historically this has been particularly true of the Roman Catholic and Orthodox Churches with miracle-working relics and icons, supernatural apparitions of the Virgin Mary or other saints,[630] and pilgrimage destinations such as Lourdes in France and Tinos in Greece where miraculous cures take place. More recently the Pentecostal movement has swept through the whole world with a strong emphasis on signs and miracles such as speaking in tongues, personal prophecies and healings.[631] An underlying assumption is that since the miracles cannot be explained by science and are beneficial for the recipients, they must be from God. But the Bible teaches that particularly at the end of time Satan will use signs and miracles to deceive the multitudes into going along with his program.

"The coming of the lawless one is according to the working of Satan, with all power, signs,

---

629 See 9:1,2, *The Bottomless Pit.*

630 Texts such as Ecclesiastes 9:5,10 ("The dead know nothing... There is no work or device or knowledge or wisdom in the grave," see also Psalms 6:5, 155:17, 146:4, Job 14:12) prove that dead people, including the saints, do not have a conscious existence before the resurrection. Therefore the miracles performed by the departed "saints" must have their origin elsewhere. While it is conceivable that God could have pity on petitioners who seek help in ignorance, in many cases demons pose as saints in order to get worship for themselves and to spin webs of deception which they use to divert people's attention from God and Jesus.

631 Pentecostal meetings often break all the rules that the apostle Paul laid out when he confronted a similar misguided emphasis on selected spiritual gifts in Corinth—more than one person speaks in tongues at once, there is no interpreter, there is disorderly confusion (1Corinthians 14:27-33). This calls into question God's presence as the source of the miracles that are performed.

and lying wonders, and with all unrighteous deception among those who perish, because they did not receive the love of the truth" (2 Thessalonians 2:9,10). The context of this passage is an exposition about "the lawless one… whom the Lord will consume with the breath of His mouth and destroy with the brightness of His coming" (v. 8); in other words, this passage refers to the period of time immediately preceding the Second Coming of Christ. Although Satan has been active all through human history, he has been restrained from fully exercising his power—"You know what is restraining, that he may be revealed in his own time" (v.6). Because of Satan's challenges, a full demonstration of both Satan's evil principles and of God's righteousness and love must take place. But God has delayed this, because billions of people all over the world do not have enough information about God to make an intelligent judgment.

However, when "the everlasting gospel" has been preached "to every nation, tribe, tongue, and people" (Revelation 14:6), then God can allow the final demonstration of Satan's principles and character. "This gospel of the kingdom will be preached in all the world as a witness to all the nations, and then the end will come" (Matthew 24:14). "You know what is restraining… for the mystery of lawlessness is already at work, only He who now restrains will do so until He is taken out of the way. And then the lawless one will be revealed" (2 Thessalonians 2:6-8).

God allows deceptive miracles, but it is important to note that the people who are deceived are those who have rejected God's truth. "God will send them strong delusion, that they should believe the lie, that they all may be condemned who did not believe the truth, but had pleasure in unrighteousness" (vs. 11,12). In these verses we see that God does not design that anyone should be lost. Deception is the final stage of a process which starts with having "pleasure

in unrighteousness," and then proceeds to a refusal to "believe the truth" about God—truth that is also a rebuke to the sin they do not want to forsake. Unfortunately for the sinner, it is the truth that condemns sin which also reveals the deceptions of the enemy of souls. When sinners reject God's Word they reject His refuge of safety. In His discourse on the end of time in Matthew 24, Jesus warned three times against deceptive miracles in the last days—"False christs and false prophets will rise and show great signs and wonders to deceive, if possible, even the elect" (Matthew 24:24, see also vs. 4,5,11).

At the same time, God's people will manifest the power of the Holy Spirit to an extent that has not been seen since Pentecost. The prophet Joel prophesied that God will pour out His Spirit and "Your sons and your daughters shall prophesy, your old men shall dream dreams, Your young men shall see visions…the sun shall be turned into darkness and the moon into blood, before the coming of the great and awesome day of the Lord" (Joel 2:28-31). "And these signs will follow those who believe: In My name they will cast out demons, they will speak with new tongues, they will take up serpents and if they drink anything deadly it will by no means hurt them; they will lay hands on the sick, and they will recover" (Mark 16:17,18).

Today rational science is skeptical of all that cannot be explained scientifically, but the very end of time will be characterized by undeniable signs, wonders and miracles. In particular, the beast from the earth of Revelation 13:11 "[will] perform great signs, so that he even makes fire come down from heaven on the earth in the sight of men. And he deceives those who dwell on the earth by those signs" (Revelation 13:13,14). What this means for God's people is that they cannot rely on miracles as proof of God's working. The Bible says that spectacular miracles will be performed through the power of Satan! How essential that we heed John's admonition, "Beloved, do not believe every spirit, but test the spirits, whether they are of God; because many false prophets have gone out into the world" (1John 4:1). "To the law and to the testimony! If they do not speak according to this word, it is because there is no light in them" (Isaiah 8:20).

16:15 Coming as a Thief

In the midst of the descriptions of the plagues, the suffering of the unrepentant, and the deceptive activity of the unholy trinity, a sober warning to God's people is interjected. **"Behold, I come as a thief. Blessed is he that watches, and keeps his garments, lest he walk naked, and they see his shame"** (Revelation 16:15).

This warning echos Jesus' admonition in Luke 12, "You yourselves be like men who wait for their master, when he will return from the wedding…Blessed are those servants whom the master, when he comes, will find watching…and if he should come in the second watch, or come in the third watch, and find them so, blessed are those servants. But know this, that if the master of the house had known *what hour the thief would come, he would have watched* and not allowed his house to be broken into. Therefore you also be ready, for the Son of Man is coming at an hour you do not expect" (Luke 12:35-40).

Jesus cautions His servants that there will be an apparent delay. It seems that they were watching faithfully through the first "watch." But as the second, and perhaps even the third watch of the night passes, there may be a tendency to feel, "My master is delaying His coming," and to fall into sin, "to beat the male and female servants and to eat and drink and be drunk" (v. 45). This is such a dangerous possibility that the apostles Peter, Paul and John all mention the need to be watchful so

that the end would not come "like a thief."[632]

The message to the Laodicean church shows that before the time of trouble the church is sleepy and indifferent, "neither cold nor hot" (Revelation 3:15). The Lord councils them, "buy from me white garments, that you may be clothed, that the shame of your nakedness may not be revealed" (v. 18). White garments represent the righteousness of Christ which is imputed and imparted to them,[633] the **"garments"** that Jesus councils His children to **"keep."**

The events leading up to the time of trouble will bring the sleepy Laodiceans to attention. Some will become a part of the 144,000 who give the final invitation, others will become a part of the great multitude that will be called out of Babylon, and unfortunately, many will choose to remain in Babylon. All will be deeply affected by the experience of living through the "great tribulation, such as has not been since the beginning of the world" (Matthew 24:21). But the time of trouble will not be over in a few days. Just one of the trumpet plagues (the fifth) continues for five months, and there are six other trumpets and seven last plagues. The stress will be unbelievable, and hopes will be raised and dashed with reports, "Look, here is the Christ…Look, He is in the desert…Look, He is in the inner rooms… False christs and false prophets will rise and show great signs and wonders to deceive, if possible, even the elect" (Matthew 24:23-26).

At that time God's people will need to **"keep their garments."** All that they are and all that they have attained is a gift of God's grace made possible through the perfect life, sacrifice and resurrection of Christ, which has been given to them freely as a robe to "wear." "I will greatly rejoice in the Lord, My soul shall be joyful in my

---

632 See 1Thessalonians 5:2-4, 2Peter 3:10, Revelation 3: 3.

633 See 3:18 *Buy from Me.*

God; For He has clothed me with the garments of salvation, He has covered me with the *robe of righteousness*" (Isaiah 61:10). To lose their garments and become naked is a symbol of spiritual defeat. The ultimate humiliation, reserved for defeated soldiers, was to be paraded naked before the populace of their conquerors.[634]

God's people are not automatically immune from defeat, even (or perhaps especially) during the time of trouble. Only through the indwelling of the Holy Spirit and deep dependence on God's Word can Christians **"Keep [their] garments"** amid the overwhelming delusions of the time of trouble. Without this, Jesus will come **"as a thief,"** revealing the nakedness and shame of their empty and meaningless profession. This is why one of the key messages to God's people is, "Here is the *patience* of the saints: here are those who keep the commandments of God and the faith of Jesus" (Revelation 14:12).

16:16 The Battle of Armageddon

"And he gathered them together to the place that in Hebrew is called Armageddon" (Revelation 16:16). The battle of Armageddon is rivaled only by the mark of the beast as a theme that piques the public interest. The mass media versions usually have nothing to do with the Biblical issues involved. The battle of Armageddon is simply the culmination of Satan's great controversy with God and his last attempt to destroy God's people before the Second Coming of Christ.[635] The history of this controversy has already been detailed in previous chapters, but an

overview will help put the battle of Armageddon into its context.

The controversy began sometime before the creation of the world when "Lucifer, son of the morning…said in [his] heart: 'I will ascend into heaven, I will exalt my throne above the stars of God…I will be like the Most High'" (Isaiah 14:12-14). "That ancient serpent, called the Devil and Satan" was "in Eden, the garden of God" where he precipitated the fall of Adam and Eve and all of their descendents afterward (Revelation 12:9, Ezekiel 28:13, Genesis 3). Not content to limit his fiendish activities to this earth, Satan imposed his presence into the heavenly councils where he brought grief and perplexity by accusing God, His government and His children "day and night" (Job 1,2, Zechariah 3:1-3, Revelation 12:10). The Book of Revelation picks up the story after the crucifixion, resurrection and ascension of Jesus, when "war broke out in heaven…and the dragon fought and his angels; and they did not prevail…and Satan, who deceives the whole world…was cast to the earth, and his angels were cast out with him" (Revelation 12:7-9), in other words, he no longer had access to heaven. "When the dragon saw that he was cast to the earth, he persecuted the woman…and to the woman were given two wings of a great eagle, that she might fly into the wilderness" (Revelation 12:13,14). This was the medieval period during which the apostate church, the "beast rising out of the sea…was given authority to continue for forty-two months…to make war with the saints and to overcome them" (Revelation 13:1,5,7 NKJV).[636] During the Middle Ages, the Roman Catholic Church utilized "holy" wars, crusades, campaigns against heretics and the inquisition to maintain her power and influence. But John saw "one of his heads as if it was wounded to death"

---

634 Isaiah 20:4, 2Samuel 10: 4,5.

635 It will be seen in chapter 20 that this is not Satan's last attempt to war against God. After the millennium, when the unrepentant have been resurrected, he will make one last desperate attempt (See 20:7-10).

636 See 2: *Thyatira* and chapter 13 for a more detailed history of the papal period.

(Revelation 13:3)—with the Protestant reformation and particularly the French and Italian revolutions, the oppressive stranglehold was broken. This allowed the great reforms of the nineteenth century (the Philadelphia period) described in chapter 3. But "his deadly wound was healed" (Revelation13:3)—the apostate religious system recovered its political power, and Satan began to put into place his plans for his last great effort.

Daniel and Jesus called the final struggle the "time of trouble such as never was" (Daniel 12:1, Matthew 24:21). The time of trouble is summarized in the pivotal text Revelation 11:18, "the nations were angry, and your wrath has come, and the time of the dead, that they should be judged, and to give the reward to your servants the prophets, and to the saints, and to those who fear your name, small and great; and to destroy those who destroy the earth." In this text we see that the time of trouble is divided into two phases. "The nations were angry" refers to the first six trumpet plagues. "Your wrath has come" refers to the seven last plagues.

The trumpets are Satan's attempt to use war and chaos to create the conditions in which he can destroy God's people and thwart God's plans. But during this time the ministry of the two witnesses (described in chapter 11) results in the winning of a great multitude who come out of Babylon—a crushing defeat for Satan.

By this time Babylon will have a new and important ally—"another beast coming up out of the earth; and he had two horns like a lamb, and he spoke like a dragon" (Revelation 13:11).[637] The United States of America began as a haven of democracy and religious liberty. But Revelation 13:11-17 predicts that the United States will enforce the agenda of the beast, including the war against the saints

The apostate American "Protestants" will set up "an image to the beast" (a union of church and state like the medieval papacy), that will deceive the multitudes "by the means of those miracles which he had power to do in the sight of the beast." It will force "them that dwell on the earth, to make an image to the beast, which had the wound by a sword, and lived" (Revelation 13:11-14). Economic pressure will be brought to bear against those who refuse to receive the mark of the beast [638] ("no one could buy or sell, except he that had the mark...of the beast" Revelation 13:17). But it is the death threat ("as many as would not worship the image of the beast should be killed" Revelation 13:15) which provokes the seven last plagues. This is the second phase of the time of trouble—"You have taken Your great power...and Your wrath has come, and the time...to destroy those who destroy the earth" (Revelation 11:18).

The plagues of sores, blood, scorching heat and darkness will throw Satan's kingdom into disarray, severing the allegiance of the masses to the Babylon religious leaders (the drying up of the river Euphrates). But Satan is not finished yet. Sending **"three unclean spirits like frogs...to the kings of the earth and of the whole world,"** the unholy trinity will **"gather them to the battle of that great day of God Almighty...and he [will gather] them together to the place that in Hebrew is called Armageddon."** In this text Satan's armies are gathered in **"Armageddon"** to fight against God's people, but the battle itself takes place in chapter 19: "And I saw heaven opened, and behold a white horse; and He that sat on him was called Faithful and True, and in righteousness He judges and makes war...And I saw the beast, and the kings of the earth, and their armies, gathered together to make war

---

637 See chapter 13:11,12 *The Beast From The Earth.*

638 In chapter 13:11-18 the mark, name and number of the beast are identified, which the beast from the earth will set up.

against Him that sat on the horse, and against His army. And the beast was captured, and with him the false prophet that worked miracles before him, with which he deceived those that had received the mark of the beast…And the rest were slain with the sword of Him that sat on the horse" (Revelation 19:11-14, 19-21).

What or where is **"the place that in Hebrew is called Armageddon?"** In order to understand the symbolism we must study three battles that took place on three mountains near the ancient Hebrew city of Megiddo.

Three Mountains and Armageddon

The above overview shows that the battle of Armageddon is much more than a military battle at a particular site in Palestine. The word "Armageddon" is unique to this scripture, and although its meaning is not perfectly clear, many scholars believe it is from the combination of the Hebrew words *har* (hill or mountain) and *Megiddon* (the city of Megiddo). The fact that Megiddo is located in the plain of Esdraelon rather than on a mountain implies the symbolic nature of the name, so the meaning should be found in Old Testament passages that deal with Megiddo and the mountains and battles associated with it. There are actually three mountains, Mt. Tabor, Mt. Moreh and Mt. Carmel, which surround Megiddo, each of which is associated with a battle and an important and miraculous victory for God's people. A review of these battles reveals the true nature of the Battle of Armageddon.

At the time when Deborah, a prophetess, was the "judge" of Israel the Canaanites under Jabin "harshly oppressed the children of Israel," enforcing their domination with nine hundred iron chariots (Judges 4:3). Deborah "called for Barak the son of Abinoam…and said to him, 'Has not the Lord God of Israel commanded, 'Go

and deploy troops at Mount Tabor…I [God] will deploy Sisera, the commander of Jabin's army, with his chariots and his multitude at the river Kishon; and I will deliver him into your hand" (vs. 6.7). Barak was afraid and said he would not go up to fight unless Deborah went with him. She agreed, but informed him that a woman would get the glory for the victory!

"Then Deborah said to Barak, 'Up! For this is the day in which the Lord has delivered Sisera into your hand. Has not the Lord gone out before you?' So Barak went down from Mount Tabor with ten thousand men following him. And the Lord routed Sisera and all his chariots and all his army" (Judges 4:15). Sisera himself was killed, not in battle, but by a simple village woman named Jael, who pierced his skull with a hammer and tent peg while he was sleeping. [639]

Deborah composed a song to commemorate the victory that shows the link to the Battle of Armageddon: "The kings came and fought… in Taanach, by the waters of Megiddo…they fought from the heavens; the stars from their courses fought against Sisera" (Judges 5:19-22). In the final battle of Armageddon real armies will be gathered to carry out the death sentence which has been pronounced against God's people, but "the stars from their courses" will fight. Angels, the "armies in heaven…on white horses" (Revelation 19:14) will fight for God's people and will utterly destroy those who are pursuing them. From this battle we learn that God's people in the Battle of Armageddon will be humble and apparently weak, but unexpectedly courageous (Deborah and Jael). However, the real victory will be a supernatural rescue from heaven ("the stars…fought").

The second mountain of Megiddo, Mt. Moreh, is the site where Gideon fought against

---

639 Judges 4:17-23.

the hoards of Midian. The Midianites were "as numerous as locusts"[640] and they "would come up with their livestock and their tents…and they would enter the land to destroy it" (Judges 6:5). The "Angel of the Lord"[641] appeared to Gideon, commanding him "Go in this might of yours, and you shall save Israel from the hand of the Midianites" (Judges 6:14). However, the victory had nothing to do with "this might of yours" and everything to do with the mighty power of God!

Gideon was first commanded to get rid of the idols in his own family (Judges 6:25-32). The assignment to go and attack the Midianites was so far beyond his own capabilities that he wondered if he was really hearing the Lord correctly, and God patiently provided miraculous signs so that he could move forward with confidence and courage (vs. 36-40). Gideon sent messengers to gather an army; 32,000 men responded, "but the Lord said to Gideon, 'The people who are with you are too many for Me to give the Midianites into their hands, lest Israel claim glory for itself against Me, saying, "My own hand has saved me" (Judges 7:2). God commanded him to send home those who were fearful, but the 10,000 who remained were still too many. God designed a strict selection process—only those who drank water "on the run" were accepted, and this resulted in an army of only 300 men! (Judges 7:1-7).

"The camp of the Midianites was…by the hill of Moreh in the valley…[Gideon] divided the three hundred into three companies, and he put a trumpet into every man's hand, with empty pitchers, and torches inside the pitchers… Then the three companies blew the trumpets and broke the pitchers—they held the torches in their left hands and the trumpets in their right hands for blowing…When the three hundred blew the trumpets, the Lord set every man's sword against his companion throughout the whole camp; and the army fled" (Judges 7:16-22).

From this story we learn that God's people in the Battle of Armageddon are totally dependent on Him, and rid their lives of every idol that might block the flow of His power. They are diligent to be sure they are hearing the Lord correctly, but when sure of His will they are fearless and ready for action. They are filled with the Holy Spirit (the torches) but they are only able to shine by being broken, as predicted by Daniel, "When the power of the holy people has been completely shattered, all these things shall be finished" (Daniel 12:7).[642] With their trust and confidence fully severed from themselves and resting in the Lord, they blow the trumpet—they proclaim God's final message to the world. The beast and his Babylonian followers are enraged, but in the face of overwhelmingly hopeless odds, the Lord wins a great victory as His enemies are routed, turn on one another,[643] and are destroyed.

The third and most prominent mountain of Meggido is Mt. Carmel. During the time of the prophet Elijah, King Ahab, spurred on by the wicked queen Jezebel, established the worship of Baal and Asherah in Israel and "Jezebel massacred the prophets of the Lord" (1Kings 18:4). God commanded Elijah to announce a drought, and then to hide by the Brook Cherith where he was fed by the birds until the brook dried up. He was then supported by a heathen widow until God told Him it was time to go confront the idolaters who ruled His people.

Elijah told Ahab, "gather all Israel to me on Mount Carmel, the four hundred and fifty

---

640 Judges 6:5, 8:10.

641 The Angel of the Lord (Judges 6:11,22) was actually the Lord Himself (vs. 14,23).

642 See sections 10: *The Shattering of the Power of the Holy People* and 11:7-10 and 11:11-13).

643 Both 16:2 *The Kings from the East* and 17:12-18 *Ten Horns and the Harlot* show that the Babylon coalition will ultimately unravel and the players will turn against one another even as they continue to pursue the "saints."

prophets of Baal and the four hundred prophets of Asherah who eat at Jezebel's table" (v. 19). The people were so confused that when Elijah called on them to decide who they would follow "the people answered him not a word" (v. 21). Elijah proposed a test: there would be two sacrifices, and the god who answered by bringing fire down from heaven would be their God. The heathen priests confidently expected that they would be able to work their usual miracles, and called upon Baal in an all-day worship service, leaping and dancing and crying out, even injuring themselves, but the humiliating impotence of their "god" was exposed—"there was no voice; no one answered, no one paid attention" (vs. 26-29).

"Elijah said to all the people, 'Come near to me'...and he repaired the altar of the Lord that was broken down" (v.30). So that everyone would know that there was no trickery, water was poured on the sacrificial animal until the water ran down over the wood, the altar, and filled up a trench around the altar. Then Elijah called upon the Lord, saying "Hear me, O Lord, hear me, that this people may know that You are the Lord God, and that You have turned their hearts back to You again.' Then the fire of the Lord fell and consumed the burnt sacrifice, and the wood and the stones and the dust, and it licked up the water that was in the trench." The people "fell on their faces; and they said, 'The Lord, He is God! The Lord, He is God!" The false prophets were seized and executed; not one of them escaped (vs. 32-40). The wicked queen Jezebel went into a rage when she saw that her priests had been killed and threatened Elijah with death. He "fled to the mountains" but God met him there and gave him new courage. In the end the soldiers who had been supporting Jezebel and her family turned against them and destroyed them (2Kings 9).

From this story we see that God's "Elijah" people will seem to be standing alone, but even a multitude of false and hostile religious leaders

standing against them will not dissuade them from challenging Babylon and appealing to the confused people to take their stand for the Lord. After winning the "great multitude" through the power of the Holy Spirit they will be threatened with death and will have to flee to the mountains. But God will fight against their enemies (who will turn upon each other at the very end) and they will be delivered.

These three incidents depict the experience of God's people through the whole time of trouble, culminating in the Battle of Armageddon. The special messengers (Deborah, Gideon and Elijah) correspond to the 144,000, who will call the people of God to come out of the slavery of idolatry and false worship. The story of Deborah shows that God's people will realize their own weakness and helplessness (a woman was the hero!). Like Gideon's army, they will be shattered so that their light can shine as they blow the trumpet. Like Elijah, they may have to hide in caves, and will be dependent on God for their very existence.[644] In each of the stories they are hopelessly outnumbered. But God will fight for them, and their enemies will be totally overthrown.

16:17-21 The Seventh Plague

"And the seventh angel poured out his bowl into the air; and there came a great voice out of the temple of heaven, from the throne, saying, 'It is done!" (Revelation 16:17). Each of the previous bowls were poured onto a specific location (the earth, the sea, the rivers, the sun, the throne of the beast, the great river Euphrates) and caused catastrophic damage in that sphere. The seventh bowl is poured **"into the air."** The air is the realm

---

644 This was also prophesied by Isaiah in the context of the Second Coming of Christ, "Who among us shall dwell with the devouring fire?...He who walks righteously...He will dwell on high; his place of defense will be the fortress of rocks; bread will be given him, his water will be sure (Isaiah 33:14-16).

Table 16.3

Revelation 6:12-17	Revelation 16:17-21
"Behold, there was a great earthquake" (v.12).	"And there was a great earthquake" (v.18).
"Every mountain and island was moved out of its place" (v. 14)	"Then every island fled away, and the mountains were not found" (v. 20).
"For the great day of His wrath has come, and who is able to stand?" (v. 17)	"The cup of the wine of the fierceness of His wrath" (v. 19).

of Satan himself who is "the prince of the power of the air" (Ephesians 2:2). In the unseen spiritual realm he directs his evil empire, attacking Christ by causing damage to His children. But with the seventh plague Satan's reign and authority come to an end, with an announcement from the throne, **"It is done."** The invisible evil government dissolves and everything connected to it falls apart, including its manifestation on earth, the **"great city"** Babylon.

"And there were voices, and thunders, and lightning; and there was a great earthquake, such as had not occurred since men were on the earth, so mighty an earthquake, and so great. And the great city was divided into three parts, and the cities of the nations fell" (Revelation 16:18,19).

This is the second time this earthquake has been mentioned. (See Table 16.3)

In Revelation 6 the context was the investigative judgment and identified the enemies of God who will be alive at the Second Coming of Christ. This passage in Revelation 16:18,19 introduces a section that details the executive judgment of these same people. By this time they have been clearly identified by their acceptance of the mark of the beast as belonging to the anti-christ politico-religious system called Babylon. The trinitarian nature of this kingdom has already been mentioned—the dragon symbolizing spiritualistic paganism, the beast representing Roman

Catholicism and the false prophet representing apostate Protestantism. This **"great city"** has, through power politics, flattery, coercion and infatuating addiction to sin, maintained authority and a tenuous unity of hate and fear. But now, with the prince of evil dethroned, the semblance of unity disintegrates into chaos—**"The great city was divided into three parts."**

"And Babylon the Great was remembered before God, to give to her the cup of the wine of the fierceness of His wrath. And every island fled away, and the mountains were not found. And huge hailstones weighing about a talent fell out of heaven on men" (Revelation 16:19-21). This passage follows the pattern of the other sets of seven: the seventh of the series introduces the theme of the section that follows.[645] In this passage the fall of Babylon is introduced, and chapters 17-19 digress from the historical time line to give the details of the identity, activity

---

645 The message to the seventh church (Laodicea) ends with "To him who overcomes, I will grant to sit with Me on My throne, as I also overcame and sat down with My Father on His throne" (Revelation 3:21). This is followed by chapters 4 and 5, the great throne room scene. With the opening of the seventh seal "there was silence in heaven for about half an hour" (Revelation 8:1). This is followed by the seven trumpets, the first "half hour" of the "hour of trial which shall come upon the whole earth" (Revelation 3:10) during which God will be "silent." The seventh trumpet announced God's reward for "[His] servants, the prophets and the saints and those who fear [His] name" and judgment on "those who destroy the earth" (Revelation 11:18). It is followed by chapters 12-14 which clearly identifies who those categories of people are.

and fate of modern Babylon as well as the joyous reaction of heaven when she falls.

With the seventh plague nature unravels; islands and mountains disappear and ninety-pound chunks of ice[646] fall out of the sky. Obviously all attacks against God's people will come to an abrupt halt.[647] In a telling demonstration of the hopeless insanity that results from consistently identifying with sin, the unrepentant turn to God, not to humble themselves in repentance, but to shake their fist at Him—**"men blasphemed God because of the plague of the hail, because that plague was exceedingly great."** By this time they finally understand that they have been on the wrong side of the great controversy. But their blasphemy of the God who died to save them and who did everything possible (including allowing the time of trouble) in order to bring them back to Himself, shows conclusively that they could never be happy in the kingdom of God where they would be in His presence forever.

---

646 About forty kilograms according to the Hebrew talent.

647 It is interesting to note that this scenario comes as no surprise to God; in the book of Job, considered to be the first book of the Bible to be written, God asks Job, "Have you seen the treasury of hail which I have reserved for the time of trouble, for the day of battle and war?" (Job 38:22,23).

"I saw a woman sitting on a scarlet beast which was full of names of blasphemy, having seven heads and ten horns...having in her hand a golden cup full of abominations" Rev. 17:3,4

Woodcut by Albrecht Durer 1498

Chapter 17

Revelation 17:1-18

17:1 And one of the seven angels which had the seven bowls, came and talked with me, saying to me, "Come here; I will show you the judgment of the great harlot that sits on many waters,

17:2 With whom the kings of the earth have committed fornication, and the inhabitants of the earth have been made drunk with the wine of her fornication."

17:3 So he carried me away in the spirit into the wilderness. And I saw a woman sitting on a scarlet colored beast, full of names of blasphemy, having seven heads and ten horns.

17:4 And the woman was arrayed in purple and scarlet, and adorned with gold and precious stones and pearls, having a golden cup in her hand full of abominations and filthiness of her fornication.

17:5 And on her forehead was a name written, MYSTERY, BABYLON THE GREAT, THE MOTHER OF HARLOTS AND ABOMINATIONS OF THE EARTH.

17:6 And I saw the woman, drunk with the blood of the saints, and with the blood of the martyrs of Jesus; and when I saw her, I wondered with great amazement.

17:7 And the angel said to me, "Why did you marvel? I will tell you the mystery of the woman, and of the beast that carries her, which has the seven heads and ten horns.

17:8 The beast that you saw was, and is not; and shall ascend out of the bottomless pit, and go into perdition; and they that dwell on the earth shall wonder, whose names were not written in the Book of Life from the foundation of the world, when they behold the beast that was, and is not, and yet is.

17:9 And here is the mind which has wisdom. The seven heads are seven mountains, on which the woman sits.

17:10 And they are also seven kings: five have fallen, and one is, and the other has not yet come; and when he comes, he must continue a little while.

17:11 And the beast that was, and is not, also is himself the eighth, and is of the seven, and goes into perdition.

17:12 And the ten horns which you saw are ten kings, which have not received a kingdom yet; but receive authority as kings with the beast for one hour.

17:13 These have one mind, and shall give their power and authority to the beast.

17:14 These shall make war with the Lamb, and the Lamb shall overcome them, for he is Lord of lords, and King of kings; and they that are with him are called, and chosen, and faithful."

17:15 And he said to me, "The waters which you saw, where the harlot sits, are peoples, and multitudes, and nations, and tongues.

17:16 And the ten horns which you saw on the beast, these shall hate the harlot, and shall make her desolate and naked, and shall eat her flesh, and burn her with fire.

17:17 For God has put in their hearts to fulfill His will, and to agree, and give their kingdom to the beast, until the words of God shall be fulfilled.

17:18 And the woman which you saw is that great city, which reigns over the kings of the earth."

17:1-5 The Great Harlot

"And one of the seven angels which had the seven bowls, came and talked with me, saying to me, 'Come here; I will show you the judgment of the great harlot that sits on many waters, with whom the kings of the earth have committed fornication, and the inhabitants of the earth have been made drunk with the wine of her fornication.' So he carried me away in the spirit into the wilderness. And I saw a woman sitting on a scarlet colored beast, full of names of blasphemy, having seven heads and ten horns. And the woman was arrayed in purple and scarlet, and adorned with gold and precious stones and pearls, having a golden cup in her hand full of abominations and filthiness of her fornication. And on her forehead was a name written, MYSTERY, BABYLON THE GREAT, THE MOTHER OF HARLOTS AND ABOMINATIONS OF THE EARTH" (Revelation 17:1-5).

This chapter is a continuation of the previous verses in chapter 16 which introduced the judgment of Babylon. Now one of the angels who had poured out the seven last plagues comes to John and offers to show him the details of the judgment of **"the great harlot who sits on many waters."** This phrase links end-time Babylon with ancient Babylon, the great oppressor of God's people and the destroyer of Jerusalem: the prophet Jeremiah referred to her as "you who dwell by many waters" (Jeremiah 51:13).

The end-time symbolic meaning of the waters, explains the angel of Revelation 17, **"are peoples, multitudes, nations and tongues"** (v. 15). This means that the Babylon of Revelation 17 is of a much larger, international scope than ancient Babylon of Jeremiah 51, but they have much in common. For example, the harlot holds a **"golden cup in her hand full of abominations and filthiness of her fornication…and the inhabitants of the earth have been made drunk with the wine of her fornication."** Ancient Babylon also "was a golden cup…that made all the earth drunk. The nations drank her wine; therefore the nations are deranged" (Jeremiah 51:7). The harlot sitting on the scarlet beast is the end-time, world-wide version of the great enemy that has been rebelling against God and warring against his people through the ages. This final manifestation of Babylon has not yet fully developed, and therefore there are some details that will only become obvious when the future arrives. But a review of the history of Babylon through the ages helps to give an idea of what to expect.

Babylon in Scripture and History

Babylon was founded in the third generation after the flood by Nimrod, the grandson of Ham who was Noah's disrespectful third son (Genesis 9:20-25, 10:6-8). "[Nimrod] was a mighty hunter before the Lord; therefore it is said, 'like Nimrod, the mighty hunter before the Lord.' And the beginning of his kingdom was Babel" (vs. 9,10). After the flood God had told Noah and his family, "Be fruitful and multiply, and *fill the earth*" (Genesis 9:1). But in rebellion, Nimrod and his followers said, "Come, let us build ourselves a city, and a tower whose top is in the heavens; let us make a name for ourselves, *lest we be scattered abroad over the face of the whole earth*" (Genesis 11:4). Thus the very foundation of Babylon was distrust of God, disobedience to His will and a desire for self to be exalted. As such it was a fitting representation of Satan's earlier rebellion in heaven ("I will exalt my throne above the stars of God...I will be like the Most High" Isaiah 14:13,14). Ultimately Babel's rebellion was such that it could not be ignored; God had to intervene in judgment, confusing their language and scattering the people.[648]

Abraham, the man chosen by God to be the father of God's faithful people, was the first person to be called out of Babylon. "The Lord God... chose Abram, and brought him out of Ur of the Chaldeans [Babylon] and gave him the name Abraham"[649] (Nehemiah 9:7). Later the king of Babylon[650] led a force of kings who attacked Sodom, where Abram's nephew Lot was living,

and took him captive. Abram "armed the three hundred and eighteen trained servants who were born in his own house and went in pursuit" and rescued Lot and his family, thus becoming the first man of God to save people out of the hands of the Babylonians (See Genesis 14).

The Old Babylonian Empire reached its height between 1800-1500 BC (from the time of the patriarchs through the exodus from Egypt). Although they made many advances in writing, art, and legal and social order, they also perfected astrology and magic. Even the famous code of Hammurabi, a masterpiece of legal legislation, was considered to be a gift from the sun god. And a number of influential epic stories such as the *Creation Story* and the *Epic of Gilgamesh*, which were a mixture of truth and error about God's creation and the flood, became some of the first written literature, thus preserving and legitimizing the fallacious narratives.

The Babylonians were conquered by the Assyrian Empire around the end of the tenth century BC (the time of Isaiah) but even then they were used by Satan against God's people. When the Assyrians conquered the unfaithful northern tribes of Israel and took them into captivity, they brought in Babylonians (among others) to take their place.[651] They became known as the Samaritans, and incorporated the worship of the Lord into their own heathen religion, creating a poisonous mixture of truth and error that was a constant snare to God's people. "They feared the Lord, yet served their own gods—according to the rituals of the nations from among whom they were carried away...They did not obey [the Lord], but they followed their former rituals. So these nations feared the Lord, yet served their carved images" (2Kings 17:33-41). This has always been the pattern of Babylon—a mixture of truth with

---

648 Genesis 11:6-9.

649 Ur was a part of what later became the Babylonian kingdom, and the Chaldeans were the religious leaders of Babylon (See Daniel 2:4).

650 In Genesis 11 the attacking king is called the "king of Shinar." Shinar is the name of the plain where the tower of Babel was built (Genesis 11:2).

651 2Kings 17:24.

enough error to make it false and deadly.

God's chosen people found Babylonian religion irresistible. For example, during the time of Jeremiah the Jewish leaders who escaped the Babylonian captivity brazenly asserted, "We will certainly...burn incense to the queen of heaven and pour out drink offerings to her, as we have done, we and our fathers, our kings and our princes, in the cities of Judah and in the streets of Jerusalem. For then we had plenty of food and were well-off, and saw no trouble. But since we stopped burning incense to the queen of heaven and pouring out drink offerings to her, we have lacked everything and have been consumed by the sword and by famine"[652] (Jeremiah 44:17,18).

In 626 BC Nabopolassar founded the neo-Babylonian empire. Determined to rule the world, he first conquered the Assyrians, destroying Ninevah in 612 BC (as described by the prophet Nahum) and then turned his attention to Judah. Because of their sinful idolatry Judah had forfeited the protection of the Lord, and He allowed Babylon to be His "rod of chastening."[653] The powerful Babylonian king Nebuchadnezzar inflicted a series of defeats upon Judah under the apostate kings Jehoiakim and Jehoiachin, taking captives which included Daniel and Ezekiel.[654] Finally, in crushing Judah's revolt during the reign of Zedekiah in 587 BC, "the king of the Chaldeans killed their young men with the sword in the house of their sanctuary, and had no compassion on young man or virgin, on the aged or

the weak...burned the house of God, broke down the wall of Jerusalem, burned all its palaces with fire, and destroyed all its precious possessions. And those who escaped from the sword he carried away to Babylon, where they became servants to him and his sons" (2Chronicles 36:17-20).

The destruction of Jerusalem and captivity of God's people by the Babylonians was considered the epitome of misery and disgrace. The psalmist wrote, "By the rivers of Babylon, there we sat down, yea we wept when we remembered Zion. We hung our harps upon the willows in the midst of it. For there those who carried us away captive asked of us a song...How shall we sing the Lord's song in a foreign land?" (Psalms 137:1-4).

But God had already prophesied the punishment of Babylon for their excesses—"When seventy years are completed, I will punish the king of Babylon and that nation, the land of the Chaldeans, for their iniquity,' says the Lord, 'and I will make it a perpetual desolation" (Jeremiah 25:12). Cyrus the Great, king of Persia, conquered Babylon by diverting the Euphrates River and marching into the city through the dry river bed on the night of Belshazzar's idolatrous banquet in 539 BC. [655] The Persians made Babylon a capital of one of their provinces, and Alexander the Great intended to make it the capital of his Hellenistic empire when he defeated the Persians in 330 BC. But he died prematurely, Babylon was repeatedly overrun by the generals who succeeded him, and the great city slowly sank into obscurity and was abandoned.[656]

Babylon's New Home

This review of the history of Babylon exposes her principles and tactics. Babylon is a religious

---

652 The "queen of heaven" was the Sumerian/Babylonian fertility goddess Inanna (Ishtar, Astarte) who was worshiped along with her son/lover Tammuz. The worship of the queen of heaven and Tammuz were condemned by Jeremiah and Ezekiel (Ezekiel 8:14, Jeremiah 7:18, 44:17-25). See Wikipedia articles "Inanna," "Tammuz," "Queen of Heaven" for more detailed information.

653 "Behold, I will send...Nebuchadnezzar the king of Babylon, *My servant* and will bring them against this land, against its inhabitants...and will utterly destroy them...And these nations shall serve the king of Babylon seventy years" (Jeremiah 25:9-11).

654 2Chronicles 36:5-10.

655 See Daniel 5.

656 Wikipedia contributors, "Babylon," *Wikipedia, The Free Encyclopedia*, http://en.wikipedia.org/w/index.php?title=Babylon&oldid=624651811, (accessed September 16, 2014).

system that contains elements of truth mixed with error, but which is at a most basic level hostile and rebellious against the revealed will of God. Religious Babylon seduces the followers of God to incorporate her pagan gods and enchanting rituals, and uses an aggressive state to capture, enslave and destroy God's people. The ancient city of Babylon disintegrated, but the mystery religion of Babylon did not fade away. Peter, sending greetings from the Christian church in Rome, wrote, "She who is in Babylon,[657] elect together with you, greets you" (1 Peter 5:13). By Peter's time pagan Rome had become the new Babylon.

"As the Romans extended their dominance throughout the Mediterranean world their policy in general was to absorb the deities and cults of other peoples rather than try to eradicate them, since they believed that preserving tradition promoted social stability. One way that Rome incorporated diverse people was by supporting their religious heritage, building temples to local deities that framed their theology within the hierarchy of the Roman religion...By the height of the empire numerous international deities were cultivated at Rome...among them Cybele, Isis, Epona, Mithras and Sol Invictus."[658]

The college of pontiffs, headed by the Pontifex Maximus, was responsible for the oversight of all the religions in the empire. "The pontifex was not simply a priest; he had both political and religious authority...The main duty of the pontifices was to maintain the *pax deorum* or "peace of the gods."[659] Even when the Roman empire became "Christian" with the "conversion" of Constantine, the emperor retained this pagan title. "Constantine showed equal favour to both religions. As Pontifex Maximus he watched over the heathen worship and protected its rights... Shortly before his death Constantine confirmed the privileges of the priests of the ancient gods."[660]

Babylon Invades the Church

Gratian, one of the last emperors in the west, refused to accept the pagan title. "Gratian's reign marks a distinct epoch in the transition of the empire from paganism to Christianity. At the time of his accession he refused the insignia of Pontifex Maximus, which even Constantine and the other Christian emperors had always accepted."[661] However, instead of abolishing the pagan office, he transferred it to Pope Damasus I! "Within a few years after the Pagan title of Pontifex had been abolished, it was revived, and that by the very Emperor that had abolished it, and was bestowed, with all the Pagan associations clustering around it, upon the Bishop of Rome...When this pagan title was bestowed on the Roman bishop, it was not as a mere empty title of honour it was bestowed, but as a title to which formidable power was annexed."[662]

"Though Paganism was legally abolished in the Western Empire of Rome, yet in the city of the seven hills it was still rampant, insomuch that Jerome, who knew it well, writing of Rome at this

657 "Babylon...allegorically, of Rome, as the most corrupt seat of idolatry and the enemy of Christianity" Thayer's Greek Lexicon, Bibleworks L.L.C. 1992-2001.

658 Wikipedia contributors, "Religion in ancient Rome," *Wikipedia, The Free Encyclopedia*, http://en.wikipedia.org/w/index.php?title=Religion_in_ancient_Rome&oldid=623982353 (accessed September 16, 2014).

659 Wikipedia contributors, "Pontifex Maximus," *Wikipedia, The Free Encyclopedia*, http://en.wikipedia.org/w/index.php?title=Pontifex_Maximus&oldid=623830253 (accessed September 16, 2014).

660 Charles Herbermann and Georg Grupp. "Constantine the Great" *The Catholic Encyclopedia* http://www.newadvent.org/cathen/04295c.htm. Accessed Sept. 16, 2014.

661 Thomas Scannell, "Gratian," *The Catholic Encyclopedia*, http://www.newadvent.org/cathen/06729c.htm, Accessed Sept. 16, 2014

662 Alexander Hislop, *The Two Babylons*, (New York: Loizeaux Brothers 1959) (First published in 1853)

very period, calls it 'the sink of all superstitions.' The consequence was, that, while everywhere else throughout the empire the imperial edict for the abolition of paganism was respected, in Rome itself it was, to a large extent, a dead letter. Symmachus, the prefect of the city, and the highest patrician families, as well as the masses of the people, were fanatically devoted to the old religion; and, therefore, the emperor found it necessary, in spite of the law, to connive at the idolatry of the Romans. How strong was the hold that paganism had in the imperial city, even after the fire of Vesta was extinguished, and state support was withdrawn from the Vestals, the reader may perceive from the following words of Gibbon:[663] 'The image and altar of Victory were indeed removed from the senate-house; but the emperor yet spared the statues of the gods which were exposed to public view; four hundred and twenty-four temples or chapels still remained to satisfy the devotion of the people, and in every quarter of Rome the delicacy of the Christians was offended by the fumes of idolatrous sacrifice.' Thus strong was paganism in Rome, even after state support was withdrawn about AD 376."

"But look forward only about fifty years, and see what has become of it. The name of paganism has almost entirely disappeared; insomuch that the younger Theodosius, in an edict issued AD 423, uses these words: 'The pagans that remain, although now we may believe there are none.' The words of Gibbon in reference to this are very striking…He expresses his surprise at the rapidity of the revolution that took place among the Romans from paganism to Christianity. 'The ruin of paganism,' he says—and his dates are from AD 378, the year when the Bishop of Rome was made Pontifex, to 395—'The ruin of paganism, in the

age of Theodosius, is perhaps the only example of the total extirpation of any ancient and popular superstition; and may therefore deserve to be considered as a singular event in the history of the human mind."[664]

"Now, how can this great and rapid revolution be accounted for? Is it because the Word of the Lord has had free course and been glorified? Then, what means the new aspect that the Roman Church has now begun to assume? In exact proportion as paganism has disappeared from without the church, in the very same proportion it appears within it. Pagan dresses for the priests, pagan festivals for the people, pagan doctrines and ideas of all sorts, are everywhere in vogue"[665]

To even suggest that the Roman Catholic Church was the continuation of Babylonian paganism seems incredible, but this is what the Book of Revelation teaches. This can be seen by comparing the woman sitting on the beast of Revelation 17 who is identified as Babylon with the beast from the sea of chapter 13, which was conclusively shown to be the papacy of the Middle Ages. (See Table 17.1)

The Beast and the Great Harlot

"So he carried me away in the spirit into the wilderness. And I saw a woman sitting on a scarlet colored beast, full of names of blasphemy, having seven heads and ten horns. And the woman was arrayed in purple and scarlet, and adorned with gold and precious stones and pearls, having a golden cup in her hand full of abominations and filthiness of her fornication. And on her forehead was a name written, MYSTERY, BABYLON THE GREAT, THE MOTHER OF HARLOTS AND ABOMINATIONS OF THE EARTH" (Revelation 17:3-5).

---

663 Hislop here refers to the monumental work by Edward Gibbon, *History of the Decline and Fall of the Roman Empire* which was published in the late eighteenth century.

664 Hislop

665 Hislop

Table 17.1

Beast of Revelation 13 (The Medieval Papacy)	Harlot and Beast of Revelation 17 (End Time Babylon)
"A beast…having seven heads and ten horns… and on his heads a blasphemous name" (v. 1).	"A scarlet beast which was full of names of blasphemy, having seven heads and ten horns" (v. 3).
"It was granted to him to make war with the saints and to overcome them" (v. 7).	"Drunk with the blood of the saints and with the blood of the martyrs of Jesus" (v. 6).
"Authority was given him over every tribe, tongue, and nation" (v. 7).	"The waters…where the harlot sits, are peoples, multitudes, nations, and tongues" (v. 15).

In 12:1,2 *The Woman* we saw that a woman represents the people of God (Israel in the Old Testament, the church in the New Testament), either pure and faithful or apostate and corrupt. In this case the woman is called **"the great harlot,"** indicating that this is a corrupt, apostate church. Here we see a powerful political entity (the **"scarlet beast"**) which is being ridden, or controlled, by a corrupt church (**"the great harlot"**). Verse five gives the names of this church—**"MYSTERY, BABYLON THE GREAT, MOTHER OF HARLOTS AND OF THE ABOMINATIONS OF THE EARTH."** Each of these names describes an aspect of the papal Roman Catholic Church.

"Mystery" is an appropriate title for the Roman Church because it considers its sacraments to be mysteries, especially the Eucharist which is the central act of Catholic worship. "The church honors the Eucharist as one of her most exalted mysteries, since for sublimity and incomprehensibility it yields in nothing to the allied mysteries of the Trinity and Incarnation. These three mysteries constitute a wonderful triad, which causes the essential characteristic of Christianity, as a religion of mysteries far transcending the capabilities of reason, to shine forth in all its brilliance and splendor, and elevates Catholicism, the most faithful guardian and keeper of our Christian heritage, far above all pagan and non-Christian religions."[666]

The title **"Babylon"** is also appropriate for the Roman Church. The apostle Peter identified Rome as Babylon (1Peter 5:13), and chapter 18, which deals with the judgment of Babylon, will show clearly that some of the prominent characteristics of the Catholic Church are those of Babylon.

She is also called the **"Mother of Harlots."** The Roman Catholic Church calls herself the "Mother Church." The Tridentine creed of Pope Pius IV, drawn up after the watershed Council of Trent, states: "I acknowledge the Holy Catholic Apostolic Roman Church for the mother and mistress of all churches."[667] In his Encyclical on Religious Unity of 1928 Pope Pius XI appealed to the various "reformers," "Let them therefore return to their common Father, who, forgetting the insults previously heaped on the Apostolic See, will receive them in the most loving fashion. For if, as they continually state, they long to be united with Us and ours, why do they not hasten

---

666 Joseph Pohle, "Eucharist" *The Catholic Encyclopedia*, http://www.newadvent.org/cathen/05572c.htm, Accessed Sept. 16, 2014.

667 http://www.catholictradition.org/Tradition/tridentine-creed.htm, Accessed Sept. 16, 2014.

to enter the church, *the Mother and mistress of all Christ's faithful?*"

This woman **"committed fornication"** (had illicit relationships) with **"the kings of the earth,"** (v. 2) which indicates a union of church and state. This of course has been the policy of the Catholic Church ever since the time of Constantine.[668] In time the church became so powerful that her law was the law of the land. This allowed her to carry out **"the abominations of the earth"**—the persecution and extermination of the "heretics" who refused to accept her dogmas.

The false doctrines that led to the abuses of the Middle Ages will be examined in 18:1-3 *Babylon is Fallen*. Although the Roman Catholic Church has expressed regret for some of her actions during that horrendous period and no longer practices them, none of the doctrines that led to those abuses have changed. This is not to say that Catholics are pagans or wicked people. According to Revelation 18:1-4, many of God's people are found in Babylon, serving Him sincerely according to their understanding of His will as it has been taught to them. However, the papal system was used by Satan to persecute God's people during the Middle Ages, and although it is apparently benign now, this chapter teaches us that it will be integrally involved in the future Babylon that will take the lead in persecuting God's people during the time of trouble.

---

668 "The official recognition of Christianity [by the state] had some unfortunate effects on the church. For the first time, the church attracted many people who lacked the dedication of the early Christians. Emperors intruded into the internal affairs of the church...But on the whole, the empire's recognition of Christianity benefited the church. The church was able to influence civil laws." "Roman Catholic Church" *World Book Encyclopedia* (Chicago, Il, 1986)

17:6-8: The Beast That Was, Is Not and Yet Is

"And I saw the woman, drunk with the blood of the saints, and with the blood of the martyrs of Jesus; and when I saw her, I wondered with great amazement" (Revelation 17:6). John had already seen a similar beast with seven heads and ten horns, which also made war with the saints and overcame them (Revelation 13:1-10). He had seen the beast from the earth set up the image to the beast, the mark and number of the beast and the death decree. But nothing he had seen up to this time caused him to **"wonder with great amazement"** as the great harlot did. John was not amazed to see beasts (which represent political entities) warring against the church. But in this vision John was seeing a woman, which in scripture represents those who are, or should be, God's chosen people. And she was taking such pleasure in killing God's people that she was portrayed as being **"drunk with the blood of the saints!"**

It is crucial that God's people will be able to discern the identity of this final great enemy during the time of the end. Jesus said that the final issues will be so deceptively confusing that "if possible, even the elect" would be deceived.[669] For this reason the angel gave a detailed description.

"And the angel said to me, "Why did you marvel? I will tell you the mystery of the woman, and of the beast that carries her, which has the seven heads and ten horns. The beast that you saw was, and is not; and shall ascend out of the bottomless pit, and go into perdition; and they that dwell on the earth shall wonder, whose names were not written in the Book of Life from the foundation of the world, when they behold the beast that was, and is not, and yet is"

---

669 Matthew 24:24.

(Revelation 17:7,8).

The angel gives the key to the identity of the woman in the identity of the beast she rides. The beast "was." In chapter 13 we saw this beast arising out of the sea, speaking blasphemy and warring against the saints for "forty-two months" (1,260 years). This was the medieval papacy in control of the nations of Europe.

But the beast "is not." The papal beast was "mortally wounded" as it first lost the allegiance of the European people during the reformation, then lost political control, especially during the French revolution, and finally was stripped of its sovereignty when it lost the papal states during the Italian revolution[670] and the pope became a "prisoner in the Vatican."

But that was not the end of the beast—in chapter 13 we saw that "his deadly wound was healed" (Revelation 13:3,12). In 1929 the Italian government signed the Lateran Pacts granting the papacy Vatican City as a sovereign state.[671] Since that time the papacy has been steadily growing in political power and influence. Major milestones include the Vatican II Council, in which the church committed itself to engaging the modern world and uniting Christendom. In 1984 the Roman Catholic Church established diplomatic relationships with the United States and formed a "holy alliance" with the US which brought down communism (See 13: *The Deadly Wound Healed*). In the description of the beast in chapter 17 there is no mention of the deadly wound, which was a major focus in chapter 13. This would suggest that the context of the vision is the time of the end, when the deadly wound is nearly or fully healed.

More specifically, the beast **"was, and is not, and will ascend out of the bottomless pit and go to perdition."** This verse uses past, present and future tenses, making it possible to establish the time frame of this vision (which is essential for establishing the identity of the eight kings of verse 10). The time frame is not the Middle Ages when the beast **"was,"** nor is it after the appearance of the antichrist who **"will ascend out of the bottomless pit."** This thought will be further developed later in this section, but for the sake of establishing the context of the angel's explanation, the beast will in the very end be personified as the antichrist, ascending **"out of the bottomless pit"** to direct the final battle against God's people. However, in this vision the antichrist is still future, and the context is that time when the beast **"is not,"** when full political power has not been completely re-established, but the "wounded" condition is no longer obvious.[672]

The addition of a new element, the harlot who is riding the scarlet beast, shows that there is a basic difference between the beast system of the Middle Ages and that of the last days. In the Middle Ages the church had its own territory (the Papal States) with their own armies, and was actively involved in the governments of the

---

670 "The Papal States were territories in the Italian Peninsula under the sovereign direct rule of the pope, from the 500's until 1870…These holdings were considered to be a manifestation of the temporal power of the pope, as opposed to his ecclesiastical primacy" Wikipedia contributors, "Papal States," *Wikipedia, The Free Encyclopedia*, http://en.wikipedia.org/w/index.php?title=Papal_States&oldid=625135797 (accessed September 17, 2014).

671 "The temporal power of the pope remained suspended until 1929, when papal sovereignty of the Holy See was recognized by treaty with the Italian Government…and a financial settlement compensated the Holy See for loss of temporal primacy." "Papacy," *Book of Knowledge*, Waverly Book Company LTD, London.

672 Confirmation of this context is found in Revelation 17:12-14. "The ten horns which you saw are ten kings who have received no kingdom as yet" (v. 12). The use of the present tense shows that in the time frame of the vision the ten kings exist but have not yet received their kingdom. This is the final united political alliance led by the "beast." "They will give their power and authority to the beast. These will make war with the Lamb and the Lamb will overcome them" (vs. 13, 14). These verses use the future tense, showing that the context is before the full authority of the beast (the antichrist). Therefore the context is after the appearance of the ten kings, but before their alliance with the antichrist.

European countries it controlled. In the last days there is an apparent separation of the religious (the church, represented by the harlot), and the political/military (represented by the scarlet beast). This is in line with the modern reality in which the church is in the background while the countries of Europe and America (the "ten horns" and the "beast from the earth") do the political and military dirty work. However, it should be kept in mind that it is the harlot who is riding the beast. Although she is in the background, the church will direct the political powers.

Beasts in prophecy have represented kingdoms and empires, and although the scarlet beast of chapter 17 is a global political power, a more personal element, the antichrist, also seems to be shown by the series of kings that are somehow related to the heads of the beast, the eighth of which is also called **"the beast." "The seven heads are seven mountains on which the woman sits… They are also seven kings…the beast that was, and is not, also is himself the eighth, and is of the seven, and goes into perdition."**

The fact that at the end of time this personal manifestation of the beast **"shall ascend out of the bottomless pit and go into perdition"** shows that this is the same entity that is one of the main players during the time of trouble. He is first introduced during the "first woe" of the trumpet plagues as the "angel of the bottomless pit" who is king over the tormenting locust army. His name is Abaddon, the destroyer, and his purpose in life is to destroy God's children (Revelation 9:11). He is seen again in Revelation 11:7, "The beast that ascends out of the bottomless pit will make war against them [the two witnesses], overcome them, and kill them." With his abbreviated title "the beast" he is a part of the unholy trinity of the sixth plague, spewing out "unclean spirits like frogs" which "are the spirits of devils, working miracles, which go forth to the kings of the earth and of the whole world, to gather them

to the battle of that great day of God Almighty" (Revelation 16:13,14). He is again present when the Battle of Armageddon takes place—"the beast, and the kings of the earth, and their armies, gathered together to make war against Him that sat on the horse [Jesus]" (Revelation 19:19).

This beast is both a political persecuting power (the scarlet beast) and a personal manifestation of Satan himself (the beast from the bottomless pit, see 11: *Satan's Impersonation of Christ*) which was predicted by Paul (the man of sin, 2 Thessalonians 2:3-10). It may be that Satan does not trust the crucial, final movements to any of his underlings. By fully possessing a human being he will be able to physically and personally direct the last events, which are so crucial for the survival of his kingdom and his life. As the following verses show, he will utilize the Babylon organization he has been perfecting since the time of Nimrod.

17:9-11 Seven Heads

"And here is the mind which has wisdom. The seven heads are seven mountains, on which the woman sits. And they are also seven kings: five have fallen, and one is, and the other has not yet come; and when he comes, he must continue a little while. And the beast that was, and is not, also is himself the eighth, and is of the seven, and goes into perdition" (Revelation 17:9-11).

The fact that this is not a simple identification is indicated by the phrase, **"Here is the mind which has wisdom."** Numerous interpretations have been suggested, each with its own problems. The first phrase, **"The seven heads are seven mountains on which the woman sits"** points to Rome, which from antiquity has been called the city built on seven hills.[673] This is consistent with the identification given above of the harlot as being the Roman Catholic Church. It is also one of the few options that would fit with verse 18, **"And the woman which you saw is that great city, which reigns over the kings of the earth."** There is no city in history that has reigned over kings as Rome has, and that was never more true than when Revelation was written.

The second phrase, **"They are also seven kings.**[674] **Five have fallen, one is, and the other has not yet come"** is more difficult. One interpretation that has been suggested is that the kings represent the progression of empires that were identified by Daniel. According to this view, the five kings which have fallen would be Babylon, Medo-Persia, Greece, Pagan Rome, and Papal Rome, with the fall of Papal Rome being the deadly wound which was received in 1798 (See 13:3 *The Deadly Wound*). This would presumably make the sixth king, the **"one"** which **"is,"** the United States, **"the beast coming up out of the earth,"**[675] which will set up the image and mark of the beast. Thus the perspective of the vision would be the time of the end, before the time of trouble. One problem with this view is that it does not have a convincing identity for the seventh empire that **"has not yet come. And when he comes he must continue a short time."** The book of Revelation does not seem to indicate another kingdom before that of "the beast" which is identified in verse 11 as being the eighth king.

Another interpretation is that the context the **"one [who] is"** refers to the time of John when he wrote Revelation. In this view the heads would represent all those empires that had a major impact on God's people. Thus the first would be Egypt which held the children of Israel in slavery, the second Assyria which conquered and led captive the northern ten tribes, the third Babylon, the fourth Medo-Persia, the fifth Greece and the sixth, the **"one [who] is"** would be pagan Rome during the time of John. A major difficulty with this theory is the identity of the seventh king, which **"must continue a short time."**[676] Moreover, we saw in the previous section that verses 8 and 12 indicate that the context is not the time of John, but the last days, after the deadly wound is healed but before the appearance of the antichrist.

Actually, the interpretations that consider the heads to be empires are problematic because the passage specifies kings, not kingdoms.[677] Furthermore, the beast **"who is of the seven"** and **"is going to perdition"** seems to be more like a person than an empire—in the New Testament only people go to perdition, not political entities. And finally, one would have to wonder why this passage would focus on ancient empires when the obvious purpose is to identify end-time Babylon.[678]

A more likely possibility takes into consideration the fact that there is no mention of the

---

673 *"The City of Seven Hills* usually refers to Rome, although there are many cities that claim to be built on seven hills" Wikipedia contributors, "List of cities claimed to be built on seven hills," *Wikipedia, The Free Encyclopedia,* http://en.wikipedia.org/w/index.php?title=List_of_cities_claimed_to_be_built_on_seven_hills&oldid=625314419 (accessed September 17, 2014).

674 The KJV and NKJV read "There are also seven Kings." Most other versions, including the ESV, NRSV, NIV and NASV read "They are also seven kings," showing that the hills and the kings are integrally related.

675 Revelation 13:11.

676 If this is Papal Rome, 1,260 years is not a very short time, and there is no accounting for the United States, which is a major player in chapter 13. If Papal and Pagan Rome are lumped together as the sixth king, this is somewhat out of harmony with Daniel which seems to consider them related but separate. Be that as it may, according to this scenario the United States or papal Rome would be the seventh king which continues **"a short time"** and the eighth, the beast, would be the future resurgent Roman power with its **"ten horns."**

677 Although the book of Daniel seems to use the words interchangeably, it makes it clear that it is doing so, which is not the case in Revelation (compare, for example, Daniel chapter seven verses 17 and 23).

678 See Appendix 7 for further discussion of this view.

scarlet beast having a "deadly wound," which was so prominent in the sea beast of chapter 13. It also considers the context, the time just before the appearance of the antichrist and the fall of Babylon. This would suggest that the whole history of the **"scarlet beast"** takes place after the deadly wound is healed.

When does this happen in history? Some commentators have seen the succession of kings as beginning in 1929, when the papacy again became a sovereign state. According to this view, the kings are the popes of the Catholic church, and at the time of this writing there have been seven popes which have "fallen" since 1929,[679] which would make the present pope, Francis, the eighth and final anti-Christ king (**"the beast"**). Since the beast who **"will ascend out of the bottomless pit and go into perdition"** arises during the fifth trumpet, this scenario is obviously incorrect.

A more likely possibility considers the fact that the healing of the deadly wound was a gradual process which may have started in 1929 but was not complete until at least the early 1960's. At that time pope John XXIII officially closed the First Vatican Council and opened the Second Vatican Council. The First Vatican Council, which began in 1868, established the principle of papal infallibility and intended to define the nature of the church, but in September 1870 the Kingdom of Italy, having already annexed the other papal territories, captured Rome which had been ruled by the papacy. Pope Pius IX suspended and never reconvened the First Vatican Council and declared himself a "prisoner of the Vatican," recognizing that the Roman Catholic Church had lost her temporal authority.

When Pope John XXIII opened the Second Vatican Council the first action was to officially end the First Vatican Council,[680] closing a painful chapter of Catholic history and opening a new one in which the council determined that the Roman Church would seek to renew the church, restore unity among all Christians and start a dialogue with the contemporary world. It could be argued that this was the true healing of the "deadly wound." If 1962 is the beginning date for counting the 7 kings, we are now living during the time described in the vision of Revelation 17; five "kings" have fallen, the current pope, Francis, is the sixth who will "reign" during the chronological context of the vision when the harlot, **"drunk with the blood of the saints,"** will gain control over the "scarlet beast." The next pope will only **"continue a short time"** and then will come the eighth king, the final antichrist.

Another credible possibility considers that the essence of the deadly wound was the loss of temporal and political power, which was manifest in the medieval church by the union of church and state in which the church used the power of the state to enforce her agenda. This kind of union of church and state was not recovered until the 1980's with the "holy alliance" between the Roman Catholic Church headed by Pope John Paul II and the United States headed by Ronald Reagan (see 13: *The Deadly Wound Healed*). In 1984 the United States appointed an ambassador to the Vatican and by 1990 the alliance had managed to topple Soviet communism, first in Poland and then in eastern Europe and Russia. This is particularly significant since Revelation 13:11,12

---

679 Pius XI 1922-39, Pius XII 1939-58, John XXIII 1958-63, Paul VI 1963-1978, John Paul I 1978, John Paul II 1978-2005, Benedict XVI 2005-2013.

680 "The outbreak of the Franco-Prussian War interrupted the council. It was suspended following the entry of the Italian Army in Rome, the so-called capture of Rome, and never resumed. It was not officially closed until decades later in 1960 by Pope John XXIII, when it was formally brought to an end as part of the preparations for the Second Vatican Council." Wikichristian contributors, "First Vatican Council" *WikiChristian*, http://.wikichristian.org/index.php?title=First_Vatican_Council, accessed Sept. 17, 2014

predicts that the final oppressive "image to the beast" will be an alliance between the United States and the Papacy. If the "holy alliance" marks the beginning of the seven kings, we are now with Pope Francis in the reign of the third king with four more to go before the final antichrist.

For further discussion of this issue see Appendix 7. Since John devoted a whole chapter to identifying this end-time entity it is obviously very important that God's people seek to understand. This requires **"A mind which has wisdom,"** and fortunately God has given a specific promise which we can claim—"If any of you lacks wisdom, let him ask of God, who gives to all liberally and without reproach, and it will be given to him" (James 1:5). This is an issue that deserves a great deal of study, prayer and discussion.

17:12-18 Ten Horns and the Harlot

"And the ten horns which you saw are ten kings, which have not received a kingdom yet; but receive authority as kings with the beast for one hour. These have one mind, and shall give their power and authority to the beast" (Revelation 17:12,13).

In chapter 16 the beast (along with the dragon and the false prophet) sent the "spirits of devils" to "the kings of the earth and of the whole world, to gather them to the battle of that great day of God Almighty" (Revelation 16:14). The ten kings of chapter 17 represent the kings which responded. Their response is depicted in Revelation 19:19, "The kings of the earth, and their armies, gathered together to make war against Him who sat on the horse [Jesus] and against His army." In chapter 17 the same scene appears, but instead of using the terms "Him who sat on the horse" and "His army" it calls them **the Lamb** and **"those who are with Him"**—"These [the beast and the ten kings] **shall make war with the Lamb, and**

the Lamb shall overcome them, for he is Lord of lords, and King of kings; and they that are with him are called, and chosen, and faithful" (Revelation 17:14). The number ten is probably symbolic, as this is a highly symbolic chapter, and ten represents a full and complete number.[681]

There is an obvious connection with the fourth beast of Daniel 7 which also had 10 horns. The horns of the fourth beast represented the barbarian tribes that took over the Roman Empire and later became the countries of Europe that were used by the Papacy to assert its power. Although the ten kings of chapter 17 are obviously not the same entities as the 10 horns of Daniel 7,[682] the European alliance of diverse nations held together by a common glue of religion appears to be the model for the final alliance. The ten kings most likely represent a one-world government headed by the beast/antichrist and consisting of the major powers of the world, united to fight the Battle of Armageddon.

Apparently the harlot riding the scarlet beast is the last-day manifestation of the religio-political entity that was symbolized in chapter 13 by the beast arising from the sea. In chapter 13 there was no distinction between the religious and the political; they were blended together in the sea beast, representing the integral union of church and state in the medieval papal system. But the distinction is emphasized in the end-time version of Babylon because of the falling out which now takes place—the political scarlet beast and the ten horns will turn against the religious harlot.

---

681 The clearest example is the Ten Commandments. See also Genesis 18:32, 24:55, 31:41, Ruth 4:2, 1Samuel 1:8, Daniel 1:12, 20, Zechariah. 8:23, Matthew 25:1,28, Luke 15:8,19:13, Revelation 2:10.

682 The main difference is that three of the ten horns of Daniel 7 were rooted out to make way for the little horn, whereas the ten kings of chapter 17 remain an integral unit. There is also the difference of the time frame. The horns of Daniel 7 appear in the sixth century AD, but the horns of Revelation 17 have a last-days context when the beast ascends out of the bottomless pit.

Through most of the time of trouble, the harlot (the religious system) will be fully supported by the masses of people—"**The waters which you saw, where the harlot sits, are peoples, multitudes, nations and tongues**" (Revelation 17:15). Chapter 16 made it clear that these "waters," symbolized by "the great river Euphrates," will be dried up (See 16:12 *The Kings from the East*). The deceived masses, disillusioned by empty promises and the grief they have suffered during the time of trouble while following their religious leaders, will finally turn against them. Satan, master manipulator that he is, will "go with the flow," and as the beast-leader of the Babylon political system he will turn the political leaders against the religious leaders—"**And the ten horns which you saw on the beast, these shall hate the harlot, and shall make her desolate and naked, and shall eat her flesh, and burn her with fire. For God has put in their hearts to fulfill His will, and to agree, and give their kingdom to the beast, until the words of God shall be fulfilled**" (Revelation 17:16,17).

At the beginning of the chapter the harlot was sitting on the seven-headed beast, obviously in control, but by the end of the chapter she is being destroyed by the antichrist beast and his allies, the ten kings. This does not mean that they have had a conversion experience; their major focus is still to "**make war with the Lamb**," but that story is not told until chapter 19. Chapter 18 gives the details of the miserable and total fall of the harlot.

"Then a mighty angel took up a stone like a great millstone and threw it into the sea, saying, 'Thus with violence the great city Babylon shall be thrown down, and shall not be found anymore." Rev. 18:21
Woodcut by Hans Holbein 1523

Chapter 18

Revelation 18:1-24

18:1 And after these things I saw another angel come down from heaven, having great power; and the earth was lightened with his glory.

18:2 And he cried mightily with a strong voice, saying, "Babylon the great is fallen, is fallen, and has become the habitation of devils, and the hold of every foul spirit, and a cage of every unclean and hateful bird.

18:3 For all nations have drunk of the wine of the wrath of her fornication, and the kings of the earth have committed fornication with her, and the merchants of the earth got rich through the abundance of her delicacies."

18:4 And I heard another voice from heaven, saying, "Come out of her, my people, that you do not partake of her sins, and that you do not receive of her plagues.

18:5 For her sins have reached to heaven, and God has remembered her iniquities.

18:6 Reward her even as she rewarded you, and double to her twice as much according to her works; in the cup which she has filled, fill to her twice as much.

18:7 As much as she has glorified herself, and lived in luxury, so much torment and sorrow give her, for she said in her heart, I sit as a queen, and am not a widow, and shall see no sorrow.

18:8 Therefore shall her plagues come in one day: death, and mourning, and famine; and she shall be utterly burned with fire, for strong is the Lord God who judges her."

18:9 And the kings of the earth, who have committed fornication and lived in luxury with her, shall mourn her, and lament for her, when they see the smoke of her burning,

18:10 Standing afar off for fear of her torment, saying, "Alas, alas that great city Babylon, that mighty city! For in one hour has your judgment come."

18:11 And the merchants of the earth shall weep and mourn over her; for no one buys their merchandise any more:

18:12 Merchandise of gold, and silver, and precious stones, and of pearls, and fine linen, and purple, and silk, and scarlet, and all thyine wood, and all manner of vessels of ivory, and all manner of vessels of most precious wood, and of brass, and iron, and marble,

18:13 And cinnamon, and incense, and ointments, and frankincense, and wine, and oil, and fine flour, and wheat, and animals, and sheep, and horses, and chariots, and slaves, and souls of men.

18:14 And the fruits that your soul lusted after are departed from you, and all things which were dainty and goodly are departed from you, and you shall find them no more at all.

18:15 The merchants of these things, which were made rich by her, shall stand afar off for the fear of her torment, weeping and wailing,

18:16 And saying, "Alas, alas that great city, that was clothed in fine linen, and purple, and scarlet, and adorned with gold, and precious stones, and pearls!

18:17 For in one hour so great riches have come to nothing." And every shipmaster, and all the multitudes on ships, and sailors, and as many as trade by sea, stood afar off,

18:18 And cried when they saw the smoke of her burning, saying, "What city is like this great city?"

18:19 And they cast dust on their heads, and cried, weeping and wailing, saying, "Alas, alas that great city, where all that had ships in the sea were made rich because of her wealth! For in one hour she is made desolate."

18:20 Rejoice over her, you heaven, and you holy apostles and prophets; for God has avenged you on her.

18:21 And a mighty angel took up a stone like a great millstone, and cast it into the sea, saying, "Thus with violence shall that great city Babylon be thrown down, and shall not be found any more at all.

18:22 And the voice of harpers, and musicians, and of pipers, and trumpeters, shall be heard no more at all in you; and no craftsman of any craft, shall be found anymore in you; and the sound of a millstone shall not be heard anymore at all in you;

18:23 And the light of a candle shall shine no more at all in you; and the voice of the bridegroom and of the bride shall be heard no more at all in you. For your merchants were the great men of the earth; for by your sorceries were all nations deceived."

18:24 And in her was found the blood of prophets, and of saints, and of all that were slain on the earth.

18:1-3 Babylon Is Fallen

"And after these things I saw another angel come down from heaven, having great power; and the earth was lightened with his glory. And he cried mightily with a strong voice, saying, 'Babylon the great is fallen, is fallen, and has become the habitation of devils, and the hold of every foul spirit, and a cage of every unclean and hateful bird. For all nations have drunk of the wine of the wrath of her fornication, and the kings of the earth have committed fornication with her, and the merchants of the earth became rich through the power of her excess" (Revelation 18:1-3).

Chapter 18 is a continuation of the elaboration on the fall of the harlot, Babylon the Great. In chapter 14 powerful messages of warning were given to the world by three angels. Now the message of the second angel, "Babylon is fallen, is fallen" (Revelation 14:8) is repeated much more forcefully by an angel **"having great power."** Although it may have been possible to ignore the message of the second angel of Revelation 14, it will not be possible to ignore this one—**"the**

earth was lightened with his glory. And he cried mightily with a strong voice."

The second angel's message "Babylon is fallen" in chapter 14 followed the first angel's message, which began, "Fear God and give glory to Him, for the hour of His judgment has come" (Revelation 14:7). As we saw in 14: *When in History?*, the judgment referred to is primarily the investigative judgment (Day of Atonement) which began in 1844. All of the three angels' messages were given at that time and brought about a great revival and awakening of interest in the Second Coming of Christ (See 3:*Missionary and Advent Movements*), but with the passage of time the impact of the messages largely faded away (See 3:15-17 *Lukewarm*).

However, when the trumpet plagues begin, the whole world will start to desperately seek help from "God." By that time the major players of Babylon the Great will already be in place, waiting only for the appearance of the beast from the bottomless pit (the antichrist) to spring into action against the saints (See 17:6-8). According to Jesus, Paul and John,[683] the delusions of that time will be overwhelming and the pressure to yield allegiance to Babylon will be almost irresistible. But God will not leave the world in darkness. He will send a mighty angel with **"great power"** (which, like the three angels of Revelation 14, represents His Spirit-filled witnesses) and the earth will be illuminated with the mighty reiteration of the message, **"Babylon is fallen."**

In chapter 17 the harlot, Babylon the Great, sitting on a seven-headed scarlet beast, was shown to be an updated, multifaceted and universal version of the seven-headed beast from the sea of chapter 13 which symbolized the Roman Catholic Church of the Dark Ages. It was during the Middle Ages that the Catholic Church perfected the doctrines that have led to her fallen state; these doctrines will form the religious foundation of end-time Babylon. In our day and age doctrine is suspect, and it is considered judgmental to criticize the beliefs of another religion. However, because of the strong emphasis both here and in chapter 14 on the "fallen" nature of Babylon, it is important to look carefully at the Catholic doctrines that have departed from the teachings of Jesus and the apostles.

The messages concerning Babylon's fallen condition are strong and detailed—**"Babylon... has become the habitation of devils, and the hold of every foul spirit, and a cage of every unclean and hateful bird. For all nations have drunk of the wine of the wrath of her fornication, and the kings of the earth have committed fornication with her, and the merchants of the earth became rich through the power of her excess...Her sins have reached to heaven"** (Revelation 18:2,3,5). There is nothing polite, diplomatic or politically correct about these messages.

Since the identity and description of Babylon are among the most prominent themes of the Book of Revelation, a somewhat lengthy and detailed exposition of Roman Catholic tradition and doctrine will now be presented. This is not intended to be self-righteous "Catholic bashing," and indeed the title "MOTHER OF HARLOTS" shows that the great harlot has daughters which are also harlots. This calls for careful self-examination on the part of the Protestant churches that have derived much of their doctrine and traditions from the "mother church." Even those who smugly consider themselves to be part of the "remnant church" should bear in mind that they are presented in chapter 3 as Laodicea, who is so disgustingly lukewarm that God is about to

---

683 See Matthew 24:21-24, 2Thessalonians 2:8-12, Revelation 13:12-17.

spew her out of His mouth![684] Thus the following is presented in humility, in order to help God's people who are in Babylon to recognize her fallen condition and heed the entreaty to **"come out of her."**

Elements of Pagan Worship

In chapter 17 we saw that the mystery religion of ancient Babylon was re-established in pagan Rome and eventually became a part of the Roman Church. Some of the elements of pagan religion which came into the church seem relatively harmless, even though not supported by any Bible teaching. However, even these "harmless" elements are a testimony to the compromises the church made in order to meet the pagan masses halfway. They also refute the claim that the "holy tradition" was handed down in an unbroken chain from the apostles to the present.

The Catholic festivals and holy days, for example, depart widely from the historical facts of the Bible, but instead are often a continuation of ancient pagan feasts. Many people know this and feel that it is unimportant, but the fact is that for most people in "Christian" countries the main contact they have with their religion is during holidays such as Christmas and Easter.

Christmas is generally the most popular feast in Christian countries and through commercialism and globalization it is becoming the primary international event of the year. "Prior to and through the early Christian centuries, winter festivals—especially those centered on the winter solstice, were the most popular of the year in many European pagan cultures...Many modern Christmas customs have been directly influenced by such festivals, including gift-giving and merrymaking from the Roman Saturnalia."[685] It is more than coincidental that the day chosen to celebrate Christ's birth, December 25, was also the pagan Roman holiday *Natalis Sol Invicti*—the birthday of the unconquerable sun.[686]

Processions are another prominent ceremony in the Catholic worship, with the public display of relics, icons, statues, or the pope himself, borne on men's shoulders on a portable throne, with all the priests and episcopates and even the statues of the saints dressed in majestic robes and crowns. Processions are unknown in the scriptures[687] but are common in pagan religions. "It was usual to carry the statue of the principal deity, in whose honour the procession took place, together with that of the king, and the figures of his ancestors, borne in the same manner, on men's shoulders."[688] The scriptures confirm the pagan connection, speaking specifically of the Babylonian gods Bel and Nebo: "They lavish gold out of the bag, and weigh silver on the scales; they hire a goldsmith and he makes it a god; they prostrate themselves, yes, they worship, they bear it on the shoulder, they carry it and set it in its place" (Isaiah 46:6,7).

The mystic keys of St. Peter which are prominently displayed during processions have a

---

684 See 3: *Laodicea.*

685 Wikipedia contributors, "Christmas," *Wikipedia, The Free Encyclopedia,* http://en.wikipedia.org/w/index.php?title=Christmas&oldid=623945581 (accessed September 18, 2014).

686 Wikipedia contributors, "Sol Invictus," *Wikipedia, The Free Encyclopedia,* http://en.wikipedia.org/w/index.php?title=Sol_Invictus&oldid=625780399 (accessed September 18, 2014).

687 When David brought the ark of the covenant to Jerusalem, as recorded in 2Samuel 6, it was in some respects like a procession, but rather than being for ceremonial display it was for the purpose of transporting the ark from its temporary site to its permanent location in Jerusalem.

688 Alexander Hislop, "The Two Babylons" (New York: Loizeaux Brothers) 1959 (First published in 1853). This classic book includes misinformation and speculation, particularly about the history of Nimrod, Semiramis and Tamuz. Nevertheless there is good and valid information in this book but it must be distinguished from that which is questionable by comparison with the Bible and other sources.

pre-Christian origin. "In Mithraism, one of the main branches of the mysteries that came to Rome, the sun god carried two keys. When the emperor claimed to be successor of the gods and Supreme Pontiff of the mysteries, the keys came to be symbols of his authority. Later, when the bishop of Rome became the Pontifex Maximus in about 378, he automatically became the possessor of the mystic keys. This gained recognition for him from the pagans…It was not until 431, however, that the pope publicly made the claim that the keys he possessed were the keys of authority given to the apostle Peter."[689]

The characteristic rituals and practices of the Catholic religion, such as the lighting of candles, making the sign of the cross, pilgrimages, the kissing of and bowing before icons, relics, and statues, the erection of personal and public altars, the use of the rosary and other ritual prayers, and liturgies and prayers for the dead, do not find support in the Bible but rest solely on the "Holy Tradition" of the church. They were, however, common practices in the heathen religions that derived from ancient Babylon.

So why does it matter if Roman Catholics and those who follow their example participate in holidays, ceremonies and rituals that have their roots in paganism, but which no are no longer directed toward the pagan gods? The problem is not so much in the origins of the ceremonies as in their purpose. God designs that His people will have a close, personal, daily relationship with Him, and this is what the human heart craves. But the Roman system seeks to fill this desire with holidays, rituals, ceremonies and pageant that promise a moment of excitement and interest but in the end leave the participants more empty and disappointed than ever.

False Doctrine of Babylon

Pagan practice finds its support in pagan doctrine. Many people today feel that doctrine is an obstacle to that which is really important, that is, worship and a personal relationship with God. But doctrine is simply a statement of what we believe about God, and it is from our belief that our worship and relationship springs. Jesus told the Samaritan woman at the well, "The true worshipers will worship the father in spirit and truth; for the Father is seeking such to worship Him" (John 4:23). No matter how much "spirit" there may be, unless there is "truth" the worship will not be that which "the Father is seeking."

One of the chief doctrines of all pagan religions is the belief in the immortal soul. The Babylonians, Assyrians, Phoenicians and Egyptians all believed that the soul has an eternal destination. Greek philosophers such as Plato made this teaching intellectually palatable, and it was through them that it came into the church (See 20: *What is a Soul?*). Since the Bible clearly teaches that not all will be saved, the doctrine of the immortal soul requires an eternal destination

---

689 Ralph Woodrow, *Babylon Mystery Religion* (Ralph Woodrow Evangelistic Association) 1993 This book includes misinformation, particularly those sections that are derived from "The Two Babylons" by Alexander Hislop, and in fact the author has since repudiated some concepts and information and has allowed "Babylon Mystery Religion" to go out of print. Nevertheless there is much good and valid information in this book but it must be distinguished from that which is questionable.

for the unsaved—everlasting hell.[690] Although many churches today attempt to moderate hell into a place of "eternal separation from God" or to postulate a "second chance" so that all will eventually be saved, the Catholic Church has staunchly held onto the concept of hell as a place of fiery eternal punishment. A few statements from the Catholic Encyclopedia summarize their doctrine:

"The Holy Bible is quite explicit in teaching the eternity of the pains of hell…No cogent reason has been advanced for accepting a metaphorical interpretation…The torments of the damned shall last forever and ever…The objection is made that there is no proportion between the brief moment of sin and an eternal punishment. But why not? Sin is an offense against the infinite authority of God, and the sinner is in some way aware of this, though but imperfectly. Accordingly there is in sin an approximation to infinite malice, which deserves an eternal punishment…Justice demands that whoever departs from the right way in his search for happiness shall not find his happiness, but lose it. The eternity of the pains of hell responds to this demand for justice. And, besides, the fear of hell does really deter many from sin; and thus, in as far as it is threatened by God, eternal punishment also serves for the reform of morals. But if God threatens man with the pains of hell, He must also carry out His threat."

"The utter void of the soul made for the enjoyment of infinite truth and infinite goodness causes the reprobate immeasurable anguish. Their consciousness that God, on Whom they entirely depend, is their enemy forever is overwhelming… Scripture and tradition speak again and again of the fire of hell, and there is no sufficient reason for taking the term as a mere metaphor…The nature of hell-fire is different from that of our ordinary fire; for instance, it continues to burn without the need of a continually renewed supply of fuel…It is meet that whoever seeks forbidden pleasure should find pain in return."[691]

This terrible misrepresentation of God's character of love is based on the false doctrine of the immortality of the soul. Although it has "deterred many from sin," in the modern age it has turned many more into agnostics or atheists. Although scripture clearly teaches that there will be a hell, it will accomplish its purpose of eradicating sin (and the souls and bodies of sinners who cling to sin—Matthew 10:28). Chapter 20 deals with this subject and examines the related scriptures in detail.

A closely related doctrine, which is also found in essentially all pagan religions, is the consciousness of the soul after death (as contrasted with the Biblical teaching that death is an unconscious nothingness awaiting the resurrection—See 6:9,10 *Souls Under the Altar* and 20: *The Soul Sleeps*). This has led to a number of

---

690 "The existence of hell can be demonstrated even by the light of mere reason. In His sanctity and justice as well as in His wisdom, God must avenge the violation of the moral order in such wise as to preserve, at least in general, some proportion between the gravity of sin and the severity of punishment. But it is evident from experience that God does not always do this on earth; therefore He will inflict punishment after death. Moreover, if all men were fully convinced that the sinner need fear no kind of punishment after death, moral and social order would be seriously menaced…If men knew that their sins would not be followed by sufferings, the mere threat of annihilation at the moment of death, and still less the prospect of a somewhat lower degree of beatitude, would not suffice to deter them from sin…It is not intrinsically impossible for God to annihilate the sinner after some definite amount of punishment; but this would be less in conformity with the nature of man's immortal soul" Joseph Hontheim, "Hell," *The Catholic Encyclopedia*, http://www.newadvent.org/cathen/07207a.htm, Accessed Sept. 18, 2014

---

691 Ibid

evils, including the worship of the saints.[692] After all, if they are still aware and concerned about what is happening on earth, why should we not seek their prayers, which, because of their holy lives, are much more effective than ours?[693] And yet the multitude of saints, with personal favorites as well as saints who have jurisdiction over particular professions or circumstances (such as St. Christopher, the saint of travelers) are simply the continuation of the worship of a pantheon of pagan gods.

The doctrine of consciousness in death has also been a major motivation for prayers for the dead. The thought of precious loved ones suffering in the fires of purgatory[694] when payment for a special mass could hasten their entrance into heavenly bliss has led to systematic and extortionate "devouring [of] widows' houses" which was so strongly condemned by Jesus.[695]

Does it really matter if people believe unbiblical doctrines such as the immortal soul and the conscious state of the dead? The real problem with these doctrines is not so much that they are not a true picture of reality but rather that they give a false and ugly picture of God. And this has always been Satan's goal: to make God so unattractive that no one would want anything to do with Him, but would turn instead to false gods that he can manipulate.

The Priesthood

Essentially every pagan religion, including ancient Babylon, has had priests who offered sacrifices to the gods. These were a counterfeit of the Old Testament sacrificial system in which priests offered sacrifices that were a "shadow" of the one great sacrifice Jesus would offer on the Cross. The book of Hebrews makes it very clear that the Old Testament shadow was done away with and Jesus is now our high priest, ministering for us in heaven. [696] There is no evidence in the book of Hebrews or anywhere else in the New Testament that the Christian Church would have a special class of priests. No one else can fulfill that role here on earth: "there is one God and one Mediator between God and men, the man Christ Jesus" (1 Timothy 2:5). All believers are "priests"[697] in the sense that they minister to those around them, directing their attention to Jesus who died for their sins.

But in the Catholic system the Lord's supper or communion is not just a memorial or commemoration of Christ's sacrifice—it is actually a renewal of His sacrifice, and a sacrifice requires a priest. The priest supposedly "creates his Creator" on the sacrificial altar and then feeds His real flesh and blood (which has been "transubstantiated" into the appearance of bread and wine)

---

692 Catholics vigorously deny that they worship the saints, preferring words such as "venerate" and "entreat." However, when they bow down and kiss the images of saints, perform liturgies and have festivals in their honor and make prayers to them, what more would be included that would constitute worship?

693 According to the Catholic Encyclopedia, "Masses 'in honor of the saints' are certainly no base 'deception', but are morally allowable, as the Council of Trent specifically declares (loc. cit. can. v); 'If any one saith, that it is an imposture to celebrate masses in honor of the saints and for obtaining their intercession with God, as the Church intends, let him be anathema." Joseph Pohle, "Sacrifice of the Mass," section "The Causality of the Mass," *The Catholic Encyclopedia*, http://www.newadvent.org/cathen/10006a.htm, accessed Sept. 18, 2014

694 The Catholic Encyclopedia article on hell referenced above refers to a subcategory of hell, "purgatory, where the just, who die in venial [minor] sin or who still owe a debt of temporal punishment for sin, are cleansed by suffering before their admission to heaven." According to Catholic theology, baptism fully atones for original sin and sins committed up to the time of baptism. But sins committed afterward must be atoned for by a combination of Christ's merit and the sinners good works (penance). If these good works have not been adequate they will be supplemented by suffering in purgatory.

695 Matthew 23:14.

696 See Hebrews 7:11-13, 8:1-6, 13.

697 "But you are a chosen generation, a royal priesthood, a holy nation, His own special people, that you may proclaim the praises of Him who called you out of darkness into His marvelous light" (1Peter 2;9, See also Revelation 1:6, 5:10).

to the worshipers, who are thereby partaking of salvation.

The Catholic Encyclopedia explains, "Jesus Christ in a wonderfully condescending manner responds to the natural craving of the human heart after a food which nourishes unto immortality, a craving expressed in many pagan religions, by dispensing to mankind His own flesh and blood. All that is beautiful, all that is true in the [pagan] religions of nature, Christianity has appropriated to itself." "The church intends the Mass to be regarded as a 'true and proper sacrifice,' and will not tolerate the idea that the sacrifice is identical with Holy Communion [the Protestant communion service]. That is the sense of a clause from the Council of Trent (Sess. XXII, can. 1): 'If any one saith that in the Mass a true and proper sacrifice is not offered to God; or, that to be offered is nothing else but that Christ is given us to eat; let him be anathema."[698]

The repudiation of the nearly incomprehensible arguments[699] which are used to "prove" the true sacrificial nature of the Mass is beyond the scope of this chapter. The Bible clearly teaches that the sacrifice on the Cross was a one-time event that is effective for all sins and for all time. "We have been sanctified through the offering of the body of Jesus Christ *once for all...He...offered one sacrifice for sins forever*" (Hebrews 10:10, 12). Suffice to say that the system of priests who hear confession, dispense forgiveness and make the performing of a false sacrifice the center of worship has been one of the most potent means of obscuring Jesus from the minds and hearts of His people.

The Catholic Church insists that the priests (as well as bishops, monks, nuns, and even deacons) must be celibate. It is admitted that this was not a requirement in the apostolic church—"We do not find in the New Testament any indication of celibacy being made compulsory either upon the Apostles or those whom they ordained."[700] Although the apostle Paul felt that being single helped him personally to focus his attention on serving the Lord,[701] he clearly stated that "the bishop must be blameless, the husband of one wife."[702] The fact that Peter and other apostles were married[703] is another example which shows that Catholic traditions such as celibacy of the priesthood do not have their foundation in apostolic teaching.[704]

Paul clearly warned, "Now the Spirit expressly says that in latter times some will depart from the faith, giving heed to deceiving spirits and *doctrines of demons...forbidding to marry*" (1Timothy 4:1-3). The news is full of shameful and disgusting revelations of gross immorality, homosexuality and child abuse among priests

---

698 Joseph Pohle, "Eucharist," *The Catholic Encylopedia*, <http://www.newadvent.org/cathen/05572c.htm>, accessed Sept. 19, 2014, Joseph Pohle, "Sacrifice of the Mass," *The Catholic Encyclopedia*, http://www.newadvent.org/cathen/10006a.htm, accessed Sept. 18, 2014

699 The Catholic Encyclopedia can be researched on-line. The article "Sacrifice of the Mass" is full of the obtuse arguments which are used to try to rationalize the illogical nature of the mass.

700 Herbert Thurston, "Celibacy of the Clergy," *The Catholic Encyclopedia* http://www.newadvent.org/cathen/03481a.htm, accessed Sept. 19, 2014.

701 See 1Corinthians 7.

702 1Timothy 3:2, 11-13.

703 "Do we have no right to take along a believing wife, as do also the other apostles, the brothers of the Lord and Cephas [Peter]?" (1Corinthians 9:5).

704 The Catholic Encyclopedia in the article "Celibacy of the Clergy" quoted above admits that the decision to marry was a matter of personal choice for hundreds of years. "This freedom of choice seems to have lasted during the whole of what we may call, with Vacandard, the first period of the church's legislation, i.e. down to about the time of Constantine and the Council of Nicaea." However, celibacy is justified with human logic such as this example, "From the earliest period, the church was personified and conceived of by her disciples as the Virgin Bride and as the pure Body of Christ, or again as the Virgin Mother (parthenos meter), and it was plainly fitting that this virgin church should be served by a virgin priesthood...The conviction that virginity possesses a higher sanctity and clearer spiritual intuitions, seems to be an instinct planted deep in the heart of man."

all over the world, as well as the efforts by the church to cover up and hide the extent of the crimes. This is not so much an indictment of the priests and leaders involved as it is of the Babylon system they have inherited.

The head of the priesthood is the pope, who, through "apostolic succession" is supposed to have inherited authority over the universal church from the unbroken chain of popes who began with the apostle Peter. Peter himself supposedly received this universal authority after his confession, "You are the Christ, the Son of the living God" when Jesus responded, "And I also say to you that you are Peter, (Greek *Petros*) and on this rock (Greek *petra*) I will build My church" (Matthew 16:16-18). This single text is insufficient evidence for such a critical doctrine, especially since the Greek words in the text, *Petros* and *petra*, are not the same, which makes it doubtful that Jesus intended to say that He was building His church on Peter. Peter never claimed for himself universal authority, and in fact he said that all Christians are "living stones being built up a spiritual house" and that "Jesus Christ…has become the chief cornerstone" (1Peter 2:4-9). Paul maintains that all the apostles and prophets are the foundation, not just Peter—"The household of God, having been built on the foundation of the apostles and prophets, Jesus Christ Himself being the chief cornerstone" (Ephesians 2:19,20). Rather than singling out Peter, Paul mentioned "James, Cephas, [Peter] and John, who seemed to be pillars" (Galatians 2:9).

In the first "universal council" in Jerusalem, it was James, not Peter, who was the obvious leader.[705] Paul, rather than deferring to an infallible pope, rebuked Peter for his errors.[706] The "unbroken succession" itself is highly suspect since there were conflicting claims by rival popes, not to mention the gross immorality and criminal behavior of some of the popes who constitute links in the chain.[707] The insistence on the universal authority of the pope has been and continues to be one of the most divisive issues in christendom.[708] Although individual popes have been great moral leaders, this does not change the fact that they preside over a fatally flawed system.

In the final analysis, the problem with the Catholic system of priests and the pope is that the attention is on their work instead of on the work of Christ. In the Old Testament era the priests were a necessary symbol of the Messiah who was to come. But now that the symbol has become a reality in Christ, the effort to symbolize Him with human priests is only a distraction from the true source of our salvation.

Salvation by Sacraments

The sacramental system of the Catholic Church uses the language of Christianity, but the means of salvation is very different. The Bible repeatedly asserts that our salvation is by faith from start to finish—"The righteousness of God is revealed from faith to faith; for it is written, 'the just shall live by faith.'" "That we might be justified by faith in Christ and not by the works of the law; for by the works of the law no flesh shall

---

705 Acts 15:6-21. After Paul, Peter, and others gave their testimonies, James was the one who made the pronouncement that was recorded and sent to all the churches.

706 Galatians 2:11-14.

707 Just one of many examples is Pope Benedict IX. "The Catholic Encyclopedia calls him "a disgrace to the Chair of Peter." The first pope said to have been primarily homosexual, he was said to have held orgies in the Lateran palace. He was also accused by Bishop Benno of Piacenza of 'many vile adulteries and murders.' Pope Victor III, in his third book of Dialogues, referred to 'his rapes, murders and other unspeakable acts. His life as a pope was so vile, so foul, so execrable, that I shudder to think of it." Wikipedia contributors, "Pope Benedict IX," *Wikipedia, The Free Encyclopedia*, http://en.wikipedia.org/w/index.php?title=Pope_Benedict_IX&oldid=617673982 (accessed September 24, 2014).

708 The most important issue in the great schism between the Eastern Orthodox and Roman Catholic Churches in 1054 (which still divides them today) was papal authority.

be justified" (Romans 1:17, Galatians 2:16). The Catholic religion, however, postulates that just as in the "old law" there were sacraments such as circumcision, animal sacrifices, rituals of ordination, etc., in the Christian dispensation there is a "new law" which specifies seven sacraments.[709] They are administered by the church, and are the means by which God dispenses His grace. Without them salvation cannot be obtained.

Although the church insists that the sacraments have their basis in faith, an examination of the most essential, baptism, shows that the sacraments are based on the works of the priest rather than the faith of the Christian. First of all, baptism is considered to be so essential that without it no one can be saved. Until very recently, even infants or embryos with their "immortal souls" which died without baptism were consigned to eternal hell.[710] However, if a priest or even a layman sprinkled them with water and said the right words before they died they would have eternal life in heaven. Obviously the infant has no faith, and in fact faith on the part of the parents was not even required.[711]

In recent years there has been furious debate within the church as it has faced harsh criticism of its stance on infant baptism. In the end the church has conceded that infants may be given entrance to heaven without the baptismal ceremony, but this concession simply underscores the underlying presupposition of baptism as well as the other sacraments: that it is a ceremony performed by a priest or his representative that leads to salvation, rather than faith on the part of the believer in what Christ has already accomplished.

Who Can Forgive Sins?

Forgiveness of sins is the heart of the gospel and the reason Jesus came to this earth and died on the Cross. "All have sinned" and "the wages of sin is death" but "if we confess our sins He is faithful and just to forgive us our sins and cleanse us from unrighteousness" (Romans 3:23, 6:23, 1John 1:9). But the Roman Catholic system of "salvation" has a "different gospel" (Galations 1:6).

Baptism, it is claimed, removes the guilt of "original sin" and of all sins committed up to that point. But according to Catholic theology, sins committed after baptism cannot be atoned for without the sacrament of penance. "Penance is a sacrament of the New Law instituted by Christ in which forgiveness of sins committed after baptism is granted through the priest's absolution to those who with true sorrow confess their sins and

---

709 "The Council of Trent solemnly defined that there are seven sacraments of the New Law, truly and properly so called, viz., Baptism, Confirmation, Holy Eucharist, Penance, Extreme Unction, Orders, and Matrimony." Daniel Kennedy, "Sacraments," *The Catholic Encyclopedia*, http://www.newadvent.org/cathen/13295a.htm, accessed Sept. 19, 2014.

710 "Hell (infernus) in theological usage is a place of punishment after death. Theologians distinguish four meanings of the term hell...The limbo of infants (limbus parvulorum), where those who die in original sin alone, and without personal mortal sin, are confined and undergo some kind of punishment" Joseph Hontheim, "Hell," *The Catholic Encyclopedia*, http://www.newadvent.org/cathen/07207a.htm, Accessed Sept. 18, 2014. This concept is refuted in Job 3:11-19 which teaches that those who "die at birth" are "quiet," "asleep," "at rest with kings and counselors of the earth" and the "stillborn child" along with "the wicked" "cease from troubling," "are at rest," and "do not hear the voice of the oppressor."

---

711 Infant baptism is justified with the claim that it is the New Testament equivalent of circumcision, which was performed on the eighth day of life. However, there was an important difference between the sacraments and the Old Testament ceremonies. These were a "shadow" of what Christ would accomplish, not life-giving rituals which imparted God's grace. Paul made this clear in Romans 4: "Faith was accounted to Abraham for righteousness. When was it accounted? While he was circumcised, or uncircumcised? Not while circumcised, but while uncircumcised. And he received the sign of circumcision, a seal of *the righteousness of the faith which he had while still uncircumcised*, that he might be the father of all those who believe" (Romans 4:9-11).

promise to satisfy for the same…It comprises the actions of the penitent in presenting himself to the priest and accusing himself of his sins, and the actions of the priest in pronouncing absolution and imposing satisfaction."[712] According to Catholic theology, the priest does not simply assure the sinner that God has forgiven him, but actually grants the forgiveness, which is then "ratified" by God. "Christ not only declared that sins were forgiven, but really and actually forgave them; hence, the Apostles are empowered not merely to announce to the sinner that his sins are forgiven but to grant him forgiveness…If their power were limited to the declaration 'God pardons you,' they would need a special revelation in each case to make the declaration valid."[713]

Since the priest himself is making the judgment, he must know the details of the sins in order to make an informed judgment. "How can a wise and prudent judgment be rendered if the priest be in ignorance of the cause on which judgment is pronounced? And how can he obtain the requisite knowledge unless it come from the spontaneous acknowledgment of the sinner… and the detailed confession of sins?"[714]

Moreover, it is claimed that since God has established the sacrament of penance, this rules out the option of the sinner going directly to God to obtain forgiveness. "For those who after baptism have fallen into sin, the sacrament of penance is as necessary unto salvation as is baptism itself for those who have not yet been regenerated' (Council of Trent, Sess. XIV, c. 2). Penance, therefore, is not an institution the use of which was left to the option of each sinner so that he might, if he preferred, hold aloof from the church and secure forgiveness by some other means, e.g., by acknowledging his sin in the privacy of his own mind. The power granted by Christ to the Apostles is twofold, to forgive and to retain, in such a way that what they forgive God forgives and what they retain God retains. But this grant would be nullified if, in case the church retained the sins of the penitent, he could, as it were, take appeal to God's tribunal and obtain pardon…It would indeed have been strangely inconsistent if Christ in conferring this twofold power on the Apostles had intended to provide some other means of forgiveness such as confessing 'to God alone'[715]…By Divine ordinance the mercy of God

---

712 Edward Hanna, "The Sacrament of Penance," *The Catholic Encyclopedia*, http://www.newadvent.org/cathen/11618c.htm, accessed Sept. 20, 2014

713 *Ibid*

714 *Ibid*

715 This and other Catholic doctrines are based upon "Holy Tradition" and can be traced to statements by the "fathers" such as Ignatius and Justin Martyr who wrote in the early centuries. However, there are at least three problems with relying on the "fathers" to provide information about the Apostolic church: 1) There is a time gap between the writings of the Apostles and those of the "fathers." Paul, for example, was probably martyred around AD 67, and had earlier said, "After my departure savage wolves will come in among you, not sparing the flock" (Acts 20:29). Peter warned, "There will be false teachers among you, who will secretly bring in destructive heresies" (2Peter 2:1). The Bible writers who wrote later (Jude, Epistles of John) acknowledge that the corruption had already entered the church (e.g. "Contend earnestly for the faith which was once for all delivered to the saints. For certain men have crept in unnoticed, who long ago were marked out for this condemnation, ungodly men, who turn the grace of our God into lewdness and deny the only Lord God and our Lord Jesus Christ," Jude 3,4, see also 1John 2:18,19, 4:1,3 2John 7-10). 2) That this corruption happened is evident from the dramatic differences between the theology of the Apostles and that of the "fathers." Paul, for example, insists that we are made right and stay right with God because of faith in what Jesus has done (Romans 5:10). In contrast, "According to Tertullian [one of the early "fathers"], 'Exomologesis [penance] is the discipline which obliges a man to prostrate and humiliate himself and to adopt a manner of life that will draw down mercy. As regards dress and food, it prescribes that he shall lie in sackcloth and ashes, clothe his body in rags, plunge his soul in sorrow, correct his faults by harsh treatment of himself, use the plainest meat and drink for the sake of his soul and not of his belly: usually he shall nourish prayer by fasting, whole days and nights together he shall moan, and weep, and wail to the Lord his God, cast himself at the feet of the priests, fall on his knees before those who are dear to God, and beseech them to plead in his behalf" (*Sacrament of Penance*, "The Catholic Encyclopedia"). 3) The earliest writings, such as Ignatius, give evidence of having been tampered with so as to be in harmony with later church doctrine.

can be obtained only through the supplications of the priests." [716]

As in the other false doctrines that have been discussed, the real problem with the doctrine of priestly forgiveness is that the focus is on the sinner's relationship with the priest, not with Christ. But Jesus expressed the desire of His heart in Matthew 11:28 when He said, "Come to Me, all you who labor and are heavy laden, and I will give you rest."

The Keys of the Kingdom

This power to forgive sins was supposedly granted to Peter and the other Apostles in Matthew 16:19, 18:18 ("I will give you the keys of the kingdom of heaven, and whatever you bind on earth will be bound in heaven, and whatever you loose on earth will be loosed in heaven") and especially John 20:21-23 ("If you forgive the sins of any, they are forgiven them; if you retain the sins of any, they are retained"). However, Jesus was actually informing the disciples of the awesome responsibility that goes along with the tremendous privileges they had received. [717] These extraordinary privileges and the commission to share them are the "keys of the kingdom."

When Jesus talked about the keys of the kingdom He was referring to the gospel of Christ's sacrifice for our sins, which is literally the difference between eternal life and everlasting destruction. The disciples were made stewards of this life-giving "key of knowledge" (Luke 11:52). Thus they (and all true believers) have

the power to bind or loose by our decisions to share what we know or to be silent, or, worst of all, to misrepresent the gospel. Souls can either hear, believe and accept the Lord (be bound in heaven) or go their way in fatal ignorance (be loosed in heaven). We can either forgive those who have done us wrong, showing them through our actions a true picture of God so that they can find forgiveness from Him, or we can retain their sins (refuse to forgive) and thus block them from knowing the truth (the gospel) of God's willingness to forgive. Jesus shows us in these texts that with the tremendous light and privilege of the gospel comes an equally serious responsibility to be faithful with what we know. One of His most scathing rebukes was to the lawyers, who had the "key" of life-giving knowledge, but refused to use it—"Woe to you lawyers! For *you have taken away the key of knowledge.* You did not enter in yourselves, and those who were entering in you hindered" (Luke 11:52).

It is evident that God was not bestowing upon a new priesthood the power to forgive sins, because there are no instances in the New Testament of anyone confessing their sins or receiving forgiveness from the Apostles or from anyone else. [718] The prodigal son confessed his sins to his father (who represented our Heavenly Father), who received him without any works of penance, putting on him a rich robe to cover his filthy garments (representing Christ's righteousness which covers our sins). Even in the Old Testament period when there was a priesthood, David showed that the sinner comes directly to God for forgiveness: "Blessed is he whose transgression is forgiven…When I kept silent, my

---

716 "Sacrament of Penance," *The Catholic Encyclopedia.*

717 In the passage in Matthew 16, Peter had just been shown by the "Father who is in heaven" that Jesus is "the Christ, the Son of the Living God" (vs.16,17). In Matthew 18 Jesus had just told the disciples how they, sinners themselves, must deal with fellow believers who have fallen into sin (vs. 15-17). In John 20 they had just encountered the resurrected Jesus, He had filled them with the Holy Spirit and given them the Great Commission ("As the Father has sent Me, I also send you") (vs. 19-22).

718 While it is true that the Apostle James wrote "Confess your trespasses to one another" (James 5:16), it should be kept in mind that this was a part of the healing prayer for the sick and involved mutual confession of sins, not one-way confession by a sinner to a priest. There is certainly nothing in this text suggesting that this is the sole means of obtaining forgiveness.

bones grew old through my groaning all the day long…I acknowledged my sin *to You*, and my iniquity I have not hidden. I said, 'I will confess my transgression *to the Lord*' and You forgave the iniquity of my sin" (Psalms 32:1-5).

John said "If we confess our sins, He [God] is faithful and just to forgive us our sins and to cleanse us from all unrighteousness" (1John 1:9). This is a direct transaction with God through Christ, with no further conditions. But according to Catholic teaching, our repentance and confession must be supplemented by works of penance in order to pay the full penalty for our sin. "After the reception of absolution in penance, there may and usually does remain some temporal debt to be discharged by works of satisfaction…If you punish your own sin, God will spare you; but in any case the sin will not go unpunished…God wants us to perform satisfaction in order that we may clear off our indebtedness to His justice… We regard it as salutary to repeat the confession, because of the shame it involves, which is a great part of penance…the oftener one confesses, the more is the [temporal] penalty reduced; hence one might confess over and over again until the whole penalty is canceled, nor would he thereby offer any injury to the sacrament…those who are in earnest about their salvation count no hardship too great whereby they can win back God's friendship."[719]

The last sentence gets to the heart of the doctrinal error. In the Catholic system God is the offended party and we must win back His friendship and satisfy His justice. But the Bible teaches that we are the ones who have estranged ourselves from God, made ourselves His enemies and rejected His love, and He is doing everything possible to win us back to Himself. "God demonstrates His own love toward us, in that while we were still sinners Christ died for us…For if when we were enemies we were reconciled to God through the death of His Son, much more, having been reconciled, we shall be saved by His life" (Romans 5:8-10).

Babylon and the Law of God

One of the most prominent features of future Babylon is her war against God's people—"I saw the woman, drunk with the blood of the saints and with the blood of the martyrs of Jesus" (Revelation 17:6). This is a continuation of the war waged by Babylon of the Middle Ages (the beast of Revelation 13) which "was granted to make war with the saints and to overcome them" (Revelation 13:7). The enmity of Babylon is simply a reflection of the wrath of her invisible ruler, the great dragon, Satan—"the dragon was enraged with the woman, and he went to make war with the rest of her offspring, who keep the commandments of God and have the testimony of Jesus Christ"(Revelation 12:17). Here we see that a major reason for Satan's rage against God's people is that they keep His commandments. As we saw in 13: *The Beast's Agenda*, Satan has always warred against God's commandments because they expose and condemn his ambition to take God's place and receive worship himself. This is why he "[persecutes] the saints of the Most High, and…[intends] to change times and law" (Daniel 7:25).

Although most of the Ten Commandments, such as prohibitions against lying, stealing and adultery, are clearly in the interest of society in general, the Catholic Church has institutionalized

---

719 "The Sacrament of Penance," *The Catholic Encyclopedia*.

the transgression of two[720] of the commandments.[721] The second commandment prohibits the making, bowing down to or serving of any "likeness of anything that is in heaven above or that is in the earth beneath or that is in the water under the earth." But Catholic churches are full of statues and images of "saints" who have died, and the Catholic people are taught to bow, kiss and offer prayers to images of the saints, and liturgies and holidays are devoted to them. Some of the images themselves have special miraculous powers so that people make pilgrimages to visit well-known images, hoping to gain a special dispensation of grace. Although theologically the miracles may be considered a manifestation of God's grace, everyone involved gives credit to the saints themselves.

Chapters 13 and 14 have already dealt with the attempt by the Papacy to change the fourth commandment by substituting Sunday for the Seventh-day Sabbath. We saw that this change will become an international issue, which will culminate in the mark of the beast and the death decree. It is interesting to note that Catholic writers have pointed to this change and its acceptance by the Protestant churches as a mark of her authority—"by keeping Sunday strictly they [Protestants] acknowledge the [Catholic] church's power to ordain feasts, and to command them under sin."[722]

Worship of the "Mother of God"

The first and second of the Ten Commandments prohibit having any other gods or making and worshiping images of anything, even if it supposedly represents God. They specifically forbid bowing down to and serving anything or anyone except God. But even though the breaking of these two commandments is perhaps the most serious and offensive of all sins,[723] they are disregarded in the Catholic (and Orthodox) worship of the Virgin Mary.

Catholics officially claim that they do not actually worship Mary, but only "venerate" or honor her for her exalted role as the mother of Jesus. But the fact is that Catholic teaching and practice is nothing short of worship. Several of the most important church holidays are in her honor, liturgies are performed and prayers are directed to her[724] and miraculous answers to prayers are attributed to her. Countless churches, shrines and altars are dedicated to her—"These shrines, which as time went on multiplied beyond calculation in every part of Europe, nearly always owed their celebrity to the temporal and spiritual favors which it was believed the Blessed Virgin granted to those who invoked her in these favored spots. The gratitude of pilgrims often enriched them with the most costly gifts; crowns of gold and precious gems, embroidered garments, and rich hangings meet us at every turn in the record of such sanctuaries...

---

720 It is interesting to note that the two longest commandments (the second and the fourth) that have the most words of explanation are the ones that are broken, as if God made a special effort to try to prevent their transgression, knowing in advance that they would be the points of attack. In her catechisms the Catholic Church has even tried to hide the second commandment, combining it with the first and then giving an abbreviated form (you shall have no other gods before Me) that completely leaves out the mention of images.

721 Breaking one of the commandments is equivalent to breaking them all (James 2:10,11).

722 "Abridgment of Catholic Doctrine" quoted in White, EG *The Great Controversy*, chapter "God's Law Immutable," Nampa, ID Pacific Press. See also www.sa-hebroots.com/catholic_admissions. php for similar statements.

---

723 The most serious warnings and threatenings in both the Old and New Testament have to do with the worship of other Gods. "He who sacrifices to any god except to the Lord only, he shall be utterly destroyed" Exodus 22:20, "If anyone worships the beast and his image...he himself shall also drink of the wine of the wrath of God which is poured out full strength into the cup of his indignation" Revelation 14:9,10.

724 In the Rosary, which is the most popular Catholic prayer, the "Hail Mary" is said 53 times, while the Lord's prayer is only said 6 times!

The special vogue of a particular shrine was due to some miraculous manifestation which was believed to have occurred there. Blood was said to have flowed from certain statues and pictures of Our Lady which had suffered outrage. Others had wept or exuded moisture. In other cases, the head had bowed or the hand been raised in benediction."[725]

Although it is admitted that much of this popular devotion is nothing but superstition, the church has done nothing to stop it, but instead has encouraged it because it is a vast source of income, and has even gone so far as to defend it as an aid to personal piety. "That popular devotion to the Blessed Virgin was often attended with extravagance and abuse, it is impossible to deny. Nevertheless we may believe that the simple faith and devotion of the people was often rewarded in proportion to their honest intention of paying respect to the Mother of God."[726]

The scriptures have even been altered to give Mary a divine role in the salvation of mankind! The first promise of a Redeemer is found in Genesis 3:15, "I will put enmity between you [the serpent] and the woman, and between your seed and her Seed. He shall bruise your head, and you shall bruise His heel." This has been changed to read, "*She* shall bruise your head, and you shall bruise *Her* heel," with "she" and "her" referring to Mary. The church admits that they have changed the scripture but defends the change because it

agrees with their exaltation of Mary.[727] And the clearest of scriptural teachings ("There is one God and one Mediator between God and men, the Man Christ Jesus" 1 Timothy 2:5) is nullified with the titles "Mediatrix" and "Co-redemptress."[728]

For centuries the church has insisted on the use of the blasphemous title "mother of God." For example, the Catholic Encyclopedia says, "Jesus is the Word made flesh, the Word Who assumed human nature in the womb of Mary. As Mary was truly the mother of Jesus, and as Jesus was truly God from the first moment of His conception, Mary is truly the mother of God."[729] In line with this is the Catholic teaching that Mary was sinless—"She is conceived without the stain of original sin…When there is question of sin, Mary must always be excepted. Mary's complete

---

725 Herbert Thurston, "Devotion to the Blessed Virgin Mary" *The Catholic Encyclopedia,* http://www.newadvent.org/cathen/15459a.htm, accessed Sept. 22, 2014.

726 *Ibid*

727 The Catholic Encyclopedia asserts, "The second point of difference between the Hebrew text and our version concerns the agent who is to inflict the mortal wound on the serpent: our version agrees with the present Vulgate text in reading "she" (ipsa) which refers to the woman, while the Hebrew text reads "He" (autos, ipse) which refers to the seed of the woman. According to our version, and the Vulgate reading, the woman herself will win the victory; according to the Hebrew text, she will be victorious through her seed. In this sense does the Bull "Ineffabilis" ascribe the victory to Our Blessed Lady. The reading "she" (ipsa) is neither an intentional corruption of the original text, nor is it an accidental error; it is rather an explanatory version expressing explicitly the fact of Our Lady's part in the victory over the serpent, which is contained implicitly in the Hebrew original. The strength of the Christian tradition as to Mary's share in this victory may be inferred from the retention of "she" in St. Jerome's version in spite of his acquaintance with the original text and with the reading "he" (ipse) in the old Latin version." Anthony Maas, "The Blessed Virgin Mary" *The Catholic Encyclopedia,* http://www.newadvent.org/cathen/15464b.htm, accessed Sept. 22, 2014.

728 "The recourse we have to Mary in prayer follows upon the office she continuously fills by the side of the throne of God as Mediatrix of Divine grace; being by worthiness and by merit most acceptable to Him, and, therefore, surpassing in power all the angels and saints in Heaven. Now, this merciful office of hers, perhaps, appears in no other form of prayer so manifestly as it does in the Rosary. For in the Rosary all the part that Mary took as our co-Redemptress comes to us" "On the Rosary, His Holiness Pope Leo XIII, September 8, 1894," http://www.newadvent.org/library/docs_le13is.htm, accessed Sept. 22, 2014

729 "The Blessed Virgin Mary," *The Catholic Encyclopedia.*

exemption from actual sin is confirmed by the Council of Trent."[730] In contrast, the scriptures are clear that "all have sinned and fall short of the glory of God—there is none righteous, no, not one" (Romans 3:23,10). Mary herself exclaimed, "My spirit rejoices in God my Savior,"[731] a clear statement that she was a sinner in need of salvation.

This is the real tragedy of the worship of Mary, as well as the other doctrines and practices of pagan origin which are so prominent in the Roman Catholic religion. In true Bible Christianity, the life, death, resurrection, mediation and return of Jesus Christ are central to every doctrine and practice, and the one great object in life is to enter into and maintain a saving relationship with God the Father, Son and Holy Spirit. But in the Catholic religion the focus is on what the church does, what the priests, bishops, and popes do, what the saints do, what the Virgin Mary does and what I do for the salvation of my soul. The Father, Son and Holy Spirit, although getting lip service, are to a great extent left out of the picture. In remembering and honoring those who are connected to God, He Himself is all too often forgotten.

To put the matter into everyday terms, if you were sick, why would you go to the mother or friend of the doctor instead of to the doctor? If your house was on fire, why would you call the mother or friend of the fireman instead of the fireman himself? The only reason would be that at some level you believed that the doctor or fireman was not really willing to help you, or that he was too busy with other things, and that he needed to be persuaded by his mother or friends who love you more than he does. But God demonstrated on the Cross that He loves you more than His own life, and would do anything for you; He doesn't need someone to convince Him to help you, and more than anything He just wants you to come to Him.

The Harlot and Her Daughters

The false doctrines that have led to the fallen condition of Babylon developed slowly and were perfected during the Middle Ages. The Protestant Reformation made major progress in overturning these errors, accepting righteousness by faith alone and the sole authority of the scriptures, and rejecting some of the worst of these doctrines, such as the mass, the priesthood, the doctrines of confession and penance, the worship of the saints and the authority of the pope and tradition. But despite this, the Book of Revelation teaches that end-time Babylon is much broader and inclusive than just the Roman Catholic Church. The title on the forehead of the great harlot is "The Mother of Harlots," indicating that she has daughters which share in her characteristics.

Certainly the Eastern Orthodox Church, although it has been at odds with the papacy for a millennium, shares almost all of her doctrines and practices. Furthermore, nearly all the Protestant churches have retained some of the Catholic doctrines that constitute the wine of Babylon, such as the immortality of the soul, eternal hell, consciousness in death, rejection of the Seventh-day Sabbath, feasts of pagan origin, and infant baptism. Even though they have these points in common, the Protestant Churches since the time of the reformers have staunchly refused to enter into communion and fellowship with the Roman Catholic Church. But according to scripture this will change, and in fact it is changing right before our eyes, as more and more Protestants and Catholics are cooperating for common social and political agendas, and even worshiping together.

What is the "glue" that is allowing Protestants

---

730 *Ibid*
731 Luke 1:47.

and Catholics to stick together despite their still considerable doctrinal differences? One of the major factors is the hyper-polarization of politics and the politicization of the church. Politics have become like team sports, with extreme partisanship and fierce rivalry that transcends the political issues, and the church has gotten caught up in this. The Catholic Church has always pushed for cooperation or even union with the state to further its agenda, but as a minority in America they have needed allies. In recent decades Evangelical Christians have also sought to influence the state on issues that are important to them such as opposition to abortion, and have found Catholics to be powerful and effective partners. Catholics and Protestants find themselves on the same "team," and these political alliances could easily evolve into the persecuting image to the beast and ultimately Babylon during the chaos and stress of the time of trouble.

Another factor is Pentecostalism,[732] a movement that has swept around the world, both in Protestant and Catholic churches. Doctrinal differences are minimized because it is an experience-oriented movement that emphasizes music, drama, speaking in tongues, personal prophecy; in other words, the worship experience. Those who share in emotional worship feel that they have unity of the Spirit, so division on the basis of doctrine seems to be a denial of the Spirit's moving and presence in the lives of their fellow worshipers, no matter what their denominational persuasion may be.

Although many Pentecostal churches are Bible based and have few differences with other Evangelical churches, there are others that make the "gifts of the Spirit" the main focus of their faith and worship. Pentecostalism has crossed all denominational barriers, and in fact has been a much more unifying force than the ecumenical movement, which is based on attempts to resolve doctrinal disagreements.

Unfortunately, it is a unity based on unscriptural elements. Speaking in tongues, for example, is found in many non-Christian religions, which shows that it is not necessarily generated by the Holy Spirit. A study of recordings of tongues by linguists has shown that it is not a known language, nor does it have the linguistic components of a true language.[733] This is in contrast to the gift of tongues as recorded in the book of Acts, which was definitely a language that could be understood by the hearers.[734] Some Pentecostals, faced with this reality, have claimed that the gift of tongues is a "heavenly language," but there is no scriptural evidence that the speaking of a heavenly language was ever a part of the experience

---

732 Pentecostalism is considered to have originated at the Azuza Temple in Los Angeles in 1906, although most of the elements, including speaking in tongues, were present in some churches much earlier. Speaking in tongues was very much of a fringe phenomena, confined to fundamentalist "holy roller" churches until the 1970's when the Pentecostal worship style, combined with contemporary music, took over the "Jesus" movement.

733 See Gerhard Hasel, *Speaking in Tongues*, (Berrien Springs, MI, Adventist Theological Society Publications) 1994.

734 Acts 2:6-11. Luke makes it a point to name the many different languages that were spoken. This, along with Acts 10:46 ("They heard them speak with tongues and magnify God") are scriptural examples in which it is possible to see the characteristics of the gift of tongues. In later instances in the book of Acts Peter either said that the gift was given in the same way as at Pentecost (ie. foreign languages, Acts 10:44-46, 11:15-17) or the nature of the gift was not specified (Acts 19:4-6). In 1Corinthians 12-14 there are verses which support both foreign languages and an unknown prayer language. But a basic principle of scriptural interpretation is that clear passages should be used to explain unclear ones.

of the early church.[735] Apparently "speaking in tongues" (not the Biblical gift, but as practiced today in Pentecostal churches) is a human capability that can be learned through modeling and coaching. As such it is not necessarily "of the devil." The problem arises when it is considered to be a "direct line to God" that does not have to be submitted to the body of Christ and the Word of God for confirmation.[736]

Likewise, personal prophecies, in which Christians who possess the "gift of prophecy" give "messages from God" to their fellow believers, often do not pass the scriptural test, which is that the predicted event must come to pass.[737] It is not at all uncommon for personal prophecies or a "word of knowledge" to fail to come to pass in the Pentecostal churches, which is not surprising since those with the "gift" often take it very casually, not realizing how serious it is to speak in the name of the Lord.

This is not to say that those who speak in tongues or give personal prophecies are wicked people or are possessed by an evil spirit; to the contrary, they are often sincere Christians who are simply following the teaching and traditions of their churches. However, the unscriptural aspects of the Pentecostal movement can be used by the devil[738] and are fast becoming the common elements that bind disparate Christian denominations together into what will become the final manifestation of Babylon.

---

735 Obviously the "tongues" spoken at Pentecost was not a heavenly language—the Greek word for tongues ("They…began to speak in tongues" Acts 2:4) is plural, showing that they were not speaking one heavenly language but many earthly languages (and the passage goes on to list the many languages spoken). It is true that Paul said, "If I speak in the tongues of men and of angels, but have not love" (1Corinthians 13:1), but this is just the first of a list of hypothetical, "ultimate" spiritual experiences which Paul himself did not have. For example, he did not "understand all mysteries and all knowledge" (v.2, compare 1Corinthians 13:9) or have "all faith" (v.2, compare 2Corinthians1:8) nor did he bestow all his goods to feed the poor (v.3, compare 2Timothy 4:15) or give his body to be burned (v.3, compare Acts 25:11). Actually, a careful study of 1Corinthians 12-14 shows that Paul was confronting the same problem that is present in Pentecostal churches today: 1) An insistence that the gift of tongues should be present in every believer who has been "baptized by the Holy Spirit" (1Corinthians 12:7-11, 30, 14:1,2,12) 2) A failure to give a message which edifies the church, but instead edifying themselves by publicly displaying their "gift" (1Corinthians 14:4-6, 12, 16, 19, 26), 3) A confusing, disorderly service which is repulsive to unbelievers (1Corinthians 14:16, 22, 23, 27,33,40). Although there are a few verses which could be interpreted as supporting unintelligible, ecstatic speech (1Corinthians14:2, 9,14), Paul speaks of them negatively and they do not overturn the clear teaching of Acts 2:6-11. Although 1Corinthians 14 is the favorite "tongues" passage, most of the verses support tongues as a foreign language that can be interpreted and understood (1Corinthians 14:5,9-11, 13). At any rate, if Pentecostal churches today carefully followed the worship guidelines given in 1Corinthians 14:26-40 there would be none of the noisy, hyper-ecstatic services that characterize some Pentecostal churches.

736 Jeremiah devotes nearly a whole chapter (Jeremiah 23:9-40) to false prophets in Israel who "speak a vision of their own heart" (v. 16). His message is summarized in vs. 31,32, verses which are very relevant today: "Behold, I am against the prophets,' says the Lord, 'who use their tongues and say, "He says." 'Behold, I am against those who prophesy false dreams' says the Lord, 'and tell them, and cause My people to err by their lies and by their recklessness. Yet I did not send them or command them; therefore they shall not profit this people at all' says the Lord."

---

737 "The prophet who presumes to speak a word in My name, which I have not commanded him to speak, or who speaks in the name of other gods, that prophet shall die. And if you say in your heart, 'How shall we know the word which the Lord has not spoken?'—when a prophet speaks in the name of the Lord, if the thing does not happen or come to pass, that is the thing which the Lord has not spoken: the prophet has spoken it presumptuously" (Deuteronomy 18:20-22).

738 There may be some validity to the idea that the deceptive activity of the beast from the earth (apostate American Protestantism, see 13:13,14 *Fire from Heaven*) is modern extreme Pentecostalism. The verse "He performs great signs, so that he even makes fire come down from heaven on the earth in the sight of men. And He deceives those who dwell on the earth, by those signs which he was granted to do" brings to mind the day of Pentecost. "Then there appeared to them divided tongues, as of fire, and one sat upon each of them. And they were all filled with the Holy Spirit and began to speak with other tongues" (Acts 2:3,4). The prophecy of Joel, which Peter quoted that day (Acts 2:16-21), obviously in its context has a last-days application, so Pentecost will be repeated. It would be just like Satan to counterfeit what he knows is coming in order to prevent many from receiving the true blessing.

18:4,5 Come Out of Her My People

"**And I heard another voice from heaven, saying, 'Come out of her, my people, that you do not partake of her sins, and that you do not receive of her plagues. For her sins have reached to heaven, and God has remembered her iniquities**" (Revelation 18:4,5).

This powerful plea will be the final call to repentance before the close of probation and the outpouring of the seven last plagues.[739] It is the same message given by the two witnesses in chapter 11, and the grand finale of the message of the 144,000 in chapter 14 (the three angels' messages). The story of this call is the heart of the Book of Revelation, dominating chapters seven, ten, eleven and fourteen. It is repeated here in chapter 18 because the great multitude escape from fallen Babylon before she is destroyed.

Their coming out is the vindication of God, who created this world to be inhabited by holy people created in His image, who ultimately will sit with Him on His throne as co-regents of the universe.[740] Satan robbed mankind of their dominion and claimed the world as his own with the human race as his subjects. In His divine wisdom the Lord gave Satan thousands of years to prove his charges against God, but the overwhelming tide of evil and destruction has more than proven that Satan is a malevolent psychopath with a blatantly false ideology. He will throw everything he has at God's people with end-time Babylon, but it will not be enough—"They overcame him by the blood of the Lamb and by the word of their testimony, and they did not love

their lives to the death" (Revelation 12:11).

God's love shining through His people will have a magnetic attraction to people who are weary of the empty lies of Babylon. Although tragically many will refuse to heed the call and will be lost, a great multitude "which no one could number of all nations, tribes, peoples, and tongues" will respond to the **"voice from heaven"** and will **"come out of her."** They will stand victorious "before the throne and before the Lamb, clothed with white robes…and they cry with a loud voice, saying, "Salvation to our God who sits on the throne, and to the Lamb" (Revelation 7:9). Their victory is Babylon's defeat, and now she comes crashing down.

18:6-8 Living in Luxury

"**Reward her even as she rewarded you, and double to her twice as much according to her works; in the cup which she has filled, fill to her twice as much. As much as she has glorified herself, and lived in luxury, so much torment and sorrow give her, for she said in her heart, I sit as a queen, and am not a widow, and shall see no sorrow**" (Revelation 18:6,7).

These and the following verses bring out an aspect of Babylon that is particularly repugnant to God—her luxurious and profligate living. The countries that are in the forefront of end-time Babylon (the United States and Europe) are the richest of any countries at any time in history, much of the wealth coming as a result of grinding the poor of the world into wretched poverty. Cheap bananas, clothes and electronics (as well as a whole raft of other consumer products) are possible because poor people in developing countries have been forced off their land to make way for multinational plantations, or have had to work in sweatshops and as field laborers for barely enough to provide a shirt on their backs and a bowl of food at the end of the day. This is a major part of **"her sins"** which **"have reached to**

---

739 The close of probation is found in chapter 15. This call to repentance is out of the order of the chronological timeline because it is part of the elaboration on the fall of Babylon.

740 Amazing as this may seem, the scriptures clearly teach that redeemed mankind will rule the universe together with Jesus Christ. See 19: *Rulers of the Kingdom*.

heaven." "Come now, you rich…you have heaped up treasure in the last days. Indeed, the wages of the laborers who mowed your fields, which you kept back by fraud, cry out; and the cries of the reapers have reached the ears of the Lord of Sabaoth. You have lived on the earth in pleasure and luxury; you have fattened your hearts as in a day of slaughter" (James 5:1-5).

A fictitious but revealing story is told about a man who was talking with the Lord. "It's such a pity that there are so many poor and starving people. Lord, why don't you feed all the hungry people of the world?" to which the Lord replied, "Why don't YOU feed all the hungry people?"[741] God has abundantly blessed the people of the "Christian" nations, but as we saw in the discussion of God's covenants with His people (see 11:19 *The Ark of the Covenant*, Appendix 9), the purpose of His blessing is so that His people can be a blessing to the world. The selfish misrepresentation of God's generous character of love by His people is one of the major reasons that so many of the world's people have rejected Christianity. "He who gives to the poor will not lack, but he who hides his eyes will have many curses" (Proverbs 28:27). The people of Babylon have lived in luxury and hidden their eyes from the poor, and the wretched of the world have cursed them for it. Nevertheless, the Lord will plead their cause—"He will bring justice to the poor of the people; He will save the children of the needy, and will break in pieces the oppressor" (Psalms 72:4). **"Therefore shall her plagues come in one day: death, and mourning, and famine; and she shall be utterly burned with fire, for strong is the Lord God who judges**

---

741 In fact, this is just what Jesus said to His disciples who came to Him concerning the needs of the multitude who had "nothing to eat. But He [Jesus] answered and said to them, 'You give them something to eat" (Mark 6:36,37). When they obeyed and brought the inadequate supply that they had He multiplied it in their hands so that it was more than enough.

her" (Revelation 18:8,9).

18:9-20 A Lament for Babylon

"And the kings of the earth, who have committed fornication and lived in luxury with her, shall mourn her, and lament for her, when they see the smoke of her burning, standing afar off for fear of her torment, saying, 'Alas, alas that great city Babylon, that mighty city! For in one hour has your judgment come" (Revelation 18:9,10). The false religious system deceived **"the kings of the earth"** so that they participated in and prospered from their illicit relationship with Babylon. However, they show their true heart in that even when the deception is revealed, they mourn (**"alas, alas"**), showing that they have not truly repented and the judgment they will receive is justified. If they could, they would continue in the sinful system, and if granted eternal life they would rebuild it again.

"And the merchants of the earth shall weep and mourn over her; for no one buys their merchandise any more: merchandise of gold, and silver, and precious stones, and of pearls, and fine linen, and purple, and silk, and scarlet, and all thyine wood, and all manner of vessels of ivory, and all manner of vessels of most precious wood, and of brass, and iron, and marble, and cinnamon, and incense, and ointments, and frankincense, and wine, and oil, and fine flour, and wheat, and animals, and sheep, and horses, and chariots, and bodies and souls of men. And the fruits that your soul lusted after are departed from you, and all things which were dainty and goodly are departed from you, and you shall find them no more at all" (Revelation 18:11-14).

God, in His lavish creation, flooded the world with rich resources that were designed to be a blessing for everyone. But the selfish desire to hoard and exploit has turned these blessings into a curse. The most grievous form of exploitation is that of making the **"bodies and souls of men,"** created in the image of God, into a commodity to be bought and sold.

We should notice that Babylon trades in both **"bodies [slaves, KJV] and souls."** Slaves are the personal property of their masters and have no choice in their behavior. Souls make their own decisions, but in the face of exploitation, poverty and despair many **"souls"** choose to take up a life of robbery, extortion, prostitution, or violence. These lifestyles will disqualify them from eternal life,[742] but the preponderance of guilt lies with those who have created the conditions that have led to a desperate choice of crime. The rich and powerful have used their power and influence to maintain, increase, and pass on their privileged status, and God will hold them responsible for the results.

The slavery of **"bodies and souls"** is not just physical slavery, human trafficking, or a life of desperate crime. It also includes the spiritual slavery that results from doctrines of fear, greed and lust that keep multitudes in chains. Religion has been one of the most potent forces keeping people in slavery to the rich and powerful. But the fall of Babylon is the opening of prison doors to "release those who through fear of death were all their lifetime subject to bondage" (Hebrews 2:15).

"The merchants of these things, which were made rich by her, shall stand afar off for the fear of her torment, weeping and wailing, and saying, 'Alas, alas that great city, that was clothed in fine linen, and purple, and scarlet, and adorned with gold, and precious stones, and pearls! For in one hour so great riches have come to nothing" (Revelation 18: 15-17). The acquisition of wealth and pleasure has been marketed internationally, and the whole world has bought into the deception that happiness

---

742 See 1Corinthians 6:9,10.

is found in what you have. However, the fall of Babylon will reveal that it is simply an illusion with no real foundation—**"for in one hour so great riches have come to nothing."**

"And every shipmaster, and all the multitudes on ships, and sailors, and as many as trade by sea, stood afar off, and cried when they saw the smoke of her burning, saying, 'What city is like this great city?' And they cast dust on their heads, and cried, weeping and wailing, saying, 'Alas, alas that great city, where all that had ships in the sea were made rich because of her wealth! For in one hour she is made desolate" (Revelation 18: 17-19). This is the attitude of those who have bought into the Babylon philosophy of self-serving, who still "don't get it," even after everything they have seen during the time of trouble. And it confirms what we have seen in other sections: that they could never be happy in the holy atmosphere of heaven where there will be no more exploitation of their fellow creatures for their own benefit. This is why God in His great wisdom and love does not grant them eternal life.

But is there a heavenly mandate for the saints to gloat over their fate? **"Rejoice over her, O heaven, and you holy apostles and prophets, for God has avenged you on her"** (Revelation 18:20). If we read this verse carefully we see that this is not God gloating because He defeated Satan and his Babylon kingdom. Gloating is a self-centered focus on ones own glory and achievements, and because He is love God actually grieves for those who are lost in the ruin of Babylon. But He also knows that as long as Babylon continues to exist, the suffering and death of His children will continue. In chapter 6:9,10 the martyrs "under the alter" cried out, "How long, O Lord, holy and true, until You judge and avenge our blood on those who dwell on the earth?" At that time they were told that they should "rest a little while longer." Now the time has come, and God invites them to "rejoice!"

18:21-24 Never Again

"**And a mighty angel took up a stone like a great millstone, and cast it into the sea, saying, 'Thus with violence shall that great city Babylon be thrown down, and shall not be found any more at all**" (Revelation 18:21). Jesus once said, "Whoever causes one of these little ones who believe in Me to sin, it would be better for him *if a millstone were hung around his neck, and he were drowned in the depth of the sea.* Woe to the world because of offenses! For offenses must come, but woe to that man by whom the offense comes!" (Matthew 18:6,7). Jesus seemed to be saying that meeting a violent death (being thrown into the sea with a millstone around your neck) would be better than facing in the judgment the reality that my actions have caused a little child to sin.

This is not to say that God has dreamed up some fiendish torture for such sinners. The essence of the judgment is a full realization of the true consequences of our sins and the damage and destruction we have caused to God's creation. Along with this will be a full revelation of the holy character of God and the sweeping requirements of His law. According to Jesus, it would be better to be killed (thrown into the sea with a millstone) than to go on to commit reprehensible sins that would be encountered again in the judgment when "the dead [will be] judged according to their works, by the things which were written in the books" (Revelation 20:12).

Thus the **"great millstone...cast into the sea"** may be more a symbol of God's mercy than of His vengeful punishment. After all, Babylon consists of men and women who have been duped and deceived by the "beast," who is Satan himself. If they were to continue on they might bring upon themselves the terrible guilt of murdering God's saints, and He wants to keep them from that, for

their own sakes as well as for the sake of the saints themselves who have suffered enough grief in the reign of sin. In mercy God answers their plea and He allows death to hide them from "the face of Him who sits on the throne" (Revelation 6:16).

"**And the voice of harpers, and musicians, and of pipers, and trumpeters, shall be heard no more at all in you; and no craftsman of any craft, shall be found anymore in you; and the sound of a millstone shall not be heard anymore at all in you; and the light of a candle shall shine no more at all in you; and the voice of the bridegroom and of the bride shall be heard no more at all in you. For your merchants were the great men of the earth; for by your sorceries were all nations deceived.' And in her was found the blood of prophets, and of saints, and of all that were slain on the earth**" (Revelation 18:22-24).

The mighty angel emphasizes that the destruction of Babylon will be complete and permanent. Sometimes when there has been a wicked, tyrannical regime which is defeated, the people are almost afraid to rejoice and celebrate because of the fear that somehow their oppressors will regain their power and return to torment them again. But God declares definitively that there will never again be another Babylon. He also makes it clear that Babylon is far more comprehensive than a particular church at a particular time in history—she is responsible for **"the blood of...all that were slain on the earth."** In the broadest sense Babylon represents the whole reign of sin, which has ravaged this planet for 6,000 years, and that reign is coming to a permanent end. "How Babylon has become a desolation among the nations!...You have been found and also caught, because you have contended against the Lord...The children of Israel were oppressed...All who took them captive have held them fast; they have refused to let them go. Their Redeemer is strong; the Lord of hosts is His name.

He will thoroughly plead their case...'A sword is against the Chaldeans' says the Lord, 'against the inhabitants of Babylon...It shall be inhabited no more forever" (Jeremiah 50:22-24, 33-35, 39).[743]

---

743 The prophet Jeremiah was given an extensive prophecy about the fall of Babylon (Jeremiah chapters 50 and 51). Although the primary application was the fall of ancient Babylon, much can be applied to end-time Babylon as well.

"Then the beast was captured, and with him the false prophet who worked signs in his presence...
these two were cast alive into the lake of fire burning with brimstone" Rev. 19:20
Virgil Solis, 1560

Chapter 19

Revelation 19:1-21

19:1 And after these things I heard a loud voice of a great multitude in heaven, saying, "Alleluia! Salvation, and glory, and honor, and power, to the Lord our God.

19:2 For true and righteous are His judgments: for He has judged the great harlot, which corrupted the earth with her fornication, and has avenged the blood of His servants at her hand."

19:3 And again they said, "Alleluia! And her smoke rises up forever and ever."

19:4 And the twenty-four elders and the four living creatures fell down and worshiped God who was seated on the throne, saying, "Amen, Alleluia!"

19:5 And a voice came from the throne, saying, "Praise our God, all you His servants, and you that fear Him, both small and great."

19:6 And I heard as it were the voice of a great multitude, and as the voice of many waters, and as the voice of mighty thunder, saying, "Alleluia: for the Lord God omnipotent reigns.

19:7 Let us be glad and rejoice, and give honor to Him; for the marriage of the Lamb has come, and His wife has made herself ready.

19:8 And to her was granted that she should be arrayed in fine linen, clean and white; for the fine linen is the righteous deeds of saints."

19:9 And he said to me, "Write, blessed are they which are called to the marriage supper of the Lamb." And he said to me, "These are the true sayings of God."

19:10 And I fell at his feet to worship him. And he said to me, "Do not do that! I am your fellow servant, and of your brethren that have the testimony of Jesus; worship God! For the testimony of Jesus is the spirit of prophecy."

19:11 And I saw heaven opened, and behold a white horse; and He that sat on him was called Faithful and True, and in righteousness He judges and makes war.

19:12 His eyes were as a flame of fire, and on His head were many crowns; and He had a name written, that no one knew, but He Himself.

19:13 And He was clothed with a robe dipped in blood, and His name is called The Word of God.

19:14 And the armies in heaven followed Him on white horses, clothed in fine linen, white and clean.

19:15 And out of His mouth goes a sharp sword, that with it He should smite the nations; and He shall rule them with a rod of iron. And He treads the wine press of the fierceness and wrath of Almighty God.

19:16 And He Has on His robe and on His thigh a name written, KING OF KINGS, AND LORD OF LORDS.

19:17 And I saw an angel standing in the sun; and he cried with a loud voice, saying to all the birds that fly in the midst of heaven, "Come and gather yourselves together to the supper of the great God;

19:18 That you may eat the flesh of kings, and the flesh of captains, and the flesh of mighty men, and the flesh of horses, and of them that sit on them, and the flesh of all men, both free and slaves, both small and great."

19:19 And I saw the beast, and the kings of the earth, and their armies, gathered together to make war against Him that sat on the horse, and against His army.

19:20 And the beast was captured, and with him the false prophet that worked miracles before him, with which he deceived those that had received the mark of the beast, and those that worshiped his image. These both were cast alive into a lake of fire burning with brimstone.

19:21 And the rest were slain with the sword of Him that sat on the horse, which proceeded out of His mouth; and all the birds were filled with their flesh.

19:1-5 Alleluia!

"And after these things I heard a loud voice of a great multitude in heaven, saying, 'Alleluia! Salvation, and glory, and honor, and power, to the Lord our God. For true and righteous are His judgments: for He has judged the great harlot, which corrupted the earth with her fornication, and has avenged the blood of His servants at her hand.' And again they said, 'Alleluia! And her smoke rises up forever and ever!'" (Revelation 19:1-3).

Heaven and earth cannot stop celebrating! Babylon has been such a persistent foe for so many millennia that to have her permanently done away with would seem almost too good to be true if it were not for the obvious **"glory and honor and power"** of our almighty God who **"has judged"** her. To say that she has **"corrupted the earth"** is a gracious understatement considering **"her fornication"** with the "kings of the earth,"[744] and the **"blood of [God's] servants"** that has been **"shed by her."**

But in the presence of God the focus cannot remain on His enemies for long—**"And the twenty-four elders and the four living creatures fell down and worshiped God who was seated on the throne, saying, 'Amen, Alleluia!' And a voice came from the throne, saying, 'Praise our God, all you His servants, and you that fear Him, both small and great!'"** (Revelation 19:4,5). The judgment of the great harlot is a foretaste of the great day when sin and death will be totally obliterated. The only trace of this terrible chapter of history will be **"her smoke [which] rises up forever and ever."** Although this phrase, borrowed from Isaiah 34:10, is not explained and does not appear elsewhere except in the parallel passage of Revelation 14:11, there is the suggestion that

744 Revelation 18:3,9.

throughout eternity there will be a memorial of smoke, which will be all that will remain of sin and sinners. Even Satan, the great originator of evil, will be "turned...to ashes" and "shall be no more forever" (Ezekiel 28:18,19).

19:6-9 The Marriage of the Lamb

"And I heard as it were the voice of a great multitude, and as the voice of many waters, and as the voice of mighty thunder, saying, 'Alleluia: for the Lord God omnipotent reigns. Let us be glad and rejoice, and give honor to Him; for the marriage of the Lamb has come, and His wife has made herself ready. And to her was granted that she should be arrayed in fine linen, clean and white; for the fine linen is the righteousness of saints" (Revelation 19:6-8).

There is remarkable similarity and contrast between verses one and six. In both verses John heard **"the voice of a great multitude...saying, 'Alleluia!"** But in verse one the rejoicing is a collective sigh of relief that the harlot is finally gone. In verse six there is irrepressible joy because the **"wife...of the lamb"** has finally **"made herself ready."** Heaven is erupting with praise, more enthusiastic than in any other part of the whole Book of Revelation.[745] At first this seems surprising, because the Second Coming, the Millennium and the final end of sin are still future. But all of those are possible only because of what is being portrayed here: **"the marriage of the Lamb."**

Many have assumed that the bride of the Lamb, referred to here as **"His wife,"** is the Christian church. But in chapter 21 an angel invited John, "Come here, I will show you the bride, the Lamb's

wife.' And he carried me away in the spirit to a great and high mountain, and showed me that great city, the holy Jerusalem, descending out of heaven from God" (Revelation 21:9,10). John then goes on to give a detailed description of the city. In these verses the Bride is New Jerusalem, the future dwelling place of the saints and of God. But in chapter 19 it says that **"His wife has made herself ready,"** which does not seem like something a city can do. Perhaps the answer lies in the fact that New Jerusalem will be the capital city of the Kingdom of God. Jesus in His parables indicates that the **"marriage of the lamb"** is the same as Christ receiving His kingdom.[746] Christ's kingdom includes the church, but it is much more—it is the whole universe, redeemed from the baleful effects of sin. Thus the Bride of Christ is the kingdom He will receive, represented by the capital

---

745 A possible rival for enthusiasm of praise is Revelation 4 and 5, when Jesus the Lamb presented His sacrifice so that the Book of Life could be opened and the judgment of the Day of Atonement could begin.

746 Jesus' parable of the wedding feast begins saying, "The kingdom of heaven is like a certain king who arranged a marriage for his son" (Matthew 22:2). Jesus went on to say that when the king sent His servants to call those who were invited they made excuses, refused to come and mistreated and killed His servants. In response the King "destroyed those murderers and burned up their city" (vs.3-7).

Likewise, in Luke 19, "A certain nobleman went into a far country to receive for himself a kingdom and to return...but his citizens hated him and sent a delegation after him saying, 'We will not have this man to reign over us.' When he returned he commanded, 'Bring here those enemies of mine, who did not want me to reign over them, and slay them before me" (Luke 19:12-27). Thus the father arranging a marriage for his son and the nobleman going to receive a kingdom have parallel themes and a similar outcome—in both cases those who should have been a part did not want to and had to be destroyed.

The nobleman who went to receive the kingdom was happy to find some of his servants faithfully doing their assigned work and ready when he returned (Luke 19:15-19). Likewise, when "the master" returns from the wedding he is pleased to find his servants faithfully watching and waiting (Luke 12:35-38). From these parallels we see that the "marriage" and "receiving a kingdom" refer to the same heavenly reality.

city, New Jerusalem.[747]

What kind of a kingdom will Jesus receive? All kingdoms consists of *territory* and property, *laws* and policies, *subjects* and rulers, and most importantly, a *king*. God's kingdom also has these elements. The **"King of kings and Lord of lords"** is, of course, Jesus (Revelation 19:16). The *territory* that Jesus receives includes this world ("the kingdoms of this world have become the kingdoms of our Lord and of His Christ" Revelation 11:15). Satan, having been cast out of heaven, claimed this world as his own. He lost his right to this world at the Cross and will lose his dominion when Jesus comes. But the territory of the kingdom includes much more than this world. Jesus is and will be "far above all principality and power and might and dominion, and every name that is named, not only in this age but also in that which is to come. And He put all things under His feet" (Ephesians 1:21,22). In other words, His kingdom includes the whole universe. There will be no rebel galaxies or dark strongholds of evil.

The *law* of this world has been the "law of sin and death" (Romans 8:2) and the policy has been like it was during the lawless time recorded in the book of the Judges, when "there was no king in Israel; everyone did what was right in his own eyes" (Judges 21:25). But the law and policy of the kingdom will be "the royal law according to the scripture, 'You shall love your neighbor as yourself'" (James 2:8).

The *subjects* of the kingdom will include all the sinless creatures of this world[748] and of the uncountable worlds throughout the universe who in their own simple or complex way serve and offer praise to the sovereign Lord. Throughout the reign of sin they have been suffering along with the human race—"For we know that the whole creation groans...for the creation was subjected to futility, not willingly, but because of Him who subjected it in hope; because the creation itself also will be delivered from the bondage of corruption into the glorious liberty of the children of God. For the earnest expectation of the creation eagerly waits for the revealing of the sons of God" (Romans 8:22, 20,21).

Rulers of the Kingdom

Within these verses in Romans 8 lies the key to understanding what has been delaying the **"marriage of the Lamb."** All of creation has been waiting "for the revealing of the sons of God." God has designed that redeemed mankind will become like Christ and will have dominion over the universe along with Him. "As many as are led by the Spirit of God, these are sons of God...and if children, then heirs—heirs of God and *joint heirs with Christ*...For whom He foreknew, He also predestined to be conformed to the image of His Son, that He might be the firstborn among many brethren" (Romans 8:14,17, 29). The fact that the saints will be joint heirs with Christ is

---

747 Daniel 7 seems to compress fifteen chapters of Revelation into five verses, with the climax occurring when Christ receives His kingdom (His Bride). The prophet saw the beginning of the great Day of Atonement ("The court was seated, and the books were opened" Daniel 7:9,10), which is the focus of Revelation four and five. Then in verse 11 ("the pompous words which the horn was speaking") he saw the blasphemous activity of Babylon (in Daniel called "the little horn") which plays such a large role in Revelation 8-16. Next he saw the destruction of Babylon ("the beast was slain and its body destroyed and given to the burning flame" Daniel 7:11), which parallels Revelation 17 and 18. Finally Daniel saw "One like the Son of Man, coming with the clouds of heaven. He came to the Ancient of Days, and they brought Him near before Him. Then to Him was given dominion and glory and a kingdom, that all peoples, nations and languages should serve Him" (Daniel 7:13,14). This receiving of the kingdom is what is called in Revelation "the marriage of the Lamb." In Daniel 7, just as in Revelation 19, it happens in Heaven after the Day of Atonement is finished and Babylon is destroyed, and before the Second Coming of Christ (which in Daniel 7 is in verse 22, "and the time came for the saints to possess the kingdom").

748 The creatures of this world have been marred by sin, but in the kingdom they will be recreated, so that "The wolf and the lamb will feed together, and the lion will eat straw like the ox...They will neither harm nor destroy on all my holy mountain," says the Lord" (Isaiah 65:25).

all the more awesome when we consider what Christ is inheriting—"God...has spoken to us by His Son, whom He has appointed *heir of all things*" (Hebrews 1:2). Revelation 21:7 makes it clear that the redeemed will receive the same inheritance—"He who overcomes *shall inherit all things.*"

John heard and saw "many angels around the throne" (Revelation 5:11). But the saints who overcome are not destined to stand around the throne of Christ;[749] they will sit on His throne with Him! "To Him who overcomes I will grant to sit with Me on My throne, as I also overcame and sat down with My Father on His throne" (Revelation 3:21). "If we died with Him, we shall also live with Him. If we endure, we shall also reign with Him" (2Timothy 2:11,12). The Book of Revelation clearly teaches that the redeemed will reign with Christ, first for a thousand years in heaven (Revelation 20:4) and then forever upon earth when New Jerusalem and the throne of God are established on the new earth (Revelation 22:3-5, 5:9,10, 21:1-3).

Despite God's promises, humans have never shown themselves fit to reign. Ever since the beginning, Adam and his descendants have been sinning and destroying rather than blessing and nurturing God's creation. Righteousness has been imputed to sinners and eternal life has been granted by grace based upon Christ's perfect life

and His atoning death on the Cross, but this does not demonstrate their fitness to reign over the universe.

However, in the midst of the time of trouble God's people will allow God to fully perfect a Christ-like character within them—"Here is the patience of the saints; here are those who keep the commandments of God and the faith of Jesus" (Revelation 14:12). It is not that they will try harder and finally "get their act together." Victory over sin and perfection of character is as much a gift of God as is repentance and forgiveness; and the conditions and events during the time of trouble will cause God's people to seek His grace and submit to Him as never before. This is the meaning of Revelation 19:8, **"His wife has made herself ready. And to her was granted that she should be arrayed in fine linen, clean and white; for the fine linen is the righteous deeds of the saints."** Imputed righteousness (justification) is based on the righteous acts of Christ, but imparted righteousness (sanctification) is demonstrated through **"the righteous deeds of the saints"** and it is these righteous deeds which show that the church has finally **"made herself ready"** to reign with Christ.

The church being ready to reign also makes it possible for Babylon to be destroyed. Babylon is not some evil entity that is so powerful that God could not protect His people from her. The Lord Himself has used His enemies to chasten and punish his people in order to bring them

---

749 Many translations of Hebrews 2:6-8 indicate that man was only temporarily to be lower than the angels. For example, the New Revised Standard reads, "What are human beings that you are mindful of them, or mortals, that you care for them? You have made them *for a little* while lower than the angels; you have crowned them with glory and honor, subjecting all things under their feet.' Now in subjecting all things to them, God left nothing outside their control. As it is, we do not yet see everything in subjection to them, but we do see Jesus, who *for a little while* was made lower than the angels, now crowned with glory and honor." Identical Greek wording for Jesus' obviously temporary state "lower than the angels" and mankind's status shows that just as Jesus was exalted "having become so much better than the angels" (Hebrews 1:4), so will be redeemed humanity.

to repentance.[750] What this punishment really amounts to is that the Lord does not continue to protect His people when they persistently reject Him.

Laodicea, the church just before the time of trouble, offers the ultimate form of rejection—lukewarm indifference—and God will allow "Babylon the Great" to rise up against her. Laodicea's experience with end-time Babylon will be like ancient Israel's experience with Babylon when they rejected God. "The Lord has sent to you all His servants the prophets, rising early and sending them, but you have not listened, nor inclined your ear to hear. They said, 'Repent now everyone of his evil way and his evil doings... yet you have not listened to Me,' says the Lord... 'Because you have not heard My words, behold I will send...the king of Babylon, My servant, and will bring them against this land" (Jeremiah 25:4-9).

However, oppression by Babylon brings God's people to their senses. "In those days and in that time' says the Lord, 'the children of Israel shall come...with continual weeping they shall come, and seek the Lord their God. They shall ask the way to Zion, with their faces toward it, saying, 'Come and let us join ourselves to the Lord in a perpetual covenant that will not be forgotten" (Jeremiah 50:4,5).

In response to their repentance God calls them to come out of Babylon so that they will not be harmed in the destruction He will bring against her. "Move from the midst of Babylon...for behold, I will raise and cause to come up against Babylon an assembly of great nations" (vs. 9,10). The redemption of God's people, although painful for them, will be complete—"The iniquity of Israel shall be sought, but there shall be none; and the sins of Judah, but they shall not be found; For I will pardon those whom I preserve" (v.20).

19:9,10 The Marriage Supper

"And he said to me, 'Write, blessed are they which are called to the marriage supper of the Lamb.' And he said to me, 'These are the true sayings of God.' And I fell at his feet to worship him. And he said to me, 'Do not do that! I am your fellow servant, and of your brethren that have the testimony of Jesus; worship God! For the testimony of Jesus is the spirit of prophecy" (Revelation 19:9,10).

The **"marriage of the Lamb"** is not the same as the **"marriage supper of the Lamb."** In Jesus' parable the servants wait for the master to return from the wedding, and then they eat together (amazingly, the master serves the servants! Luke 12: 35-40). The parallel to the wedding, the "receiving of the kingdom," takes place in heaven while the saints are still on earth sharing the gospel and being persecuted (see Daniel 7:13,14, 15-27). The marriage supper comes later, after Christ returns, when "many will come from east and west, and sit down with Abraham, Isaac, and Jacob in the kingdom of heaven" (Matthew 8:11).

This verse gives a clue as to who will be present at the feast. "Abraham, Isaac, and Jacob" represent those of God's people throughout the ages who believed God's promises and will be saved because of their faith, either in the Savior to come or the Savior who has come. "Abraham believed God, and it was accounted to him for righteousness...Those who are of faith are sons of Abraham...So then those who

---

750 For example, "Babylon was a golden cup in the Lord's hand" (Jeremiah 51:7). "I will send and take all the families of the north' says the Lord, 'and Nebuchadnezzar the king of Babylon, My servant, and will bring them against this land" (Jeremiah 25:9). "The Lord will bring the king of Assyria upon you and your people...The Lord will whistle for the fly that is in the farthest part of the rivers of Egypt, and for the bee that is in the land of Assyria...The Lord will shave with a hired razor, with those from beyond the River, with the king of Assyria...Assyria, the rod of My anger and the staff in whose hand is My indignation. I will send him against an ungodly nation, and against the people of My wrath" (Isaiah 7:17,18,20, 10:5,6).

are of faith are blessed with believing Abraham" (Galatians 3:6-9).

Some have taught that only those who "believe in the name of Jesus" will be saved, quoting Peter's words to the Jewish rulers concerning "the name of Jesus Christ of Nazareth, whom you crucified, whom God raised form the dead…Nor is there salvation in any other, for there is no other name under heaven given among men by which we must be saved" (Acts 4:10-12). But the fact that Abraham, Isaac and Jacob will be saved (not to mention the long list of faithful in Hebrews 11) shows that believing in the name of Jesus simply means believing in Jesus, whether one has heard His name or not. Since God is One, when the Father sends the Holy Spirit in the name of Jesus it is the same as sending Jesus Himself. Although the Holy Spirit was sent with special power and a new ministry after the resurrection of Christ, He has been sent (in the name of Jesus) to all people at all times,[751] and many have responded to Him and will be present at the **"marriage supper."**

Besides the men and women of God's chosen people, another class is mentioned—"many will come from east and west" (and the parallel passage in Luke 13:29 includes those from the north and the south). In other words, God has His people everywhere. In the Bible the east signifies such peoples as the Moabites, Edomites, and Midianites,[752] the west is the land of the Philistines, Tyre, and Greece,[753] to the North are the Assyrians, Babylonians, Gog and Magog, and the king of the North,[754] and to the south are Sodom, Egypt, the Amalekites, and the king of the South.[755] These are nations who have been the traditional enemies of God's chosen people, outside of the promises and covenants, and yet God will consider where they were born, the circumstances of their lives, and how they have responded to the moving of His Spirit. "I will make mention of Rahab [Egypt] and Babylon to those who know Me; Behold, O Philistia and Tyre, with Ethiopia: 'This one was born there'.… The Lord will record, when He registers the peoples, 'This one was born there'" (Psalms 87:4,6). Indeed, the parable of the wedding feast indicates that it will be those from the "highways and hedges" who will fill the banquet hall rather than the more favored "who were invited."[756]

"A certain king arranged a marriage for his son, and sent out his servants to call those who were invited to the wedding, and they were not willing to come" (Matthew 22:2,3). The invitation may have involved being born into a Christian family or community, or being given a persuasive gospel invitation. But the response of many of these invited ones shows that God's kingdom was not their priority—"They were not willing to come." Some were involved in accumulating material goods and businesses, others were busy with their social interactions and some, being offended, attacked the servants who delivered the invitation.[757] Their rejection disqualified

---

751 Many scriptures show that the Holy Spirit was very active in Old Testament times, for example, "Create in me a clean heart, O God, and renew a steadfast spirit within me. Do not cast me away from your presence, and do not take Your Holy Spirit from me" (Psalms 51:10,11). "Where can I go from Your Spirit? Or where can I flee from Your presence?" (Psalms 139:7). "I will give you a new heart and put a new Spirit within you;…I will put My Spirit within you and cause you to walk in my statutes…(Ezekiel 36:26,27). See also Genesis 6:3, Exodus 31:3, Numbers 11:24-29, 14:24, 24:2, 27:18, Deuteronomy 34:9, 1Samuel 10:1-11, 16:11-13, 19:20-24, 2Kings 2:9-15, 1Chronicles 12:18, 2Chronicles 15:1,2, 20:14-17, 24:20, Nehemiah 9;19,20,30, Job 33:3,4, Psalms 106:32,33, 143:10, Proverbs 1:22,23, 20:27, Isaiah 30:1, 44:1-5, 48:16, 59:21, 63:9-12, Ezekiel 3:24, 11:5, 39:28,29, Daniel 5:11, Micah 2:7, 3:8, Haggai 2:4,5, Zechariah 4:6, 7:12.

752 Isaiah 11:14, Judges 6:3.

753 Isaiah 11:14, Daniel 8:5,21.

754 Jeremiah 25:9, Ezekiel 16:46, 30:2,14,15, Zephaniah 2:13, Daniel 11:40.

755 Ezekiel 16:46, Genesis 13:1,3, Numbers 13:29, Daniel 11:40.

756 Luke 14:15-24, Matthew 22:1-14.

757 Luke 14:18-20, Matthew 22:3-6.

them from being a part of the marriage supper—"None of those men who were invited shall taste my supper" (Luke 14:24). Next "the poor and the maimed and the lame and the blind" were invited—those who had enough problems that they recognized their need. The Apostle Paul identified this dynamic—"For you see your calling, brethren, that not many wise according to the flesh, not many mighty, not many noble, are called. But God has chosen the foolish things of the world to put to shame the wise, and God has chosen the weak things…the base things…the things which are despised…that no flesh should glory in His presence" (1Corinthians 1:26-31).

However, no matter where they were found, even from "the highways and hedges," all had to pass inspection. "But when the king came in to see the guests, he saw a man there who did not have on a wedding garment. So he said to him, 'Friend,[758] how did you come in here without a wedding garment?' And he was speechless. Then the king said to the servants, 'Bind him hand and foot, take him away and cast him into outer darkness; there will be weeping and gnashing of teeth.' For many are called, but few are chosen" (Matthew 22:11-14).

The requirement of the wedding garment brings the parable full circle back to Revelation 19—**"To her it was granted to be arrayed in fine linen, clean and bright, for the fine linen is the righteous acts of the saints."** Christ forgives us freely, having borne our sins on the Cross, but He never leaves us as we are: "For this is the will of God, your sanctification" (1Thessalonians 4:3). Sanctification is not a matter of "trying to be good;" it is God's initiative, His power and His grace which makes it possible. On the other hand, it does not happen automatically; we must allow Him to do this work, and this will feel like we are trying as hard as we possibly can to do what is right. This is expressed in many scriptural admonitions. "*Submit* to God. *Resist* the devil" (James 4:7). "*Strive* to enter through the narrow gate" (Luke 13:24). "*Be even more diligent* to make your call and election sure" (2 Peter 1:10). "*Make every effort* to be found spotless, blameless and at peace with Him" (2 Peter 3:14). The balance is found in Paul's admonition, "*Work out* your own salvation with fear and trembling; for it is *God who works in you both to will and to do* for His good pleasure" (Philippians 2:12,13). Jesus said, 'Without Me you can do nothing," but Paul insists, "I can do all things through Christ who strengthens me."[759]

Those who have lived in darkness, without the church or God's Word, immersed in false teaching, will not have known much of the will of God, but that which they have known through the Spirit will be required of them. And those who have lived in the light of God's Word and the church have an even higher standard. "That servant who knew his master's will and did not prepare himself or do according to his will shall be beaten with many stripes. But he who did not know, yet committed things deserving of stripes shall be beaten with few. For everyone to whom much is given, from him much will be required; and to whom much has been committed, of him they will ask the more" (Luke 12:47,48).

The "stripes" (blows or beatings) take place in this life as we endure the trials and tribulations of living in a world of sin. God allows trials as a small part of the school or discipline He has designed for each of His children. "If you endure chastening, God deals with you as with sons; for what son is there whom a father does not chasten?" Through the influence of blessings, trials,

---

758 The king still considered him to be His friend, even though he was disqualified to partake of the wedding supper!

---

759 John 15:5, Philippians 4:13.

and faith experiments we grow up in Christ "till we all come to the unity of the faith and of the knowledge of the Son of God, to a perfect man, to the measure of the stature of the fullness of Christ" (Hebrews 12:7, Ephesians 4:13). This is the work God is doing in His saints, and our cooperation with His work opens the way for an experience we do not want to miss—**"Blessed are those who are called to the marriage supper of the Lamb!"**

19:11-13 Christ on a White Horse

"And I saw heaven opened, and behold a white horse; and He that sat on him was called Faithful and True, and in righteousness He judges and makes war. His eyes were as a flame of fire, and on His head were many crowns; and He had a name written, that no one knew, but He Himself. And He was clothed with a robe dipped in blood, and His name is called The Word of God" (Revelation 19:11-13).

In chapter four John saw "a door standing open in heaven" and was able to witness events taking place in the heavenly sanctuary. This time heaven itself is opened—the invisible judgment taking place there is finished, and Jesus, no longer as a Lamb, but as a man of war is leading a very visible invasion of planet Earth. The unholy trinity gathered the "kings of the earth...to the battle of that great day of God Almighty"[760] in a final effort to exterminate the people of God. But Jesus will not abandon His people. "Christ, having been offered once to bear the sins of many, will appear a second time, not to deal with sin, but to save those who are eagerly waiting for him" (Hebrews 9:28).

The return of Christ in glory is the precious

and often ignored promise that fills the scriptures. "Enoch, the seventh from Adam, prophesied...saying, 'Behold, the Lord comes with ten thousands of His saints, to execute judgment on all'" (Jude 14,15). "Our God shall come, and shall not keep silent; a fire shall devour before Him, and it shall be very tempestuous all around Him." (Psalms 50:3-5). "All the tribes of the earth will mourn, and they will see the Son of Man coming on the clouds of heaven with power and great glory" (Matthew 24:30). "I will come again" (John 14:3). "He will appear a second time" (Hebrews 9:28). "Looking for the blessed hope and glorious appearing of our great God and Savior Jesus Christ" (Titus 2:13). These are just a small fraction of the verses which speak of the coming of Christ in glory.

In Revelation 6:2, Christ rode into the world on a white horse "conquering and to conquer" and "a crown was given to Him," the crown of victory (Greek *stefanos*). Now the victory has been won and **"on His head were many crowns,"** but these are the crowns of rulership and authority (Greek *diadema*), showing that He has "taken [His] great power, and reigned" (Revelation 11:17), as the "great voices in heaven" proclaimed, "The kingdoms of this world have become the kingdoms of our Lord and of His Christ, and He shall reign forever and ever!" (v. 15). The **"robe dipped in blood"** is an image from Isaiah 63 which shows that Jesus is not making a "courtesy call" when He returns. "I have trodden them in My anger, and trampled them in My fury; their *blood is sprinkled upon My garments, and I have stained all My robes. For the day of vengeance is in My heart*" (Isaiah 63:3,4).

"His name is called the Word of God." The second person of the Trinity "humbled Himself and became obedient to the point of death, even the death of the cross" (Philippians 2:8), and throughout the Book of Revelation Jesus has been represented as the sacrificial Lamb. However, at

---

760 Revelation 16:14.

His coming His name emphasizes the fact that He is the eternal God—"In the beginning was the Word, and the Word was with God, and the Word was God…. All things were made through Him, and without Him nothing was made that was made" (John 1:1-3). Now He is returning to claim that which is His own.

"And the armies in heaven followed Him on white horses, clothed in fine linen, white and clean" (Revelation 19:14). No doubt this verse includes the myriad of angels who have surrounded His throne and will accompany Him from heaven. But the fact that these **"armies in heaven"** are **"clothed in fine linen, white and clean"** is a reference to verse 8 where the angel explained that **"the fine linen is the righteous acts of the saints."** In chapter 7 we saw that the saints, "who are coming out of the great tribulation and washed their robes and made them white in the blood of the Lamb…are before the throne of God, and serve Him day and night,"[761] in other words, by faith they are **"in heaven"** even as they endure the time of trouble. In chapter 14 these same saints are shown again having an in-Heaven-while-still-on-earth experience as they "follow the Lamb wherever He goes."[762] They have **"followed Him"** by faith, but now as He comes they follow Him by sight as He turns the tables on their foes, who have been poised to strike against them.

"And out of His mouth goes a sharp sword, that with it He should smite the nations; and He shall rule them with a rod of iron. And He treads the wine press of the fierceness and wrath of Almighty God. And He Has on His robe and on His thigh a name written, KING OF KINGS, AND LORD OF LORDS" (Revelation 19:15,16). As we saw in chapter 12, ruling with **"a rod of**

iron"** is an image taken from Psalms 2. "Why do the nations rage, and the people plot a vain thing? The kings of the earth set themselves, and the rulers take counsel together, against the Lord and against His anointed, saying, 'Let us break their bonds in pieces and cast away their cords from us" (Psalms 2:1-3). This verse exposes the underlying attitude which makes it impossible for the "kings" and "rulers" of this world system to be a part of the eternal kingdom: they are unwilling to submit to the **"King of kings."** To them the kingdom principles of loving God and neighbor are "bonds" and "cords" which would gall them forever; there is no alternative except the **"rod of iron"**—"You shall break them with a rod of iron; You shall dash them to pieces like a potter's vessel" (v. 9). The fatal power of sin over the lives of those who will not submit to God is shown by the incredible fact that even after all that the ungodly have experienced through the time of trouble and particularly the seven last plagues, they are still fighting against God until the bitter end.

19:17-21 The Supper of the Birds

"And I saw an angel standing in the sun; and he cried with a loud voice, saying to all the birds that fly in the midst of heaven, 'Come and gather yourselves together to the supper of the great God; that you may eat the flesh of kings, and the flesh of captains, and the flesh of mighty men, and the flesh of horses, and of them that sit on them, and the flesh of all men, both free and slaves, both small and great" (Revelation 19:17,18).

What a pathetic contrast there is between the **"marriage supper of the Lamb"** (v.9) and **"the supper of the great God!"** In the former, "many will come from the east and the west, and will take their places at the feast with Abraham, Isaac and Jacob in the kingdom of heaven" (Matthew 8:11

---

761 Revelation 7:14,15, see 7: *In Heaven while on Earth* footnote 280 for commentary on the translation.

762 See 14:2-5 *Representatives of the Lamb.*

NIV). "The Master...will gird himself and have them sit down to eat and will come and serve them" (Luke 12:37). "In Your presence is fullness of joy; At Your right hand are pleasures forevermore" (Psalms 16:11).

However, for those who have stubbornly refused the offer there is only the fearsome prospect of being themselves the "main course"—for the birds and beasts who will feast on them! Their final fate shows that in its eternal results sin is the great equalizer. In this life there is a vast gulf between the honor and homage bestowed upon kings, captains, and mighty men and the contempt and dishonor shown to the **"small...and slaves."** But they will all be equal in the bellies of the birds.

"And I saw the beast, and the kings of the earth, and their armies, gathered together to make war against Him that sat on the horse, and against His army" (Revelation 19:19). This verse is linked directly to Revelation 16:13,14, which portrays "the spirits of devils, working miracles, which go forth to the kings of the earth and of the whole world, to gather them to the battle of that great day of God Almighty." This is the Battle of Armageddon, the final attempt to exterminate God's people (See 16:16 *The Battle of Armageddon*). However, in making war against the saints, they are actually making **"war against Him that sat on the horse,"** in other words against Jesus, the One who said, "Inasmuch as you did it to one of the least of these My brethren, you did it to Me" (Matthew 25:40).

Jesus never told His followers to defend themselves—to the contrary, He taught that we are to "turn the other cheek." He told Peter, "Put your sword in its place, for all who take the sword will perish by the sword" (Matthew 5:39, 26:52). Paul counseled, "Do not avenge yourselves, but rather give place to wrath; for it is written, 'Vengeance is Mine, I will repay' says the Lord" (Romans 12:19). Now the day has come for the Lord to

answer the prayer of the "souls under the altar" who cried out, "How long, O Lord, holy and true, until You judge and avenge our blood on those who dwell on the earth?" (Revelation 6:10). Now Jesus, who has been despised and rejected, is coming, and the "lawless one" and his followers will be "consumed by the breath of His mouth and destroyed with the brightness of His coming" (2 Thessalonians 2:8).

"And the beast was captured, and with him the false prophet that worked miracles before him, with which he deceived those that had received the mark of the beast, and those that worshiped his image. These both were cast alive into a lake of fire burning with brimstone" (Revelation 19:20). As we saw in chapters 11:7-10 and 17:6-8, **"the beast"** in his final manifestation is not just an antichrist political system, but is an actual manifestation of Satan as he carries out his final deception by pretending to be Christ. Apparently Satan will fully possess a human being and appear as "the lawless one" who, "according to the working of Satan, with all power, signs, and lying wonders" will deceive "those who perish" (2 Thessalonians 2:9,10). He is the last of the eight final kings of "Babylon the Great"—"the beast that was, and is not, is himself also the eighth, and is of the seven, and is going to perdition" (Revelation 17:11).

The **"false prophet"** is the miracle-working leader of the American Church-state alliance (See 16:13 *The Unholy Trinity*). These two have been the heads of the final "one-world government" which will unite during the time of trouble and seek to enforce the worship of the beast through the mark and number of the beast. But now these two are the "first fruits" of those who will be destroyed in the lake of fire.

19:21 The Second Coming

"And the rest were slain with the sword of Him that sat on the horse, which proceeded

out of His mouth; and all the birds were filled with their flesh" (Revelation 19:21). Although the focus of these verses is on the destruction of the unrepentant, we should not forget that this is the Second Coming of Christ, which is the event that the church has been waiting for ever since He went to heaven and promised to return.

The angel at His ascension promised, "This same Jesus, who was taken up from you into heaven, will so come in like manner as you saw Him go into heaven" (Acts 1:11), in other words, personally and visibly. Jesus Himself promised, "As the lightning comes from the east and flashes to the west, so also will be coming of the Son of Man be" (Matthew 24:27). He then mentioned the supper of the birds—"For wherever the carcass is, there the eagles [or vultures as a number of translations read] will be gathered together" (v. 28).

Jesus listed the physical signs which will accompany His coming: "Immediately after the tribulation of those days the sun will be darkened, the moon will not give its light, the stars will fall from heaven, and the powers of the heavens will be shaken" (v. 29). In Luke He adds, "On the earth distress of nations with perplexity, the sea and the waves roaring" (Luke 21:25). John in Revelation 6 mentions these same signs and adds, "There was a great earthquake...and every mountain and island was moved out of its place" (Revelation 6:12-14). Jesus concludes, "Then the sign of the Son of Man will appear in Heaven, and then all the tribes of the earth will mourn,[763]

and they will see the Son of Man coming on the clouds of heaven with power and great glory. And He will send His angels with a great sound of a trumpet, and they will gather together His elect from the four winds, from one end of heaven to the other" (Matthew 24: 29-31).

Paul describes the same event in 1 Thessalonians 4:16,17: "For the Lord Himself will descend from heaven with a shout, with the voice of an archangel and with the trumpet of God. And the dead in Christ will rise first. Then we who are alive and remain shall be caught up together with them in the clouds to meet the Lord in the air." "For the trumpet shall sound, and the dead will be raised incorruptible, and we shall be changed" (1 Corinthians 15:52).

Thus even though the details are not spelled out in Revelation 19, we can see from these other verses of scripture that at this point in the timeline 1) The **"kings of the earth"** and the rest who have rejected God will be gathered against God's people, 2) Signs will appear in the sun, moon, and stars and there will be chaotic shaking of the heavens, roaring of the sea, and a tremendous earthquake, 3) The sign of Jesus' coming will be followed by Jesus Himself coming on the clouds with His angels, 4) The unrepentant will be destroyed "by the brightness of His coming," 5) The "dead in Christ" will be resurrected, 6) They along with the living righteous will be given new, incorruptible bodies and will be gathered by the angels to be with Jesus.

This will be the day when Jesus fulfills His promise to His followers, "Let not your heart be troubled; you believe in God, believe also in Me. In My Father's house are many mansions; if it were not so, I would have told you. I go to prepare a place for you. And if I go and prepare a place for you *I will come again and receive you to Myself*; that where I am, there you may be also" (John 14:1-3).

---

763 John described this mourning in Revelation 6:15, "The kings of the earth, the great men, the rich men, the commanders, the mighty men, every slave and every free man, hid themselves in the caves and in the rocks of the mountains, and said to the mountains and rocks, 'Fall on us and hide us from the face of Him who sits on the throne and from the wrath of the Lamb!' This verse describes exactly the same group (kings of the earth, etc.) who "were killed with the sword which proceeded from the mouth of Him who sat on the horse," showing that these two passages are describing the same event, the Second Coming of Christ.

As the time of the Second Coming approaches there will be an accelerating of events that will finally become an earth-shattering blur as the final, momentous acts of God take place one after another (see the chart that follows). Now, as the world teeters on the brink of eternity, it is time to make sure we are ready. "Remember therefore how you have received and heard, and hold fast, and repent. If therefore you do not watch, I will come upon you as a thief, and you will not know what hour I will come upon you" (Revelation 3:3).

Accelerating Toward The Second Coming

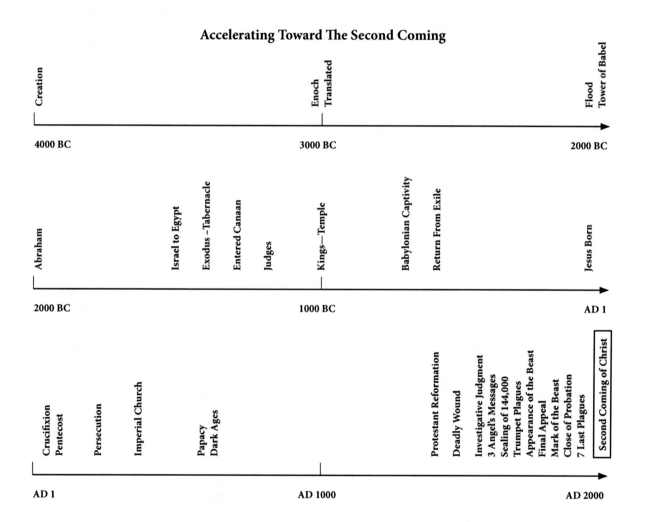

"I saw an angel coming down form heaven, having the key to the bottomless pit and a great chain in his hand. He laid hold of the dragon... and he cast him into the bottomless pit." Rev. 20:1-3
Woodcut by Albrecht Durer 1498

Chapter 20

Revelation 20:1-15

20:1 And I saw an angel coming down from heaven, having the key of the bottomless pit and a great chain in his hand.

20:2 And he laid hold on the dragon, that ancient serpent, who is the Devil, and Satan, and bound him a thousand years,

20:3 And cast him into the bottomless pit, and shut him up, and set a seal on him, so that he would not deceive the nations any more, until the thousand years were fulfilled. And after that he must be loosed for a little while.

20:4 And I saw thrones, and they sat on them, and judgment was given to them. And I saw the souls of those that were beheaded for the witness of Jesus, and for the word of God, and who had not worshiped the beast, or his image, and had not received his mark on their foreheads, or in their hands; and they lived and reigned with Christ a thousand years.

20:5 But the rest of the dead did not live again until the thousand years were finished. This is the first resurrection.

20:6 Blessed and holy is he that has part in the first resurrection. On such the second death has no power, but they shall be priests of God and of Christ, and shall reign with him a thousand years.

20:7 And when the thousand years are completed, Satan will be released from his prison,

20:8 And shall go out to deceive the nations which are in the four quarters of the earth, Gog, and Magog, to gather them together to battle, the number of whom is as the sand of the sea.

20:9 And they went up on the breadth of the earth, and surrounded the camp of the saints, and the beloved city; and fire came down from God out of heaven, and devoured them.

20:10 And the devil that deceived them was cast into the lake of fire and brimstone, where the beast and the false prophet are, and shall be tormented day and night forever and ever.

20:11 And I saw a great white throne, and Him that sat on it, from whose face the earth and the heaven fled away; and there was found no place for them.

20:12 And I saw the dead, small and great, standing before God; and the books were opened. And another book was opened, which is the Book of Life. And the dead were judged out of those things which were written in the books, according to their works.

20:13 And the sea gave up the dead which were in it, and Death and Hades delivered up the dead which were in them; and they were judged every man according to their works.

20:14 And Death and Hades were cast into the lake of fire. This is the second death.

20:15 And whoever was not found written in the Book of Life was cast into the lake of fire.

20:1-3 Satan Bound for 1000 Years

"And I saw an angel coming down from heaven, having the key of the bottomless pit and a great chain in his hand. And he laid hold on the dragon, that ancient serpent, who is the Devil, and Satan, and bound him a thousand years, and cast him into the bottomless pit, and shut him up, and set a seal on him, so that he would not deceive the nations any more, until the thousand years were fulfilled. And after that he must be loosed for a little while" (Revelation 20:1-3).

Satan will be personally directing the final events of the Battle of Armageddon by possessing a man who is called "the beast." Along with the "false prophet," the beast will be "cast alive into the lake of fire," but this is not the end of Satan, who, as a spirit being, can abandon the body of the beast and would still like to cause mayhem and destruction. But he will not be permitted to do this. He will be **bound [for] a thousand years** in **the bottomless pit.**

In 9:1,2 *The Bottomless Pit* we saw that the bottomless pit (translated "the abyss" in other versions) was first mentioned in Genesis 1 as the chaotic, formless condition of the earth before creation (Genesis 1:2 Greek Septuagint). It also refers to the place where demons can be confined when they are cast out of people. In Luke 8:31 the demons begged Jesus not to send them to the abyss. In the same story in Mark 5:10 the demons

begged Jesus not to send them "out of the country" and again in Matthew 8:31 they begged that they could go into a herd of swine. Comparing these texts, it is evident that the abyss is the place of confinement where demons are not permitted to possess and torment anyone. This goes along with Jesus' description of demons who are cast out of a person: "When an unclean spirit goes out of a man, he goes through dry places, seeking rest, and finds none" (Matthew 12:43). Peter described this "homeless" condition: "God did not spare the angels who sinned, but cast them down to hell [the Greek word *tartarus* is unique to this scripture] and delivered them into chains of darkness, to be reserved for judgment" (2Peter 2:4).

Considering all these scriptures together, we see that the **"bottomless pit"** where Satan (and undoubtedly his demons with him) will be chained is simply the earth in its chaotic condition following the catastrophic events associated with the Second Coming of Christ. Satan will be chained in the sense that he will not be permitted to leave the earth and there will be no one there to tempt—the rebellious will be dead and God's followers will be in Heaven.

The chaotic earth is described in Jeremiah 4:23-26. "I beheld the earth, and indeed it was without form and void;[764] and the heavens, they had no light. I beheld the mountains and indeed they trembled, and all the hills moved back and forth. I beheld, and indeed there was no man, and all the birds of the heavens had fled. I beheld, and indeed the fruitful land was a wilderness, and all its cities were broken down at the presence of the Lord, by His fierce anger." Isaiah 24 gives a similar picture, "Behold, the Lord makes the earth empty and makes it waste…The inhabitants of the earth are burned…The earth is violently broken, the earth is split open, the earth is shaken exceedingly…It shall come to pass in that day that the Lord will punish on high the host of exalted ones, and on the earth the kings of the earth. They will be gathered together, as prisoners are gathered in the pit and will be shut up in the prison; after many days they will be punished." (Isaiah 24:1,6,19,21,22). The "many days" which are mentioned are the thousand years that Satan will be bound. But during that time, while Satan is chained to a depopulated earth, the redeemed will be in Heaven as **"priests of God and of Christ, and shall reign with Him a thousand years"** (Revelation 20:6).

20:4,5 The First Resurrection

"And I saw thrones, and they sat on them, and judgment was given to them. And I saw the souls of those that were beheaded for the witness of Jesus, and for the word of God, and who had not worshiped the beast, or his image, and had not received his mark on their foreheads, or in their hands; and they lived and reigned with Christ a thousand years. But the rest of the dead did not live again until the thousand years were finished. This is the first

resurrection"** (Revelation 20:4,5).

John saw the righteous raised to life in **"the first resurrection."** At first glance it may appear that only the martyrs (**"those that were beheaded for the witness of Jesus"**) are resurrected. But John first saw a general overview of all who will live during the Millennium (**"I saw thrones, and they sat on them, and judgment was given to them"**) and then the vision focuses in and gives him a view of the martyrs (**"those that were beheaded"**), especially those who had gone through horrors of the time of trouble (**"who had not worshiped the beast, or his image, and had not received his mark"**). Just as in the judgment in chapter 6, the martyrs are given an "honorable mention" because of the special devotion they have displayed (see 6:9,10 *Souls Under the Altar*).

This scene obviously takes place at the Second Coming of Christ, because in 1 Thessalonians 4:16 Paul says that "the Lord Himself will descend from heaven with a shout, with the voice of the archangel, and with the trumpet of God. And the dead in Christ will rise first." "For as in Adam all die, even so in Christ all shall be made alive. But each one in his own order: Christ the firstfruits, afterward those who are Christ's at His coming… in a moment, in the twinkling of an eye, at the last trumpet. For the trumpet will sound, and the dead will be raised incorruptible, and we shall be changed." (1 Corinthians 15:22,23,52).

In Revelation 20 this is called **"the first resurrection."** There is also a "second resurrection," which takes place after the 1000 years—**"but the rest of the dead did not live again until the thousand years were finished."** Jesus also mentioned these two resurrections: "The hour is coming in which all who are in the graves will hear His voice and come forth—those who have done good, to the *resurrection of life*, and those who have done evil, to the *resurrection of condemnation*" (John 5:28,29).

Those who are resurrected, as well as the

---

764 Jeremiah uses the identical language of Genesis 1:2 which described the chaotic state of the earth before creation when "the earth was without form and void, and darkness was over the face of the deep [abyss]."

righteous who are alive at His coming (**"who had not worshiped the beast, or his image, and had not received his mark"**) will **"live and reign with Christ a thousand years"** before the **"rest of the dead"** are resurrected. What is the purpose of this thousand-year **"reign"**? We might consider this period to be an orientation to eternal life. God at the resurrection will "transform our lowly bodies that they may be conformed to His [Jesus'] glorious body" (Philippians 3:21) but there is no indication that He is going to "download" new minds. Many of us will be woefully lacking in the concepts and principles of heaven. Considering how warped our minds have been by the life of sin we have experienced and how little we really know of what it means to love the Lord with all our heart and our neighbors as ourselves, a thousand years is not really such a long time to learn all that we will need to know in order to carry out the elevated and glorious "job description" that God has prepared for us. Fortunately we will have a universe of angels and holy beings and God the Father, Son and Holy Spirit to be our teachers!

A major part of our preparation will be to thoroughly learn how noxious and destructive sin has been. We will gain this understanding through a work that we will do during the **"thousand years"**—**"judgment was given to them."** Paul said, "Do you not know that the saints will judge the world?…Do you not know that we shall judge angels?" (1Corinthians 6:2,3). Apparently "the saints" will examine **"the books"** which contain the records of the lives of those who were not a part of the first resurrection, because **"the dead [will be] judged out of those things which were written in the books, according to their works"** (Revelation 20:12).

This does not mean that the saved will decide who will have eternal life—that will already have been decided by God, which is why they will have had a part in the first resurrection. But those who are given eternal life will have the opportunity to be fully satisfied that God's judgment has been just and righteous. They will be able to see not just the behavior but also the history and circumstances that have shaped the lives of those who rejected God, to a degree that will far surpass any reality TV program! They will see how sin has ruined lives and marred the image of God in humanity, and will understand why those who were not granted eternal life could never be happy in a holy universe. No doubt there will be some surprises and even grief concerning those who were not a part of the first resurrection. In this work of judgment all questions will be settled "and God will wipe away all tears from their eyes" (Revelation 21:4).

20:7-10 Satan Released

"And when the thousand years are completed, Satan will be released from his prison, and shall go out to deceive the nations which are in the four quarters of the earth, Gog, and Magog, to gather them together to battle, the number of whom is as the sand of the sea. And they went up on the breadth of the earth, and surrounded the camp of the saints, and the beloved city; and fire came down from God out of heaven, and devoured them. And the devil that deceived them was cast into the lake of fire and brimstone, where the beast and the false prophet are, and shall be tormented day and night forever and ever" (Revelation 20:7-10).

For 1,000 years Satan will look upon the wreckage he has brought about with his rebellion. But at the end of the thousand years he will have a chance to prove that he is still the same old unrepentant devil. **"And when the thousand years are completed, Satan will be released from his prison, and shall go out to deceive the nations"** (Revelation 20:7,8). His release will take place when the unrepentant are resurrected and he again has someone (**"the nations"**) to tempt.

"But the rest of the dead [the unrepentant] **did not live again until the thousand years were finished"** (Revelation 20:5).

"The rest of the dead" are called **"Gog and Magog."** This is a reference to Ezekiel chapters 38 and 39, which speaks of "Gog of the land of Magog, the prince of Rosh, Meshech and Tubal" (Ezekiel 38:2). This passage describes the most massive alliance of all time from all corners of the world—"Persia, Ethiopia, and Libya are with them, all of them with shield and helmet; Gomer and all its troops, the house of Togarmah from the far north and all its troops—many people are with you" (vs. 5,6). They come against God's people who have been saved from captivity—"In the latter years you will come into the land of those brought back from the sword and gathered from many people on the mountains of Israel, which had long been desolate; they were brought out of the nations, and now all of them dwell safely" (v.8). They devise a plan to attack God's people in their apparently defenseless **"camp"**—"Thoughts will arise in your mind, and you will make an evil plan: you will say, 'I will go up against a land of unwalled villages, I will go to a peaceful people, who dwell safely, all of them dwelling without walls, and having neither bars nor gates…You will come up against My people Israel like a cloud, to cover the land. It will be in the latter days that I will bring you against My land, so that the nations may know Me, when I am hallowed in you, O Gog, before their eyes" (vs. 10,11, 16).

This scenario is portrayed in Revelation 20 as Satan going out **"to deceive the nations"** (the resurrected unrepentant) and leading them to **"surround the camp of the saints, and the beloved city."** Although John does not mention New Jerusalem descending from Heaven to the earth until chapter 21, this has apparently happened by the time the 1,000 years are over. The resurrected unrepentant, who have been sleeping in the grave since they died, do not have a clue

as to what has been happening through the ages, and Satan is able to dupe them into believing that they can take over the **"beloved city."** John here gives the short version—**"fire came down from God out of heaven, and devoured them."** But then he elaborates and shows that the unrepentant will actually face the great final judgment at this point, coming face to face with the God they have scorned and rejected. They will also experience the horror of seeing their own lives in review in graphic detail from the **"books…and… the book of life"** that will be **"opened"** as they stand in petrified awe before the **"great white throne."**

20:11-15 The White Throne Judgment

The work of investigative judgment by the saints in heaven during the thousand years is a precurser to the final executive judgment that takes place **"when the thousand years are over."**

"And I saw a great white throne, and Him that sat on it, from whose face the earth and the heaven fled away; and there was found no place for them. And I saw the dead, small and great, standing before God; and the books were opened. And another book was opened, which is the Book of Life. And the dead were judged out of those things which were written in the books, according to their works And the sea gave up the dead which were in it, and Death and Hades delivered up the dead which were in them; and they were judged every man according to their works. And Death and Hades were cast into the lake of fire. This is the second death. And whoever was not found written in the Book of Life was cast into the lake of fire" (Revelation 20:11-15).

During the thousand years the saved will be satisfied that God's judgments have been an expression of both justice and love. But **"the** dead" who have just been raised in the second resurrection will stand before the **"great white throne."** The **"books"** will be **"opened"** and they will come face to face with **"those things which were written in the books."** How this will happen technically with billions of people all at once is not made clear—perhaps it will be something like the experience people have when they almost die, and the events of their life "pass before their eyes" in a moment of time. At any rate, after seeing the facts concerning their lives, those who could not be saved will have to admit that God has been more than fair and His judgment of them is just. "We shall all stand before the judgment seat of Christ." "At the name of Jesus every knee should bow, of those in heaven, and of those on earth, and of those under the earth, and that every tongue should confess that Jesus Christ is Lord to the glory of God the Father." (Romans 14:10, Philippians 2:10,11).

Those whose names are not **"found written in the Book of Life"** will be **"cast into the lake of fire."** This brings up one of the most misunderstood concepts in the Bible: the doctrine of hell and the second death. Some have felt that God's nature of love excludes the possibility of His destroying anyone, and that the many references such as this one are either metaphorical or threats designed to encourage good behavior.

In recent years many have believed that hell is simply eternal separation from God, and the fire and torment that are mentioned represent the mental agony of those who will not be in His presence. Others have persisted in the more traditional view that the fires of hell are literal, and that the "immortal souls" of those who do not repent will be subject to fiery torment of some kind for all eternity. The medieval church depicted this suffering in graphic detail, with writers such as Dante and artists like Hieronymus Bosch creating an explicit and terrifying prospect for those who would dare to refuse God's love and mercy.

This passage clearly teaches that not everyone will be found written in **"the Book of Life."** These unfortunates will be **"cast into the lake of fire"** which is called the **"second death."**[765] Jesus referred to both the first and the second death in Matthew 10:28: "Do not fear those who kill the body [the first death] but cannot kill the soul. But rather fear Him who is able to destroy both soul and body in hell." The destruction of both body and soul is what is referred to in Revelation as the second death, and hell (*gehenna*)[766] is the **"lake of fire."** Some have taught that Jesus' words refer to the time of death, but the first death of the body clearly cannot be a time when both soul and body would be destroyed in hell, since the bodies (and souls) of the unrepentant are resurrected at the end of the thousand years.

It is clear from this verse that the soul in hell suffers the same fate as the body in hell (God will "destroy both soul and body in hell"). Does the body go on living, perhaps separated from God for eternity? Obviously not: "For behold, the day is coming, burning like an oven, and all the proud, yes all who do wickedly will be stubble. And the day which is coming shall burn them up, says the Lord of hosts, that will leave them neither root nor branch…You shall trample the wicked, for they shall be ashes under the soles of your feet" (Malachi 4:1,3). The fate of the body is total annihilation, and according to Jesus, that which happens to the body also happens to the soul.

This is clearly taught in Ezekiel 18:4: "Behold,

---

765 See also Revelation 2:11, 20:6, 21:8.

766 "The word derives its meaning from the Hebrew ge-hinnom (the valley of Hinnom) which was a pit into which refuse was dumped, a site which had long been contemptuously regarded in the Hebrew mind, as when Josiah dumped the filth of Jerusalem (II Kings 23:10) to be burned, and in which the bodies of executed criminals were tossed." *Zondervan Pictorial Bible Dictionary*, (Grand Rapids, MI, Zondervan Publishing, 1973). Use by permission of Zondervan www.zondervan.com.

all souls are Mine, the soul of the father as well as the soul of the son is Mine. The soul who sins shall die." Some have argued that "soul" in the Old Testament has a different meaning than in the New Testament, but James confirms Ezekiel's words, "He who turns a sinner from the error of his way will save a soul from death" (James 5:20). Peter taught the same thing, quoting Moses, "The Lord your God will raise up for you a prophet like me from your brethren [Jesus]. Him you shall hear in all things, whatever He says to you. And it shall be that *every soul who will not hear that Prophet shall be utterly destroyed* from among the people" (Acts 3:22,23). Souls are not immortal; they can die, and soul death is what is meant by the second death.[767]

What Is a Soul?

Actually, most of the misconceptions about hell reflect a basic misunderstanding of what the soul is. Many believe that the Bible teaches that man has an immortal soul,[768] but of the 458 instances in which the word "soul" is used in the Bible[769] there is not a single mention or intimation that man has a soul that is immortal. In fact, the Bible clearly teaches that it is God "the King of kings and Lord of lords, who alone has immortality" (1 Timothy 6:16). We can only have immortality if God gives it to us; it is not an intrinsic part of our nature.

The account of the creation of man in Genesis 2:7 shows what a soul is. "And the Lord God formed man of the dust of the ground, and breathed into his nostrils the breath of life; and man became a living soul.[770] The combination of dust (physical body) plus the breath of life (spirit) created a soul. The soul is simply the whole person, and the word soul is used repeatedly in both the Old and New Testament for person or life.[771] When a person dies the opposite happens; the breath of life returns to God, the body becomes dust again and the soul ceases to exist. "If He should gather to Himself His Spirit and His breath, all flesh would perish together and man would return to dust" (Job 34:14,15).[772]

Nor is there any indication that the "spirit" or "breath of life" is an intelligent entity, the "real inner person" which has an existence apart from the body. This idea is from Greek philosophy and gradually pervaded Christian theology, but it is foreign to Biblical thought. The Biblical soul is the whole person: the body, mind, heart, emotions, personality, inner self, that which seeks after God or turns away from Him. Peter made it clear, speaking of the resurrection of Jesus, that it is the soul, not just the body, that is resurrected. "Concerning the resurrection of the Christ...His soul was not left in Hades [the grave], nor did His flesh see corruption" (Acts 2:31). When a person dies (the first death) the soul (whole person)

---

767 This is taught in one of the most well-known texts of the Bible, John 3:16, "Whoever believes in [God's only begotten Son] shall not perish." This shows that whoever does not believe will perish.

768 Many have taught that because God made man in His image, man must have an immortal soul. However, the Bible does not specify what it means to be made in the image of God. In fact, man does not share the most basic characteristics of God: omnipotence (all powerful), omniscience (all knowing) and omnipresence (present everywhere). Therefore it is presumptuous to select a characteristic of God, such as His immortality, and assert categorically that this is what it means to be made in the image of God, especially when God specifically says that He alone has immortality (1Timothy 6:16).

769 This statistic is based on the King James Version of the Bible.

770 The Hebrew word for soul here is Nephesh, the same word that is used consistently in the Old Testament for soul.

771 For example, "Man is also chastened with pain on his bed, And with strong pain in many of his bones, so that his life abhors bread, and his soul succulent food." (Job 33:19,20). "And I will say to my soul, 'Soul, you have many goods laid up for many years; take your ease; eat, drink, and be merry'" (Luke 12:19).

772 See also Ecclesiastes 12:6,7.

sleeps in the grave,[773] awaiting the resurrection. The resurrection is the rising out of the grave of the soul. And in the case of the unrepentant, it is this resurrected soul that is destroyed in hell.

"The Lord preserves all who love Him, but all the wicked[774] He will destroy" (Psalms 145:20). "The wicked shall be no more; indeed you will look carefully for his place but it shall be no more…into smoke they shall vanish away" (Psalms 37:10,20). "Those who war against you shall be as nothing, as a nonexistent thing" (Isaiah 41:12). "You have destroyed the wicked; You have blotted out their name forever and ever…Even their memory has perished" (Psalms 9:5-8). These texts and many more emphasize the complete obliteration of those who are destroyed, with no hint of an inner spiritual entity that continues to live on.

Since God "alone has immortality," He is the source of all life. This means that there is no such thing as an independently immortal soul

---

773 Paul, speaking of those who would be resurrected, called them "those who have fallen asleep" (1 Thessalonians 4:13). When Stephen was stoned, "he fell asleep" (Acts 7:60). Jesus, speaking of Lazarus, said "Our friend Lazarus sleeps, but I go that I may wake him up." Then His disciples said, 'Lord, if he sleeps he will get well.' However Jesus spoke of his death, but they thought that He was speaking about taking rest in sleep. Then Jesus said to them plainly, 'Lazarus is dead' (John 11:11-14). Daniel shows where they sleep: "Many of those who *sleep in the dust* shall awake, some to everlasting life, some to shame and everlasting contempt" (Daniel 12:2). Jesus made it clear that sleeping in the dust is the same as being in the grave: "The hour is coming in which all who are in the graves will hear His voice and come forth—those who have done good, to the resurrection of life, and those who have done evil, to the resurrection of condemnation" (John 5:28,29).

774 The Old Testament frequently uses the Hebrew word *rasha*, often translated wicked, to characterize those who do not follow God. The basic meaning is "guilty one" in contrast to "righteous one." This does not mean that the wicked are sinners and the righteous are not; Christians are declared to be righteous because of their faith in the perfect righteousness of Jesus, who took their guilt upon Himself. The wicked could become righteous instantaneously by repenting of their sins, confessing to God and accepting His forgiveness (1 John 1:8,9). For this reason this commentary uses "unrepentant" instead of "wicked" (except when quoting the Bible) to show that the "righteous" have the same intrinsic nature and have exhibited the same types of behavior as the "wicked."

---

separated from God—the soul must be continually receiving life from God or it will cease to exist. It is inconceivable that God would continually infuse life into souls that were eternally separated from Him in hell.

An Act of Righteousness and Love

The judgment which results in the destruction of the unrepentant is an act of righteousness. God has extended His mercy, he has pleaded with those who have turned away from Him, but through the choices of their lives the unrepentant have demonstrated that they do not want what God wants to give them: Himself forever. Heaven, in the overwhelming presence of a pure and holy God, would be eternal torment—even when they see Him coming they call out for the mountains and rocks to hide them from His face (Revelation 6:16). When God puts an end to sin He will grant what they will really want: destruction, which is the only way they can be separated from God in that day when "all the earth [and the whole universe as well] shall be filled with the glory of the Lord" (Numbers 14:21). For this reason it is not just an act of righteousness but also an act of love when God pronounces the sentence, "These [who do not know God] shall be punished with everlasting destruction from the presence of the Lord and from the glory of His power" (2 Thessalonians 1:8,9).

Jesus, looking down the span of history to the great day of judgment, spoke in Matthew 25:31-46 of the same scene that is presented in Revelation 20: "When the Son of Man comes in His glory, and all the holy angels with Him, then He will sit on the throne of His glory. All the nations will be gathered before Him, and He will separate them one from another." Just as in Revelation, they will be judged "according to their works"—did they feed the hungry, clothe the naked, visit the sick, or did they instead turn away from Jesus in the person of those in need? (vs. 35-45). "Then He will also say to those on the left hand [who had not had compassion on the needy], 'Depart from Me, you cursed, *into the everlasting fire* prepared for the devil and his angels'...And these will go away *into everlasting punishment*, but the righteous into eternal life" (vs. 41,46).

These last verses have caused some to believe that the unrighteous will be tormented forever ("everlasting fire...everlasting punishment"), but a comparison with other scriptures shows that they actually teach just the opposite.

Eternal Fire

Jesus said that the unrighteous would go "into everlasting fire prepared for the devil and his angels" (Matthew 25:41). In the book of Jude there is actually an example which shows what everlasting or eternal fire is. "Sodom and Gomorrah, and the cities around them in a similar manner to these, having given themselves over to sexual immorality and gone after strange flesh, are set forth as an example, suffering the vengeance of eternal fire" (Jude 7). The story of the wickedness of Sodom and Gomorrah is recounted in Genesis 19. Lot, the only righteous man in the city, was saved out of it with his family, and "the Lord rained brimstone and fire on Sodom and Gomorrah from the Lord out of the heavens. So He overthrew those cities...and behold, the smoke of the land...went up like the smoke of a furnace...when God destroyed the cities of the plain" (Genesis 19:24-29). Obviously the "eternal fire" which destroyed Sodom is not still burning—it was not quenched or put out; it continued to burn until it had completely done its work of destruction.[775] In the same way the "eternal fire" which will destroy the unrepentant

will destroy them forever. They do not burn eternally; the results are eternal.

This interpretation is verified by the fact that the "everlasting fire" that Jesus spoke about in Matthew 25:41 is "prepared for the devil and his angels." This means that the fire will do the same thing to unrepentant people that it does to the devil. The fate of Satan is described in Ezekiel 28. The "king of Tyre [Satan][776]...became filled with violence within and sinned" and so was "cast as a profane thing out of the mountain of God" (vs. 12, 16). God said of him (using His perspective of the future, as if it has already happened), "You defiled your sanctuaries by the multitude of your iniquities...Therefore I brought fire from your midst [this is the "everlasting fire" mentioned in Matthew 25:41]. And I turned you to ashes upon the earth in the sight of all who saw you. All who knew you among the peoples are astonished at you; You have become a horror *and shall be no more forever*" (vs. 18,19).

Satan will be annihilated eternally; he will not live to be tortured forever in hell, and by no means will he be in charge of hell, directing its torment as he is popularly depicted. As the great instigator of sin, his destruction will be more fearsome than that of any other being (**"tormented**

---

775 This is also the meaning of the phrase "unquenchable fire" in Matthew 3:12 and Luke 3:17.

776 It is obvious that this passage is speaking of Satan, rather than the literal king of Tyre, because 1) He had already talked about the earthly ruler of Tyre in vs. 1-10 under the name "the prince of Tyre." 2) The "king of Tyre" was "in Eden, the garden of God" (vs. 13), was "the anointed cherub who covers," "walked back and forth in the midst of fiery stones" (v. 14) and was on "the mountain of God" (v. 15).

day and night" Revelation 20:10)[777] but even he will finally be reduced to nothingness and "shall be no more forever."

Jesus called the "everlasting fire" which completely destroys the devil and the unrepentant "everlasting punishment" (Matthew 25:41,46). Again, this does not mean punishment that continues forever, but rather punishment that has everlasting results. The apostle Paul made this clear in 2Thessalonians 1:7-10: "The Lord Jesus [will be] revealed from heaven with His mighty angels in flaming fire taking vengeance on those who do not know God, and on those who do not obey the gospel of our Lord Jesus Christ. These shall be *punished with everlasting destruction from the presence of the Lord and from the glory of His power, when He comes in that Day."*

The Soul Sleeps Until the Resurrection

The Bible clearly teaches that the first death is a sleep[778] in which there is no consciousness.[779] The sleeping dead will "wake up" with the resurrection, either the **"first resurrection"** at the Second Coming of Christ, or the **"second resurrection"** which takes place 1000 years later. At that time the dead will be judged,[780] and those who are not found written in the Book of Life will be cast into hell (**"the lake of fire"**) which will totally annihilate them, both body and soul.

Most churches teach that the soul goes straight to heaven or hell at the time of death, but this is illogical in light of the judgment. If God gave them their reward when they died, what would be the purpose of the judgment? Would he drag people out of hell so that he could give them their sentence and then throw them back in? Would He find out in the judgment that some who had gone to heaven or hell had ended up in the wrong place? Would the resurrection and judgment be a time to give those already in hell a body so that they could feel physical as well as mental and spiritual pain?

Moreover, this theory is also unbiblical. 1Thessalonians 4:13-18 makes it clear that it is not at the time of death, but at the resurrection of the dead when "those who have fallen asleep" will rise with the righteous living and "meet the Lord in the air. And thus we shall always be with

---

777 This text which states that the devil "will be tormented day and night forever and ever" appears at first glance to contradict the passage in Ezekial 28. However, it seems to be a shorthand version of Revelation 14:11 which states that "the smoke of their torment ascends forever and ever; and they have no rest day or night, who worship the beast." It is the smoke, or memorial of their torment, which rises forever. Their torment is a lack of rest, which is transitory, day and night (this phrase refers to a period of time that seems endless but actually does finally end, see Genesis 8:22, Psalms 32:4, 42:3, Revelation 12:10). They do not rest during the time when they "worship the beast and his image" (It does not say that they have no rest who *worshiped* the beast, as it would if it was referring to a permanent condition which was caused by a previous act). The torment has a permanent result, complete and total destruction, the only trace of which will be the permanent memorial of smoke. This interpretation is confirmed by the fact that Babylon will likewise be "utterly burned with fire," "shall not be found anymore," but "Her smoke [like that of annihilated sinners] rises up forever and ever" Revelation 18:8,21, 19:3.

778 John 11:11-14, see also Luke 8:52-55, Daniel 12:2, Acts 7:59,60, 1Thessalonians 4:13-17, John 6:39,40,44, Job 3:11-19, Jeremiah 51:39,57.

779 For example, "The living know that they will die, but the dead know nothing...Their love, their hatred and their envy have now perished...There is no work, or device or knowledge or wisdom in the grave" (Ecclesiastes 9:5,6,10). See also Psalms 6:5, Psalms 115:17, Psalms 146:4, Job 14:12.

780 John 12:48, Acts 17:31, Romans 2:15,16, Romans 14:10-12, 1Corinthians 4:4,5, 1Corinthians 6:2,3, 2Timothy 4:1.

the Lord." "When Christ who is our life appears, *then* you also will appear with Him in glory" (Colossians 3:4). Paul, in anticipation of his execution ("the time of my departure") said, "Finally, there is laid up for me the crown of righteousness, which the Lord, the righteous Judge, *will give to me on that Day*, and not to me only but also *to all who have loved His appearing*" (2Timothy 4:7,8). Jesus Himself said, "*I will come again* and receive you to Myself" (John 14:3). None of these statements make any sense if the disembodied soul goes immediately to God at the time of death.

It is sometimes asserted that Jesus' comment to the thief on the cross (Luke 23:43) is proof that people go to heaven as soon as they die, but a consideration of the original language[781] shows that the thief, like everyone else, will await the resurrection. The story of the rich man and Lazarus (Luke 16: 19-31) has also been used to support the idea that people go to heaven or hell as soon as they die, but a careful study of what

the text actually says[782] shows that this view is not consistent. The point is that neither these texts nor any others in scripture show that people go straight to heaven when they die. And there

---

781 Jesus' statement to the thief on the cross, "Assuredly, I say to you, today you will be with Me in Paradise" (Luke 23:43) is often pointed to as proof that the dead go to paradise as soon as they die. But Jesus Himself made it clear that He did not go to paradise that day—two days later, after His resurrection, He told Mary Magdalene "I have not yet ascended to My Father" (John 20:17). Actually the confusion is a simple matter of punctuation. The original Greek, which was written without punctuation, reads "*Amin soi lego simeron met'emou esi en to paradeiso*" (truly indeed to you I say today with me you will be in the paradise). If the comma, which was added later by editors, was placed after "today" rather than before it, the statement would simply mean "today I tell you that you will be with me in paradise." Some have theorized that paradise is some pleasant resting place, but not in the presence of God. However, Revelation 2:7 makes it clear that paradise is where the Tree of Life is, and Revelation 22:1-3 shows that the Tree of Life is before the throne of God.

782 "There was a certain rich man who was clothed in purple and fine linen and fared sumptuously every day. But there was a certain beggar named Lazarus, full of sores, who was laid at his gate... So it was that the beggar died and was carried by the angels to Abraham's bosom. The rich man also died and was buried. And being in torments in Hades, he lifted up his eyes and saw Abraham afar off, and Lazarus in his bosom. Then he cried and said, 'Father Abraham, have mercy on me, and send Lazarus that he may dip the tip of his finger in water and cool my tongue; for I am tormented in this flame.' But Abraham said, 'Son, remember that in your lifetime you received your good things, and likewise Lazarus evil things; but now he is comforted and you are tormented.... Then he said, 'I beg you therefore, father, that you would send him to my father's house, for I have five brothers, that he may testify to them, lest they also come to this place of torment.' Abraham said to him, 'They have Moses and the prophets; let them hear them.' And he said, 'No, father Abraham; but if one goes to them from the dead, they will repent.' But he said to him, 'If they do not hear Moses and the prophets, neither will they be persuaded though one rise from the dead'" (Luke 16:19-31).

The most obvious explanation of this passage is that this was a well-known story which Jesus used to make a point, but that not every detail was intended for instruction. This would be in keeping with His previous story of the unjust steward (Luke 16:1-13). The point of the story of the rich man and Lazarus was that miracles, including the resurrection of the dead (which actually happened with Jesus' friend Lazarus!) would not be convincing to those who will not accept the testimony of the scriptures (hence Jesus said "let them hear Moses and the prophets").

Some readers, however, insist that the story should be taken literally. But even a literal interpretation does not support the idea that the soul goes to everlasting heaven or hell at the time of death. Assuming the story to be literal, we notice that both the rich man and Lazarus had bodies—the rich man wanted water for his tongue—and he wanted Lazarus to bring it with his finger. Physical bodies could not be present until after the resurrection.

The rich man did not seem to know that thousands of years had passed and that his brothers had long since died. This would be consistent with the fact that the dead sleep in the grave and know nothing of the passing of time. Abraham did not bother to explain to him the irrelevant details of all that had happened while he had been asleep. He simply informed him that there was no "second chance" of salvation after death, no way to pass from hell to heaven, and no intercession, even on the part of the "saints" (such as Lazarus) which could alter their fate. Consistent with the words of Jesus, the rich man had been thrown "into the everlasting fire prepared for the devil and his angels" (Matthew 25:41). The fire would do its work of destruction, leaving "neither root nor branch" (Malachi 4:1), and like the devil, the rebellious angels, and the multitudes of unrepentant people who will be there with him, he "shall be no more forever" (Ezekiel 28:19).

are no scriptures which indicate that sinners go immediately to hell where their souls live in misery, awaiting the resurrection and judgment that would consign them to even more torment for all eternity. See also 6:9,10 *Souls Under the Altar*.

Love Based on Fear?

Many Christians are afraid to let go of the idea of a hell of eternal torment, fearing that there would be no motivation for the sinner to turn away from his sin if the consequences were "simply" an end to his existence. But there is nothing simple about the final destruction of the unrepentant. It will be a fearsome experience when the fullness of their guilt will be in vivid contrast with the full revelation of the glory and holiness of God. But even more basic is the fact that fear does not motivate love. "We love Him because He first loved us,"[783] not because we are afraid of Him.

The use of fear to force obedience is actually the very opposite of God's character. It is the beast who threatens those who "would not worship the image of the beast to be killed" (Revelation 13:15).[784] It was godless Nebuchadnezzar who proclaimed that "whoever does not fall down and worship shall be cast immediately into the midst of a burning fiery furnace" (Daniel 3:6). Most Christians today are appalled by the torture that was inflicted on

"heretics" by the church during the Inquisition of the Middle Ages, but this was only the logical extension of the doctrine of eternal hell. If God will torment forever those who reject Him, why shouldn't their torture start now, in this life, especially since before death there is the possibility of repentance? If eternal hell is true, God is even more unjust than the inquisitors, since He, according to this doctrine, tortures without a possibility of repentance and reprieve.

The human concepts of love, mercy and justice are a faint reflection of the divine characteristics, but nevertheless are based upon them. Therefore, ideas and practices which violate the human conceptions of love, mercy and justice are usually a violation of the divine reality. The concept that God would create man, knowing in advance that he would sin, and then consign him to an eternity of punishment when he did sin violates all standards of love, mercy, and even justice. Our God-given sense of justice rejects the notion of "cruel and unusual punishment." Those governments that submit their criminals to torture are considered barbaric; how much worse would be one which not only continued the torture for the entire lifetime of the offender, but devised ways to prolong the life of the transgressor so that his torment could continue. And yet this blasphemous charge has been leveled against God by His church! Moreover, with the traditional understanding of the resurrection of the ungodly, God is made to be even more of a monster. Not content with the torture of the "soul" that they have been experiencing since death, God arranges to reunite them with a physical body so that their eternal torment will be even more intense! It is no wonder that in consideration of this gross injustice, the majority of those who live in the traditionally Christian countries of Europe have rejected all religion and faith in God, who has been so badly misrepresented.

---

783 1John 4:19.

784 At first glance it would seem that both the beast and God threaten coercive punishment, the beast as quoted above in Revelation 13:15 and God in Revelation 14:9,10 "If anyone worships the beast...he himself shall also drink of the wine of the wrath of God...and he shall be tormented with fire and brimstone in the presence of the holy angels." But there are some basic differences. The beast threatens coercive punishment in this life to those who do not obey him. God warns of eternal consequences (destruction) that will be executed after death in the judgment. The true emphasis of God's warning is not the pain the unrepentant will experience, but eternal life that they will miss. In other words, Satan's threats are all about the behavior that he wants to force us to perform. God's warnings are about the blessings that He doesn't want us to miss.

Sin Finally Finished

It is not God's purpose with hell to give people what they deserve. One of the most basic aspects of His character is that He *does not* give sinners what they deserve, but rather tries to find ways to bring them to salvation, taking upon Himself the punishment they deserve. Hell is not a way of "getting back at" sinners, but is simply a way of bringing an end to sin and suffering.

If hell were for eternity, sin would never come to an end. But thank God, sin and evil will not be immortalized. **"Death and Hades"** will be **"cast into the lake of fire."** All forms of death will be eradicated. This includes the first death—there will be no more people sleeping in the grave, oblivious to the reality of God. It also includes the living death of separation from God that the Apostle Paul describes as "dead in trespasses and sins" (Ephesians 2:1). And the second death, destruction of the soul, will also be abolished—no one will ever again face the wages of sin, because sin and everything connected with it will be destroyed. "For He [Christ] must reign till He has put all enemies under His feet. The last enemy that will be destroyed is death" (1Corinthians 15:25,26).[785]

God will create "a new heaven and a new earth" where "no more death, neither sorrow, nor crying, neither shall there be any more pain; for the former things have passed away" (Revelation 21:1,4). These "former things," which God promises will not exist, would exist in hell if hell were a place or condition of eternal punishment or separation.

The **"second death"** is a "fire that shall never be quenched" (Mark 9:45)—no one will put it out until it has consumed everything that can die, both body and soul. "The elements will melt with fervent heat; both the earth and the works that are in it will be burned up" (2Peter 3:10). With sin permanently abolished, God will then renew His creation—"We, according to His promise, look for new heavens and a new earth, in which righteousness dwells" (v. 13). There will be no dark corner of the universe where sin, suffering and death will continue. Everyone and everything will forever be in harmony with God.

Since God will not force the unrepentant to love Him, but He will bring an end to all sin, there must be a hell, and sinners will be destroyed. But even this destruction is so foreign to God's nature (He is "not willing that any should perish but that all should come to repentance" 2Peter 3:9) that it is called His "strange act" (Isaiah 28:21). God's great heart of love pleads with every soul to turn away from the destruction of hell, to allow their names to be **"written in the book of life"** so as to avoid being **"cast into the lake of fire."** "Therefore I will judge you, O house of Israel, every one according to his ways,' says the Lord God. 'Repent, and turn from all your transgressions, so that iniquity will not be your ruin. Cast away from you all the transgressions which you have committed, and get yourselves a new heart and a new spirit. For why should you die, O house of Israel? For I have no pleasure in the death of one who dies,' says the Lord God. 'Therefore turn and live!" (Ezekiel 18:30-32).

---

785 Those who claim that death is simply separation from God and the second death of hell is eternal separation overlook the fact that death itself (including separation from God) will be destroyed.

"He carried me away in the spirit to a great and high mountain, and showed me the great city,
the holy Jerusalem" Rev. 21:10
Matthew Merian 1630

Chapter 21

Revelation 21:1-27

21:1 And I saw a new heaven and a new earth, for the first heaven and the first earth had passed away; and there was no more sea.

21:2 And I, John saw the holy city, New Jerusalem, coming down from God out of heaven, prepared as a bride adorned for her husband.

21:3 And I heard a loud voice out of heaven saying, "Behold, the tabernacle of God is with men, and He will dwell with them, and they shall be His people, and God Himself shall be with them, and be their God.

21:4 And God will wipe away all tears from their eyes; and there shall be no more death, neither sorrow, nor crying, neither shall there be any more pain; for the former things have passed away."

21:5 And He that sat on the throne said, "Behold, I make all things new." And He said to me, "Write, for these words are true and faithful."

21:6 And He said to me, "It is done. I am Alpha and Omega, the Beginning and the End. I will give to him that is thirsty of the fountain of the water of life freely.

21:7 He that overcomes shall inherit all things; and I will be his God, and he shall be My son.

21:8 But the fearful, and unbelieving, and the abominable, and murderers, and fornicators, and sorcerers, and idolaters, and all liars, shall have their part in the lake which burns with fire and brimstone, which is the second death."

21:9 And there came to me one of the seven angels who had the seven bowls full of the seven last plagues, and he talked with me, saying, "Come here, I will show you the bride, the Lamb's wife."

21:10 And he carried me away in the spirit to a great and high mountain, and showed me that great city, the holy Jerusalem, descending out of heaven from God,

21:11 Having the glory of God; and her light was like a most precious stone, like a jasper stone, clear as crystal.

21:12 And it had a wall great and high, and had twelve gates, and at the gates twelve angels, and names written thereon, which are the names of the twelve tribes of the children of Israel.

21:13 On the east, three gates; on the north, three gates; on the south, three gates; and on the west, three gates.

21:14 And the wall of the city had twelve foundations, and on them the names of the twelve apostles of the Lamb.

21:15 And he that talked with me had a golden reed to measure the city, and the gates of it, and the wall of it.

21:16 And the city lies foursquare, and the length is as great as the breadth. And he measured the city with the reed, twelve thousand stadia. The length and the breadth and the height of it are equal.

21:17 And he measured the wall thereof, one hundred forty-four cubits, according to the measure of a man, that is, of an angel.

21:18 And the building of the wall of it was jasper, and the city was pure gold, like clear glass.

21:19 And the foundations of the wall of the city were adorned with all manner of precious stones. The first foundation was jasper; the second, sapphire; the third, chalcedony; the fourth, emerald;

21:20 The fifth, sardonyx; the sixth, sardius; the seventh, chrysolyte; the eighth, beryl; the ninth, topaz; the tenth, chrysoprase; the eleventh, jacinth; the twelfth, amethyst.

21:21 And the twelve gates were twelve pearls; every one of the gates was of one pearl. And the street of the city was pure gold, like transparent glass.

21:22 And I saw no temple therein, for the Lord God Almighty and the Lamb are its temple.

21:23 And the city had no need of the sun or of the moon to shine in it, for the glory of God gives it light, and the Lamb is its lamp.

21:24 And the nations of those who are saved will walk in its light, and the kings of the earth bring their glory and honor into it.

21:25 And the gates of it shall not be shut at all by day; indeed, there shall be no night there.

21:26 And they shall bring the glory and honor of the nations into it.

21:27 And there shall not enter into it anything that defiles, or causes abomination or a lie, but only they which are written in the Lamb's Book of Life.

21:1 New Heaven and Earth

"And I saw a new heaven and a new earth, for the first heaven and the first earth had passed away; and there was no more sea" (Revelation 21:1). The hope of a new order of existence is what makes the concept of eternal life desirable. If we had to spend eternity living as we do now with pain, suffering, loss, and shallow, empty and negative relationships, not to mention the constant harassment of the devil, eternal life would truly be the eternal hell that many Christians believe in. But the believers through the ages "all died in faith, not having received the promises, but having seen them afar off, were assured of them, embraced them, and confessed that they were strangers and pilgrims on the earth...They desired a better, that is a heavenly country" (Hebrews 11:13,16).

The "lake of fire" which will destroy the unrepentant at the final judgment is the cleansing fire that prepares the earth for being made new. "The heavens will pass away with a great noise, and the elements will melt with fervent heat; both the earth and the works that are in it will be burned up...Nevertheless, we, according to His promise, look for new heavens and a new earth in which righteousness dwells" (2 Peter 3:10,13).

The destruction of the unrepentant will be the last abhorrent reminder of sin, ushering in the new reality. "For as the new heavens and the new earth which I will make shall remain before Me, says the Lord, so shall your descendants and your name remain...All flesh shall come to worship before Me' says the Lord. 'And they shall go forth and look upon the corpses of the men who have transgressed against Me. For their worm does not die, and their fire is not quenched. They shall be an abhorrence to all flesh" (Isaiah 66:22-24). Fortunately, the worms will not die and the fire will not be quenched until they have done a total and complete job of removing every trace of sinners and the effects of sin. This is emphasized by the fact that **"there was no more sea."** In both Daniel and Revelation the sea is the symbolic source of the fearsome enemies that persecute God's people (Daniel 7:3, Revelation 13:1).

God Himself will comfort His people of every sorrow that may result from remembering the sin experience, especially the pain associated with the memories of those who have perished. **"And God will wipe away all tears from their eyes; and there shall be no more death, neither sorrow, nor crying, neither shall there be any more pain; for the former things have passed away."** (Revelation 21:4). "For behold, I create new heavens and a new earth; and the former shall not be remembered or come to mind" (Isaiah 65:17). This is not to say that God will perform some kind of brainwashing technique, but everything about the new creation will be such as to delight the heart and mind, and drive out the negative memories of sin. There is no doubt, however, that there will be enough remembrance of the terrible epoch of evil that no one will ever want to be involved with it again. "Affliction will not rise up a second time" (Nahum 1:9).

A world without pain or sorrow is so out of the realm of human experience that God reiterates the promise with a personal guarantee:

"And He that sat on the throne said, 'Behold, I make all things new.' And He said to me, 'Write, for these words are true and faithful" (Revelation 21:5).[786]

21:2,3 Earth, Capital of the Universe

"And I, John saw the holy city, New Jerusalem, coming down from God out of heaven, prepared as a bride adorned for her husband. And I heard a loud voice out of heaven saying, "Behold, the tabernacle of God is with men, and He will dwell with them, and they shall be His people, and God Himself shall be with them, and be their God" (Revelation 21:2,3).

Sometimes when there has been a naughty child in the classroom the teacher will make him sit in the seat closest to the teacher's desk in order to keep an eye on him and keep him out of trouble. Other times naughty children have to stay in their room away from everyone else as a punishment. Fortunately, neither of these scenarios are the reason for God establishing His capital on earth with redeemed mankind.

God's purposes for humanity are from eternity, and these include our reigning with Him and sitting with Him on His throne. "God... has saved us and called us with a holy calling... according to His own purpose and grace which

---

786 Even though God revealed many unbelievable things to John, it is those that have to do with the awesome privileges that God has planned for his people which called forth His personal guarantee. In chapter 19 the angel speaks of the blessing which will come to those who have been invited to the marriage supper of the Lamb, "And he said to me, 'These are the true sayings of God" (Revelation 19:9). Again, in the verse under consideration, after promising to make all things new the angel says, "These words are true and faithful." And in chapter 22 the angel reveals that God's servants "shall see His face, and His name shall be on their foreheads...and they shall reign forever and ever.' Then he said to me, 'These words are faithful and true" (Revelation 22:4-6). Perhaps He makes these guarantees because we intuitively know how entirely unworthy of these privileges we are.

was given to us in Christ Jesus *before time began*" (2 Timothy 1:9). "He chose us in Him *before the foundation of the world*, that we should be holy and without blame before Him in love" (Ephesians 1:4). The twenty-four elders, as representatives of redeemed mankind, "sang a new song, saying, 'You [God]...have redeemed us... and have made us to our God kings and priests; and *we shall reign on the earth*" (Revelation 5:9,10. See 19:*Rulers of the Kingdom*).

One of the cardinal attributes of God is His omnipresence; He fills every place at the same time. However, the promise, **"He will dwell with them...God Himself will be with them,"** indicates that the earth will be the site of a visible manifestation of God, where His creation will gather before Him.

"New Jerusalem" on planet earth will be the capital of the universe! Here the "mansions" that Jesus told His followers that He was going to prepare for them will be located, no doubt **"coming down from God out of heaven"** with the holy city (John 14:2). Jesus' promise to His followers was, "Where I am, there you may be also" (v. 3).

The city is called **"the bride, the Lamb's wife"** because it represents the whole kingdom of God, which is the inheritance of Jesus (see 19: 6-9 *The Marriage of the Lamb*). It is now in heaven, and there it will be the home of the saved during the 1000 years. But after the millennium the holy city will descend out of heaven to earth. **"And he carried me away in the spirit to a great and high mountain, and showed me that great city, the holy Jerusalem, descending out of heaven from God"** (Revelation 21:10). It will rest upon a desolate earth, broken by the great events associated with the Second Coming of Christ, and for this reason it is called "the camp of the saints" (Revelation 20:9). But after the great white throne judgment and the cleansing of the earth by fire the redeemed will spread out over the earth made new, and will come to visit the city.

"The gates of it shall not be shut at all by day; indeed, there shall be no night there. And they shall bring the glory and honor of the nations into it" (Revelation 21:25,26).

21:6,7 The Inheritance of the Overcomers

"And He said to me, "It is done! I am Alpha and Omega, the Beginning and the End. I will give to him that is thirsty of the fountain of the water of life freely. He that overcomes shall inherit all things; and I will be his God, and he shall be My son" (Revelation 21:6,7).

When Jesus promises that **"he who overcomes shall inherit all things,"** He is not talking about a meager inheritance. Besides their "mansions" in the city the saints will also have country homes which they shall build, and gardens which they shall plant, recalling the idyllic life in the Garden of Eden. "They shall build houses and inhabit them; they shall plant vineyards and eat their fruit...and My elect shall long enjoy the work of their hands" (Isaiah 65:21-23).

All of this speaks of a very real existence. God said, **"Behold, I make all things new,"** not "I make all new things." This suggests that there is not a completely different order of **"things"** in the kingdom of God, but that they are made new in a way that takes away every trace of the effects of sin. The popular notion of the saved as being like cherubs floating around on clouds playing harps has as little support in scripture as the notion that eternal life will be a continual "gazing at the beatific vision" or becoming "a note in the eternal heavenly choir."

The physical, mental, emotional and social as well as the spiritual aspects of mankind will reach their highest expression. John said, "When He [Jesus] is revealed, we shall be like Him" (1 John 3:2). Jesus after His resurrection had a real physical body and ate real food in the presence of

His disciples (Luke 24:36-43). The fact that "the wolf shall dwell with the lamb, the leopard shall lie down with the young goat, the calf and the young lion" (Isaiah 11:6), and "everyone shall sit under his vine and under his fig tree" (Micah 4:4) indicates that the physical creation that delights us now will be even more delightful when it is renewed. Since the "elect shall long enjoy the work of their hands," it will not be like an endless vacation with nothing to do—fascinating projects will challenge our physical as well as mental abilities.

"The earth shall be full of the knowledge of the Lord" (Isaiah 11:9). Secrets of God's creation and a true understanding of science will keep our minds continually expanding. Even in this life positive emotions such as "love, joy, [and] peace" are "the fruit of the Spirit" (Galatians 5:22), but this is only a foretaste of what our emotions will be with the absence of the darker feelings of grief, sorrow, anger and jealousy. "You will show me the path of life; In Your presence is fullness of joy; At Your right hand are pleasures forevermore" (Psalms 16:11). This is no monastic existence; even as the Hebrew meaning of Eden was "pleasure,"[787] so Eden restored will bring the most intense pleasure and delight.

"Many…will sit down with Abraham, Isaac and Jacob in the kingdom of heaven" (Matthew 8:11). This verse shows that both individuality and satisfying social interactions will continue to be a source of pleasure and fulfillment. When the disciples met Jesus after the resurrection they were able to recognize Him by His mannerisms[788] and related to Him as the friend they had known. Likewise, although the redeemed will have new bodies "conformed to His glorious body" (Philippians 3:21), we will still retain our personalities and relate to our friends and loved ones, as well as to an eternally expanding "circle of friends." Best of all, we will interact with others without the suspicions and misunderstandings that mar relationships here.

The redeemed will enjoy the ultimate spiritual experience of being in the immediate presence of God, the source of everything. "The throne of God and of the Lamb shall be in [New Jerusalem]; and His servants shall serve him. And they shall see His face; and His name shall be in their foreheads" (Revelation 22:3,4). Jesus spoke of the Holy Spirit as being an internal spring of water—"The water that I shall give him will become in him a fountain of water springing up into everlasting life." "If anyone thirsts, let him come to Me and drink. He who believes in Me, as the scripture has said, out of his heart will flow rivers of living water.' But this He spoke concerning the Spirit, whom those believing in Him would receive" (John 4:14, 7:37-39). We experience this internal presence of God through the Holy Spirit in this life ("God has put his Spirit in our hearts as a deposit, guaranteeing what is to come" 2Corinthians 1:22), but our sinful human natures get in the way of our receiving God's Spirit in its fullness. We find ourselves crying out with the Psalmist, "My soul thirsts for You; my flesh longs for You in a dry and thirsty land where there is no water. So I have looked for You in the sanctuary to see Your power and your glory" (Psalms 63:1,2). In contrast, in the new earth we will be fully satisfied—**"I will give of the fountain of the water of life freely to him who thirsts."**

We are actually extremely limited in our ability to comprehend the meaning of the promise, **"He that overcomes shall inherit all things,"** because our priorities and desires are so shaped by our own sinful natures and the sin which permeates our society around us. But the promises given to those that overcome in chapters two and

---

787 Strong's Exhaustive Concordance, World Bible Publishers.
788 Luke 24:30,31.

three give an idea of what will be important to us then and there. Jesus promised that we will eat from the tree of life, eat of the hidden manna, have a new name written on a white stone, have the morning star, be clothed in white garments, be a pillar in the temple of God, have the name of God and the holy city written on us, and sit with Jesus on His throne. While these may seem a bit intangible now, they will turn out to be awesome privileges and an unending source of joy.

21:8 The End of Evil

"**But the fearful, and unbelieving, and the abominable, and murderers, and fornicators, and sorcerers, and idolaters, and all liars, shall have their part in the lake which burns with fire and brimstone, which is the second death**" (Revelation 21:8). The Book of Revelation goes to great length to show that evil will come to a permanent end, and in fact the beginning, history and end of sin is the great theme of the whole Bible. Chapter 21 is where God guarantees that the eternal life He offers will not be marred by people who refuse to let go of sin.

Included are those who break the first half of the Ten Commandment law which has to do with love and loyalty for God ("**idolaters**"), as well as those who break the second half which forbids relating in destructive ways to others ("**murderers, sexually immoral,…all liars**"). Those who refuse to believe despite the evidence that God has given ("**the…unbelieving**") will not be present, no matter how admirable or apparently moral their lives have been; they have the "seed" of sin, which would eventually bear all the other wicked fruits. The "**cowardly**" are also left out; this group is especially relevant to the time of trouble, which is such a major focus of Revelation. Many will receive the "mark or the name of the beast or the number of his name" because they will be afraid of the economic sanctions or the

death threat. But this fear itself shows a basic lack of trust, which would eventually lead back to sin.

Although many particular types of sin that seem heinous to us are not mentioned,[789] the angel specifically mentions "sorcerers"—those who have had a personal relationship with Satan and his bewitching magic. This promise is particularly relevant considering the deceptive signs and miracles that will be a part of the final events.[790] Sadly, this will include many who believe that their supernatural spiritual abilities came from God. "Many will say to Me in that day, 'Lord, Lord, have we not prophesied in Your name, cast out demons in Your name, and done many wonders in Your name?' And then I will declare to them, 'I never knew you; depart from Me, you who practice lawlessness!'" (Matthew 7:22,23).

The redeemed, in contrast, are those who have repented of sin; in other words, they have wanted to obey God and are sorry they have violated His will. Jesus paid the penalty for their sins and guarantees that through His grace, in the new earth free from temptation, they will not spoil the perfection of God's kingdom. Those who are content to continue breaking God's law cannot have a part because they would eventually bring back the whole reign of sin. It is for this reason only that God declares, "**there shall not enter into it anything that defiles, or causes abomination or a lie, but only they which are written in the Lamb's Book of Life**" (Revelation 21:27). Despite His deep love for them, their exclusion is the only way to guarantee that "**there shall be no more death, neither sorrow, nor crying, neither shall there be any more pain; for the former things have passed away**" (Revelation 21:4).

---

789 The apostle Paul gives extensive lists of sins that will result in exclusion from God's eternal kingdom such as 1Corinthians 6:9,10 and 2Timothy 3:1-5.

790 Revelation 13:13,14, 16:14, 19:20.

21:9-21 The Holy City

"And there came to me one of the seven angels who had the seven bowls full of the seven last plagues, and he talked with me, saying, 'Come here, I will show you the bride, the Lamb's wife.' And he carried me away in the spirit to a great and high mountain, and showed me that great city, the holy Jerusalem, descending out of heaven from God, having the glory of God; and her light was like a most precious stone, like a jasper stone, clear as crystal" (Revelation 21:9-11).

The detailed description of New Jerusalem emphasizes again the reality of the Kingdom of God. There is nothing in the description to support the highly symbolic interpretations that are sometimes given. The corresponding section in the chiastic structure, the church on earth (chapters two and three), is basically literal and descriptive, which suggests that this section is fairly literal as well.

The first thing John noticed was the light that radiated from the city, "like a most precious stone, like a jasper stone, clear as crystal." There is no consensus as to exactly what precious stones are referred to here or in the stones that make up the twelve foundations of the city (verses 19,20). At any rate, today's jasper (a form of chalcedony) is not transparent and comes in a variety of colors. Most Bible dictionaries suggest that the form mentioned in the Bible is green, which would go along with the fact that God on his throne "was like a jasper" and the rainbow glow around his throne was "in appearance like an emerald" (Revelation 4:3). What is clear from this passage is that whatever the color, the whole city will glow with the radiance of God Himself.

"And it had a wall great and high, and had twelve gates, and at the gates twelve angels, and names written thereon, which are the names of the twelve tribes of the children of Israel. On the east, three gates; on the north, three gates; on the south, three gates; and on the west, three gates" (Revelation 21:12,13).

The only other place in the Book of Revelation where the twelve tribes of Israel are mentioned is chapter seven, the sealing of the 144,000. We saw there that the tribes did not represent literal descendents of the patriarchs, but rather spiritual Israel, and the individual tribes represent the different characters and personality types (as described in Genesis 49) of those who are a part of spiritual Israel. The unusual listing of the tribes left out Dan and Ephraim, the two tribes that were leaders in idolatry, showing that the 144,000 who are called to give the final message to the world, will include all kinds of people, except for those who are worshipers of other gods (See 7:4-8, *The Tribes of Israel*).

In this passage it is not clear whether the same listing would apply for entrance to New Jerusalem. In the listing of the gates in Ezekiel 48:30-34 the original twelve patriarchs are named (with Joseph rather than his sons Ephraim and Manasseh). What is apparent is that all who are a part of the redeemed will have full access to the city, each with a designated gate for "his tribe." There will be no second-class entrance based on race, caste or achievement. Actually, if there were a "servant's entrance" it would be the most honorable since the "class system" of God's kingdom is that "whoever desires to be great among you, let him be your servant" (Matthew 20:26).

"And the wall of the city had twelve foundations, and on them the names of the twelve apostles of the Lamb. And he that talked with me had a golden reed to measure the city, and the gates of it, and the wall of it. And the city lies foursquare, and the length is as great as the breadth. And he measured the city with the reed, twelve thousand stadia. The length and the breadth and the height of it are equal. And he measured the wall thereof, one hundred

forty-four cubits, according to the measure of a man, that is, of an angel. And the building of the wall of it was jasper, and the city was pure gold, like clear glass" (Revelation 21:14-18). The new capital of the universe will dwarf anything ever seen on earth. For example, Washington DC has an area of about 468 square miles. But New Jerusalem will have an area of either about 120,000 or 2,000,000 square miles, and it will be either 350 or 1,400 miles high![791] Obviously the means of travel will be much different than what we have now!

The fact that the twelve apostles have their names written on the foundations of the future capital of the universe shows that the very existence of the heavenly kingdom has its basis in the gospel commission which Jesus gave the apostles before He left the earth, "Go therefore and make disciples of all the nations, baptizing them in the name of the Father and the Son and of the Holy Spirit" (Matthew 28:19). This is not to say that the Kingdom of God is established by human effort. It has been established by the sacrifice of Jesus, and everything is built upon what He accomplished on the Cross—"For no other foundation can anyone lay than that which is laid, which is Jesus Christ" (1 Corinthians 3:11). Paul clarified the relationship between the church, the apostles and Jesus: "You are no longer strangers and foreigners, but fellow citizens with the saints and members of the household of God, having been built on the foundation of the apostles and prophets, Jesus Christ Himself being the chief cornerstone" (Ephesians 2:19,20).

God in His wisdom has left it to His disciples, as vessels and tools of the Holy Spirit, to bring people to Christ and this is the sense in which the apostles are foundational in the Kingdom of God. Jesus said, "Go into all the world and preach the gospel to every creature" (Mark 16:15). The apostles were the first to take the gospel to the world, and their work laid a foundation for the labor and sacrifices of countless other faithful Christians. Peter acknowledged the importance of each believer's witness when he admonished us to be "looking for and *hastening* the coming of the day of God" (2 Peter 3:12), showing that we can "hasten" the Second Coming by aggressively bringing the gospel to the world. All who are looking forward to the heavenly kingdom, dissatisfied by this world of sin and sorrow, should identify with Paul who said, "We are God's fellow workers...you are God's building. According to the grace of God which was given to me, as a wise master builder, I have laid the foundation, and another builds on it" (1 Corinthians 3:9,10).

"And the foundations of the wall of the city were adorned with all manner of precious stones. The first foundation was jasper; the second, sapphire; the third, chalcedony; the fourth, emerald; the fifth, sardonyx; the sixth, sardius; the seventh, chrysolyte; the eighth, beryl; the ninth, topaz; the tenth, chrysoprase; the eleventh, jacinth; the twelfth, amethyst. And the twelve gates were twelve pearls; every one of the gates was of one pearl. And the street of the city was pure gold, like transparent glass" (Revelation 21:19-21).

God is extravagant in His use of shades of beautiful color, so that the shimmering walls and gates will catch and accentuate the light that radiates from God on His throne. In the Old Testament sanctuary service the priest wore a breastplate upon which a similar arrangement of precious stones were set, each one engraved with the name of one of the tribes of Israel. Again, the emphasis is on the individuality and diversity of those who are a part of the kingdom. The heavenly kingdom is not characterized by bland

---

791 According to the Zondervan Pictorial Bible Dictionary, the Greek "stadia" is about 606 feet, so 12,000 stadia would be about 1,400 miles. It is not clear from the text if the 1400 miles refers to each side or to the whole wall (perimeter).

uniformity, even though all are "conformed to the image of His Son" (Romans 8:29). Everything about heaven is designed to stir up interest, capture the imagination and satisfy the love of beauty.

21:22-25 The Lord Is the Temple

"**And I saw no temple therein, for the Lord God Almighty and the Lamb are its temple. And the city had no need of the sun or of the moon to shine in it, for the glory of God gives it light, and the Lamb is its lamp. And the nations of those who are saved will walk in its light, and the kings of the earth bring their glory and honor into it**" (Revelation 21:22-24).

The temple on earth was an arrangement necessitated by sin, because it was impossible for mankind to have direct contact with God—"I will set My tabernacle among you, and My soul shall not abhor you" (Leviticus 26:11). Sinful man, who would have been destroyed by the glory of God's direct presence, confessed his sinfulness over the innocent victim in the hands of the "holy" priest, both of whom represented Jesus. The sin was transferred to the victim, and the priest carried the "sin" (the blood of the victim) into the presence of God. The blood was sprinkled, wiped and poured on the sanctuary furnishings and furniture, showing that God took upon Himself the guilt of the sinner. Thus the lawbreaker could have indirect contact

with God and in the interaction could be made clean so that he was no longer guilty before God. However, with sin eradicated there will be no need for a mediator. Just as we have been coming directly to Jesus, so we will come directly to "**the Lord God Almighty.**"

In the Old Testament sanctuary system only the high priest could come into the Most Holy Place, where the visible glorious presence of God made candles or other sources of light unnecessary. The holy city itself is constructed in a perfect cube, just like the Most Holy Place of the sanctuary,[792] and like the Most Holy Place, has no need for any other source of light besides the glory of God. This indicates that New Jerusalem, the home of the redeemed here on planet Earth, will be the "Most Holy Place" of the universe, the place where "**all the nations**" shall come and bask in the immediate presence of "**the Lord God Almighty and the Lamb**"—"**And the nations of those who are saved will walk in its light, and the kings of the earth bring their glory and honor into it. And the gates of it shall not be shut at all by day; indeed, there shall be no night there. And they shall bring the glory and honor of the nations into it. And there shall not enter into it anything that defiles, or causes abomination or a lie, but only they which are written in the Lamb's Book of Life**" (Revelation 21:24-27). These verses describe an existence beyond our comprehension. But the last two chapters of Revelation tell us enough about it to know that we wouldn't want to miss it!

---

792 "The inner sanctuary was twenty cubits long, twenty cubits wide, and twenty cubits high" (1 Kings 6:20).

"Behold I am coming quickly, and My reward is with Me, to give to every one according to his work" Rev. 22:13

Matthew Merian 1630

Chapter 22

Revelation 22:1-21

22:1 And he showed me a pure river of water of life, clear as crystal, proceeding out of the throne of God and of the Lamb.

22:2 In the middle of the street of it, and on either side of the river, was the tree of life, which bore twelve manner of fruits, and yielded her fruit every month. And the leaves of the tree were for the healing of the nations.

22:3 And there shall be no more curse, but the throne of God and of the Lamb shall be in it; and His servants shall serve him.

22:4 And they shall see His face; and His name shall be in their foreheads.

22:5 And there shall be no night there, and they need no lamp, nor light of the sun; for the Lord God gives them light. And they shall reign forever and ever.

22:6 And he said to me, "These sayings are faithful and true; and the Lord God of the holy prophets sent his angel to show to his servants the things which must soon take place."

22:7 "Behold, I am coming quickly. Blessed is he that keeps the sayings of the prophecy of this book."

22:8 And I John saw these things, and heard them. And when I had heard and seen, I fell down to worship before the feet of the angel which showed me these things.

22:9 Then said he to me, "See, do it not. For I am your fellow servant, and of your brethren the prophets, and of those who keep the sayings of this book. Worship God!"

22:10 And he said to me, "Do not seal the sayings of the prophecy of this book, for the time is at hand.

22:11 He that is unjust, let him be unjust still; and he that is filthy, let him be filthy still; and he that is righteous, let him be righteous still; and he that is holy, let him be holy still."

22:12 "And, behold, I am coming quickly, and my reward is with me, to give every one according as his work shall be.

22:13 I am Alpha and Omega, the beginning and the end, the first and the last."

22:14 Blessed are they that do His commandments, that they may have the right to the tree of life, and may enter in through the gates into the city.

22:15 For outside are dogs, and sorcerers, and fornicators, and murderers, and idolaters, and whoever loves and makes a lie.

22:16 "I, Jesus, have sent My angel to testify to you these things in the churches. I am the Root and the Offspring of David, and the bright and morning star."

22:17 And the Spirit and the bride say, "Come." And let him that hears say, "Come." And let him that is thirsty come. And whoever will, let him take the water of life freely.

22:18 For I testify to every man that hears the words of the prophecy of this book, if anyone shall add to these things, God shall add to him the plagues that are written in this book.

22:19 And if anyone shall take away from the words of the book of this prophecy, God shall take away his part out of the Book of Life, and out of the holy city, and from the things which are written in this book.

22:20 He who testifies these things says, "Surely I am coming quickly." Amen. Even so, come, Lord Jesus.

22:21 The grace of our Lord Jesus Christ be with you all. Amen.

22:1 The River of Life

"And he showed me a pure river of water of life, clear as crystal, proceeding from the throne of God and of the Lamb. In the middle of its street, and on either side of the river, was the tree of life, which bore twelve fruits, each tree yielding its fruit every month. The leaves of the tree were for the healing of the nations" (Revelation 22:1,2). The description of the river and tree of life is an obvious reference to Ezekiel 47 in which the prophet also saw a river proceeding from the temple, with trees on its bank with healing leaves. (See Table 22.1)

The passage in Ezekiel 47 gives details that are not presented in the "outline sketch" of Revelation 22. First of all, the water increases the more it flows—it starts ankle-deep and ends up "too deep, water in which one must swim, a river that could not be crossed" (v. 5). Secondly, wherever the water from the temple flows, it brings healing—it is flowing into the deadly brine of the Dead Sea, and "when it reaches the sea its waters are healed" (v. 8). Thirdly, it brings new life to living things that are somehow dead—"every living thing that moves, wherever the rivers go, will live" (v. 9).

Table 22.1

Ezekiel 47	Revelation 22:1,2
"Water, flowing from under the threshold of the temple...It was a river" (vs. 1,5).	"A pure river of water...proceeding from the throne of God" (v. 1).
"There were very many trees on one side and the other" (v. 7).	"On either side of the river was the tree of life... each tree" (v. 2).
"They will bear fruit every month" (v. 12).	"Each tree yielding its fruit every month" (v. 2).
"Their leaves [will be] for medicine" (v. 12)	"The leaves of the tree were for the healing of the nations" (v. 2).

This picture should be considered along with the symbolic meaning of water in the book of Revelation—"the waters which you saw...are peoples, multitudes, nations and tongues" (Revelation 17:15). Add to this Jesus' description of living water: "He who believes in Me, as the Scripture has said, out of his heart will flow rivers of living water." But this He spoke concerning the Spirit" (John 7:38,39).

Putting this all together, it is possible that the **"river of water of life, clear as crystal, proceeding from the throne of God and of the Lamb,"** besides being a literal geographical feature of New Jerusalem, represents a continuing ministry of those who have been called out of "every nation, tribe, tongue and people." They will go out from the throne of God, filled with the Holy Spirit, to bring healing to the universe which has been wounded by sin.

This is not to say that there are other sinful worlds, but there is no question that the effects of sin have not been limited to this earth. In the heavenly councils, "when the sons of God came to present themselves before the Lord, Satan also came among them" (Job 1:6).[793] Until Satan and his fallen angels were defeated by Jesus' life, death and resurrection and "cast out" of heaven, they were a full-time plague to the unfallen beings—"the accuser of our brethren...accused them day and night" (Revelation12:7-10). Just as Satan caused havoc on this earth, he caused it in the heavenly realms, so much so that John heard "a loud voice saying in heaven...'Rejoice, you heavens, and you who dwell in them...for the accuser...has been cast down" (vs. 10-12). "For we know that the whole creation groans and labors with birth pangs together until now...The creation itself also will be delivered from the bondage of corruption into the glorious liberty of the children of God" (Romans 8:22,21).

The whole universe has been traumatized by sin and the sophistry of the one who was once "the anointed cherub who covers" (Ezekiel 28:14). Those who have lived through the sin experience and emerged victorious will, through the influence of the Holy Spirit, be like a healing stream bringing refreshing, life-giving comfort to the wounded creation. God is the great source of everything, and His nature is reflected in the law of the universe—selfless love, receiving in order to give. Redeemed human beings, created in the image of God and the recipients of the greatest outpouring of grace, will have the most to give.

22:3-5 The Face of God

"And there shall be no more curse, but the throne of God and of the Lamb shall be in it; and His servants shall serve him. And they shall see His face; and His name shall be in their foreheads." (Revelation 22:3,4). No one on earth except Jesus has ever seen God's face.[794] Moses, who had the closest relationship with Him of anyone who ever lived, wanted to see God's glory. God granted him to see his "back," but told him, "you cannot see My face; for no man shall see Me, and live" (Exodus 33:18-23).

It is sin that makes it impossible for man to look upon God, whose holiness is incompatible with sin: "Your sins have hidden His face from you" (Isaiah 59:2). "For our God is a consuming fire" (Hebrews 12:29). The apostle Paul describes God as "He...who alone has immortality, dwelling in unapproachable light, whom no man has seen or can see" (1Timothy 6:16). Because of this, God has always revealed Himself visibly in

---

793 It is clear that this is not talking about an earthly council, because Satan, when asked "From where do you come?" replied, "From going to and fro on the earth" (Job 1:7).

794 The exception would be Adam and Eve before the entrance of sin. There are those such as Enoch and Elijah who have been translated to heaven, and presumably they have the same privileges there that we will have when we are resurrected or translated.

an indirect way, as "the Angel of the Lord"[795] or "the Son of God"[796] and most importantly, as Jesus ("He who has seen Me has seen the Father" John 14:9). "God…has shone in our hearts to give the light of the knowledge of *the glory of God in the face of Jesus Christ*" (2Corinthians 4:6).

Even the veiled revelation of God's glory had an overwhelming effect on those who saw Him. When "the Angel of the Lord appeared" to Samson's parents, Manoah, the father, "said to his wife, 'We shall surely die because we have seen God!" (Judges 13:22,23). Daniel, seeing a vision of the Son of God, said of himself, "No strength remained in me, for my vigor was turned to frailty in me and I retained no strength…I turned my face toward the ground and became speechless… nor is any breath left in me" (Daniel 10:8,15,17). When Paul saw a vision of Jesus on the Damascus road he was blinded and so traumatized that "he was three days without sight, and neither ate nor drank" (Acts 9:8,9).

It is not God's purpose to traumatize people with His presence, and for this reason He is constantly trying to prepare His people for a full revelation of His glory. He does this by giving the Holy Spirit to live in our hearts, making us accustomed to His character and holiness. God said through Ezekiel, "I will not hide My face from them anymore; for I shall have poured out My Spirit on the house of Israel', says the Lord God" (Ezekiel 39:29). Through repentance and prayer we receive His righteousness, and this prepares us to see His face—"He shall pray to God, and He will delight in him, he shall see His face with joy, for He restores to man His righteousness" (Job 33:26).

All this is preparation for the day when God will show Himself in His full glory. To those who have not allowed Him to prepare them, His glory will be too much—they will be "destroy[ed] by the brightness of His coming" (2Thessalonians 2:8). "But to you who fear My name the Sun of Righteousness shall arise with healing in His wings" (Malachi 4:2). The "Sun of Righteousness" will bathe the whole earth with radiant glory—**"And there shall be no night there, and they need no lamp, nor light of the sun; for the Lord God gives them light. And they shall reign forever and ever"** (Revelation 22:5).

22:6-15 I Am Coming Quickly

"And he said to me, 'These sayings are faithful and true; and the Lord God of the holy prophets sent his angel to show to his servants the things which must soon take place.' 'Behold, I am coming quickly. Blessed is he that keeps the sayings of the prophecy of this book" (Revelation 22:6,7). Over 1,900 years ago Jesus said, **"I am coming quickly!"** To give added emphasis, He repeats it three times in this last chapter of Revelation. He promises that He is coming with a reward—**"Behold, I am coming quickly and My reward is with Me, to give to every one according to his work"** (Revelation 22:12). Finally, Jesus' last words in the book of Revelation are, **"Surely I am coming quickly"** (Revelation 22:20). We have to wonder, considering that nearly two thousand years have passed, what does **"I am coming quickly"** mean? Has Jesus had an unexpected delay? Have we, the church, failed to "get our act together" so He could come? Is the promise just a carrot being dangled before us to keep us perpetually motivated to follow the Christian life?

It seems clear that the apostles expected Jesus to return within their lifetimes. The apostle Paul included himself in the "we" who would see the coming of the Lord, saying, "Then *we* who are alive and remain shall be caught up together with them in the clouds to meet the Lord in the air"

---

795 Judges 6:22, Genesis 32:30.

796 Daniel 3:25.

(1Thessalonians 4:17). John said, "It is the last hour; and as you have heard that the Antichrist is coming, even now many antichrists have come, by which we know that it is the last hour" (1John 2:18). James said, "Establish your hearts, for the coming of the Lord is at hand…the Judge is standing at the door!" (James 5:8,9). Peter said, "The end of all things is at hand; therefore be serious and watchful in your prayers…for the time has come for judgment to begin" (1Peter 4:7,17).

Peter himself confronted this issue, referring to "scoffers [who] will come in the last days…saying, 'Where is the promise of His coming?…All things continue as they were from the beginning of creation" (2Peter 3:3,4). He points out that the wicked antediluvian world was finally destroyed by a universal flood, and that our present wicked society has a rendezvous with fiery judgment "in which the heavens will pass away" (vs.5-7, 10). But the Lord will bring this about at the right time, and for God this will be neither too early nor too late.

In fact, the passing of what we consider to be a long period of time is meaningless in God's view. He is not concerned with how much time has passed, but rather how ready the world is for Him to come. "Beloved, do not forget this one thing, that with the Lord one day is a thousand years, and a thousand years as one day" (2Peter 3:8). If God had said, "I'm sending Jesus in a couple of days," we would not understand, but it would be consistent with His frame of reference where two days could be as 2,000 years. "The lord is not slack concerning His promise, as some count slackness, but is longsuffering toward us, not willing that any should perish, but that all should come to repentance" (v. 9).

For the church, this long wait is analogous to the forty years that the children of Israel wandered in the wilderness before entering the Promised Land. The sentence that they would not enter was given after 12 spies returned from spying out the land and 10 of them reported that the people of Canaan were too strong for them to defeat. God had already told them that he would fight for them and would even send hornets to drive out the corrupt idolaters who lived there (Deuteronomy 7:20, Joshua 24:12). However, despite the miracles they had seen in coming out of Egypt, the people still did not have the faith to believe that God could give them victory.

Sending in the 12 spies was a test, and their response showed that they failed the test, that they were not ready for the trials that would be involved in entering the Promised Land where powerful enemies were determined to hold on to their territory. The spies, presumably the most courageous warriors they could find, fled before the inhabitants of the land, and this was a preview of the disastrous defeat which would have occurred if God had allowed them to enter then and there. The wilderness wandering that God prescribed, rather than being a punishment, was a time to test them and to increase their faith so that they would finally be ready. As they were about to enter the promised land Moses said, "The Lord your God led you all the way these forty years in the wilderness, to humble you and test you, to know what was in your heart, whether you would keep His commandments or not" (Deuteronomy 8:2).

Likewise, the Second Coming of Christ is not simply a matter of Jesus appearing in the sky one day. Before He comes the world must go through the time of trouble and the fearsome events that are portrayed in the Book of Revelation. The world (including the church) is no more ready for the time of trouble than the children of Israel were ready to enter the Promised Land. Unpleasant and discouraging as the two thousand years of "wilderness wandering" have been, they have been a necessary preparation for the events that will precede the Second Coming.

This gets to the heart of the matter. Although

people are being saved and lost all the time, the final events (which are the subject of most of the Book of Revelation) have the potential for bringing about the greatest mass movement for the acceptance of the gospel in all of human history. But the corresponding danger is that almost everyone could be swept away in the last-day deceptions. That which makes the difference is the response of God's people, who have been given the role of being His messengers to the world.

This does not mean that God is waiting for His people to "finish the work" and then Jesus will come. "He [God] will finish the work and cut it short in righteousness" (Romans 9:28). The great harvest, depicted in chapter 14, is a work that only God can do: "On a cloud sat One like the Son of Man…and in His hand a sharp sickle…and *He who sat on the cloud* thrust in His sickle on the earth, and the earth was reaped" (Revelation 14:14-16). Only God, through His Holy Spirit, can change a human heart so that it is fit to be a part of His harvest. But the "Lord of the harvest" has, in His divine wisdom, appointed His church to be "laborers" in His harvest field with a small but essential role that He will not do for us.

Jesus said, "The harvest truly is great, but the laborers are few; therefore pray the Lord of the harvest to send out laborers into His harvest" (Luke 10:2). In a sense the last great harvest is like every other harvest. Only God can make a seed germinate and grow, and only He can send the vital sunshine and rain. But unless the "laborers" plant the seeds in the ground there will not be a harvest. And the laborers are responsible for chasing away birds, pulling weeds and removing rocks from the field (Matthew 13:3-23).

Peter characterizes the role of God's people as "looking for and hastening the coming of the day of God" (2Peter 3:12). The fact that the day can be "hastened" indicates that although His

coming is inevitable, it is not on an absolute, pre-ordained date. Whether He comes sooner or later depends on the response of people who know Him and tell others about Him. "This gospel of the kingdom will be preached in all the world as a witness to all the nations, *and then* the end will come" (Matthew 24:14). God provides the message, prepares the way and sends the Spirit, but He doesn't do the preaching. Angels are pictured as giving the great messages, but they symbolize men, women and children who have experienced God's grace and are impelled to share it, even in the face of opposition and the threat of death.

Final Warnings

"Now I, John, saw and heard these things. And when I heard and saw, I fell down to worship before the feet of the angel who showed me these things. Then he said to me, 'See that you do not do that, for I am your fellow servant, and of your brethren the prophets, and of those who keep the words of this book. Worship God" (Revelation 22: 8, 9).

Seeing the splendor and glory of the kingdom, John was overwhelmed and fell at the feet of the heavenly messenger. This provoked the first of a series of final warnings whose importance is underlined by the fact that they are among the final impressions that God wants to leave us with in Revelation and in the whole Bible.

Perhaps most critical is the admonition that we are not to worship anyone or anything besides God. To human logic and experience it seems reasonable to try to more effectively get Jesus' attention by appealing to His friends, His mother or to the angels who surround Him. But there is not the slightest hint of worship being directed to the 24 elders, the four living creatures or the "angels around the throne" (Revelation 5: 11). To the contrary, they emphatically insist, **"Worship God!"**

That this is a difficult lesson to learn is shown both by the one billion Catholics and Orthodox who worship the saints (in spite of the clear scriptural prohibition)[797] as well as by the fact that John had to be told twice not to do this himself—here in chapter 22 and in chapter 19. When the angel messenger implied that John was invited to "the marriage supper of the Lamb," he "fell at his feet to worship him. But he [the angel] said to [John], 'Do not do that! I am your fellow servant, and of your brethren who have the testimony of Jesus. Worship God!'" (Revelation 19:10). It is Satan and his cohorts who want worship for themselves—"The world...worshiped the dragon... and they worshiped the beast...As many as would not worship the image of the beast [were] to be killed" (Revelation 13:3,4,15). When we direct our worship to anything or anyone that is created we spoil the love relationship that our Creator wants to have with His creatures.

"And he said to me, 'Do not seal the sayings of the prophecy of this book, for the time is at hand" (Revelation 22:10). The second warning is directed to John and to other religious teachers who would follow him. Revelation is a difficult book, and the natural tendency is to "seal the words" by teaching that the prophecies are too difficult to understand or have no relevance to us today. But this is a sure way to miss the blessing that God has prepared for us—"Blessed is he that reads, and they that hear the words of this prophecy, and keep those things which are written therein" (Revelation 1:3). Religious leaders who do not feel that they have a full or complete

understanding of Revelation should not be afraid to encourage their "flock" to study for themselves. We can trust the Holy Spirit to teach us what we need.

Finally there is a warning for each one who reads the Book of Revelation. **"For I testify to every man that hears the words of the prophecy of this book, if anyone shall add to these things, God shall add to him the plagues that are written in this book. And if anyone shall take away from the words of the book of this prophecy, God shall take away his part out of the Book of Life, and out of the holy city, and from the things which are written in this book"** (Revelation 22: 18, 19).

No doubt this verse has discouraged would-be "editors" of Revelation through the centuries, who would have liked to change the book to make it say what they wanted it to say. But notice that the warning is **"to every man that hears the words of the prophecy of this book."** There is a risk involved in understanding the prophecies of Revelation. As long as they are obscure and controversial they are simply food for religious argument and speculation. But when the meaning of Revelation becomes clear, it is obvious that its messages call for radical change. This may involve the change of long-held doctrinal positions or even church affiliation. But at an even more basic level, Revelation calls for a change of life. Luke-warm spiritual indifference is shown to be seductive but fatal (Revelation 3:16). So is the legalistic complacency that assumes that "Jesus has taken care of my sins through His sacrifice, so I don't really have to worry about obedience." In contrast, Revelation presents "those who keep the commandments of God and the faith of Jesus" (Revelation 14:12).

One of the most prominent themes of Revelation is that God is calling a great multitude to come out of spiritual Babylon. But the experience of God's chosen people who were

---

797 Orthodox and Catholics insist that they do not worship saints or angels, but rather venerate and honor them. But they bow before them (Greek *proskineo*), which is exactly the kind of worship that is prohibited and condemned both in the Ten Commandments (Exodus 20:5) and in Revelation (Revelation 9:20, 13:8,12,15, 14:11, 19:10, 22:8,9). Of the 60 times that this word is used in the New Testament, all refer either to worship of God and Jesus or to false worship.

captives in Babylon is very instructive. When the Persians conquered Babylon, King Cyrus freed the Israelites to return to Israel, but most of them chose to stay.[798] In Babylon they had a comfortable, prosperous life, in contrast to the rigors of returning and rebuilding the ruins of their ancestral homeland. After so long in the land of captivity their friends, families and businesses were in Babylon, and it seemed like too much of a sacrifice to leave. This is the danger for those who **"hear the words of the prophecy of this book."** The easy, comfortable course of action is to **"add to these things"** or **"take away from the words of the book,"** in other words, to pick and choose the parts of the message of Revelation that allow me to stay as I am. But this is fatal. **"if anyone shall add to these things, God shall add to him the plagues that are written in this book. And if anyone shall take away from the words of the book of this prophecy, God shall take away his part out of the Book of Life, and out of the holy city, and from the things which are written in this book."**

Now Is the Time

"And he said to me, 'These sayings are faithful and true; and the Lord God of the holy prophets sent his angel to show to his servants the things which must soon take place.' 'Behold, I am coming quickly. Blessed is he that keeps the sayings of the prophecy of this book" (Revelation 22:6,7). God gave the Book of Revelation for **"His servants"** who need its instructions in order to play their part in the final events. The curious, sensation-seeking people of this world will continue to find Revelation to be a confusing maze of symbols and cryptic messages, or support for their favorite conspiracy theory. But for those who seek the Lord with

all their heart, Revelation will be an open letter of comfort and encouragement during the dark days ahead.

The angel said to Daniel, "Shut up the words, and seal the book until the time of the end; many shall run to and for, and knowledge shall increase…Many shall be purified, made white, and refined, but the wicked shall do wickedly; and none of the wicked shall understand, but the wise shall understand" (Daniel 12:4,10). The angel who brought the Revelation to John emphasized that the "time of the end" when "the wise shall understand" could be any time, now that Jesus has won the victory, gone to heaven and sent His Spirit. **"And he said to me, 'Do not seal the sayings of the prophecy of this book, for the time is at hand"** (Revelation 22:10). Now is the time for God's people to study the prophecies, learn their privileges and duties, clarify their mission to a lost world, and go forth as white horses, with Jesus holding the reins, "conquering and to conquer" (Revelation 6:1).

"Blessed are they that do His commandments, that they may have the right to the tree of life, and may enter in through the gates into the city" (Revelation 22:14). Other versions read, "Blessed are those who wash their robes." Both versions have support in ancient manuscripts and in extra-biblical references. Both themes are also integral messages of the Book of Revelation. The remnant who overcome are described as "they who keep the commandments of God" (Revelation 12:17, 14:12). They are also described as those who "washed their robes and made them white in the blood of the Lamb" (Revelation 7:14). Our fitness for heaven is the blood-washed robe of Christ's righteousness. The result of wearing it is that we "keep the commandments of God."

Perhaps God in His wisdom has allowed both of these essential themes to be preserved in the very last message of the very last book of the Bible. It is our choice now to let Him wash our

---

798 See Ezra 2, especially verses 64,65.

robes and to give us the power to keep His commandments. Jesus is ready and eager to come live in us, transform us from the inside out, and walk with us on a thrilling and satisfying adventure that will last forever. But now is the time to make that choice. Jesus "stands at the door and knocks," waiting for us to "open the door" so He can "come in" (Revelation 3:20). We put Him off at our own peril. All too soon the time for decisions will be over, and many who have closed their ears to the pleading of the Spirit will end up on a path that will leave them out of the kingdom. **"For outside are dogs, and sorcerers, and fornicators, and murderers, and idolaters, and whoever loves and makes a lie…He that is unjust, let him be unjust still; and he that is filthy, let him be filthy still; and he that is righteous, let him be righteous still; and he that is holy, let him be holy still. And, behold, I am coming quickly, and my reward is with me, to give every one according as his work shall be"** (Revelation 22:15, 11,12).

22:16-21 Come!

"I, Jesus, have sent My angel to testify to you these things in the churches. I am the Root and the Offspring of David, and the bright and morning star. And the Spirit and the bride say, 'Come.' And let him that hears say, 'Come.' And let him that is thirsty come. And whoever will, let him take the water of life freely" (Revelation 22:16,17).

Jesus expressed His deepest desire, a desire that impelled Him to "empty Himself," leave heaven, and take upon Himself the sins of the whole world,[799] with the invitation: "Come to me, all you who labor and are heavy laden, and I will give you rest" (Matthew 11:28). Jesus ends the revelation of Himself with a similar personal appeal to all **"who thirst." "The Spirit,"** who comes in Jesus' name, says, **"Come!"** So does **"the bride,"** symbolizing the whole kingdom of God, all the angels and "living creatures" who have been watching with intense interest as the great controversy between good and evil unfolds on planet earth. And Jesus urges those of us **"who hear,"** who have already responded to Jesus' invitation, to join our voices, inviting those around us to **"Come!"**

"The Revelation of Jesus Christ" was not given simply to be a source of prophetic information. It is, rather, an appeal to come to Jesus, so that He can take away our guilt and shame, wipe away every tear, satisfy every thirst with the water of life and every hunger from the tree of life. Jesus pleads to each one of us personally, "Hear what the Spirit says!"[800]

"He who testifies to these things says, 'Surely I am coming quickly.' Amen. Even so, come, Lord Jesus!"

"The grace of our Lord Jesus Christ be with you all. Amen" (Revelation 22: 20,21).

---

799 Philippians 2:7,8.

800 Revelation 2:7, 11, 17, 29, 3:6, 13, 22.

Appendix 1
The Literary Chiasm

Kenneth Strand developed the concept of the chiastic literary structure of Revelation.[801] Strand's division of the sections of the chiasm (excluding the prologue and epilogue) are shown in Table App1.1

Table App1.1

I—A1	II—B1	III—C1	IV—D1	V—C2	VI—D2	VII—B2	VIII—A2
1:10-3:22	4:1-8:1	8:2-11:18	11:19-14:20	15:1-16:17	16:18-18:24	19:1-21:4	21:5-22:5

Although the discovery and development of this literary structure was a major step forward in the understanding of Revelation, there are a number of problems with the division of the sections as it is presented by Strand. The problems stem from an attempt to make a chiastic pair of the woman clothed with the sun of chapter 12 and the harlot of chapter 17. Although this pairing seems intuitive, it necessitates a distortion of the chiastic structure with the following problems:

1) It is not a true chiasm of the eight divisions. Section III is paired with V, and IV is paired with VI, even though some of the scriptural links are weak. In order to maintain a semblance of the chiastic structure, sections III and IV are joined together as a unit and V and VI are joined together:

C1-D1   C2-D2
B1   B2
A1   A2

2) Although Strand contends that each section should begin with a sanctuary scene (with sanctuary imagery such as the throne, the Lamb, the four living creatures, 24 elders, sanctuary furniture, etc.), his section VI does not begin with any sanctuary imagery, only "a loud voice…out of the temple" which is actually a part of the previous section.

3) An obvious sanctuary scene, 14:1-5, is ignored rather than being used as a beginning marker of a new section.

---

801 See Frank Holbrook, editor, *Symposium on Revelation—Book I*, (Biblical Research Institute, Review and Herald 1992). Strand's chiastic structure was included in a commentary on the book of Revelation by C. Mervynn Maxwell (C. Mervyn Maxwell, *God Cares 2*, Nampa, ID Pacific Press, 1985)

4) The strong links between chapters 12, 13 and chapter 14, and the obvious and clear division of themes between chapter 13 and 14 are ignored.

The division of the chiasm is of more than academic interest. It is the division of the book into two halves that defines the overall theme of the book. Strand, with his division between chapters 14 and 15, sees the first half of the book as history and the second half as future prophecy. This of course necessitates making the substance of the first half historical, specifically, the seals and trumpets (which comprise more than a third of the book). In order to support the historical views of the seals it necessitates making the crucial fourth and fifth chapters some kind of "inauguration" (either of Christ's priestly ministry or of His kingly reign) which took place just after the resurrection and ascension. This claim is made despite the strong evidence that these chapters represent the introduction of the antitypical Day of Atonement (see Appendix 2). The historical view also necessitates fantastic, implausible interpretations (especially in the trumpets), the assignment of historical significance to obscure historical events, or glossing over of details of the prophecies in order to make historical applications of the seals and trumpets. Most modern historicist commentaries have simply chosen to generalize these sections, calling them historical but refusing to assign dates or events.[802]

I have suggested the division shown in Table App1.2

Table App1.2

I—A1	II—B1	III—C1	IV—D1	V—D2	VI—C2	VII—B2	VIII—A2
1:10-3:22	4:1-8:1	8:2-11:19	11:19-13:18	14:1-14:20	15:1-18:24	19:1-20:15	21:1-22:5

---

802 Another problem with dividing the book between chapter 14 and 15 with the first half historical is that it makes the Book of Revelation primarily a history book with an addendum about the time of trouble rather than a guidebook for navigating earth's final events as this book maintains.

The problems which are solved by this division are:

1) A true mirror-image chiasm of every section is presented:

```
        D1   D2
      C1       C2
    B1           B2
  A1               A2
```

2) Every section begins with a sanctuary scene, and every sanctuary scene in the book is the beginning of a section.

3) The links between corresponding sections are stronger, especially in III—VI and IV—V.

This division divides the book in a different place (between chapters 13 and 14), which demands a reconsideration of the themes of the two halves and of the overall theme of the book. Since the theme of the climax of the first half in chapter 13 is the culmination of Satan's efforts to destroy God's people and the climax of the second half in chapter 14 is the culmination of God's program to bring the "everlasting gospel" to the world, the division into historical and future halves does not follow. The overall theme is the great controversy between God and Satan concerning sin, and God's ultimate victory and the eradication of sin from the universe.

Progression of Sanctuary Scenes

The progression of the sanctuary scenes that introduce each of the chiastic sections of Revelation helps to clarify the meaning of the book. Except for the prologue and epilogue, each of the 10 chiastic sections is introduced by a scene from the heavenly sanctuary, which at first glance appear to be a random sampling of items of sanctuary furniture such as the altar of incense or of individuals who participate in the sanctuary drama such as the 4 living creatures and the 24 elders. However, a careful study of the sanctuary scenes shows that the particular mix of furniture and individuals coincide with the progression of the yearly Old Testament sanctuary ceremonies which prefigured the sanctuary activity that has been taking place in Heaven since the ascension of Jesus and the institution of His priestly ministry.

1) The first sanctuary scene, which introduces the seven churches, is found in Revelation 1:12-15. John saw Jesus dressed in "a garment down to the feet" which was the robe used by the priest in their daily ministration in the sanctuary (Exodus 28:4, 31). He saw Jesus walking among seven golden lampstands, which suggest the seven lamps that illuminated the Holy Place (the first room) of the sanctuary. This scene depicts the ongoing ministry of Jesus for His church that began when He returned to heaven after His crucifixion and resurrection, analogous to the "daily" ministry of sacrifices and ceremonies in the Old Testament sanctuary. It corresponds perfectly with the messages to the seven churches (Revelation chapters 2 and 3) that portray the history of the church through the centuries, from the time of John until the final events.

2) The second sanctuary scene (Revelation 4:1-5:14) which introduces the seven seals begins with a vision of a "door open in heaven," the door separating the Holy Place (first room) from the Most Holy Place (second room, see 4:1 *A Door Open in Heaven*). John saw "seven lamps of fire" which again suggests the lamps in the Holy Place, but he also saw the throne of God, which corresponds to the mercy seat that was on top of the ark of the covenant in the Most Holy Place (Hebrews 9:5). The time during the ongoing sanctuary service that there was ministry that took place in both rooms of the temple was the Day of Atonement, and this is in harmony with the extensive imagery and symbolism that indicate

that this section depicts the introduction of the antitypical Day of Atonement (see 4: *The Day of Atonement*).

3) The third sanctuary scene (Revelation 7:9-8:5) introduces the seven trumpets. Again John saw items from the Holy Place (the golden altar, Revelation 8:3,5) and the Most Holy Place (the throne, the censer, Revelation 7:9, 8:3, Leviticus 16:12, Hebrews 9:3,4), showing that this section is a continuation of the Day of Atonement. An "angel" (who represents Christ) is seen ministering with a golden censer, taking incense from the golden altar to offer with "the prayers of the saints" (Revelation 8:3,4). This corresponds to the second stage of the Day of Atonement when the High Priest, carrying a golden censer, brings the blood of the sacrifices "inside the veil" (into the Most Holy Place, Leviticus 16:12-16). This phase of the service was the last opportunity for the people to "afflict [their] souls and do no work at all" (Leviticus 16:29,30), in other words, to demonstrate their repentance and faith. In the Book of Revelation this last chance for repentance happens during the seven trumpets with the ministry of the two witnesses.

4) The fourth sanctuary scene (Revelation 11: 15-19) introduces the war in heaven and the oppression of the "saints" by the beast. The focus is exclusively in the Most Holy Place and specifically on the ark of the covenant which contained God's law, the Ten Commandments. The Law of God is the standard of judgment so this scene is very appropriate considering that this section exposes Satan, his rebellion, and his agents which "should be judged" (Revelation 11:18).

5) The fifth sanctuary scene (Revelation 14:15) introduces the vision of the 144,000 and the three angels' messages. The vision continues in the Most Holy Place but instead of viewing the ark and the law, it focuses on the throne of God which in the Old Testament sanctuary service was called the mercy seat (Exodus 25:17-22,

Leviticus 16:2). This emphasis fits with the portrayal in this section of the final message of mercy that will go to the world (the three angels' messages).

6) The sixth sanctuary scene (Revelation 15:1-8) introduces the "end of probation" and the seven last plagues. John saw the sanctuary opened and "filled with smoke" so that "no one was able to enter the temple" (Revelation 15:5-8). In three passages in the Old Testament the temple was filled with smoke and in each case the priests finished their ministry and left the sanctuary (Exodus 40: 33,34, 2Chronicles 5:13,14, 1Kings 8:10,11). This represents the third phase of the Day of Atonement services in which the priest left the Most Holy Place, came out of the temple, and sacrificed a burnt offering for himself and for the people who had been "afflicting their souls" throughout the whole ceremony (Leviticus 16:23,24, 29,30). He no longer offered the blood of the sacrifices and there was no longer an opportunity for anyone to come to the sanctuary to confess their sins. This symbolism is appropriate for this section in which the opportunity for forgiveness has ended (the end of probation) and God is concerned with protecting His faithful children with the seven last plagues.

7) The seventh sanctuary scene (Revelation 19: 1-8) introduces the Second Coming of Christ, the binding of Satan during the millennium and the final judgment of the impenitent. This scene is unique in that unlike every other sanctuary scene in which it is explicitly mentioned that John "saw" the sanctuary articles and individuals, in this scene John apparently did not see anything; he heard "a loud voice of a great multitude from heaven" and "a voice from the throne." He somehow knew that "the twenty-four elders and the four living creatures fell down and worshiped God who sat on the throne" but there is no mention that he saw them. In the Old Testament Day of Atonement this corresponds to the final

stage that takes place away from the sanctuary; the scapegoat was taken out into the wilderness, the bodies of the sacrificial animals were taken "outside the camp" to be burned, and all involved washed their clothes and bodies and "came into the camp" (Leviticus 16:21-28). Likewise, in this section of Revelation the beast, the false prophet and finally the impenitent are burned and Satan is first bound and finally burned, bringing the history of sin to an end.

8) The final sanctuary scene (Revelation 21:2-5,22) introduces the "new heaven and new earth." Since every trace of sin and sinners has been eliminated, there is "no temple…for the Lord God Almighty and the Lamb are its temple" (Revelation 21:22). John saw New Jerusalem which will be a perfect cube, just like the Most Holy Place of the sanctuary, but instead of being a symbol of the presence of God, "the tabernacle [actual presence] of God" will be "with men, and He will dwell with them" (Revelation 21:3).

Thus we see that the sanctuary scenes that introduce the chiastic sections correspond to the themes of those sections. They present a progression that follows the ancient Hebrew ceremonial year, beginning with the daily ministry throughout the centuries of church history, progressing to the beginning of the Day of Atonement (the judgment in heaven), the beginning of the time of trouble (the golden censer), then moving from the Holy to the Most Holy Place as everyone on earth makes a decision for or against the Lord, and then out of the temple with the close of probation and finally to the end of the temple and into the immediate presence of God. This progression of the sanctuary scenes is another verification of the meaning of the various scenes that are presented in Revelation, beginning at the time of John and moving progressively to the eradication of sin and to the eternal kingdom of God.

Appendix 2

Revelation 4,
Judgment or Inauguration?

Chapters four and five set the stage and are crucial to the understanding of the first half of the Book of Revelation. There has been ongoing debate as to whether these chapters 1) are simply a view of heaven, 2) constitute the coronation/ inauguration of Jesus into his priestly/kingly ministry after the resurrection and ascension, or 3) introduce the pre-advent investigative judgment (the position taken by this book).

The coronation/inauguration interpretation has received increasing support in recent years (for example *Revelation of Jesus Christ* by Ranko Stefanovic)[803]. This view will be addressed in three parts: 1) the evidence that chapters 4-6 portray the pre-advent "investigative" judgment, 2) answers to the criticisms of this position, and 3) objections to the coronation theory.

Evidence for Pre-Advent Judgment

First of all, the themes and language of chapters four and five borrow heavily from the two most prominent "investigative judgment" passages of the Old Testament: Daniel 7 and Ezekiel 1-10.

Daniel 7 clearly refers to the pre-advent judgment when "the court was seated and the books were opened" (Daniel 7:9). Parallel language and themes suggest that Revelation 4 and 5 are dealing with the same subject. (See Table App2.1)

---

803 Ranko Stefanovic, *Revelation of Jesus Christ* (Berrien Springs, MI Andrews University Press, 2002)

Table App2.1

Daniel 7	Revelation 4,5
"I watched till thrones were put in place…the Ancient of Days was seated…His throne was a fiery flame" (Daniel 7:9).	"Behold, a throne was set in heaven, and One sat on the throne…Around the throne were twenty-four thrones" (Revelation 4:2,4).
"The court was seated and the books were opened" (Daniel 7:10).	"Who is worthy to open the book?…The root of David has prevailed to open the book" (Revelation5:2,5).
"A thousand thousands ministered to Him; ten thousand times ten thousand stood before Him" (Daniel 7:10).	"I heard the voice of many angels…and the number of them was ten thousand times ten thousand, and thousands of thousands" (Revelation 5:11).
"One like the Son of Man…He came to the Ancient of Days, and they brought Him near before Him. Then to Him was given dominion and glory and a kingdom" (Daniel 7:13,14).	"In the midst of the throne…stood a Lamb as if it had been slain…And He came and took the book out of the right hand of Him that sat on the throne (Revelation 5:6,7).
"The greatness of the kingdoms under the whole heaven shall be given to the people, the saints of the Most High" (Daniel 7:27).	"You…have made us to our God kings and priests; and we shall reign on the earth." (Revelation 5:9,10).

The first 10 chapters of the book of Ezekiel also have many parallel elements with Revelation 4 and 5 (See Table App2.2).

Table App2.2

Ezekiel 1-10	Revelation 4,5
"Four living creatures…each had the face of a man…the face of a lion…the face of an ox…the face of an eagle" (Ezekiel 1:5-10).	"Round about the throne were four living creatures…the first…was like a lion, the second…like a calf, the third…had a face like a man, and the fourth…was like a flying eagle" (Revelation 4:6,7).
"The likeness of the firmament above the heads of the living creatures was like the color of an awesome crystal stretched out over their heads" (Ezekiel 1:22).	"Before the throne was a sea of glass, like crystal" (Revelation 4:6).
"Above the firmament over their heads was the likeness of a throne…on the likeness of the throne was a likeness with the appearance of a man high above it" (Ezekiel 1:26).	"Behold, a throne set in heaven, and One sat on the throne." (Revelation 4:2).
"Like the appearance of a rainbow in a cloud on a rainy day, so was the appearance of the brightness all around it" (Ezekiel 1:28).	"There was a rainbow around the throne" (Revelation 4:3).

This section in Ezekiel depicts the investigative judgment of God's people during the time they were being sent into Babylonian exile. "Do you see what they are doing?…You will see greater abominations…Go in, and see the wicked abominations which they are doing there…Have you seen what the elders of the house of Israel do in the dark, every man in the room of his idols? For they say, the Lord does not see us, the Lord has forsaken the land…etc…Have you seen this? Therefore I also will act in fury" (Ezekiel 8:6-18). The striking parallels in themes and language would suggest that Revelation 4,5 is also dealing with investigative judgment. The investigation in Ezekiel is followed by the sealing of the faithful on their foreheads, which leaves the unmarked to be slain (Ezekiel 9). This is what happens in Revelation 7 with the sealing of the 144,000 "on their foreheads" followed by the destructive judgments of the trumpets on "those men who do not have the seal of God on their foreheads" (Revelation 7:3, 9:4).

There are also close links with another investigative judgment chapter, Revelation 14, which contrasts those who worship the beast (chapter 13) with the 144,000 who "are without fault before the throne of God" (Revelation 14:5). The process that culminates in their final victory begins on earth with the announcement, "Fear God and give glory to Him, *for the hour of His judgment has come*" (Revelation 14:7). The heavenly scene of Revelation 14 mirrors Revelation 4 and 5. The Lamb, who is the central figure in Revelation 5 (vs. 6-12), also opens the scene in 14:1. The throne is in both scenes (4:2-6, 14:3,5), the four living creatures and the 24 elders are present (4:4,7, 14:3), there are harpers playing harps and singers singing songs (5:9, 14:3). Even the themes are the same: giving glory to him who created all things (4:11, 14:7) and the redemption of people from "every nation, tribe, tongue and people" (5:9, 14:6). Since the "hour of His

judgment" is a primary theme of chapter 14, it would also be a central theme of chapters 4 and 5.

A prominent symbol of Revelation 4 and 5 is the throne. Thrones are very strongly linked to judgment in both the Old and the New Testaments—Daniel 7 has already been mentioned. Other references include Psalms 122:3-5 and Proverbs 20:8. "The tribes go up, the tribes of the Lord to the Testimony of Israel…for thrones are set there for judgment." "A king who sits on the throne of judgment scatters all evil with his eyes" See also 2 Samuel 22:28, Proverbs 15:3, 1 Kings 14:22, 15:11.

Jesus said of His followers, "But you are those who have continued with Me in my trials, and I bestow upon you a kingdom…that you may…sit on thrones judging the twelve tribes of Israel" (Luke 22:28-30). Jesus will sit on a throne to judge—"When the Son of Man comes in His glory…Then He will *sit on the throne of His glory*. All the nations will be gathered before Him, and He will separate them one from another…then the King will say to those on His right hand, 'Come, you blessed of My Father, inherit the kingdom…Then he will say to those on the left hand, 'Depart from Me, you cursed, into the everlasting fire prepared for the devil and his angels" (Matthew 25:31-46).

The fact that the throne of God is the most prominent feature of this section points to a "Most Holy Place ministry" rather than a "daily" ministry. Some expositors have pointed out that the seven lamps (Revelation 4:5) are in the Holy Place, and have theorized that the throne that John saw is analogous to the table of showbread which was also in the Holy Place, with the two stacks of bread symbolizing the Father and the Son on their throne. But there are a number of problems with this view. First of all, there is no Bible evidence that the table of showbread symbolized God on His throne so the theory is a matter of speculation. Moreover, all the other articles in the sanctuary were symbols of a phase of God's salvific activity, not of God Himself. For that matter, the use of bread or anything else to represent God is a violation of the second commandment and would seem especially inappropriate in light of the Roman Catholic mass which is the heart of the false doctrinal system that "takes away the daily sacrifice" (Daniel 8:10, 11:31), in which the priest "creates his Creator" by "transubstantiating" bread into God. Finally, it seems rather odd that God the Father would be sitting on the table-of-showbread "throne" in the Holy Place for 1813 years while the ark and the mercy seat were sitting empty in the Most Holy Place waiting to be occupied.[804] More satisfactory is the view that the "door open in heaven" (Revelation 4:1) was the door between the Holy and the Most Holy place and John could see both rooms as the ceremonies of the Day of Atonement began.

The phrase in Revelation 4:1, "after these things" (Greek *meta tauta*) indicates that the scenes in chapters 4 and on follow chronologically after the seven churches. It is true that this phrase is used in other parts of Revelation to indicate a movement from one theme to another, but in Revelation 4:1 the phrase is used twice, first to change the scene and then to indicate the chronology. The progression of the church through history followed by the investigative and executive judgment is in harmony with this. But to go from the period of the church after the end of the first century back sixty-plus years to Christ's coronation is not in chronological order.

Another prominent symbol in Revelation 4 and 5 are eyes: the lamb has seven eyes (Revelation 5:6), and the "four living creatures" who are "around the throne" are "full of eyes in front and in back…around and within"

(Revelation 4:6,8). Eyes symbolize the Lord's ability to distinguish in judgment those who are righteous from those who are not: "The Lord is in His holy temple, the Lord's throne is in heaven; His eyes behold, His eyelids test the sons of men. The Lord tests the righteous" (Psalms 11:4-7). "A king who sits on the throne of judgment scatters all evil with his eyes" (Proverbs 20:8, see also 2 Samuel 22:28, Proverbs 15:3, 1Kings 14:22, 15:11).

The fact that this scene has imagery from both the Holy Place (the seven lamps of fire) and the Most Holy Place (the throne) suggests the Day of Atonement, the only day in the ceremonial year in which the priest ministered in both rooms.

The chiastic structure links chapters 4 and 5 with chapters 19 and 20, which are the key executive judgment chapters. This suggests that chapters 4 and 5 also have a judgment theme.

Answers to Objections

Much has been made of the fact that the Greek words for judgment do not appear in chapters 4 and 5. This is a little strange since those who object have no problem considering the seven trumpets to be judgments, even though the words for judgment do not appear there either. The fact is that the words for judgment almost never appear in the first half of the Book of Revelation. The thirteen instances of the use of the Greek words for judge and judgment are all either in the second half of the linguistic chiasm (from 14 on) or refer to events which will take place at that time (6:10 and 11:18). The words are used in connection with the meting out of punishments (executive judgment), not the investigation phase of judgment. The two instances (14:7 and 20:4) which relate to an investigative phase include within their context the executive phase (14:17-20, 20:11-15).

---

804 Daniel 7:9,10 implies that God's mobile throne (with its fiery wheels) moves from the Holy to the Most Holy Place rather than God moving from one throne to another.

Obviously the phrase "investigative judgment" does not appear in the Bible, but the concept is everywhere, as has been pointed out in chapter 5. The typology is from the Day of Atonement, and in the passages in Leviticus 16 and 23, where the ceremonies of the Day of Atonement are described, the words "judge" or "judgment" never appear. So why should we consider it significant that they do not appear in Revelation 4 and 5?

The objection is made that the proving of worthiness and acclamations of praise found in the drama of taking the sealed scroll in Revelation 5 are not found and do not fit in Old Testament judgment passages including the Day of Atonement. However, Revelation 4 and 5 includes a concept that never appeared in the Old Testament type: a challenge that there was no one worthy of carrying out the Day of Atonement ceremony. In the type, the priest offered sacrifices first for his own sin, but in the antitype this was clearly irrelevant because the antitypical priest (Christ) was Himself the sinless offering. Thus there is a new aspect and we could expect a new and unique response.

The fact is that we would not expect a challenge to Christ's right to rule after His sinless life, perfect death and victory over the grave. The usurper of the throne was clearly defeated. However, we would certainly expect a challenge that sinful humanity could be redeemed, and this is the point of the investigative judgment. The challenge is answered, not by the appearance of the Lion of the tribe of Judah or the Root of David (both symbols of sovereign rule), but by the Lamb as if it were slain (the symbol of redemption). We would certainly expect celebration of the fact that the whole purpose of Christ's incarnation, death and resurrection, that is, the redemption of humanity, was finally going to be accomplished.

Chapters 4 and 5 do not give a comprehensive view of the investigative judgment, they simply set the scene for the judgment (which is carried out in chapter 6). These chapters correspond to Daniel 7: 9,10 where "the judgment was set" and where we also see the "thousand thousands" who no doubt are also celebrating the giving of "dominion and glory and a kingdom" to "One like the Son of Man."

The objection is made that in Revelation 4 and 5 only one book is mentioned, whereas in Daniel 7 it is "books," and that in Revelation 4 and 5 the book is not yet opened. But notice that in Revelation 20, which clearly depicts the judgment, the real focus is on one book, the Book of Life, and the other books are peripheral—"The dead were judged…by the things which were written in the books…and anyone not found written in the Book of Life was cast into the lake of fire" (Revelation 20:12,15). This was the thought that made John weep much—that neither he nor any of his beloved brethren could be redeemed unless the Book of Life could be opened. The other books (for example, the book of the Law) have essential information, but they do not have the information about the individuals' responses to God that will be the evidence that will allow them to saved. Chapters 4 and 5 establish the right to open the Book of Life. It is in chapter 6 that it is actually opened (presumably with the other necessary books).

The objection has been raised that if Revelation 4,5 describes the beginning of the investigative judgment in AD 1844, then everything that follows Revelation 5, including the seven seals, the seven trumpets, and the ministry of the two witnesses of Revelation 11, would occur after the year 1844. That is the position that this book has taken (with the exception of the obvious flashback scenes in chapters 12 and 13). There are serious problems with trying to apply the seals and trumpets to the progression of history, so much so that modern commentators are generally unwilling to assign specific dates or events.

It is also claimed that the literary arrangement of Revelation shows that the structural composition of the first half of the book focuses on the historical Christian era, rather than on the eschatological period. I see the clearest literary arrangement to be the chiastic structure. When the chiasm is correctly laid out (as in chapter 1 and appendix 1), it shows that there are eight sections (plus prologue and epilogue) which divide between chapters 13 and 14. This means that there are two climaxes rather than just one, with chapter 13 being the climax of the first half and chapter 14 the climax of the second half. This division does not support the two halves of the book as being history and future, but rather that the book is divided into the two sides of the great controversy, Satan's challenge and God's victory. Within this context chapters 4 and 5 depict Satan's challenge to the opening of the Book of Life, an attempt to prevent the investigative judgment from taking place. It is from the Book of Life that Christ presents the evidence that God's children have believed and can be saved, and in chapter 5 Satan (the "strong angel" v. 2) attempts to stifle that evidence.

Problems with the Enthronement Interpretation

Probably the most serious problem with considering chapters 4 and 5 to be the coronation and enthronement of Christ is that the Lamb is never pictured on the throne. It has been suggested that the scroll "in the right hand of Him who sat on the throne" (Revelation 5:1) means that the scroll is sitting on an extended couch-like throne on the right side, so taking it from the hand must

mean sitting on the throne.[805] This is unconvincing, especially in light of the fact that in verse 13 and later in chapter 7, after the enthronement has supposedly taken place, the praise is to "Him who sits on the throne, *and* to the Lamb, forever and ever." "Salvation belongs to our God who sits on the throne, *and* to the Lamb" (Revelation 5:13, 7:9, 10). This would be a time when the worshipers should mention that both the Father and the Lamb are sitting on the throne if the point of the chapters was the enthronement. There is no question that Jesus did sit upon the throne upon His ascension, but this does not seem to be a chapter that emphasizes His enthronement.

According to the coronation scenario the book is sitting on the couch/throne to the right of "the one who sat on the throne" and the Lamb comes and sits there, taking the book. But the Greek of verse 7 *kai ilthen kai eilhfen ek tis dexias tou* uses the preposition "*ek*," which signifies motion away, so it would either show motion taking the book away from the throne (which would not seem to support sitting on the throne), or, more likely, as all English and modern Greek translators have rendered it, motion taking the book away from the right hand. This is in contrast to the use of the preposition *en* (in, on) when Paul clearly speaks of Jesus sitting on the throne, *ekathisen en dexia toy thronou* (seated at the right hand of the throne, Hebrews 8:1). In other passages, when Jesus and the other New Testament writers referred to His future sitting on the throne at the right of God they omitted the definite article *tis* (*kathou ek dexion mou*, Mark 12:36, Acts 2:34, Heb. 1:13), showing that the reference was to the right in general (as in direction) rather than to something specific on the right (as in the right hand). In other words, the original Greek does not seem to support the

---

805 Stefanovic p. 201.

depiction of the Lamb sitting down on the right side of the throne, but rather of taking something (the book) from the right hand.

Since the text doesn't say that the Lamb sits on the throne, and most translators have rendered the scroll as being in the right hand rather than on the right side, it seems presumptuous to formulate a doctrine of enthronement when there is only an assumed sitting on the throne.

There is essentially no parallel language between chapters four and five and such coronation texts as 2 Kings 11, 2 Samuel 2 and 5, 1 Kings 1, 2 Kings 23 or the prototype in Deuteronomy 17. This calls into serious question the enthronement interpretation, since Revelation is built upon themes identified by parallel language and allusions from the Old Testament. With such clear parallels to the investigative judgment texts as have been shown above and none for the coronation passages, the enthronement interpretation is difficult to sustain.

The idea that the sealed book of Revelation 5 could be analogous to the Deuteronomy 17 copy of the law that the king was supposed to "write for himself" (v. 18) upon his inauguration is interesting. That book was to be copied by the king so that he could "read it all the days of his life, that he may learn to fear the Lord His God and be careful to observe all the words of this law and these statutes." It is a tremendous leap to the idea that this book represents some kind of "eternal covenant, the revelation of God's salvific acts on behalf of humanity, a record of the cosmic controversy, symbolic of the sum and substance of God's plan and purpose for the human race and the entire universe" as has been maintained.[806] There seems to be a lack of scriptural evidence. There are only the few sketchy references to a book ever being given to a king, the main one

being at the coronation of Joash (2 Kings 11:12), and in none of the texts is there any exposition of its significance beyond instruction in the law. To confidently assert a linkage between the Deuteronomy 17 book of the law and the sealed book of Revelation 5 seems presumptuous.

Even more difficult to grasp is the connection between the sealed book of Revelation 5, the sealed visions of Isaiah 29, the law which is sealed "among my disciples" in Isaiah 8 and the book of the law in Deuteronomy 17.[807] The idea that God sealed his law so that it was unavailable or incomprehensible to his people because of their sins is not scriptural. The law is always wide open to saint and sinner alike, even when God "hides His face" (Isaiah 8:17). Certainly there is no consensus among theologians concerning the meaning of the phrase "bind up the testimony, seal the law among my disciples." Therefore it would not be wise to make this verse an essential link in the interpretation of Revelation 5.

The concept of worthiness is the focus of the heavenly praise in chapter 5. But the acclamations do not focus on the kingly titles the "Lion of the tribe of Judah" and the "root of David," but rather "worthy is the Lamb who was slain." "You are worthy...for You were slain, and have redeemed." The focus is not on Christ's worthiness to be the ruler of history, as would be symbolized by His royal inauguration, but on His ability through His sacrifice to rescue those who would otherwise be judged and condemned to death. The pre-advent judgment seems to be the most appropriate context for this praise of the slain Lamb's worthiness because the only reason anyone will be pronounced worthy of eternal life in the judgment is Christ's sacrifice for their sins.

To sum up the objections to the coronation theory, we should note that 1) there are few if any

---

806 Stefanovic, Ranko *Revelation of Jesus Christ* (Berrien Springs, MI Andrews University Press, 2002) p. 196

807 Stefanovic p. 169-172.

scriptural links to the passage in Deuteronomy 17 or to other coronation texts, 2) According to Deuteronomy 17, the king of Israel was to write a copy of the law; it was not presented to him, 3) The application and key importance of this text is questionable since there are no clear examples of it being carried out in the coronations of the kings of Israel, 4) It is highly questionable that the book of the law could in any way be considered a sealed book. 5) It is a tremendous, unsubstantiated leap from a copy of the law of Moses which the king was to use to help him rule properly to "the scroll of God's eternal covenant—the revelation of His salvific acts on behalf of humanity…a record of the cosmic controversy, symbolic of the sum and substance of God's plan and purpose for the human race and the entire universe."

In conclusion, more evidence and clearer links need to be shown in order to sustain the interpretation of Revelation 4 and 5 as the Day-of-Pentecost coronation of Christ in the heavenly sanctuary, especially in the face of the obvious links to the pre-advent judgment.

Appendix 3
Kings of the North and South

Daniel 11:40-45 describes a war "at the time of the end," the last battle in a war between the King of the North and the King of the South that has been raging for 2,300 years. Evidence given in 9: *The Locust Army* suggests that this last battle is the same war described in the seven-trumpet plagues of Revelation 8-11. A study of the war through the centuries makes it possible to identify the end-time players.

Daniel 11 seems at first to be very confusing, referring to "he" without making it clear whether "he" is the King of the North, the King of the South or someone else. The vision also seems to give very detailed descriptions of specific rulers but then skims over vast stretches of history with no mention of the events that took place. Three principles help to make sense of this confusing chapter.

First and most important, chapter 11 is parallel with the visions of Daniel chapters 2, 7 and 8.[808] The metal image of chapter 2 provides the basic outline of a progression through the empires that have oppressed God's people (Babylon, Persia, Greece, Pagan Rome and Papal Rome). Chapters 7 and 8 fill in more details, showing that the emphasis of the visions is on the papal period of the Middle Ages when the saints are persecuted,

that there is an attempt to change God's law, and that there is an attack on the "daily sacrifices." We would also expect chapter 11 to progress through the same empires and focus on the same persecution and attacks. Locating these events in the vision helps to give some general structure and time frames.

Secondly, as the vision moves from one empire to the next there is a detailed description of the first kings of each empire, which helps to verify the transition. But the vision skims over all but the most important of later events of the empires.

Finally, there are "landmarks" within the vision, the most important of which are "Cyrus, king of Persia" (10:1) at the beginning of the vision, the "time of trouble such as never was" (12:1) at the end of the vision, and "the prince of the covenant" (Jesus) in verse 22. This shows that the vision begins with the Persian Empire under Cyrus and moves through the Greek Hellenistic Empires and has reached the pagan Roman Empire by verse 22. The vision then continues from pagan Rome through papal Rome to the end of time. Other important landmarks include Daniel 11:4 ("His kingdom shall be broken up and divided toward the four winds of heaven"). A comparison with Daniel 8:8 shows clearly that this is the division of the Greek Empire after the death of Alexander the Great. Also Daniel 11:31 ("they shall take away the daily sacrifices"), when

---

808 See chapter 13: *The Beast from the Sea* for an explanation of the repeated progression of history in the prophecies of Daniel 2 and 7. See 14: *When in History* for a brief overview of Daniel 8.

compared with Daniel 8:11, is clearly the time of papal supremacy during the Middle Ages.

From these observations it is obvious that the Kings of the North and South are not static entities, but will change and evolve through the course of history.

The vision was given to Daniel after the fall of Babylon "in the third year of Cyrus king of Persia" (Daniel 10:1) which coincided with "the first year of Darius the Mede" (Daniel 11:1). Darius was the ruler of the Persian province of Babylon during the reign of Cyrus the Great (who conquered Babylon in 539 BC). "Behold, three more kings will arise in Persia, and the fourth shall be far richer than them all...He shall stir up all against the realm of Greece. Then a mighty king shall arise who shall rule with great dominion, and do according to his will" (Daniel 11:2-4).

These verses set the pattern for the whole vision. There are a number of phases in the vision, just as in Daniel's previous visions—Persia, Greece, pagan Rome, and papal Rome. In each phase there are amazingly accurate details of the first few years, and the remainder of the phase is skipped over quickly. The "three more kings... in Persia" who arose after Cyrus were Cambyses, False Smerdis, and Darius I. The fourth who would "stir up all against the realm of Greece" was the immensely wealthy Xerxes (Ahasuerus, the husband of Esther in the Bible) who launched a series of attacks against Greece, with disastrous defeats at Salamis and Plataea in 480 and 479 BC.

The narrative then skips over the remaining eight kings of Persia down to the time of Alexander the Great ("a mighty king," v.3) who defeated Darius III in 331 BC and established the Greek (Hellenistic) Empire. And as in chapter 8, where Alexander, under the figure of a goat with a great horn which is broken with four horns coming up to take its place, so here "His kingdom shall be broken up and divided toward the four winds of heaven, but not among his posterity...

His kingdom shall be uprooted, even for others" (v.4). Alexander died of a fever in Babylon at the age of 32 and the Greek Empire, rather than going to his offspring, was carved up into four Hellenistic (Greek-speaking) kingdoms, which included the Seleucid ("King of the North") kingdom in Syria and the Ptolemaic ("King of the South") kingdom in Egypt.

With remarkable accuracy Daniel highlights in verses 5-15 the history of the first few kings of the North and South during the Hellenistic period, so accurately, in fact, that many commentators have concluded that it must have been written after the events had taken place.[809] See, for example, *God Cares vol. 1* by C. Mervyn Maxwell[810] for a review of some of the historical details of the Seleucid and Ptolemaic kings and how they relate to the prophecies of Daniel 11.

Verse 16 marks an important transition. The Hellenistic Kings of the North and South have been attacking each other through verse 15, but now a new power comes into the picture: "But he [the new power] who comes against him [the King of the North] shall do according to his own will, and no one shall stand against him. He shall stand in the Glorious Land with destruction in his power" (Daniel 11:16). The most destructive power in the vision of Daniel 7 was the fourth beast, Rome. Likewise, in chapter 8 the "little horn which grew exceedingly great toward the south, toward the east and toward the Glorious Land...[which] cast down some of the host and some of the stars to the ground and trampled

---

809 Most commentators agree on the identities of the Kings of the North and South through the Hellenistic period, but disagreement begins in verse 14. An exception are those who see the "abomination of desolation" in verse 31 as the reign of Antiochus Eipiphanes (reigned 175-164 BC). This interpretation ignores the fact that Jesus said that the abomination of desolation was still future in His day (Matthew 24:15). See footnote 116 on chapter 3: *The Day of Atonement, 2300 Days* for more details.

810 Maxwell, C. Mervyn, *God Cares Vol. 1* (Nampa, ID Pacific Press 1985)

them" (Daniel 8:9) was also Rome. From history we know that the power which conquered the Seleucid kingdom (the King of the North) and stood "in the Glorious Land" (Palestine) was Rome. Pompey was the Roman general who conquered Palestine in 66 BC and he briefly shared in the rulership of Rome, but Julius Caesar defeated him and greatly increased the power of the Roman Empire (details of his reign are found in verses 17 and 18).[811] Now there was a new King of the North.

"There shall arise in his place one who imposes taxes on the glorious kingdom" (v.20). This was Caesar Augustus who took power after the assassination of Julius Caesar. His imposing of taxes is even mentioned in Luke 2:1 at the time when Jesus was born—"a decree went out from Caesar Augustus that all the world should be registered" ("taxed," KJV).

"In his place shall arise a vile person" (v.21)—Augustus was succeeded by Tiberius and the series of emperors who followed, including such "vile persons" as Nero, Hadrian, Decius, Diocletion and other cruel tyrants who caused God's people so much grief. During the reign of the pagan Roman emperors the "prince of the covenant," Jesus, was "broken" and the Jewish nation "swept away...with the force of a flood" (v.22), a reference to the crucifixion of Christ in AD 31 AD and the destruction of Jerusalem in AD 70.

"And after the league (Hebrew *chabar*, joining or binding together, union, alliance) is made with him, he shall act deceitfully, for he shall come up and become strong with a small number of people" (v. 23). During the reign of Constantine

(ruled 312-337 AD) the union of church and state was formed ("the league") which paved the way for the medieval Papacy.[812] This was symbolized in the multi-metal image of Daniel 2 as the legs and feet of iron mixed with clay, where two materials that ordinarily do not mix were mixed together. In the vision of the beast empires of Daniel 7 "the league" is symbolized by the horns (divisions) of the fourth beast (Rome) that are dominated by the "a little horn [the papacy]... different from the first ones...whose appearance was greater than his fellows " (Daniel 7:8,24,20).

Just as the little horn of Daniel 7 and 8 began small and developed into the major power which opposed God's people, so here the new King of the North, the Papacy, begins "with a small number of people" and "comes up and becomes strong." "He shall enter peaceably, even into the richest places of the province" (v. 24). The popes became the effectual rulers of Rome ("the richest places") and eventually of Western Europe, gaining power "peaceably"—they did not fight their own wars but got others to fight for them (See chapter 2: *Thyatira*).

During the portion of the vision (vs. 16-24) that represents the reign of the Roman emperors (27 BC-AD 476) and the early Papacy, the King of the South is not mentioned. This is consistent with history—Rome conquered the Ptolemaic kingdom of Egypt in the Battle of Actium in 31 BC and Egypt became a Roman province. But starting in AD 632 a new power arose in the South, Islam, represented in verse 25 by a new King of the South. "He [the King of the North,

---

811 Consistent with the pattern of the vision, details are given of the first Roman emperors, including Julius Ceasar's relationship with Cleopatra ("the daughter of women" v. 17), his Mediterranean campaign to consolidate his power ("he shall turn his face to the coastlands" v. 18) and his murder by Brutus and Cassius in 44 BC ("a commander will put an end to his insolence" v. 18).

812 "The league" could also refer to the loose union of tribes that came to be the Holy Roman Empire, represented by the ten toes of the image of Daniel 2 and the 10 horns of the fourth beast of Daniel 7. Both the union of church and state under Constantine in the east and formation of the Holy Roman Empire in the west took place in the same time frame (fourth through sixth centuries) and had the same results—a corrupt church whose dogmas and decrees were enforced by an oppressive state.

the medieval Papacy] shall stir up his power and his courage against the King of the South with a great army. And the King of the South shall be stirred up to battle with a very great and mighty army, but he shall not stand." Islam was the southern power that had conquered the Middle East, parts of Spain and was threatening the eastern Christian Byzantine Empire. The last straw was when the Seljuk Turks began to interfere with pilgrims traveling to Jerusalem. Pope Urban II urged the European leaders to carry out the first crusade from AD 1096-1099. The Turks opposed them "with a very great and mighty army" but ultimately they were conquered and the crusaders "liberated" Jerusalem ("he shall not stand").

The Muslims gradually regained control of the Holy Land over the next two hundred years despite two more crusades. In 1201 "Pope Innocent III persuaded many French nobles to take part in [the fourth Crusade]. The crusaders bargained with the Venetians to take them by ship to the eastern Mediterranean. But when they got to Venice they could not pay the costs. The Venetians said they would transport the crusaders to the Holy Land if the crusaders helped them attack the Byzantine Empire...They seized Constantinople after a fierce battle...The Venetians and crusaders divided Byzantine territory and riches among themselves...It was an expedition for economic and political gain. The real victors were the Venetians...The crusaders never reached the Holy Land, and much of it remained in the hands of the Muslims."[813]

This fourth crusade is mentioned in verses 29-31—"At the appointed time he [the King of the North as represented by the crusaders] shall return and go toward the south; but it shall not be like the former or the latter. For ships from

Kittim [the Venetians][814] shall come against him,[815] therefore he shall be grieved and return in rage against the holy covenant, and do damage... they shall take away the daily sacrifices, and place there the abomination of desolation" (vs. 29-31). The crusaders did "return in a rage...and do damage"—the sack of Orthodox Constantinople not only contributed to the defeat of Eastern Christianity by the Muslims, but also left a wound and schism between Orthodox and Catholics that continues to this day. But worse was to come. After the debacle of the fourth crusade the Papacy turned its attention to "heretics" closer to home, setting up the most abominable, desolating institution of all times—the Inquisition.

Pope Innocent III, who ordered the fourth crusade, presided over the Papacy at the zenith of its power. The doctrines that obscured the plan of salvation had been developing for centuries (the taking away of the daily sacrifices—See chapter 14: *The Daily Sacrifice*). The death decree against those who would not accept the Catholic system of worship was codified in the Inquisition which he set up in 1229—the abomination of desolation (See 2: *Thyatira*, 10: *The Abomination of Desolation* and Appendix 10). All of this was predicted in verses 30 and 31—"he shall...return in rage against the holy covenant, and do damage... then they shall take away the daily sacrifices, and place there the abomination of desolation."

The focus of Daniel 11:29-39 is on the King of the North, the medieval Papacy, which "shall exalt and magnify himself above every god, shall

---

813 "Crusades," *World Book Encyclopedia*, World Book Inc. (Chicago, IL, 1986)

814 Kittim is a general term for all islanders or people of the coastland of the Mediterranean Sea (See Strongs Concordance or other Bible dictionary), and in fact the Greek Septuagint translates it as Romaioi—Romans, which at that time referred to all Italians (including Venetians).

815 English translations make it sound like there is an attack by the "ships of Kittim" against the King of the North. But the Hebrew does not say "come against him"—the word *bow* simply means come, enter or come in. A literal, word-for-word translation might be "enter ships of Kittim, disheartened he turns back."

speak blasphemies against the God of gods, and shall prosper" (v. 36)[816]. The persecution of God's people, particularly the reformers, is also predicted—"The people who know their God shall be strong, and carry out great exploits. And those of the people who understand shall instruct many; yet for many days[817] they shall fall by sword and flame, by captivity and plundering" (vs. 32,33).

In the meantime the King of the South has again dropped out of the picture with no mention of him in verses 31-39. This is consistent with the long decline of the Ottoman Empire as a world power after the crusades, so that by the end of World War I Islam was essentially impotent as a political and military force.

The extensive focus of Daniel 11 on the King of the North as the medieval Papacy (vs. 23-39) is consistent with the visions of Daniel chapter 7 (the four beasts, and the "little" horn which "shall speak pompous words against the Most High" and "shall persecute the saints"[818]), of chapter 8 (the ram, the goat, and the "little" horn which "cast down some of the host," takes away "the daily sacrifice" and sets up "the transgression of desolation"[819]) and of Revelation 13 (the beast which rises out of the sea and "opened his mouth in blasphemy against God" and "to make war with the saints"[820]). All of these visions identify and focus on the persecuting papal power of the Middle Ages. A comparison of the four visions show that they have many elements in common, confirming their identity and filling out details

not found in any one vision by itself. (See Table App3.1)

The point of these comparisons is that since these four passages obviously describe the same power, it is possible to learn details from one passage to fill in gaps in the others. This is important because it is from Revelation 13 that we learn the identity of the end-time persecuting powers.

At the "time of the end" the King of the South reappears ("the King of the South shall attack him"), and it will be this offensive that provokes the extreme reaction of the King of the North who "shall come against him like a whirlwind" (v. 40). Here is predicted the resurgence of militant Islam (the King of the South) with a powerful, coordinated end-time attack against the King of the North that ushers in the time of trouble.[821]

By this time the King of the North has evolved again. Revelation 13 reveals that the Papacy would suffer a "mortal wound." This was fulfilled with the Protestant reformation, the arrest of Pope Pius VI in 1798 and the loss of the papal territories in 1870, reducing the ability of the Papacy to manipulate governments (See 13:3 *The Deadly Wound*).[822] But "his mortal wound was healed"—the Papacy regained its prestige and influence (See 13: *The Deadly Wound Healed*). In addition, Revelation 13 reveals that the Papacy was to gain a new end-time ally—the "beast coming up out of the earth"—the United States of America (see 13:11,12 *The Beast from the Earth*)—which "exercises all the authority of the first beast [the Papacy] before him, and causes the earth and those who dwell therein to worship

---

816 The parallel passage in the vision of Daniel 7 is verse 7 "He shall speak pompous words against the most high" and in the vision of chapter 8 verses 10-12 "He even exalted himself as high as the Prince of the host and by him the daily sacrifices were taken away... He cast truth down to the ground. He did all this and prospered."

817 The "many days" are the 1,260 days of Daniel 7 and Revelation 12—See chapter 12 "*One Thousand Two Hundred Sixty Days*.

818 Daniel 7:25.

819 Daniel 8:9-14.

820 Revelation 13:1-10.

---

821 In chapter eight we saws that the time of trouble has two parts— the seven trumpets (chapters 8-11), which are Satan's attempt to defeat God's people, and the seven last plagues (chapters 15-19), which are God's rescue of His people.

822 The mortal wound is alluded to in Daniel 11:36: "Then the King [of the North] shall do according to his own will...and shall prosper till the wrath has been accomplished, for what has been determined shall be done."

Table App3.1

Daniel 7 Little Horn	Daniel 8 Little Horn	Daniel 11 King of the North	Revelation 13 First Beast
"It had ten horns, and another, a little one greater than his fellows" (vs.8,20).	"A little horn which grew exceedingly great" (v. 8).	"He shall come up and become strong with a small number of people" (v. 23).	"I saw a beast rising up out of the sea, having…ten horns' (v. 1).
"He shall speak pompous words against the Most High" (v. 25).	"He even exalted himself as high as the Prince of the host" (v. 11).	"He shall exalt and magnify himself… and shall speak blasphemies against the God of gods" (v. 36).	"He opened his mouth in blasphemy against God" (v. 6).
"He shall persecute the saints of the Most High" (v. 25).	"It cast down some of the host and some of the stars to the ground, and trampled them" (v. 10).	"They shall fall by sword and flame, by captivity and plundering" (v. 33).	"It was granted to him to make war with the saints and to overcome them" (v. 7).
"He shall persecute… for a time, times and half a time" (v. 25).	"It refers to many days in the future" (v. 26)	"For many days they shall fall by the sword" (v. 33)	"He was given authority to continue for forty-two months' (v. 5).
"He shall intend to change times and law" (v. 25).	"By him the daily sacrifices were taken away, and the place of His sanctuary was cast down" (v. 11).	"Shall defile the sanctuary fortress; then they shall take away the daily sacrifices" (v. 31)	"To blaspheme…His tabernacle" (v. 6)
"The same horn was making war against the saints, and prevailing" (v. 21)	"An army was given over to the horn… He did all this and prospered" (v. 12).	"The king shall do according to his own will…and shall prosper" (v. 36).	"All the world marveled…saying, 'Who is like the beast? Who is able to make war with him?" (vs. 3,4).

the first beast" (Revelation 13:11,12). The United States will be the military and religious supporter of the Papacy, "bringing fire down from heaven" (false miracles) and "causing as many as would not worship the image of the beast to be killed" (persecution) (Revelation 13:13-15).

From these comparisons it appears that at the time of the end there will be an attack by militant Islam against Europe, the United States, or both ("the King of the South shall attack him" Daniel 11:40). The northern forces will retaliate— their armies "with chariots, horsemen and with many ships shall enter the countries, overwhelm them, and pass through" (Daniel 11:40).

All of chapter 11 has been quite literal, more so than any of the other prophecies of Daniel, thus there is no reason to consider the description of this last phase of the war to be symbolic. When Daniel writes that "He [the King of the North] shall also enter the Glorious Land," this would indicate that the last war will be centered in the Middle East. Specific countries which have modern counterparts are mentioned—"Edom, Moab, and the prominent people of Ammon…Egypt shall not escape…the Libyans and Ethiopians shall follow at his heels" (vs. 41-43). Apparently the headquarters of the King of the North will be in Palestine, perhaps at Jerusalem—"And he shall plant the tents of his palace between the seas [the Dead Sea and the Mediterranean Sea] in the glorious holy mountain" (v. 45). Some kind of development will enrage the northern forces into a murderous frenzy of destruction—"But news from the east and the north shall trouble him; therefore he shall go out with great fury to destroy and annihilate many" (v. 44).[823] However, despite the vast military machine of the northern countries, they will ultimately fail—"Yet he shall come to his end, and no one will help him" (v. 45).

As we saw in chapter 9, there are clear linkages between the final King of the North and the locust armies of Joel and Revelation 9. A likely scenario is that the initial attack ("At the time of the end the King of the South shall attack him" v. 40) will be a strike by militant Islam, and this corresponds to the first four trumpets. The counterattack ("And the king of the North shall come against him like a whirlwind, with chariots, horsemen, and with many ships; and he shall enter the countries, overwhelm them, and pass through" v. 40) would be military retaliation by European and American forces and corresponds to the fifth and sixth trumpets.

This war is followed by "a time of trouble such as never was since there was a nation" (Daniel 12:1) which corresponds to the seven last plagues. Finally Jesus will come to rescue His people—"And at that time your people shall be delivered, every one who is found written in the book. And many of those who sleep in the dust of the earth shall awake, some to everlasting life, some to shame and everlasting contempt. Those who are wise shall shine like the brightness of the firmament, and those who turn many to righteousness like the stars forever and ever" (Daniel 12:1-3).

---

823 This verse could correspond to the sixth trumpet, in which a 200 million-man army kills a third of mankind (Revelation 9:13-19).

Appendix 4
The Secret Rapture

Many Evangelical Christians today believe that the present "dispensation" (phase of God's activity) is the "time of the Gentiles."[824] They teach that those who are faithful Christians now will be secretly "raptured"—that God will take them to heaven before the great tribulation. This is supposed to be followed by a seven-year time of trouble which will be God's dispensation for the conversion of the Jews and those "Gentiles" who were not converted and raptured before the time of trouble.

This theory has been popularized by books and movies such as the "Left Behind" series which portray a sudden disappearance of Christians, snatched away from the driver's seat of cars, from airplanes or out of their beds. The sealing of the 144,000 is, according to this theory, the conversion of Jews, who then become witnesses during the time of trouble. Those who were true and faithful Christians will have been raptured and will look on from the safety of heaven.

While this is a nice theory, and most Christians would love to escape the great tribulation, the Bible does not teach this anywhere. First of all, Jesus clearly taught that there will be a great tribulation at the end of time: "For then there will be great tribulation, such as has not been since the beginning of the world until this time, no, nor ever shall be (Matthew 24:21). Jesus said that there would be increasing turmoil leading up to the great tribulation: wars and rumors of wars, famines, pestilences and earthquakes, persecution and hatred directed at believers, deceptive false prophets, widespread lawlessness, and finally the "abomination of desolation" and then the great tribulation (Matthew 24:4-21). But Jesus did not say that at some point before things get too bad the true Christians would be taken away; He said, "He who endures to the end shall be saved" (Matthew 24:6).

The Greek word for tribulation is *thlipsis*, which is used in the New Testament to describe the difficult experiences that God's people endure in this world, not those that they escape. For example, Jesus said, "In the world you will have tribulation" (John 16:33). Paul assures us that "we must through much tribulation enter into the kingdom of God" (Acts 14:22). John himself, while writing the book of Revelation, was a "companion in the tribulation and kingdom and patience of Jesus Christ" (Revelation 1:9). Paul goes so far as to say that "we also glory in

---

824 Dispensationalists point to texts such as Luke 21:24, "And Jerusalem will be trampled by Gentiles until the times of the Gentiles are fulfilled" as evidence that God has different plans for saving the Gentiles and the Jews. According to this theory, God's plan for the Jews during the Old Testament was that they would be saved because they were obedient in keeping the law. During the "dispensation" for the Gentiles people could be saved by grace through faith. The Jews would have another chance to be saved during the time of trouble after the "rapture" of the church. During this time the converted Jews would preach the gospel to the other people who had been "left behind."

tribulations, knowing that tribulation produces perseverance, and perseverance character, and character hope" (Romans 5:3,4). There are no scriptures that hold out the promise that Christians will somehow avoid tribulation.

This is the main problem with the theory of the secret rapture: there are no scriptures that clearly teach it. Rather than emerging as a doctrine from the clear teaching of the Bible, the theory of the secret rapture is presented and then texts are given which supposedly support it. Many of these texts actually teach the exact opposite of the secret rapture.

Among the favorite "rapture" texts are those like Matthew 24:40,41: "Two men will be in the field; one will be taken and the other left. Two women will be grinding at the mill; one will be taken and the other left." The scenario that is presented is that people will be going about their everyday activities when some will be "taken" to heaven and the others "left" behind to experience the time of trouble.

However, a careful reading shows that the story of those "taken" and "left" is another way of emphasizing the previous verses—"For as in the days before the flood, they were eating and drinking, marrying and giving in marriage [going about their everyday activities] until the day that Noah entered the ark, and did not know until the flood came and *took them all away*, so also will the coming of the Son of Man be. Then two men will be in the field, one will be taken and the other left" Matthew 24:38-40.[825] It was the flood that took them all away to destruction, not the ark taking them to a place of safety. In the Genesis account it is clear: "Every living thing on the face of the earth was wiped out; men and

animals and the creatures that move along the ground and the birds of the air were wiped from the earth. *Only Noah was left*, and those with him in the ark"[826] (Genesis 7:23 NIV).

This understanding is in harmony with the parallel passage in Luke 17: 34-37. Jesus again said, "Two men will be in the field, the one will be taken and the other left." The disciples wondered where they would be taken to—"And they answered and said to Him, 'Where, Lord?' So He said to them, 'Wherever the body [dead body, NIV] is, there the eagles [vultures, NIV] will be gathered together.'" In other words, the ones taken are those who are destroyed, whose bodies become food for the birds, as described in Revelation 19:17,18, which portrays the Second Coming of Christ and the "feast of the birds."[827] The ones who are left are "we who are still alive, *who are left* until the coming of the Lord" (1 Thessalonians 4:15 NIV).[828]

Rapture theorists insist that Christ's coming is in "two installments," first in secret before the time of trouble (which they claim will coincide with the resurrection of the righteous) and then visibly at the end of the time of trouble. They point to texts like 1 Thessalonians 4:13-18 and 1 Corinthians 15:50-54 as being "rapture" texts and Matthew 24:27-31 as being a "visible coming"

---

825 The Greek for took ("the flood came and *took* them all away") is *airo*, which means "take up, raise up." Thus in the original language it is obvious that it is the wicked who are "taken up" (and destroyed), not the righteous.

826 The Hebrew for left ("only Noah was left") is *shaar*, which means "to remain, be left behind." Thus in the original language it is obvious that it is the righteous who, like Noah, are "left behind" (to meet Jesus), not the unrepentant or the Jews.

827 "Then I saw an angel standing in the sun; and he cried with a loud voice, saying to all the birds that fly in the midst of heaven, 'Come and gather together for the supper of the great God, that you may eat the flesh of kings, the flesh of captains, the flesh of mighty men, the flesh of horses and of those who sit on them, and the flesh of all people, free and slave, both small and great." (Revelation 19:17,18).

828 This is a favorite "rapture" text, supposedly referring to the Jews and undecided who will be converted during the time of trouble. But note that Paul included himself and those who are faithful among the "we who are alive and remain." He gives no indication that there is another group more faithful who went to heaven first.

text. But a simple comparison of these three texts shows that 1) the rapture happens at the same time as the resurrection of "those who sleep in Jesus," 2) the resurrection, far from being secret, is a very audible event with "a shout," "the voice of the archangel," and "the last trumpet," and 3) the last "loud trumpet call" takes place when Christ appears in His visible glory. There is no place in these texts for a secret rapture.

Moreover, Revelation 20:4,5 teaches clearly that the "first resurrection" (which, according to 1 Thessalonians 4:13-18 and 1 Corinthians 15:50-54 coincides with the rapture of the living righteous) takes place at the Second Coming of Christ and the beginning of the millennium, not secretly seven years earlier. A study of the other "rapture passages" shows that none of them teach that the righteous will be secretly taken to heaven before the time of trouble.[829]

The Book of Revelation provides the most comprehensive outline of the developments at the end of the age, and believers in the rapture theory have tried to find the "rapture event" in Revelation. They have focused on Revelation 4:1,2, "After this I looked, and, behold, a door was open in heaven. And the first voice which I heard was like a trumpet talking with me, which said, 'Come up here, and I will show you things which must take place after this.' And immediately I was in the spirit; and, behold, a throne was set in heaven."

Just reading the text, it seems like there is nothing to discuss; the obvious meaning is that John in vision was invited to see and hear the scenes in heaven that he wrote about in

Revelation. But rapture theorists point out that there is movement from earth to heaven in the command, "Come up here," and that the church, which was the focus of chapters 2 and 3, is not mentioned in the rest of Revelation. Therefore, according to their reasoning, this text must mean that the church will go to heaven before the time of trouble.

We should notice first of all that the church is not mentioned in Revelation 4:1,2, so it is speculative to maintain that those verses portray the rapture of the church. In fact, even in chapters 2 and 3 there is no mention of the universal church, only of the specific churches (of Ephesus, Smyrna, etc.). According to the historicist method of interpretation, these churches represent the progressive history of the church through the centuries, ending with the lukewarm Laodicean Church, and Laodicea is certainly not going to be raptured!

This book has taken the position that chapters 4-7 represent the investigative judgment that takes place in heaven before the "close of probation" and the seven last plagues. Individuals cannot be taken to heaven until they have been judged, so Revelation 4:1,2 which introduces the preliminary events before the actual judging takes place in chapter 6, could not be the rapture event.

Furthermore, the church does appear in later chapters: it is called "the saints" (Revelation 13:7,10, 14:12). Paul in 1 Corinthians 14:33 mentions "the churches of the saints," which shows that wherever the saints are, there the church is. And the saints are very much on earth in the Book of Revelation until they go to heaven at the Second Coming and spend the millennium there (Revelation 20). This is the rapture that Paul talked about in 1 Thessalonians 4:17; there is no mention of a rapture 7 years earlier in Revelation or anywhere else in the Bible.

This is not just an academic matter. No doubt

---

829 So-called rapture passages include John 14:1-3, Romans 8:19, 1 Corinthians 1:7,8, 15:51-53, 16:22, Philippians 3:20,21, 4:5, Colossians 3:4, 1 Thessalonians 1:10, 2:19, 4:13-18, 5:9, 5:23, 2 Thessalonians 2:1, 1 Timothy 6:14, 2 Timothy 4:1, 4:8, Titus 2:13, Hebrews 9:28, James 5:7-9, 1 Peter 1:7,13, 5:4, 1 John 2:28-3:2, Jude 21, Revelation 2:25, 3:10, 4:1,2. This list is cited in Revelation Unveiled by Tim LaHaye (Zondervan 1999). None of them say that the righteous will be taken to heaven before the time of trouble.

during the chaos of the beginning of the time of trouble many Christians will believe that the rapture has already taken place and they have been left behind. Satan will exploit their belief that their faith was inadequate, tempting them to either give up in despair, or to try to follow the "road map" of the left-behind scenario, which he will manipulate.

The Rapture and the Propehcy of Daniel 9 (70 Weeks)

Much of the confusion concerning the time of trouble, the role of the Jews, and the so-called secret rapture has to do with a misunderstanding of the prophecy of seventy weeks of Daniel 9. This prophecy was an explanation given by the angel Gabriel to Daniel to help him understand the prophecy of 2,300 days found in Daniel 8 that he had seen earlier, and specifically to understand a cryptic conversation that he had heard—"How long will the vision be, concerning the daily sacrifices, and the transgression of desolation, the giving of both the sanctuary and the host to be trampled underfoot?' And he said to me, 'For two thousand three hundred days, then the sanctuary shall be cleansed." (Daniel 8:13,14). This prophecy is explained in 14: *When in History* and in Appendix 5. Briefly, Daniel understood the 2,300 days to be 2,300 years, and, believing that His beloved city would not be restored for thousands of years, he "fainted and was sick for many days" and was "astonished by the vision" (Daniel 8:27). Gabriel came later (Daniel 9) to explain the vision, but did so indirectly with the prophecy of seventy weeks.

In answer to Daniel's earnest prayer, the angel Gabriel was sent to him so that he could "consider the matter, and understand the vision" (Daniel 9:21-23). "Seventy weeks [490 days] are determined for your people and for your holy city, to finish the transgression, to make an end of sins, to make reconciliation for iniquity, to bring in everlasting righteousness, to seal up vision and prophecy, and to anoint the most Holy" (v. 24). In other words, Daniel's people, the Jewish nation, were being given a 70 week period of "probation" to turn from their sins and "to anoint the Most Holy," Jesus. The 70 weeks were "determined" (literally, cut off) from the total 2,300 days.

This time period was to start with "the going forth of the command to restore and build Jerusalem" (v. 25), which was given by the Persian king Artaxerxes in 457 BC[830] (Ezra 7:12-26).[831] The time was divided into three phases. "From the going forth of the command to restore and build Jerusalem until Messiah the Prince, there shall be *seven weeks*, and *sixty-two weeks*; the street shall be built again and the wall, even in troublesome times. And after the sixty-two weeks Messiah shall be cut off, but not for Himself...Then He shall confirm a covenant with many for *one week*, but in the middle of the week He shall bring an end to sacrifice and offering" (Daniel 9:25-27). Seven weeks is apparently the time in which "the street shall be built again and the wall," in other words, the rebuilding of the city. Then there would be sixty-two weeks in which to carry out the requirements of the probation (to finish transgression, etc.), which would

---

830 See Zondervan Pictorial Bible Dictionary (Grand Rapids, MI 1973) p. 579. A number of historical and archeological sources identify the first year of the reign of Artaxeres as 464 BC. His decree was enacted in the seventh year of his rule (Ezra 7:8).

831 There were actually three decrees given. The first by Cyrus (Ezra 1:1-4) allowed for the building of "the house of the Lord God of Israel." The second decree by Darius (Ezra 6:1-12) again allowed for the building of the temple after it had been halted by opponents. The third decree was by Artaxerxes (Ezra 7:11-26). However, it was only under the decree of Artaxerxes that provision was made for the building of the walls and city, as specified by the prophecy of Daniel 9:25 (See Nehemiah 2:1-9)

take place "in troublesome times"[832]. Then during the final week "the Messiah shall be cut off, but not for Himself." The physical impossibility of carrying out all of this in seventy literal weeks suggests the use of the day-for-a-year principle, which, when applied, provides one of the most strikingly accurate prophecies of the Bible.

The "seven weeks and sixty-two weeks," "until Messiah the Prince," (49 years plus 434 years for a total of 483 years of prophetic time), when added to 457 BC reaches to the year AD 27, and indeed in that year John the Baptist lowered Jesus into the waters of the Jordan river "to anoint the Most Holy" (vs.25,24).[833] This signaled the beginning of the seventieth week (the final seven years), and the prophecy specifies that "in the middle of the week," which would be 3 1/2 years later, "He shall bring an end to sacrifice and offering," being "cut off, but not for Himself." Right on cue, in AD 31 Jesus provided the ultimate sacrifice, bringing to an end the sacrificial system which had been a "shadow" of the "one sacrifice for sin forever" (Hebrews 10:1,12). The end of the sacrificial system was confirmed when "the veil of the temple was torn in two from top to bottom" (Matthew 27:51), signifying the end of the temple ministry with its sacrifices.

The Jews still had half a week of probation, the time that the apostles preached exclusively to the Jews. But in AD 34 the Jews sealed their rejection of Jesus by stoning Stephen, the first Christian martyr, and the disciples "were scattered and went everywhere preaching the word"[834] (Acts 8:4).[835] Just a few years later the final specification of the prophecy was fulfilled; the Romans, "the people of the prince who is to come" did come in AD 70, and because of "the overspreading of abominations" they did "destroy the city and the sanctuary" and "[made] it desolate" (Daniel 9:26,27).

This remarkably accurate prophecy is an amazing testimony to the divine origin of the Bible. But many dispensationalist commentators, rather than accepting the application of the seventieth "week" to the ministry of Jesus, instead insert a 2,000 year gap and apply it to the anti-Christ! They insist that the final "week" will take place at the end of time, a seven-year time of trouble during which the Jews will be saved.

The prophecy reads, "And after the sixty-two weeks Messiah shall be cut off, but not for himself; And the people of the prince who is to come shall destroy the city and the sanctuary. The end of it shall be with a flood, and till the end of the war desolations are determined. Then He shall confirm a covenant with many for one week; but in the middle of the week He shall bring an end to sacrifice and offering" (Daniel 8:26,27). Those who believe in the rapture and the end-time role for the Jews insist that the "He" who "shall confirm a covenant with many for one week" is "the prince who is to come"—the anti-Christ. Since this anti-Christ appears in the last days, and the seventy weeks began over four hundred years before Christ, obviously there would have to be a gap somewhere (they say between the

---

832 The inter-testament period was a very "troublesome time" for the Jews as they were repeatedly overrun by the Hellenistic Seleucid and Ptolemy kingdoms (the King of the North and King of the South) and finally conquered by the Romans.

833 The baptism of Jesus is dated by Luke as "the fifteenth year of the reign of Tiberius Caesar." Luke carefully gives several other historical events to define this date (See Luke 3:1,2.). Although there are some disagreements, the most likely dating is the fall of 27 AD (See *SDA Bible Commentary* on Luke 3:1, Hagerstown, MD Review and Herald, 1980).

834 Although the Jews were disqualified by their rejection of Christ to be the chosen people of God, salvation is still available to any individual of the Jewish race in the same way it is for all other people: by faith in Jesus (See Romans 11, esp. vs. 23,24).

835 Shortly afterward God directed Peter to preach the gospel to Cornelius and his family, who became the first baptized gentiles, and the apostles realized that "God has also granted to the Gentiles repentance to life" Acts 11:18.

sixty-ninth and the seventieth week) and a part of the time "determined" for the Jews would be at the time of the end. However, this view disregards the fact that the whole passage has been about the "Messiah." Jesus is the "He" who confirmed the "everlasting covenant" (Isaiah 24:5), and the mention of "the prince who is to come" is parenthetical.

Unfortunately the Jews did not fulfill the terms of their "probation." As a nation they rejected the Messiah, and as a result they were rejected as being the chosen people to bring the gospel to the world[836] (although Paul makes it clear in Romans 9-11 that individual Jews can be saved like anyone else).

The "prince who is to come" is obviously a Roman, since it is his "people" who were to "destroy the city and the sanctuary" (which the Romans did in AD 70). It was the *Roman* Catholic Papacy which headed the church during the apostasy of the Middle Ages, and although the Papacy received a "mortal wound" (Revelation 13:3), "the mortal wound was healed" (See chapters 13 and 17 for details of the recovery of the papal supremacy). In chapter 17 it is clear that Satan himself will be the final manifestation of the anti-Christ power, and he will personally lead the struggle to destroy God's people in the Battle of Armageddon. All of this is prophesied to take place, but it has nothing to do with the final "week" of the seventy-week prophecy, which was fulfilled with the life and sacrifice of Jesus.

This analysis of the 70-week prophecy of Daniel 9 shows that the 70 "weeks" have all been completed. There is no 7-year period (the "last week") left to be fulfilled for the Jews. Individual Jews can be saved just like anyone else, but they will never again be the chosen people, and the church will not be "raptured" away to heaven leaving the Jews behind to convert the world. The 144,000 who will do that work, are spiritual Israel (See 7:4-8, *The Tribes of Israel*).[837] They are sealed before the time of trouble and they will be protected by God (although they will suffer many trials and tribulations and some will be martyrs). They will be raptured along with those who have accepted their message when Jesus comes "on the clouds of heaven with power and great glory. And He will send His angels with a great sound of a trumpet, and they will gather together his elect from the four winds, from one end of heaven to the other" (Matthew 24:30,31).

---

836 Jesus gave the parable of the vinedressers (who represented the Jews) who refused to give the fruits of the vineyard to the owner (God), mistreating and killing His servants and finally His Son. He ended the parable with the statement, "Therefore I say unto you, the kingdom of God will be taken from you and given to a nation bearing the fruits of it" (Matthew 21:33-46).

837 It should be kept in mind that the 144,000, who are sealed in their foreheads and protected in the midst of the trumpet plagues (Revelation 9:4), are not Jews who will be converted during the time of trouble. 1) They are sealed before the plagues begin (Revelation 7:1-8) whereas the rapture theorists contend that the Jews will be converted during the time of trouble. 2) They "were not defiled with women, for they are virgins" (Revelation 14:4), which indicates that they have not been involved in false religious systems (See chapter 14:1-5). 3) They are sealed out "of all the tribes of the children of Israel" (Revelation 7:4), whereas the Jews are descendents of the tribes of Judah, Benjamin and Levi (1Kings 12, esp. verses 19-24, 2Kings 17, esp. v. 18). In chapter 7 we saw that Israel is now spiritual Israel, and includes all who are true "children of Abraham," having the faith of Abraham (Romans 4:9-16). Paul makes it clear that many Jews will be saved (Romans 11), along with "the fullness of the Gentiles...and so all [spiritual] Israel will be saved" (Romans 11:25,26). But there is nothing in scripture to indicate that the Jews will ever again be God's chosen people.

Appendix 5
The 2,300 Days of Daniel 8

In Daniel 8 the prophet was shown a vision of a ram that represented the Medo-Persian Empire, followed by a goat that represented the Greek Empire, first under Alexander the Great (a "notable horn") and then as the divided Hellenistic kingdoms ("four notable horns"). Finally a little horn that became huge, representing first pagan and then papal Rome, attacked the "daily sacrifices" and the "sanctuary." This vision parallels and covers the same span of history as the visions of chapter 2 (the multi-metal image), chapter 7 (the four beasts and the little horn) and chapter 11 (the Kings of the North and South), with each separate vision providing a slightly different perspective and additional details.

After presenting the span of history, Daniel 8:13 asks a crucial question: "How long will the vision be?" Verse 14 gives what at first appears to be a cryptic answer: "For 2,300 days, then the sanctuary shall be cleansed." At this time the sanctuary in Jerusalem was in ruins, and Daniel and many of the Jewish people were in captivity in Babylon, hoping that God would make it possible for them to return and rebuild the temple and Jerusalem. It was obvious from the sweeping context of the vision, with the rise and fall of three empires, a major attack on the daily sacrifices and the cleansing of a sanctuary that had not even been built yet, that 2,300 days (just over 6 years) was not nearly enough time for all of that to happen. The vision began

in Daniel's day with "the kings of Media and Persia" but was to extend "to the time of the end" (Daniel 8:20, 17). No doubt Daniel understood the day-for-a-year prophetic principle, and the thought that the temple would not be "cleansed" or restored for 2,300 *years* was so overwhelming that "I, Daniel, fainted and was sick for days...I was astonished by the vision" (Daniel 8:27).

The angel Gabriel had been sent to Daniel to interpret the vision to him—"Gabriel, make this man understand the vision" (Daniel 8:16). Gabriel had carefully explained the identity of the ram and the goat, and had elaborated on the destructive activity of the great horn. But he did not explain the meaning of the statement, "For two thousand three hundred days [literally evenings and mornings]; then the sanctuary shall be cleansed." He had only said, "The vision of the evenings and mornings which was told is true" (v. 26). But this was the crucial point that Daniel felt that he needed to understand, and it caused him great distress—"I was astonished by the vision, but no one understood it" (v. 27).

Chapter 9 is a continuation of Daniel 8. As Daniel later reviewed the prophecies of Jeremiah concerning the restoration of the temple and Jerusalem he learned that "the number of the years specified by the word of the Lord through Jeremiah the prophet, that He would accomplish seventy years in the desolation of Jerusalem" (Daniel 9:2). There was a huge discrepancy between the 70 years of Jeremiah and the 2,300 years that his vision had indicated, and Daniel likely feared that the continuing unfaithfulness of his people had caused God to prolong the time. Daniel humbled himself and appealed to God's great mercy—"Then I set my face toward the Lord God to make request by prayer and supplications, with fasting, sackcloth and ashes, and I prayed to the Lord my God, and made confession" (v. 3).

In answer to his prayers God sent "the man [angel] Gabriel whom I had seen in the vision at the beginning" (Daniel 9:21). His stated purpose was to help Daniel to "understand the vision" (v. 23), in other words, to complete the explanation of the vision that he had begun in chapter 8. Two important points should be kept in mind: 1) Gabriel's purpose in returning was to finish the explanation of the vision in chapter 8 (and the portion that Daniel had not understood was the 2,300 days and the cleansing of the sanctuary), and 2) Daniel's main concern had to do with his people, the Jews, and his city, Jerusalem.

In Gabriel's interpretation of the vision of chapter 8 he had used two different Hebrew words for vision, and these help us understand what he was explaining in chapter 9. The first word, *chazon*, was used to talk about the vision as a whole—"How long will the vision [*chazon*] be concerning the daily sacrifices and the transgression of desolation, the giving of both the sanctuary and the host to be trampled underfoot?" (Daniel 8:13).

The second word for vision, *mareh*, was used to talk about the aspect of the vision which had to do with the two thousand three hundred days—"And the vision [*mareh*] of the evenings and mornings which was told is true" (v. 26).

It was the *mareh* (the meaning of the 2,300 days) that Daniel had not understood, so God sent Gabriel to him again—"Gabriel, whom I had seen in the vision [*chazon*] at the beginning,

being caused to fly swiftly, reached me about the time of the evening offering. And he informed me and talked with me and said, 'O Daniel I have now come forth to give you skill to understand... therefore consider the matter and understand the vision [*mareh*]" (Daniel 9:21-23). Notice that Daniel referred to a vision in which Gabriel had appeared "at the beginning," in other words, the vision of Daniel 8. Notice also that when Gabriel said that he wanted to help Daniel "understand the vision," he had not used the word for the whole vision (*chazon*) but instead he had used the word *mareh* that referred to the part of the vision concerning "the evenings and mornings" (the 2,300 days).

From this it is obvious that it was the 2,300 days that Gabriel specifically wanted to explain. But strangely, rather than talking about the 2,300 days, he explained that there would be "seventy weeks [which] are determined [literally 'cut off']"[838] for your people [the Jews]" (v. 24). This addressed Daniel's main concern (for his people and his city), but since Gabriel's purpose was to explain the meaning of the 2,300 days, the obvious implication is that the seventy weeks (490 days) that were cut off for the Jews were cut off from the 2,300 days. This means that the starting point for the seventy weeks would also be the beginning of the 2,300 days.[839]

---

838 "This verb appears only in the passive stem (Niphal), and only in Daniel 9:24, the famous "seventy weeks" passage. In rabbinic Hebrew the root ptk basically means "cut," hence the translation "decreed" in most versions. (See Marcus Jastrow, Dictionary of the Targtimin, the Talmud Babli and Yerushalmi, and the Midrashic Literature, I, Pardes, 1950, p. 513.)."

839 The prophecy of seventy weeks was no doubt given to reassure Daniel that his people, the Jews, would not have to wait for the completion of the 2,300 years to return from Babylon.

The 2,300 days are prophetic days[840] in which each prophetic day represents one year, so when the angel mentioned 70 weeks he was actually referring to 490 years which were "determined" for the Jews.[841] The 490 years were to begin with "the going forth of the command to restore and build Jerusalem" which was given by Artaxerxes in 457 BC (Daniel 9:25, Ezra 7:6-8, 12-26, 6:14).[842] The longer period of 2,300 years would also start in 457 BC. Some simple arithmetic shows that the 2,300 years ended in AD 1844. At that time the cleansing of the sanctuary, (which is the same as the "investigative judgment") would begin.

Admittedly, the vision of Daniel 8 with the

---

840 The day-for-a-year principle is obvious from the prophecies of Daniel. For example, the seventy weeks (490 days) of Daniel 9 was to start with "the command to restore and build Jerusalem" (which was in 457 BC) and would extend "until Messiah the Prince," Jesus (Daniel 9:25). The prophecy of 2,300 days in chapter 8 began with "the kings of Media and Persia" (the Persian kings reigned in the 6th and 5th centuries BC) and would extend "to the time of the end" (Daniel 8:20,17). The prophecy of "time, times and half a time" (1,260 days) in chapter 7 began at the time of the breakup of the pagan Roman Empire and extended "until the time came for the saints to possess the kingdom" (Daniel 7:22). All these prophecies started in ancient times and continued the number of *years* the prophecy specified in *days*. Other scriptural support for this principle is found in Numbers 14:34, Ezekiel 4:5,6, Job 10:5, Psalm 77:5.

841 For more information about the 70 weeks prophecy see Appendix 4 *The Secret Rapture.*

842 There were three decrees concerning the Jews returning from their captivity in Babylon. The first was by Cyrus (Ezra 1:1-4) given in 536 BC, which only concerned building the temple. The 69 weeks (483 years) of the prophecy which were to extend "until Messiah the Prince" would only reach to 53 BC starting from 536 BC, long before "the Messiah," Jesus. Darius issued the second decree in 520 BC (Ezra 4:24, 6:1-12) so the 69 weeks would only extend to 37 BC, also before the Messiah. Moreover, the decree of Darius only provided for building the temple. The third decree was given by Artaxerxes. The text of the decree is in Ezra 7:12-26 and it allowed the Jews to do "whatever seems good to you and your brethren to do…whatever is commanded by the God of heaven" (Ezra 7:18,23) which could include restoring Jerusalem and the wall, as specified in the prophecy. The "going forth of the command" occurred when Ezra left Babylon with the decree and went to Jerusalem "in the seventh year of King Artaxerxes" (Ezra 7:7). This has been archaeologically proven to be 457 BC (see *Zondervan Pictorial Bible Dictionary,* [Grand Rapids, MI Zondervan Publishing, 1973] p. 579). Sixty-nine weeks, starting from 457 BC, extends to AD 27, the year Jesus was "anointed" at His baptism (Messiah means anointed).

2,300 days is one of the most challenging in scripture to understand. What follows is another approach that may clarify some points. The time period designated by 2,300 "evenings and mornings" (Hebrew *ereb boqer*) in Daniel 8:14,26 is at first frustrating because no beginning point is given. A careful study of chapter 8 and 9 together shows that chapter 9 (the prophecy of 70 weeks) is an explanation of chapter 8 that includes the beginning point for both prophecies. It is perhaps somewhat clearer if the two prophecies are studied starting with chapter 9 first and then applying it to chapter 8.

1. The "seventy weeks [which] are determined for your [Daniel's] people [the Jews]" extend "from the going forth of the command to restore and build Jerusalem until Messiah the Prince [Jesus]" (Daniel 9:24).

2. The "command to restore and build Jerusalem" could be the decree of Cyrus, Darius or Artaxerxes (Ezra 6:14). Cyrus reigned after defeating Babylon from 536-529 BC. Darius reigned from 521-486 BC. Artaxerxes reigned from 465-423 BC.

3. "Until Messiah" could refer to Jesus' birth (4 or 3 BC), His baptism (AD 27) or His crucifixion (AD 31).

4. Seventy literal weeks (490 days) obviously do not extend from the 5th or 6th century BC until the time of Christ, but 490 *years* is the appropriate time frame.

5. The 490 years specified could only fit with the decree of Artaxerxes, because the decree "in the first year of Cyrus (536 BC)" plus 490 years extends to 46 BC, and the decree in "the second year of the reign of Darius (Ezra 4:24)" plus 490 years extends to 30 BC, both of these dates being significantly before the Messiah.

6. The prophecy of Daniel 9 actually specifies that from the decree to rebuild Jerusalem until the Messiah will be "seven weeks and sixty two weeks" (a total of 69 weeks or 483 days/years).

7. Artaxerxes' decree "went forth" in the seventh year of his reign, 457 BC (Ezra 7:6-9, 11-25).

8. 457 BC plus 483 years extends to AD 27, the year of Christ's baptism.

9. That these are the right dates is confirmed by the following 2 points:

   A. The 483 years would extend until "the Messiah," which means the anointed one. Jesus was anointed to his ministry at his baptism.

   B. In the midst of the next week (the 70th week) the Messiah was to be "cut off but not for Himself" (Daniel 9:26), a phrase that refers to His death on the cross for sinful humanity. This event would "bring an end to sacrifice and offering," in other words, it would end the sacrificial system. This also took place with the sacrifice of Jesus, as evidenced by the torn curtain in the temple (Matthew 15:38). Jesus was indeed crucified "in the middle of the (70th) week" in AD 31, 3 ½ years after His baptism in AD 27.

10. The time prophecy of 70 weeks/490 years was not an isolated prophecy, but is directly related to another prophecy:

   A. According to Daniel 9:24, the 70 weeks were determined, literally "cut off." So the 490 years were cut off from another longer period of time.

   B. The explanation by Gabriel concerning the 70 weeks was given so that he could "understand the vision" (Daniel 9:22,23), in other words, as an explanation of a previous vision. The question is, what period is the 70 weeks cut off of, and what vision was Gabriel explaining with the 70 weeks?

11. The same angel, Gabriel, had appeared in the vision of chapter 8, and had been given the command, "Gabriel, make this man understand the vision" (Daniel 8:16). But he had not

succeeded in his mission—at the end of the vision Daniel admitted, "I was astonished by the vision, but no one could understand it" (Daniel 8:27).

12. Gabriel had successfully explained most of the vision of chapter 8 concerning Persia, Greece, the little horn and the desolation of God's people and the place of His sanctuary. The only part of the vision that wasn't explained was the part about the "evenings and mornings," in other words, the 2,300 days (Daniel 8:26).

13. The obvious conclusion is that the 70 weeks prophecy was an explanation of the 2,300 days. It would be logical to use one time prophecy to explain or clarify another.

14. The mystery of the 2,300 days was its starting point. A starting point was given in the 70 weeks prophecy (the decree to rebuild Jerusalem). This would also explain what the 70 weeks were cut off from—they were the part of the 2,300 days that applied to the Jews.

15. The 70 weeks prophecy remarkably confirmed that the "days" in these prophecies refer to years. This is also confirmed by the fact that the 2,300 days were to extend from the time of the Persian Empire until "the time of the end" (Daniel 8:17, 19-26).

16. With a starting date of 457 BC, the 2,300 years extend to AD 1844.[843]

17. A careful comparison of the visions of Daniel chapters 8 and 7 shows that they are covering the same empires and the same events. The little horn of chapter 8 is the same as the little horn of chapter 7.

18. In chapter 7 the little horn would rise up after the demise of the Roman Empire (the end of the 5th century AD) and would exercise oppressive authority for "a time, times and half a time." A comparison with Revelation 12:6, 13-17

---

843 When calculating keep in mind that historians never count a year "0"; 1BC goes directly to 1 AD.

shows that time, times and half a time is the same as 1,260 days. Again, the time frame shows that these are years rather than literal days. Starting in the early 6th century AD, the 1,260 years would extend until the end of the 18th century.

19. After the 1,260 years the judgment would begin—"the court shall be seated (Daniel 7:25,26, 8-11, 21,22).

20. The link between the end of the 2,300 years in chapter 8 which initiated the cleansing of the sanctuary and the end of the 1,260 years of Daniel 7 followed by the judgment are obvious—these are the same event. Thus the cleansing of the sanctuary that begins in 1844 is the judgment that takes place in Heaven.

21. This is the judgment that is announced in Revelation 14:6, "The hour of His judgment has come."

22. Obviously this is an invisible judgment, not the time when individuals will stand before the throne, because the angel announces to people living on earth that the hour of judgment has already come (the Greek word is *hilthen*, it came).

23. The obvious question over 160 years later is, what is taking so long? Does God need so much time to make up His mind? But, as we saw in chapter 14,

A. The judgment is not for God's sake, but for the sake of the rest of the universe who will have to live for eternity with the results.

B. There is a lot involved in the judgment, including the vindication of God Himself.

C. One of the most important and time-consuming aspects is the preparation of the witnesses (the parallel is the book of Job where Job was a witness for God against accusations and claims by Satan).

24. Why is this important?

A. Satan's attacks are increasingly vicious and seemingly successful as we approach the end of time because "the devil has come down to you having great wrath because he knows that he has a short time" (Revelation 12:12). The knowledge that we are in the very last phase of history helps God's people have the courage to hold on.

B. The knowledge that prophecies given over 2,000 years ago show that the judgment is proceeding right now is a powerful incentive for people who have been spiritually indifferent to wake up and make a decision concerning God's invitation.

Appendix 6
Jesus Did Not Establish Sunday

It has been taught that Jesus established Sunday as the day of worship, a memorial of His resurrection. According to this view, He taught by example, meeting with His disciples on the first day of the week for communion and worship. Some have gone so far as to suggest that every time Jesus met with His disciples after the resurrection was on a Sunday.

The first meeting was early on the morning of the first day with Mary Magdalene and "the other Mary" (Matthew 28:9,10, Mark 16:9-11, John 20:11-18). After resting in the tomb on Sabbath, Jesus took the very first opportunity to meet with those who were seeking Him, even before He ascended to heaven (John 20:17). He gave them work to do for unbelievers—"Go to My brethren and say to them, I am ascending to My Father and your Father." "And when they [the other disciples] heard that He was alive and had been seen by her, they did not believe" (John 20:17, Mark 16:11).

Later that afternoon Jesus met again with two disciples on the road to Emmaus (Luke 24:13-35, Mark 16:12,13). Although they had heard the report of the women, they still did not believe. He rebuked them ("O foolish ones, and slow of heart to believe in all that the prophets have spoken" Luke 24:25) and gave them a Bible study ("Beginning at Moses and all the prophets He expounded to them in all the Scriptures the things concerning Himself," v. 27). As soon as

they recognized Him "He vanished from their sight" (v. 31) before they had a chance to worship Him or even eat with Him.

Later that night[844] Jesus appeared to His disciples (John 20:19-23, Luke 24:36-49, Mark 16:14-20) in the upper room "where the disciples were assembled for fear of the Jews" (John 20:19). Notice that they were not assembled for a worship service. "He rebuked their hardness of heart because they did not believe those who had seen Him after He had risen" (Mark 16:14), and proved to them that He was alive by showing them His hands with the marks of the nails. "But while they still did not believe," He asked for food and ate in their presence in order to prove that he was not "a spirit" (Luke 24:36-43). Then He gave them their job description: "As the Father has sent me, I also send you" (John 20:21). "Go into all the world and preach the gospel to every creature" (Mark 16:15). There is no record of any worship, prayers or communion service in any of these three meetings with His disciples on the day of His resurrection.

"After eight days," presumably also on a Sunday night,[845] Jesus met again with His

---

844 This was actually the second day of the week according to the Jewish method of reckoning days "from evening to evening" (Leviticus 23:32).

845 John 20:26. The Jews used inclusive reckoning, which means that any part of any day is counted as a day.

disciples. But rather than instituting a new day of worship, His visit was for the purpose of meeting with the one disciple who was still an unbeliever—Thomas. Because he had been absent on the previous occasion, he had declared, "Unless I see in His hands the print of the nails...I will not believe" (John 20:25). After seeing with his eyes and feeling with his fingers, Thomas expressed his belief, "My Lord and My God!" But Jesus, in a rebuke which sums up his attitude toward all the unbelievers He met with on each of His "Sunday meetings," said "Because you have seen Me, you have believed. Blessed are those who have not seen and yet have believed" (vs. 28,29).

The picture that emerges is that the meetings with His disciples on Sundays were 1) the earliest opportunity He had to meet with them after His resurrection, 2) Not a meeting of those who in faith believed, but rather a meeting with unbelievers, 3) Not a time of worship, prayer or communion, but rather to rebuke their lack of faith and prove that He was alive, 4) A time to give them their instructions for the work He wanted them to do.

Besides these meetings on Sunday Jesus met with His disciples several other times on other days. He met with them on an unspecified day in Galilee at "the mountain which Jesus had appointed for them" (Matthew 28:16). There is nothing in the text or context that would hint that this was on the first day of the week or any other specific day. This is the first time that it is recorded that His disciples worshiped Him[846]— "When they saw Him, they worshiped Him" (v. 17). He then gave them "all authority...in heaven and on earth" and told them to go to "all nations, baptizing them in the name of the Father and of the Son and of the Holy Spirit, teaching them to observe all that I have commanded you" (v. 19).

Jesus also met with His disciples on a beach in Galilee (John 21:1-23). Again the day is not specified, but this meeting would certainly not support the idea that Jesus changed the Sabbath to Sunday and met on that day, since the fishing, hauling in of heavy nets, building fires and cooking were all forbidden on the Sabbath.

Jesus' final meeting with His disciples was the day of His ascension (Acts 1:1-11). This meeting took place forty days after His resurrection (v. 3) so it was probably on a Thursday and definitely not on a Sunday. According to this account, "He presented Himself alive after His suffering by many infallible proofs, being seen by them during forty days and speaking of the things pertaining to the kingdom of God" (Acts 1:3). Very few of these meetings are recorded in the Scriptures, but there is the clear implication that they were throughout the period of time and not limited to the five Sundays during that period. This is supported by John's comment that "Jesus did many other signs in the presence of His disciples which are not written in this book" (John 20:30).

The statement that "every time Jesus met with His disciples was on a Sunday" is simply not in harmony with the facts of Scripture. Moreover, it is an attempt to establish a doctrine by Biblical examples, rather than clear Scriptural teaching, and in fact it is not even in harmony with the clearest Biblical examples. Paul himself had a meeting with Jesus on the road to Damascus (Acts 9:1-19, 22:1-16, 26:9-18). Although in three places he describes this meeting in detail, even telling the place and the time of day,[847] he says nothing about it being on the first day of the week. John is the other apostle who had a meeting with Jesus, while in exile on Patmos. He did

---

846 Mary Magdalene and "the other Mary" worshiped Him when they met Him at the tomb (Matthew 28:9), but there is no record that His disciples worshiped Him during any of the Sunday meetings.

847 "As I journeyed and came near Damascus at about noon" (Acts 22:6).

specify that it was "on the Lord's day," but there is nothing in the Bible that would indicate that this was the first day of the week. In his gospel, which he apparently wrote at about the same time, he consistently refers to "the first day of the week" (John 20:1,19), not the "Lord's day." It is true that in the second century the church began to apply this term to Sunday, along with many other imaginative ways they used to try to distinguish themselves from the Jews and thus avoid persecution.[848] However, in the Bible this phrase finds application either as the Sabbath (Jesus said, "the Son of Man is Lord even of the Sabbath" Matthew 12:8) or the Second Coming of Christ ("So also the Son of Man will be in His day" Luke 17:24).

There is only one instance recorded in the Bible in which the early church met on the first day. "Now on the first day of the week, when the disciples came together to break bread, Paul, ready to depart the next day, spoke to them and continued his message until midnight" (Acts 20:7). Since days were considered to be "from evening to evening"[849] the portion of the first day that would include midnight would be what we consider to be Saturday night. The most likely scenario is a Saturday night sermon which continued after the regular Sabbath worship, with Paul setting out on his journey Sunday morning. At any rate, this night-time meeting could not be considered the regular pattern of worship, because it took place under unusual circumstances, since Paul was leaving them the next day and would never see them again. Even the "breaking of bread" did not take place until after midnight,[850] which is not a pattern that churches follows today.

It is sometimes asserted that Paul referred to Sunday worship service collections of offerings for the poor in 1Corinthians 16:1,2. "Now concerning the collection for the saints…On the first day of the week let each of you lay something aside, storing up as he may prosper." However, the Greek word *par' eavto* (by yourself) shows that this was an individual work, not a "passing the plate" as today's Christians might imagine from modern worship services. On the first day of the week, before they spent all their money on other things, the Christians were to lay aside "by themselves" something for the poor "that there be no collections when I come" (v. 2).

Some, in their attempt to tear down the Biblical Sabbath, go so far as to say that Jesus broke the Sabbath in His healing of the sick, his command to the healed paralytic to "take up your bed and walk" (John 5:8) and by allowing his disciples to "thresh" grain by rubbing it in their hands as they walked through the wheat fields (Matthew 12:1-8). This argument flies in the face of one of the most basic premises of the gospel: if Jesus had broken any part of the law, including the Sabbath, He could not have been our substitute and Savior.[851] It is true that Jesus violated the Sabbath of the Pharisees, but this Sabbath was a perversion of the Sabbath of the Lord, which Jesus clarified, magnified and obeyed, giving an example of true Sabbath keeping. When the Pharisees accused Him of breaking the Sabbath He did not say, "It is lawful to do whatever you want on the Sabbath." He said, "It is lawful to do good on the Sabbath" (Matthew 12:12).

Jesus consistently upheld the law of God and condemned those who would try to minimize its claims. "Do not think that I came to destroy the Law of the Prophets. I did not come to destroy

---

848 See 1:10 *The Lord's Day* and 2:1-5 *First Love.*

849 Leviticus 23:32, Mark 1:21, 29-32.

850 Acts 20:11.

851 Jesus is able to be our substitute because He committed no sins, therefore His sinless life could be credited to our account and His sacrifice could pay the legal debt of our sin. But if He had broken any commandment, including the Sabbath, He would not have had a perfect life to credit to us, and His death would only have paid the price for His own sins.

but to fulfill. For assuredly, I say to you, till heaven and earth pass away, one jot or one tittle will by no means pass from the law till all is fulfilled" (Matthew 5:17,18). It is sometimes argued that "all [was] fulfilled" on the Cross, therefore the law could pass away. But all has not been fulfilled because sin is still very much with us, and therefore the law is still needed to condemn sin. Moreover, "heaven and earth" have not "passed away" as the verse specifies.

"Whoever therefore breaks one of the least of these commandments and teaches men so, shall be called least in the kingdom of heaven, but whoever does and teaches them, he shall be called great in the kingdom of heaven" (Matthew 5:17-19). The Sabbath itself would certainly not be considered "one of the least of these commandments." One third of the words of the Ten Commandments are taken up by the Sabbath command. And although none of the Ten Commandments were just "for the Jews," the Sabbath commandment shows within itself that it predated the Jewish people. It begins with the words, "Remember the Sabbath day" and mentions "the seventh day" of Creation when "God rested," showing that it has been in effect since the beginning of time.[852] It is ironic that the one commandment that God charged His people to remember is the one most Christians have forgotten.

It has been claimed that the law of the Old Testament was fulfilled by Jesus (true), so New Testament believers do not have to obey the law (no scriptural support). According to this teaching, all except the Sabbath commandment were re-instituted by being mentioned by Jesus or the Apostles, but because there is no direct mention of the Sabbath in the New Testament, this shows that it was changed. However, there are actually several New Testament verses that make it clear that the Sabbath is very much a part of the new covenant "law of liberty" (James 1:25). In three passages Jesus said that He is Lord of the Sabbath.[853] The book of Hebrews clearly states, "There remains, then, a Sabbath-rest for the people of God" (Hebrews 4:9). And the direct quotation of the Sabbath commandment is used repeatedly to identify the God of the New Testament believers. For example, when the people of Lystra tried to worship Paul because of the miracles he performed, he rebuked them, saying, "Men, why are you doing these things? We also are men with the same nature as you, and preach to you that you should turn from these useless things to the living God, who *made the heaven, the earth, the sea, and all things that are in them*" (Acts 14:15). This is a direct quotation of Exodus 20:11, the commandment, "Remember the Sabbath day, to keep it holy." See also Acts 4:24 and Revelation 14:7.

It is obvious that the Sabbath was not changed by Jesus or the Apostles because there is no Biblical record of a Sabbath controversy. The abolishing of circumcision, which was not even as central to Jewish faith as the Sabbath, provoked a firestorm of controversy which resounds in the book of Acts and the letters of Paul.[854] There is no way that the Sabbath could have been quietly abandoned; any attempt to replace it with Sunday would have been met with extreme hostility by the Jews, and the complete absence of any New Testament controversy about the Sabbath is compelling proof that it was not even an issue. It is true that the "Jerusalem Council" (Acts 15)

---

852 In Exodus 16, before the Ten Commandments were given, God specified that manna was not to be gathered on the Sabbath. When some of the people gathered on the Sabbath, "The Lord said to Moses, 'How long do you refuse to keep My commandments and My laws?" This proves that God's laws in general and the Sabbath in particular were in force before the giving of the Ten Commandments on Mt. Sinai.

853 Matthew 12:8, Mark 2:28, Luke 13:16.

854 Acts 11:1-18, 15:1-29, Romans 2:25-29, 4:9,10, 1Corinthians 7:19, Galatians 2, 5:1-14, 6:12-15.

did not specify that "Gentiles who are turning to God" would have to keep the Sabbath, only requiring that they "abstain from things polluted by idols, from sexual immorality, from things strangled, and from blood" (v. 20). But the fact is that the council did not deal with any of the Ten Commandments, only those aspects of the ceremonial law that would prevent Jewish Christians from having social interactions with Gentile Christians.[855] The Sabbath does not appear as an issue until the third decade of the second century,[856] by which time Christians were trying to disassociate themselves from the Jews in order to avoid persecution (See 2:1-5 *First Love*).

When God abolished circumcision,[857] animal sacrifice,[858] and the Levitical priesthood,[859] He made it perfectly clear in the New Testament that He was doing so. But there is no hint in the New Testament that the Sabbath has been done away with. To the contrary, the evidence is that Jesus and the Apostles kept the Sabbath,[860] and that the Sabbath would be important until the end of time and even in eternity.[861]

The most common argument against keeping the Sabbath is that this proves that one is "under the law" rather than "under grace." But this argument is inconsistent. Almost all Christian denominations recognize the Ten Commandments as valid for Christians, not as a means of salvation but as a witness against sin. When we honor parents, refrain from adultery or suppress our covetous desires for things that do not belong to us, our actions are empowered by grace, because we cannot of ourselves obey God's law (Romans 8:7). So why is it that when it comes to obeying the Sabbath commandment this is somehow proof of legalism?

The real reason that most Christians accept nine of the commandments but reject the Sabbath is that the Sabbath is the one law that general society does not accept. Everyone agrees that murder, stealing and even idolatry are wrong, but keeping the Sabbath puts one radically out of step with the rest of society. The purpose of the law is to reveal our sin, but the majority of Christians do not want a law that tells them that working on the seventh day is a sin—the social and economic consequences are too great. And so most attempt to ignore the issue, convincing themselves that all the hundreds of denominations that have sanctified Sunday for all these centuries couldn't be wrong. But anyone who has read this far needs to face the fact that there is no evidence in the Bible to support the change of the Sabbath. We would do well to heed Peter's declaration; "We ought to obey God rather than men" (Acts 5:29).

---

855 Other aspects of the health laws, such as clean and unclean meats, were not such a problem since the Jews could recognize and refuse them, but they could not tell if a particular piece of meat they were served had been drained of blood or offered to idols. Likewise, the Jews would consider it particularly offensive to associate with those who were involved in homosexuality, incest, sex with prostitutes, or other sexual immorality which might be culturally acceptable in the Gentile societies. It was assumed that those non-ceremonial aspects of the law that still applied would be learned—"For Moses has had throughout many generations those who preach him in every city, being read in the synagogues every Sabbath" (Acts 15:21).

856 The Epistle of Barnabas, dated by the majority of the scholars between AD 130 and 138, was written by a pseudonymous Barnabas, probably at Alexandria where the conflict between Jews and Christians was particularly acute. See Samuel Bacchiocchi, *From Sabbath to Sunday* (Berrien Springs, MI, Biblical Perspectives) p. 218

857 Galatians 5:1-12, 6:12-15.

858 Hebrews 10:1-14.

859 Hebrews 7:9-24.

860 Luke 14:16, Acts 17:2, 18:4.

861 Matthew 24:20, Isaiah 66:22,23.

Appendix 7
The Seven Heads of the Beast of Revelation 17

The identification of the seven heads of the beast of Revelation 17 has been a controversial issue, with various theories that include the caesars of the first century, the succession of kingdoms that oppressed God's people through the ages, and the end-time popes culminating with the antichrist.

The context of the vision is an elaboration of the sixth and seventh of the seven last plagues of chapter 16, namely, the "Battle of Armageddon" and the fall of Babylon. The vision begins when an angel takes John to the wilderness to see "the judgment" of a gorgeously arrayed harlot sitting on a scarlet beast.

There are obvious similarities between the seven-headed scarlet beast of chapter 17 and the seven-headed sea beast of chapter 13, but the new feature of chapter 17 is that there is a harlot riding the scarlet beast. This may emphasize the difference between end-time Babylon and the medieval Papacy (the sea beast) which was an integrated religious and political entity. The last-day manifestation (the harlot riding the scarlet beast) seems to indicate some kind of separation, with the religious entity (the harlot) riding or controlling the political entity (the scarlet beast) until the final end when the horns of the scarlet beast (ten last kings) turn on the harlot and destroy her (Revelation 17:12-18).

A number of commentators assert that the heads of the beast represent seven consecutive world empires which oppressed God's people, starting with either Egypt or Babylon and progressing until the final oppressive government (last-day Babylon), which will take the lead in the last efforts to destroy God's people. The seven heads of the beast are considered consecutive or sequential; in other words, they are not all an active part of the beast at the same time.

However, there is evidence that the heads of the beasts are a flexible symbol with multiple meanings. The angel starts by explaining, "The seven heads are seven mountains [or hills] on which the woman sits" (v.9). In verse 18 the woman is interpreted as being "that great city which reigns over the kings of the earth," which the reader in John's day would certainly have understood to be Rome (and indeed there has never been a city in history which has ruled over such an extensive empire, both as ancient pagan Rome and as religious Catholic Rome). The seven hills of Rome were very famous and are still used as an identifying feature, even in general encyclopedias. Thus the symbol of the heads as hills seems to be used in order to identify (without naming) Rome as the great harlot.

Then the angel identifies the heads as "seven kings" (v. 10). This seems to be a change of symbolism rather than two ways of saying the same thing. Especially if the "kings" were considered to be world empires, it would not fit the facts of history to consider the seven hills to be synonymous with seven world empires going back to Egypt or Babylon—verse 9 says that the harlot sits on seven hills, not one of the seven. In what way could the great harlot (the apostate Christian church) be considered to be "sitting" on Babylon, Medo-Persia, etc?

The flexible use of symbols can also be seen in the ten horns. In the final manifestation of the beast (chapter 17:12) they are 10 last day kings, whereas in Daniel 7 they are 10 barbarian tribes involved in the breakup of the Roman Empire. In chapter 13 the horns have crowns and in chapter 12 they do not, so apparently their exact meaning can change with the specific context.

The heads-as-empires theory asserts that the scarlet beast is the final oppressive empire and is represented by one of the heads. The other six heads represent previous empires. But it is hard to make a list of empires fit the specifications of the vision. The lists of empires in the book of Daniel (chapters 2, 7, 8, and 11) are Babylon, Medo-Persia, Greece, pagan Rome and papal Rome. What empires would constitute the sixth, seventh and eighth heads? Starting with previous oppressive empires gives enough heads (Egypt, Assyria, Babylon, Medo-Persia, Greece, Pagan Rome, Papal Rome, scarlet beast). But the angel said that the seventh "king" would "continue a short time." How could the 1,260 years of papal supremacy be considered "a short time?"

Moreover, the scarlet beast is not the only seven-headed beast; the dragon of chapter 12 and the sea beast of chapter 13 also have seven heads. Are these heads also successive oppressive empires? The evidence does not seem to support this theory. For example, in chapter 12 the dragon does not seem to be tied to a specific kingdom at all, being present both at the birth of

Jesus (v. 4, where the human agents were Herod, the Jewish leaders and pagan Rome) and again in the "wilderness" pursuing the "woman clothed with the sun" (the remnant church) during the 1,260 years of Papal supremacy (vs. 13-17). Then in chapter 16 the dragon shows up again at the very end of time as a part of the unholy trinity. So if the heads of the dragon represented kingdoms there would be two or even three represented: pagan Rome, papal Rome and the end time manifestation. But if papal Rome is represented by the dragon, how can it also be represented by the sea beast in chapter 13? And in chapter 16 the dragon and the "beast" are spewing out unclean spirits at the same time (vs. 13), so how can they represent successive kingdoms?

Perhaps looking for the heads to be successive kingdoms doesn't fit very well for the dragon. The context of chapter 12 seems to be an elaboration of the "war in heaven" rather than an exposition of a particular phase of a succession of earthly empires. The seven heads of the dragon would more likely represent the fullness of Satan's activity or agents.

There are also difficulties in trying to apply the heads of the sea beast of chapter 13 to a succession of empires. The focus of the sea beast seems to be on the papal period, but with a special emphasis on the head that received a deadly wound. The deadly wound is more than simply the arrest of Pope Pius VI in 1798, and includes the Protestant Reformation on through the French Revolution and the loss of papal territories in 1870. An interesting observation is that throughout the most damaging phases of the deadly wound the Roman Catholic Church in no way ceased to exist, nor was it on the verge of disappearing. One aspect, her ability to maintain political and military control of Europe, was severely damaged, but other aspects of her existence, activity and agenda continued and even grew during this period. If the heads were successive phases of the beast, when a head received a deadly wound the whole beast would nearly die, but in history the deadly wound only damaged one aspect of the papacy, while the other aspects prospered. This implies that the heads of the sea beast are concurrent aspects or characteristics of the Papacy, not successive phases or kingdoms.[862]

The interpretation that the heads of the sea beast are aspects of the Papacy is also suggested by the fact that the sea beast is a composite of the four beasts of Daniel 7. The sea beast reflects aspects of these four kingdoms (the mouth of a lion, the feet of a bear, the body of the leopard, the horns of the monster) and the seven heads and ten horns constitute all the heads and horns of the four beasts. Within this composite, where do Egypt and Assyria fit in as two of the heads, as has been suggested? This again calls into question the theory of the heads as progressive kingdoms.

In fact, the angel of Revelation 17 does not say anything about kingdoms. "The seven heads are…seven kings" (vs.9,10). It has been asserted that kings and kingdoms could be interchangeable, referring to this usage in the book of Daniel. But in Daniel the writer makes it very clear that the words "king" and "kingdom" are being used interchangeably (2:37, 39, 7:17, 23). No such clarification exists in Revelation, and in fact in Revelation 17:12 it is very clear that the Greek usage is specific in its distinction between kings and kingdoms ("The ten horns which you saw are ten *kings* who have received no *kingdom* as yet"). Evidence is lacking to prove that the angel meant seven kingdoms when he referred to the seven heads as seven kings.

Actually, the eighth head/king seems much more like a person than an empire: "The beast that was, and is not, is himself also the eighth, and is of the seven, and is going to perdition." Although perdition (Greek *apoleia*) means destruction and could theoretically be applied to a kingdom or government, there are no New Testament instances of this word being used for anything besides people (for example, 2 Peter 3:7 "The day of judgment and *perdition of ungodly men*").

There are a series of texts in Revelation which reveal a relationship between the beast, the bottomless pit and going to perdition. These texts seem to show that the beast goes beyond its political and organizational characteristics and as the eighth head the beast acquires personal characteristics at the very end of time. The first reference is in Revelation 9, the fifth trumpet, which mentions "the angel of the bottomless pit." The angel's name, Apollyon, is a form of the word for perdition (Revelation 9:11). The bottomless pit is a term that seems to refer to the chaotic demonic realm (Revelation 9:1-3, Luke 8:31). Section 8: *Are the Trumpets Past or Future?* presents evidence that the trumpets are end time events, the progressive release of the "four winds of strife" (Revelation 7:1), which take place after the sealing of the 144,000 and before the close of probation. If so, the "angel of the bottomless pit" would no doubt be the same as "the beast from the bottomless pit" who also appears at the end of time.

The bottomless pit is then linked to "the beast" who wars against the two witnesses in chapter 11 ("the beast that ascends out of the bottomless pit will make war against them" v. 7). In chapter 17:8,11 the beast is again seen coming out of the bottomless pit, making war against "the Lamb… and those who are with Him." It is announced that he will go to perdition (destruction), and this happens in chapter 19 when the beast leads the kings and armies of the earth in their last great struggle against Jesus at His Second Coming. The beast goes to perdition by being cast into the lake

---

862 Some possible aspects of the papacy which could be represented by the seven heads of the sea beast are given in Appendix 11.

of fire (19:19,20). It is apparent from the context (chapter 17-19 being an elaboration of chapter 16, the Battle of Armageddon) that this beast of chapters 17 and 19 is the same beast which in chapter 16 was sending evil spirits out to the kings of the earth to gather them for the battle that then takes place in chapter 19. In chapter 16 the unclean spirits come out of the mouth of the beast, the dragon and the false prophet, the unholy trinity (vs. 13,14). Since the Holy Trinity is a triad of persons, we would expect that the counterfeit unholy trinity would also be persons rather than empires, governments or systems.

All of this activity by the beast sounds like a very personal manifestation of Satan, which is also described in 2Thessalonians 2, the impersonation of Christ by Satan (the final antichrist). The antichrist seems to fit very well with the personified beast in the above passages, and without this application we are left with no mention in Revelation of this very important, personal, last hour attack by Satan.

The point of this as it relates to Revelation 17 and the heads of the beast is that if the eighth king is a person, Satan's counterfeit manifestation of Christ, and since the eighth king is "of the seven," it would follow that the seven kings are also a succession of persons. The seven last popes would be good candidates since the heads are also seven hills, which points to Rome. Although there could be other suggestions, a series of world empires doesn't seem to fit.

It has been suggested that the chronological context of the angel's explanation, "five have fallen, one is…(Revelation 17:10) must be the time of John because angelic explanations are given in a context the prophet and the first-century readers could understand, including the chronological context. But it should be kept in mind that the angel gave three markers of the chronological context, and none of them fit with the first century AD. As we saw above, the seven heads

are seven kings, "five have fallen, one is," so the chronological context of the vision is the reign of the sixth king who "is." The angel also explained that "the beast that you saw was, and is not, and will ascend out of the bottomless pit and go to perdition" (vs. 8). The use of the past, present and future tenses show that the chronological context of of the vision is the time in which the beast "is not." This does not fit at all with the context of John's day if the heads are interpreted as being consecutive empires, because the Roman empire was at the peak of its power at that time. But it does fit into the last-day context of the time when the deadly wound which destroyed the Papacy's military and political power is nearly healed and the antichrist is about to appear to lead end-time Babylon into a new round of persecution of the saints.

An additional indication of the chronological context is found in verses 12-14, which state, "the ten horns which you saw are ten kings who have received no kingdom as yet, but they receive authority for one hour as kings with the beast. They are of one mind, and they will give their power and authority to the beast. These will make war with the Lamb." The ten kings exist within the time frame of the prophecy ("The ten horns… *are* ten kings") but their power is still limited ("who have received no kingdom as yet"). In the future they will "give their power…to the beast." The ten kings obviously did not exist at the time Revelation was written, but they do fit if the context of the prophecy is the time after the healing of the deadly wound and before the appearance of the antichrist.

In fact, this is one of the primary features of the beast of chapter 17, as contrasted with the sea beast of chapter 13: there is no mention of the deadly wound. This appears to be a major implied theme of chapter 17: that the deadly wound, which was a primary feature of the sea beast of chapter 13, has healed and the harlot, in control of the beast as a political entity (and finally with the whole system being led by the personified eighth-king beast) will again make war on "the Lamb…and those who are with Him" (vs. 14).

With this understanding it is plausible that the series of heads/kings are the popes who have reigned since the healing of the deadly wound. If the healing of the deadly wound took place with the opening of the Second Vatican Council (see 17:9-11 *Seven Heads*), the current pope, Francis I, would be the "one [who] is," the head/king at the time of the vision of Revelation 17 when the woman is "drunk with the blood of the saints" (Revelation 17:6). In other words, the reign of the current pope will see the initiation of the persecution of God's people. The next (seventh) pope would be the one "who must continue a short time," followed by the antichrist.

Alternatively, if the full healing of the deadly wound was manifest in the "holy alliance" in which the United States and the Papacy formed an alliance that brought down Soviet communism (see 13: *The Deadly Wound Healed* and 17:9-11), Pope Francis would be the third "king," with four more to go before the antichrist.

In conclusion, the theory that the seven heads of Revelation 17 are the final series of popes does seem rather unbelievable. However, it seems to fit the specification of the prophecy better than the interpretation that considers the heads to be a series of world empires starting from ancient times.

Appendix 8
Job and the Great Controversy

Many books and articles have been written about the book of Job and the pain and suffering he endured, trying to analyze how we should deal with pain and loss. But the book of Job is only secondarily concerned with the problem of pain. It is really about God's problem. It may seem strange to think that God could really have problems, considering that He is the sovereign Creator, all-powerful, all knowing, and present everywhere. However, the book of Job shows that God not only has a problem but a dilemma.

The book starts with a brief sketch of Job. He is blameless and upright, besides being very wealthy. Despite his great wealth he fears God and ministers diligently to his family and community (Job 1:1-5, 29:12-17).

Unknown to Job, a great council is taking place in heaven as the "sons of God"[863] gather. But there is a discordant element—Satan appears among them. In answer to Gods question, "From where do you come?," Satan says that he has come from planet earth, and that he in fact is the ruler of earth, going where he pleases and doing what he pleases.[864] This of course is not what God created the earth for—when He created man He gave him dominion over the earth, to rule it and subdue it (Genesis 1:26-28). But at the dawn of creation Satan stole the earth from Adam and Eve[865] and became their ruler, infecting them with his sinful character.

However, God is not willing to concede that Satan completely and exclusively rules the earth. He points to Job who is "a blameless and upright man, one who fears God and shuns evil" (Job 1:8). We see here that God does not have a problem with Job. He is not seeking to develop his character or teach him lessons—God is answering a serious challenge by Satan. If God were to concede the earth to Satan (and presumably end His involvement in its affairs), the suffering that we now see would be nothing in comparison. Therefore He tells Satan that He has someone who has not submitted to his evil principles, that planet earth still has humans who are loyal to God.

Satan does not accept the evidence of Job's character and behavior. He accuses God of buying Job's loyalty by blessing him with wealth and protecting him from harm—"So Satan answered the Lord and said, 'Does Job fear God for nothing? Have You not made a hedge around him, around his household, and around all that he has on every side? You have blessed the work of his

---

863 Job 38:4-7 reveals that the sons of God are heavenly beings who existed before the creation of the world.

864 Job 1:6,7, 2:1,2. In Ezekiel 28:14 we see that the phrase "walking back and forth" indicates occupying a rightful position.

865 Satan alluded to his ownership of the earth when he offered to give it to Jesus (its Creator!) if only He would bow down and worship Satan (Matthew 7:8,9).

hands, and his possessions have increased in the land. But now, stretch out Your hand and touch all that he has, and he will surely curse You to Your face!" (Job 1:11).

This creates a dilemma for God. He can protect His friend Job, in which case Satan will claim that he was right, that the earth really does belong to him, despite the presence of a few "good" people that God has bribed into serving Him. Or He can remove His protection, in which case Satan will unleash his destructive rage upon Job to prove that Job doesn't really serve God out of anything but self-interest.

Because the stakes are so high—the whole human race—God allows Satan to move against Job, although He still puts some limits on how far he can go (Job 1:12, 2:6). Satan acts quickly, first destroying all of Job's possessions and children. Then, after demanding from God permission to touch Job's body, he destroys his health and leaves him in abject pain and misery (Job 1:13-22, 2:7-10).

The majority of the book consists of dialogues between Job and his "friends." At first they are shocked and silent, but little by little they develop their core argument—that pain and suffering come upon those who sin and rebel against God, and that Job's affliction proves that he is a wicked sinner, whether he admits it or not.

Job consistently maintains that he has done nothing to deserve the kind of suffering he is experiencing. On the one hand he expresses faith in God—he knows that his Redeemer lives and that even if God slays him he will still trust in Him (Job 13:15, 19:25-27). On the other hand he accuses God of hiding from Him and beseeches Him to come tell him what he has done and why he is being punished (Job 23). His three friends are not able to overturn Job's insistence that he is innocent. At this point a younger friend, Elihu, speaks up in God's defense, telling Job that he is

wrong to accuse God in order to justify himself (Job 32-37).

Then God Himself shows up to speak to Job "out of the whirlwind" (Job 38:1). Although this is one of the most extensive narratives by God in the Bible, many readers have been frustrated, expecting God to say things related to the issue at hand, which is that He has allowed Satan to devastate Job's life. But at first glance it seems that God ignores Job's pain and complaints, and simply tells him, "I am the Creator, I am wise and powerful, I have made many amazing animals and you can't understand Me. I know what I'm doing and you need to simply submit to my sovereignty." Although this is all true, it is not very satisfying. However, a careful reading shows that God in His answer to Job actually gives important insight into the issues of the great controversy and the reasons for the pain and suffering that fills the earth.

God begins by pointing to His creation, that was so perfect and wonderful in the beginning that "the sons of God shouted for joy" (Job 38:4-7). He describes how He maintains the order of the universe, keeping the sea in its place, causing the sun to rise and bringing light to the earth, controlling the seasons, keeping the heavenly bodies in their orbits and providing rain at the right time and in the right amount (Job 38:8-38). In effect He says to Job, "You can't imagine what chaos there would be if I were not constantly controlling My intricately balanced creation."

Then God comes to the heart of his message to Job about His great dilemma—that the creation has been defiled by the effects of sin that resides in the hearts of the creatures He loves. To illustrate the problem He uses specific animals as examples. He points first to two animals that kill other creatures and eat their dead bodies—lions and ravens. That this is not a part of God's plan is made clear by the fact that in the New Earth "the lion shall eat straw like the ox"

(Isaiah 11:7) and "there shall be no more death" (Revelation 21:4). But even though these creatures have been warped by the effects of sin and live completely out of harmony with God's plan and intention in creation, they are still totally dependent upon Him. He still opens His hand to "satisfy the appetite of the young lions" and "provide food for the raven when its young ones cry to God" (Job. 38:39-41). God, in love and mercy, gives life and provides for His creatures which do not do what He wants, and this includes sinners and even Satan! Jesus underscored this amazing truth with His statement, "[God] makes the sun rise on the evil and the good, and sends rain on the just and on the unjust" Matthew 5:45.

God then gives a description of six animals that have the very characteristics of humans that make it difficult for God to reach them and bring them out of sin and into harmony with Him. Wild goats and deer hide so effectively that one cannot know where and how they bear their young. The wild donkey is so independent that it scorns the care of a human owner, finding its own food in the desert. The wild ox refuses to submit its great strength to a master. The ostrich is so stupid that she can't even care for her own young. The horse has no fear, and is even attracted to the battle that puts its life at risk. And finally, the eagle loves blood and dead things, and makes its home on high where it cannot be reached. (Job 39:1-30).

These are the characteristics of sinful humanity. We hide from God, we reject His offers to care for us, we refuse to submit to His sovereignty, we are blind to our own stupidity, we are not afraid of the dangers that can kill us and we love the things that lead to death. God challenges Job to tell Him how he would relate to sinners if he were God and had the infinite power that God has at His disposal. "Have you an arm like God? Or can you thunder with a voice like His? Then adorn yourself with majesty and splendor and array yourself with glory and beauty. Disperse the rage of your wrath; look on everyone who is proud and bring him low; tread down the wicked in their place. Hide them in the dust together, bind their faces in hidden darkness" (Job 40:11-13). Is this how Job would handle the problem of sin and sinners? God has not done this; instead of overwhelming us with His "majesty and splendor...glory and beauty," He "made Himself of no reputation, taking the form of a bondservant...He humbled Himself" (Philippians 2:7,8). Instead of "treading down the wicked in their place" He "is long-suffering toward us, not willing that any should perish but that all should come to repentance" (2Peter 3:9). Job, in His complaints against God, has questioned God's judgments and actions, and God asks him the pointed question, "Would you indeed annul My judgment? Would you condemn Me that you may be justified?" (Job 40:8).

Now God comes to the real dilemma—behind the rebellion of sinful humanity there is the originator of sin, Satan. It is Satan who has brought sin and suffering into the world, and he is the direct cause of Job's problems. By presenting two creatures that do not now exist on earth, God shows the difficulty of dealing with "the ruler of this world."[866]

Behemoth is "the first of the ways of God" (this invites a comparison with "Lucifer, son of the morning" Isaiah 14:12). He has a "tail like a cedar, bones like beams of bronze, ribs like bars of iron...the river may rage, yet he is not disturbed; He is confident, though the Jordan gushes into his mouth, though he takes it in his eyes or one pierces his nose with a snare" (Job 40:15-24). Job should consider how difficult it would be for him to move Behemoth out of his place in the river. God has a similar dilemma; Satan has taken up residence "in the river" of this earth, and most of its inhabitants are his loyal subjects. It is no

866 John 12:31, 14:30, 16:11.

simple matter for God to get rid of him, especially since His goal is to save as many of Satan's followers as possible.

Finally God points to Leviathan, a creature most like the fire-breathing dragon of mythology, whose "breath kindles coals, and a flame goes out of his mouth" (Job 41:21). God first reminds Job that Leviathan cannot be controlled ("Can you put a reed through his nose, or pierce his jaw with a hook?...Lay your hand on him; remember the battle—never do it again!" Job 41:2, 8). He cannot be reasoned with ("Will he make many supplications to you? Will he speak softly to you?" Job 41:3,4). He will not cooperate ("Will he make a covenant with you? Will you take him as a servant?" Job 41:4). He is dangerous to be around ("Will you play with him as with a bird, or will you leash him for your maidens?" Job 41:5). On the other hand, if you decide that you want to get rid of him he is hard to kill ("Can you fill his skin with harpoons, or his head with fishing spears?... Indeed, any hope of overcoming him is false" Job 41:7,9). There are no chinks in his armor ("His rows of scales are his pride, shut up tightly as with a seal...that no air can come between them;[867] they are joined one to another, they stick together and cannot be parted" Job 41:15-17). There is no chance of changing his heart ("His heart is as hard as stone, even as hard as the lower millstone" Job 41;24). He is not afraid of anything ("On earth there is nothing like him which is made without fear" Job 41;33) and he leads a host of others who are like him ("He is king over all the children of pride" Job 41;34).

For us, like Job, it is easy to say, "Why does God allow evil? Why doesn't He put an end to pain and suffering?" God's answer is that it is not as easy as it seems, even for God. He has a world full of people like the animals He mentioned, who hide from Him, who think they don't need Him, who refuse to submit to him, who don't think clearly, who foolishly have no fear of the consequences of their actions, and who love the things of death. And planted firmly in the midst of the river of humanity is the great rebel, "the king over all the children of pride."

It is tempting to think that God should just exercise His sovereign power and put a stop to it once and for all. If this would bring an effective and final end to sin, no doubt God would do this. But knowing what it really takes to rid the universe of sin, God has utilized a different strategy. "For God so loved the world that He gave His only begotten Son, that whoever believes in Him should not perish but have everlasting life" (John 3:16). "We were reconciled to God through the death of His Son" (Romans 5:10).

No one wants sin and suffering to end more than God, and in the end " there shall be no more death, neither sorrow, nor crying, neither shall there be any more pain; for the former things have passed away...Behold, I make all things new" (Revelation 21;4,5). Until then, we who find ourselves suffering from the effects of sin should ask God to help us see things from His perspective. If we could gain some insight into the reality "behind the scenes," we might share in Job's experience. After hearing God's words, he finally said, "I have uttered what I did not understand, things too wonderful for me which I did not know...I have heard of You by the hearing of the ear, but now my eye sees You" (Job 42:3-5).

---

867 The word for air is spirit, showing that Satan is impervious to the influence of the Holy Spirit.

Appendix 9
The Everlasting Covenant

Beginning in Genesis, God made a series of "everlasting covenants" with His people. These covenants were agreements that God made with people He had chosen to be His special representatives. His purpose was not to show favoritism to His chosen people, but rather to develop them into a "picture of God" that would attract those around them to come to God. In order to accomplish this, each of the covenants had four elements. The *promise* of the covenant was that He would bless His people so that they in turn could be a blessing and an example to those around them. The *requirement* of the covenant was His law, which is a reflection of His character, demonstrating the holiness that is an integral aspect of His nature. The *provision* for failure to meet the requirements of the law was the sacrifice of Christ, symbolized in the Old Testament covenants by animal sacrifices. The *sign* of the covenant was a visible symbol of the agreement, which had within it some relationship to the essence of the covenant.

Covenant with Noah

The first covenant that was actually called a covenant was with Noah.[868] Through the offspring of Cain sin had proliferated in the world, and finally the faithful descendents of Seth, (the "sons of God") began to intermarry with the lawless descendents of Cain (the "daughters of men," Genesis 6:2).[869] "Then the Lord saw that the wickedness of man was great in the earth, and that every intent of the thoughts of his heart was only evil continually" (v. 5). This condition threatened to totally extinguish the holy line that was supposed to bring forth the "seed of the woman," the Messiah, who would crush the serpent's head (Gen. 3:15).

In order to cleanse His creation, God intended to bring "floodwaters on the earth to destroy from under heaven all flesh in which is the breath of life" (Genesis 6:17). But to preserve the human race as well as animals, God chose Noah, "a just man, perfect in his generations" who "walked with God" to "establish [His] covenant" (Genesis 6:9,18). The first element of the covenant, God's blessing to mankind, was to preserve Noah and His family (and through them the

---

868 God made a covenant with Adam and Eve after they sinned, but the word "covenant" is not used.

869 This unclear passage has led to endless speculation, much of it revolving around the fact that the phrase "the sons of God" apparently refers to angels in some passages such as Job 1:6, 38:7. However, it seems incredible that angels would impregnate humans, especially in light of Paul's statement that angels are "spirits" (Hebrews 1:7), Jesus' comment that spirits do not have flesh and bones (Luke 24:39), and His statement that the angels "neither marry nor are given in marriage" (Matthew 22:30). The New Testament uses the phrase "sons of God" for human beings who are filled and led by His Spirit (Romans 8:14,19, Galatians 3:26). Thus it probably refers to the faithful descendants of Seth, in contrast to the lawless descendants of Cain.

knowledge of God) and to cause him to be "fruitful and multiply, and fill the earth" (Genesis 9:1). He also promised that "never again shall there be a flood to destroy the earth" (Genesis 9:11). This is the purpose of all of the covenants: that the knowledge of God would be preserved and would spread throughout the earth.

The second element, His requirements, was that people "shall not eat flesh with its life, that is, its blood," and that they should not "shed man's blood" (Genesis 9:5,6). These requirements, although not comprehensive, struck at the very essence of the sin of the pre-flood society, who ravaged the earth with their violent disregard for the sanctity of life.[870]

The third element, God's provision to save those who violate His requirements, was implied indirectly by the fact that Noah "built an altar to the Lord, and…offered burnt offerings on the altar" (Genesis 8:20). This prefigured and symbolized the sacrifice of Christ, which makes it possible for God to forgive sins. When Noah had offered sacrifices, God declared His mercy and willingness to forgive—"I will never again curse the ground for Man's sake, although the imaginations of man's heart is evil from his youth, nor will I again destroy every living thing as I have done" (Genesis 8:21).

The fourth element was the sign of the covenant. "And God said, 'This is the sign of the covenant which I make between Me and you, and every living creature…I set My rainbow in the cloud and it shall be for *the sign of the covenant* between Me and the earth" (Genesis 9:13). There was an obvious relationship between the sign of the covenant and the promised blessing of the covenant. God had promised not to destroy the world with another flood, and the rainbow was present when it rained, reminding mankind

that rain would never again result in universal destruction. "It shall be, when I bring a cloud over the earth, that the rainbow shall be seen in the cloud; and I will remember My covenant which is between Me and you…The waters shall never again become a flood to destroy all flesh" (Genesis 9:14-16).

God called this covenant "the everlasting covenant between God and every living creature of all flesh that is on the earth" (Genesis 9:16). This does not mean that there would be an eternal need for a guarantee that God would not destroy the world with a flood. The phrase "everlasting covenant" is used in each of the covenants, and means that the covenant will apply until it has fulfilled its purpose, in this case, until there are "new heavens and a new earth in which righteousness dwells" (2Peter 3:13).

Covenant with Abraham

Unfortunately, after the flood the human race returned to their sinful ways, again threatening to obliterate the holy line from which the "seed of the woman," the Messiah, would come. Indeed, God had to call Abram, the man He had chosen, out of Babylon (Ur of the Chaldees) because his family had started to serve false gods.[871] God made a covenant with Abraham, which again included the four elements.

First, the blessing to mankind was that through Abraham, and specifically "in [his] seed all the nations of the earth shall be blessed" (Genesis 12:3, 22:18). Paul makes it clear in the book of Galatians that this seed refers to Jesus Christ.[872]

The second element, obedience to the law, was the reason God chose Abraham for His

---

870 Genesis 6:11-13.

871 Genesis 11:28-12:4, Nehemiah 9:7, Joshua 24:2,3.

872 "Now to Abraham and his Seed were the promises made. He does not say, 'and to seeds,' as of many, but as of one, 'and to your Seed,' who is Christ" (Galatians 3:16).

covenant—"For I have known him [Abraham], in order that he may command his children and his household after him, that they keep the way of the Lord, to do righteousness and justice, that the Lord may bring to Abraham what He has spoken to him." "Abraham obeyed My voice and kept My charge, My commandments, My statutes, and My laws" (Genesis 18:19, 26:4,5).

God's provision to save those who violate His requirements (which in every covenant points to the sacrifice of Jesus on the Cross) was prefigured by the altars for sacrifice that Abraham built wherever he settled,[873] but even more powerfully in the drama of the sacrifice of Isaac.[874]

The sign of the Abrahamic covenant was circumcision—"You shall be circumcised in the flesh of your foreskins, and it shall be a sign of the covenant between Me and you" (Genesis 17:11). This unusual and seemingly barbaric sign actually had a close relationship with the blessing God was promising in the covenant—that through "Abraham's seed" (Jesus) all the families of the world would be blessed. The Hebrew word for seed (*zera*) is the same word used for semen (See Leviticus 15:6, for example) which issues from the same organ that is circumcised. Thus this "sign in the flesh" was a continual reminder that someday the true seed would come.

As in the covenant with Noah, God promised Abraham that He would "establish My covenant between Me and you and your descendants after you in their generations, for an everlasting covenant" (Genesis 17:7). In this case "everlasting" meant until the promise was fulfilled, and since Christ was the promised seed, circumcision was no longer an appropriate practice after

Christ. Paul went so far as to declare that "if you become circumcised, Christ will profit you nothing" (Galatians 5:2), both because circumcision had become a way by which the Jews attempted to establish their own righteousness, and because it denies the reality that the true seed has come.

The "Old" Covenant

God promised Abraham that his descendants would be "as the sand of the sea" and would be "a great nation," and that they would inherit the land of Canaan (which was located at the crossroads of the earth). This was to be fulfilled in the nation of Israel, which God called out of slavery in Egypt. God made a covenant with them at Mt. Sinai, which is often called the "old covenant."[875]

God declared His purpose in selecting them, that they would be a blessing to the world—"You shall be a special treasure to Me above all people, for all the earth is Mine, and you shall be to Me a kingdom of priests and a holy nation" (Exodus 19:5,6). The role of a priest is to mediate between sinful man and God, in order to bring the sinner close to God. God intended to sanctify (make holy) the nation of Israel so that they could be priests to the world. He would place them where they could have the greatest exposure, and bless them to such an extent that the whole world would take notice.

In this covenant God gave the most detailed exposition of His requirements. "The Lord… wrote on the tablets the words of the covenant, the Ten Commandments" (Exodus 34:28). He also gave His law in a more concise form, quoted by Jesus nearly 1,500 years later—"You shall love the Lord your God with all your heart, with all your soul, and with all your strength" and "you shall love your neighbor as yourself"

---

873 Genesis 12:7,8, 13:18.

874 God's demand that Abraham sacrifice his son Isaac led to one of the most powerful pictures of the sacrifice of Christ—Isaac was Abraham's "only beloved Son," God provided a substitute for the one condemned to die, and by faith Isaac was resurrected from the dead (Genesis 22, Hebrews 11:17-19).

---

875 The Bible never actually uses the phrase "old covenant," but the fact that a "new covenant" is mentioned implies that there must be an old one. See Hebrews 8:13.

(Deuteronomy 6:5, Leviticus 19:8). He also gave an expanded version, the "law of Moses," which gave details of how the law would apply to an agricultural nation of former slaves who were being established as a theocracy in the midst of hostile, heathen nations.

In one of the greatest blunders of all time, the people, awestruck by the overwhelming presence of God as he thundered out the Ten Commandments, told Moses that they did not want to hear the voice of God anymore, but that he should "go near and hear all that the Lord our God may say, and tell us all that the Lord our God says to you, and we will hear and do it." (Deuteronomy 5:27). Not realizing the absolute holiness the law required, or the abject sinfulness of the human heart, they totally miscalculated their own inability to meet the requirements of the law.

God had anticipated this, and along with the law he gave the third element, the provision for sin in the sacrificial system—"An altar of earth you shall make for Me, and you shall sacrifice on it your burnt offerings and your peace offerings, your sheep and your oxen. In every place where I record My name I will come to you, and I will bless you" (Exodus 20:25). These sacrifices, a "shadow" of the true sacrifice and ministry of Christ, made it possible for the sinful children of Israel to be acceptable to a holy God—"I will set My tabernacle [the place of sacrifice] among you and My soul shall not abhor you" (Leviticus 26:11).

The sign of the covenant was the Sabbath—"Therefore the children of Israel shall keep the Sabbath...as a perpetual covenant. It is a sign between Me and the children of Israel forever" (Exodus 31:16, 17).[876] It was a sign of the blessing God wanted to give the world through His chosen people—that they would be a "holy nation" and a "kingdom of priests"—"My Sabbaths you shall keep...It is a sign between Me and you...that I am the Lord who sanctifies you" (Exodus 31:13).[877]

The two reasons God gave for keeping the Sabbath show why it is an appropriate sign of His covenant. "Remember the Sabbath day...for in six days the Lord made the heavens and the earth" (Exodus 20:8-11). The Sabbath is a memorial of God's creation, and for hopelessly sinful human beings, holiness requires an act of creation ("Create in me a clean heart, O God" Psalms 51:10). Holiness is not an alteration, modification or improvement of the present condition, but requires creative activity on the part of God that is as miraculous as His word which said "Let there be light' and there was light" (Genesis 1:3).

The Ten Commandments are repeated in Deuteronomy and are nearly identical except for the reason for keeping the Sabbath. "Observe the Sabbath day, to keep it holy...and remember that you were a slave in the land of Egypt and the Lord your God brought you out from there by a mighty hand and by an outstretched arm, therefore the Lord your God commanded you to keep the Sabbath day" (Deuteronomy 5:12-15). Thus the Sabbath is also a memorial of redemption, symbolizing the rest that God's people enjoy when they are no longer slaves of sin. Far from being a symbol of human effort or "works of the law," the Sabbath symbolizes God's creation and redemption, which are the only way that God's people can be a "kingdom of priests and a holy nation."

Right from the start the children of Israel broke the covenant. Even while Moses was on Mt. Sinai receiving the stone tablets of the Ten Commandments, the people were at the base of

---

876 "Hallow my Sabbaths and they will be a sign between Me and you, that you may know that I am the Lord your God" (Ezekiel 20:20).

877 "Sanctify" is the Hebrew word *"qadash"* which means to consecrate or set apart as holy.

the mountain crafting a golden calf and engaging in licentious worship (Exodus 32:5,6). Their long and continual history of rebellion followed by repentance when they suffered the painful consequences of their sin showed that they had not really entered into the covenant that God had made with them. And so Moses, just before he died, made a "revised version" of the covenant, which really captured the essence of the "old covenant" mentality of the children of Israel.

"These are the words of the covenant which the Lord commanded Moses to make with the children of Israel in the land of Moab, *besides* the covenant which He made with them in Horeb" (Deuteronomy 29:1). We see from this verse that this covenant was not just a repetition of the Sinai (Horeb) covenant—it recognized the reality that they had not kept His covenant. The "words of the covenant" included highly detailed instructions governing every area of life (eg. Deuteronomy 10-26). They were to be hand-written on large stones ("You shall set up for yourselves large stones, and whitewash them with lime. You shall write on them all the words of this law" Deuteronomy 27:2,3,8). Half of the tribes of Israel were to stand on Mount Gerizim to pronounce a blessing on those who obeyed the law ("All these blessings shall come upon you and overtake you, because you obey the voice of the Lord your God"). The other half of the tribes were to stand on Mount Ebal and pronounce a curse on those who disobeyed ("Cursed is the one who does not confirm all the words of this law") (Deuteronomy 27:11- 28:68).

The blessings (abundance of children, animals, food, victory over enemies, financial and national success) were strong positive incentives to obey. The curses, on the other hand, were very strong negative incentives to be feared—poverty, defeat, disease, famine, national ruin and being scattered all over the world where they would be persecuted, sold into slavery and killed. "All

nations would say, 'Why has the Lord done so to this land? What does the heat of this great anger mean?' Then people would say, 'Because they have forsaken the covenant of the Lord God of their fathers, which He made with them when He brought them out of the land of Egypt; For they went and served other gods, and worshiped them" (Deuteronomy 29:24-26).

This was a performance-based covenant that reflected the people's focus on externals—it did not include the Ten Commandments written and spoken by God, nor was it placed inside the ark of the covenant, and it condemned their rebellious refusal to enter into His heart covenant. "So it was, when Moses had completed writing the words of this law in a book, when they were finished, that Moses commanded...'Take this book of the law, and put it beside the ark of the covenant of the Lord your God, that it may be there as *a witness against you*; for I know your rebellion and your stiff neck...I know that after my death you will become utterly corrupt and turn aside from the way which I have commanded you" (Deuteronomy 31:24-29).

Essentially this covenant spelled out the consequences of not entering into the true heart covenant that God always wanted for His people. Although this is the kind of covenant that the legalistic human nature wants to enter into, God cannot accept this as anything more than a temporary arrangement on the way to a true covenant of love, and in fact it was this covenant that was "nailed to the cross" (Colossians 2:14).[878] But even in the midst of this harsh covenant, God

---

878 No doubt it was the Moab covenant that the Apostle Paul had in mind when he wrote in Colossians 2:14, "Having wiped out the handwriting of requirements that was against us, which was contrary to us. And He has taken it out of the way, having nailed it to the cross." Notice that the covenant at Moab was handwritten on a whitewashed stone and was to be beside the ark as "a witness against (them)." Jesus on the Cross fully repudiated obedience as a means of salvation.

pleaded for the hearts of His people—"For this commandment which I command you today is not too mysterious for you, nor is it far off…but the word is very near you, in your mouth and in your heart, that you may do it…I have set before you life and death, blessing and cursing; therefore choose life, that both you and your descendants may live, that you may love the Lord your God, that you may obey His voice, and that you may cling to Him, for He is your life and the length of your days" (Deuteronomy 30:11-20).

The New Covenant

The new covenant was given because God's people had not entered into the covenant He gave them at Sinai. The new covenant was basically the same as the old—it is "the everlasting covenant"—but it must be an internal spiritual reality rather than an external code of behavior.

Even in the Old Testament period God announced that He was going to make a new covenant. "Behold, the days are coming when I will make a new covenant with the house of Israel and the house of Judah" (Jeremiah 31:31). It was not that God had made a faulty covenant, but His people were faulty in their understanding and keeping of the covenant. "For if that first covenant had been faultless, then no place would have been sought for a second. Because *finding fault with them* He says: 'Behold, the days are coming, says the Lord, when I will make a new covenant" (Hebrews 8:7,8).

The surprising thing is that the new covenant is almost exactly the same as the "old covenant." God still designs that His people shall be a blessing to the world ("God…made us sufficient as ministers of the new covenant," 2Corinthians 3:6), although His people now include anyone who is willing. Peter, writing to believers scattered all over the world, including Gentile believers "who once were not a people but are now the people of God," said "You are a chosen generation, a royal priesthood, a holy nation, His own special people, *that you may proclaim the praises of Him* who called you out of darkness into His marvelous light" (1Peter 2:9,10).

Again, His requirement is His law, but instead of being written on stone tablets, "This is the covenant that I will make with the house of Israel after those days,' says the Lord, 'I will put my laws in their mind and write them on their hearts" (Hebrews 8:10). The big difference is that there is no longer a middleman; God will not talk to "Moses" and then have the prophet or priest talk to His people. In the new covenant there is direct interaction between God and His people. "I will be their God, and they shall be My people. None of them shall teach his neighbor, and none his brother, saying, 'Know the Lord,' for all shall know Me, from the least of them to the greatest of them" (Hebrews 8:10,11). The requirements of the new covenant are to be internalized. "God… made us sufficient as ministers of the new covenant, not of the letter but of the Spirit; for the letter kills, but the Spirit gives life…We all, with unveiled face, beholding as in a mirror the glory of the Lord, are being transformed into the same image from glory to glory, just as by the Spirit of the Lord" (2Corinthians 3:6,18).

The new covenant, just as the old, makes provision for the breaking of God's law, but with a reality rather than a shadow. In the old covenant the sacrifices pointed forward to the great sacrifice Christ would make on the Cross. In the new covenant the sacrifice has already been accomplished. Instead of looking forward by faith, we now look back by faith to the "one sacrifice [offered] for sins forever" (Hebrews 10:12). As the writer of Hebrews makes clear, it was this sacrifice which made effective all the previous sacrifices that had prefigured it[879]

Naturally, the fulfilling of the great sacrifice of Christ negated the need for the "shadow" sacrifices, as well as the priests and the ceremonies connected with them. "For the law, having a shadow of the good things to come and not the very image of the things, can never with these same sacrifices, which they offer continually year by year, make those who approach perfect...but in those sacrifices there is a reminder of sins every year" (Hebrews 10:1,2). "For the priesthood being changed, of necessity there is also a change of the law" (Hebrews 7:12).[880] In the new covenant, rather than a sacrifice, there is a memorial ceremony, the Lord's Supper, which symbolizes what Christ has done.[881] "This cup is the new covenant in My blood. This do as often as you drink it, in remembrance of Me. For as often as you eat this bread and drink this cup, you proclaim the Lord's death till He comes" (1 Corinthians 11:25,26).

The New Testament does not clearly say what the sign of the new covenant is.[882] However, the fact that the new covenant offers the same blessing to the world through God's chosen people (who are now the church), has the same law (but written on the heart instead of tables of stone), and has the same sacrifice (but as a reality rather than a shadow), suggests that the Sabbath, with a deeper spiritual meaning, is also the sign of the new covenant.

This is supported by the third and fourth chapters of Hebrews, in which God's rest on the Sabbath is presented as a continuing reality for those who believe the gospel. "Therefore, since a promise remains of entering His rest, let us fear lest any of you seem to have come short of it...For we who have believed do enter that rest...There remains therefore a rest (Greek *Sabbitismos*, the keeping of the Sabbath) for the people of God. For he who has entered His rest has himself also ceased from his works as God did from His" (Hebrews 4:1-3, 9,10). With the law written in the heart, the Sabbath becomes a true sign of God's creative and redemptive work that he has accomplished and is accomplishing in us through the sacrifice, resurrection and ministry of Jesus. The new covenant Christian "has ceased from his works," in other words, his own futile efforts to make himself acceptable, to live a holy life and to minister to a lost world. Instead he allows God to "work in [him] both to will and to do for His good pleasure" (Philippians 2:13) so "that the righteous requirements of the law might be fulfilled in us who do not walk according to the flesh but according to the Spirit" (Romans 8:4). Although the new covenant Christian does labor diligently, his labor is directed at knowing God—"Let us know, let us pursue the knowledge of the Lord," "Let us therefore make every effort to enter that

---

879 "He is the Mediator of the new covenant, by means of death, for the redemption of the transgressions under the first covenant" (Hebrews 9:15).

880 The context of this section in Hebrews makes it clear that this is not the Ten Commandment law that is changed, but the law concerning the establishment and duties of the Levitical priesthood.

881 The Catholic Mass, which is considered to be a repetition of the sacrifice of Christ, denies the reality that "we have been sanctified through the offering of the body of Jesus Christ once for all" (Hebrews 10:10).

882 The Lord's Supper is not the sign of the covenant, because it is the memorial of the sacrifice, which was the third element of the covenant.

rest" (Hosea 6:3, Hebrews 4:11 NIV).[883]

The new covenant is called the everlasting covenant, essentially the same as all the rest of the covenants—"May the God of peace...make you complete in every good work to do His will... through the blood of the everlasting covenant" (Hebrews 13:20,21). It was this covenant that was brought into focus when "the temple of God was opened in heaven, and the ark of His covenant was seen in His temple" (Revelation 11:19).

In the book of Daniel, Satan's enmity against the covenant was manifested through the activity of the "King of the North" who "shall be moved against the holy covenant; so he shall do damage...and show regard for those who forsake the holy covenant...He shall corrupt with flattery those who do wickedly against the covenant" (Daniel 11:28, 30, 32). The "King of the North" who wars against the covenant turns out to be none other than "the beast," whose destructive activity is featured in Revelation 13.

The climax of the great controversy theme of Revelation is found in chapters 12-14. There it is seen that the four elements of the everlasting covenant are the great issues of the final struggle, with each coming under fierce attack by the dragon, "that serpent of old" who hates Christ's people and the message they have for the world, His law, His sacrifice, and the sign of His covenant.

---

883 In recent years a "new covenant" theology has been developed by dispensationist theologians (those who believe that God has a different plan for the salvation of people at different periods or "dispensations"). They theorize a radical disconnect between the way of salvation for the Jews during the Old Testament period (based on keeping the law) and salvation in the New Testament (only believe). This theology ignores the fact that salvation in the Old Testament was also by grace, since all the children of believing Abraham will be saved through faith in the Savior to come, just as New Testament believers are saved by faith in the Savior who has come.

Today there are some who call themselves Christians who follow the old covenant and others who follow the spurious "new covenant." These are in contrast to the true new covenant Christians. For example, many Christians perform ritual prayers and hear the scriptures as a part of a liturgical ceremony which "saves" them (old covenant). The "new covenant" Christian knows that he "doesn't have to" pray or read the scriptures in order to be saved, so he does so when he "feels like it." The true new covenant Christian knows that prayer and the word of God are the life of his soul, so they are a regular part of his life whether he feels like it or not. The old covenant fundamentalist keeps standards of diet, dress and behavior because these are God's requirements and if he breaks them he will "go to hell." The "new covenant" Christian "knows" that he is not saved by behavior so he doesn't worry about rules and standards. The true new covenant Christian doesn't want anything in his life that will get in the way of the closest possible relationship with the Lord or misrepresent his Savior in any way, and this is reflected in his diet, dress and behavior. Some old covenant "believers" distribute books and give Bible studies because this is a necessary part of their "salvation." The "new covenant" Christian "knows" that he is not saved by witnessing so he doesn't worry about it. The true new covenant Christian knows that spreading the Gospel is Jesus' highest priority, so it becomes his highest priority too. And so the understanding (or misunderstanding) of the covenant is played out in every phase of the Christian life.

Appendix 10
The Abomination of Desolation and Daniel 12

The abomination of desolation is one of the major signs given by Jesus to help His disciples recognize and understand the final events. He said, "Therefore when you see the abomination of desolation spoken of by Daniel the prophet, standing in the holy place (whoever reads, let him understand), then let those who are in Judea flee to the mountains...For then there will be great tribulation, such as has not been since the beginning of the world until this time, no, nor ever shall be" (Matthew 24:15-21).

Jesus here refers to the "great tribulation" (called the "time of trouble" by Daniel) that

is mentioned in Daniel chapter 12.[884] Daniel

---

884 Although some commentators have insisted that the primary application of the great tribulation of Matthew 24:21 is the 1,260 years of papal persecution from AD 538 until 1798, there are problems with this interpretation. 1) Jesus said this tribulation would be greater than any other "since the beginning of the world until this time, no nor ever shall be." The "time of trouble" of Daniel 12:1 is also the greatest "since there was a nation even to that time" and is clearly just before the Second Coming when God's people "shall be delivered" and when "those who sleep in the dust shall awake" (the resurrection). The fact that both are the greatest trouble or tribulation of all time rules out their being different events, so both take place just before the Second Coming. 2) The people who saw the sign of the great tribulation (the abomination of desolation, Matthew 24:15) were to flee for their lives so as not to be trapped by sudden developments. Although this kind of flight could apply to the tribulation connected with the destruction of Jerusalem or to the final time of trouble, it could hardly apply to the papal persecution which developed gradually over a period of hundreds of years, 3) The prophecy continues, specifying that "immediately after the tribulation of those days the sun will be darkened and the moon will not give its light; the stars will fall from heaven, and the powers of the heavens will be shaken. Then the sign of the Son of Man will appear in heaven." (Matt. 24:29,30). It has been claimed that these signs were fulfilled by the darkening of the sun and moon on May 19, 1780 and the falling of the stars on November 13, 1833. But this interpretation is problematic for two reasons: First of all, Jesus presents the signs as coming in quick succession (sun and moon will be darkened, stars will fall, powers of heaven will be shaken, and *then* the sign of the Son of man will appear in heaven). There is no sense that this is a process that takes place over the span of more than 230 years. Moreover, Jesus specified that the signs would begin "immediately *after* the tribulation of those days," whereas the dark day took place 18 years *before* the tribulation ended in 1798 (see 13: *The Deadly Wound*). Thus the main application of these signs is at the end of the great tribulation that takes place just before the Second Coming of Christ.

describes in chapter 11 a war between the King of the North and the King of the South that spans more than 2,500 years, from the time of the Persian Empire until the "time of the end" when there will be a final vicious struggle. "At that time Michael [Jesus][885] shall stand up...and *there shall be a time of trouble such as never was since there was a nation, even to that time*. And at that time your people shall be delivered, every one who is found written in the book. And many of those who sleep in the dust of the earth shall awake, some to everlasting life" (Daniel 12:1,2). Daniel's linking of the "time of trouble such as never was" to the resurrection shows that the abomination of desolation that Jesus referred to, which was a signal for God's people to "flee to the mountains," and which would come just before the "great tribulation," takes place during the "time of the end" just before the Second Coming of Christ and the resurrection of the just.

However, if we compare Matthew 24 with the parallel passage in Luke 21 we find not only a clue as to what the abomination of desolation is, but also that it applies to more than one event. Jesus said, "But when you see Jerusalem surrounded by armies, then know that its desolation is near. Then let those who are in Judea flee to the mountains...for there will be great distress in the land and wrath upon this people, and they will fall by the edge of the sword, and be led away captive into all nations. And Jerusalem will be trampled by Gentiles until the times of the Gentiles are fulfilled" (Luke 21:20-24). This verse obviously talks about the destruction of Jerusalem that took place in 70 AD. Compare it with Matthew 24:15,16 (See Table App10.1).

Table App10.1

"When you see Jerusalem surrounded by armies, then know that its desolation is near. Then let those who are in Judea flee to the mountains..." Luke 21:20,21	"Therefore when you see the abomination of desolation....standing in the holy place..., then let those who are in Judea flee to the mountains" Matthew 24: 15,16

---

885 See 12:7-9 *Michael Casts Satan Out*

In these verses we see that in some sense "Jerusalem surrounded by armies" and threatened with destruction is equivalent to "the abomination of desolation." We also see that there are at least two chronological contexts: the destruction of Jerusalem in AD 70 and the great time of trouble at the time of the end. In other words, Jesus seems to be indicating that we should look for multiple applications in the interpretation of the abomination of desolation.[886]

Jesus said that we should recognize "the abomination of desolation spoken of by the prophet Daniel." In the book of Daniel the abomination of desolation is mentioned three times.

1. The abomination of desolation is mentioned in Daniel 9 within the context of the 70 weeks (490 years) of probation that was given to the Jewish nation—"Seventy weeks are determined for your people and for your holy city" (Daniel 9:24). This probationary period ended with the "Messiah, the Prince" (Jesus) who was to be "cut off, but not for Himself" (on the cross He was "cut off" for sinful humanity). "He [the Messiah] shall confirm a covenant with many for

one week;[887] but in the middle of the week He shall bring an end to sacrifice and offering" (through His sacrifice Jesus brought the sacrificial system to an end). "And the people of the prince who is to come [the Romans] shall destroy the city and the sanctuary…and in their place shall be an abomination that desolates" (Daniel 9:27 NRSV). In these verses the abomination of desolation is linked to the destructive judgments which the Jews suffered after their rejection of Christ, particularly the destruction of the temple and Jerusalem by the Romans in AD 70, as predicted by Jesus in Luke 21:20. For further explanation of the 70 week prophecy see appendix 4.

2. The second reference to the abomination of desolation is within the detailed outline of the history of the great war between the "King of the North" and the "King of the South" in Daniel 11 (see 9: *Kings of the North and South* and Appendix 3 for details). Briefly, the Kings of the North and South are two opposing forces, both enemies of the people of God. They appeared after the division of the Greek Empire established by Alexander the Great (Daniel 11:3,4), with the northern Seleucid kingdom (in present Syria and Turkey) and the southern Ptolemy kingdom in Egypt. As the prophecy progresses, the King of the North evolves into the Roman Empire and later the papal Roman Empire, opposed by the southern Muslim empires. God's true people, first in Palestine, later primarily in Europe, were caught between these opposing forces. As the stream of history reaches the Middle Ages the angel explains, "And forces shall be mustered by

---

886 Multiple applications are also expected because of the nature of the question Jesus was answering. In response to Jesus' statement that the temple would be destroyed, the disciples had asked, when will these things be? And what will be the sign of Your coming, and of the end of the age?" The disciples were actually asking three questions, about events that they mistakenly assumed would happen at about the same time.

1. "When will these things be?" "These things" referred to that which He had been talking about, the destruction of the temple and Jerusalem in 70 AD by the Roman army under Titus.

2. "What will be the sign of your coming" Here the disciples were asking for signs of the Second Coming of Christ.

3. "[What will be the sign of] the End of the Age?" In other passages Jesus used the phrase "the End of the Age" to refer to that last period of time when the angels would judge and separate the righteous from the wicked (the investigative judgment).

Jesus gave them a blended reply that answered all three questions at once—in other words, there are three applications to the prophecy Jesus gave in Matthew 24, including three applications of the abomination of desolation. See 10: *Clues in Matthew 24* for a more detailed examination of this prophecy.

---

887 This "week" (seven years in prophetic time) included the 3 ½ years of Christ's ministry plus the 3 ½ years up to the stoning of Stephen, during which the gospel was offered exclusively to the Jews. At the end of their probationary period "a great persecution arose against the church…and those who were scattered went everywhere preaching the word" (Acts 8:1-4). The Jews had sealed their rejection of the Messiah and lost their chance to be God's chosen people. For further explanation of the 70 week prophecy see Appendix 4.

him [the King of the North], and they shall defile the sanctuary fortress; then they shall take away the daily sacrifices, and place there the abomination of desolation" (Daniel 11:31). The abomination of desolation mentioned here is the persecution of true Christians who would not accept the papal system, culminating in the Inquisition.

3. The third reference is in Daniel 12. In response to the final attacks of the King of the North (Daniel 11:40-45), Michael (Christ) "stands up" (finishes his work of mediation) which ushers in "a time of trouble such as never was since there was a nation" (Daniel 12:1). "At that time [God's] people shall be delivered" and "many of those who sleep in the dust of the earth shall awake" (the Second Coming and resurrection) (v. 2). Daniel "heard," but "did not understand" and asked the angel, "My lord, what shall be the end of these things?" (v. 8). The angel informed him that "from the time that the daily sacrifice is taken away, and the abomination of desolation is set up, there shall be one thousand two hundred and ninety days. But blessed is he who waits, and comes to the one thousand three hundred and thirty-five days" (vs. 11,12).

This controversial verse deserves careful study. It mentions the abomination of desolation; is it referring to the abomination of Daniel 9 and Luke 21 that took place when the pagan Roman Army surrounded Jerusalem and the holy temple, threatening them with destruction? Is it referring to the abomination of Daniel 11:31 in which the Papacy of the Middle Ages used the power of the state (the Inquisition) to persecute the "remnant" of believers? Or does it refer to the abomination of desolation that Jesus said would appear just before the "great tribulation such as has not been since the beginning of the world" (Matthew 24:21)? Or could it refer to all of them?

There is some evidence that could link the abomination of desolation and the prophetic periods of 1,290 and 1,335 days with the destruction of Jerusalem. As mentioned above, Jesus in Matthew 24 and Luke 21 linked the abomination of desolation that was the signal for Christians to flee for their lives with "Jerusalem surrounded by armies."[888] In the war that resulted in the destruction of Jerusalem, the city was first surrounded by armies in October-November AD 66 when the forces of the Roman commander Cestius besieged the city in response to rioting and insurrection by Jewish zealots (Josephus *Wars* 2:19:4). But "Cestius was not conscious either how the besieged despaired of success…he retired from the city, without any reason in the world" (Josephus *Wars* 2:19:7). The zealots pursued his troops, inflicting heavy losses; but this retreat gave those Christians who remembered the words of Jesus an opportunity to "flee to the mountains." The next year general Vespasian and his son Titus led armies against the Jews, first conquering Galilee and the Judean towns and cities and finally putting Jerusalem under siege. Infighting among various factions of zealots, which resulted in the burning of the food supplies within Jerusalem, led to indescribable suffering and the city finally fell in July, AD 70. The fall of Jerusalem was approximately 1,335 days from when it was first surrounded by armies in November 66, which could be considered a fulfillment of the 1,335 days that were predicted to follow the abomination of desolation in Daniel 12:11,12.[889] This scenario would make the abomination of desolation the appearance of the army of Cestius outside the city walls of Jerusalem.

---

888 Matthew 24:15-21, Luke 21:20,21.

889 The detailed account of the siege of Jerusalem by Josephus is not linked to many specific dates so the exact significance of the 1,290 days is a matter of speculation. It could possibly refer to the burning of the food supplies which resulted in "the power of the holy people [being] completely shattered," followed by "all these things [being] finished." (Daniel 12:7). The blessing pronounced on "he who waits and comes to the one thousand three hundreds and thirty-five days" could simply mean that anyone who did not die in the siege at least saved his life when the city fell to the Romans.

There is also a possible application of Daniel 12:11,12 to the medieval Papacy. First of all, the major parallel prophecies of Daniel 2, 7 and 8 all focus their greatest attention on the Papacy (the legs of clay and iron of the image of Daniel 2, the "little" horn of Daniel 7 and the horn of Daniel 8).

Moreover, the two time periods of Daniel 12:11,12 (1,290 days and 1,335 days) could be extensions of the "time, times and half a time" of verses 6 and 7, which refers to the period of papal oppression in the Middle Ages: "And one said to the man clothed in linen who was above the waters of the river, 'How long shall the fulfillment of these wonders be?' Then I heard the man clothed in linen…[He] swore by Him who lives forever, that it shall be for a time, times and half a time; and when the power of the holy people has been completely shattered, all these things shall be finished" (Daniel 12:6,7). The period "time, times and half a time" also appears in Daniel 7:25; the "little horn" (the medieval Papacy) "shall speak pompous words against the Most High, shall persecute the saints of the Most High, and shall intend to change times and law. Then the saints shall be given into his hand for a time and times and half a time." This period is the same as the 1,260 days, time, times and half a time, and 42 months of Revelation 12:6, 12:14 and 13:5. These all refer to the long centuries during the Middle Ages when the Papacy controlled the nations of Europe and used them to persecute the saints (see 12: *1,260 days*).

There are also linguistic links between the 1,260 day (and possibly by extension the 1,290 and 1,335 day) periods in Daniel 12 and the activity of the medieval Papacy. In Daniel 12:6 the angel asked, "How long shall the fulfillment of these wonders be? (the answer was "time, times and half a time"). A slight variation of the Hebrew word "wonders" (*pele*) is also found in Daniel 11:36 "Then the king [of the North, the Papacy] shall do according to his own will: he

shall exalt and magnify himself above every god, shall speak *marvelous things* against the God of gods." The same word is found in Daniel 8:24 "His [the medieval Papacy] power shall be mighty, but not by his own power; He shall destroy *fearfully*." Both of these verses refer to the unprecedented activity of the medieval Papacy, so when in Daniel 12:6 the angel asked, "How long shall the fulfillment of *these wonders* be?" the answer "time, times and half a time" could refer to the destructive "wonders" of the medieval Papacy, which not only persecuted the saints but also destroyed the true understanding of God and His plan of salvation.

Just a few verses later in Daniel 12:11 the angel informs Daniel, "From the time that *the daily sacrifice is taken away, and the abomination of desolation is set up*, there shall be one thousand two hundred and ninety days." There is a clear linguistic parallel here with the medieval papal activity in Daniel 11:31, "And forces shall be mustered by him [the King of the North or Papacy], and they shall defile the sanctuary fortress; then *they shall take away the daily sacrifices and place there the abomination of desolation*."

Historically the three time periods have been considered by some commentators to have an applications related to the medieval Papacy. The first and most basic time period (time, times and half a time or 1,260 prophetic days) refers to the 1,260 years of papal political and military supremacy. This could be considered to begin in AD 538 when the Byzantine armies of Justinian expelled the last Arian tribe from Rome, freeing the Papacy to expand its base of power. An important marker of the end of papal supremacy is 1798, exactly 1,260 years later, when Pope Pius VI was arrested by the armies of the French Revolution.

"From the time that the daily sacrifice is taken away and the abomination of desolation is set up, there shall be one thousand two hundred an ninety days" (Daniel 12:11). If this period is considered to overlap the 1,260 years, but starting 30 "days" (years) earlier, it would begin in AD 508. In that year Clovis the Frank made Roman Catholicism the official religion of his kingdom, the first union of church and state for the Roman Catholic Church. The Franks went on to become France, the "first son" and main protector and enforcer of the medieval Papacy.

"Blessed is he who waits, and comes to the one thousand three hundred and thirty-five days" (Daniel 12:12). If this period begins simultaneously with the 1,290 days (years) in AD 508, it extends to 1843-44, which is the date of the termination of the 2,300 evenings/mornings of Daniel 8:14. At this time the judgment began, "a judgment [that] was made in favor of the saints of the Most High, and the time came for the saints to possess the kingdom" (Daniel 7:23, see 3: *Day of Atonement, 2300 Days*).

According to this scenario, the abomination of desolation of Daniel 12:11, also referred to by Jesus in Matthew 24:15, is the conversion of Clovis the Frank.

The previous two applications of the 1,290 and 1,335 day prophecies (fall of Jerusalem and medieval Papacy), while conceivable, do not seem very convincing. There is evidence that the primary application of the two time periods of Daniel 12:11,12 is to the very end of time. Most importantly, Jesus mentioned the "abomination of desolation, spoken of by Daniel the prophet" as a sign just before the "great tribulation, such as has not been since the beginning of the world until this time, no, nor ever shall be" (Matthew 24:15,21). There is no other mention of the abomination of desolation in the book of Daniel besides that in Daniel 12:12 that could possibly have its context during the final "great tribulation."

Moreover, the angel told Daniel in 12:13, "You shall rest, and will arise to your inheritance at the end of the days," referring to his resurrection at the coming of Christ. The phrase "at the end of the days" uses the same word for days (*yome*) that is used in verses 11 and 12 (1,290 days, 1,335 days). This word is not used for the prophetic time periods in Daniel in which a day represents a year ("Time, times and half a time" Daniel 7:25, 12:7, "Two thousand three hundred evenings and mornings," Daniel 8:14, "seventy weeks" Daniel 9:24). Although "the end of the days" could conceivably refer to the end of the age, it is not used in this way elsewhere in Daniel[890] and the implication is that Daniel would "arise" at the end of the 1,290 and/or 1,335 days just mentioned in the previous verse.

Daniel had heard two angels having a conversation in which they asked, "How long shall the fulfillment of these wonders be?" with the answer, "a time, times, and half a time." But then Daniel, who "heard [but] did not understand" asked "My lord, what shall be the end of these things?"(v. 8). We should note that Daniel had a different interest from that of the angels. They asked about "these wonders" which, as we saw above, probably refers to the activity of the medieval Papacy. But Daniel wanted to know about "the end of these things." The Hebrew word translated "the end" (*achariyth*) can be translated "after part," "latter part" or "latter time." Thus it appears that Daniel was most interested in the final portion of the prophecy, when "many shall run to and fro and knowledge shall increase," when "those who... turn many to righteousness [shall shine] like the stars forever and ever," when "Michael stands up" and "many of those who sleep in the dust of the earth shall awake," and when his "people shall be delivered" (Daniel 12:1-4). After telling

---

890 In other passages Daniel refers to "the end" rather than "the end of the days," for example, "For He is the living God, and steadfast forever; His kingdom is the one which shall not be destroyed, And His dominion *shall endure to the end* (Daniel 6:26), "For at the appointed time the end shall be" Daniel 8:19), "for the end will still be at the appointed time (Daniel 11:27),

him that the words "are sealed till the time of the end" (v. 9) the angel informed him, "from the time that the daily sacrifice is taken away, and the abomination of desolation is set up, there shall be one thousand two hundred and ninety days. But blessed is he who waits, and comes to the one thousand three hundred and thirty-five days" (v. 11,12) The implication is that these are time periods that would take place at "the end of these things." This interpretation is supported by the fact that individuals could "wait and come to" (v. 12) the fulfillment of these periods, which they could not if they applied only to the long centuries of the Middle Ages.

The natural question would be, if these time periods refer to events still future, what are they? Again the key is in the starting point: "And from the time that the daily sacrifice is taken away, and the abomination of desolation is set up, there shall be one thousand two hundred and ninety days. Blessed is he who waits, and comes to the one thousand three hundred and thirty-five days" (Daniel 12:11,12). The taking away of the daily sacrifice is mentioned explicitly in Daniel 11:31 and most clearly in Daniel 8:11,12: "He [the Roman Catholic "horn" power] even exalted himself as high as the Prince of the host [Jesus Christ]; and by him the daily sacrifices were taken away and the place of His sanctuary was cast down. Because of transgression, an army was given over to the horn to oppose the daily sacrifices and he cast truth down to the ground. He did all this and prospered." The taking away of the daily sacrifice here refers to the false doctrinal system developed by the papal church that nullified the sacrifice and mediation of Christ (see 14: *The Daily Sacrifice*). The Protestant Reformation restored to a great extent the true teaching about Christ and the righteousness by faith that we have in Him, but Revelation 13 predicts that Protestant America will create an "image to the beast," in other words, Protestants will adopt the false teachings and practices of Catholicism at the end of time that will again obscure the true gospel of Christ's sacrifice and mediation.

Besides the taking away of the daily sacrifice, the abomination of desolation is also a sign of the beginning of the two time periods of Daniel 12:11,12. The clearest picture of what the abomination of desolation entails is connected with the destruction of Jerusalem (Daniel 9:27, Luke 21:20). There we see that it is the threat of violence posed by the enemies of God's people—submit or perish. This was also the case in the Middle Ages; the Papacy "[took] away the daily sacrifice" by developing a system of false doctrine and then "set up the abomination of desolation" by persecuting those who refused to submit to the papal authority, culminating in the Inquisition.[891] This will also be the case in the final crisis when the "beast coming out of the earth" will create an "image of the beast" and then use coercive force (the mark of the beast and the death decree, Revelation 13:14-17) to try

to force everyone to "worship the image of the beast" (v. 15).

Will it be possible to recognize the final abomination of desolation and thus know the beginning of the time period of 1,290 days (and presumably by extension the 1,335 days)? In the application of the prophecy to the destruction of Jerusalem it was possible to know when Jerusalem was "surrounded by armies," and although the Christians may not have been able to predict exactly what was going to happen and when, they did know when to flee so as to save their lives. The abomination of the papal period was a part of prophetic time, came on gradually, and has been identified only in hindsight. The abomination of the last days will be more like the destruction of Jerusalem in that it will involve literal time and dramatic, rapid events. The most obvious events are those found in Revelation 13:11-18, specifically, the image, mark and number of the beast and the death decree against those who refuse to worship the image of the beast. No doubt God will give His people wisdom at that time, not to predict the date of the coming of Christ (which Jesus assures us is not to be known, Matthew 24:36), but in order to recognize the signs, to know what to do and especially when to flee, and to be able to take heart that the great tribulation is almost over and Jesus will soon appear.

---

891 Some interpreters insist that the abomination of Daniel 12:11 and Daniel 11:31 ("They shall take away the daily sacrifices, and place there the abomination of desolation") is of a different nature than that of Daniel 9:27, contending that since the abomination is closely associated with the taking away of the "daily" (*tamid*), that the abomination of desolation is the false doctrinal system that replaced the daily. But the fact that the two are closely associated does not mean that one is the opposite of the other. The daily was taken away by the false doctrines that were established; in other words, the taking away of the daily was the establishment of false doctrine. True doctrine was not first taken away and then replaced by false doctrine.

The meaning of prophetic language should be consistently applied unless there is clear evidence of a change of meaning, which in this case there is not. This implies that the abomination of desolation of the Middle Ages was analogous to the coercive power of the Romans that threatened God's people when Jerusalem was under siege. Thus the abomination of the Middle Ages would be the coercive state power that enforced the false doctrinal system that took away the daily sacrifice.

Further evidence is found in Daniel 8:13, which is closely related to Daniel 11:31. Instead of the *abomination of desolation* it refers to the *transgression of desolation*, using similar language: "How long will the vision be, concerning the daily sacrifices and the transgression of desolation?" The "transgression of desolation" in this verse makes reference to verse 12, "Because of transgression, an army was given over to the horn to oppose the daily sacrifices." Here we see that the transgression of desolation involves an army, implying coercive force to enforce the taking away of the daily. This links Daniel 8:13 (and the parallel 11:31) to the obvious military application of the abomination of desolation in Daniel 9:27 and to Luke 21:20, but does not support the idea of the transgression (or abomination) of desolation being a doctrinal system.

Finally, this theory can be tested by applying it to Jesus' statement in Matthew 24. "Therefore when you see [the false doctrinal system developed by the Roman Catholic Church in the Middle Ages], then let those who are in Judea flee to the mountains. Let him who is on the housetops not go down to take anything out of his house…And pray that your flight may not be in winter or on the Sabbath. For then there will be great tribulation, such as has not been since the beginning of the world until this time, no, nor ever shall be." The inadequacy of this interpretation is obvious. Whatever the abomination of desolation is, Jesus made it clear that it would be a sign so sudden and dramatic that Christians could recognize it and immediately flee from their homes leaving all their belongings behind. This does not describe a doctrinal system that developed over the course of hundreds of years, nor does it harmonize with medieval history if the abomination of desolation is considered to be the conversion of Clovis the Frank in AD 508.

Appendix 11
The Sea Beast and the Beasts Of Daniel 7

John saw a beast rising out of the sea in Revelation 13 that is the prototype for the final persecuting power in chapter 17. The beast from the sea was a terrifying composite of three ferocious animals, a leopard, a bear and a lion, and it had ten horns. These are the same animals which "came up from the sea" in the vision of Daniel 7. Daniel saw a lion with eagle's wings, a bear raised up on one side with three ribs in its mouth and a four-headed leopard with four wings. He then saw a fourth "dreadful and terrible" beast with iron teeth and ten horns. Adding all of the heads and horns of Daniel's four animals together yields the seven heads and ten horns of the beast that rises out of the sea in Revelation 13. This implies that the sea beast somehow embodies a combination of the characteristics of the animals of Daniel 7.

The vision of the four wild animals of Daniel 7 is itself parallel to the vision of Daniel 2, in which Nebuchadnezzar, the king of Babylon, saw an enormous image made of four different metals. In order to identify the beast from the sea of Revelation 13 it is necessary to understand Nebuchadnezzar's dream of the four-metal image, the parallels it has with the four animals of Daniel 7, and the relation that these four animals have with the beast from the sea.

Daniel was a member of the royal family of Judah and had been taken captive by the Babylonians where he was put in a school to learn to be a royal adviser ("the wise men, the astrologers, the magicians and the soothsayers" Daniel 2:27). One night Nebuchadnezzer, the king of Babylon, had a terrifying dream which he was unable to remember when he woke up. God enabled Daniel to see and to interpret the dream, which was of a giant image of a man with a golden head, silver chest, brass belly, iron legs, and feet of iron mixed with clay. Daniel explained that Nebuchadnezzer (as king of the Babylonian Empire) was the head of gold. "But after you shall arise another kingdom inferior to yours; then another, a third kingdom of bronze, which shall rule over all the earth. And the fourth kingdom shall be as strong as iron…that kingdom will break in pieces and crush all the others" (Daniel 2:39,40).

The fourth iron kingdom would eventually be divided—"As the toes of the feet were partly of iron and partly of clay, so the kingdom shall be partly strong and partly fragile…They will mingle with the seed of men; but they will not adhere to one another" (Daniel 2:42,43). In the grand finale, "A stone was cut out without hands, which struck the image on its feet of iron and clay, and broke them in pieces…The God of heaven will set up a kingdom which shall never be destroyed…It shall break in pieces and consume all these kingdoms, and it shall stand forever" (Daniel 2:34, 44).

This vision shows in outline form the history of the world empires that ruled over God's people from the time of Daniel when Babylon ruled until the end of time when God will set up His eternal kingdom. The vision portrays a seamless succession of empires, not a disjointed jumping from one time frame and geographical location to another. As such the identity of the kingdoms should be obvious from the facts of history.

The Wild Animals of Daniel 7

The metal image with its succession of empires is paralleled by the succession of wild animals that Daniel saw rising out of the sea in the vision of Daniel 7. A simple review of history in any encyclopedia reveals that the Babylonian Empire (the head of gold of chapter 2 or the lion of chapter 7) ruled the middle east from about 625-539 BC and its greatest king, Nebuchadnezzar, conquered Palestine and destroyed the Jewish temple. Stories of the Babylonian victory and rule over God's chosen people are found in the books of Jeremiah, Ezekiel, Daniel, 2Kings and 2Chronicles.

Babylon was defeated by the Medo-Persian Empire (the breast of silver, the bear) with Cyrus the Great as its first king in 539 BC. Stories about how the Persian Empire ruled over God's people are found in the books of Daniel, Esther, Nehemiah and Ezra. The Persian Empire was defeated at the battle of Arbela in 331 BC by the Greeks led by Alexander the Great. After his death the Greek Empire (the belly of brass, the leopard) was divided among his four generals (thus the leopard had four heads), with the divisions becoming rival Hellenistic kingdoms. Their rule was during the period between the Old and New Testaments, and is chronicled in the apocryphal books of Maccabees. The Hellenistic kingdoms were gradually defeated by the Romans (the legs of iron, the fourth terrible beast), which

"devoured, broke in pieces, and trampled."[892] The oppressive Roman rule, including its role in the crucifixion of Christ and persecution of the apostolic church, is found in the New Testament.

In the late third century the Roman Empire was divided into two halves (thus the image had two legs), the eastern empire, with its capital at Constantinople, and the western empire with its capital at Rome. In the fifth and sixth centuries the Western Roman Empire was overrun by barbarian tribes, who eventually became the countries of Europe. In a political sense, they were a continuation of Rome, although divided, and in the image this is represented by the fact that the iron continues in the feet, divided into ten toes.

But a new element is added—the iron is held together by clay. All the other kingdoms were represented by pure metals, so here the mixture of iron and clay represents a mixed, divided kingdom that is held together with something unusual. In several passages of scripture clay is used to represent God's people,[893] and in Jeremiah 18:4-6 clay represents God's people in religious apostasy. We can conclude that the feet and toes represent the continuation of the Roman Empire, but as a mixture of religious (clay) and political (iron) power, in other words, the "Holy Roman Empire."

This scenario correlates with the ten horns of the fourth fearsome beast of Daniel 7—"The ten horns are ten kings who shall arise from this kingdom" (Daniel 7:24). Note the seamless progression from the imperial Roman Empire to the ten-horns power. Also note that there is an unusual element among the ten horns—a "little" horn, "different from the first ones" which "shall rise after them" (vs. 25, 24).

In Daniel 7 the horns receive more attention than all of the other animals. Verse 24 shows that

---

892 Daniel 7:19.

893 Isaiah 64:8,9, Jeremiah 18:4-6, Lamentations 4:2, Romans 9:21.

these ten kingdoms[894] were not originally part of the Roman Empire, but came up later and became a part of it. This agrees perfectly with the history of the breakup of the Western Roman Empire. The empire came to an official end in AD 476 when the Germanic chieftain Odacer forced Romulus Augustulus, the last Roman emperor, from the throne. This was followed by a chaotic stage in which the barbarian tribes from the north, which are represented by the ten horns, fought among themselves for control of the Roman territory.

Verse 24 continues, "And another shall rise after them; He shall be different from the first ones." "I was considering the [ten] horns, and there was another horn, a little one, coming up among them, before whom three of the first horns were plucked out by the roots. And there, in this horn, were eyes of a man, and a mouth speaking pompous words...He shall speak pompous words against the Most High, shall persecute the saints of the Most High, and shall intend to change times and law. Then the saints shall be given into his hand for a time and times and half a time" (Daniel 7:8,24,25).

Like the clay in the feet of the image, this little horn "shall be different." The difference is that instead of simply having a political agenda, it also has a religious agenda. It speaks "against the Most High." It "persecutes the saints" and in fact its reign for "a time, times and half a time" constitutes a severe crisis for the church (see Revelation 12:13-17). Worst of all, it tampers with God's ordinances—"He shall intend to change times and law" (v. 25).

History reveals that the medieval Papacy was the political power that was "different" from the previous powers in Rome in that it was purportedly religious rather than political. However, the Papacy ultimately achieved political power over the tribes that became the countries of Western Europe. The armies of Justinian, the emperor of the Eastern Roman Empire, defeated the Arian tribes that opposed Roman Catholicism (the three horns that were plucked out by the roots to make way for the little horn).[895] The pope allied himself with the "converted" Franks (another of the ten tribes, who became the French nation) and eventually brought most of Europe under his control as the "Holy Roman Empire." Although this was a gradual process with a number of set-backs, AD 538 holds special significance[896] as the year when the armies of Justinian expelled the last of the opposing barbarian tribes from the city of Rome. This year can be used as a starting point for the "time, times and half a time" of papal political authority, the 1,260 year reign of the "little horn" (see 12, *One Thousand Two Hundred and Sixty Days*).

We should keep in mind that although the book of Revelation focuses on the activity of the medieval Papacy in a very negative way, this does not mean that the Roman Catholic Church was worse than other powers and people of that time. It was a brutal era; kings, empires, and other religions committed atrocities every bit as heinous as those of the papal system. But Revelation

---

894 A comparison verses 17 and 23 of Daniel 7 shows that Daniel uses the words "kings" and "kingdoms" interchangeably.

895 The three tribes that were destroyed by the papal allies were the Heruli (AD 493), the Vandals (AD 534) and the Ostrogoths (AD 553) Smith, Uriah *Daniel and the Revelation* (Hagerstown, MD Review and Herald Publishing 1972), p. 128

896 There are a number of significant dates in the establishment of the political power of the papacy. In AD 476 the last western Roman emperor, Romulus Augustulus, was deposed and the territory of the western empire was overrun by "barbarian" tribes who were followers of Arian Christianity and who were considered heretics by the Roman Catholic Church. In AD 508 the Franks became the first of the barbarian tribes to accept the Catholic religion, becoming the military allies of the papacy. In AD 533 the powerful Byzantine emperor Justinian issued a decree declaring the pope to be the head of all the Christian churches. In AD 538 the armies of Justinian drove the Ostrogoths out of Rome, leaving the effective authority in the hands of the Papacy. See Smith, Uriah, *Daniel and the Revelation*.

does not expose them because their actions were not done in the name of Jesus. In a number of passages God says that he acts "for My name's sake, that it should not be profaned in the sight of the Gentiles" (Ezekiel 20:22), and this applies to His exposing of the corruption of the apostate church. Jesus, in describing the corruption which He predicted would come into the church, said "an enemy has done this" (Matthew 13:28). The "enemy" is not the Catholic Church, the pope or church leaders and certainly is not the Catholic people who often have a close personal relationship with Christ. The enemy is Satan, and God's purpose in exposing the fall of the church during the Dark Ages is to prepare us for the future, when the majority of the Christian church will become Babylon, the enemy of God's people.

The table and diagram below summarize the visions of Daniel 2 and 7. Keep in mind that the beast from the sea of Revelation 13 is a composite of the beasts of Daniel 7. This will become important when we compare the characteristics of the sea beast with the characteristics of the ancient empires. (See Table App11.1)

Like a Leopard

It is significant that the sea beast takes aspects of the wild animals of Daniel 7 to form a composite beast—the seven heads and ten horns each represent important aspects of the medieval Papacy. Although the Book of Revelation does not specify what the heads represent, a study of the empires represented by the heads gives some characteristics that fit remarkably well with the characteristics of the Papacy of the Dark Ages. Keep in mind that this extensive study of the characteristics of the medieval Papacy is not so that we can understand history, but rather so that we will be able to recognize the "Babylon" power of the last days.

The beast from the sea was **"like a leopard,"** in other words, in general it most closely resembled the empire represented by the leopard. In Daniel 7 the leopard was the symbol of the Greek Hellenistic Empire. It is not surprising that the sea beast, which symbolizes the European Roman Catholic "Empire," would be most like the Greek Empire, since Greek culture, values

Table App11.1

Image of Daniel 2	Beasts of Daniel 7	Empire Represented
Head of Gold	Lion	Babylonian Empire
Breast of Silver	Bear	Medo-Persian Empire
Belly of Brass	Leopard	Greek Hellenistic Empire
Legs of Iron	Terrible Beast	Pagan Roman Empire
Feet of Iron and Clay	Ten Horns and Little Horn	Papal Roman Empire

Daniel 2   **Daniel 7**

Babylon

Persia

Greece

Pagan
Rome

Papal
Rome

Judgment

God's
Kingdom

and philosophy form the foundation of European culture.

The first and most obvious feature of the leopard of Daniel 7 is that it is the only animal that has four heads. This aspect is also emphasized in Daniel's other visions. In chapter 8 Greece is symbolized by a goat with one huge horn, representing Alexander the Great. But "when he was strong, the great horn was broken; and for it came up four notable ones toward the four winds of heaven" (Daniel 8:8). This represents the breakup of the Greek Empire into warring kingdoms after the death of Alexander. Likewise, in chapter 11, "a mighty king...of the realm of Grecia [Alexander]...shall rule with great dominion" but when "his kingdom shall be broken, [it] shall be divided toward the four winds of heaven" (Daniel 11:2-4). Out of this division arose the King of the North and the King of the South, the warring Hellenistic kingdoms in Syria and Egypt that fought each other for more than 200 years (Daniel 11: 5-15).

Thus a primary characteristic of the Greek Empire (and the Greek people in general from antiquity until modern times)[897] is to divide into factions which war with one another, all the while maintaining a common culture and identity. And indeed this is a primary characteristic of the sea beast, the medieval Catholic Church. From the time it became the official church of the Roman Empire there was fighting among the various Patriarchates, often brutal and to the death. The church eventually split into the

Eastern Orthodox and the Roman Catholic Churches, bitterly accusing and opposing and even fighting against each other, but all the while considering themselves to be estranged parts of the same body with nearly identical doctrines and teachings. Moreover, the image of Daniel 2 with its iron toes held together by clay accurately pictures the European Catholic Empire that "will not adhere to one another" (Daniel 2:43)—the individual European nations have constantly warred against one another even while bound together by the common Catholic faith.

Each of the four heads of the leopard represents a characteristic of the Greek Hellenistic Empire that is also a characteristic of the papal church of the Middle Ages. One prominent characteristic of the Hellenistic Empire was a highly developed system of pagan mythology, with the gods and goddesses of Olympus, who were in many ways like humans, entering into the daily lives and affairs of men. Greek mythology told the intricate details of their origins and lives, and Greek art, particularly sculpture, was focused on depictions of these gods and goddesses.

In like manner, the Roman Church early adopted the worship of the saints. Prayers and liturgies were offered to them, seeking their intervention in the problems and affairs of men. Like the Greek gods, the various saints had "specialty areas" (such as Saint Christopher, the patron saint of travelers). Volumes of literature were devoted to their lives and deeds, legends developed around their miracle-working powers, and churches were lavishly decorated with art and sculpture depicting them.

A second characteristic of the Greek Empire was Greek philosophy, which was developed by such brilliant men as Plato and Aristotle into a system that became the foundation of western civilization. Although Bible writers utilized some Greek terminology, most notably the *Logos* (the "Word" of John 1), the Greek concept of the

---

897 Some of the primary examples of Greek factions warring against each other include the Peloponnesian wars between the Greek city-states (most notably Athens and Sparta), the wars between the Hellenistic kingdoms, the division of Constantinople into four "sports clubs" that at one point destroyed half the city and killed 30,000 people (the "Nika riots" of AD 531), the iconoclast-iconodule controversies of the 8th and 9th centuries, the factions who after the war of independence murdered Ioannis Kapodistrias, the first prime minister, and the brutal civil war between communists and royalists after World War II.

corruptible body inhabited by a pure immortal soul was in sharp contrast to the Hebrew concept of God uniting matter and spirit to create the soul, and the Christian concept of the resurrection of the body. However, beginning even before Christ with the allegorical interpretations of the Old Testament by Philo of Alexandria, there was an attempt to harmonize Hebrew/Christian thought with Greek philosophy. This effort was continued by Justyn Martyr, Clement of Alexandria, Origen, and the "Cappadocian fathers,"[898] who succeeded in synthesizing the Hebrew/early Christian concepts of God, Christ and man with the Greek philosophies of Plato and the Stoics. This synthesis of Greek, Hebrew and Christian philosophy laid the foundation for the theology of the Catholic and Orthodox Churches, most notable the doctrine of the immortal soul.

A third characteristic of the Greek Empire was Hellenism, the pervasive Greek culture that was dominant from the Mediterranean all the way to India. Unlike previous world empires, which simply conquered in order to exploit but left local culture basically intact, the Greek language, architecture, philosophy and culture were incorporated into and came to dominate that of the defeated nations. Even when the divided Greek Empire was defeated by the Romans, its advanced culture still prevailed, shaping and transforming the comparatively crude culture of the early Romans.

Likewise, the Roman Catholic Church developed a Catholic culture that was pervasive wherever it was the dominant religion. Catholic festivals such as Christmas, Easter and days to celebrate the saints replaced local festivals, and the church even determined the weekly patterns of eating, fasting, and rest. The laws of the church became the law of the land. The church and its

activities were at the center of social life, and the priests and monks were among the most influential people in society.

Unlike the earlier Babylonian and Persian Empires, the Greek Empire did not disappear when it was defeated. Because the Hellenistic kingdoms were divided, the Romans slowly took over their territory, but through the dominant and advanced Hellenistic culture the Roman Empire was heavily influenced. This was especially true in the Eastern Empire after the capital was moved to Constantinople, and with the collapse of the Western Roman Empire the Greek Empire was essentially reborn and continued for another 1000 years as the Christian Byzantine Empire, established by Constantine the Great. A fourth characteristic of the sea beast was the Greek/Byzantine model of Christianity.

The primary feature of Byzantine Christianity was the union of church and state. Beginning with Constantine in the early fourth century, the emperor was integrally involved in the affairs of the church.[899] Laws were passed giving special privileges to the "official" church, and exponents of opposing views were suppressed or even killed. "Justinian (527-565), more fully than any of the eastern emperors, succeeded in making himself master of the church...The church was now practically a department of the state."[900] The Papacy followed this same policy during the centuries of its supremacy, but took it a step farther: rather than the church being a department of the state, the state became the agent of the church.

To summarize, **"the beast which [John] saw was like a leopard"**—the four headed leopard of Daniel 7, the heads of which stand for the

---

898 Basil of Caesarea, Gregory of Nazianzus and Gregory of Nyssa.

899 For example, the first general council of the church, held in Nicaea in 325, was called by Constantine in order to deal with the Arian controversy, which threatened the unity of the church and thus the stability of the empire.

900 Walker, Williston *A History of the Christian Church* (News York, C. Scribner, reprint available from Amazon.com) pg. 154.

four main characteristics of the Greek Empire: a strong influence from paganism, an underlying doctrinal foundation in Greek philosophy, a pervasive, universal Catholic culture, and the union of church and state.

Feet Like a Bear

Another prominent feature of the composite sea beast was that **"his feet were like the feet of a bear."** The feet, or paws of a bear are the means by which he applies his great strength to seize prey or to maul foes.[901] In political terms this corresponds to administrative or executive power, so the executive power of the sea beast is like that of the bear, which in Daniel 7 represented the Persian Empire. The strength of the Persian Empire (as depicted in the book of Esther, which gives the most insight into the Persian system) was its high degree of administrative organization[902] and the detailed and permanent nature of its laws.[903]

The administrative structure of the Catholic Church began to develop as early as the second century.[904] Before this, in the early church, each member was expected to contribute to the worship of the church, with local elders and deacons who had been appointed to provide leadership and direction.[905] Jesus Himself commanded that there would not be dictatorial authority by church leaders—"You know that the rulers of the Gentiles lord it over them, and those who are great exercise authority over them. Yet it shall not be so among you; but whoever desires to become great among you, let him be your servant" (Matthew 20:25, 26). But by the second century local leadership had been developed into a system of hierarchical rulership with a regional bishop. This system evolved through the centuries into the complex system of canon law with the pope at the head of a highly organized and rigidly controlled hierarchy, which is able to effectively wield both religious and political power on a worldwide basis.

One of the most notable features of the Persian system was that their laws were considered infallible and unchangeable, particularly when sealed by the king.[906] Likewise, the Catholic Church considered its rulings and laws that it formulated in church councils to be infallible, and in fact one of its prime teachings is that the church, being the body of Christ, can never err. Beyond this, "Roman Catholics believe that the pope is infallible in matters of faith and morals. This means they believe that the pope cannot possibly commit an error when he speaks ex cathedra, or by virtue of his office."[907]

In summary, the fifth "head" (characteristic) of the sea beast is its administrative power and unchangeable laws, symbolized by **"the feet of a bear."**

The Mouth of a Lion

The sea beast also had a mouth **"like the mouth of a lion."** In Daniel 7 the lion represented

---

901 See 1Samuel 17:34-37.

902 Esther 3:12-15, 8:9-14.

903 Esther 1:13,15, 19, 4:11, 16, Daniel 6:8,12,15.

904 The "Catholic Church developed its distinguishing characteristics between AD 160 and 190. The hitherto relatively independent congregations were now knit into an effective union. The power of the bishops was greatly strengthened, a collection of authoritative New Testament Scripture recognized and a creed formulated. Comparatively loosely organized Christianity now became a rigid corporate body, having recognized official leaders, and capable not merely of defining its faith, but of shutting out from its communion all who did not accept its creed or its officers…'About AD 50, he was of the church who had received baptism and the Holy Spirit and called Jesus, Lord; about AD 180, he who acknowledged the rule of faith [creed], the New Testament canon, and the authority of the bishop" Walker pgs. 59,60

905 1Corinthians 14:26-33, 1Timothy 3:1-13, Titus 1:5-9.

906 Esther 1:19, Daniel 6:8,12,15.

907 "Pope," *The World Book encyclopedia*, (Chicago, IL 1986).

the Babylonian Empire. The mouth is the part of the body that speaks, and according to Daniel 2, the ones who spoke for Babylon in a religious sense, the "mouthpiece" of their religion, were "the magicians, the astrologers, the sorcerers and the Chaldeans," in other words, the Babylonian priesthood.[908] "Herodotus, the world traveler and historian of antiquity, witnessed the mystery religion and its rites in numerous countries and mentions how Babylon was the primeval source from which all systems of idolatry flowed."[909] The mystery religion of Babylon was characterized by its priests with their highly developed ritual magic.

It is surprising how much ritual magic resembles the liturgy of the Roman Church. "To work most magic, the magician sings or speaks special words in a certain order. These magic words are called incantations or spells. Some incantations form prayers to demons, spirits or other supernatural forces. Magic actions accompany the words spoken in performing much magic... Magic objects include things with supposed supernatural powers."[910]

The Catholic priesthood in their liturgies use just such special, highly ritualized words and actions in order to "create" the actual body and blood of Christ. Even though no change has taken place in the bread and wine that can be detected, they insist that each mass is a renewal of the sacrifice of Christ, and that "The whole Christ, flesh and blood, body and soul, Divinity

and humanity, is really present."[911] It is considered that the eating and drinking of these is an actual partaking of salvation, and this ritual is the central act of the Catholic faith, and in fact the core of the Catholic religion.

In addition, miraculous powers are attributed to icons and relics (holy objects such as the bones and clothing of the saints, pieces of the "true cross," etc.), as well as to holy places, which are destinations for pilgrims. The priests, monks and nuns who officiate and administer these "mysteries" serve an equivalent role to the priests of the ancient mystery religions.

The sixth "head" (characteristic) of the sea beast is the system of priests who use ritual magic, symbolized by the **"mouth of a lion."**

Ten Horns

The sea beast also had ten horns. In Daniel 7:7 the prophet saw "a fourth beast, dreadful and terrible, exceedingly strong. It had huge iron teeth; it was devouring, breaking in pieces, and trampling the residue with its feet...*and it had ten horns.*" This beast symbolized the Roman Empire, which was characterized by its powerful and brutal military prowess. The highly organized Roman legions, with their advanced military strategy and weaponry and well-developed road system were able to quickly extend their power to crush all rebellion or resistance.

The Papacy was the successor to the line of Roman emperors in the west. Although the church did not always have its own army, it controlled the armies of those countries that were under its domination. Thus the Franks and later the Holy Roman Empire and Spain became the military arm of the church. The nations of Europe that put their armies at the disposal of the papal

908 Daniel 2:2,27, 4:7, 5:11.

909 Ralph Woodrow, *Babylon Mystery Religion* (Riverside, CA.) Pg.4. This book includes misinformation, particularly those sections that are derived from "The Two Babylons" by Alexander Hislop, and in fact the author has since repudiated some concepts and information and has allowed "Babylon Mystery Religion" to go out of print. Nevertheless there is good and valid information in both this book and in "The Two Babylons" but it must be distinguished from that which is questionable.

910 "Magic," *World Book Encyclopedia*, (Chicago, IL 1986)

911 Joseph Pohle, "Dogmatic Theology" *The Catholic Encyclopedia* http://www.newadvent.org/cathen/14580a.htm, Accessed 10-21-2014

church in order to carry out its agenda are represented by the ten horns of the sea beast.

The seventh head and the ten horns of the sea beast represent the military might of the Papacy, operating through the countries of Europe that were under its authority, and it is this head that suffered a "deadly wound." Revelation 13:3 informs us that "the deadly wound was healed." The beast with its healed military head is called Babylon in the Book of Revelation and is depicted in Revelation 17 as a harlot riding a scarlet beast with the same seven heads and 10 horns as the beast from the sea of Revelation 13. Last-days Babylon is an international confederation of of powers that has the same characteristics of the sea beast described above, and like the medieval Papacy it will "make war with the saints" (Revelation 13:7), so much so that the harlot is "drunk with the blood of the saints" (Revelation 17:6).

We invite you to view the complete
selection of titles we publish at:

www.ASPECTBooks.com

Scan with your mobile
device to go directly
to our website.

Please write or email us your praises, reactions,
or thoughts about this or any other book we publish at:

ASPECT Books

www.ASPECTBooks.com

P.O. Box 954
Ringgold, GA 30736

info@ASPECTBookscom

ASPECT Books titles may be purchased in bulk for
educational, business, fund-raising, or sales promotional use.
For information, please e-mail:

BulkSales@ASPECTBooks.com

Finally, if you are interested in seeing
your own book in print, please contact us at

publishing@ASPECTBooks.com

We would be happy to review your manuscript for free.

CPSIA information can be obtained
at www.ICGtesting.com
Printed in the USA
FSOW02n2328190116
15734FS